ASQUITH

ASQUITH

Portrait of a Man and an Era

by

ROY JENKINS

CHILMARK PRESS

New York

All rights reserved under International and
Pan-American Copyright Conventions

Published in New York by Chilmark Press, Inc.
and distributed by Random House, Inc.

Library of Congress Catalog Card Number: 65-14596

© Roy Jenkins, 1964

Printed in Great Britain

PREFACE

This book, planned in the autumn of 1959, has taken a whole Parliament (and a long one) to complete. In the course of these five years I have accumulated many debts of gratitude. The biggest is to Lady Violet Bonham Carter, who has been consistently helpful. Still more than for her help, however, I am grateful for her tolerance. The book grew into something she did not entirely like, into a view of her father which, while to my mind far from unfavourable, is in some respects equally far from her own. Confronted with this development she did not hesitate to argue with me, and occasionally to register a strong protest. But she did not attempt to force her interpretation on me.

The book leans heavily on three supports: the collection of Asquith Papers, the ownership of which has recently been transferred from Balliol College to the Bodleian Library; other, mainly published, sources which have become available since the appearance of the official biography by J. A. Spender and Cyril Asquith in 1932; and the letters, hitherto unused, which Asquith wrote to Miss Venetia Stanley (later Mrs. Edwin Montagu) between 1910 and 1915. The unattributed quotations in chapters 17, 21 and 22 are from this last source.

For facilitating my use of the first source I am grateful to Mr. J. N. Bryson, formerly librarian of Balliol College, and to Mr. D. S. Porter, of the Department of Western Manuscripts at the Bodleian. In connection with the second source I owe a particular debt to Sir Harold Nicolson, of whose incomparable *King George V* [Constable] I have made extensive use, by quotation and in other ways; to the late Lord Beaverbrook, some of whose views I seek to controvert, but who was unfailingly helpful to me, and to the Beaverbrook Canadian Foundation, for permission to make substantial quotations from both *Politicians and the War* and *Men and Power*; to the late Lord Hankey for his highly informative *The Supreme Command* (Allen & Unwin), from which I have quoted; and to Mr. Wayland Young, who kindly made available to me passages from the diary of his mother, Lady Scott. I am also indebted to many others whose works I have consulted, referred to, and discussed.

For her part in making the third source available I am grateful to Mrs. Milton Gendel (formerly Miss Judy Montagu), who also provided a photograph of her mother.

Others who gave particular help included Mrs. C. F. G. Masterman, Sir Alan Lascelles, Mrs. Anthony Henley, Mr. Randolph Churchill and Lady Elliot of Harwood. Mr. Anthony King (Fellow of Magdalen College, Oxford) and Mr. Philip Williams (Fellow of Nuffield College) read the manuscript and made suggestions (most of which were accepted) of great value. My secretary, Mrs. Church, typed the whole book and did much wearing work upon the references. Mr. Mark Bonham Carter combined, with remarkable resilience and finesse, the roles of publisher, grandson, literary executor and general consultant. To all these and to others—for the list is not exhaustive—I am very grateful.

Acknowledgment is also due, and is gladly made, to:

Her Majesty the Queen for permission to quote from certain letters written by or on behalf of King Edward VII and King George V; and to Viscount Knollys where these letters were written by his grandfather;

The Chartwell Trustees for permission to quote from certain letters of Sir Winston Churchill;

The Earl of Rosebery for permission to quote an unpublished letter from his father to Asquith;

Messrs. A. D. Peters & Co. for permission to quote from Hilaire Belloc's *Sonnets and Verses* (Duckworth);

Messrs. Eyre & Spottiswoode for permission to quote from Margot Asquith's *Autobiography* and *More Memoirs*;

Messrs. Elliot & Fry, Ltd., for the photograph of Lord Rosebery facing page 65 and Messrs. Bassano, Ltd., for permission to reproduce it;

and the Radio Times Hulton Picture Library for permission to reproduce the remaining photographs facing page 65 and those facing pages 128, 160, 161, 352, 353, 448, 449 and 481.

ROY JENKINS

Combe, August 1964

CONTENTS

A.   A2

CONTENTS

ILLUSTRATIONS

CHAPTER I

FROM YORKSHIRE TO BALLIOL

1862-75

Herbert Henry Asquith was born in the small Yorkshire woollen town of Morley on September 12th, 1852. He was the second son of Joseph Dixon Asquith, a minor employer in the woollen trade. Three daughters were born to the family later, two of whom died early. Such a casualty rate amongst children was not unusual at the time, but physical infirmity or ill-fortune was a marked characteristic of the family, affecting all of its members except for Herbert Asquith,[1] who was always notably robust, and his sister Evelyn. Joseph Asquith died suddenly at the age of thirty-five, having twisted an intestine in a game of village cricket. He had enjoyed no intensity of life to set against its early end. " I gather from local and family tradition," his second son wrote many years later, " that (my father) was a cultivated man, interested in literature and music, of a retiring and unadventurous disposition, and not cut out in the keen competitive atmosphere of the West Riding for a successful business career."[a]

Emily Asquith, his wife, was a much stronger personality. She was a woman of wide interests, considerable cultivation, and unusual

---

[1] Herbert (or, as a child, Bertie) was the Christian name by which Asquith was known throughout the first forty years of his life. But his second wife called him Henry, and so did the few friends of his middle and later years who addressed him by his first name. Any reference to " Herbert " by the time of his premiership came as a faint echo from a distant past. The change was not widely noticed, for there have been few major national figures whose Christian names were less well known to the public. " H. H. Asquith " was throughout his chosen designation, and his almost invariable signature, except for occasional abbreviations to " H.H.A. ".

13

conversational power. She is described as having " a biting turn of phrase and humour."[b] But she spent most of her life lying on a sofa, suffering from a mixture of bronchitis and heart weakness. Despite these afflictions, she survived her husband by twenty-seven years, and both because of this fact and of her other attributes had a far greater influence upon Herbert Asquith than did his father. In particular, she gave him a habit of omnivorous reading.

The third physically unfortunate member of the family was the elder son, William Willans Asquith. He was only a year older than Herbert, and the two boys, intellectually well-matched, were the closest of companions for much of their early lives. But at the age of sixteen the elder one received a severe kick on the spine during a school game. He was slow to recover and had to leave school. Thereafter Herbert was always ahead of his brother, although William's intellectual achievements remained considerable. But the growth of his mind was not matched by that of his body. The kick was responsible for his height never increasing beyond 5 feet 1 inch. After leaving Oxford he went to Clifton as a schoolmaster and remained there for the whole of his active career. He never married, and died in 1918.

The circumstances of life of this rather frail family were those of modest comfort. Croft House, where the children were born, was a solidly built dwelling of dark Yorkshire stone, with six or seven bedrooms, three or four living-rooms and a good staircase. It had nothing of even the most minor magnate's residence about it and was in no way set apart from the surrounding community. Yet, in a characteristic West Riding way it was at once half urban and half rural. It commanded a good view looking towards Leeds across the scarred industrial landscape. Both geographically and socially it was a little indeterminate. The mills were at the back door but the countryside was at the front; and it might have been the house of a small manu-facturer like Joseph Asquith, or of a school-teacher, or of a non-con-formist minister or of a local tradesman who had decided to move half a mile away from his shop. Herbert Asquith's principal Morley memories were of walking round the town at the head of a procession of children to celebrate the end of the Crimean War in 1856, and of regular, stiffly-attired, Sunday visits to Rehoboth Chapel, the local home of a Congregationalist sect and very much the centre of his parents' lives.

In 1858 the Asquiths removed about ten miles north-west to the village of Mirfield. Life here followed much the same pattern as at Morley and the change made little difference to the children. At neither place did Herbert and his brother go to school. They were looked after by a nursery maid and taught by their mother.

After two years at Mirfield Joseph Asquith died suddenly. He left little money and the family were henceforth dependent upon their mother's father, William Willans. Willans was the head of a wool-stapling business in Huddersfield. He came from the same Puritan, petty-bourgeois background as Joseph Asquith, but he was more energetic and, by this time, a good deal more prosperous. He was an important civic figure in Huddersfield, and in 1851 he had narrowly missed election to Parliament as Radical member for the borough. He established the Asquith family in a house a short distance from his own, and undertook the education of the two boys. For a year they were sent as day-boys to Huddersfield College, and then went on to a small mixed boarding school run by the Moravian order[1] at Fulneck, almost in the suburbs of Leeds.

This school kept rather oddly timed terms and the two Asquiths arrived there at the beginning of August, 1861 (with no prospect of even a day's holiday until September), shortly before Herbert's ninth birthday. From here he began to write his first letters to his mother, and filled them with expressions of rather resigned distaste. " We do not like the place at all," he wrote on August 6th, " for besides having nothing to do such dreadful smoke comes over from Pudsey that it makes everything quite black. . . . I do not like either masters or boys. . . . " However, he was sufficiently composed to finish the letter with the dignified ending: " With best love to all, believe me ever to remain, Your affte. son H. H. Asquith."[c] The boys never got to like the school; but the teaching was said to have been quite good.

The next family unheaval occurred only two years later, when William Willans died. The Huddersfield connection died with him,

1 The Moravians, a highly disciplined Protestant sect with a strong missionary bent, trace their origin back to 1457 when a group of peasants in the Kingdom of Bohemia retired to a remote Moravian village, and there established a *Unitas Fratrum*. After 1620 they were forced underground in Bohemia, and only attracted the name Moravian when groups of them began to emigrate early in the eighteenth century. They first came to Yorkshire in 1742. The boarding school at Fulneck existed from 1801 to 1884.

and Emily Asquith, with her daughter, left Yorkshire for the softer climate of St. Leonards, in Sussex. The two boys went to London to live with their uncle, John Willans, who had taken over responsibility for their education.[1] They arrived there in January, 1864, but within a year John Willans and his wife moved back to the north. Herbert Asquith, still only twelve, went with his brother as paying guests, first to a family in Pimlico and then to a " dispensary doctor " and his wife in Liverpool Road, Islington. That was the end for them, both of a close Yorkshire connection and of any effective home background. They went as day-boys to the City of London School, then in Milk Street off Cheapside. Their lives alternated between the City and, after the move to Islington, a typical mid-Victorian residential dependency of commercial London. It was a physical environment very similar to that which Joseph Chamberlain, born in Broad Street and brought up in Highbury, had experienced ten years earlier.

Only the physical background was similar, for the City of London School, despite the commercial bent of much of its teaching and of most of its pupils, offered to some the opportunity of a classical education of the highest quality, and this was most eagerly seized upon by Herbert Asquith. The school had been re-founded by the Corporation of London about thirty years previously and had 650 boys by the time Asquith entered. It offered no advantage of surroundings. The buildings were undistinguished and cramped, and there was no playing field. For games—never of much interest to Asquith—the boys went on half-holidays to Victoria Park in Bethnal Green. The number of masters was small and Asquith was at first taught in a class of sixty. But the quality of some of them was enough to make up for this. The most notable, and the one who did most to facilitate Asquith's academic success, was the new headmaster, Edwin Abbott, who arrived in 1865. He had himself been a boy at the school and had then gone to Cambridge, where he had been Senior Classic in 1861, the year before the pre-eminent Jebb. In Asquith's own words: " He was a Cambridge scholar of the most finished type in days when that type produced some of its most brilliant specimens."[d] He was also a remarkably gifted teacher, although he himself discounted the view that he had done much for Asquith. His main contribution, he insisted, was to excuse him from handwriting and book-keeping in the fifth form, and from

[1] Financial responsibility was later divided between him and his three younger brothers. All four of the uncles were later repaid by the Asquiths.

mathematics in the sixth form. " There was nothing left but to place before him the opportunities of self-education and self-improvement," Abbott wrote; " simply to put the ladder before him, and up he went."*e*

Yet, despite Asquith's rapid and seemingly effortless progress up this ladder of classical academic attainment, it was not in this field that his most outstanding quality lay. " As a classical scholar," his official biographers have perceptively written, " (he) was rather strongly and finely competent than freakishly endowed. What his tutors discerned was the application of an extra-ordinarily muscular intelligence to a subject for which it had a marked sympathy rather than the uncanny specialised aptitude of a Jebb or a Murray."*f* Where his ability was almost unique was in the use from an early age of a resonant, elaborately constructed, yet beautifully balanced and lucid English diction. Dr. Abbott has testified that his speeches in the school debating society exhibited all the *gravitas* and massive precision which were later to become recognised as the most notable Asquithian oratorical characteristics. The opening sentences of a prize-winning encomium upon the original founder of the City of London School, which he composed and declaimed at the age of seventeen, provide a fair sample of the measured maturity of tone which apparently came naturally to him:

" In acknowledging our obligations to the heroes of the past," he announced, " it is always a relief to be able to desert the commonplace of eulogy, and to point to the fabric built upon their self-denying efforts as the best memorial at once of their greatness and of our gratitude. The great man whom we commemorate today, could his spirit hear the tribute of our praise, would I am sure rejoice that we should turn from the obscure details of his career, to dwell in preference upon those after-fruits which have crowned with an honourable immortality the name of John Carpenter."*g*

At the end of 1869 Asquith won a Classical Scholarship at Balliol. At that time only two were awarded each year, and as the reputation of the college was already very high it would have been a great achievement for any boy, and was particularly so for one from a relatively unknown school which had never previously gained a Balliol scholarship. He was captain of the school at the time, and was riding confidently and even a little complacently upon a high tide of early success. In his academic work his contempt for what he regarded as inferior disciplines outside the main stream of traditional learning had the paradoxical effect of making him rigidly specialised. A contemporary recorded that " he had little interest in any subject except Classics and English," and that he spent his mathematics hours composing Greek verses, his chemistry hours in making " irreverent jests " and his German hours in diverting the master from the teaching of such an unimportant language.[h] This being the bent of his mind—and given the fact that he was never intellectually very tolerant—it was an advantage to him that he spent his schooldays in the crowded heart of the capital rather than in some cloistered academic grove. In the latter surroundings he might have grown up a classical pedant with little comprehension of the mid-nineteenth century world around him. In London, " generally taking a little stroll in Cheapside after lunch, but (getting) awfully knocked about during it," as he expressed it in a letter to his mother, such detachment was much more difficult. And Asquith's interest in everything touching the conduct of public affairs was always strong. He went frequently to the House of Commons and heard some of the great parliamentary reform debates of the mid-sixties. He wrote meticulous accounts of them to his mother, and even practised some amateur analysis of the division lists. He went also to meetings of the City Court of Common Council at Guildhall and, more frequently, to the Law Courts. Here his early sense of fastidious discrimination was exercised to the full.

" I have just returned from the Court of Queen's Bench where the Lord Chief Justice[1] is presiding," he wrote to his mother at the age of twelve. " One of the Counsel had just made a very agitated address to the jury, and at its conclusion a witness was put into the box whose evidence, being that of an illiterate man on an uninteresting subject, I did not care to hear. The man in question was a foreman or something of that kind of a shipping or dock company. I want to hear the Chief Justice sum up, and so I shall go to the Court again on the conclusion of this."[i]

Asquith's intellectual superiority did nothing to detract from the firmness of his radicalism. He disapproved strongly of Robert Lowe's position on the franchise; he went to the Crystal Palace to attend a demonstration of welcome to Garibaldi; he spent part of a Founder's Day holiday attending a Reform League meeting in support of Irish Church disestablishment—having spent the other part of it listening

[1] Sir Alexander Cockburn.

to a lecture on Christianity and progress at the Congregational Union; and he noted with approval that when he heard Archdeacon Wordsworth preach " a regular defence of the Irish Church " in Westminster Abbey, many of the congregation walked out in the middle. " Poor Dean Stanley sitting opposite the pulpit had the pleasure of being cursed in his own Abbey,"*j* he added. The mystical aspects of religion never meant much to Asquith,[1] but at this stage of his life, and indeed for many years afterwards, he was a great listener to sermons. But so he was to almost any form of oratory. The presentation of ideas, perhaps more than their formulation, constantly exercised his mind.

Nevertheless the impact upon Asquith of the London of the 'sixties was not all associated with oratory or the higher arts of government. Walking up Ludgate Hill to school one morning in 1864 he came upon the bodies of five murderers, hanging with white caps over their head, outside Newgate. Half an hour before they had been publicly executed, and their corpses were still available for inspection. On another, less macabre occasion he inspected, in a Fleet Street booth, the " fattest lady in the world." And towards the end of his schooldays he began, with a great sense of daring, to go to plays. Forty-seven years later, after driving past " the rather squalid little house " in Liverpool Road where he had lodged, he recorded in a letter his memory of this departure:

" I remember vividly the guilty sense of adventure with which I slipped out early one evening to pay my first visit to the theatre, and the care which I took to cover my tracks on my return. We had been brought up to regard the theatre as one of the devil's most damnable haunts; I am sure my mother had never entered one in her life, and her scruples were fully shared by the old Puritan couple—a Dispensary Doctor and his wife—with whom I lodged. I must have been quite 16 when I took the plunge; the play was a now forgotten one of Robertson's called " Dreams," and the heroine's part was taken by Miss Madge Robertson— now Mrs. Kendal—whom I regarded with true moon-calf devotion. *Ce n'est que le premier pas qui coûte*, and after a time I became an habitual play-goer, *i.e.* by careful economy I saved up in the course of a fortnight the 2/- needed for a seat in the pit, and

[1] Although in later life he came to enjoy the liturgy and prayers of the Church of England.

in order to secure a place in the front row I have often stood out-side the door for one or even two hours."[k]

In another letter, two days' later, he reverted to the impression made upon him by Miss Robertson. " I believe that Mrs. Kendal . . . was the first woman I at all idealised," he wrote: " she was not really beautiful, but had a most alluring voice, and to a callow novice in the pit seemed almost more than human. But of course she was as remote as a star from one's daily life."[l]

The end of Asquith's schooldays meant the temporary end of his life in London. The summer of 1870 was the transition period. In July, a few days after the outbreak of the Franco-Prussian War, he was delivering his already quoted address at his last City of London Founder's Day, and receiving all the acclamation due to an unusually successful boy at the pinnacle of his school career. In October, when the French Empire had fallen and German troops had invested a Republican Paris, he went to Oxford.

It was not only Asquith's first term as a Balliol undergraduate. It was also Benjamin Jowett's first term as Master of the college. Jowett, the most famous of Victorian Oxford figures, had been balked of this ambition sixteen years earlier when Dr. Scott had been elected over his head. This defeat was the beginning for Jowett of nearly decade of chagrin, controversy and bitterness, but it led to no such diminution of energy as had afflicted his almost equally notable contemporary, Mark Pattison, in similar circumstances.[1] By 1864 Jowett had established his supremacy in Balliol and had far more influence upon the affairs of the college than his rival in the Master's Lodging. His election (on September 7th, 1870) was such a foregone conclusion that the occasion for it—Scott's appointment to the Deanery of Rochester—arose directly out of a plot between Gladstone and Robert Lowe the Chancellor of the Exchequer, to make a vacancy for him.

Asquith, who was later to be regarded as the epitome of the Balliol man, therefore arrived at the college at the beginning of its most renowned Mastership. But the conjunction of events was not as signi-ficant as it looks. Balliol's period of distinction began long before Jowett became Master and almost equally long before his influence became predominant. The change from an old foundation with un-distinguished buildings and a Scottish connection into a great forcing

[1] Pattison was defeated for the Rectorship of Lincoln in 1851.

20

house of late nineteenth and early twentieth century politicians, administrators, ecclesiastics and men of letters began with Bishop Parsons, who was elected in 1798. It continued apace under " the Old Master," Henry Jenkyns, whose reign lasted from 1819 to 1854. This undistinguished High Church Tory, notable principally for his small white pony, was an improbable figure to preside over a great period of reform and rehabilitation, yet somehow or other he allowed it to happen under him.

" No College in Oxford," H. W. C. Davis was able to write of this period several decades later, " has parted with the old tradition to the same extent as Balliol."*m* And he went on to explain that he meant by this that Balliol had anticipated of its own free will most of the reforms which were imposed upon the rest of the University, first by the Royal Commission of 1854, and then by that of 1877. By its attitude to religious tests, to married tutors, to open scholarships, and above all, perhaps, by its eagerness to pull down its old buildings, the college showed its resolute modernity. Its intellectual climate was eclectic, humanist, and a little worldly. It held that men were greater than theories and that action was of more value than contemplation. This approach, as a prelude to the great position which Balliol men were to occupy in the world in the latter part of the century, began to produce outstanding academic results from the 'thirties onwards. Between 1837 and 1896, when there were approximately twenty colleges in the University, Balliol won thirty-four of the sixty Ireland Scholarships—the most coveted classical award.

The pre-eminence of Balliol therefore began well before Jowett had made his mark. Furthermore, his elevation to the Mastership reduced rather than increased the influence which he might have had upon Asquith. Asquith read his freshman's essays to him, received his weekly battels in his presence, and met him also at occasional breakfast parties or even upon that great nineteenth century Oxford institution —an intellectual walk. But he was never his pupil. And even if he had been, it is doubtful if Jowett's influence upon Asquith would have been as great as upon many other young men. In the first place Asquith was never open to wide masculine intellectual influence. His mind and his ambitions, from a very early age, were too firmly and securely set for that. And partly for this reason there was probably never great natural sympathy between the two men. Jowett, perhaps with a touch of snobbery, preferred those whose natural talent was in danger of being

obscured by a frivolous or *fainéant* overlayer, which he could strip off
or at least render innocuous. At a later stage he was more interested in
Margot Tennant, Asquith's second wife, than he ever was in Asquith
himself; and he got more satisfaction out of his relations with Lord
Lansdowne, who told Miss Tennant, "had it not been for him, I
would have done little with my life,"[n] than out of those with Asquith.
For Asquith needed no one to make him do a great deal with his life.
And he expressed his own feelings towards Jowett, at a time when the
latter was thought to be dying,[1] with a notable detachment and coolness:

> "I am afraid poor old Jowett is dying," he wrote in a private letter
> of October 26th, 1891. "It seems but the other day that my wife
> and I were staying with him. We had a very pleasant party: not
> too large and well assorted.... It is already difficult to conceive
> of the Oxford in which, partly by sympathy and partly by
> antagonism, he was formed.... Jowett, in his day, did probably
> more than any other single man to let some fresh air into the
> exhausted atmosphere of the common rooms, and to widen the
> intellectual horizon of the place. In my time he was already looked
> upon, by the more advanced spirits, as an extinct volcano, and even
> a bit of a reactionary.... He never at any time (I should think)
> had anything definite to teach...."[o]

The Balliol volcano of Asquith's day who was in no danger of
extinction was T. H. Green. This austere, reserved philosopher had
come up to Balliol as a Commoner from Rugby in 1858. He had no
great gift either of classical scholarship or of lucidity of expression, but
after his First in Greats and his election to a fellowship in 1862, and then
to a tutorship in 1866, he made his own brand of neo-Hegelian thought
the dominant intellectual influence, certainly in Balliol and perhaps in
the University as a whole. He had great personal influence and
gathered a strong band of disciples around him. Although he worked
amicably with the Master his teaching was the beginning of a revolt
against Jowett's method. He had neither the eclecticism nor the intellectual grace of the Master, and he taught his young men what he
wanted them to believe. He died young, but his values and outlook,
handed down first through his pupil and biographer, R. L. Nettleship,
and then through many others, persisted in Balliol almost to the present
day.

[1] In fact he survived for another two years.

Asquith was close to Green. He was taught by him, and he approved of his politics (unlike those of Jowett, about which he was often inclined to complain), for Green was both an active and an ardent Liberal, and served for a time as a member of the Oxford City Council. Yet Asquith was never fully under his influence. This was partly again due to his natural resistance to such a process, and partly to his lack of interest in speculative thought. He summed it all up quite neatly fifty years later, expressing at once his respect for Green's personality and intellect and his own innate distrust of any philosophical *schema*:

Between 1870 and 1880 Green was undoubtedly the greatest personal force in the real life of Oxford. For myself, though I owe more than I can say to Green's gymnastics, both intellectual and moral, I never " worshipped at the Temple's inner shrine." My own opinions on these high matters have never been more than those of an interested amateur, and are of no importance to anyone but myself.[p]

Asquith's " interested amateurishness," did not apply to his general work at Oxford. From the day when he arrived in Balliol in October, 1870, and established himself in rooms at the top of Staircase IV he worked with a steady and proficient ease which brought results of almost unbroken excellence. He achieved a clear First in Honour Moderations in the spring of 1872 and was *proxime accessit* for the Hertford Scholarship that same year. In 1873 he was also *proxime* for the Ireland, with Henry Broadbent, a notable scholar who was later Librarian of Eton, the winner. That in itself would have been a reason more for congratulation than for disappointment, but when he again achieved the same position in the following year, with the margin then so narrow that the examiners took the unusual step of awarding him a special consolation prize, his *proxime* position looked a little too much of a habit. In the summer term of 1874 he was the only Balliol man to get a First in Greats and he added to this the achievement of being bracketed with Broadbent as the winner of the Craven Scholarship. In the autumn of that year he was elected, with Andrew Bradley, the Shakespearian scholar, to a prize fellowship of Balliol.

Asquith's academic successes, which were striking without being sensational—a quarter of a century later his eldest son, Raymond, was to repeat them with the addition of the elusive Ireland and an All Souls fellowship—were achieved on the basis of a moderate and controlled amount of work. They were the product neither of erratic genius nor of excessively concentrated plodding. They left him plenty of time for other activities, and even in his last term before Greats he spent several hours a day sailing on the Thames near Godstow, and also went over to Woodstock to speak for St. John Brodrick against Lord Randolph Churchill. But his main occupation outside his work, as might have been foretold from his schoolday interests, was the Oxford Union. He made his maiden speech there early in his first term, and from then onwards he spoke in almost every political debate, mostly putting forward the orthodox advanced Liberal point of view with his own peculiar combination of lucidity, force and precision. Herbert Warren, later President of Magdalen, who knew him well, believed that he spoke as effectively at the Union as he ever did. He occupied most of the important offices of the Society. As Treasurer he was a notable innovator, introducing smoking and the provision of afternoon tea into the Society's rooms. He justified these new arrangements on the slightly sententious ground that they would encourage under-graduates to do an hour's daily reading outside their subject, and offered the novels of Trollope as an example of what he regarded as suitable material. In spite of these reforms, he did not succeed easily to the Presidency of the Union. He was defeated at his first attempt, and did not get the chair until the final term of his last year. For most under-graduates this would have been a burden in his Schools term, but Asquith took it all in his stride.

His social life at Oxford was only moderately active. In his second term his elder brother, retarded by ill-health, joined him at Balliol, and they lived together in a single set of rooms, a most unusual arrange-ment at the time and one which suggests an attachment to the familiar (and to economy) rather than a great branching out. But he had a fairly wide range of friends and acquaintances both in his own college and outside. In Balliol his main associates were Alfred Milner, Andrew Bradley, Herbert Warren, Charles Gore (later Bishop, first of Birming-ham and then of Oxford), A. R. Cluer (later a County Court judge), Thomas Raleigh (later a notable Indian civil servant), and W. P. Ker, Churton Collins and W. H. Mallock (all of whom achieved some dis-tinction as literary critics). Outside the college his principal friends were Herbert Paul of Corpus, who became an outstanding journalist and sat for a short time in the House of Commons as Liberal member for Edinburgh, and Henry Broadbent, already mentioned as a scholar. They were all men of considerable intellectual worth, and some of them, notably Milner, Bradley and Gore, were to achieve positions of commanding influence. But they were in no sense a group of *jeunesse dorée*. They were not a glittering set within the University, who spread fashions and started legends, as did the young men with whom Raymond Asquith was to mingle a generation later. They provided Asquith with a group of moderately close friends (although with none of them did real intimacy—if it ever existed—persist throughout his life), against which agreeable background he could achieve his university triumphs, but they did not launch him into the world of nineteenth century power or social distinction.

His first taste of this came immediately after he ceased to be an undergraduate, when he spent the summer and early autumn of 1874 coaching the son of the Earl of Portsmouth, and moving between his two country houses, Hurstbourne Park in Hampshire and Eggesford in Devon. "I thus obtained a glimpse of a kind of life which was new to me,"[q] he recorded. At Lord Portsmouth's he met politicians like Lord Carnarvon, who was then Colonial Secretary, and fashionable men of letters like Lord Houghton.

This interlude over he returned to Balliol and spent the first year of his fellowship in residence. But he did not continue this habit. He wished to be a lawyer and not a don, because the law was the accepted door, for young men without position, into the world of power and politics. This meant London and not Oxford. For the remaining six years of his fellowship it was merely a small but useful source of income to him. He left Oxford finally at the end of the summer term of 1875, and although he retained for the University a deep and almost romantic attachment, unusual in one whose later life was to be so strikingly successful, he never lived again within the city.

CHAPTER II

A STRUGGLING BARRISTER

1875-86

After leaving Balliol in June, 1875, Asquith spent six weeks as a member of a reading party at St. Andrews. Most of his close Oxford associates were there, and the expedition later came to assume for him the glow of a long-remembered Indian summer to his university life. But it also contained some seeds of the future. It was his first visit to Scotland and it took him, by chance, into the heart of the constituency which he was to represent in the House of Commons for thirty-two years. All around him, during this long vacation, lay the rolling countryside of East Fife and the electors who, with their children, were to be faithful to him throughout the long years of his mounting success—but not afterwards.

Even nearer at hand were the links of the Royal and Ancient St. Andrews Golfing Society, and Asquith there made his first acquaintance with the only non-sedentary game which was ever to arouse his interest. It was a useful acquaintanceship, for although golf was then so little developed that he and his modest-living student companions were able to hire the services of the British open champion to carry their clubs, the game was to become an almost essential accompaniment to Edwardian politics. In the heyday of Asquith's career, there was hardly a politician of note who did not seek his relaxation (and in some cases attempt to transact a part of his business) upon a golf links. Balfour was at least as addicted to the game as was Asquith himself, and Lloyd George even built himself a house alongside one of the best-known Surrey courses.

The Scottish holiday over, Asquith went to London and moved into rooms at the imposing address of 90 Mount Street, Mayfair. He had been eating his dinners in Lincoln's Inn for his last few years at Oxford, and he came to London for nine months' work in chambers before his call to the bar. He had been accepted as a pupil by Charles Bowen, one of the most distinguished of nineteenth-century legal minds, and he began work with him in the last days of October. Bowen, apart from being the son of a country parson and a Rugbeian, had a similar background to Asquith's own. He had been a scholar and fellow of Balliol and President of the Union. He had won all the University prizes and was Jowett's favourite pupil. Unlike Asquith, however, he was a notable athlete with poor health. He once exhibited the former prowess by the curiously unmodern feat of jumping a cow as it stood in a field, and the latter weakness led to frequent periods of long convalescence and an early death before the age of sixty. But by that time he had been successively a *puisne* judge for three years, a lord justice of appeal for eleven, and a law lord for one. He was also a notable wit, although many of his verses and recorded remarks now seem to suffer from the contrived facetiousness which came only too easily to Victorian classicists in their lighter moments.

When he accepted Asquith, Bowen had recently made his reputation in the interminable case of the Tichborne Claimant, and was Junior Counsel to the Treasury, or " Attorney-General's devil." He also had a large general practice, and was at the height of his success as an advocate; three years later, at the age of forty-four, he went straight from the junior bar to the bench. A short period as a pupil therefore gave Asquith a little experience of almost all branches of Common Law work. It also gave him a modified admiration for this perfect example of a Balliol man of the previous generation. His admiration was modified because Bowen's supremely refined intelligence was not muscular enough for his own taste; and because he was irritated by the latter's inability to delegate work—a capacity which was always highly developed in Asquith himself—and which resulted in most of the pupils' drafts being completely re-written by Bowen. Despite this, and despite his removal to another set of chambers immediately after his call to the bar in June, 1876, Asquith remained on terms of close acquaintanceship with Bowen. Sixteen years later, as Home Secretary, he gave the judge his last public appointment.

The chambers in which Asquith established himself were at 6, Fig Tree Court. The other occupants were two almost equally junior men who had also been pupils of Bowen's. In these surroundings he spent seven extremely lean years. The tide of success which had flowed strongly from his last years at school to his acceptance in chambers as distinguished as Bowen's, suddenly ceased to run. He was without legal connections, there was no one in the chambers from whom work might filter down to him, and he had no money of his own. Placed as he was, indeed, the whole venture of going to the bar, rather than remaining at Oxford or seeking some public service employment, was a hazardous gamble. And it was a gamble which brought no early winnings. For at least five years after his call, his professional earnings were negligible. His reaction was not to withdraw disappointedly or even, as might have been expected from Jowett's view of him as above all a determinedly ambitious young man[1], to meet setback with caution. On the contrary, he doubled his stake. In August, 1877 he got married.

His wife was Helen Melland, the daughter of a Manchester doctor. Asquith had known her since 1870, when he was eighteen and she only fifteen. They had met at St. Leonards-on-Sea, while Asquith was staying with his mother and she with some neighbouring cousins. Throughout his time at Oxford occasional vacation meetings on the South Coast were supplemented by a growing correspondence. She was Asquith's first love, and for many years his only one. " The first *real* one," he wrote later, after referring to his already mentioned non-real, schoolboy attachment to Madge Robertson, " . . . was Helen who afterwards became my wife. I showed the same constancy which has since been practised by my sons, and waited from about 18 to 25 (hardly ever seeing her in the interval)."[a] During 1874 they became secretly engaged, and in the autumn of 1876 Asquith went to Manchester to try to turn this clandestine arrangement into an open one. Dr. Melland, a well-established physician of commanding presence who survived to the age of 98, responded to Asquith's approach with a combination of courtesy and caution. But two months later he gave his consent by letter. " Although I have not had any opportunity of becoming better acquainted with you personally," he wrote, " I have been able to make certain enquiries which have satisfied me that I may give my consent to your becoming engaged to my daughter. I have the fullest conviction that your industry and ability will procure for you in due time that success in your profession which has attended you in your past career."[b] If the standard was to

[1] " Asquith will get on ; he is so direct," had been the Master of Balliol's summing up (Spender and Asquith, *Life of Lord Oxford and Asquith*, 1, p. 35).

be "industry and ability," it would have required a very exacting father-in-law to fault Asquith.

Miss Melland's position and fortune were not such that there could have been any question of a man with Asquith's ambitions marrying her for worldly reasons. But she was not so penniless that the change of circumstances meant any reduction in his standard of living. With her income of a few hundred pounds a year, with the money from his Balliol fellowship still continuing, and with chance earnings from lecturing and journalism, which he began increasingly to seek, they were able to move at once into a spacious, white-walled, early nineteenth century house in what was then John Street, and is now Keats Grove, Hampstead. Here, surrounded by a large garden and looking across the street to John Keats's old house, they lived what Asquith's official biographers insist was a simple, but agreeable and placid married life.

Placidity, indeed, was constantly stressed by Asquith himself as the keynote both of his wife's character and of the satisfaction which he derived from the marriage. This is a recurring theme of his writing about the relationship his wife wanted not only after and during the marriage, but even before it took place. " I am more than ever convinced," he wrote to his mother in January, 1877, " that H's health and happiness depend upon a speedy marriage and the chance of a quiet home, where she can be properly looked after and cared for."[c] But he was equally insistent that " a quiet home " and a simple unpretentious domesticity was what he, too, required. Yet an element of doubt remains as to whether Asquith, even at this stage in his career, did not secretly hanker after a more tense relationship and a more dramatic way of life. There was always in his character a surprising but strong streak of recklessness. It made him go to the bar instead of seeking a safer occupation. It made him marry before he had an assured income. It was later to make him enter Parliament before he had an established practice. And it made him, in the early 'eighties, when his briefs were still rare, spend nearly £300 (equivalent to at least £1200 today) on a diamond necklace for his wife. It must, from everything that is known of her character and pattern of life, have been almost the last thing that she wanted.

In appearance Helen Asquith was tall, brown-haired and very good-looking in a quiet featured way. The impression which survives of her is of an unambitious woman, with a calm and quietly assured character. "Hers was a beautiful and simple spirit,"[d] Haldane recorded in his autobiography. Her husband wrote: " She had one of those personalities which it is almost impossible to depict. The strong colours of the palette seem to be too heavy and garish: it is difficult to paint a figure in the soft grey tints which would best suit her, and yet she was not neutral or negative. Her mind was clear and strong, but it was not cut in facets and did not flash lights, and no one would have called her clever or " intellectual ". What gave her her rare quality was her character, which everyone who knew her intimately (Haldane for instance) agrees was the most selfless and un-worldly that they have ever encountered. She was warm, impulsive, naturally quick-tempered, and generous almost to a fault. . . . "[e]

Asquith was right about the difficulties of depiction. The picture he gives is not altogether clear. But there is no doubt that he lived contentedly with her for many years; and the talent of so many of their children was such that she must surely have contributed sub-stantially to the strain.

The first of these children, Raymond, was born in 1878. Partly on the basis of an effortless academic record which surpassed even that of his father, he left the memory of a figure of almost legendary talent when he was killed in 1916. The second son, Herbert (or Beb as he was known in the family) was born three years later. He followed his father and brother in becoming President of the Union, but not in their quality as classical scholars, although he made a minor reputation as a poet and novelist. The third son, Arthur (or Oc), born in 1883, was the least intellectual of the family. But he achieved distinction as a war-time soldier, reached the rank of Brigadier-General at 31, and was recommended for the Victoria Cross.

In 1887 Helen Asquith's only daughter, now Lady Violet Bonham Carter, was born. The conventions of her time and *milieu* denied her any opportunity for academic achievement, but she developed a political knowledge and oratorical power which have made her one of the outstanding women of her generation. The last child was Cyril, born in 1890. His academic record was still more memorable than that of his older brother.[1] Like Raymond and Herbert he went to the bar and rose to become a Lord of Appeal Ordinary before his relatively early death in 1954.

[1] The freemasonry of intellectual success within which Asquith family relations came to be conducted is perfectly summed up by the note which

At least three of these children were by any standards exceptional and the other two were in no way negligible figures. The one quality which their father failed to transmit to any of them (except to Violet, to whom it was of least use) was the sustained ambition which comes from a desire to influence the development of events. Here, perhaps, their mother's character played its part.

With the growth of his family—at least until 1883—greatly exceeding that of his practice, and with his Balliol fellowship expiring in 1881, Asquith's need for additional income became intense. At first his search for this had mainly to take the form of examining and teaching, and not at a particularly elevated level. For a few years he marked papers set by the Oxford and Cambridge Board for examinations at the public schools, and reviewed the work, amongst many others, of George Curzon at Eton and Austen Chamberlain at Rugby. Then he taught himself the rudiments of economics (a subject for which his sceptical and strictly non-mathematical mind gave him neither great affinity nor particular aptitude) in order that he might pass on the teaching of Marshall and Jevons to University Extension Classes at Wimbledon and Clapham and other suburbs. He also lectured in the law to audiences of would-be solicitors. In 1880 he gave a course in Chancery Lane on the law of insurance and carriage by land.

None of this work was either well-paid or intellectually stimulating to Asquith. He was not a natural teacher, for his lucidity was unmatched by any insistent desire to impart knowledge or to open the minds of others. Even as a political speaker he neither sought nor needed any very close relationship with his audience, and as an advocate he was always a little impatient (and consequently unskilled) in dealing with the whims of juries—and even of judges. He was therefore not sorry when it became possible to tilt the balance of his income-raising efforts towards writing, which had the additional advantage of being more remunerative. His attempt at publication within the field of his profession was unsuccessful however. He did a

---

Cyril received from Raymond when in 1908) he followed him (and his father) in winning the first Balliol scholarship:
> Dear Cyril,
>   Fancy you being as clever as—
>   Raymond.

lot of work in preparation of a manual on the law of carriage by sea, but was frustrated by the publication, before he was ready, of a definitive text-book on the subject, and consequently abandoned his own labours.

As was his habit. he met the setback with equanimity; and it was, in any event, balanced by the growth of an intimate connection with two leading weekly papers. The first was the *Spectator,* then under the joint editorship and proprietorship of Richard Holt Hutton and Meredith Townsend. They were an incongruous couple,[1] but they worked smoothly together and produced a successful paper, Liberal in politics but literary in much of its content, and almost all written by themselves. What was not written by them was written by a very few outside contributors, of whom Asquith was probably the most constant. His association with the paper was sufficiently close that when one or other of the two editors went away, he frequently moved in and helped to put the paper together. He wrote for them upon what he described as " almost every kind of topic—political, social, literary, economic,"*f* but the two essays which he chose subsequently to re-publish*g* were both on severely classical subjects—The Art of Tacitus and The Age of Demosthenes.

Asquith's *Spectator* period lasted for ten years. It began, tentatively, even before his call to the bar, and it continued, perhaps with lessening intensity towards the end, until 1886, the year of the Home Rule split in the Liberal Party. Although Hutton had hitherto been a Gladstone man almost without reserve, the paper then took a firmly Unionist line against the Prime Minister, and Asquith thought that political divergence on an issue of such importance made it necessary for him to sever his connection. A few years later the Hutton-Townsend partnership ended and the *Spectator* passed under the control of St. Loe Strachey with whom Asquith was on friendly terms, but with whom he agreed on little beyond free trade. He never renewed his contributions.

[1] " Ostensibly they had nothing in common," Asquith wrote of them: " Townsend, with his courtly Anglo-Indian air, tapping his snuff-box, and walking up and down his room, emitting dogmatic paradoxes: Hutton, more than short-sighted, looking out on external things through a monocle with an extra-powerful lens, and talking with the almost languid, donnish air of one who had in the old days breakfasted with Crabbe Robinson, and sat at the feet of Arthur Clough." (*Memories and Reflections,* I, p. 68.)

Helen Melland, Asquith's first wife

The young Home Secretary—Asquith in 1894

At the end of the 'seventies, Hutton and Townsend, as well as using Asquith's work themselves, had introduced him to the *Economist*. The *Economist* was then jointly edited by Palgrave and Lathbury but continued to live under the shadow of Walter Bagehot who had died, still in the editorial chair, only in 1877. Asquith's work for this paper became more regular than for the *Spectator*, but the connection (as it appears from his subsequent writings about the period[h]) was a more work-a-day and less enjoyable one for him. He was retained at a salary of £150 a year, and in return for this he wrote, almost every week, one of the paper's two leading articles. He found no difficulty in striking the note of rational radicalism which was called for by the paper's tradition. This connection came to an end in 1885, but because of the growth of his work at the bar and not of any political disagreement.

The first turning point in his legal career came in 1883. Until then he was short of money, under-employed, and full of surplus intellectual energy. The first shortage, as has already been indicated, led to no great privation. His way of life in Hampstead may have been simple but it was not such as to cut him off from social contacts with those he then knew or wanted to know. Nor did it preclude regular visits to the theatre and fairly frequent journeys abroad, sometimes with and sometimes without his wife. With his wife he went mostly to Germany and Switzerland, but with male companions, often at Easter time, he used to go further south, to Provence, to the Riviera and to Tuscany. His friends were almost all the old ones of Oxford days, although Mark Napier, the son of a diplomat peer and another occupant of the chambers in Fig-Tree Court, became a close one and a frequent visitor to Hampstead.

Then, in 1881, Asquith's intimacy with Haldane began. This was a friendship of great importance which lasted throughout the middle years of his life. R. B. Haldane, at this stage, was a rather clumsy young Scotsman of twenty-five. He came of nonconformist stock like Asquith himself, but his family were much more firmly established in the upper ranks of the middle class, and he had the advantage of some private money. Instead of going to Oxford (the Anglican influence of which was feared by his father) he had studied at Edinburgh, Göttingen and Dresden and had acquired in the course of these wanderings a strong and persistent taste for rather cloudy metaphysics. This was alien to the bent of Asquith's own mind, which was always more lucid and less speculative than Haldane's. But there were many other things which bound them together. Haldane had come to London in 1877 and had gone to the Chancery bar. Although his first success came a little earlier than Asquith's (he was earning £1,000 a year by 1883), when they first met he was almost equally briefless. They both shared a deep interest in politics, and an attachment to the moderate left of the Liberal Party. Here Asquith's interest was perhaps the greater, for Haldane, who stated bluntly in his *Autobiography* that Asquith " from the beginning ... meant to be Prime Minister," was probably more concerned with the law for its own sake and not merely as a stepping stone to politics. For neither was he as well endowed as Asquith. His diction was even cloudier than his metaphysics, and as he himself freely admitted he had "no attractive presence" and "a bad voice." Despite these deficiencies, and the fact that he was four years younger, he was at this time a little further ahead than Asquith, not only in the law but also in politics.

He was the first secretary of the Eighty Club, which took its name from the year of Gladstone's second accession to power. It was originally composed of a group of young Liberals with radical and mildly imperialist leanings who had begun meeting under the leadership of Albert (later 4th Earl) Grey, the grandson of the Reform Bill Prime Minister, but who later found him too erratic and seceded to found the club on their own. It was not only a dining club, which entertained guests ranging from George Meredith to Charles Parnell, but also an organisation providing speakers for meetings in the country. Asquith became a member about a year after its foundation, having recently met Haldane at dinner in Lincoln's Inn. A few months afterwards Haldane, "most uncharacteristically" as Asquith put it, fell ill and went to stay with his new friend in Hampstead for a long period of semi-convalescence. This visit established their intimacy. Thereafter for many years they dined together several times a week, travelled abroad in each other's company, consulted together on every political issue, and on many legal ones too. The friendship was the closest which Asquith ever developed with any man.

Haldane was also a great favourite with Asquith's family. His exuberance and generosity of spirit, aided rather than hindered by physical characteristics which tended always to make him a faint figure of fun, produced strong private charm of a kind which was as accessible to children as to adults. Lady Violet Bonham Carter, in an article which she contributed to *The Times* on the centenary of his birth[i] has testified to its effect upon herself and her brothers. She also told of an occasion—a striking example of surplus intellectual energy—when Haldane got a rare brief (concerning the alleged infestation of some property by rats), and both he and her father, who had not received one of his own for months, sat up for nearly a whole night at Hampstead, preparing every possible ramification of the case.

Behind this exuberance of Haldane's there was a deep intellectual curiosity and seriousness of purpose. At this stage he found these characteristics matched by Asquith's own, although as the form in which he recorded this indicates, he came to believe that there was later a change in Asquith. " He had as fine an intellectual apparatus, in the way of grasp and understanding," Haldane wrote, " as I ever saw in any man. In his earlier political days he was a very serious person. I remember once passing along the Horse Guards with him. He touched my arm and pointed to the figure of John Bright walking in front of us. ' There,' he said, ' is the only man in public life who has risen to eminence without being corrupted by London Society '."[j]

There was intended to be a dark hint for the future in Haldane's recollection of this remark, but at the time at which it was made, if there was any corruption of Asquith taking place it was Haldane himself, as much as anyone, who was doing it. It was he rather than Asquith who had a gourmet's taste and was already becoming a large buyer of fine clarets and champagnes. It was he too who had the greater knowledge of Europe and of the political and even the social world at home.

Asquith began to catch up only after the improvement of his legal prospects in 1883. This occurred as a result of the appointment, after an interval, of R. S. Wright to Bowen's old job as Junior Counsel to the Treasury. Wright, although he did not know him well, immediately asked Asquith to become his " devil." The offer was enthusiastically accepted, and Asquith moved from the ungrateful chambers in Fig Tree Court to join Wright at 1, Paper Buildings, where he remained until his final retirement from the bar in 1905.

Wright was like Bowen in being a Balliol man, a classicist, a favourite of Jowett's—who died in his house—and in proceeding subsequently straight from the junior bar to the bench. But he was unlike him in being a plodding, eccentric introvert rather than a captain-of-the-school figure with splendid all-round gifts. He was not much in court, and his normal routine was to sit all day in his chambers with a tall hat on his head and a briar pipe in his mouth, working almost continuously from six in the morning until nine at night, except for breakfast and dinner visits to the Reform Club.

There is no evidence that Asquith ever achieved any real friendship with Wright, but the connection was nevertheless immensely valuable to him. It gave Asquith a political as well as a legal *entrée*. Wright worked closely to the Attorney-General, Sir Henry James, to whom he owed his own appointment,[1] and this agreeable, urbane and pleasure-loving Whig, who was Gladstone's favourite law officer, soon recognised Asquith's quality and established with him an ease of relationship which was possible for neither of them with the intermediate Wright.

One of Asquith's first tasks for the Attorney was almost perfectly suited to his abilities and his interests. By 1883 the Bradlaugh case had dragged on for three years, destroying the effectiveness of the Parliament and draining away a sizeable proportion both of the energy and the authority of the Prime Minister. Gladstone had decided to try to end the matter by passing an Affirmation Bill, and he asked James for a memorandum on the legal and constitutional significance of the parliamentary oath. By a protracted process of devolution Asquith was asked to prepare this. The result, after much effort on his part, was a highly authoritative survey, written in his own peculiar combination of lucid and architectonic English. James was delighted to be able to produce (with suitable acknowledgment) such an impressive product of someone else's labour,[2] and the Prime Minister who admired lucidity in others and an architectonic style in every one, was fully satisfied. Thereafter Asquith had the confidence of James and the notice of Gladstone—whose memory was soon afterwards fortified by hearing him speak at a dinner of the Eighty Club.

---

[1] James no doubt thought that there would be advantages in securing an assistant whose qualities were so nearly the opposite of his own. Wright continued to work with James after he had ceased to be Attorney-General, and in 1886, fortified by Sir Charles Russell, the foremost advocate of the day, who had succeeded as Attorney and was later to be Lord Chief Justice of England, they proceeded jointly to give Sir Charles Dilke some of the worst professional advice that any man can ever have received.

[2] He kept the manuscript and—a characteristic gesture—gave it as a wedding present to Asquith's second wife.

For a year or two these new connections brought Asquith more in the way of political opportunities and legal promise than of real rewards. In 1884 he wrote and had published by the Liberal Central Association a short guide for election agents to the Corrupt Practices Act which placed the first limit on the expenses of candidates and which James had just piloted through the House of Commons. By 1885, however, he was beginning to secure some briefs of his own. These came mainly from solicitors who used regularly to instruct Wright, and had got to know Asquith in this way; but as these solicitors included firms who acted for several of the big railway companies—which at that time were both prosperous and litigious—they offered a connection of great potential value. Then, when the general election of December, 1885, produced its usual crop of disputed returns, Asquith found that his corrupt practices manual was yielding more than royalties and that he was retained in almost all cases as junior counsel for the Liberal candidate. By the spring of 1886, at the age of 33, and with ten years' standing as a barrister, he was at last able to earn a moderate income and occupy most of his time by professional work.

CHAPTER III

A SURE THRUST TO FAME

1886-90

Asquith gave himself no opportunity to consolidate this long-awaited and modest legal success. In July, 1886, within a few months of the briefs and fees beginning to arrive, he became a Member of Parliament.

The connection between politics and the law was then much more intimate than it is today. Almost every leader of the bar sought and achieved a period in the House of Commons as an essential step in his career. This applied not only to men like Sir William Harcourt, Sir Henry James or Sir Hardinge Gifford (later Lord Halsbury), who had strong views on matters of policy and who attached as much or greater importance to political as to legal advancement. It applied also to those whose interest was primarily legal, to men like Sir Charles Russell (the prototype of a fashionable advocate), Sir Richard Webster and Sir Horace Davey. This was partly because the road to legal preferment then lay much more directly through politics. There were vast fees to be earned by the law officers; the Lord Chancellorship was a highly coveted position; the office of Lord Chief Justice was known as " the Attorney-General's pillow " (both Russell and Webster laid their heads upon it); and a high proportion of appeal and *puisne* judges were men who had sat for a short time in the House of Commons and had been appointed during one of their party's periods of office.

Parliament was therefore regarded as a natural place for an established barrister to go. But it was also regarded as a presumptuous and dangerous one for a junior with an insecure position—particularly if he had no private fortune. It fitted in with and was likely to improve the practice of a sought-after Queen's Counsel. It could more easily damage that of a little known member of the outer bar, whose one strength ought to be that of complete availability. In fact, Asquith's experience ran contrary to the accepted rule and he probably improved his earning power by going into the House of Commons. But it was difficult for him to foresee this, and by his action in 1886 he ran a big risk of losing what he had built up in the previous three years.

He did so at the insistent prompting of Haldane, who, without a family and a little more secure at the bar, had already taken the same step a few months earlier. He had been elected for the East Lothian or Haddington division at the general election of December, 1885. This election was the first to be fought under the extended franchise in the counties, which had been introduced in 1884, and the new distribution of seats, which became law in the spring of the following year. It was delayed for some months to allow the latter measure to come into operation. The second Gladstone Government had been defeated on the Budget in June and had made way for a minority administration under Lord Salisbury. This Conservative Government held office during six months of complicated manoeuvre and realignment on the Irish question, the net result of which was that Parnell delivered much of the Nationalist vote in the large English towns to the Conservatives, and Gladstone became committed to Home Rule.

Partly as a consequence of this short-lived Irish flirtation with Lord Salisbury, the Liberal majority was much smaller than had been expected. And it was by no means clear how much of it would accept Gladstone's conversion to Home Rule. What was certain was that there was a majority in the new House of Commons for other aspects of the Liberal programme. When Jesse Collings moved his "three acres and a cow" amendment to the address at the end of January, the Conservative Government was heavily defeated, and Gladstone became Prime Minister for the third time. The Whig opponents of Home Rule, represented by Hartington, Goschen and Henry James, refused to serve. The Radical Unionists (to give them a title they had not then assumed) doubtfully accepted office, although Gladstone committed the major mistake of not giving their leader, Joseph Chamberlain, an office from which he would have been reluctant to resign. In March, when the details of the Home Rule Bill were before the Cabinet, both he and G. O. Trevelyan left the Government. The prospects of the bill were further weakened at the end of May when John Bright declared his opposition. On June 8th, 1886, the second reading was defeated by 343 to 313. 93 members who had been elected as Liberals voted against the Government, and Gladstone

39

advised an immediate dissolution of the six-month-old Parliament.

These were the circumstances in which Asquith fought his first election. One of the dissident 93 was Boyd Kinnear, the member for East Fife. He was a local laird, a writer of some note, and a radical; he had followed Chamberlain rather than Hartington into the division lobby against the Prime Minister. But this fact did not propitiate the local Liberal Association, who were firmly Gladstonian. They passed a vote of no confidence in Boyd Kinnear and called for a new candidate. They needed one in a hurry, and Haldane, established as member for the neighbouring county and with family connections extending over most of the eastern half of the Scottish Lowlands, was able to put forward Asquith's name. The East Fife Association met on June 26th and decided by a large majority to offer him the nomination. The invitation was received and accepted on the following day, a Saturday. Polling was then only ten days away, and the strictest Sabbatarianism was necessary upon two of them. There has not often been more of a shot-gun marriage between a member and his constituency.

East Fife was then a peculiarly isolated part of Eastern Scotland. Although its southern flank comes within ten miles of the centre of Edinburgh, the Forth Bridge had not been built, and access was only by ferry. On the north, the Tay Bridge, leading to Dundee, which had collapsed while a train was crossing on a stormy night in 1881, had not been replaced. Within the constituency the only effective means of transport was by horse-drawn carriage, which did little to ease the problems of a candidate who had to attempt a whirlwind campaign. There was no central town, for St. Andrews and Cupar, although geographically included, were electorally distinct in the separate constituency of St. Andrews Burghs. Most of the population—engaged in fishing, farming, a little mining and the dying industry of hand-loom weaving—lived in scattered townships and villages. Ladybank and Auchtermuchty were the biggest of them.

The tradition of the constituency was firmly Liberal. The undivided county had not returned a Tory since 1832, and Boyd Kinnear in the new East division had obtained a big majority in 1885. In the 1886 election he stood again, although this time of course as a Liberal Unionist and, in accordance with the agreement made between Salisbury and the Liberal Unionist leaders, without Conservative opposition. Asquith's task was to secure a sufficient majority of regular Liberal voters to outweigh the Conservatives who came to the aid of Kinnear.

This was by no means an insuperable one, for many Tories, whatever their leaders might say, were reluctant to vote for a man who only six months before had fought under the dangerously radical banners which Chamberlain was then fashioning for his supporters. And in his wooing of the Liberal electors Asquith had the advantages of the Scottish prestige of Gladstone, who was campaigning only a few miles away in Midlothian; of the natural allegiance of the constituency; and of his own unusual gifts of speech and argument. At this election the first two were probably the more powerful, for in the time available he could address only a few scattered meetings, and some of these were as hostile at the end as they had been at the beginning. The liabilities he had to overcome were those of being an unknown, " carpet-bagging " Englishman[1]. But the advantages more than outweighed them and he was returned by the modest majority of 2,862 to 2,487. Thereafter, until 1918, his majorities were fluctuating and mostly small, but never disappeared.

Throughout Scotland the policy to which Asquith had committed himself (in his election address he said he was an " advanced Liberal " and an uncompromising Home Ruler) did reasonably well, but in England there was a heavy swing against Gladstone. The overall results gave 316 seats to the Conservatives and 78 to the Liberal Unionists, as against 191 to the Gladstonians and 85 to the Irish Nationalists. Lord Salisbury, who succeeded immediately as Prime Minister, had a large majority if the Liberal Unionists voted with him and a small one if they abstained. If they voted against him he would have been out, but in a Parliament dominated by Irish questions there was little danger of their doing so. Nevertheless they were not part

---

[1] It was not then as great a disadvantage in the circumstances to be an Englishman as it would be today, when English members for Scottish seats are very rare birds indeed. Apart from Asquith himself, John Morley, Augustine Birrell and Winston Churchill, to cite only Liberal politicians of the first prominence, all sat for Scottish constituencies during the next twenty-five years. Birrell sat for the other part of the County of Fife, and on one occasion in about 1900 when he and Asquith and Haldane had climbed to the top of a hill near the Firth of Forth which commanded a wide view over both Fife and East Lothian, he turned to the others and exclaimed: " What a grateful thought that there is not an acre in this vast and varied landscape which is not represented at Westminster by a London barrister! " (*Memories and Reflections*, I, p. 105.)

of the Government and their leaders continued to sit on the front opposition bench.

Asquith's first Parliament therefore presented the bizarre spectacle of Chamberlain and Hartington, two of the firmest upholders of the Government's policy on the main issue of the day, sitting alongside the leader of the opposition, and often attacking him bitterly from the same despatch box at which he had just spoken.[1] Opposite, for a short time, sat Lord Randolph Churchill, who at 37 had forced his way to the leadership of the House, but who lasted barely six months before his precipitate resignation from the Government. He was succeeded as leader by W. H. Smith and as Chancellor of the Exchequer by Goschen, the first of the Liberal Unionists to serve under Salisbury. As the Parliament wore on, Arthur Balfour, who was appointed Chief Secretary for Ireland in 1887, became an increasingly dominant member of the Government. He amazed the Irish by the ruthlessness of his policy and the House by the tenacity of his debating; his *sobriquet* changed from Pretty Fanny to Bloody Balfour.

Asquith succeeded from the first in making the maximum of impact upon the parliamentary scene with the expenditure of the minimum of effort. Surprisingly, his background of achievement, relatively much less great in 1886 than it had been in 1876, did him far more good in Parliament than it had done him in his early years at the bar. The House of Commons, always tritely said to be contemptuous of outside reputations, showed that it did not mind provided the fame was not genuine. For Asquith did not really have an outside reputation in 1886. But the House treated him from the first as though he did. The point is neatly put by his official biographers, " It was often said of Asquith," they wrote, " . . . that he was never a member of the rank and file. From the start he assumed the manner of a front bencher and the House accepted him at his own valuation."[a]

He made no speech until he had been a member for nearly nine months. The occasion he then chose was a full-dress debate on a

[1] Asquith described the exact allocation of seats in the following terms: " Mr. Gladstone sat opposite the box in the leader's place, with Sir W. Harcourt or Mr. John Morley on his left to act as a kind of buffer. Occupying the seats nearest the gangway were the Liberal Unionist chiefs—Lord Hartington, Mr. Chamberlain, Sir Henry James, Mr. Heneage. On the other side of Mr. Gladstone were the old colleagues who had remained faithful to him." (*Memories and Reflections*, I, p. 117).

motion to give precedence over all other business to an Irish Crimes Bill. It was Balfour's first major debate as Chief Secretary. Asquith delivered his maiden speech to a full House late on the third night, March 24th, 1887. It made a profound impression. Haldane refers to it in his *Autobiography* as "a brilliant maiden speech (which) · turned towards him the attention of the public as well as the Liberal leaders in the House."[b] Immediately afterwards Asquith wrote to his wife:

> *House of Commons,*
> *24 March 1887*
>
> My dearest love,
> I must just send you a line to say that I took the plunge tonight about 10.30 before a good house, and spoke for about half an hour. I was listened to very well & everyone says it was a great success. Joe Chamberlain who followed was very polite and complimentary—In haste
> Ever yr. own husband,
> *Herbert*

Read now, the speech is remarkable more for the note of authority which crept into the phrasing than for the argument, powerful and sustained though that was. Asquith succeeded in assuming—and this is perhaps the main characteristic of a front-bench style—that the interest of a statement lay in the fact that he was making it, and not merely in its own inherent wisdom. His words were obviously carefully prepared, which was not often the case with his later speeches, even on major issues. Both qualities are illustrated by the following passage:

As to the prevalence of crime, having regard to these admitted facts, I say deliberately that this is a manufactured crisis. We know by experience how a case for coercion is made out. The panicmongers of the press—gentlemen to whom every political combination is a conspiracy, and to whom every patriot is a rebel—were the first in the field. They have been most effectively assisted on the present occasion on the other side of the Channel, by the purveyors of loyal fiction and patriotic hysterics, wholesale, retail and for exportation. The truth, whatever truth there is in the stories, is deliberately distorted and exaggerated. Atrocities are fabricated to meet the requirements of the market with punctuality and despatch; and when the home supply fails, the imagination of the inventive journalist wings its flight across the Atlantic and he sets to work to piece together the stale gossip of the drinking saloons in New York and Chicago, and ekes it out with cuttings from obscure organs of the dynamite press.[c]

This successful beginning led to no unleashing of Asquith's parliamentary tongue. He continued throughout the Parliament to speak only two or three times a year,[1] mainly on Irish questions, although occasionally on other ingredients of " advanced Liberalism "—the payment of Members of Parliament or the removal of a religious qualification for the Lord Chancellorship, both of England and of Ireland. But he never did any parliamentary drudgery, and Harcourt in 1890 wrote to Morley complaining of " Asquith who will never do a day's work for us in the House."[d] Even with Harcourt, however, who was a great complainer, there is no evidence that this fastidiousness ever did him any real harm. He spoke in the country rather more often than he did in the House (this indeed was what provoked Harcourt, who had disliked one of his platform pronouncements), and he was skilful in choosing his occasions so as to produce a considerable impact.

One of his first and most striking successes of this sort was at the Nottingham meeting of the National Liberal Federation in October, 1887. The issue within the party at the time was the possibility of Liberal reunion, and Asquith came out firmly against making too many concessions to the dissidents. " It was a very good thing to do what they could to recover the lost sheep. Henry IV had said that Paris was worth a Mass. But they might pay too high a price even for the capitulation of Birmingham."[e] And he went on, speaking in the presence of Gladstone, to pay a tribute to him which showed that, when necessary, he could indulge fully in the art of rhetorical peroration. " (His) presence at our head," Asquith said, " is worth a hundred battalions. To the youngest it is an inspiration, to the oldest an example, to one and all a living lesson of devotion, hopefulness and vitality.

[1] Rather oddly, in the circumstances, he recalls in the chapter in his memoirs entitled *Parliamentary Novitiate*, Charles James Fox's advice that the way to become a good House of Commons speaker was to speak every night on every subject. (*Memories and Reflections*, I, p. 110). But this was in relation to Balfour. Presumably he thought, quite rightly, that he himself needed neither the advice nor the practice.

Let us rejoice that one survivor of the heroic age of English politics has entered on the last struggle of a life spent on the battlefields of freedom; and let us, lesser men of a later day, be proud that in such an enterprise and under such omens we are permitted to obey his summons and follow when he leads."*f* The applause was naturally tumultuous, but the more critical minds were also impressed. " Eloquent and powerful," was Morley's comment.

In Parliament at this time Asquith worked closely with a group of five or six near contemporaries. These included Haldane, Edward Grey and Arthur Acland, who had all come into the House in 1885, and Tom Ellis and Sydney Buxton, who had arrived at the same time as Asquith. Although Asquith was by no means the senior, either in age or in parliamentary experience, it was under his leadership, Haldane testifies, that the group drew together. Its members shared a common outlook on most questions of the day, and tried to fill in some of the gaps in Liberal policy which resulted from Gladstone's pre-occupation with Ireland. Occasionally this brought them into mild conflict with the leadership. Haldane and Grey, in particular, were inclined to pursue a very independent course in the division lobbies, but Asquith was usually more cautious, partly, Haldane rather felinely suggested, because " he had fewer views of his own than most of us."*g* However, he abstained from voting in support of the Opposition's attack on the Attorney-General in March 1889 for his activities as advocate for *The Times* before the Parnell Enquiry,[1] and, together with the other Liberal lawyers who had done the same, incurred another portion of Harcourt's wrath. " These are the gentlemen," the latter wrote, " who call out for ' more vigour.' The truth is, what they like is to stand by with their hands in their pockets and order the front bench to do all the fighting and then abuse them for their pains."

With Harcourt the group never had very close or easy relations. He was too much of a Parliamentary " bruiser," always more interested in tactics than in ideas, for their tastes. But with Morley, whose more intimate contact with Gladstone gave him much of the status of first lieutenant, they felt a greater affinity. In many ways, indeed, they looked to him as their political mentor, and he was a frequent guest at the dinners which (rather obscurely calling themselves the " Articles

[1] See *infra*, pp. 48-50. Asquith may have been influenced by his own involvement in the case (although on the other side), as well as by professional solidarity.

Club ") they began to hold in 1888, sometimes at the Savoy Hotel and sometimes at the National Liberal Club. " We young Liberals looked up to him with deep respect," Haldane wrote.

This respect helped to keep the group from getting too far out of touch with the official leadership of the party. But in many ways the affinity upon which the group thought it to be based was a false one. Morley had the glamour of a great literary reputation and the intellectual attraction of a subtle and cultivated mind. But his political outlook was basically different from that of the group. They were social reformers. Haldane, Acland and Ellis were all deeply interested in education; Buxton, who sat for Poplar, was much concerned with sweated labour and housing; and Asquith shared the interests of his friends. On all these matters Morley's outlook was strictly Gladstonian. His concern with what his chief rather incredulously and distastefully described as " construction " was always minimal.

In addition the group soon began to develop imperialist leanings. They were as opposed to Little Englandism abroad as they were to a purely negative Liberalism at home. In Haldane's case, and to some extent in Asquith's too, this sprang from the nature of their legal practices. They were much involved in arguing Colonial appeals before the Privy Council. This gave them a close interest in the systems of government and practices of life in what Dilke had called Greater Britain; and it divided them sharply from Morley, who was every bit as much of a Little Englander as Harcourt. It also made them draw closer to Lord Rosebery, who was their other favourite guest at the Savoy Hotel or National Liberal Club dinners, and who had been an active participant in the affairs of the Imperial Federation League since soon after its inception in 1885. In 1889 Asquith joined the League, and provoked some further displeasure. " Spencer was very angry about Asquith joining the Imperial League," Harcourt wrote, " and said he was greatly disappointed in him."[h]

Haldane and Asquith also organised a series of dinners which, while still rigidly masculine, were less austerely political in purpose than those of the Articles Club. These took place annually at the Blue Posts inn, off Cork Street, and the normal practice was for the two hosts to invite four prominent politicians, and four other men who were eminent for other reasons. Rosebery recorded in his diary for an evening in 1889: " Dined with Asquith and Haldane at the Blue Posts. Sate (sic) next A. Balfour. Took John Morley on to the

National Liberal Club Reception."[i]   Other politicians who attended included Chamberlain, Randolph Churchill, Grey and Carson. Amongst the non-politicians were Bowen, Burne-Jones, Alfred Lyall and Russell Lowell. These dinners continued until 1892. They indicated both that the hosts had a parliamentary position which enabled them to command the attendance of important guests and that they were anxious to enlarge their social circle. In Asquith's case, in particular, there was room for this. Throughout the late 'eighties he continued to live quietly in Hampstead, although in 1887 he moved to a larger, more modern, less attractive house at 27, Maresfield Gardens, off Fitzjohn's Avenue. He was a figure of note in the House of Commons, but he moved in no general society. Almost the only women he knew were the wives of his Oxford and legal friends, a restriction made greater by the fact that so many of these friends were bachelors.

Asquith's practice at the bar, as already indicated, benefited rather than suffered from his election to Parliament. But it took no bound forward during his first few years in the House. Since his call he had been a member of the North-Eastern circuit, which was centred on Leeds and which he had chosen, there being no obvious alternative, on the slender ground of his old Yorkshire connection. He had always been a half-hearted circuit-goer, for he had no taste for the criminal and jury work which it involved; and, particularly after his election, his practice was almost entirely in London and on the civil side. Much of his work was in the appellate courts. It was an unexciting, moderate sized, high quality practice. In 1888 he began to take pupils, and one of the first, John Roskill, later a judge, recorded that " before he took Silk in 1890 he was not in a very large practice and often gave his pupils Wright's papers as well as his own." Roskill added that " his clients were of the best."[j]   They yielded him £1,500 or £2,000 a year.

Most of Asquith's legal (as opposed to his political) work at this time brought him no public notice of any sort. There were occasional exceptions arising out of his rare forays to the Central Criminal Court. In 1889 he unsuccessfully defended Cunninghame Graham, the Scottish laird and Labour M.P., who, with John Burns, was charged with unlawful assembly as a result of the events of " Bloody Sunday " in Trafalgar Square; and in the following year—a rather less liberal cause—he successfully prosecuted Vizetelly, the English publisher of Zola's novels, for the offence of obscene libel.

His next major advance came suddenly and dramatically in February, 1889, when he was junior counsel to Sir Charles Russell before the Parnell Commission of Enquiry. As long previously as April 18th, 1887, *The Times* had published a facsimile print of a letter dated 1882 and apparently signed by Charles Stewart Parnell, in which the Irish leader expressed his approval for the Phoenix Park murder of Frederick Burke, the permanent under-secretary in the Dublin Castle administration. Although this was damaging to the Nationalist cause, Parnell contented himself at the time with a House of Commons announcement that the letter was a forgery and did not take up the challenge of the editor of *The Times* to test the matter in a libel action. In July, 1888, F. H. O'Donnell, who had been an Irish member of the previous Parliament and who was also implicated in the charges made by *The Times*, took such an action. In the course of the case, which O'Donnell lost without the London jury troubling to leave the box, further letters which were still more damaging to Parnell were read out. His reaction to these was still (and probably wisely) to avoid the English law courts, but to make a personal statement in the House of Commons demanding that a Select Committee be set up. The Government countered with the quite different offer of a Commission of three judges (all of them known Unionists) charged with enquiring not merely into the alleged forgeries but into all the accusations against the Nationalist Party made by *The Times*—in other words, into almost the whole recent course of Irish history. This procedure, as strongly opposed by the Liberals as by the Nationalists, had eventually to be accepted. The Attorney-General, free then to engage in private practice as well as official duties, was briefed by *The Times*. Parnell countered with Russell and Asquith. The selection of Asquith was made more on political than on legal grounds and was influenced by the strong speech against the composition and terms of reference of the Commission which he had made in the House.

The work of the Commission was above all else a marathon. It began sitting on September 18th, 1888 and took evidence on 128 days. The crux of the matter, the question of the forged letters, was not reached until the sixth month. It then took Russell only two days to demolish Pigott, the purveyor of the letters to *The Times*. With his cross-examination still incomplete, Piggott fled to Paris, leaving behind him two confessions which were in many respects discrepant but which were agreed in admitting that all the letters purporting to be from Parnell were forgeries. A week later he shot himself in a Madrid hotel.

Parnell's vindication was complete. For a short time he became almost a popular hero with the British public. The city of Edinburgh made him a freeman; the Liberal Party gave him a standing ovation in the House of Commons; and even *The Times* formally withdrew all the charges which were based upon the letters. Although the Commission was to drag on for another year, only one point of major interest remained to be elucidated. This was how a newspaper of the standing of *The Times* had ever come to accept and publish documents of such outstanding importance from so obviously tainted a source.

The vital witness on this point was C. J. Macdonald, then the manager of the paper—Buckle was editor. Asquith has described in his own words what happened when the examination-in-chief of this witness was complete:

It would of course naturally have fallen to Russell to cross-examine him; and I was never more surprised in my life than when, just as the court rose for lunch, he turned to me and said: " I am tired: you must take charge of this fellow." I protested, but in vain, and I was left to the critical task of conducting the cross-examination: a task all the more formidable because my leader, the greatest cross-examiner at the English Bar, sat there throughout and listened. I got on to what proved to be an effective and even a destructive line of attack, and in the course of a couple of hours or so made the largest step in advance that I ever took in my forensic career. Russell, who throughout had not interrupted by suggestion or otherwise, was unmeasured in his appreciation of every successful point, and when I finished almost overwhelmed me with the generosity of his praises and his congratulation. It was a moment that will never fade from my memory . . .[k]

What Asquith had established in the course of this cross-examination, apart from his own reputation as an advocate, was that Macdonald had undertaken no investigation of the authenticity of the letters, and had behaved throughout with a credulity which would have been childlike had it not been criminally negligent. Roskill wrote that Asquith " often said that Macdonald was the easiest witness he had ever demolished, for his prejudices had literally obscured an honest, if limited, understanding "[l]; but easy or not there can be no doubt that

Asquith's interrogation of him, unprepared though it was, was conducted with a mounting and deadly precision.

The crisis of the enquiry over, Russell and Asquith abandoned regular attendance at its now dreary proceedings. Asquith for the first time in his career, found himself flooded with briefs. Less than a year later, again prompted by Haldane, who was taking the same step himself, he decided to apply for silk, and was admitted as a Queen's Counsel in February, 1890, at the age of 37.

As a silk Asquith was an immediate and considerable success. Some barristers build up large practices as juniors which they fail to maintain when they are called within the bar. With him the reverse was the case. The few months after the Macdonald cross-examination apart, he was much busier as a Queen's Counsel than he ever had been as a junior—and his fees were of course much larger. His income rose to about £5,000 a year.

He was also in the happy position that the occasion which had made his legal reputation had in addition improved his political standing. In the days of the " union of hearts " it was a great advantage within his party for a Liberal M.P. to have played a leading part in unmasking the anti-Irish machinations of *The Times*. And the prospects of the party itself had been improved by Parnell's vindication. The by-election results were encouraging, and up to the summer of 1890 the chances of a great Home Rule majority, whenever the dissolution came, looked strong. So were Asquith's prospects of a major post in the Government which would give effect to the policy. He was indulging in no foolish day-dreaming when he told Roskill, one evening about this time, that he would not accept a judgeship, but wished to be Home Secretary.

CHAPTER IV

A WIDER STAGE

1890-92

This untroubled prospect and calm advance of all the aspects of Asquith's life did not continue without interruption. The autumns of 1890 and 1891 each brought upheaval, the one public and the other private. In November, 1890, the O'Shea divorce suit, in which Parnell was cited as co-respondent, was heard. Parnell's easy assurances that nothing damaging against him would emerge proved unfounded. Gladstone declined to act as a censor of morals—such a role would have been inappropriate as he had known about Parnell's relationship with Mrs. O'Shea since the early 'eighties—but he was forced by Nonconformist opinion to make it known to the Irish that Parnell's continued leadership would make his own position impossible. The " union of hearts " was then dissolved in the bitter wranglings of Committee Room Fifteen. The Nationalists split into 26 " Parnellites " and 44 " anti-Parnellites." The cohesion of the Home Rule forces was greatly damaged, and so were the prospects of the Liberal Party at the following general election. The tide of by-election successes ceased to flow, and the chances of a decisive majority faded. By Christmas Morley reported that never in his life had he seen Gladstone so depressed.[a]

This change in the outlook affected Gladstone far more than it did Asquith. The latter was not an old man and he was rarely accused of being in a hurry. Nor, firmly " Parnellite " though he was,[1] did he

[1] After Parnell's death Asquith wrote: " I still regard him—measured by his opportunities and his achievements—as one of the half-dozen great men of action of this century. Napoleon stands by himself. . . . But the only other of this age that I would rank higher than Parnell are Abraham Lincoln, Bismarck, and (perhaps) Cavour." (Letter to Margot Tennant, written in October, 1891). And he consistently took the view that, had he been an

suffer from an Irish obsession. A setback, both to Home Rule and to his party's immediate prospects, did not greatly affect the assumptions on which his life was based.

The second upheaval, occurring in September, 1891, was of a quite different order. On August 13th of that year he took his wife and children to Lamlash in the Isle of Arran for a Scottish holiday. A week later his second son fell ill with influenza. Two days after this Helen Asquith was infected. It was assumed that her illness was the same as her son's. In consequence five days elapsed before a doctor was called in. His diagnosis was not influenza but typhoid. The son recovered but the mother did not. After three weeks of fluctuating illness she died on Friday, September 11th. On the Monday she was buried in the local churchyard. On the Wednesday Asquith returned to Hampstead with his five children, the oldest of them twelve and the youngest eighteen months. Apart from a bare record of events the only comment which he commited to the brief diary which he kept at the time was " *infelix atque infaustum iter,*" written in the margin against the date of the departure for Lamlash.

Such austere classicism of expression now suggests a certain want of feeling. But there is no reason to suspect this. A Roman reserve was always natural to Asquith. He fought against any expression of his stronger feelings. He even failed to convey them to Raymond, then nearly thirteen, and a certain persistent constraint in the relationship between father and son set in as a result. But of course the feelings existed. No one could fail to have been deeply affected by the drama of his wife's illness on the lonely Scottish island, culminating in the removal of the mother of his five young children. But neither the circumstances nor the consequences were necessary to enhance the tragedy. He was bound to his wife by nearly twenty years of unforced intimacy, and he never spoke of her, either before or after her death except in terms of affection and admiration. At the same time there is inevitably the suspicion that a certain incompatibility, if not of temperament at least of way of life, had developed between them by 1891. The frankest available account of their latter day relationship is contained in a letter which he wrote to Mrs. Horner (later Raymond Asquith's

---

Irishman, he would have been with John Redmond in supporting Parnell, and not with Justin Macarthy in opposing him.

mother-in-law) on the first anniversary of his wife's death. Mrs. Horner had never known her and Asquith began with a series of moving and convincing tributes to her sweetness and generosity of character.[1] Then he continued with an account of her attitude to his expanding horizons:

She cared little for society, shrank from every kind of publicity and self-advertisement, hardly knew what ambition meant. She was more wrapped up in her children than any woman I have ever known. To me she was always perfect, loyal, sympathetic, devoted; not without pride in such successes as I had; but not the least anxious for me to " get on," never sanguine or confident, and as a rule inclined to take a less hopeful view of things. I used sometimes to reproach her with her " pessimism." What has happened to me lately would have given her little real pleasure; indeed, I doubt whether, if she had been here, I would have taken such a step. She was the gentlest and best of companions, a restricting rather than a stimulating influence, and knowing myself as I do I have often wondered that we walked so evenly together. I was only eighteen when I fell in love with her, and we married when we were little more than boy and girl. In the cant phrase our marriage was a " great success "; from first to last it was never clouded by any kind of sorrow or dissension; and when the sun went down it was in an unclouded sky.

Could such an unclouded relationship have persisted indefinitely, in view of Asquith's thrusting ambition on the one hand, and his wife's complete lack of interest in worldly success on the other? His view, expressed in the letter, that had she lived he might not have accepted Cabinet office in the following year may perhaps be dismissed as permissibly exaggerated. But what is certain is that in the twelve months or so before her death both his pattern of existence and his outlook on life were changing sharply. The main change in the pattern was his movement into a wider social sphere. At first this took the form merely of his attendance at a large number of House of Commons dinner parties, and of a growing intimacy with some Conservative members who were both socially and politically prominent—Randolph Churchill, Arthur Balfour, Alfred Lyttelton, George Curzon, St. John Brodrick. A little later the invitations which he received and accepted were for private house dinner parties or for Saturdays to Mondays in

[1] These were quoted in ch. II. (see page 30 *supra*.).

the country, and came not from politicians, Conservative or Liberal, but from fashionable hostesses—Mrs. Grenfell (later Lady Desborough), Lady Ribblesdale, and Mrs. Horner herself.

The change in his outlook was in part a reflection of these new opportunities and in part a natural mellowing. The rather austere young Hampstead lawyer was giving way to the successful, early-middle-aged politician. The man who had spoken of Bright's incorruptibility in terms so slighting of almost every other political figure was changing into someone who could refer to himself with pride as belonging to " the laxer of the two schools " so far as social relations between politicians of different parties were concerned. The undergraduate who had become engaged to almost the first girl he had ever met was beginning to discover a wide circle of women friends. And with this discovery went a rather excessive reaction against " political " conversation which was to remain with him for the rest of his life. In the 'seventies and early 'eighties his main pleasure was political discussion, but in July, 1892, he could write to Mrs. Horner: " Yesterday I lunched with J. Morley, but our talk was of elections and majorities and savoured too much of the shop to be worth reporting." The point of Haldane's somewhat loaded remark that " in his earlier political days (Asquith) was a very serious person " was beginning to make itself felt—although it must be said that Haldane's own social evolution in the 'nineties followed very much the same course.

Helen Asquith was always a reluctant participant in these new activities. Margot Tennant, whom Asquith had first met in the spring of 1891 and who was later to be his second wife, subsequently wrote of this subject in terms which perfectly illustrated the point even if they were hardly a tribute to her own tact:

" I found out from something he (Asquith) said to me that he was married and lived at Hampstead and that his days were divided between 1, Paper Buildings and the House of Commons. . . . When I discovered that he was married, I asked him to bring his wife to dinner, which he did, and directly I saw her I said:

" ' I do hope, Mrs. Asquith, you have not minded your husband dining here without you, but I rather gathered Hampstead was too far away for him to get back to you from the House of Commons. You must always let me know and come with him whenever it suits you'."[b]

Miss Tennant recorded further encounters with Helen Asquith:
" I was anxious that she should care for me and know my
friends," she wrote, " but after a week-end spent at Taplow with
Lord and Lady Desborough, where everyone liked her, she told me
that though she had enjoyed her visit she did not think that she
would ever care for the sort of society that I loved, and was
happier in the circle of her home and family. When I said that she
had married a man who was certain to attain the highest political
distinction, she replied that that was not what she coveted for him.
Driving back from Hampstead where we had been alone together
I wondered if my ambition for the success of her husband, and
other men, was wrong. She came several times to see me in
Grosvenor Square and took me to hear her husband in the Law
Courts, where he and Lord Russell of Killowen were engaged on
the famous case of the baccarat scandal. We were accompanied
by her son Raymond, and in a desire to amuse this lovely little
boy I remember that I fluttered my pocket handkerchief on to
the heads of those sitting below us from the gallery."[c]

A growing difference of tastes between Asquith and his first wife
cannot therefore be doubted. Had she lived some conflict must have
developed between his social proclivities and her preference for the
old, quiet Hampstead life. No doubt the strength of his attachment to
her and the calmness of her character would have made the conflict
containable. But it would have been there.

Helen Asquith's death altered all this. At a time when the external
features of his life were already changing rapidly, Asquith was left to
find a new domestic framework as well. He was emotionally bereft,
but he was also, unwillingly, free. The old pattern of his life was
broken in nearly all its aspects. The new one was to bear little relationship to it. The transition was not without its difficulties.

With the problem of the children Asquith had the immediate help
of his wife's sister, Josephine Armitage, who was at Lamlash (as was
his own brother) when the death occurred. But Mrs. Armitage had
a family of her own at Altrincham, in Cheshire, and was not therefore available for long. " My chief care for the moment," he wrote to
Mrs. Horner on September 22nd, " is to find someone who can take
charge of my house and my little children . . ." His rapidly expanding
and largely uncommitted income at least meant that he had no problem
of money, and was able to employ housekeepers, nannies and nursery

maids on a lavish scale. On this basis he went back to Maresfield Gardens, and Raymond and Herbert, after a week or so, returned to their private school at Lambrook. Towards the end of 1892 he finally abandoned Hampstead, and moved himself into an apartment at 127, Mount Street, only a few doors away from his old rooms as a law student, and the children to Surrey. First he rented, on George Meredith's recommendation, a rather pretty house on Box Hill, near Dorking. Meredith was a near neighbour there, and Asquith used to call on him during most of his week-end visits to the children. When this house ceased to be available Asquith moved the children to the less attractive surroundings of a redbrick villa near Redhill. There he continued to visit them frequently, usually spending an evening and a night away from London. These arrangements lasted until his second marriage in 1894, by which time Raymond and Herbert were at Winchester, and Arthur at Lambrook.

For a few weeks after his return from Arran Asquith was disabled by a combination of grief and domestic responsibility from playing much part in politics. Apart from the pressure of household arrangements, most of his time was occupied by letter-writing and by reading; he read four Balzac novels, Moltke's *Franco-German War*, Rose's *Ignatius Loyola*, and Bishop Wordsworth's *Reminiscences*. He missed that autumn's meeting of the National Liberal Federation at Newcastle-upon-Tyne, where Gladstone went on October 2nd, rather unenthusiastically to proclaim the general radical programme, which was subsequently known by the name of that city.[1] None of the lieutenants, influenced partly no doubt by the decline in the electoral prospect, were much more enthusiastic than their leader, and Asquith wrote of " a sawdust programme " supported only by " a rattle of Harcourtian fireworks." But whatever the quality of the programme, which ranged from Welsh church disestablishment to triennial parliaments and the payment of members, it was the one on which the increasingly

---

[1] His want of enthusiasm apparently led to no great restraint of presentation. Sir Philip Magnus wrote: " It was noticed at Newcastle that while he was attacking the House of Lords, his arms were raised higher and higher, as though they sought to invoke the wrath of Heaven, while his knees sagged lower and lower, until it seemed as though they must end by touching the boards. The performance was not one over which he would have wished his biographer to linger, and he did not linger long over it himself." (*Gladstone*, p. 396).

imminent election had to be fought, and during the months of preparation for the contest Asquith was again active at meetings throughout the country.

From November, 1891, indeed, he was active in all respects—legal, political and social. He still avoided much speaking in the House of Commons, although on April 27th, 1892 he took his first parliamentary stand on an issue about which he was long to remain almost passionately committed—that of opposition to women's suffrage.[1] But he was busy in every other way. He was building up his practice, sometimes by activities like going to Oldham to earn fifty guineas by advising the Corporation on their rights and liabilities in connection with a new sewerage scheme, and more occasionally (for his practice was always a fairly humdrum one) by appearing in a notable *cause célèbre* like the Berkeley peerage case. He was conferring and corresponding with Morley and Rosebery and Harcourt, and sometimes with Gladstone himself. And his engagement books were full of dinner and week-end commitments—at Taplow Court with the Grenfells, at Easton Grey near Malmesbury with the Graham Smiths (a sister and brother-in-law of Margot Tennant), at Mells Park near Frome with the Horners, and at a number of other houses.

Parliament was dissolved on June 29th, and the results mostly came in during the second week of July. East Fife was one of the early returns, and Asquith was re-elected with a majority reduced by 82. "I had a hardish fight at the end," he wrote to Mrs. Horner, "the Kirk, who is a vigorous old lady, scratching and kicking at me like a muscular virago." By Sunday, July 10th, he was back in London, having spent Friday night in Glasgow, where Margot Tennant's brother was a candidate, and Saturday in Arran, visiting his wife's grave in the little churchyard at Lamlash.

Despite his slightly disappointing result, Asquith was more fortunate than Gladstone, who in Midlothian found that an 1886 majority of more than 4,000 had melted away to one of 690. The overall

[1] Apart from speaking, he joined with nineteen other members in sending out an all-party whip against the private member's bill which was before the House. The most notable of the other signatories were Sir Michael Hicks-Beach, Joseph Chamberlain, Henry Chaplin, Lord Randolph Churchill, George Curzon, Sir William Harcourt, Sir Henry James, Henry Labouchère and A. J. Mundella. Haldane and Grey were equally committed on the other side.

result was 273 Liberals, 81 Nationalists and one Labour member against 269 Conservatives and 46 Liberal Unionists. The majority for Home Rule was a slightly ramshackle one of 45. It was less than had been hoped for but it was enough to make a change of government almost certain.

Nevertheless Lord Salisbury did not resign at once but waited to meet Parliament. This meant several weeks of uncertainty and rumour-mongering. " We live here at present under very demoralising conditions," Asquith wrote on July 25th. " First there was the daily ebb and flow of the election returns, and now that we have got into power (after a fashion) our whole world is engaged in constructing imaginary ministries. ... The town is pretty full again and there is a kind of Indian summer of a season but the atmosphere is heavy with politics. Nothing is too absurd to be said and believed, as e.g. that Mr. G. has had a fit (or is going to take a peerage) or that Rosebery has gone off in a yacht to the North Pole."

Lord Salisbury's decision not to resign also meant that there had to be an amendment to the address around which the anti-Government forces could coalesce, an 1892 equivalent of Jesse Collings's 1886 " three acres and a cow " motion. The view was that such an amendment should be moved from the back benches, and Gladstone fixed on Asquith as the most suitable person to perform this task; Thomas Burt, the Northumberland miners' leader who had been in the House since 1868, was to be the seconder.

Asquith received Gladstone's formal invitation on August 2nd. Unusually, he was at the Old Bailey conducting a criminal case when the letter came, but he appears to have been aware of his selection beforehand and to have assumed that it carried with it the near certainty of a seat in the new Cabinet. He wrote to Mrs. Horner on August 1st:

" I suppose, as you say, I ought to feel satisfied and happy. When I was a boy I used to think that to get into the Cabinet before one was 40 was, for an Englishman who had to start on the level of the crowd, the highest height of achievement. I shall not be 40 until September so the odds are (between you and me) that I shall have the chance, at any rate, of bringing off this dream of young ambition. ... Still I have not, as I know I am never likely to have, what I really want ... Do you know those fine lines in M. Arnold's ' Buried Life ' how

From the soul's subterranean depths upborne
Come airs and floating echoes that convey
A melancholy into all our day.
. . . ' Is the man going mad? ' I hear you ask. Certainly this is not
a proper state of reflection for a ' successful politician ' who has
been chosen to turn out a Government and who is supposed (by
the newspapers) to be jostling vigorously in the scramble for
' high office '. . . . "

What is surprising about this letter is not Asquith's layer of melancholy (which did not prevent his accepting the task with alacrity and
discharging it with dexterity) but his assumption, well-founded though
it proved, that the moving of this amendment carried with it a place
in the Cabinet. Certainly the precedent of 1886 did not suggest this.
All that poor Collings got then was a rather grudging offer of the
parliamentary secretaryship to the Local Government Board and a
suggestion by Gladstone—which was one of the reasons for the
estrangement of Chamberlain—that he should take a cut in the salary.
Nor was Asquith at all inclined by nature to be a man who counted
his chickens before they were hatched. Yet it is difficult to see on what
his confidence could have been based. Admittedly there had been
encouraging conversations with Morley during the preceding year, and
he had even sought and received Balfour's advice, very much in
accordance with his own predictions, that he should hold out for a
political and not a law office. But all this, even encouragement from
one so close to the fount of power as Morley, was not the same as a
firm offer from the Prime Minister himself, who had been recorded in
Rosebery's diary for May 28th as being " averse to giving Asquith
Cabinet office."[d] Gladstone indeed was always loath to break what he
called the " old rule " of not putting men into the Cabinet until they
had first served in junior office, and this had helped to confine Dilke
(although not Chamberlain) to an under-secretaryship in 1880, despite
the fact that he had previously enjoyed with Harcourt conversations
very similar to those of Asquith with Morley.

Asquith, however, was more fortunate. On August 8th, in the last
speech which he was ever to make from a back bench of the House of
Commons, he moved his amendment of no confidence, and three
days later saw it duly carried by a majority of 40. Salisbury then
resigned at once, and the Queen, having taken the exceptional step
of announcing in the *Court Circular* that she had received his resigna-

tion " with great regret," reluctantly gave her commission to Gladstone on August 13th. On the following afternoon, a Sunday, Asquith was in Brooks's Club when one of the Prime Minister's secretaries arrived and handed him a letter:

SECRET   *Hawarden Castle,*
Chester   1 C(arlton) G(ardens),
Aug. 14. 92

My dear Asquith

I have the pleasure of writing to propose that you should allow me to submit your name to Her Majesty for the office of Home Secretary.

I have understood that you are willing to quit your practice at the bar and in consequence I find myself able to offer this just and I think signal tribute to your character abilities and eloquence.

Believe me

Very faithfully yours

W. E. Gladstone[e]

Although he **has** written that he was determined not to enter the Government unless it contained " a strong infusion of new blood " Asquith apparently rested on his conversations with Morley and showed no hesitancy at this stage. " I replied at once, gratefully accepting the Prime Minister's proposal . . .", he wrote. And, indeed, from the point of view of the inclusion of his friends, the new Government was a satisfactory one to him. Acland was Vice-President of the Council. Edward Grey was under-secretary at the Foreign Office and Sydney Buxton under-secretary at the Colonial Office. Tom Ellis was Deputy Whip. Rosebery had been offered the Foreign Secretaryship, although his acceptance could not be secured until August 15th,[1] and Morley

---

[1] " So be it—R," was the apparently self-abnegatory telegram which he then sent to Gladstone after an interview with the Prince of Wales. Secure in the knowledge that the Queen would make great difficulties if he were not at the Foreign Office, Rosebery had been peculiarly unforthcoming, even by his own standards. But the Queen was not alone in thinking his presence essential. " Without you the new Government would be ridiculous, with you it is only impossible," was the comment of Harcourt, who had rather truculently accepted the Exchequer. Within two years he was probably wishing that the Government had been a ridiculous one.

was to be Chief Secretary for Ireland. Of Asquith's close associates, only Haldane was left out.

The Queen was at Osborne, and the new ministers went there on August 18th to receive the seals of office. Crossing in the steamer from Portsmouth they passed another boat carrying the outgoing Conservative ministers to the mainland, and hats were raised in silent salute. Silence, indeed, was the main feature of the whole day's proceedings, for the new Privy Councillors (Asquith, Acland, Bryce and Henry Fowler) were sworn in and they and the old ones then received their seals without the Queen saying a word to any of them. Four of the senior ministers—Rosebery, Spencer, Kimberley and Harcourt—were later given audiences, but to judge from Harcourt's experience, these did not constitute a very notable breach in her taciturnity.[1] Asquith returned to London without any conversational contact, but the Queen thought him "an intelligent, rather good-looking man." A week or so later he was again summoned to Osborne, this time to dine and sleep, and to be given an opportunity to make more of a personal impression. He took it successfully and the Queen recorded in her journal that she "had a conversation with Mr. Asquith whom I thought pleasant, straightforward and sensible." She added, in a typical royal attempt to attach familiar bearings to a new face: "He is a very clever lawyer, who was with Sir H. James."*

Asquith's achievement in becoming a member of this Cabinet—and in a post which was his first choice—was a formidable one. He was younger than any of his colleagues, he was without inherited wealth or influence, he had been in the House of Commons only six years, and he had addressed it on little more than a dozen occasions. Nor is there any doubt that the achievement gave him great and understandable satisfaction. His occasional bouts of melancholy, of sadness for the death of his wife, and of yearning for some fulfilment that never was on land or sea, were doubtless completely genuine. But they existed alongside a strong desire for worldly success and for the ability to exercise the powers which he knew he possessed. "Do you re-

[1] " When he went in to have his audience the Queen said, ' How do you do, Sir William, I hope you are well?' W.V.H. replied and added, ' I hope, Madam, you will feel that our desire is to make matters as easy and as little troublesome to you as we can possibly do.' She bowed, but said nothing and then asked, ' How is Lady Harcourt? Terrible weather is it not? and so oppressive?' And that was all! " (Gardiner, *op cit*.II, p. 185).

member," he wrote to Mrs. Horner two months after he had taken office, " . . . the Theban, somewhere in Herodotus, who says . . . that of all human troubles the most hateful is to feel that you have the capacity of power and yet you have no field to exercise it. That was for years my case and no one who has not been through it can know the chilly, paralysing, deadening depression of hope deferred and energy wasted and vitality run to seed. I sometimes think it is the most tragic thing in life."

Tragic or not, it was an affliction which was not for many years again to worry Asquith. He had achieved a major political position at an early age. With his older colleagues he spent the autumn of 1892 preparing for the first parliamentary session of the new Government, which did not begin until February of the following year.

CHAPTER V

MR. GLADSTONE'S HOME
SECRETARY

1892-4

Asquith was a successful Home Secretary—" the best of the century "
is the unqualified judgment of Gladstone's latest biographer[a]—in an
unsuccessful Government. His success came partly from his skill as a
parliamentary orator. He had always been good in this respect, but the
practice which office imposed made him better. By the end
of the Parliament he was the one minister who could be depended upon
never to make a bad speech, and he often went further and achieved a
devastating debating force. He never had the emotional range of
Gladstone or the electrifying effect of Randolph Churchill at his best,
but he had a consistent power of pungent, almost unanswerable
argument.

As a departmental chief, in addition to his obvious quality of quick
comprehension, he was cool and decisive. He had an intellectual self-
confidence which left him in little doubt about the rightness of his own
decisions. His energies were devoted not to re-considering his actions
but to demonstrating their wisdom, sometimes in an unconciliatory
way. On top of this he had a moderate, but not excessive, taste for
innovation. He liked to move, but in well-tried directions. He was not
a man for producing a stream of imaginative ideas, some of them as
bad as others were good. There was never a danger of his being swept
off his feet by some attractive but reckless plan. All in all he was an
almost perfect minister from the civil servant's point of view, and was
recognised as such by the two successive permanent under-secretaries
who served him at the Home Office. But he was also much more than
this. He was respected by his colleagues for his counsel in Cabinet and
for the strength which he gave to the Government in the House; and

63

he inspired confidence amongst uncommitted opinion in the country.

One of his first administrative decisions concerned the right of public meeting in Trafalgar Square—a subject with a good deal of explosive political force behind it. After the troubles of 1887 (which had led to Asquith's defence of Cunninghame-Graham at the Old Bailey), Henry Matthews, Home Secretary in the outgoing Government, had authorised the Commissioners of Metropolitan Police to issue an order banning all meetings in the Square. There was doubt about the legal validity of the order, but it was accepted without challenge for the time being, despite the grumbling of the Liberal opposition and the resentment of left-wing opinion in London. This opinion, radical as well as socialist, looked to the new Government to put the matter right without delay. Within two days of Asquith's taking office, the matter had been raised in the Press and he had received a polite but firm letter from William Saunders, the radical M.P. for Streatham, stressing the importance which " the advanced electors of London " attached to a quick settlement of the matter. It also became known that, in any event, the Metropolitan Radical Association proposed to hold a meeting in November and, if necessary, to test the ban in the courts.

Lushington, the permanent under-secretary at the Home Office, wrote a memorandum in favour of maintaining the *status quo*, which, as the Lord Chancellor pointed out, was " not much use as no-one knew whether it could be maintained "; the Queen caused her secretary to write agitatedly asking what were Asquith's intentions; and Harcourt, whom Asquith consulted as a former Home Secretary, wrote from Derby, where he was engaged in a " vexatious contest " for his re-election, suggesting that in certain circumstances Mr. Gladstone had best be consulted. This was bad advice, for Gladstone's reply was likely to be uninterested, cloudy, and tinged with annoyance that the new Home Secretary could not make his own decisions without disturbing the Prime Minister's Irish brooding. Wisely, Asquith did not take it. Instead he set W. H. Eldridge, a barrister whom he trusted and knew to have good trades union contacts, to find out whether a compromise solution might be acceptable to the labour leaders, and if so, exactly what form it might take. Such an approach Asquith believed to be necessary both because there was a genuine conflict between the unrestricted right of meeting and the interests of local shop-keepers, 'bus and cab-drivers, etc., and because he was

Asquith in Hyde Park with his daughter Elizabeth, *c.* 1900

Left, Lord Rosebery
Right, Sir Edward Grey

Below, Arthur Balfour

anxious to establish for himself and the Government a reputation for responsibility and firmness which would not be helped by an unconditional removal of the ban.

Eldridge's report was favourable. A limited right of meeting would be accepted by all the interested parties except for the Social Democratic Federation, and they could be ignored because they were " only really Mr. Hyndman." Asquith therefore proceeded along these lines and worked out a solution by which meetings could be held in daylight on Saturday afternoons, Sundays and bank holidays, provided that the police were given previous notice and their regulations as to the approach route of any procession were accepted. When a deputation from the Metropolitan Radical Federation waited upon him on October 19th he announced this solution to them, not as a tentative offer but as a firm decision, and immediately afterwards gave it general publicity. It was accepted both by the deputation and by general London opinion, and has stood until the present day.

Asquith's solution of this potentially tiresome problem was regarded as the first success of the Government and earned him a spate of congratulation. Rosebery, who was always rather a radical in London, was particularly forthcoming. " To have pleased *The Times* and the *Star* and indeed everybody," he wrote, " may rank with the achievements of Hannibal in crossing the Alps or of Orpheus charming his miscellaneous congregation." The Queen, however, did not respond with the other members of this miscellaneous congregation, but informed the Home Secretary of her dislike and distrust of the new arrangement.

Asquith's next major decision made him less popular with radical opinion, and so far from giving the Government another triumph, led to its first parliamentary storm. In January, 1893, the Parnellite rump, under the leadership of John Redmond, raised an agitation for the release of fourteen Irish " dynamiters," who had been imprisoned since the early 'eighties. The Government's majority was such that pressure from any part of its normal support was a serious matter. Nevertheless, Asquith's review of the sentences, conducted on the austere principle that no valid distinction could be drawn between crimes of violence committed for political motives and those committed for more personal reasons, decided that no remission was desirable. " The result of my examination," he wrote, " was that I was left without a shadow of doubt as to the guilt, or as to the propriety of the conviction and sentence, of any one of the prisoners."[b]

The Parnellites pressed the matter to the extent of putting down an amendment to the address at the opening of the Government's first session of Parliament, and Asquith had to reply, on February 9th, in his maiden speech as a minister. This he did in an early example of what was later to be known as his "sledge-hammer" technique. In a long speech, he reviewed each of the cases with a devastating and unyielding logic. It was an impressive first appearance at the despatch box, but it was received with an equal if not greater enthusiasm on the other side of the House as on his own. "Mr. Arthur (Balfour) rushed up to dinner immediately afterwards in one of his rare moods of *ringing* enthusiasm," Mrs. Grenfell wrote to Asquith, "and told us all about it, nearly word for word—and then I got this scribbled line from another of their side ' I know it will interest you to hear that Asquith stepped this evening into the ranks of the *very few*, the five or six men, one is proud to reckon as compatriots. His speech was magnificent, of the greatest ability and highest courage....' I am so overjoyed and proud to hear them all *overflowing* with admiration, so proud of my little square-inch of your dear friendship," she concluded.

The speech was also admired on the Government benches. Its arguments made it easier for some radicals to vote against the amendment. But Justin McCarthy, the leader of the anti-Parnellite Nationalists, who also had to vote for the Government if it was to survive and produce its Home Rule Bill, complained publicly that Asquith had "shut the gates of mercy with a clang"; and John Morley, without dissenting from the Home Secretary's line, told him privately[c] that he might have been less "*cassant.*"

Asquith's next big speeches in the House (but he was not now so successful at avoiding minor ones as he had previously been: in the summer of 1893 he wrote complaining of "nearly 9 hours at the H. of C. . . . (sitting) hour after hour through dreary discussions on Supply") were on February 23rd when he introduced a Welsh Suspensory Bill, designed to pave the way for Welsh Church Disestablishment, and on April 14th when he intervened in the eight-day debate on the second reading of the Home Rule Bill. His speech on the first occasion was notable chiefly for the fact that he provoked the wrath of the Queen, who wrote to Gladstone complaining that Asquith had "admitted" that the Welsh bill was merely a first step to the disestablishment and disendowment of the Church of England.

Gladstone sent the letter on to Asquith with the characteristic comment: "The enclosed is in no way formidable except that it will entail on me the necessity of writing rather a long letter." He added: "Her Majesty's studies have not yet carried her out of the delusive belief that she is still by law the 'head' of the Church of England."[d] The Welsh Bill was not proceeded with at this stage owing to the rapacious demands on time made by the Irish one.

Asquith's connection with the Home Rule Bill was not an intimate one. He had not been a member of the Cabinet committee (Gladstone, Morley, Spencer, Herschell, Campbell-Bannerman and Bryce) which drafted it, but his name was printed on its back because of his departmental position. Partly for this reason and partly because of his debating strength he was asked to speak on second reading. But once he had done so, and delivered what *The Times* described as "perhaps as good a case for his clients as anyone who had yet spoken on the same side," his responsibilities were mostly at an end. Gladstone, indeed, was himself so indefatigable throughout the long committee stage that even Morley, let alone ministers less directly concerned, was largely overshadowed. Nevertheless Asquith had to be present throughout most of this parliamentary struggle, magnificent as a last display of Gladstone's fighting powers but dismal because of the general conviction that ultimate failure was inevitable. His attendance was dictated not only by the narrowness of the Government's majority but also by the practice of the time, which demanded from ministers a much more constant House of Commons attendance on subjects other than their own than is usual today.[1]

The bill completed its slow progress through the House of Commons early on the morning of September 2nd, when it received a third reading by a vote of 307 to 267. Six days later the peers refused it a second reading by 419 to 41, proportionately the worst showing, on a major question, which any Government has ever made in the House of Lords. Gladstone was for an immediate dissolution on the issue, but he could not carry his colleagues with him. They thought that, in the phrase of the time, "the cup had to be filled up" with English rather than Irish legislation before the electorate could be appealed to with any hope of success; and Asquith, despite the fact

---

[1] "When I am ill," said Harcourt, "I am in bed. When I am not, I am in the House of Commons"; but he was an even more assiduous parliamentarian than most of his contemporaries.

that an Employers' Liability Bill,[1] to which he had devoted great effort during the session, had been so mangled by the Lords that abandonment seemed the better course, fully agreed with the majority of the Cabinet. Gladstone was therefore forced to acquiesce, although the combined result of the Lords' vote and his colleagues' reaction to it was a fatal blow to his last political hopes. His premiership continued for another six months, but its purpose and authority came effectively to an end on September 8th, 1893.

Asquith was occupied during part of that summer and autumn with a particularly nasty " law and order " incident. A protracted coal strike in the North of England led to sporadic rioting and some damage to property in parts of the West Riding of Yorkshire. The local magistrates asked for police reinforcements. Asquith transmitted their requests to other local police forces and also, in his capacity as head of the Metropolitan force, sent 400 London policemen to the area. This led to no improvement in the situation, and the magistrates began to send repeated requests to the Home Office for the use of troops. On September 3rd the Home Secretary sanctioned such an application, and a platoon of the Queen's Own Yorkshire Light Infantry was present at Featherstone colliery, near Wakefield, four days later. Asquith's own account of what then occurred is as follows:

A magistrate was present with the troops; he made no fewer than seven appeals to the crowd, who were armed with sticks and bludgeons, to discontinue the work of destruction, much valuable property being already ablaze; the Riot Act was read; a bayonet charge was unavailingly made; and as the defensive position held by the small detachment of soldiers (fewer than thirty men) was becoming untenable, and the complete destruction of the colliery was imminent, the magistrate gave orders to the commander to fire. Two men on the fringe of the crowd were unfortunately killed.[e]

The two Coroner's juries which held inquests on the dead men came to different conclusions. The one thought that there had been sufficient reason for the troops to open fire, the other not. The incident was first raised in the House of Commons on September 20th, the day before the adjournment after the continuous sittings of the summer.

[1] It was designed to get rid of the last traces of the doctrine of common employment, by which a workman was inhibited from suing an employer for injury suffered as a result of the negligence of a fellow employee.

Asquith gave a firm reply insisting that the responsibility for the preservation of order lay with the local authorities and that it would have been wrong, with the less adequate information at his disposal, to have refused their requests. He did not attempt to judge between the conflicting verdicts of the two juries. For this purpose, and to investigate the whole matter, he set up a Special Commission composed of Bowen, Haldane, and Sir Albert Rollit, a Tory M.P. and solicitor. This Commission heard evidence at Wakefield and produced a report which was notable to the public for completely exonerating the magistrates, officers and troops, and to lawyers for formulating with great precision the respective duties of the civil and military authorities at times of public disorder.

This was not the end of the matter. Had Asquith not been so "*cassant*" he might have chosen a less intellectually distinguished but more politically appeasing Commission. But that was not the way his mind worked. He saw no harm in appointing his closest friend as the one "left-wing" member, or his old master as the chairman, because it did not occur to him that they could be other than impartial, and he did not see why it should occur to others either. It was an example of his persistent tendency to be a little too concerned with what may be called "Athenæum opinion" and not sufficiently concerned with a more general and less urbane public. In any event "Featherstone" pursued him throughout the middle years of his career and earned him a measure of working class unpopularity much as "Tonypandy" did with Winston Churchill nearly a generation later. "Why did you murder the miners at Featherstone in '92?" someone shouted at him at a meeting many years afterwards. "It was not '92, it was '93," was his characteristic reply.

The cool determination with which he discharged most of his judicial duties at the Home Office did not extend to his decisions about the reprieve of murderers. To say that he was an "abolitionist" Home Secretary would be to misunderstand either the state of public opinion at the time or Asquith's desire to run ahead of it. He was not a man for the pursuit of hopeless causes. But he disliked the death penalty, both because of its presumptuous finality and because of its ghoulish associations; and his responsibility for the exercise of the prerogative of mercy caused him great unease. One of the most difficult cases concerned a man who was hanged at Liverpool Jail on January 4th, 1893. The nature of the crime was not such as to raise the question of a reprieve, but there was persistent doubt as to identity. Was the man who was to be hanged the murderer? Asquith wrote Mrs. Horner an anguished letter on January 3rd, but he did not halt the processes of the law. Later, he told his daughter, he received a letter from the priest who had taken the condemned man's last confession, telling him that he had nothing with which to reproach himself. When this story was published by Lady Violet Bonham Carter,*f* some time after her father's death, it aroused a storm of Roman Catholic protest. The letter was not left amongst Asquith's papers.

Gladstone resigned as Prime Minister on March 3rd, 1894. He had been in dispute with his colleagues since January 9th, when in an argument with Lord Spencer about the size of the naval estimates he had been supported only by Shaw-Lefevre, the First Commissioner of Works. He had then retired to Biarritz for three weeks, but showed no desire to give way while there. Nor did the other ministers. Asquith recorded in his diary for January 13th: " Lunch with Harcourts. Talk with H. and Loulou.¹ We agreed that we could make no proposals. Best chance to trust to time and Atlantic breezes." But the main result of the Atlantic breezes, according to Sir Algernon West, was to produce in Gladstone a growing conviction that all his colleagues, except Shaw-Lefevre, were " mad and drunk." The real cause of the dispute, of course, was something deeper than the question of economy in naval expenditure. Had this been the only point at issue Harcourt would hardly have found himself opposed to the Prime Minister. But on Gladstone's side there was the constant desire to embroil the Government in a struggle to the death with the House of Lords over Ireland. " After breakfast to A. Morley's,² where was A. West just back from Biarritz with Mr. G's latest," Asquith wrote in his diary for February 7th. " He proposes an immediate dissolution—pretext being action of H. of Lords on our Bills; we all agreed that this is madness."³ On the side of the other ministers there was the growing conviction that Gladstone was no longer either physically or mentally capable of presiding over the Government. The " gradual closing of

¹ Lewis (later 1st Viscount) Harcourt, Sir William's son by his first marriage.

² Former Chief Whip and then Postmaster General.

³ Accusations of insanity were freely exchanged between the Prime Minister and his Cabinet at this stage.

the doors of the senses," which he had first mentioned in 1892, was gathering momentum.

Asquith wrote later that " Mr. Gladstone's resignation was entirely his own act "*g* and this was no doubt formally true. But Asquith himself, like most other ministers, had come to the conclusion by early January that it was time for the act to be committed. His admiration for Gladstone had been unconfined. To the end of his life he thought him the greatest man with whom he had ever worked. But he knew how rapidly Gladstone's judgment was failing. In consequence, he made no attempt to cling to the Grand Old Man during this Lear-like period. His relations with Gladstone had been based on high mutual respect, but hardly upon great personal intimacy. And this was a time when those who had been far closer, Morley particularly, and Rosebery too, were convinced that the moment for resignation had come.

Gladstone at last made his decision known to his colleagues on February 27th, and on March 1st he attended his final Cabinet and made his last speech in the House of Commons. What happened at this Cabinet—the " blubbering Cabinet " as Gladstone subsequently referred to it—was described by Asquith many years later: " Before the Cabinet separated, Lord Kimberley (the senior member), who was genuinely moved, had uttered a few broken sentences of affection and reverence, when Harcourt produced from his box and proceeded to read a well-thumbed MS of highly elaborated eulogy. Of those who were present there are now few survivors; but which of them can forget the expression of Mr. Gladstone's face, as he looked on with hooded eyes and tightened lips at this maladroit performance? "*h*

Asquith wrote to Gladstone a day or two later, and was proud of the letter which he received in reply. " The future is in my mind a clouded picture," it ran: " but I am glad that the prolongation of my political life has given me an opportunity of helping the arrangements under which you have taken your stand in political life. I well remember the impression made upon me by your speech at the Eighty Club, the first time I ever saw or heard you. It has since been, of course, deepened and confirmed. Great problems are before us: and I know no one more likely to face them, as I hope and believe, not only with a manly strength, but with a determined integrity of mind. I most earnestly hope that you may be enabled to fulfil your part, which will certainly be an arduous one."*i*

The succession was not a certain one. In spite of the naval estimates,

Gladstone, had he been asked, would have recommended the Queen to send for Lord Spencer. But he was not asked. And, indeed, biased and bitter though the Queen had been in most of her later dealings with him, this omission was neither unconstitutional nor unreasonable. It was not desirable that a Prime Minister who was in effect being forced out by colleagues who venerated his past, but no longer trusted his judgment, should be allowed to choose his own successor. Spencer would have been a most inadequate choice. The "red earl" as he was known (owing to the colour of his beard rather than the nature of his political views) had no great powers either of intellect or leadership, and no following in the Liberal Party. Spencer commended himself to Gladstone because he was an old Whig aristocrat whom he had known for many years, and one of the very few in this category who had not deserted him over Home Rule.

The more serious claimants were Harcourt and Rosebery. The former—the Great Gladiator as he was sometimes called in those enthusiastic days—was nearly twenty-five years Rosebery's senior and had a much wider experience of office. Furthermore, he had the advantage of being in the Commons. A peer Prime Minister, as Salisbury showed, was then by no means impossible, but it was faintly ludicrous for the head of the Government to sit in a House in which he could muster only 41 supporters. In addition, Harcourt's "Little England" views were more popular in the Liberal Party than Rosebery's imperialism. For all these reasons, Harcourt would almost certainly have been the choice of a majority both of Liberal members of Parliament and of the party's active supporters in the country. Against this Rosebery had three sources of strength, two of them useful and the third decisive. The Queen wanted him; the Liberal press was on the whole on his side; and his Cabinet colleagues, while not perhaps burning with enthusiasm at the prospect of his leadership, were clear that, as the head of a tottering Government, he was much preferable to Harcourt.[1]

Asquith was one of the firmest of the "Roseberyites." He was a friend, and was in close agreement with him on matters of foreign policy, though on home policy, he claimed, he sided as often as not with Harcourt. Asquith's essential objection to Harcourt, like that of most of the other ministers, was based on temperament rather than

[1] The Queen sent for him on her own initiative, and would no doubt have done so in any event. But had the views of his fellow ministers been different he might have failed to form a Government.

72

policy. " And yet, to tell the naked truth," he wrote, " he was an almost impossible colleague, and would have been a wholly impossible chief."*j* Nevertheless, Asquith's firmness of view did not make him as important an influence as is suggested by Harcourt's biographer.[1] It was Morley, co-lieutenant and close ally of Harcourt's since the late 'eighties, who was the Brutus of the occasion, and who veered at the crucial moment to Rosebery—although he was soon to veer back again. But not before the decision had been taken. The new Prime Minister kissed hands on March 4th, and was soon expressing his usual distaste for his new office.

He made few Cabinet changes, saying that the Government's hold on life was hardly such as to make them worth-while. The most notable was the promotion of Lord Kimberley to the Foreign Office, an event which began John Morley's process of switching back to the anti-Rosebery camp. Harcourt became leader of the House of Commons as well as Chancellor of the Exchequer, after making certain conditions about access to Foreign Office information. Asquith remained Home Secretary.

<hr />

[1] Gardiner, *op cit.*, II, p. 269, says that Asquith and Acland are said to be the only Commons members of the Cabinet who were against Harcourt.

CHAPTER VI

A NEW WIFE AND A DYING GOVERNMENT

1894-5

Asquith's first important act under the new Government was to re-marry. This he did at St. George's, Hanover Square, on Wednesday, May 10th, 1894. His second wife was Margot Tennant, the daughter of a rich, partially self-made Liberal baronet, who had established himself as a territorial figure in the Scottish Border country, and whose numerous children had erupted into social prominence with unusual force.

This second wedding was very different from Asquith's first, in Manchester, seventeen years previously. The Cabinet postponed its meeting in order not to clash with the ceremony. Apart from the bridegroom, three Prime Ministers, Gladstone representing the past, Rosebery the present, and Balfour the future, signed the register. The pavements from Grosvenor Square to Hanover Square, according to the memoirs of the bride, " were blocked with excited and enthusiastic people." Her old nurse was unsuccessfully offered first £10 and then " anything you like " for a ticket of admission to the church by a gentleman with a gardenia. " I must see Margot Tennant married," he had said.[a] Haldane, as best man, struck an almost pedestrian note.

Asquith had first met Miss Tennant, as has been mentioned, in 1891, a few months before the death of his first wife. She has left a vivid description of this first encounter:

> The dinner where I was introduced to my husband was in the House of Commons and I sat next to him.[1] I was deeply impressed by his conversation and his clear Cromwellian face. I thought then, as I do now, that he had a way of putting you not only at your

---

[1] She also wrote: " I had never heard of him, which gives some indication of how much I was wasting my time."

74

ease but at your best when talking to him which is given to few men of note. He was different to the others and, although un- fashionably dressed, had so much personality that I made up my mind at once that this was the man who could help me and would understand everything.

After dinner we all walked on the Terrace and I was flattered to find my new friend at my side. Lord Battersea chaffed me in his noisy and flamboyant manner, trying to separate us, but with tact and determination his frontal attack was resisted and my new friend and I retired to the darkest part of the Terrace where, leaning over the parapet, we gazed into the river and talked far into the night.

Our host (Lord Battersea) and his party—thinking that I had gone home and that Mr. Asquith had returned to the House when the division bell rang—had disappeared; and when we finished our conversation the Terrace was deserted and the sky light.

It never occurred to me that he was married, nor would that have affected me in any way. . . . Mr. Asquith and I met a few days later dining with Sir Algernon West . . . . and after this we saw each other constantly.[b]

By October, 1891 they had begun a regular exchange of long, frequent and intimate letters. And by the end of the year, Miss Tennant having left for a two months' visit to Egypt in early Novem- ber, Asquith was writing to Cairo: " You tell me not to stop loving you, as if you thought I had done or would or could do so. Tenny- son speaks somewhere of the ' sin which practice burns into the blood,' and there are other things besides sins which are burnt into the blood, not to be washed out either by change or circumstance or acts of will. We have a trying time before us: at least I have: but before it begins I entreat you never to doubt that, locked and buried though it may be, your place is always sacred and always your own . . ."

Nor was this letter out of keeping with at least one layer of Miss Tennant's own feelings. After her much described first meeting with Asquith, she had said to her sister, Lady Ribblesdale: " Asquith is the only kind of man that I could ever have married—all the others are so much waste paper! " Lady Ribblesdale replied: " He would never have proposed to you," and Miss Tennant recorded that " this remark of hers hurt me: and I pondered over it in my heart."[c] But pondering

75

in her heart did not mean that she quickly reached finality in her mind, and for nearly two and a half years after the autumn of 1891, despite the fact that she was already 27 at the beginning of her period of indecision, she havered between marriage and non-marriage.

Asquith therefore passed his first, highly successful years as Home Secretary in a state of constant emotional stress. Despite a great deal of advice, notably from Rosebery and Randolph Churchill, about the unwisdom of the course he was proposing, he does not appear to have wavered in his desire to marry Margot Tennant. " I can conceive of no future of which you are not the centre, and which is not given, without a shadow of doubt or a shiver of fear to you alone," he wrote in the summer of 1892. Miss Tennant exhibited no similar constancy of purpose. The choice was perhaps a more difficult one for her. When she came to know Asquith she was a leading figure both in the Leicestershire hunting world and in that part of London society which prided itself upon its intellectual interest and adventurousness. She moved around the hunting counties displaying an unusual talent for borrowing horses and for reckless riding; and she moved around the country houses in which " The Souls "[1]—as she and her friends were known—used to congregate, playing pencil and paper games and indulging in an endless series of heart-searching conversations.

Wherever she went she became the centre of attention. Her *forte*, especially on a first meeting, was the unexpected, provocative remark. She told the Duke of Beaufort that his unique blue and buff hunting colours, although pretty for women, were unsporting for men; her reward was a portrait inscribed " Hark Halloa! ". She told Lord Randolph Churchill that he had " resigned more out of temper than conviction," and was repaid with an invitation to meet and sit

---

[1] " The Souls " like most coteries, had a membership which was slightly blurred at the edges; but amongst the central figures were Arthur Balfour, George Curzon, George Wyndham, Harry Cust, St. John Brodrick, Lord Pembroke, Lady Granby (later Duchess of Rutland), the Duchess of Sutherland, Lady Windsor (later Lady Plymouth) and Lady Brownlow. Miss Tennant, writing many years later, referred to the group, in terms which confirmed more than they denied: " The Souls was a foolish name given by fashionable society to myself and my friends . . . Since those days there has been no group in society of equal distinction, loyalty, and influence. . . . None of us claimed any kind of superiority or practised any sort of exclusion." (*More Memories*, p. 147).

next the Prince of Wales at a supper party, which she attended wearing what most of the women present thought was her nightgown. She told General Booth (of the Salvation Army) that he did not believe in hell any more than she did, and then knelt with him, praying, on the floor of the railway compartment in which they were travelling. She hinted to Lord Tennyson that she thought he was dirty and got him to give her a long reading from " Maud " and " The Princess."

Miss Tennant was spontaneous and stimulating in her approach with all sorts of people, but she liked particularly to know the great and famous, and if possible be more in their confidence than anyone else. When Randolph Churchill rashly asked her if she knew any politicians, " I told him that with the exception of himself I knew them all intimately." When Gladstone (during his brief, third premiership) came to luncheon with her parents in Grosvenor Square, her father's eager anticipation of the visit made her " afraid he might resent my wish to take Mr. Gladstone up to my room after lunch and talk to him alone." But the resentment, if it existed, was overcome, and Gladstone was duly led away.

It was not only politicians who formed her court. Her *Autobiography* contains an account of a knockout literary victory over Lady Londonderry. Before " a circle of fashionable men and women " an argument had developed about the merits of a new volume of essays by John Addington Symonds, Miss Tennant taking a view hostile to their style and content. Lady Londonderry was sufficiently nettled by this view (or perhaps by the manner in which it was expressed) to say eventually, " I am afraid you have not read the book."

" This annoyed me," Miss Tennant's account continued; " I saw the company were enchanted with their spokeswoman, but I thought it unnecessarily rude and more than foolish. I looked at her calmly and said: ' I am afraid, Lady Londonderry, you have not read the preface. The book is dedicated to me '."[d]

Presented with a stage, Miss Tennant always wished to be at its centre:

" At the time I was engaged to be married," she recorded in a later volume of memoirs, " my mother took me to Paris, and Monsieur Worth made me several beautiful dresses. Knowing that I was devoted to dancing, he devized a rainbow-coloured gauze gown reaching to the floor which he insisted upon giving to me. It was of immense width, but of such soft material that the gauze clung closely to my figure. He superintended every fitting, and when the dress was finished I asked that all the women who had worked upon it should come downstairs and that I would dance to them. . . .

"When M. Worth returned to the fitting-room accompanied by the smiling sempstresses, he held his hands behind his back. Inspired by my beautiful dress and feeling in high spirits, I danced as I had never danced before, and was so busy manipulating the yards of stuff in my ample skirts that I noticed nobody. But when I sat down breathless and excited, I looked round and saw that the room was full of people, and Worth flung an enormous bouquet of artificial roses at my feet."[e]

Alongside her eagerness for attention, Margot Tennant possessed a remarkable ability not merely to shock but also to captivate and even inspire. Her success as a lion hunter owed at least as much to the co-operation of the lions as to her own intrepid determination. Gladstone would not have required much luring to her room in Grosvenor Square. He was always delighted to talk to her, and soon after his eightieth birthday he even wrote her a poem, although verse was not his happiest medium.[1] Of the other Prime Ministers who attended her wedding, Rosebery was an old friend, but one whose affection had been temporarily dimmed by a press rumour, published in the autumn

[1] When Parliament ceases and comes the recess,
And we seek in the country rest after distress,
As a rule upon visitors place an embargo,
But make an exception in favour of Margot.

For she brings such a treasure of movement and life,
Fun, spirit and stir, to folk weary with strife,
Though young and though fair, who can hold such a cargo
Of all the good qualities going as Margot?

Up hill and down dale, 'tis a capital name
To blossom in friendship, to sparkle in fame;
There's but one objection can light upon Margot,
Its likeness in rhyming, not meaning, to *argot*.

Never mind, never mind, we will give it the slip,
'Tis not *argot*, the language, but *Argo*, the ship;
And by sea or by land, I will swear you may far go,
Before you can hit on a double for Margot."

of 1891, that he was engaged to be married to her. Her enthusiasm for denying the rumour was not, in his view, as great as his own, or as it should have been—not particularly because she wished it to be true, but because she thought a joke was none the worse for being a public one. But Balfour, perhaps because he never read the newspapers, was totally unaffected by a similar rumour about himself and Miss Tennant, and remained on close and easy terms with her for many years. He may have expressed his enthusiasm less effusively than Gladstone[1] but there is no doubt that he admired her wit and valued her friendship. So, in a less intimate way, did Salisbury. Alfred Milner proposed marriage to her in 1892 and when his offer was refused, so his latest biographer informs us, became " Asquith's life-long, devoted enemy."

Such a woman would probably have found it difficult to make up her mind about any marriage. This indeed had been the case before she met Asquith, and she had havered her way, fickle, demanding and difficult to please, through nearly ten London seasons, a host of minor suitors and a long-drawn-out, quarrelsome and mutually unsatisfactory love affair with Peter Flower, the younger brother of the Lord Battersea who had introduced her to Asquith. Flower was a great figure in the hunting field and on the race course, a man who combined striking good looks, physical recklessness and intellectual immaturity in about equal proportions. To Margot Tennant he appeared one-dimensional. For a person of her adventurousness Asquith undoubtedly offered an impressively broad avenue of escape from the circumscribed and febrile arena of her previous emotional experiences, and from the persistent sterility of this affair with Flower in particular. But marriage with Asquith posed big problems. "It is not possible," the Master of Balliol (one of her most successfully captured lions) wrote to her, " to be a leader of fashion and to do your duty to the five children."*

Miss Tennant's position was complicated by the fact that, as a leader of fashion, she was at least as self-made as was her father as a Border landlord. It was her own wit and daring, constantly and exhaustingly exercised, which gave her the prominent and coveted

[1] On one occasion Miss Tennant was foolish enough to suggest to him that he was sufficiently self-contained that he would not greatly mind if all his close women friends—Lady Elcho, Lady Desborough, one or two others, and herself—were all to die. " I think I should mind if you *all* died on the same day," he replied after a pause for reflection.

position which she occupied. She was the least securely established of any of the women Souls. Even without the problem of the five children, could she assimilate a husband who, however talented and successful and even socially malleable he might be, had shared nothing of her life and friends of the previous ten years? An added difficulty was the fact that, rich though her father had become, there was no question of limitless money being available for her. She had too many brothers and sisters. Her extravagance could have done with the support of a rich husband. It was likely to be a heavy burden upon Asquith's ministerial salary or his earnings at the bar.

On top of all this there was the sharp, almost violent difference in temperament between herself and her prospective husband. She wrote about it as a family difference between herself and her step-children, but it was quite as deep between herself and Asquith.

" Tennants believed in appealing to the hearts of men," she wrote, " firing their imagination and penetrating and vivifying their inmost lives. They had a little loose love to give to the whole world. The Asquiths—without mental flurry and with perfect self-mastery—believed in the free application of intellect to every human emotion; no event could have given heightened expression to their feelings. Shy, self-engaged, critical and controversial, nothing surprised them and nothing upset them. We were as zealous and vital as they were detached and as cocky and passionate as they were modest and emotionless. They rarely looked at you and never got up when anyone came into the room. If you had appeared downstairs in a ball-dress or a bathing-gown they would not have observed it and would certainly never have commented upon it if they had. . . . They were devoted to one another and never quarrelled. . . Perfectly self-contained, truthful and deliberate, I never saw them lose themselves in my life and I have hardly ever seen the saint or hero that excited their disinterested emotion. When I thought of the storms of revolt, the rage, the despair, the wild enthusiasms and reckless adventures of our nursery and schoolroom, I was stunned by the steadiness of the Asquith temper."[9]

There were therefore plenty of reasons why Margot Tennant might have hesitated over the marriage. And hesitate she certainly did, keeping Asquith for two years on a see-saw of alternating hope and despair. In the early summer of 1892 it seemed as though he might quickly succeed. Then in August, after the formation of the Government, he went for the first time to Glen, the Tennant home in Peeblesshire where she had lived most of her life. Here she not only took him to the grave of her sister who had died in 1886, and made him indulge in the almost unbelievably un-Asquithian behaviour of kneeling with her on the grass and praying together, but also sent him away " very sad at heart," with the " candle of hope " nearly blown out. Then it revived again before flickering once more after a Sunday at Balliol. " I was rather depressed when I went to bed last night," Asquith wrote in the following year " and lay awake . . . thinking of what you told me about your interview with the old Master." This, however, appeared to be only a momentary flicker, for he concluded the paragraph: " But our talk in the train this morning made me a different man." A few months later he was once more cast down, and there was even a faint trace of exasperation in his letters: " I daresay my feelings are made rather morbidly sensitive just now, and my mental vision where you are concerned is dislocated by the strong conviction I have that this is, for good or bad, a most critical time in both our lives. I dread more than I can tell having to go back (and for always) to where we were two months ago. . . ." But a short time afterwards he was once again elated: " And this afternoon as I sat on the Treasury Bench, answering questions, I got your telegram and read it furtively, and crammed it hastily into my trousers pocket, until I could get out of the House and read it over and over again in my little room."

And so it went on until a short time before their marriage. The engagement when it was finally agreed upon and announced was a short one. Miss Tennant had at last suppressed her fears about the five children, and overcome the state of mind which she described as " groping as I had been for years to find a character and intellect superior to my own, I did not feel equal to facing it when I found it." And Asquith, for the moment, had undoubtedly achieved what he wanted. He had reversed the pattern followed by many men of being rather discontented with one woman, and then, when an opportunity for fresh choice presented itself, proceeding to marry someone who was as similar as possible to his first wife. Instead, he claimed complete happiness while his first marriage lasted, but followed this up by the early acquisition of a second wife who was in almost every respect the direct opposite of Helen Asquith. The marriage which he began in Hanover Square in his forty-second year and on a high tide of worldly success was to be quite different, both emotionally and socially, from that which seventeen years before he had entered upon in Didsbury Parish Church.

His wedding gave the new Government one of its few hours of harmony. The Rosebery Cabinet was a singularly unhappy one in which to serve. Within eight days of its formation the Prime Minister made what Asquith described as his *faux pas* in the House of Lords and incensed the radical wing of the party and their Irish supporters by suggesting that Home Rule could not be achieved until a majority of the English members in the House of Commons were in its favour. This " predominant partner " approach was to provide the Unionists with one of their most convenient lines of defence over the next twenty years; and its enunciation by the head of a Liberal Government helped to provoke a radical revolt in the House of Commons on the following day. Labouchère moved an amendment to the address calling for the almost complete abolition of the House of Lords veto and carried it by a majority of two, the opposition abstaining. To be defeated on such an occasion was an unusual and humiliating experience for a Government. Resignation was avoided by the expedient of voting down the amended address and bringing in a new one in its place; but it was an inauspicious beginning.

Relations between Rosebery and Harcourt quickly deteriorated. Harcourt was busy preparing (with the help of Alfred Milner who was chairman of the Board of Inland Revenue) and then piloting through the House of Commons his famous " death duties " Budget. This measure—paradoxically the only notable achievement of the administration over which he presided—was distasteful to Rosebery. There is dispute as to how much opposition the Prime Minister offered in the Cabinet (" we spent dreary hours listening to H(arcourt) reading out typewritten discourses on the Budget," he later recorded[h]) but what is certain is that he wrote a hostile memorandum to Harcourt, who replied in uncompromising and even bitter terms,[1]

[1] The tone of the exchange may be gauged from a passage in which Harcourt, replying to a suggestion of Rosebery's that the whole landowning class would be alienated from the Liberal Party, wrote: " If it be so, the Liberal Party will share the fate of another party which was founded 1,894 years ago, of which it was written that it was ' hard for a rich man to enter into the Kingdom.' I think it is highly probable that there are many young men who will go away sorrowful because they have great possessions."

and that he made little attempt to present a united front to the Queen. " With regard to the Budget, it is practically passed," he wrote to her on July 13th, " and it would be impossible now to make any change in its provisions. Lord Rosebery is himself inclined to take a somewhat gloomy view of its effect on the class to which he himself belongs."[i]

Henceforward the Prime Minister and the leader of the House of Commons were barely on speaking terms. They communicated only by means of papers circulated in red despatch boxes or by cold exchanges across the Cabinet table. This rupture extended to policy. There were in effect two Governments. Harcourt occupied himself with his Budget (with which interference from the House of Lords was still regarded as unthinkable), with the new issue of local option (in licensing), and with a constant nagging watch upon Lord Kimberley, designed to exorcise any trace of a " forward policy " from the Foreign Office. When Rosebery threw the question of the relations between the two Houses into the centre of politics, Harcourt stood consciously (and unnaturally) aloof from the whole issue, and when Lord Spencer wrote to remonstrate with him, he replied, blandly but surprisingly, " As you know I am not a supporter of the present Government."[j]

Asquith, although a natural "Roseberyite," wrote that " on the merits of most of the points at issue I was disposed to side with Harcourt." But this feeling about the merits was more than balanced by his conviction that Harcourt's personal behaviour was intolerable. " His lack of any sense of proportion," he wrote, " his incapacity for self-restraint, and his perverse delight in inflaming and embittering every controversy, made co-operation with him always difficult and often impossible. Cabinet life under such conditions was a weariness both to the flesh and to the spirit."[k] Like a number of other ministers Asquith tried to get on with his departmental work and avoid being too much embroiled in the quarrel. Rosebery always wrote to him on terms of close friendship and even complicity (" 67 ton guns are from time to time being discharged from a certain fortress in the New

---

(Gardiner, *op cit.*, II, p. 284). Against this part of the memorandum Rosebery wrote: " No, it is the young men who are to inherit great possessions who will suffer. So this refined innuendo is beside the mark." (Crewe, *Lord Rosebery*, II, p. 467).

Forest[1] at the devoted Kimberley. . . . I did wish you had been in Mount Street on Saturday. I received orders from the C. of E. on the subject of poor M.[2] on Friday afternoon . . .") and Asquith fully reciprocated this friendliness. But he was more concerned at this stage with completing his successful tenure of the Home Office than with taking sides and attempting to drive the Liberal Party in one direction or the other.

During the fifteen months between the retirement of Gladstone and the fall of the Government three aspects of Asquith's work attracted most attention. The first was a thankless attempt to bring the Welsh Disestablishment Bill to a stage at which it was ready for slaughter by the House of Lords. The bill had been introduced and then abandoned because of the Home Rule Bill in 1893, and the procedure was repeated, still more perfunctorily on this occasion, in the short session of 1894, when Harcourt's Budget swallowed up most of the available time. In 1895, however, it was given a higher priority, and itself became the main consumer of parliamentary days. But it made very slow progress. Asquith had to deal not only with determined opposition and obstruction from the Unionists, but also with sporadic cross-fire from Welsh Liberals who thought the Government was not going far enough. Lloyd George, who had been first elected in 1891 and whose political interest in those days was primarily sectarian, was prominent and extreme amongst these. It was Asquith's first contact with him.

It was also Asquith's first experience of trying to push a big, controversial bill, inch by inch, through the House of Commons. As could have been foreseen, he discharged this duty with skill and urbanity, but he did not enjoy the manoeuvring which it involved and he did not warm during the process to the Welsh nonconformists whose interests he was serving. The frequent and long-winded deputations from Welsh members he found even more trying than the almost endless sittings in the House, and a certain antipathy towards the Welsh temperament, which in later life (even before 1916) he

[1] Harcourt built a house called Malwood, near Lyndhurst, in 1883. It was designed in what was sometimes called the " parliamentary style " and bore a strong resemblance to Highbury which Joseph Chamberlain had built a few years earlier. At the end of his life Harcourt inherited (from his nephew) the old family mansion of Nuneham, near Oxford, and died there. But he always greatly preferred Malwood.

[2] Arnold Morley, the Postmaster General.

never made much effort to conceal, may well have begun with his troubles over the Disestablishment Bill. After twelve nights in committee and remarkably little progress, " it was with a sigh of relief," Asquith wrote, " that, when the Government was defeated on another issue, I laid down my thankless task."[1]

Asquith was simultaneously occupied with a less sterile legislative task. This was a Factories and Workshops Bill, which rounded off one of the most constructive aspects of his work at the Home Office. Within a few months of his appointment he had carried through a substantial strengthening of the Factory Inspectorate, including the notable innovation of appointing the first women inspectors. A year later he again increased the establishment of this division of his department and appointed another two women, the first two having already proved themselves successful. In addition he set up six committees to enquire into some of the most notorious " dangerous trades " of the period, such as chemicals, pottery and paint, and generally gave a higher priority, in respect both of his own attention and of the allocation of the most talented civil servants, to the industrial side of the Home Office's work than had hitherto been the practice.

The Factories Bill, which he introduced in March, 1895, contained a mixed bag of provisions. A necessary minimum of space for each person employed was laid down. New rules for the reporting and investigation of accidents were made and a new standard of protection against moving machinery was ordered. Fire escapes for all industrial premises were stipulated. Restrictions were placed on overtime working, and docks and laundries were brought for the first time within the scope of factory legislation. Although a complicated and far-ranging measure it was not regarded as controversial in a strict party sense. The committee stage was taken not on the floor of the House of Commons, but in what was then called the Grand Committee on Trade. As a result the progress of the Factories Bill was not blocked by the Welsh Church Bill. Even so, it was still in committee when the Government resigned on June 24th. The new Government agreed to assist its passage, however, and on July 6th, the day before the dissolution, it went through all stages in the House of Lords and received the royal assent.

Asquith's most notable foray into general politics during this period was in the debate on the address at the beginning of the 1895 session. In addition to dealing with an amendment affecting the Home Office he

85

also replied to a much wider-ranging one moved by Chamberlain which accused the Government of wasting the time of the House by putting before it measures which were known to have no chance of passing into law. Instead of "filling up the cup" with grievances against the House of Lords, Chamberlain argued, the Government should proceed to lay before Parliament any constitutional proposals which it had in mind. The object of the amendment was to expose the split between Rosebery and Harcourt on House of Lords reform, but for Chamberlain, with his past support of Welsh disestablishment and his past attacks on the peers, it was rash ground to choose.

Asquith used the opportunity presented by this unusual lowering of Chamberlain's parliamentary guard to hammer him mercilessly. "Now, Sir," he concluded, "I should be glad to know, and the House would be glad to know. . . . what my right honourable friend[1] thinks has happened to the cup which was nearly full in 1885 (when Chamberlain had himself originated the phrase), and how he explains that in his view the House of Lords, which, as he told the electors then, had ' sheltered every abuse and protected every privilege for nearly a century ' has become, as he apparently thinks it has, the last refuge of popular liberty?"*m* "Asquith's speech last night was a splendid success," Harcourt wrote to his son with one of the bursts of generous enthusiasm which compensated for much of his tiresomeness. "He knocked Joe into a cocked hat. Even the Tories admit that the latter was nowhere. . . . I don't think I have ever heard a speech which created so great an effect in the House."*n*

The Government had a good debating spring, for both Harcourt himself and Henry Fowler, the new Secretary of State for India, achieved successes almost as notable as Asquith's, the former with a denunciation of bimetallism and the latter with a defence of the Indian cotton duties. Unpromising though the subjects sound, these achievements raised the stock of the Government, and Harcourt was able to write triumphantly to the Chief Whip of " our insolent foes (going) chapfallen to eat their addled Easter eggs."

The triumphs did not long continue. The Government had very small majorities on many of the Welsh Church divisions in May and early June. But defeat came, in a thin House (Asquith like many others was paired), on the unexpected issue of a motion to reduce Campbell-Bannerman's salary because of deficiencies in the supply of cordite.

[1] As he rather surprisingly still called Chamberlain.

Had the Cabinet wished to fight back and get the House to reverse this decision they could no doubt have done so. Alternatively they could have asked for a dissolution. But after a four hour discussion ministers decided against either move. Divided on so many other issues, Rosebery and Harcourt were united in agreeing that, for a weak Government, they had run their course, and that it was time to go. Asquith did not originally agree with them—only Ripon and Tweedmouth did—but like the rest of the Cabinet he came into line. Rosebery resigned that evening and left it to Salisbury, for whom the Queen immediately sent, to arrange for the dissolution of Parliament. Asquith handed over his seals to Sir Matthew Ridley with the secure knowledge that he had scored an outstanding success during his thirty-four months of office.

CHAPTER VII

OUT OF OFFICE

1895-1902

The election of 1895 was a disaster for the Liberals. There was no unity of policy. Morley fought on Home Rule. Harcourt fought on local option. And Rosebery, insofar as he fought at all, did so on the House of Lords. His interventions on this or any other issue took place before the dissolution of Parliament. Once the campaign had properly begun, the convention that peers should not interfere in elections coalesced with his distaste for much of his party to make him give the widest possible berth to the scene of the contests. He hired a yacht and sailed round the North of Scotland, calling occasionally at remote fishing ports to receive, with mixed feelings, news of the mounting disasters.

Asquith had a hard campaign, fought without his wife who was ill in London, but his result—a majority increased from 294 to 716 —was much better than the general run of Liberal performance. This was not primarily due to his record as a minister or to his effectiveness as a campaigner. The Scottish lowlands as a whole, which had failed to swing to the Liberals in 1892, compensated by refusing to swing against them in 1895. Campbell-Bannerman, the only other member of the late Cabinet with a constituency in this area, also improved his majority. But in England the Liberal toll was severe. Harcourt was beaten at Derby and Morley at Newcastle-on-Tyne. Harcourt's reverse occurred sufficiently early in the staggered election of those days for him to switch rapidly to West Monmouthshire, where local option was more popular, and secure his return there without any break in parliamentary service. But Morley remained out until the late autumn when he too retired to a haven in the Celtic fringe— Montrose Burghs.

Rosebery brought himself to write a short note of regret to Harcourt after the Derby result, but his real feelings were better expressed in a letter which he wrote to Asquith on July 22nd. After commiserating with him on the " insolent set made at you in the way of heckling," and congratulating him on his " admirable temper and composure," he added: " I think it would do one of our defeated colleagues infinite good to stand for East Fife. My only interest has been in individual elections like yours, for the general catastrophe was under the circumstances certain and inevitable. We may indeed congratulate ourselves that we are not more completely pulverised."

Even so, the defeat was bad enough. The Liberals were reduced from 274 to 177. Lord Salisbury's majority was 152, and the new Government, the first in which the Liberal Unionist leaders accepted office, showed every sign of being a long-lived one.

This meant that Asquith had to make major dispositions in his pattern of life. His political prospects had greatly advanced during the lifetime of the Liberal Government. In a party rent by faction he was the only man of note of whom no-one spoke ill. This was not because he was a weak figure without a clear-cut position. His moderate Roseberyite views were well known, but many of those who did not accept them nevertheless thought that the best hope for the future of the Liberal Party lay with him. " You need not mind any of the quarrels," Sir William Harcourt said to Margot Asquith . . . " your man is the man of the future."[a] Mr. Gladstone believed much the same; so did Lord Spencer; and so, more predictably, did Lord Rosebery.

From 1895 onwards Asquith believed that, without some unforeseen ill chance, he would one day be leader of the Liberal Party. But he was in no great hurry to hasten that day, partly because he was by nature a patient man, and partly because he would have suffered considerable personal inconvenience from becoming leader early in a long period of opposition. It would have involved devoting all his time to a salary-less occupation, and this he could not afford. His second marriage brought him £5,000 a year, but it also brought him a pattern of expenditure which precluded full-time politics unless his party were in office and he was paid another £5,000 a year as a minister.

In the autumn of 1894 he had taken a lease on 20, Cavendish Square, and this remained his London house, with the exception of the years in Downing Street, until 1920. It was a spacious and comfortable house, but inconvenient to run—all the food had to be brought from a mews kitchen across the courtyard at the back,—and upon the scale at which it was maintained, extremely expensive. There were normally fourteen servants in the house, including a butler and two footmen, who were occupied with a continuous round of luncheon and dinner parties. In addition to the fourteen there were a coachman and boy in the stable. Until the Wharf, near Abingdon, was acquired nearly twenty years later, the Asquiths had no regular house out of London, so that expense at least was spared. But they usually took a house in Scotland for the later summer and early autumn; and Mrs. Asquith's resumption of hunting soon after their marriage led to considerable expenditure which ended only when she finally sold her horses in 1906.

Even without the new lavishness which came with his second marriage, Asquith would have remained dependent on his professional earnings. He had five children—four of them boys—to educate, and after the age of about forty any return to the austerity of his early Hampstead days would have been most unwelcome to him. His marriage to Margot meant that his total family expenditure was much higher; but even had this not taken place he would still have had to return to the bar. He could never have afforded to be a full time politician in opposition. In 1888, well before the death of his first wife, he had told his pupil John Roskill that, if he achieved his immediate ambition of becoming Home Secretary in the next Government, his firm plan, when he was again in opposition, was to return to practice. At that time, no doubt, he could not foresee how near and how quickly he would approach the leadership, but his declaration of intention was important because it then involved a sharp break with tradition. No former Cabinet Minister had ever previously appeared in a supplicatory role before judges. The distinction was a fine one, for former law officers had frequently done this. In 1886, for example, Sir Henry James and Sir Charles Russell, each a former Attorney-General, had both appeared in the Dilke case. But neither had served in the Cabinet, nor did any law officer until 1912, when Asquith himself included Sir Rufus Isaacs, then Attorney-General. They were not therefore Privy Councillors, for this political honour was then granted sufficiently sparingly that it was in effect confined to the Cabinet.[1] And

[1] There were occasional exceptions. When Chamberlain unavailingly tried to persuade Dilke to accept the Irish Office without the Cabinet in 1882 he argued that " it carried with it the Privy Council " and he was probably

the point of the loose convention which Asquith was preparing to break was that, as a Privy Councillor, he would be of higher rank than most of the judges before whom he was likely to appear, and that this might be damaging both to his own dignity and even to the whole established system of precedence. In fact, when he broke the convention relatively little notice was taken and no dire consequences followed, either for himself or anyone else. Since then there has never been any question of the right of lawyers to return to practice from the Cabinet, although the numbers who have wished to do so have been surprisingly small; Simon in the 'twenties and Shawcross in the 'fifties have been the most notable examples.

In the autumn of 1895 Asquith therefore returned to 1, Paper Buildings and began his final period of practice, which was to last a solid decade. He had lost some ground as a result of his absence and new leaders had established themselves. Russell had become Lord Chief Justice, and Carson and Edward Clarke had succeeded as the most formidable jury advocates. More significantly from Asquith's point of view, Haldane and C. A. Cripps (later Lord Parmoor) had taken the leading places in appeals to the Judicial Committee of the Privy Council and cases before the Railway Commission. This was the type of work on which, together with House of Lords appeals, Asquith's practice became increasingly concentrated.

After a short interval he achieved a position roughly equal to that of Cripps and Haldane. But he never rose above this. His jury appeal, in spite of his political success, remained woefully deficient. He never became a fashionable advocate, and he appeared in few cases which attracted much public interest. One of the exceptions was *Powell v. Kempton Park Racecourse Company*, and here he was engaged, during the several stages of a long-drawn-out battle, in arguing the abstruse proposition that an unroofed enclosure adjoining a race-course was a

---

speaking with Gladstone's authority, although G. O. Trevelyan, who accepted the job after Dilke's refusal, did not get the honour. And in 1856, a still more pertinent exception, Palmerston made Stuart Wortley, who had already acquired a Privy Councillorship, his Solicitor General. In 1902, Haldane, a member of the Chancery Bar, who had never held office although he was a more prominent member of Parliament than most of those who had, was made a right honourable in the Coronation honours. But this was after Asquith's break with tradition.

" place kept and used for betting " within the meaning of the Act of 1853, rather than in any dramatic destruction of witnesses or deployment of evidence. He never again spent as widely-publicised a day in court as that on which he had dissected Macdonald of *The Times* before the Parnell Commission in 1888. As a result his legal work was notably lacking in that aura of anecdote which surrounded the careers of Russell or Carson, or F. E. Smith or Marshall-Hall, or even Haldane —if only because of the last-named's verbal convolutions.

From the layman's point of view, Asquith's practice was, quite simply, a dull one, efficiently but undramatically conducted, without an undue expenditure of effort, and probably not of absorbing interest even to Asquith himself. But it yielded an income which, over the decade from 1895, fluctuated between £5,000 and £10,000 a year. He was never poorer, and sometimes much better off, than when in office. As a mark of success as a barrister his earnings may be considered high without being sensational; but they might have been markedly higher had he not been devoting a substantial part of his energies to politics.

Even upon politics, however, Asquith's expenditure of effort in the years after 1895 was in no way prodigal. Although he now had the concentrated front bench responsibilities associated with being one of the only six members of the late Cabinet left in the Commons, he returned so far as possible to the pattern of parliamentary attendance which he had followed between 1886 and 1892. In the session of 1896 he spoke eighteen times, but voted in only 124 divisions out of 419. In 1897 he spoke on 28 occasions, and voted once more in 124 divisions —out of a total 375. Many of his House of Commons speeches were on major occasions, and he supplemented them, as in the previous period, by occasional well-chosen platform engagements in the country. Nevertheless, his parliamentary economy did not pass without some comment, although this mostly took the form of regret that he was not more available rather than of a feeling that anyone who was so occupied outside was of little use to the Liberal Party. " But I do find that Grey is hopeful," Arthur Acland wrote to Asquith on January 20th, 1899 in a letter which began by complaining about the laziness of Harcourt's leadership, " and that you and he may do a good bit (in the H. of C.) if you have time to spare from law and society, and he from his country pursuits. . . ."[b]

The edge of criticism here, of course lay more in the suggestion of

Asquith's pre-occupation with society than of his immersion in the law. Insofar as there was a basis for the suggestion it arose partly, but by no means entirely, out of his second marriage. Several years before this took place he was living a life (while a minister) in which it was possible, as he recorded perhaps more with surprise than pleasure, to lunch three times in one week in the company of Balfour's friend, Lady Elcho, and also to sit next to her twice at dinner. But a week of such concentrated social activity was more unusual for him in the early 'nineties than at the end of the decade. Until 1894 Asquith gave very few luncheon or dinner parties of his own and went to no balls. After his marriage he was no less active as a host (or perhaps as a hostess's husband) than as a guest, and, in addition, his summer nights were often rounded-off by brief, non-dancing visits to the balls of the season. His wife has testified that this worldy activity was only of superficial interest to him, and there is certainly force in her parallel view that his outlook and actions were never influenced by any desire to stand well in the drawing-rooms of London. Why then, did he choose to spend so much time in them? The answer is partly that this was the sort of life he thought he had settled for when he married Margot, and partly that, when not engaged in the actual business of law or politics, he increasingly enjoyed feminine rather than masculine company, and frivolous rather than serious conversation; and this was the easiest way to find it.

Margot Asquith herself was a specialist in conversation which was both feminine and frivolous, and it might have been expected that her husband's desires in this direction would be satisfied at home. But she was perhaps a better performer in public than in private. And although their marriage forged a strong and lasting bond of intellectual and political loyalty between them, and was also a considerable success from the point of view of Margot's relations with the Asquith children, its early years were overshadowed by her persistent ill-health. In May, 1895, her first confinement resulted in a few days of great fear for her life, the loss of the child, and her condemnation, as a result of phlebitis, to three months of prostration.

She was by no means entirely solitary or consistently cast down during these months,[1] but it was obviously a dismal and trying period,

[1] In her *Autobiography* (I, p. 289) she describes a visit from Harcourt on June 21st: "I had seen most of my political and other friends—Mr. Gladstone, Lord Haldane, Mr. Birrell, Lord Spencer, Lord Rosebery, the Arch-

particularly when the general election took away from London not only her husband but most of her other friends as well. And at the end of it she was far from recovering her full health. " For many years after my first confinement," she wrote, " I was a delicate woman." Her disease was regarded as neurasthenia, and its worst manifestation was a persistent and almost complete sleeplessness. " Not the least sorrowful part of having neurasthenia " she continued, " is that your will-power, your character and your body are almost equally affected by it." And again: " No one who has not experienced over any length of time real sleeplessness can imagine what this means . . . insomnia is akin to insanity."[c]

There were occasional periods of relief. She enjoyed " bouts of health golfing in Scotland and hunting in Leicestershire," and at the beginning of 1897 she managed a successful confinement and her daughter Elizabeth was born.[1] In addition she always had great buoyancy of spirit, at least in public. But her troubles continued for a long time. All her pregnancies were difficult ones. Her son Anthony— Asquith's last child—was born in 1902, but, in addition to the misfortune of 1895, she lost two other children at birth—in 1899 and 1907. Her ill-health, according to her own testimony, continued for so long that " in the year 1908, when my husband became Prime Minister, I went to St. Paul's Cathedral and prayed that I might die rather than hamper his life as an invalid."[d]

The effect of all this was private rather than public. Margot did not become a recluse. Nor was there any question of a foundering of the marriage or a rupture of relations between herself and Asquith. But it did mean that the fulfilment he found was not as complete as he had perhaps hoped for before the marriage took place. It was not only that her illness made her difficult to live with. He probably expected that she would in any event be that. Rather was it that it

---

bishop of Canterbury, John Morley, Arthur Balfour, Sir Alfred Lyall and Admiral Maxse—and was delighted to see Sir William Harcourt." This visit took place on the evening of the Government's defeat on the cordite vote, and Harcourt only just got back into the House in time. But John Morley, who had unexpectedly joined Harcourt at her bedside, was still with her—and unpaired—when the division took place.

[1] 1897–1945. In 1919 she married the Roumanian diplomat Prince Antoine Bibesco.

made her less exhilarating and satisfying—which he had certainly not expected.

During these years towards and around the turn of the century Asquith's appearance underwent a great change. When the Liberal Government left office he was 42. He still looked a young man. Although he was always of rather stocky build he was not particularly heavy and his features were clear cut. His hair was fair and rather neat. He retained something of his Oxford and Hampstead air of ingenuous earnestness.

At first the main change in his appearance which resulted from his marriage was a considerable smartening-up of his dress. Left to himself he was always indifferent to clothes, but Margot thought them more important. Her account of their first meeting stressed his virtues despite the fact that he was "unfashionably dressed." And in their early letters there were occasional mocking remarks—from both sides—about the inelegance of his suits and hats. For a short time this was corrected. Their marriage photographs show that on this day at least he was fully presentable; and in the picture facing p. 64 which was taken in the summer of 1898 and shows Asquith walking with his daughter Elizabeth, he had even achieved a certain glossiness.

It was a short-lived quality. This photograph was a transitional one. His features were still young but they had become plump. A few years later the youth had gone. He put on much more weight, his face became not merely full-cheeked but heavy-jowled, and his hair became quite grey and, apparently, much looser in texture. By 1902 or '03 his appearance was that of a man well-advanced in middle-age. And with this advance there went the final abandonment of any attempt at elegance. Either Margot had ceased to care or, in this respect, he had revolted against her influence. His clothes were mostly the conventional ones for the occasion—although both on the golf course and in Scotland he preferred blue serge to tweed—but were baggy and carelessly worn. His hair was allowed to grow much longer, and he visited the barber with reluctance. In general his appearance became rather shaggy and he assumed that look of dignified, benevolent slovenliness, which was how he was to be best remembered. It is well expressed by the photograph opposite p. 320, which shows him in Whitehall in the early years of the Liberal Government of 1905. Thereafter he did not change much until well after the end of his premiership.

CHAPTER VIII

A DISMAL OPPOSITION
1895-9

The troubles which had beset the Liberal Party in government and during the general election showed no sign of diminishing in the new Parliament. Before it had even met Rosebery communicated to Lord Spencer his "irrevocable decision not to meet Harcourt in council any more." Harcourt received the news from Spencer. Asquith received it direct from Rosebery in a letter dated August 12th. This referred to "the contingency which we foresaw" having arrived, and made it clear that the proscription meant there could be no full meetings of former Liberal ministers, and that Rosebery wished all his colleagues to know what he had written in his letter to Spencer: "Had we boxes I would circulate it in a box!"

"Let me say one word quite frankly to you," he concluded. "I am more than willing to stand aside, if that should be judged best for the party. Nor does it seem easy to see how in our shattered condition the party can be led by a peer. But what would be worse, and indeed worst, would be that the party should be led by a Commons Castor and a peer Pollux who disagree on every subject and communicate on none."

For a man of such notoriously bad temper Harcourt took the proscription with remarkable equanimity. He referred to it as "a damned piece of impertinence" but, according to Lord Spencer, these were "the only bitter words used by him." Perhaps he was as reluctant as Rosebery to make any further attempts at co-operation, but was delighted that the responsibility for the break should rest so obviously on the other side. For a brief moment, at this stage, the possibility of an Asquith leadership was discussed, but as Harcourt showed no disposition to retire—why should he have played Rosebery's game for him?—the proposal lapsed.

It was accepted that for the time being the 1894 arrangement should persist. Harcourt would lead in the Commons and Kimberley in the Lords, while Rosebery would retain the titular leadership of the whole party, although his lack of any contact with Harcourt obviously made this role almost meaningless. Demoralisation followed rapidly and inevitably from this situation. Harcourt himself, with his old trouper's persistence, plodded on from the front bench, but there was hardly any one to support him. " Asquith went off to Scotland for good yesterday," he wrote to his wife on August 15th. " Campbell-Bannerman will not return from Marienbad. Bryce only is left, and he is off this week to the Cape. Acland is ill and Fowler shows up rarely."[a]

At the end of the month Parliament adjourned until February, and the Liberal Party was given an interval for re-grouping. It made little use of the opportunity. In January Asquith spent twenty-four hours with Rosebery at Mentmore and made a determined effort to move him into a more co-operative position. He did not succeed. " You did not convince me the other evening, nor I you," Rosebery wrote on January 29th. " I act as an obstacle, real or apparent, to the unity of the Liberal Party," he continued. " I am therefore bound in the interests of the party and its unity to offer some remedy or alternative, and thus I offer to take a back seat, nay, if necessary, to retire from politics, at any rate for a time. What more can I do? " But this was not what Asquith wanted, and he kept the knowledge of Rosebery's nearness to resignation to as narrow a circle as possible.

In the following August Rosebery drew up and circulated to his colleagues a memorandum which gave political and not merely personal shape to his discontents.

" There will be I suppose this autumn calls for a definite Liberal policy," he began. " Any such calls will be in my opinion premature, and, as far as I am concerned, futile. . . . It is impossible for the Liberal Party to remain nailed to the innumerable political propositions lightly accepted by Mr. Gladstone for the promotion of his Irish policy. The party needs to make a new start and to shed much of this—which may be desirable in the abstract or may not—but which by its bulk and multifarious aggressiveness constitutes an encumbrance—not an inspiration or assistance. . . . I believe that the best chance for the Liberal party lies much more in reaction from the present government than in any gospel of its own. The present government is the first Tory government since 1867: weakly and distractedly Tory no doubt, but compelled to be Tory by the brute force of its majority. . . . This is an immense advantage to the Liberal party, because it forces real Liberals back to that party, and helps on the process which all true Liberals must have at heart—the restoration of the Liberal party to what it was in richness, variety and strength before 1886."*b*

This was the clearest outline of his political attitude given by Rosebery during these years, and it contained one strand of thought—that of hope for the restoration of the pre-1886 balance—which was later to separate him sharply from Asquith. The memorandum was also a prelude to his resignation, although it did not state this, and his mind, at least as to timing, may easily not have been made up when he wrote it. But at the end of September Gladstone suddenly emerged from retirement. In the last public speech of his life, at Liverpool, he delivered a great denunciation of the Armenian massacres, accompanied by a demand for British intervention against the Turks. This Rosebery chose to treat not only as a last speech but as " the last straw on his back." His personal relations with Gladstone had remained perfectly friendly —and continued so—but he regarded the G.O.M.'s final policy demand as totally unacceptable, and its promulgation as further undermining his own position. In fact Harcourt was just as opposed to Gladstone's demands as was Rosebery[1] but, unlike Rosebery, he was not worried that they would enable " discontented Liberals to pelt him with (Gladstone's) authority." Nor was he looking for an excuse to resign. But Rosebery was, and on October 6th he wrote to Ellis, the Chief Whip, announcing laconically that " the leadership of the party, so far as I am concerned, is vacant."

No one appears to have been consulted beforehand. Asquith was due to stay with Rosebery at Dalmeny for an Edinburgh meeting on Friday, October 9th, and he received two letters from him on the Wednesday, both dated Tuesday, the 6th. The first, written before the letter to Ellis, made no reference to it and was concerned mainly with travel arrangements. The second, by a later post, excused the brevity of the first one by his having been " occupied to the last moment with a letter to Ellis, of which I am afraid you will disapprove," and which could not be described in " a letter about trains." After pegging his resignation to Gladstone's speech, Rosebery concluded:

[1] Asquith, surprisingly, had gone furthest towards them by suggesting the severance of diplomatic relations with Turkey.

" From the bottom of my heart I can say that one of my deepest regrets in coming to that decision is the political severance with yourself, for your loyalty and friendship are one of my few bright associations with the last two years. I hope that, very soon, you will replace me."

Asquith arrived at Dalmeny on the Thursday morning, a few hours after the daily newspapers which carried the first news of the resignation. He was in time to join a curious luncheon party at which the future Lord Northcliffe, whom Rosebery described as " an interesting young man " and who had come for an interview, was also present. Rosebery noted that Asquith " behaved as always extremely well, but complained a little of no one having been consulted." The following evening, supported by H. H. Fowler as well as by Asquith, Rosebery delivered his resignation address to an audience of 4,000 in the Empire Theatre, Edinburgh. " It went off well enough," he noted, " indeed too well—as the Empire Theatre was so conversational to speak in that I lasted for nearly two hours." In the course of the two hours, as might have been expected in the circumstances, he paid a notably warm tribute to Asquith, including the following passage, hackneyed by then in its prediction of ultimate political success but interesting in its attribution of qualities: " Those who say that[1] must know Mr. Asquith very little, because consummate and considerable as are his powers of brain, in my opinion his head is not equal to his heart, and it is that rare combination of head and heart which, in my judgment, if my prophecy be worth anything, will conduct him to the highest office in the State."

The meeting over they returned to Dalmeny. On the following day, the Saturday, Margot arrived, and she and Asquith spent that day and the next with Rosebery until, on the Sunday evening, he left for Newmarket and they returned to Glen. Asquith and Rosebery remained on terms of affectionate friendship—Asquith usually stayed at Dalmeny or Mentmore once or twice a year and Rosebery wrote a letter of congratulation whenever Asquith made a particularly notable speech—but except for a brief moment in 1902 there was no further political collaboration between them. That chapter was effectively over. Asquith regretted its end, but he accepted it more realistically than did either Grey or Haldane who continued until 1905 to look upon

---

[1] That Asquith had not been in as " hearty association " with Rosebery as he might have been. Who did? Or was Rosebery merely displaying his over-sensitive egocentricity even in his introduction to the tribute?

Rosebery as in some sense their true leader and to believe that he might again be Prime Minister.

In the outside world Rosebery's going caused a great stir. He always obtained the maximum dramatic effect from his actions, and the voluntary resignation of a party leadership by a man of 49 who had held it for only fifteen months of government and eighteen months of opposition would at any time be a remarkable event. But Harcourt at least took it in his stride. " For my part I really do not see what is changed except ' that there is a Liberal the less '," he wrote to Morley on October 26th. " Of course the reasons given by Rosebery for bolting are not the true ones," he added. " I believe he funked the future which he saw before him . . . that he did not know what to say and so took up his hat and departed."[c1]

In the sense that the public standing of the Liberal Party at the time was hardly such that it could afford the loss of a single notable figure Harcourt's comment was complacent—although in his position he would have needed a superhuman breadth of view not to be glad to see the back of Rosebery. But in the sense that the change made little immediate practical difference he was undoubtedly right. Rosebery had done nothing for the party since he had ceased to be Prime Minister. The leadership in neither House of Parliament was affected, and no question of appointing a new titular leader for the party as a whole was raised. Harcourt was so much the superior of Kimberley, not only in political experience (as he had been of Rosebery) but in popular impact too (as he had not been) that he now necessarily appeared before the public as the real leader. But he made no attempt to secure formal recognition for this reality. On the contrary he reacted rather casually to the new circumstances. " One advantage of the situation," he wrote, " is that I feel altogether absolved from speechification. I have happily discharged my double barrel to my constituents, which is all that is obligatory."[d]

So he retired for the rest of the autumn and early winter. But he took the opportunity in November, again in a private letter to Morley, to deny any animosity towards Asquith. " Every effort has been made by the mischief-makers to cause ill blood between me and Asquith,"

[1] Harcourt at this stage seemed preoccupied by hat-seizing departures. " For my part," he wrote about himself four days later, also to Morley, " if I did not think it currish to bolt in the presence of difficulties, I should take up my hat and say good-bye." (Gardiner, *op cit.*, II, p. 422.)

he wrote. "I have had every reason to rely on his good faith and good will, and never allow myself to be influenced by gossip."*e*

The only immediate effect of Rosebery's resignation was to give a further twist to the already rapid spiral of Liberal demoralisation. Politics were not wholly in the doldrums. Domestically this may have been so. The third Salisbury Government had little that was constructive to propose in the field of home legislation; and indeed, so weak was its impetus in this direction, that even the distracted Liberal opposition was able to bury its first major venture—the Education Bill of 1896, designed to relieve the position of the voluntary schools—in what Harcourt called "the bog of Hansard." But externally it was a period of movement and innovation. Joseph Chamberlain, his energies pent up by a decade of political transition—determined to give no support to the Liberals, unwilling to join the Conservatives—had at last found his way back to office as Colonial Secretary.

Almost the first result, although an unintentional one, of his forward colonial policy, was the disastrous Jameson Raid into the territory of the Transvaal which took place over the Christmas and New Year of 1895–6. Asquith wrote of the enterprise in terms of lofty and mocking disapproval:

An adventure more childishly conceived or more clumsily executed it is impossible to imagine, and it resulted in immediate and ignominious failure. Dr. Jameson and his fellow filibusters (together with their secret cipher) were captured by the Boers. They were handed over with perhaps superfluous magnanimity, by President Kruger to the Imperial authorities, and having done by their blundering folly as great a disservice as it was possible to render, not only to the Uitlanders but to the best interests of the Empire, were, on their arrival in England, acclaimed and fêted by a section of London society as the worthy successors of Drake and Raleigh.*f*

Yet he allowed Margot to go a long way towards lining up with this "section of Society." "Dr. Jim (Sir Starr Jameson) had personal magnetism, and could do what he liked with my sex," she wrote. "My husband and I met the Doctor first—a week or ten days before his trial and sentence—at Georgina Lady Dudley's house; and the night before he went to prison he dined with us alone in Cavendish Square."*g*

This last statement, if her recollection was correct, is a striking example both of her ability to hunt even the most unsuitable lions and of the absence of publicity for private events in those days. Jameson, together with his collaborators, stood his trial at the Old Bailey between the 20th and the 29th of July, 1896. On the last day he was sentenced by Lord Chief Justice Russell to fifteen months' imprisonment and was sent that evening to Wormwood Scrubs. The Asquith dinner must therefore have taken place on the night of the 28th, when Jameson was poised between acquittal and punishment and when the attention of the whole country was concentrated upon him. It is astonishing in these circumstances, when even the Government thought his conviction highly necessary, that a prominent Liberal should have dared to ask him to dinner. It is rather as though, had the circumstances made it possible, Bonar Law had decided on the day after the Dublin Easter Rebellion to organise a little private party for Patric Pearse or James Connolly. It is even more astonishing that Jameson should have wished to accept the invitation for that particular evening. Surely, however great may have been Margot's charm and however impressive Asquith's reputation, he would have preferred to spend it with some of the many who regarded him as a wronged hero.

Mrs. Asquith related another incident about the Jameson events which, although also without corroboration, is inherently more probable. Of more significance than the guilt of Jameson was the complicity first of Cecil Rhodes (which no one was greatly inclined to doubt), and secondly of Joseph Chamberlain (which many people were inclined to suspect). To enquire into the first and if possible to avoid enquiry into the second of these matters, the Government proposed the appointment of a House of Commons Select Committee. Chamberlain moved to set it up on the day Jameson was sent to prison, but the proposal lapsed with the end of the parliamentary session a fortnight later, and the Committee did not begin work, after re-constitution, until the new session in February, 1897. The incident which Mrs. Asquith described related to July, 1896:

" I remember opening the front door of 20 Cavendish Square to Mr. Chamberlain one morning about that time, and showing him into my husband's library," she wrote. " At the end of a long visit I went into the room and said:

' What did Joe want, Henry? ' To which he answered:

' He asked me if I would serve on the Committee of Inquiry into the responsibility of the Jameson Raid—they call it " the

Rhodes Commission "—and I refused.' I asked him why he had refused, to which he answered: ' Do you take me for a fool? ' "[h]

It is not clear why Asquith should have reacted so violently against this proposal. Neither then nor subsequently did he believe in Chamberlain's guilt. " Nothing could have been more prompt or correct than the steps at once taken by Mr. Chamberlain. . . ." he wrote many years later of the Colonial Secretary's immediate reaction to Jameson's enterprise. " His condemnation of the Raid was severe and uncompromising . . . and both Lord Rosebery and Sir William Harcourt paid public tributes to the admirable manner in which he had handled the situation."[i] And there were plenty of other " fools " who responded to equal or lesser pressure. Chamberlain got Harcourt and Campbell-Bannerman, amongst former Liberal ministers, to serve on the Committee, and they were both curiously compliant in not following up the lines of enquiry which might have proved damaging to the Colonial Secretary, without in consequence suffering any loss of standing in the Liberal Party.[1] Perhaps Asquith, with his steadily developing belief in an economy of intellectual effort, was merely reacting against spending six months upon an enquiry which he thought likely to be politically disappointing.

It would be easy to exaggerate Liberal bitterness against Chamberlain at this stage. The older generation of leaders—Harcourt and Morley—never entirely lost the personal friendship with him which they had established upon the basis of political agreement in the 'eighties. And even in the late 'nineties this was accompanied by surprising if occasional shafts of political sympathy. " I have great confidence in Chamberlain's humanity," Morley wrote to Asquith in a letter dealing with South Africa and dated December 21st, 1897. " He has real feeling about ill-treatment of natives and will do as much as anybody to keep the brutes of colonists in order in these matters. . . . When you write to Milner be sure to convey to him all good wishes from me."[j] Asquith and his contemporaries, on the other hand, had barely known Chamberlain in his Liberal days, but they were eager to get to know him better in his Unionist ones. On June 11th, 1898, for example, a well-assorted political luncheon party, composed of the

---

[1] Against the view that a more resolute pursuit of the contents of the " Hawksley telegrams " might have unmasked Chamberlain, must be set the careful exoneration of him which is one of the main themes of Lady Pakenham's (now Lady Longford), *Jameson's Raid*, published in 1960.

Asquiths, Haldane, Edward Grey, Augustine Birrell and Chamberlain with his third wife and daughter Beatrice, assembled in the Cheshire Cheese off Fleet Street, and was a great success. Both sets of Liberals, the older Gladstonians and the younger imperialists, regarded Chamberlain as a most formidable foe. But they had no wish, in spite of 1886 and subsequent events, to destroy him politically—a wise tolerance, as things turned out, from the point of view of the future of the Liberal Party.

A more significant relationship for the politics of colonial affairs in the years leading up to the South African War, was that between Alfred Milner and many of the Liberals, and particularly Asquith. Milner was appointed by Chamberlain to succeed Sir Hercules Robinson as High Commissioner in South Africa in March, 1897. He quickly became the instigator and instrument of a tough policy towards the Boers, but he went out with the blessings of the Liberal Party—of which he was in general a supporter—as well as of the Government. Asquith, who had known him since Balliol, presided at a great dinner of farewell, at which Chamberlain, Balfour and Morley spoke, and to which Rosebery and Harcourt (united for once) sent warm messages. After his arrival at the Cape Milner used Asquith as his main channel of communication with the Liberal Party and wrote him long, frequent and confidential bulletins of information and argument. That there was little of an " imperialist " intrigue about this correspondence is shown by Morley's desire to use it as a vehicle for his own good wishes. But as time went on Milner became more inclined to suggest that what he wrote should be shown " to Grey and Haldane and no one else." There is little doubt that Asquith's views on the approach of the Boer War were influenced by Milner's letters, Germanically voluminous though they were for his taste.

Before the war became imminent the Liberal Party suffered another upheaval. On December 8th, 1898, Harcourt wrote a long letter to Morley, rehearsing his grievances since the retirement of Gladstone, and announcing that he was not prepared to continue as leader. Morley replied on December 10th with equal publicity, telling Harcourt that all his complaints were more than justified, and that the surprise was that he had continued to put up with the situation for so long. On December 14th the correspondence was published in the newspapers.

Asquith was ignorant of these transactions until he received the news in a letter from Harcourt on the morning of the 13th. The body of this letter was cool and calm, but attached to it was a less calm and longer postscript which pin-pointed Rosebery's letter to Spencer of August, 1895, as "the key to the whole situation," but refused to mention its author by name, referring to him darkly throughout only as "he" or "him." Asquith at once treated the situation created by Harcourt's decision as one of major crisis for the Liberal Party. He put off his appointments in the Law Courts and set out to find Ellis, the Chief Whip, whom he had "not seen for months."[1] He located him with some difficulty at his house in Cowley Street, Westminster, and showed him Harcourt's letter. Then he went across to the House of Lords where Haldane was arguing a case and took him out into a corridor in order to read the letter to him.[2] With both Ellis and Haldane, Asquith was more concerned to discuss the future rather than any question of putting back the past. They were "each of them strong that . . . (Asquith) was the proper successor."

While he was talking to Haldane, Asquith accidentally encountered Morley who was on his way to some committee. He remonstrated with him about Harcourt's action—not then knowing how deeply implicated Morley was in the whole business—and discovered both how useless this was and what were the exact plans for publication. "We had an unsatisfactory and not very agreeable interview, though we parted on perfectly friendly terms," Asquith recorded. His next task was to reply to Harcourt's letter. He expressed his disapproval of the decision and of the way in which it had been taken. But he did so sufficiently agreeably for Harcourt to reply on the following day in a distinctly more friendly tone than he had struck in his first letter. This second Harcourt letter to Asquith contained the following notable passage:

[1] This, together with Asquith's comment when he received Harcourt's letter that "no word of any sort or kind (except a letter announcing Lou-Lou's engagement) had passed between him and me during the autumn" does not say a great deal for the cohesiveness of the Liberal opposition during parliamentary recesses.

[2] Quite reasonably in the circumstances Asquith took no notice of the last sentence of Harcourt's letter which said: "I must beg you to treat this communication *as absolutely secret* until the public announcement which must be immediate."

One of my strongest feelings is a regard for the character and dignity of the House of Commons. It depends mainly on maintaining the authority and position of the leaders on both sides. A leader of opposition who finds his whips speaking and voting against him[1] cannot maintain that respect which is due to his position, still less when he finds the organisation of the party working against him in the country.[2] One of these days—and that an *early* day—you will have cause to be grateful to me for having vindicated the authority of the leader.[k]

That night Asquith went to Leicestershire to see his wife, and returned to London on the following morning—Wednesday, December 14th. He had two problems on his mind at this stage. The more immediate but lesser one was what he was to say in Birmingham on the Friday evening, when he was due to address a public rally at the close of a meeting of the National Liberal Federation.[3] The greater problem was whether, if the pressure were sufficiently strong, he should allow himself to be pushed into the vacant leadership. He had sedulously spread around the view that he could not afford it. Spencer, for instance, wrote to him on Christmas Eve: " As to yourself I heartily wish that you could lead the opposition; I consider that you are the right man for the post, at the same time I feel that the party cannot ask you to sacrifice your family and private interests. . . ."[l] And Asquith himself, after noting the strong opinions of Ellis and Haldane in his favour, recorded:

From the first this was not my own view. On personal grounds it is impossible for me without a great and unjustifiable sacrifice of the interests of my family to take a position which—if it is to

[1] Ferguson and MacArthur, assistant Liberal whips with Roseberyite leanings, had apparently done this on one or two occasions.

[2] This was a reference to the persistent influence of Rosebery, and of his strongly committed organ, the *Daily News*, upon certain parts of the Liberal machine; and also, perhaps, to the fact that Ellis did not do as much to counteract this as he might have done.

[3] Both Harcourt and Morley wrote in their public exchange as though some challenge to Harcourt's leadership had been likely to emerge at this meeting; but as in the outcome a proposal at the meeting that Harcourt should be asked to reconsider his decision was not pressed on the ground that it would interfere with the prerogatives of the parliamentary party, this does not seem very plausible.

be properly filled—would cut me off from my profession and leave me poor and pecuniarily dependent. On public and party grounds, I doubt whether at this moment and under existing political conditions, I would not render as good service as second in command as in the position of leader. From every point of view I thought that the best choice our party could make was Campbell-Bannerman.[1m]

Yet his contemporary writings[2] give the impression that at this stage he was wavering. He was unusually worried about his speech at Birmingham—which, despite the disarray of the Liberal Party, was delivered to a packed Town Hall and then to an overflow meeting—and took the precaution both of writing it out, and of choosing " matter (which was) not very inspiring." No doubt the circumstances would have made it necessary for any prominent figure in the party to speak circumspectly, but Asquith seemed additionally anxious to say nothing which would commit him either to accepting or refusing the leadership. He got back to London on the Saturday morning and Ellis and Haldane lunched with him in Cavendish Square. " There was much discussion between us as to the possibility of my leaving the Bar and leading the party, but we all agreed that in the first instance the leadership ought to be offered to Campbell-Bannerman, whom I and all would loyally support."

That luncheon probably decided Asquith against taking the leadership. If Ellis and Haldane had put a pistol to his head by taking the view that Bannerman was impossible, Asquith might have been prepared to say yes. But they did not. And when a letter from Fowler in much the same sense arrived on the Monday morning, Asquith decided that he could write with a good conscience to Bannerman (who was in bed with a cold in Scotland) and urge him to accept the rather thankless burden. " My object in writing to you," he stated, " is to say at once, and without any ambiguity, that I earnestly hope you will see your way to take the lead. . . ."[n] On the Wednesday Bannerman's reply reached Cavendish Square. It was warm and friendly,

[1] If Asquith were to exclude himself, Bannerman became almost inevitable. Harcourt and Morley apart, there were only two other ex-Cabinet ministers—Fowler and Bryce—left in the Commons. Neither was *papabile*.

[2] The main source is an 1,800 word memorandum of events—unusually long for Asquith—which he wrote immediately before Christmas. (*Asquith Papers*, IX, ff 109–28).

and dealt pithily and sensibly with Harcourt; but although it implied that he would accept the leadership, it did not say so:

How much more dignified and easier it would have been if the big man had written a simple note to Ellis, alleging advancing years, failing sight, loss of Lou-Lou, etc., etc. as reason for not going on. I never knew a more gratuitous bungle than the whole thing. But we can laugh over it at our leisure. . . . The situation is hideous. I can honestly reciprocate every word you say. I am not my own candidate, and will do my best to help another far more merrily than I should ask help for myself. I really do not know what may come of it, and can only hope that the weeks as they pass may have a settling effect.

But the big salmon will always be sulking under his stone, and ready for occasional plunges which will not always be free from a sinister intention. . . . I have no doubt that we poor ex-Cabinets at least shall have no difficulty, whoever may be nominal leader, in holding together and steering straight.⁰

A day or so later, however, Campbell-Bannerman told Tweed-mouth, who visited him in Scotland, that " if his doctor allowed him " he would accept the leadership. By the New Year this authority (who had to be written to in Vienna) had been prevailed upon not to object, and there remained only the problem of arranging the formalities of election. No one doubted that once the other ex-ministers had made their offer to Campbell-Bannerman, and he had accepted it, the arrangement would also be accepted without challenge by the party as a whole. The only point at issue was how large a circle of front-benchers was to be consulted before the general party meeting. Tweedmouth (who had some standing as an ex-Chief Whip) wanted a prior meeting of all front-bench men, but this was strongly resisted by Campbell-Bannerman himself, who wrote to Asquith on January 2nd arguing that it was quite wrong to interpose another circle of authority between the Shadow Cabinet (which was restricted to communicant " ex-Cabs " as he called them) and the back-benchers. Asquith wrote back on January 3rd concurring with Campbell-Bannerman's view, but saying that he was also opposed to Fowler's idea of a meeting of all the surviving members of the late Cabinet. " Who is entitled to issue such a summons? " he asked. " Are the three principal members[1] to

[1] Rosebery, Harcourt and Morley.

be included or omitted? And is there any member of it, in either House, who wishes to see it assembled again for any purpose under Heaven? "*p*

These opinions upon which Asquith and Campbell-Bannerman concurred were very austere ones. They restricted the electing body to four men, of whom one was the new leader, and another his only possible rival. In the outcome Campbell-Bannerman was forced to modify them to the small extent of agreeing to a general front-bench dinner.

In other ways, too, the new leader began on a firmly traditional course—which may in part have been a result of his feeling that the Liberal Party, so battered from both right and left, needed continuity rather than change, and a reminder that it had known better days and would perhaps soon know them again. " As to its scene," he wrote to Asquith on January 17th about the forthcoming party meeting, which had been arranged for February 6th, " my disposition is all for the Reform Club. Anything else would be a confession of weakness and decadence. Why should we lose our hold on so excellent a property? And as a matter of fact I believe more of our men (certainly the best of them) belong to it than any other. . . . The alternative is a Committee Room, which would be to sink to the level of the Irish, who do not profess to have any home in London."*q*

Campbell-Bannerman was also eager to create a sense of unity, cohesion and even cosiness amongst those who were left in the Shadow Cabinet. They could at least all congratulate each other on not having treated the party as badly as in their different ways Rosebery, Harcourt and Morley had done. This was a constant theme of the correspondence of Spencer, Fowler, Bannerman and (to a lesser extent) Asquith with each other.

For the future of the party the crucial factor was the development of relations between the last two. Previously they had never had close contact with each other beyond that involved in sitting first in a Cabinet and then in a Shadow Cabinet together. Their official inter-course had been perfectly agreeable but they were in no sense friends. Neither in London nor in Scotland did they move in the same social world. They belonged to different wings of the party. Asquith, largely because of his Roseberyite affiliations, was by this stage thought of as the strong man of the right. Campbell-Bannerman, beyond having supported him for the premiership in 1894, was in no sense a Roseberyite. He had some leanings towards the Little Englandism of Harcourt and Morley, but within the Liberal Party he was basically a man of the centre, loyal to the Gladstonian traditions although more concerned with keeping the party together than with any ideological considerations. He was sixteen years Asquith's senior (which meant that he could not be a long-term rival) and, although both shrewd and cultivated, he was manifestly his intellectual inferior, a less accomplished parliamentarian, and not as well-known a national figure. But he was respected by his colleagues and popular with the rank and file of the Liberal Party.

Could he and Asquith work smoothly and closely together? They began excellently, with a warm and frequent exchange of letters written in mutual confidence. Asquith was at such pains to avoid any suggestion that he was not whole-heartedly behind the new leader that, when influenza prevented his attending Campbell-Bannerman's eve-of-session dinner on February 3rd, he concluded his apology by writing: "If a list of the guests is sent to the papers it might be as well to treat me as constructively present, and include my name. Otherwise we may have some nonsense about a ' diplomatic indisposition'!"*r* Then in April, when the sudden death of Tom Ellis at the age of forty dealt the party yet another blow, they successfully surmounted the crisis together. After some initial hesitancy, they agreed to the appointment of Herbert Gladstone, who had been under-secretary to Asquith at the Home Office. By the early summer of 1899 it looked as though the Liberal Party might at last be approaching a calmer and more successful period. Perhaps after all the loss of Rosebery and Harcourt had been blessings in disguise. As leaders they had each of them been disruptive as well as lazy.[1] Things might now go better. And when Rosebery stood out against the new spirit of closing the existing ranks by attending a dinner of the City Liberal Club on May 5th and appealing again for a new party embodying all the pre-1886 Liberal elements, Asquith sat down on the following day and wrote him a long and vigorous letter of remonstrance:

[1] Harcourt was diligent in a parliamentary sense, but he was lazy in a policy sense. As Arthur Acland had written to Asquith on January 20th, 1899, making a contrast with Harcourt's practice: "The great strength of Mr. G. and of Chamberlain has been that they were always . . . planning and gathering files of information from others with a view to the future." (*Asquith Papers*, IX. 164–172).

6th May, 1899   *20 Cavendish Square, W.*

My dear R,

I am writing in the spirit of friendship: otherwise I should remain silent.

I have read, and re-read, your speech of last night, and the effect upon me—for I have not compared notes with other people, except for two minutes with Spencer—is very depressing.

I do not dwell upon what you say as to the " decay " of Parliamentary Liberalism—though I think a kinder and more appreciative phrase might have been employed to describe the uphill endeavours of a small minority fighting against overwhelming odds and exposed to the recurrent loss of former leaders.

But the main and most serious question suggested by your speech is—what are to be the lines of reconstruction of the Liberal Party of the future? You revert to the *status quo* of '85 as the possible and desirable point of a new departure, with the supplement of a due admixture of " imperialism."

This of course to the ordinary intelligence means (1) a repudiation of H(ome) R(ule), either as an immediate or as an ultimate aim of Liberal policy, and (2) a condonation of the constant and malignant activity of the small faction (numerically) but (electorally and politically) the powerful conjugation of ex-Liberal forces which from '86 to '99 have been in Parliament our most formidable and relentless foes and in the country the most militant and effective ally of the regular and normal Tory army.

Can it be supposed that Hartington and Chamberlain, and those whom they represent and lead, will find in the existing condition of things, or in any probable or possible remoulding of what is, any tempting inducement to abandon their present allies and return to the old camp? And if, as I think, their recantation is the vainest of dreams, what new principle of reconstruction do you offer to our own party—the men who in bad times and under discouraging conditions, and with every social influence arrayed against them, have stuck to the ship and supported their party? They are to surrender at discretion in order that, perchance, the spectacle of their compliance may—through pity or contempt—reconvert the apostates.

III

I am—I believe—an Imperialist in your sense and agree with you that the homage which the present government have paid to Imperialism is in the nature of lip-service and not (apart from the hysterics of rhetoric) a real devotion. But what will be said—and not without plausible argument—is that you are seeking to reconstruct the Liberal Party—or to create its successor—on the basis of an amalgam of Unionism and jingoism. This seems to me to offer to the doubting middle voters the maximum of inducement to remain or become Tory, and the minimum of motives to join our own ranks.

I have spoken frankly, and I know that you won't misinterpret my motives, or question my real friendship and affection.
Always yours,

H.H.A.[8]

The force of this letter was somewhat reduced by the fact that, after he had written it, Asquith decided not to send it. But he kept it carefully amongst his papers, with the inscription " not sent " upon the envelope, and it depicted clearly the wide political gulf which had opened between him and Rosebery at this time, and his own agreement with Campbell-Bannerman that the important task was to rally those elements in the Liberal Party which had remained faithful. While this agreement lasted there was hope for the Liberal Party. But it did not last for long.

CHAPTER IX

LIBERAL IMPERIALISM AND THE BOER WAR

1899-1902

The issue which destroyed this delicate, new-found sense of Libera unity, and sent Asquith temporarily back into the arms of Rosebery was the war in South Africa. The Boer ultimatum, which precipitated its outbreak, was delivered on October 9th, 1899 and fighting began three days later. This was no storm out of a clear sky. South Africa had been in a state of sustained crisis since the previous February; and in June, Chamberlain, in what he regarded as a most critical speech in Birmingham, had made the country face the possibility of war and had talked of how, " having undertaken this business (the protection of the ' Uitlanders ' in the Transvaal) we will see it through."[a]

At this preliminary stage, however, and even to some extent throughout the first phase of the war itself, the Liberal differences were containable. Although Chamberlain made a correct prognosis when he wrote in July that if it came to war " the Government could rely upon the vast majority of its own supporters and a minority of the opposition," Asquith and the other potential members of this minority showed no desire to commit themselves in advance; and this was in spite of the fact that Milner, still writing voluminously to Asquith, was far more in favour of forcing the issue than was Chamberlain. On June 20th the Colonial Secretary had invited Campbell-Bannerman to a private interview and had tried—unsuccessfully—to get his support for a show of force, presenting this not as a prelude to war but as a substitute for it. The only result was that on June 28th the Liberal leader publicly reaffirmed the opposition to military preparations which he had announced eleven days before.

There was no indication at this stage that Asquith disagreed with his chief. On September 2nd he went out of his way to express to his constituents his disapproval of "irresponsible clamours which we hear from familiar quarters for war." He saw no problem which could not be solved by " firm and prudent diplomacy "; and while Campbell-Bannerman might not have given as much stress to the firmness as to the prudence, they were still in reasonably close step with one another.[1]

The decisive event for Asquith was the Boer ultimatum. " From it," his official biographers say, " . . . he ' dated as the Mohammedans do from the Hegira '."[b] And as he himself put it nearly two years later: " We (the Liberal Imperialists) held and still hold that war was neither intended nor desired by the Government and the people of Great Britain, but that it was forced upon us without adequate reason, entirely against our will."[c] It was in many ways an odd event to treat as an absolute determinant of attitude, especially by one who regarded Chamberlain's diplomacy as indefensible, for it merely anticipated a British ultimatum which had been approved by the Cabinet on September 29th, and was in the process of delivery by the extraordinarily dilatory method of mail steamer. But this was not fully known at the time, and for the moment Asquith's view about the outbreak of hostilities did not separate him from Campbell-Bannerman.[2] The

[1] After this meeting, which he described as having taken place " in a small upper room in Leven in the presence of about 100 females, with a small sprinkling of the other sex," Asquith wrote to express the hope that Campbell-Bannerman would agree with his speech. But he added: " It would be a mistake to suppose that our people—as a whole—are at all strongly pro-Boer. I talked to one or two representative Liberals before I spoke—Free Church ministers and such—and was rather surprised to find how anti-Kruger and bellicose was their frame of mind." (*Campbell-Bannerman Papers*, 41210, 171-4).

[2] During the period leading up to hostilities, and the first few days after their outbreak, what separated Campbell-Bannerman from his colleagues, much more than any difference of political outlook, was the English Channel. As was his usual habit he had been at Marienbad since the beginning of August, but was persuaded with great difficulty by Herbert Gladstone (assisted by Asquith) to cut short his holiday and start for England about September 24th. Owing to the state of Lady Campbell-Bannerman's health, he explained, he then travelled back by the shortest stages heard of since the development of railways. One day's journey took him only from Frankfurt to Mainz. When he got to Brussels he read a several days' old copy of *The Times* and decided that the situation had improved sufficiently for him to stay there. He got to London on October 3rd, but went back to Paris on the 7th

Liberal leader, in his first speech after the recall of Parliament on October 17th, spoke of the Boers as having " committed an aggression which it was the plain duty of us all to resist," and joined with Asquith in abstaining on an unofficial Liberal amendment to the address (moved by Philip Stanhope) censuring the Government's conduct of the negotiations.

Nevertheless, even at this stage, Campbell-Bannerman's underlying attitude to the problem of South Africa was not the same as Asquith's. Bannerman claimed that he was " anti-Joe, but never pro-Kruger," and his behaviour throughout made the claim a perfectly reasonable one. Even so, his relatively simple character and non-metropolitan outlook made him much less impatient of the slow and wily stubbornness of " Oom Paul " than was Asquith, with his smooth-working Balliol intellect. Furthermore, if Campbell-Bannerman did feel any hostility towards Kruger it was more than balanced by his distrust of Milner. He believed him to be an opinionated and dangerous man of doubtful judgment. He was nervous of his close relations with Asquith, and he scoffed at what he called the *religio Milneriana*, a spiritual disease to which he believed Liberal intellectuals, and especially Liberal Balliol intellectuals, to be highly susceptible.

Campbell-Bannerman's abstention on the Stanhope amendment was therefore dictated more by a desire to avoid difficulties with his colleagues than by any firm conviction that it was a mistaken motion. As a manoeuvre for holding together the Liberal Party his inaction was manifestly a failure. It may have left him united with Asquith, Fowler, Grey and Haldane, but it separated him from 135 Liberal members (of a total of 186) who went into the lobby with Stanhope For a man resolved to lead from the centre—or indeed for any leader—this was obviously a dangerous situation.

Rosebery made matters worse by two provocative speeches at the

---

to fetch his wife. He was still there when war broke out, and was then delayed at Calais by a Channel storm on October 13th. As a result the Shadow Cabinet could not meet until October 14th, two days after fighting had begun and five days after the Boer ultimatum. The whole episode illustrated the truth of his description of himself, in his leadership acceptance speech as of " an easy-going disposition."

end of the month, in one of which he seemed to lay the blame for the war more on Gladstone (for his Majuba Hill policy in 1882) than on Chamberlain. The result of all this was that Campbell-Bannerman decided he had gone too far towards propitiating the Liberal Imperialists. He accordingly began a slow movement back towards a more anti-war position. A new note was discernible in his speeches in Manchester on November 8th and in Birmingham on November 24th. " I felt sure that he would have to drop down on our side and he has done it," Morley wrote to Harcourt. " C-B has cut the painter of the dinghy in which Rosebery, Grey and Fowler[1] may drift off by themselves," was Harcourt's comment.[d]

Campbell-Bannerman's new tack took him towards the arms of these two sulking Achilles whose resignations less than a year before had opened the way to his leadership. But Harcourt could never sulk for long. He was full of political energy during the autumn of 1899 and eager to capture Campbell-Bannerman for the anti-war cause. Morley—much more of a natural sulker—remained more difficult to propitiate. "Remember," he said to Asquith when they were washing their hands in the Athenaeum one day later in the war, " that in this matter, I am not, and never have been, a follower of C-B."[e]

It was not merely towards Harcourt and Morley that Campbell-Bannerman was taken by his shift of position. On the extreme " Little England " (or perhaps " Little Wales ") wing of the party Lloyd George was already mounting his campaign of virulent opposition to the war which was to endanger his seat, his law practice and even his life, but which was also to launch him as a national figure. For him there was no question of holding a delicate balance between the intransigence of Kruger and the impatience of Milner. He saw the Boers as a God-fearing, liberty-loving people, a sort of South African equivalent of the radical hill-farmers of Wales, whose independence was threatened by the greed of the Rand financiers and the arrogance of Chamberlain's colonial policy. By one of the great ironies of history he made his reputation as a man of the left by this starry-eyed championing of a community now almost universally regarded as the most reactionary in the whole world.

Of more immediate importance to Campbell-Bannerman than the activities of Lloyd George and the few who went the whole way

[1] Asquith still remained remarkably free from criticism.

116

with him were the views of established Liberal parliamentary figures. The majority of these were unsympathetic to the Liberal Imperialists. In this category were Bryce, the fourth of the remaining " ex-Cabs ", Sir Robert Reid, who had been Attorney-General at the end of the last government, and a large part of the solid centre of the party in the House of Commons, men who were individually undistinguished but important to any leader's authority. In the House of Lords also there were few "Roseberyites." The handful of Whig peers who had not become Unionists in 1886 mostly remained faithful to the full Gladstonian tradition. The three most notable members of the front opposition bench—Spencer, Kimberley and Ripon—were all at least as anti-war as Campbell-Bannerman.

Outside Parliament the position was rather different. Rosebery still had a powerful hold not only on uncommitted opinion but also on many of those who were active in the Liberal Party machine. His vain and perverse character contained a streak of almost magical attraction, both private and public, which is impossible to recapture from his writings or the records of his behaviour, but the existence of which cannot be doubted. " I sometimes think that the reason why Rosebery attracts so much attention," Grey wrote, " is that the genius in him lifts him up so that he is conspicuous in the crowd, a head taller than it. . . . It's as if God dangled him amongst us by an invisible thread."*f* On his carefully-spaced public appearances people were always eager to see him—not unnaturally if he appeared before them in such a remarkable way. When he spoke at Glasgow in 1902, a crowd of 5,000 were in the hall; but 32,000 had applied for tickets.

Nor was Rosebery the sole strength of the Imperialists. Asquith principally, but Grey and Haldane to a substantial extent too, commanded great respect within as well as outside the party. There was no clear split between a moderate mass of Liberal voters and an extreme group of party activists. None of the leading Liberal Imperialists seem to have had the slightest difficulty in convincing their constituency associations of the rightness of their point of view. Indeed they implied (but perhaps this is always a favourite gambit for members with loyal associations) that they might have been under some pressure had they gone the other way.

Campbell-Bannerman himself provided some support for this view by recording, after a short visit to Dunfermline in his own constituency in early December, 1899, that " for the moment there is a coldness."

To some extent the Imperialists may have been helped by the Liberal press, which was broadly on their side. The exceptions were the *Manchester Guardian* and, somewhat more marginally, the evening *Westminster Gazette*. But the *Daily News*, which amongst London dailies counted as the official Liberal organ, was under the editorship of E. T. Cook and was violently pro-Milner. And so too, after November, 1899, was the *Daily Chronicle*. In that month H. W. Massingham, the pro-Boer editor, was dismissed and most of his editorial staff went with him. Thereafter it too followed what may be loosely called an Asquithian policy.

As a result the anti-imperialist wing of the party began to look around for a way of redressing the balance. They thought of starting a new national morning newspaper but decided that the cost— estimated at £250,000—was prohibitive. Then, at the beginning of 1901, they succeeded in effecting a palace revolution within the *Daily News*. George Cadbury, the Quaker Birmingham chocolate-maker was brought in, and the " cocoa-press," which lasted in some form for the next fifty-nine years, was born. Cook and his Imperialist staff were dismissed, just as Massingham and his lieutenants of the *Daily Chronicle* had been dismissed fifteen months earlier, and this paper, in the words of Halévy, then became " Puritan as well as Radical." Party schism produced an uncertain climate for Liberal journalists.

The balance which Campbell-Bannerman tried to strike was an almost impossible one. Whatever he said or did he was certain to offend an important and apparently indispensable section of his sadly debilitated party. During the autumn of 1899 and the early part 1900 he had very little room for manoeuvre. The war went so badly for England that only mad dogs like Lloyd George ventured out into the winter chill. But in the early spring Lord Roberts began to reverse the tide of Boer victories. In March Ladysmith was relieved and Bloemfontein occupied. In May a similar pattern was followed with Mafeking and Johannesburg. The victories made the political situation in Britain more fluid and increased Campbell-Bannerman's difficulties. " I follow with languid interest," Harcourt wrote with unconvincing cynicism in June, " the triumph of our arms and the dissolution of our Party."*g*

In July the Liberals approached an apotheosis of disorganisation. Sir Wilfred Lawson moved a " pro-Boer " amendment to a Government motion and was supported in the division lobby by Bryce,

Morley, Reid, Labouchère, Lloyd George and 25 others. Grey spoke strongly the other way and took a total of 40, including Asquith, Fowler and Haldane, into the Government lobby with him. Campbell-Bannerman with only 34 followers could do nothing more inspiring than to abstain. His leadership appeared to be reduced to a nullity.

This Liberal disarray, combined with the mistaken belief that the war was already won, prompted the Government to decide upon a dissolution of Parliament on September 17th and an election in early October. Chamberlain was the decisive figure both in pressing for the election and in conducting it when it came. His campaign showed some signs of megalomania and an unflagging determination to capitalise in his favour every ounce of patriotic feeling. He relentlessly damned all sections of the opposition, making no attempt to distinguish between those who had supported the war and those who had not. One of his chief objects, Garvin has informed us, " was to break the Liberal Imperialists," whom he regarded as a menace to the true imperialist vote.[h] He was instinctively hostile to a centre position in politics, something which he himself had determinedly leapfrogged in his violent transition from left to right.

Chamberlain accordingly proclaimed, and made the principal slogan of the election, " that a seat lost by the Government is a seat gained by the Boers," and worried very little when a careless telegraphist caused it to be published in a still harsher form.[1] The only exception that he made, even privately, was Grey. (" The election) has been fought with the greatest malignity by the baser sort on the other side," he wrote with splendid self-righteousness to his wife on October 14th, " and their disgraceful proceedings have only been repudiated by one single man, that is Sir Edward Grey. They are a bad lot. . . ."[i]

---

[1] The remark was originally made by the Mayor of Mafeking. Chamberlain quoted it, with attribution, in a speech at Tunstall, Staffordshire, on September 27th. At that stage it did not attract great publicity. A few days later he was asked to send a message to the Heywood division of Lancashire and repeated the phrase, this time without attribution. In transmission it was changed to " A seat lost to the Government is a seat sold to the Boers." The new version produced an even sharper storm of Liberal protest than the original would have done, but the protesters, quite naturally, were not greatly mollified when a correction was published. In any case, on innumerable Unionist posters, the slogan was soon appearing as " a vote for a Liberal is a vote for the Boers."

Asquith he lumped with the rest, and given his standards of judgment, he was right, for the ex-Home Secretary was particularly scathing in exposing Chamberlain's own electioneering methods.

This was the first " Khaki election." It was viciously fought, but compared with its successor in 1918 it was notably unsuccessful in swinging a great body of votes to the Government side. The most that it did was to prevent the swing away which might otherwise have occurred and which was then regarded as the natural pattern of events. But the state of the Liberal Party might easily have achieved that, without any " patriotic " appeal working in the other direction. At the general election of 1895 the Unionist majority was 152. Between then and 1900 it was reduced by by-election losses—all of them occurring before the outbreak of the war—to 130. As a result of the Khaki election it was increased to 134. This gave the Unionists a firm hold on the new House of Commons. Their share of the popular vote was less impressive. They secured only 2,400,000 as against the Liberals' 2,100,000. As was pointed out at the time, the " Boers " had polled surprisingly well.

The fact that they had all been equally subject to the rasp of Chamberlain's tongue might have been expected to bind the different Liberal factions together. But in politics defeat is usually divisive. Each faction blames the other for what has gone wrong. The Imperialists obviously believed that the Liberal Party might have done better had the centre and left not opened themselves to Chamberlain's " unpatriotic " charges—however unjustifiable they thought his electioneering methods to be. Asquith could support this belief by pointing to the fact that in East Fife his majority had risen from 716 to 1,431, while in the Stirling Burghs, only about 30 miles away, Campbell-Bannerman fell back from 1,127 to 630. Asquith, his official biographers tell us, took his own result as signifying constituency " approval of the line that he had hitherto taken on the war," while Campbell-Bannerman, we learn from the equivalent source, could only treat his " as a set-back which he frankly confessed was a complete surprise to him," but might have something to do with a turnover of the Roman Catholic vote on the schools question.

Throughout the country, however, while the Liberal Imperialists mostly did somewhat better than the generality of their party, the difference was not so decisive as to leave no ground for dispute. The extreme " pro-Boers," who were at this stage almost as critical of

Campbell-Bannerman as were the Imperialists,[1] countered by arguing that if the leadership had not compromised themselves by accepting the annexation of the two republics as inevitable,[2] the party could have fought back more enthusiastically and effectively. In addition, the centre of the party had a more concrete cause of grievance than the right. In July a Liberal Imperial Council had been set up, with R. W. Perks, who was member for Louth and Fowler's law partner, as the leading figure. The Imperialist front-benchers held aloof from its activities, but were inevitably regarded as sympathetic to its objects. Immediately before the election it issued a list of 56 Liberal candidates —including of course Asquith, Grey and Haldane—whom it regarded as worthy of the fullest support. This proceeding, with the implied proscription of the remainder, naturally aroused considerable resentment. And the offence was made worse when the Council responded to the defeat by publishing a manifesto (the style of which should at least have made it clear that Asquith had nothing to do with the drafting) declaring that " the time has arrived when it is necessary to clearly and permanently distinguish Liberals in whose policy with regard to Imperial questions patriotic voters may justly repose confidence from those whose opinions naturally disqualify them from controlling the action of an Imperial Parliament of a world-wide community of nations."

Campbell-Bannerman reacted strongly and immediately. On October 21st he wrote to Harcourt saying: " I have sent to the Press a letter in denunciation of the Perks manifesto, which carries mischievous audacity beyond toleration, but I think the manifesto is a happy incident, as showing quiet Liberals through the country something of

[1] The lines of dispute were as usual a little blurred, but the following is a rough guide to the position:

(a) the right of the Liberal Party, while critical of Chamberlain's diplomacy, believed that the Boers had caused the war by their ultimatum, and that the only tolerable outcome was British annexation of the Transvaal and the Orange Free State:

(b) the centre thought that the British Government was more responsible for the outbreak of the war, but accepted that, it having started, British annexation of the two republics was bound to follow:

(c) the left believed that the Boers were broadly right.

[2] Campbell-Bannerman, paradoxically, accepted the need for this earlier than did Asquith.

the spirit of the men we have to deal with."*j* All the typical signs of reaction to a really bitter intra-party dispute were present in this statement. But Campbell-Bannerman did not feel that he could then leave it entirely to " quiet Liberals " to make their disapproval felt. On November 15th he spoke at Dundee and delivered a strong attack on the Liberal Imperialist Council and an equally strong encomium of Harcourt and Morley. By an unfortunate slip of the tongue he referred to the Council as the Liberal *Unionist* Council. This slip in turn aroused great bitterness. Its modern equivalent would be for a prominent Labour Party spokesman to refer to the right wing of that party as wishing to behave as MacDonald did in 1931.

The immediate post-Khaki election period was therefore one of mounting disunity within the Liberal Party. Campbell-Bannerman's intention throughout these months was to hold the balance between the different sections of his followers. At Dundee, acting against the advice which Asquith had given him in a friendly letter of November 13th, he made some sort of overture—although a rather clumsy one —towards Rosebery. In December he had to deal with an offer from Harcourt to rejoin the Shadow Cabinet, and told him, in effect, that it would be inopportune. Both in that month and in January he threw his weight against any Liberal motion for the recall or censure of Milner. He also claimed that both then and in the summer of 1901, when the position became still more strained, he retained good personal relations with Asquith. He often complained about the machinations of " Master Haldane " or " Master Grey," but he never gave Asquith this disapproving title or put him in quite the same category.

Yet even if their relations remained reasonably good they could hardly be called close. In the weeks after the election Campbell-Bannerman exchanged frequent and friendly political letters with Harcourt, the man whose flouncing resignation had pushed him into the leadership. There were no equivalent exchanges with Asquith, who was nominally his first lieutenant. But when they saw each other, which was fairly frequently while the House was sitting and most infrequently when it was not, they were always able to speak easily and amicably. Asquith's position throughout was that of a committed Imperialist, but a moderate one whose influence upon the others, both ostensibly and in fact, was restraining.

Over the turn of the century, from December 1900 to the spring of 1901, the internal party situation became a little easier. Before Christmas the Imperialists joined with impressive enthusiasm in supporting a Lloyd George motion which was in effect a personal censure of Chamberlain for allowing his family firms to benefit from war contracts. This led to a bitter debate, and the fact that Grey and Haldane—who both spoke—drew a large part of the acrimony on to their own heads helped to silence suspicions that the Liberal right was preparing to do a Whig shuffle across to the Unionists. After Christmas there was the lull caused by the death of the Queen on January 22nd and then a remarkably amicable meeting of the National Liberal Federation at Rugby at the end of February.

This easier period came to an end on May 24th—the date of Milner's return to England on leave. Whatever effect he may have had in South Africa he never failed to be the enemy of conciliation within the Liberal Party. From the moment of his arrival a new and more dangerous phase of the Liberal Imperialist dispute began. Grey went down to Southampton to meet him. Fowler attended a Claridge's banquet which Chamberlain gave in his honour, and listened, with approval it was assumed, to a notably intransigent speech. This provoked Morley to denounce Milner as an " imitation Bismarck," and Bryce to use equally strong but less pithy language. Then Grey replied to Morley at Berwick-on-Tweed. Campbell-Bannerman attempted one conciliatory speech, claiming that apart from a few unimportant people and a few unimportant issues there was basic Liberal unity on South Africa. This produced more derision than conviction.

A fortnight later, he swung decisively away from emollient platitude, and at a dinner of the National Reform Union on June 14th, delivered his most memorable and controversial statement of the war. Boer resistance was then carried on by guerilla methods. They had no effective army in the field, but almost every isolated farmstead had become an armed blockhouse. British troops were trying to complete their conquest by destroying the farm buildings and shepherding the Boer population into concentration camps. Campbell-Bannerman, speaking at the Holborn Restaurant before a predominantly " pro-Boer " audience, which included Harcourt and Morley, was discussing these methods. " A phrase often used," he said, " was that ' war is war,' but when one came to ask about it one was told that no war was going on, that it was not war. When was a war not a war? When it was carried on by methods of barbarism in South Africa."[k]

As is often the case when a phrase which will live in history has been fashioned the newspapers hardly noticed it on the first morning. But on the second morning they were loud in their denunciations, and many of Campbell-Bannerman's normal supporters in the centre of the party agreed with the editors in thinking that he had gone too far. Asquith, upon the basis of the first day's reports, had written his leader a letter of remonstrance. He was however courteous and even friendly in tone and put much of the blame on Morley:

SECRET   *20 Cavendish Square, W.*
                                                        15th June, 1901
My dear CB,
    I have read—with more regret than surprise—the report of last night's dinner. Through no fault of yours, the proceedings were turned into an aggressive demonstration by one section of the party, J.M.'s 'impromptu,' in particular, being of the most challenging description.
    I am very glad I was not there, and I shall do all I can to discourage reprisals, but I do not know with what success. It is a 'regrettable incident.'
                                       Yours ever,
                                                H. H. Asquith[l]

On the third day after the speech, Campbell-Bannerman explained to the House of Commons that he had intended no calumny against the army. But he also repeated, in relation to the system of warfare, the offending word, " barbarism." Haldane rose later in the debate to rebuke his leader for its use and to dissociate himself from him; and in the division which followed fifty Liberals showed their disapproval by abstention.

At this stage, Asquith, who had been amongst the fifty, moved for the first time into the leadership of the Imperialist (and, as it had now clearly become, anti-Campbell-Bannerman) wing. Hitherto, although he had always been regarded as the strongest man amongst them, he had left the running to Grey or Haldane or Fowler. In his constituency he had spoken clearly, but outside it, both in the House and in the country, he had tried to avoid the issue. But on June 20th he dined with the South Essex Liberals at the Liverpool Street Hotel and took the opportunity to reply moderately but strongly, not so much to Campbell-Bannerman himself as to those like Morley and Labouchère who had been encouraged by the leader's apparent lurch leftwards to mount a whole series of new attacks on the Imperialists:

"I am speaking not for myself alone," Asquith said, "but for a large number of my colleagues in the House of Commons and for a still larger body of Liberal opinion outside. Those, I say, who have taken that view may be right or they may be wrong. That is not what I am concerned to argue; time will decide. We have never sought to make the holding of that view the test of the political orthodoxy of our fellow Liberals, and I hope that we never shall. But that makes it all the more necessary for me to say in the plainest and most unequivocal terms, that we have not changed our view, that we do not repent of it, and that we shall not recant it."

Thus there began what Henry Lucy described as the process of "war to the knife and fork" within the Liberal Party. Where the South Essex Liberals stood on the issue is not known, but there were many people outside who were delighted with Asquith's speech. Fowler wrote on June 23rd a letter of great enthusiasm, congratulating Asquith on his "defence of the true Liberalism." "We must smash the talk about secession (that is what Harcourt, Labouchère and Co. desire)," he significantly continued. "*We* represent the majority of the Party. We are loyal to its principles and traditions. . . . "[m] At this stage the Liberal taste for dispute by public banquet began to get out of control. It was decided to hold another dinner to Asquith in recognition of his speech at the Liverpool Street Hotel. The process looked unending, but it was not allowed to continue without protest. On June 28th forty Liberal M.P.s wrote a joint letter to Asquith explaining that, despite their regard for him, they would not come to the dinner because they saw its purpose as disruptive. The letter was organised by Reginald McKenna, later to be one of Asquith's closest Cabinet colleagues, and Charles Hobhouse, who became Financial Secretary to the Treasury. Amongst the signatories were George Whiteley and the Master of Elibank, both of whom were to serve as Chief Whip under Asquith.

A day later there arrived a letter of protest from Lord Kimberley who had been Rosebery's Foreign Secretary. "I am much concerned," he wrote, "that you are to attend a dinner, which I am told is to be the occasion of a further demonstration against the recent speeches of C.B. and others on the South African situation."[n] Then, on July 10th—

the dinner was to be on July 19th—Campbell-Bannerman himself wrote, in direct and pressing terms. " Will you let me appeal to you," he said, " to get it (the dinner) postponed to a later time when all the Party will join in it, and when it will have lost all that tinge of sectional feeling which undoubtedly will cling to it now."^o

This appeal was written on the day after a special party meeting which Campbell-Bannerman, following the announcement of the dinner plans, had felt it necessary to summon in order to strengthen his authority. At this meeting he secured a unanimous vote of confidence and the solace, such as it was, of supporting speeches of varying enthusiasm from Harcourt, Grey and Asquith. They all said that they wished him to continue as leader, but the last two made it quite clear that this was only so long as, on the central issue of the day, they were not expected to follow his lead. Nevertheless the party meeting had slightly strengthened Campbell-Bannerman's position, and in his winding-up speech he had stressed that what he had objected to were not honest differences of view but separate organisations established for the purpose of " perpetuating and accentuating " these differences.

Such an organisation he undoubtedly regarded as being behind the dinner. Asquith nevertheless did not respond to his appeal to postpone it. " I have communicated with those who are responsible for the dinner," he wrote on the same day that he had received Campbell-Bannerman's letter, " and I find the arrangements are too far advanced to make postponement possible except at the cost of enormous inconvenience to people in all parts and countless explanations and misunderstandings." He added, that in the circumstances, he " would not take amiss the abstention of many of (his) friends," but hoped that " those who are coming will be allowed to do so without any suspicion of ulterior motives."^p

Campbell-Bannerman fortunately interpreted this letter as meaning that Asquith could not postpone the dinner ("no one more than Asquith himself wishes the Asquith dinner to be given up," he wrote to a friend at the time), and this view is endorsed by Asquith's official biographers.^q But it is contradicted by a letter which Grey wrote to Asquith on July 12th. " I have seen Rosebery . . .", he wrote, " I told him about C-B's letter and that you and some of us were very annoyed at such a move being made; and that the suggestion of a dinner of union at which he should preside could not be entertained. . . . " The contradiction would have been more direct, of course, had the letter been from Asquith to Grey; but relations of the closest confidence existed between the two men and there is no reason to think that Grey misrepresented Asquith's position to Rosebery. In the next passage of the same letter, Grey suggested that Asquith's mood at the time was more intransigent than Campbell-Bannerman allowed for, but that there was a deliberate arrangement by which he should stand a little aloof from the other Liberal Imperialists. Rosebery, it appears, told Grey that he did not want " to put the fat in the fire before the dinner was held." Grey passing this comment on to Asquith said: " I thought personally that making the fat frizzle could not hurt us, but that I thought it would be better that you should not be privy to any letter he (Rosebery) wrote." [r]

On the other hand Asquith had written back to the forty Liberal M.P.s in most conciliatory terms, saying that he entirely understood their attitude, but stressing that the dinner was no secessionist move: " Having differed from our friends upon one question, we are told that before long we shall be found in general agreement with our opponents. This is an illusion which in my opinion cannot be too promptly and effectively dispelled." To achieve this, he insisted, would be his main purpose at the dinner. The probability seems to be that Asquith was not averse to using the dinner as a show of his own strength as against that of Campbell-Bannerman, that he could not in any event have put it off without letting down his Imperialist associates, but that he was a little nervous that it might take on too extremist a tone.

In addition, however far he himself might have been from secession, he saw a danger that many important Liberal supporters might do precisely this unless they could be assured of the strength of the moderate wing. Lord Durham[1]; for instance, wrote to Asquith from Newmarket on July 2nd saying that he wished to attend the dinner as " a silent supporter." " I hate politics," he continued; " but, of course, am interested in the future of Liberalism. . . . But, I shall not assist, with my money, an opposition which does not recognise its duty to the Empire in preference to a desire to make itself disagreeable to the present Government." [s]

So the plans for the dinner proceeded. Then, at the last moment, Rosebery threw an extraordinarily timed spanner into the Liberal

[1] 1855–1928, the grandson of "Radical Jack." His letter sounded as though he might have inherited more of the wealth than of the radicalism of his forbear.

Imperialist works. When asked to preside at the dinner he had declined, perhaps wisely from everybody's point of view. And when asked to speak at the annual meeting of the City Liberal Club at lunch-time on the same day he had also declined, accompanying this latter refusal with an anti " methods of barbarism " manifesto which was published in *The Times* on July 17th. Then, unnecessarily and unexpectedly, he had turned up at the luncheon meeting after all and had delivered a provocative, headline-catching speech. The result was, as a *Times* leader commented the next day, that " the attention of the public, which was fixed beforehand on the late Home Secretary, has been suddenly turned to the late Prime Minister."

The Liberal Party, Rosebery said, must " start with a clean slate as regards those cumbersome programmes with which (it was) over-loaded in the past." As for himself: " I must plough my furrow alone. That is my fate, agreeable or the reverse; but before I get to the end of that furrow it is possible that I may find myself not alone." This intervention led even Grey to deliver a sharp public remonstrance. It had been made at so ill-chosen a time as to suggest that some hidden vein of jealousy of Asquith's leadership of the Liberal right must suddenly have risen to the surface of Rosebery's complex character. Why otherwise should he have departed, in a manner so likely to steal Asquith's thunder, from his normal practice of giving weeks of prior build-up to his infrequent speeches? Yet on the following day he was writing to Asquith, blandly, admiringly, but without apology or apparent embarrassment:

> *The Durdans,*
> *Epsom*
> *July 20 1901*

My dear A,

I have just finished reading the banquet speeches,[1] each and all of them with admiration. But yours is by far your finest and most complete speech, and you know how greatly I admire all your speeches. It seems to me faultless, and will I think rank as one of the memorable speeches of our time.

The others too were all excellent. I hope with all my heart that you and your following will be able to control the Liberal party in the right direction. Indeed I think you may, for you have

[1] Grey presided and Fowler also spoke.

Sir Henry Campbell-Bannerman

Asquith: about 1904

the cream of the ability of the party, and your banquet has wiped out the National Reform Union.

One word more. There will be attempts (I see them beginning) to separate you and me. I do not mean politically for that can take care of itself, but in regard to personal friendship. Do not let them succeed, for our friendship is one of my most prized possessions.

Please give Margot my heartiest congratulations on your triumph, which I hope will cheer your suffering girl.[1]

Yours,

AR.

This letter is made more puzzling by the fact that it is difficult to believe that Rosebery could greatly have approved of Asquith's "banquet speech." It was in sharp—perhaps deliberate—contrast to his own oration of a few hours before. Rosebery, to justify his continued detachment, had described the attempt to paper over the Liberal cracks as "organised hypocrisy." Asquith had tried to reconcile his conflicting views about the desirability of the dinner by stressing the underlying unity of the party and attempting to turn attention away from the South African quarrel to the less contentious ground of home policy. Liberal Imperialism, he insisted, must be linked with a policy of radical reform for "Little England." The non-pejorative use of the term "Little England" was in itself something of an emollient to the other wing of the party, and the speech as a whole smoothed some of the feathers which had been ruffled by the preparations for the dinner. "A dangerous corner was thus turned," Asquith's official biographers commented.[t] But the stretch of road which came into sight did not look particularly promising. The temporary discord between Rosebery and the other leading Liberal Imperialists did nothing to bring them closer to Campbell-Bannerman; it merely made the disarray of the Liberal Party look even more complete. The prospect of a return to power seemed almost infinitely remote. "Some day if you are as long-lived as many of our tough politicians have been," Arthur Acland (no doubt trying to strike a cheerful note) wrote to Asquith, "there will be changes and even perhaps

[1] Violet Asquith had been dangerously ill with infantile paralysis for the previous week, a great additional strain upon Asquith at this difficult time.

a Liberal Government though it is difficult to see what it could do in such a Tory country as England now is."*u*

This was not quite the nadir of Liberal fortunes. With Parliament in recess the later months of 1901 passed fairly quietly, although one or two shots were exchanged between the leaders of the two factions in their autumn speeches. The noise of these was soon drowned in the vast rumble of advance publicity which Rosebery succeeded in building up for a speech which he was to deliver to the Chesterfield Liberal Association on December 16th. For several weeks beforehand the newspapers were full of contradictory rumours about what he was going to say; but they all agreed that he was going to say something which would give a new twist to politics. When the day came he succeeded in giving two new twists. On South Africa he outflanked his Liberal Imperialist lieutenants from the left. He had never fully shared their enthusiasm for Milner, and this enabled him to come out more firmly for a negotiated peace as opposed to unconditional surrender than they had been prepared to do. At the same time, he opened up a new cause of Liberal schism. The party was not only told once again to " clean its slate " but was also instructed to put away its " fly-blown phylacteries." Not surprisingly in view of its almost total lack of meaning the significance of this latter phrase was not at first appreciated. Campbell-Bannerman, indeed, was sufficiently encouraged by the note of conciliation on South Africa to call upon Rosebery in the following week and seek a rapprochement. He was quickly disillusioned, for during this interview Rosebery made it clear to the Liberal leader (as he was to do to the public in a speech at Liverpool on February 14th) that by " fly-blown phylacteries " he meant most of the Newcastle programme, and in particular, Home Rule for Ireland. " (I) stated definitely that I could have nothing further to do with Mr. Gladstone's policy," Rosebery recorded in his own note of the interview.*v*

This was an impossible position for Bannerman. Apart from his own convictions, which were strong on the subject, he had just publicly re-committed himself to the old policy on Home Rule in a speech at Dunfermline. He automatically excluded co-operation with Rosebery on these terms. " But where are the acolytes?," he wrote to J. A. Spender on January 1st, 1902. "Ronald F. (Munro Ferguson, the former Scottish whip) is making speeches calling on Liberals to elect between R. and me who are irreconcilably at variance on the war.

Haldane tramps in his heavy way along the same path. I believe Grey also will follow it. Will Asquith? I never hear anything of or from him."[1]*w*

In fact " the acolytes " were more firmly with Rosebery than for some time past. Grey wrote to Campbell-Bannerman on January 2nd threatening to repudiate his leadership unless he fully accepted the views on the South African War which Rosebery had put forward at Chesterfield. But at least this was an old issue. Even more depressingly for Liberal unity, Haldane wrote to Asquith from Scotland on January 5th raising the new issue. He was vehemently in favour of Rosebery moving from the generality of " fly-blown phylacteries " to an explicit anti-Home Rule statement provided that it was held up for a month or so—which was precisely what happened. " The feeling is pretty strong up here that such a declaration ought to come," he concluded.

Asquith was more cautious, but he was moving in the same direction. He made no attempt to prevent the widening of the Liberal gap during that winter. On January 14th he made an intransigent speech saying that the Boers must be convinced " of the finality of the result and the hopelessness of ever renewing the struggle," and he suggested to the Liberal Unionists that Rosebery's policy of the " clean slate " might make it easier for them to re-enter the party. On January 23rd he abstained from voting on the main opposition amendment to the Address, despite the fact that he had been closely involved in deciding upon its compromise wording.

Then, on March 1st, a week after Rosebery had written to *The Times* explicitly and even brutally repudiating Campbell-Bannerman's leadership,[2] Asquith explained his own position in a long open letter

---

[1] This last sentence is strong evidence against the view, sedulously fostered by Spender himself in his biographies both of Campbell-Bannerman and of Asquith, that throughout even the periods of greatest strain relations between his two subjects remained both close and friendly. And there were other indications of acerbity at this stage. " Whoever may propose the amendment to the Address it will certainly not be Asquith," Bannerman wrote early in January. (Spender, *Campbell-Bannerman*, II, p. 22).

[2] Campbell-Bannerman, unwisely some of his friends judged, had asked in a speech at Leicester on February 19th (notable also for a firm pinning of his colours to all the old Liberal masts) whether Lord Rosebery spoke from " the interior of our political tabernacle or from some vantage ground

to his constituents. Like almost all of his pronouncements this was moderate in form. But it leaned heavily towards Rosebery in substance, and amounted to a considered repudiation of Campbell-Bannerman by the man who was nominally his first lieutenant in the House of Commons. He commended the Chesterfield speech and said that it defined a common ground upon which, at this stage of the conflict, the great majority of Liberals were able to meet. In late December this might have been conciliatory. But in early March, when the leader of the party had made it quite clear that it was not ground upon which he could stand, it was the reverse. Asquith then dealt with Home Rule. He did not disavow Gladstone, but he said that even his " magnificent courage, unrivalled authority and unquenchable enthusiasm " had been unable to overcome the repugnance of a large majority of British people to the question of a Dublin Parliament. And in the eight years which had elapsed since 1893 their opinion had hardened:

If we are to be honest, we must ask ourselves this practical question. Is it to be part of the policy and programme of our party that, if returned to power, it will introduce into the House of Commons a bill for Irish Home Rule. The answer, in my judgment, is No. . . . Because the history of these years . . . has made it plain that the ends which we have always had, and still have, in view —the reconciliation of Ireland to the Empire and the relief of the Imperial Parliament (not as regards Ireland alone) from a load of unnecessary burdens—can only be attained by methods which will carry with them, step by step, the sanction and sympathy of British opinion. To recognise facts like these is not apostasy; it is common sense.

In addition, in the last days of February, the Liberal Imperialist Council was replaced by the much more formidable Liberal League. Rosebery was president, and Asquith, Grey and Fowler were vice-

---

outside." Rosebery wrote immediately to *The Times* giving his answer " at this moment of definite separation." " Speaking pontifically within his ' tabernacle ' last night, (Sir Henry) anathematised my declarations on the ' clean slate ' and Home Rule. It is obvious that our views on the war and its methods are not less discordant. I remain, therefore, outside his tabernacle, but not, I think, in solitude."

presidents. The policy object of the League was to promote Liberal Imperialist ideas and the doctrine of the " clean slate." Its organisational object was less clear. Rosebery said it was to prevent " his friends being drummed out of the Liberal Party." There were others who feared it might have more aggressive and schismatic tendencies. These fears were encouraged when the Liberal organiser in the Home Counties was appointed chief agent of the League, with the suggestion that part of his job might be the promotion of candidatures.

Campbell-Bannerman, who for several weeks past had believed a split was as likely as not and had concerted plans with the Chief Whip as to what to do when it occurred, made it clear that the promotion of candidatures would be for him the breaking point. Asquith at least had no desire to force such a rupture. In a speech at St. Leonards-on-Sea on March 14th he announced that " he would have nothing to do with any aggressive movement against his fellow-Liberals, he would have nothing to do with any attempt to destroy or weaken the general organisation of the party."

Almost accidentally this speech marked the turning point in the Liberal Party's quarrels. During the latter part of March most of the Liberal members associated with the League fell into line with Asquith's limited interpretation of its functions. But the more significant pressures towards Liberal unity came from outside. On March 24th the Government presented to Parliament a highly controversial Education Bill. On April 14th Sir Michael Hicks-Beach introduced his last budget, which included a proposal for a duty at the rate of 1/- a bushel on imported corn. On May 12th the South African War ended in the the Peace of Vereeniging. On May 23rd even Lord Rosebery made a speech of unity. After nearly eight years of Liberal schism a new era in politics was beginning.

CHAPTER X

THE OPPOSITION REVIVED

1902-5

Following close behind these other changes there came a change in the premiership. On July 10th, 1902, Lord Salisbury resigned and was succeeded by his nephew, Arthur Balfour. Balfour held office for three years and five months, and his period at 10, Downing Street is now commonly regarded as one of failure—almost of disaster. From an electoral point of view it was. Not only did it lead up to a massacre of Unionists at the 1906 general election, but it was punctuated by a constant series of by-election defeats. These underlined the narrow basis of support upon which Balfour was operating, as did the unusual number of policy resignations from his Cabinet. In this way he lost the two dominant personalities of the Government, Chamberlain and Devonshire (as Hartington had become), as well as a Chancellor of the Exchequer, a Secretary of State for India, and one for Scotland, and a Chief Secretary for Ireland. All but the last of these resignations arose out of the tariff reform issue, which Chamberlain threw into the centre of politics in May, 1903, and which caused Balfour to equivocate for the remainder of his premiership.

In spite of electoral weakness, internal schism, and tergiversation at the top on what appeared the most important issue of the day, the Government was in reality one of significant achievement. In his three and a half years Balfour accomplished more than his uncle had done in the preceding seven. He concluded the entente with France, he set up the Committee of Imperial Defence, and he pushed through the Education Bill of 1902. All three of these changes had a powerful long-term effect upon the development of the country.

The Education Bill was controversial for reasons which are now difficult fully to comprehend. Asquith described it as a piece of " reactionary domestic legislation," and his view was shared by almost every Liberal and by many Unionists as well. Only in a sectarian sense was it reactionary; educationally it was on balance progressive. But the politics of education were in those days dominated by sectarian questions, and Haldane, with a remarkable indifference to the frequency of his disagreements with the party leadership, was almost unique amongst Liberals in thinking that a national system of secondary education and the concentration of educational responsibility upon the major local government units—the country councils and county boroughs—was well worth the loss of the old school boards and the provision of ratepayers' money for the voluntary schools. It was this last provision, in spite (or perhaps because) of the fact that it was certain to lead to an improvement in the standards of the Anglican and Roman Catholic Schools, which aroused the Nonconformists and hence the Liberal Party. It also disaffected Joseph Chamberlain, who, in spite of everything which had happened since 1886, could not quite forget that it was the cause of non-sectarian education which had first given him national prominence. "I told you that your Education Bill would destroy your own party," he wrote gloomily to the Duke of Devonshire. "It has done so. Our best friends are leaving us by scores and hundreds, and they will not come back."[a] Chamberlain, however, did not choose to desert the Government on the issue. He merely allowed it to be one of a number of influences which sent him sulkily off to spend the winter of 1902-3 in South Africa. But as his musings while there led to his resignation on a still more explosive issue in the following September the fissiparous effects of the Education Bill upon the Unionist Party were not negligible.

Still more important was its unifying effect upon the Liberal Party. There have indeed been few bills which served a greater variety of useful purposes. Thanks largely to the cool nerve of Balfour himself it was law by the end of the year and began immediately to improve British education. But the act of passing it greatly weakened the Government, which had been long enough in power. And the act of opposing it greatly strengthened the Liberal Party, the persistent feebleness of which had unbalanced politics since 1886.

Asquith, like Rosebery and (a little more doubtfully) Grey, did not share Haldane's non-partisan position on the bill. He took a full and even a leading part in the opposition to it. He spoke frequently in the House on the subject and he shared the platform with Campbell-Bannerman at several of the major demonstrations which were organised outside. On these occasions he committed himself fully against all the main provisions of the bill and not merely against the rate subsidy for voluntary schools. " To sum the matter up," he said at the St. James's Hall in London on November 19th, " you have here a bill which absolutely upsets and revolutionizes the existing system of education. It abolishes the School Boards and establishes in place of them a non-representative authority." Yet the education controversy, along its traditional sectarian lines, was never one in which Asquith felt deeply involved or completely at home. There was too much Celtic excitement on his own side and too much intellectual force on the other for this to be so. The part he played in opposition to the 1902 Act was less important for its own sake than as a prelude to the fiscal controversy which began in the following year. This second controversy completely engaged Asquith's political attention, and was perfectly suited to his combination of talents. It was also central to the re-establishment of his position with the Liberal Party as a whole. The educational prelude meant that when the fiscal issue exploded upon the country he was already well-placed to take the lead in opposition to Chamberlain. A year earlier it would have been more difficult for him.

This explosion occurred on May 15th, 1903. On that evening Chamberlain used the familiar platform of the Birmingham Town Hall to divert the stream of English politics. He had returned to England in March with his temper no better than it had been when he left in November. His grievance about education might have faded, but it was more than replaced by his discovery that Ritchie, the new Chancellor, was determined to repeal the 1/- duty on corn which Hicks-Beach had introduced in the previous budget and which Chamberlain believed could be used for a limited experiment in imperial preference. Three weeks before the Birmingham speech the budget announcing this repeal had been introduced. Balfour was trying to hold the Cabinet together on the basis of acceptance of the budget on the one hand and a summer of enquiry into imperial preference on the other. Chamberlain on May 15th made it abundantly clear that there was no question of his waiting for the results of the enquiry and that he would interpret the compromise exactly as he liked.

" You can burn your leaflets," he had told the Liberal Chief Whip. " We are going to talk about something else." The confident arrogance of this statement was more than justified by the effect of the Birmingham speech. With an almost contemptuous ease, Chamberlain there set himself to show that, although Balfour might be Prime Minister, it was he who determined the course of politics. He began by dismissing the current subjects of dispute. In South Africa his " party weapons had become a little rusty " and he had returned in no mood to excite himself about matters like the Education Bill or temperance reform. Perhaps, he added sardonically, " the calm which is induced by the solitude of the illimitable veldt may have affected my constitution." The " constitution " of the Empire, he believed, was also in grave danger of being affected. Unless it could be held together by material ties, which meant preferential duties, it would inevitably disintegrate. The country had to choose between the fostering of imperial unity and " an entirely artificial and wrong interpretation which has been placed upon the doctrines of Free Trade by a small remnant of Little Englanders of the Manchester School who now professed to be the sole repositories of the doctrine of Mr. Cobden and Mr. Bright."

He also advocated retaliatory duties against foreign countries, and this second proposal led later to his placing increasing reliance, as a prop to his argument, on the depressed condition of British trade.[1] For the moment, however, it was the imperial argument which was to the fore, and Chamberlain made no effort to soften the conflict of ideas which was involved. " If you are to give a preference to the colonies," he said in the House of Commons a few days after Birmingham, " you must put a tax on food."

Asquith's reaction to the Birmingham speech was immediate. " On the morning of the 16th May, 1903," his wife records in her autobiography, " my husband came into my bedroom at 20 Cavendish Square with *The Times* in his hand. ' Wonderful news today,' he said, ' and it is only a question of time when we shall sweep this country'. Sitting upon my bed he showed me the report of a speech made at Birmingham the night before by Mr. Chamberlain."[b] This appraisal of the situation, which was to prove quite accurate, greatly increased Asquith's interest in politics. At Doncaster on May 21st he delivered the first direct reply to Chamberlain, and in the House of Commons during that summer he tried hard and effectively to widen the breach

[1] " Agriculture . . . has been practically destroyed," he rather extravagantly declared at Greenock on October 7th. " Sugar has gone, milk has gone, iron is threatened, wool is threatened. The turn of cotton will come. . . . "

between the Colonial Secretary and the other members of the Cabinet. This tactic paid excellent dividends. On September 9th Chamberlain sent a letter of resignation to Balfour, which a week later was accepted by the Prime Minister, who had in the meantime performed a balancing operation by shedding three Free Trade ministers, including the Chancellor of the Exchequer.[1] This development not only weakened the Government but also made it certain that Chamberlain, relieved of any restraints, would keep the issue, so disruptive for the Unionists and so unifying for the Liberals, continuously on the boil. It had become his only political *raison d'être*.

After his resignation Chamberlain at once embarked upon a programme of provincial meetings, expounding and amplifying his proposals. During that autumn he spoke at Glasgow, Greenock, Newcastle, Tynemouth, Liverpool, Cardiff, Newport and Leeds. Asquith also took to the platform. On October 8th he went to Cinderford in the Forest of Dean and there replied closely to the case which Chamberlain had deployed on Clydeside on the two previous nights; and he followed this up during the next month with important speeches at Newcastle, Paisley and Worcester, each of which was a direct refutation of Chamberlain's arguments. These speeches were all reported at length in the principal London and provincial newspapers, and the exchange assumed something of the nature of a gladiatorial contest, watched with close interest by politically conscious people throughout the country. Both sets of speeches were then collected and quickly published in pamphlet form. Chamberlain's cost 1/- and were entitled *Imperial Union and Tariff Reform*. Asquith's cost only 6d. (there were fewer of them) and were entitled *Trade and the Empire: Mr. Chamberlain's Proposals Examined*.

Between them the two pamphlets rehearse most of the arguments of this old controversy. Chamberlain had the advantage of the initiative; Asquith was always in the position of replying to him rather than developing a positive case of his own. Chamberlain also had the

[1] A fortnight afterwards the Duke of Devonshire, whom Balfour had not intended to lose, insisted on following these Free Traders. He provided at least one exception to the categories of men whom Mrs. Asquith thought to be peculiarly susceptible to the heresies of protection. " This caught on like wild fire," she wrote, " with the semi-clever, moderately educated, the Imperialists, Dukes, Journalists and Fighting Forces." (*Autobiography*, II, p. 53).

advantage of being a greater master of the isolated memorable phrase. But in other respects Asquith was on top. He was always at his best defending a well-prepared position and picking out with a deadly destructiveness the intellectual weaknesses in a hastily prepared enemy attack. And this was the position in this dispute.[1] Chamberlain, whose powers were perhaps already a little in decline, argued his case with most of his habitual clarity and with as many facts as he could assemble. But he did not carry Asquith's intellectual guns. He knew no economics, and his command over the rules of logic was by no means as complete as that of his adversary. Nor was his knowledge of the factual background to the discussion always as reliable as Asquith's. Here the latter's voluminous memory and well-ordered mind was of great value. Despite the many other calls on his time he always gave the impression of being thoroughly prepared, in the sense not of carefully turned phrases but of stores of readily available information. A striking example is given by his official biographers. Chamberlain asserted that after the repeal of the Corn Laws in 1846 the price of wheat during the next ten years was higher on the average than in the period preceding repeal. Asquith was immediately able to point out that repeal, while passed in 1846, did not take effect until 1849; that in the middle 'fifties prices were artificially raised by the Crimean War; but that between 1849 and 1853, the only years from which fair deductions could be drawn, the trend was sharply downwards.[c]

After a few weeks of this relentless shadowing Chamberlain began to show signs of nervous exasperation. At Cardiff, on November 20th, he fell back on that familiar resort of the intellectually worsted and claimed that Asquith was a remote lawyer with no business experience. Asquith replied sharply (if a little implausibly) that he would " gladly defer to businessmen who understood and applied the rules of arithmetic." This exchange was remembered and when the Chamberlain pamphlet came out at the end of the year Mrs. Chamberlain sent Asquith a copy inscribed " From the Wife of a Man of Business— M.E.C."—a gesture which combined good humour and prickliness in about equal proportions.

Asquith's activities in this campaign did a good deal to restore his

[1] It is not without irony that the two issues on which the Liberal Party re-established its unity were both essentially conservative ones: the desire to *preserve* the 1870 *status quo* in education; and the desire to *preserve* the Cobdenite *status quo* in fiscal policy.

relations not only with the Liberal Party generally but with Campbell-Bannerman in particular. Bannerman had also been unusually active that autumn, making at least five platform speeches as against his normal ration of two. These had all dealt principally with the tariff reform issue, but in a way quite different from Asquith's. They had not been directed so determinedly at the centre of Chamberlain's argument, and they had not attracted quite the same degree of attention. But the leader showed no jealousy of his lieutenant. " Wonderful speeches," he wrote in November. " How can these fellows ever have gone wrong? "[d1] The praise was genuine and it was easy for Campbell-Bannerman to give it, for as its expression implies, he always treated Asquith as in a different category from himself, in no way subject to direct comparison.

The new issue also made House of Commons relations easier. There was no question any longer of Campbell-Bannerman and Asquith leading different Liberal factions into different lobbies. Instead they could sit united watching Balfour turn and twist (and on a series of famous occasions in March, 1905 resort to the expedient of leading all his followers out of the House) in a desperate and skilful attempt to avoid the complete disintegration of his party. Nor did the Licensing Bill, the other great issue of the 1904 session, create any difficulty for the Liberals. This measure provided that where a licence was withdrawn, not because of misconduct, but on grounds of public policy, compensation should be paid; it was denounced by an united opposition as a brewers' charter and a typical piece of Tory legislation.

Yet it would be a mistake to imagine that after Chamberlain's Birmingham speech the Liberal leadership was miraculously freed of all friction and distrust. Differences had gone too deep for sudden healing. What happened in 1903 was that they were driven beneath the surface, but this was a great improvement on the previous position. In one sense, though, the apparently helpful issue of free trade provided a fresh cause of dissension. Amongst the Unionist majority in the House of Commons were a substantial group of " free-fooders " as they came to be called. A few of these carried their opposition to Chamberlain to the extent of joining the Liberal Party. The most

[1] The speeches were Asquith's alone, but the " fellows " included his Liberal Imperialist associates, for whom (with the possible exception of Haldane) he seemed to be earning a sort of collective absolution.

notable was Winston Churchill,[1] who crossed the floor in May, 1904; and the others included Sir Edgar Vincent (later Lord D'Abernon) and Sir John Poynder (later Lord Islington). But they were unrepresentative of the much greater number of Unionists who agreed with them on the issue but who did not elevate it above all other political questions. Education was an obstacle for some of these. Lord Hugh Cecil, for instance, combined a violent attachment to free trade with a high Anglican approach to voluntary schools. Even so, he was too much of a Cecil extremist to be typical. He wrote to Asquith in December, 1903, suggesting an amendment to the address which, he thought, would procure 30 Unionists in the Opposition lobby and 100 abstaining. But the men whom this was designed to catch were more cautious than he was himself. Nevertheless the prize of obtaining their support remained a dazzling one for the office-hungry Liberals. Herbert Gladstone as Chief Whip was instructed to explore the possibility of enticing them with unopposed returns in their constituencies, but he found the local Liberals reluctant to co-operate. Campbell-Bannerman, always sensitive to rank-and-file opinion, did not push him as far in this direction as some of the Liberal Imperialists would like to have gone.

Campbell-Bannerman's position on this whole matter was delicate. The education issue apart, he himself was the biggest single obstacle to co-operation with the Unionist free-fooders. Some of them might have been prepared to eject Balfour in favour of a Devonshire or a Rosebery or even an Asquith Government, but certainly not for a Campbell-Bannerman one. "Methods of barbarism" was still too fresh in their minds for that. In addition, Bannerman's speeches always stressed that the full radical programme was the only effective alternative to protection, and this too made co-operation more difficult. Lord James of Hereford (as the former Attorney-General had become) wrote to Asquith on December 21st, 1903, pointing out these obstacles.[e]

Campbell-Bannerman himself was perfectly aware that if the

[1] Despite the fact that he might have been considered a portmanteau representative of all the categories which Margot Asquith thought most susceptible to the tariff reform bug. He was "moderately educated" even if not "semi-clever," and he was nearer to being at once an imperialist, a duke, a journalist, and a member of the fighting forces than almost any other man in England (see p. 138 *n.*, *supra*).

Liberal Party was seeking an " opening to the right " his leadership stood in the way. This did not mean that he overtly opposed such a development. Indeed we are told by J. A. Spender that " he was foremost in plans for conciliating these people, and joined cheerfully in discussing the various ways of eliminating himself."*f* In any event he was rather doubtful towards the end of 1903 whether he could long continue as leader. His wife's health, never good, had been so bad that autumn that they had been unable to pay their normal two months' visit to Marienbad; and his own buoyancy had suffered greatly from this deprivation On October 29th Herbert Gladstone had written an important letter to Asquith from Hawarden:

> Possibly you may already possess this information. In any case I think it right to make sure that you know it. When I saw C-B. at Belmont we had a long talk about the future. He told me that so far as he was concerned in the event of a change of government he did not think that he would be able to take any part which involved heavy and responsible work. A peerage and some office of dignity like the Presidentship (*sic*) of the Council would be what he would like.*g*

This letter should be remembered when considering the attitude towards the future premiership taken by the Liberal Imperialists during this and subsequent years.

Doubts about his own physical capacity for the leadership did not pre-dispose Campbell-Bannerman in favour of those who were in effect saying that they would not co-operate with the Liberal Party so long as he was in command. He wrote to Asquith on December 26th in distinctly cool terms about the Unionist Free Traders: " James says the most of them would support the Gov. on any amendment to the address. Will our people in the country think this ' good enough ' to withdraw candidates in favour of these gentry? . . . We are ' the man on horseback '; and while everything should be done to make things easy for them, it is they who must draw closer to us, however distasteful."*h* Asquith did not dissent from this view. " I quite agree with what you say about our relations with the Free-fooders," he replied on December 28th. " They look very well in the shop window, but I fear that in most constituencies their voting strength is negligible."*i*

During 1904 and 1905 Campbell-Bannerman's enthusiasm for the premiership revived somewhat; and with this revival the issue of co-operation with the dissident Unionists might easily have become the cause of fresh dispute between him and Asquith. Fortunately, growing disillusionment with the determination of the dissidents combined with the strength which the Liberal Party had begun to show at by-elections to avoid this. For a few months after Chamberlain's resignation there were fears that his initiative was improving the popularity of the Government. All the new ministers who had to seek re-election were returned without difficulty, and the Liberals even lost a seat at Rochester. But by the summer of 1904 and on through 1905 the picture was quite different. There hardly seemed to be a safe Conservative seat left in the country; and the need of the Liberal Party for allies declined accordingly.

For the Liberal Imperialists this new confidence did not settle the question of the leadership. Their concern for Campbell-Bannerman's health remained at least as great as his own; and Haldane and Grey often did not even bother to operate behind this cloak.

One of Asquith's reactions to Chamberlain's new policy was to attempt to use it as a lever to get Rosebery back into active politics. In July, 1903, he tried unsuccessfully to persuade him to join a free trade committee, and in December he asked him to attend a political dinner, with the same result. Early in the autumn, however, Haldane and Grey, at Dalmeny, persuaded him to be a little more forthcoming, although hardly in the direction of Liberal unity. Haldane, writing from the New Club in Edinburgh, sent Asquith an excited account of this interview on October 5th:

(1) R.(osebery) has embodied in a secret memorandum[1] his reasons why he will *not* form a Govt. . . .

(2) R. will not enter a S(pencer) ministry. He expressed the utmost contempt for S.

(3) R. reiterates that he is going to work with all his strength for an A(squith) ministry. He admits that he has been too remiss, and has telegraphed to arrange 3 more meetings—in London (East

[1] This was dated September 30th and is published in full in Crewe's *Rosebery* (II, pp. 585–87). It shows Rosebery at his most self-pitying. He complained that he had only a few real followers. He suffered from the grave disadvantage of not being in the House of Commons. His memory, his hearing and his powers of application were fading. He had fallen into a solitary habit of life which he could not easily break, and he was sure that a return to office would mean a return of sleeplessness.

End), Leicester and Edinburgh. He finally admitted that a Spencer compromise might be necessary to get C-B from the House of Commons. Grey and I said that we would not serve under C-B either as P.M. or as leader in the H. of C.

This is what passed, and it was very definite. I left it to Grey and he was like a rock. You must lead us accordingly.*j*

Grey sent his own account two days later. It conflicted at no point with Haldane's, but it made more explicit their joint view that an Asquith premiership could not immediately be achieved. Grey had told Rosebery that they should aim only at making Asquith leader of the House of Commons. Otherwise "it would be urged upon you and your friends that it would be ungenerous and unnecessary to insist upon jumping over Spencer too...."*k*

Asquith's replies to these letters are not available. They were probably brief and non-committal. He rarely wrote long letters to men, and there is no evidence that he was making the running against Campbell-Bannerman. But neither did he resist the pressure which came from Haldane and Grey, who were, and remained, his closest political friends and associates. There is no reason why he should have done so, particularly in view of the intelligence which he received from Herbert Gladstone at the end of the same month.

There were no further important developments in relation to the leadership until the late summer of 1905. By then the Unionist Government's hold on life was slender. In July Balfour had persuaded his own supporters that it was right to carry on only by warning them, at a private meeting, that the state of foreign affairs made an immediate change undesirable. In August King Edward coincided with Campbell-Bannerman at Marienbad and greatly improved his relations with the Liberal leader. In June he had been doubtful about dining with him at the house of Lord Carrington, although in the event this encounter had gone well.*l* Two months later in Bohemia the King's friendliness and hospitality was such that, as soon as the royal party had departed, Campbell-Bannerman's doctor ordered him to bed for 48 hours. As a consolation for this strain on his digestion, Bannerman, as he wrote to Herbert Gladstone and to several others, had the King's assurance that he "must soon be in office and very high office."

Whether or not the Chief Whip passed this information on to the Liberal Imperialists they decided within a week upon concerted action.

Haldane was the instigator. As he described it in his *Autobiography*: " I went to Asquith at a country house he and his wife had taken at Glen of Rothes in the north-east of Scotland. Grey had a fishing at Relugas, only about fifteen miles off. After consultation, Asquith and I decided to go over and confer with Grey."*m* This meeting, which led to the so-called "Relugas compact," took place in the first days of September, 1905. The essence of the compact was that unless Campbell-Bannerman took a peerage and left the leadership in the Commons to Asquith none of the three would serve under him. The idea of a Spencer premiership appeared to have been dropped; and within a fortnight it was made still less likely by Spencer's serious illness.

Haldane, who had the closest relations with the court, was deputed to convey the news of the compact to King Edward, and if possible to secure his support. On September 12th, after his return to his house at Cloan, he accordingly wrote a long letter to Lord Knollys, the King's secretary. He referred to his having heard that Campbell-Bannerman was " greatly gratified by the kindly notice taken of him at Marienbad by the King," as well as to another development which might have precipitated the Relugas meeting. The Liberal Imperialists had hoped for some time that Campbell-Bannerman would agree to go to the Lords on a change of Government. " But we have within the last few days been made aware that this course will not be acceptable to a certain section of the party. They are not, for the most part, men whose names carry weight with the public. But they are vocal and energetic and have access to Sir H.C.B." This section of the party had to be combated on policy even more than personal grounds. That would be the object of the triumvirate laying down conditions without which they would not serve:

What is proposed is that Asquith should, in as friendly and tactful a way as possible, and without assuming that Sir H.C.B. is adverse, tell him of the resolution we have come to. We are none of us wedded to prospects of office. To Asquith and me they mean pecuniary sacrifice. This we do not shrink from in the least, but we ought not to make sacrifices uselessly. Grey delights in his new work as Chairman of the North-Eastern Railway. But we are all ready to do our best cheerfully under Sir H.C.B. provided we have sufficient safeguards. What we would try to bring about is that, if the situation arises, and Sir H.C.B. is sent for, he should propose to the King the leadership in the House of Commons with the

145

Exchequer for Asquith, either the Foreign or Colonial Office for Grey, and the Woolsack for myself. As to this last I am merely recording for you the wish of the others.[n]

Even so, this precision about the distribution of offices, as opposed to the question of Bannerman going to the Lords, went further than had been agreed. Grey, for instance, wrote to Asquith on October 2nd, still from Relugas, setting out his views in his usual rather ill-ordered way:

I adhere to the opinion that it is too soon to put a pistol to CB's head. If he shows himself willing to discuss the formation of the next Govt. he should be told what we think and feel. But we want it to come to him in a friendly way and not as if we were trying to force him in a way which he might think premature and unfriendly. . . . My feeling is quite friendly and loyal to him, but I don't mean to go into a Govt. unless the spokesman of the Govt. in one House of Parliament is yourself or Rosebery; and the latter alternative is apparently not a possible one under present conditions. I think it is too soon in any case to stipulate for definite offices.[o]

By this time, however, Haldane was launched on the next stage of the plan. He accepted that Grey was somewhat lukewarm and wrote in his *Autobiography*: " Asquith and I were more practical than Grey, who hated having to make any move." He was equally undiscouraged by the reply he received from Knollys, who wrote only on his own behalf, for the King did not reach Balmoral from his Marienbad expedition until September 25th, but who did not hesitate to advance arguments which ran directly counter to Haldane's own:

"I venture to ask you, and those whose names I have just mentioned (Asquith and Grey), would not you be better able to advance the interests of those questions, to which you rightly attach so much importance, as well as the welfare of the Country and the Liberal Party, by joining Sir H.C.B's Government, even if he remained in the House of Commons, than by holding aloof and making yourselves powerless to moderate the dangerous influence which might be brought to bear upon him?[p]

Haldane's response to this discouragement was to write to Asquith on September 27th:

What now is essential is 1) that you should see H.C.B. as soon as possible—within hours of his being back if practicable. Balmoral leaks curiously,[1] and it would be bad not to get the first word; 2) that this should be kept absolutely from Rosebery until it is communicated fully to H.C.B. His interest would be to wreck it. *q*

Haldane also arranged to visit Balmoral soon after the King's return. He arrived there on October 5th and sat next to his host at dinner that evening. On the following day he wrote again to Asquith:

I think that the King will ask C.B. to Sandringham in November and say that he doubts, from recent observation, whether anyone but a young man can be both P.M. and leader in the H. of C.— with the increasing business. This leaves it open to C.B. to think that Ld. S. may be sent for, and later on will enable the King to suggest a peerage to H.C.B.....*r*

The fear which Haldane had expressed in a previous letter to Asquith that Campbell-Bannerman " might with some semblance of justification allege a Court intrigue " did not seem entirely misplaced.

After his Balmoral visit, which lasted three days and included another long private talk with the King, Haldane arranged for Asquith to meet him in Edinburgh. As he put it in his *Autobiography:* " I left the Castle with the feeling that there was no more for me to do, and that the next step must be taken by Asquith when he saw C-B."*s*

Campbell-Bannerman could never be seen very early in the autumn. Asquith did in fact obey Haldane's rather excited advice of September 27th—he called at Belgrave Square within hours of his leader's return to England. But this was not until November 13th, and the interview which then took place was by no means entirely satisfactory to the Liberal Imperialists. The most immediate account of it comes from Mrs. Asquith's diary:

On Monday ... Henry came into my bedroom at Cavendish Square, where I was having my hair washed, and told me that he had seen Sir Henry Campbell-Bannerman.

Hearing this I could not wait, but tying a shawl round my head ran down to the library, where I sat down on one of the leather armchairs. Henry walked up and down the room and told me all he could remember of his talk with C.B.

He found him in his library in Belgrave Square looking at a newspaper called *The Week's Survey,* which he asked Henry if he

[1] Or was it " furiously "? The passage is not easy to decipher.

had ever heard of. Henry replied that he had not. They then proceeded to discuss Russia and Germany. Henry was glad to find him sound on Germany. He dislikes the Kaiser and thinks him a dangerous, restless, mischief-making man.

Suddenly he said that he thought things looked like coming to a head politically, and that any day after Parliament met we might expect a General Election. He gathered that he would probably be the man the King would send for, in which case he would make no phrases but would consent to form a government. Henry said: " C.B. then looked at me and said: ' I do not think that we have ever spoken of the future Liberal Government, Asquith? What would you like? The Exchequer, I suppose? '— I said nothing—' or the Home Office?' I said, ' Certainly not,' At which he said: ' Of course if you want legal promotion what about the Woolsack? No? Well then, it comes back to the Ex-chequer. I hear that it has been suggested by that ingenious person, Richard Burdon Haldane, that I should go to the House of Lords, a place for which I have neither liking, training nor ambition. In this case you would lead the House of Commons. While Lord Spencer was well and among us, nothing under Heaven would have made me do this! Nothing except at the point of the bay-onet '." . . . I could see that the impression left upon Henry's mind while he was telling me of this conversation was that it would be with reluctance and even repugnance that Campbell-Banner-man would ever go to the House of Lords.

C.B. then asked my husband who he thought best fitted for the Home Office; to which Henry replied that that depended upon who would have the Woolsack, and added: " ' For that, my dear C.B., there are only two possible people, Haldane or Reid, and went on to say that Reid had told him in past days that he did not fancy leaving the House of Commons: " in which case," said Henry, " why not give him the Home Office and Haldane the Woolsack? " C.B. answered, " Why not *vice versa*? "

When Henry told me this—knowing as I do that Haldane had set his heart on being Lord Chancellor, I was reminded of George Eliot's remark, " When a man wants a peach it is no good offering him the largest vegetable marrow," but I merely said that I hoped Haldane would not stand out if Reid desired the Woolsack. He went on to tell me that C.B. had then said:

" There are two more delicate offices we've not mentioned
Asquith—the Colonial and the Foreign Office? "

Henry said he thought Edward Grey should have the Foreign
Office; C. B. answered that he had considered Lord Elgin for this,
but Henry was very strong upon Grey. He said that he was the
only man, and that it was clear in his mind that Grey's appointment
as Foreign Minister would be popular all over Europe. He ex-
patiated at great length and convincingly on Grey's peculiar
fitness for a post of such delicacy.

C.B. said he wanted him for the War Office, but Henry told me
—having been unshakable upon this point—he felt pretty sure he
had made an impression, as C.B. ultimately agreed that Lord
Elgin would do well in the Colonial Office.

Henry ended our talk by saying to me:

" I could see that C.B. had never before realised how urgently
Grey is needed at the Foreign Office and I feel pretty sure that he
will offer it to him."[t]

A few days later there was another meeting between Asquith and
Campbell-Bannerman, but on the second occasion Grey was also
present and it was policy—in relation to Ireland—and not personalities
which was discussed.[1] At this meeting a compromise approach to
Home Rule was worked out, to which Campbell-Bannerman gave
expression in a speech at Stirling on November 23rd. Full self-government for Ireland remained the objective of the Liberal Party, but
the Nationalists were given clear notice that in the next Parliament
Home Rule would not be given the priority of 1886 and 1892. It
would have to wait its turn, and in the meantime the Irish were
advised to accept any degree of devolution they could get, " provided
it was consistent with and led up to (the) larger policy."

In this way the only likely remaining source of pre-election policy
dissension between Campbell-Bannerman and the Liberal Imperialists
was disposed of. But Rosebery remained unaware of the agreement
which Asquith and Grey had reached with Campbell-Bannerman, and
proceeded completely to misinterpret the Stirling speech. In a speech
of his own at Bodmin on November 25th he referred to it as " the

[1] On November 25th, however, during a Wiltshire week-end, Asquith
sent Campbell-Bannerman a letter of exceptional length, almost the whole
of which was devoted to a determined advocacy of Haldane's claims to
the Woolsack. (*Campbell-Bannerman Papers*, 41210, 247–52).

hoisting of the flag of Irish Home Rule," and announced " emphatically and explicitly and once for all that I cannot serve under that banner." Rosebery intended the Bodmin speech to mark his " final separation " from Campbell-Bannerman. In fact, its greater significance lay in marking his final separation from Asquith and Grey, both of whom reacted with some impatience to such a maladroit performance at that particular time.

The timing was especially unfortunate, because although no one knew whether Balfour would resign or dissolve, or exactly when he would act, he clearly could not much longer avoid doing one thing or the other. His position had been further weakened during November by the National Union of Conservative Associations insisting, against his advice, on passing a " whole-hog " tariff reform resolution. But although the Liberals were eager for office many of them were frightened about accepting it before a dissolution. "I am strongly against our taking office, if Balfour resigns now," Grey wrote to Asquith on November 24th. " He ought to be made to carry on till January when a dissolution can take place."[u] Herbert Gladstone wrote in the same sense on the same day.

Asquith at first shared these fears. " The storm signals are flying, and everything points to an early break-up," he told Campbell-Bannerman in his letter of November 25th. " It is obviously right that these people should themselves dissolve, and that the Liberal Party should not be compelled to form a Government until the country has given its decision, and the composition of the new Parliament is ascertained."[v] But when Campbell-Bannerman wrote from Scotland a week later saying that he, like Morley and Lord Ripon, was strongly in favour of acceptance, Asquith did not persist in his opposition.

He received this letter on the morning of Saturday, December 2nd. It was by then widely known that Balfour was to resign on the following Monday or Tuesday, and the new situation involved Asquith in a sudden and costly change of plan. He was about to leave for Egypt, where he had been briefed by some members of the family of the ex-Khedive at a fee of 10,000 guineas—by far the biggest he would ever have received. It was clear he could not go. He cancelled his passage, returned his brief, and prepared for the next and most important phase of his life. But what was to happen to the "Relugas compact"?

CHAPTER XI

THE RADICAL DAWN

1905-6

Campbell-Bannerman left Scotland for London by the night train on Sunday, December 3rd, and arrived only a few hours before Balfour's Monday afternoon resignation. It had required urgent telegrams from Morley and Herbert Gladstone to bring him south even then. From Euston he went straight to his recently acquired house in Belgrave Square, and passed the day there in a series of interviews. He saw Asquith and Grey together early, and found "there was no difference worth thinking of between him and them." This was because they again discussed policy—and mainly Ireland—rather than the allocation of offices and the arrangements for leadership in the two Houses.

On these latter matters Asquith and Grey were united in wishing the objects of the Relugas compact to be achieved, but divided on the amount of pressure they were prepared to apply to this end. Whatever he may have thought in September, Asquith was clear from the beginning of these December discussions that he could not coerce Campbell-Bannerman by threatening to stand out from the Government. His reasons for this change of position were most firmly set out in a letter which he wrote to Haldane (urging him to accept office) three days later:

The conditions are in one respect fundamentally different from those which we, or at any rate I, contemplated when we talked in the autumn. The election is before and not behind us, and a Free Trade majority, still more an independent majority, is not a fact but at most a probability.

I stand in a peculiar position which is not shared by either of you.

If I refuse to go in, one of two consequences follows either (1) the attempt to form a Govt. is given up (which I don't believe in the least would now happen) or (2) a weak Govt. would be formed entirely or almost entirely of one colour.

In either event in my opinion the issue of the election would be put in the utmost peril. It would be said that we were at issue about Home Rule, the Colonies, the Empire, etc., etc., and the defections of the whole of our group would be regarded as conclusive evidence. The *tertius gaudens* at Dalmeny[1] would look on with complacency. I cannot imagine more disastrous conditions under which to fight a Free Trade election.

And the whole responsibility, I repeat, would be mine. I could not say, after the offers made to Grey and you,[2] that our group had been flouted, and the only ground I could take would be that I and not C-B must from the first lead the new H. of Commons. I could not to my own conscience or the world justify such a position.

If the election were over, and Free Trade secure, different considerations would arise.[a]

Grey saw the matter differently. The most moderate of the three at Relugas in September, he now became the most intransigent in London in December. This was partly because he was the least interested in office, and partly because of a certain awkward inflexibility in his character. As Arthur Acland had written about him to Asquith five years earlier: " I think he is a man rather to see difficulties than to help people over them. . . . "[b] In any event Grey went back to Campbell-Bannerman at ten o'clock on the night of the same Monday, " all buttoned up " as the latter described him, and firmly told the Prime Minister-elect that unless he went to the House of Lords he (Grey) would accept no office.

This move of Grey's was foolish as well as intransigent. Campbell-Bannerman, his biographer tells us, was " greatly wounded and surprised " by this interview. But he was only worried by it because he thought that Asquith as well as Haldane must be a party to the ultimatum. For Haldane—" Schopenhauer " as he derisively called him—he had at this stage neither affection nor respect. He was determined not to give him the Woolsack and would have been quite

[1] Rosebery, irritation at whose Bodmin performance helped to make Asquith more conciliatory towards Campbell-Bannerman during these negotiations.

[2] p. 156 *infra*.

happy not to have him in the Government at all. Grey he regarded as much more useful, but, as his conversation with Asquith on November 13th had shown,[1] by no means indispensable. Asquith himself he did regard as nearly indispensable, and would have been hesitant about trying to form a Cabinet without him.

Grey, however, unlike Campbell-Bannerman, knew perfectly well by the time of his Monday night interview, that Asquith was not with him in his ultimatum. He did not resent this. " If you go in without me eventually," he had written earlier that day, " I shall be quite happy outside and I shan't think it the least wrong of you. . . ."[c] But he did not comprehend that without Asquith to give it force his ultimatum was likely to be more irritating than persuasive. Campbell-Bannerman was in fact undecided about a peerage when Grey saw him. He was by no means confident about facing Balfour in the House of Commons, and in addition the advice of his Viennese doctor, on whom he leant heavily, was against the double burden.[2] Grey turned what might have been an easy personal adjustment into a major political choice.

On the following morning Campbell-Bannerman went to Buckingham Palace to kiss hands. In the event he failed to secure his sovereign's hand for this symbolic act, but the King did not fail to slip in an expression of his own view that a peerage might be best for the new Prime Minister's health. This did nothing to make the proposition more agreeable to Campbell-Bannerman. He merely assumed (and not without foundation) that Haldane had been intriguing with the King. Was Asquith a party to the plot? Campbell-Bannerman had seen him early that Tuesday morning before the visit to the palace, had told him of Grey's attitude on the previous night, had expressed his own fears that he might be thought lacking in courage if he went to the Lords, and had asked for Asquith's views. Margot Asquith recorded in her diary the account which her husband gave her of his reply:

[1] p. 149 *supra*.
[2] " I am sure that those who are persuading you to remain in the House of Commons are not your true friends—I beg your pardon, in that direction —and that they do not think of your precious health as the most important matter," Dr. Ott wrote on December 9th (Spender, *op cit.*, II, p. 199). This letter was of course too late to affect Campbell-Bannerman's decision, but it referred back to an earlier agreement, to which Lady Campbell-Bannerman was a party, that " for your precious health it would be best for you to go to the House of Lords besides occupying the Government."

Henry answered that the position was almost too delicate and personal for them to discuss; but C.B. pressed him to say frankly everything that was in his mind. Henry pointed out what a fearful labour C.B. would find the combination of leading the House and being Prime Minister, as they were practically two men's work; that no one could possibly accuse him of being a coward; that the House of Lords was without a leader, and that it was placing him (Henry) in a cruel and impossible position if under the circumstances Edward Grey refused to take Office; he was his dearest friend as well as supporter, and to join a Government without such a friend would be personal pain to him, as they had never worked apart from one another.[d]

This was strong moral pressure, but it did not sound like an ultimatum; and the fact that it was not became completely clear when Campbell-Bannerman again saw Asquith soon after his return from the King, formally offered him the Exchequer, and received an unconditional acceptance. This acceptance more than outweighed the delicate pressure of the previous interview. As soon as he had received it Campbell-Bannerman telegraphed to Lord Cromer in Cairo and offered him the Foreign Office. This was an extraordinary move. Cromer was a great pro-consul, but he had no experience of British politics, he had never been a Liberal, and within two years he was to become an active (although moderate) Unionist. He was Grey's first cousin, but this in the circumstances was a doubtfully conciliatory consideration. Fortunately, after twenty-four hours' thought, he refused the offer on the ground of weak health.

That evening before dinner Asquith went to Hatfield, to keep (with almost excessive social meticulousness) an engagement to join a Salisbury house party. Margot was there already, having arrived with her step-daughter Violet during the afternoon; and the fullest account of the events of the next few days comes from her diary.[1] On this first evening of the visit she found her husband " profoundly anxious." He was apparently unaware of the Prime Minister's offer to Cromer, but he had seen Grey again before leaving London and had found him

[1] There is a certain confusion of dates in these diary passages. Mrs. Asquith speaks in one place of the Hatfield visit having begun on Wednesday, December 6th, and in another of the Wednesday being the second day of the visit. It seems most likely that they went to Hatfield on the Tuesday, and returned finally to London on the Friday morning (December 8th).

as adamant as ever—" in an uncompromising three-cornered humour." The chances of getting him to join seemed remote, and Asquith's pleasure at office must have been considerably reduced by the separation from his friends which seemed likely to be involved. But he did not brood. " That night at dinner at Hatfield," Margot wrote, " my husband looked worn out, and I admired him more than I could say for throwing himself into the social atmosphere of a fancy ball, with his usual simplicity and unselfcentredness." *e*

The next morning the Asquiths motored to London for the day. Asquith went to see Campbell-Bannerman in Belgrave Square and Margot went to their own house in Cavendish Square, where Herbert Gladstone came and gave her all the news. Asquith, as he told his wife that evening, when they had both returned to Hatfield, attempted a direct appeal to the Prime Minister:

I said, " It is no use going over the ground again, my dear C.B. I make a personal appeal to you, which I've never done before; I urge you to go to the House of Lords and solve this difficulty." *f*

Campbell-Bannerman received this appeal in a friendly but non-committal way. His wife was arriving from Scotland that evening. When she came he would consult her and be guided by the result. And that was the end of the interview.

Lady Campbell-Bannerman's advice, conveyed over dinner, was decisively given for a policy of " no surrender,"[1] and thereafter the Prime Minister's mind was not in doubt. He was unable to convey his decision to Asquith that evening, but he told Morley and Tweedmouth, who called at Belgrave Square after dinner. He also discussed with them certain alternative possibilities for the Foreign Office—Cromer's refusal had arrived. Here Morley, despite what he was later to write about the " unedifying transactions " of the Liberal Imperialist group, played an important part in urging Campbell-Bannerman to hold the door open to Grey. He scoffed at the Prime Minister's other suggestions for the post, and he later wrote warning him against " light-weights " and pointing out that " the F.O. is a terribly weak place in your armour." *g*

Asquith meanwhile was back amongst the Hatfield festivities. But only for a short time. On the Thursday morning he again travelled

[1] The fact that she put it in terms of defiance is a good indication of how self-defeating Grey's move had been.

to London and went once more to Belgrave Square. On this occasion his wife recorded him as reporting:

He (Campbell-Bannerman) looked white and upset and began like a man who, having taken the plunge, meant to make best of it. He spoke in a rapid, rather cheerful and determined manner: "I'm going to stick to the Commons, Asquith, so will you go and tell Grey he may have the Foreign Office and Haldane the War Office."*h*

Asquith duly conveyed these offers. He saw Grey, but failed to shake his intransigence. As soon as Asquith had left him, he wrote a letter of definite refusal to Campbell-Bannerman. This covered not merely the Foreign Office but any participation in the Government. He even raised again the difficulty of separation from Rosebery.

Haldane was a more flexible proposition. Unlike Grey, he had been balked of the office which he coveted, but he had a livelier sense of political ambition. In some aspects of his temperament Grey was like Rosebery. He loved creating situations in which he could say no. Haldane was much more like Asquith. On his own terms if possible, he preferred the occupancy of the seats of power to the sterile pleasure of watching his inferiors try to fill them. Perhaps for this reason Asquith did not think it as necessary to see him as it had been to see Grey—despite the fact that he was available in London and, indeed, had Grey staying with him at his flat in Whitehall Court.

Instead, Asquith went to the Athenaeum in the early afternoon and wrote Haldane a long letter for delivery by hand. The central part of this letter has already been quoted as an exposition of Asquith's own reasons for accepting office.[1] The beginning may now be added: "I was empowered this morning to offer the Foreign Office to E. Grey, and an offer of the War Office will soon be on its way to you." And the end: "I write this now, because I see no chance of seeing you today as I have to go to the country,[2] and that you may have these considerations in your mind when you receive C.B.'s offer. I don't want in the

[1] See pages 151-2 *supra*.
[2] A defensively generalised expression, for Haldane knew perfectly well where Asquith was staying, and disapproved of his being away. "To make things worse," he wrote in his *Autobiography* (p. 168), "Asquith and his wife proceeded to keep an engagement to stay with the Salisburys at Hatfield. . . . Asquith came to town indeed during the day, but it was difficult to see him as much as the circumstances required."

least to attempt to influence your judgment; your position and Grey's, as regards this particular point, are necessarily different from mine. But I need not say what an enormous and immeasurable difference your co-operation would make to me. Whatever happens nothing can change our affection and confidence."*

This letter was handed to Haldane at four o'clock, when he was presiding over a committee meeting at the Imperial Institute in South Kensington. At the same time he was given a letter from Campbell-Bannerman. This, somewhat confusingly, offered him not the War Office but the Attorney-Generalship. It added, however, that if he did not want that (which he did not) the Prime Minister would make other proposals " involving Cabinet rank."[1] After his meeting Haldane drove home to Whitehall Court, calling on the way on Lady Horner, Asquith's old correspondent of the early 'nineties, at Buckingham Gate. Lady Horner, he subsequently recorded, was a decisive influence turning his mind towards acceptance. But he still regarded himself as bound not to accept unless he could also change Grey's mind. It was not difficult for him to see Grey. When he got home to Whitehall Court he found him lying on a sofa in his library " with the air of one who had taken a decision and was done with political troubles." Haldane talked to him for some time. Then, at Grey's suggestion, they walked to Arthur Acland's rooms in St. James's Court. They were with him from 7.30 to 8.15 and " he poured into (them) arguments about destroying the prospects of the Liberal Party." When they left they went to the Café Royal and dined together in a private room. There, when they had finished their fish—perhaps because he missed the rest of it Haldane was very precise about the stage of the meal which had been reached—Grey agreed that it was his duty to accept office, provided that Haldane were included in the Cabinet.

Armed with this news Haldane left Grey at dinner and rushed off to Belgrave Square in a hansom cab. Campbell-Bannerman came out from dinner to see him. He responded with pleasure to the news that Grey's mind had changed and offered Haldane first the Home Office and then, surprised at his preference, the War Office. By ten o'clock on that Thursday night Haldane had returned to report to Grey in Acland's rooms. The matter was finally settled the next morning when Grey called upon the Prime Minister.

[1] In those days the phrase carried its natural meaning—membership of the Cabinet. Today it is a polite euphemism for exclusion from that body.

The Asquiths, at Hatfield, were cut off from these final moves. After sending off his letter to Haldane Asquith had returned there on the Thursday evening thinking that there was little chance of moving Grey.[1] " When Henry arrived I saw at a glance that it was all up," Margot recorded. On the following morning when they travelled up to King's Cross and opened *The Times* in the train they read the report of Grey's refusal as the last word. But at Cavendish Square Asquith received a brief note from Haldane, written on the previous evening, telling him that Grey had agreed to " reconsider his position." On reading this he went off to find Haldane. By twelve he knew that everything was satisfactorily arranged.

The filling of the other offices proceeded smoothly, and the Cabinet list was ready for the King on that same Friday, December 8th. Although only five of its members had ever held Cabinet office before it was a Government of unusual talent. It contained at least five ministers of outstanding intellectual quality: Asquith, Haldane, Morley (Secretary of State for India), Birrell (President of the Board of Education) and Bryce (Chief Secretary for Ireland). In addition there were men such as Lloyd George (President of the Board of Trade), Crewe (Lord President), John Burns (Local Government Board), Winston Churchill (under-secretary for the Colonies), and Grey, whose gifts differed widely both from those of the " intellectuals " and from each other, but which were at least equally remarkable.

There was no question of the Cabinet being, in the phrase Asquith had used to Haldane, " all of one colour." The strict Gladstonian tradition was represented by Ripon (Lord Privy Seal) and Herbert Gladstone (Home Secretary) as well as by Morley and Bryce. The Prime Minister's own outlook was closely reflected by that of the

[1] Sometime on that Thursday indeed he wrote the following note to Campbell-Bannerman:

SECRET   20 *Cavendish Square, W.*
                                              7 *December,* 1905
My dear CB,
    I deeply regret both your decision and E. Grey's.
    On the assumption that both are irrevocable, Crewe seems to me for many reasons the best man for the F.O.
                        Yours,

                                                    H.H.A.
(*Campbell-Bannerman papers,* 41210, 253)

Lord Chancellor, Loreburn, and the Secretary of State for Scotland, John Sinclair. In addition, Lloyd George and John Burns were both regarded as men of the " new left," although the latter quickly developed into an outstandingly conservative minister. The " moderates " were represented not only by the famous three of the Relugas compact but also by Crewe, by Fowler,[1] who was a vice-president of the Liberal League, by Lord Carrington[2] (later Marquess of Lincolnshire), who was one of King Edward's closest friends,[3] and by Lord Elgin,[4] to whom *The Times* gave the accolade of saying that he had never made a partisan speech. Lord Tweedmouth (the former Chief Whip, who soon became insane) as First Lord of the Admiralty, and Sydney Buxton as Postmaster-General completed the Cabinet.

The new ministers went to Buckingham Palace to receive their seals of office on the Monday afternoon. It was a day of exceptionally thick fog (even by Edwardian standards), and the atmosphere became even blacker while they were with the King, so that many of them had great difficulty in finding their way to their departments. The Liberal Imperialists were particularly unlucky. Haldane, Grey and Fowler left the Palace together in a hired brougham, but had to abandon it in the Mall. Grey spent an hour walking from there to the Foreign Office. Fowler merely succeeded in finding his way back to Buckingham Palace. And Haldane, clutching his seals in a bag, felt his way, as he rather curiously put it, " along the horses' heads," until he arrived, exhausted and muddy, at the War Office, then in Pall Mall.

Asquith, on his own, did rather better, and arrived in reasonably good order at the Old Treasury building on the corner of Whitehall and Downing Street. The department which he arrived to command was one which had changed little since the days of Gladstone's first premiership. It had not grown at all; and in 1905, despite there being temporarily two joint permanent secretaries, the cost of salaries was actually lower than it had been in 1872. There were only twenty-two

[1] Chancellor of the Duchy of Lancaster.
[2] President of the Board of Agriculture.
[3] The King testified to his friendship for Carrington by telling Campbell-Bannerman that he looked " upon Charlie as a brother " and asking for him to be made Lord Chamberlain. The Prime Minister fell in with this suggestion, but Carrington refused, on the ground of health, and became a Cabinet Minister instead. (Sir Sidney Lee, *King Edward VII*, II, p. 446).
[4] Secretary of State for the Colonies.

first division clerks (or administrative class civil servants as they would now be called), and the total staff of the department, messengers included, was barely 200.

The two permanent secretaries were as firmly Gladstonian as was the establishment. Sir Edward Hamilton, in charge of finance, had been one of the G.O.M's secretaries over many years, and Sir George Murray, in charge of administration, had also served as a private secretary during Gladstone's fourth government. They held joint office throughout Asquith's time at the Exchequer and constituted a solid official front in favour of the old, nineteenth century view of the functions of the Treasury. Its role was to enforce economy upon other departments rather than to initiate policy of its own. So long as this view prevailed, and particularly if there were no great revenue changes to be made, the Treasury was rather a dull department over which to preside. It carried high prestige, but unless the Chancellor had some outside functions, as with Harcourt who was leader of the House of Commons in 1894-5,[1] it did not necessarily give him a commanding position in the Government.

Asquith's two immediate predecessors, Austen Chamberlain and Ritchie, had been far from occupying such a position. But Asquith himself had a role much more analogous to that of Harcourt. He was deputy leader of the House, under a leader who, however firmly he had clung to his seat in the Commons, was by no means the most indefatigable of parliamentarians. Asquith was encouraged to range widely over the whole field of policy. His position was indeed much stronger than Harcourt's. So far from having been passed over for the premiership by a younger man, he was universally regarded as Campbell-Bannerman's natural and inevitable successor. Even those who had been most strongly opposed to Liberal Imperialism did not believe that they could, or should, keep Asquith out of the first place for long. They had no alternative leader of his generation to put forward. They held, together with the bulk of the party, that it would be intolerable to reward Campbell-Bannerman for his years of service in opposition by superseding him on the threshold of office. They believed too that he was the most unifying leader under whom the Government could make a start. But, with the habitual confidence of

[1] Harcourt's position would in any event have been dominating because of the impact of his "death duties" budget; but budgets of such importance rarely came more than once in a generation.

Lloyd George watches the scene

Margot Asquith crosses Parliament Square

The Ulster Revolt: Sir Edward Carson and Bonar Law lead the way

those fresh to power, they saw long years of office stretching ahead, and there were few who thought that Campbell-Bannerman, 69 and old for his age, was likely to be there for more than the first two or three. Asquith, at 53 and with a constitution which required no austerity of life to keep it unimpaired, could look forward with a quiet confidence to the premiership. His advance always owed little to chance. From this stage in his career it would have required quite exceptional ill luck to deprive him of the foremost place.

In these circumstances the Chancellor's traditional residence, 11 Downing Street, next door to the Prime Minister, would have been a more than usually appropriate place for him to live. But he did not occupy it. Margot thought it too small for the family and told her father that she would have "to farm out" either her own or her stepchildren as there was no room for both a nursery and a schoolroom. Sir Charles Tennant responded by offering to pay her the rent which she and her husband had been hoping to get for 20, Cavendish Square and which they had been looking to as a small compensation for the replacement of Asquith's bar earnings by a ministerial salary of £5,000. This offer enabled them to continue to live in the greater spaciousness of Cavendish Square and to lend 11, Downing Street to the Home Secretary, who had no London house of his own.[j]

The Government of 1905, unusually for those of this century (the 1922 Conservative Government and the 1931 National Government are the only others in the same category), faced an election as soon as it was formed. There could be no question, despite the by-election victories of the previous two years, of governing through the 1900 House of Commons. The old parliament met only for dissolution.

The opening salvo of the election was fired on December 21st, when Campbell-Bannerman addressed a large Albert Hall meeting, but the campaign generally did not start until immediately after Christmas. Asquith began with a programme of outside engagements and did not go to East Fife until a few days before polling. But he did not speak with the frequency which most modern political leaders would consider necessary, and he did not plan his meetings to cover the country. In the fortnight beginning on December 29th he spoke at Sheffield, Huddersfield, Stockton-on-Tees, Oakham, Henley-on-Thames, Perth and an unidentifiable place described as Lensham. During the period of this tour the one issue which threatened to cause difficulties within the Liberal Government was that of Chinese labour in the Transvaal. The recruitment and mass importation of Chinese coolies for work in the goldmines of the Rand, authorised by a Colonial Office ordinance of 1904, was widely regarded as the most unsavoury aspect of the aftermath of the war in South Africa. " They have brought back slavery to the British Empire," Lloyd George proclaimed.

The issue looked a splendid election weapon for the Liberal Party. But, not untypically of such weapons, it proved a dangerous one to handle. In his Albert Hall speech Campbell-Bannerman announced that orders had been given " to stop forthwith the recruitment and embarkation of coolies in China." This was received with acclaim by the audience and was taken to mean that no more Chinese would embark for South Africa. Most of the Cabinet, and particularly the lawyers, received the statement with a good deal less enthusiasm. What was to happen to the 14,000 licences for importation which had been issued during November but which, in most cases, had not already been taken up? Were they to be revoked, and if so, how could the action be made legal except by retrospective legislation? And was the British taxpayer then to be involved in compensating the mine-owners for the losses they would suffer from the Government's change of policy? Asquith was strongly against both of these courses and took the lead in urging the Prime Minister to re-interpret his pledge in accordance with the demands of " practicability " and to say that it meant that there would be no further recruitment, but no more than that. The matter was finally settled at a Cabinet on January 3rd, with Campbell-Bannerman good humouredly but a little reluctantly falling into line. It was an early example of the power within the Government of the Chancellor of the Exchequer.

This re-interpretation produced some radical grumbling, and when the new Parliament met several members—and notably Hilaire Belloc, whose liberalism was always most intense when it could be allied with his savage hatred of the " gallant Albus," " fair young Wernhers " and " tall Goltmans " of international Jewish finance[1]—complained

[1] In the same month that this debate took place (February, 1906) Belloc produced one of his most viciously satirical poems against those whom he thought had done well out of the South African bloodshed:

> We also know the sacred height
> Up on Tugela side,
> Where those three hundred fought with Beit
> And fair young Wernher died.

about the softness of the Government towards the Rand magnates. By then the main problem was not new importations but what was to be done with the 47,000 Chinese already in South Africa. With the Liberal Party firmly committed to immediate self-government for the defeated Boers there was obviously a good deal to be said against imposing a solution from Whitehall. This was Asquith's view, and it was justified by the fact that by June, 1907, the Transvaal took its own decision in favour of sending the Chinese home. The experiment in semi-slavery had by then proved such a failure that not even the mine-owners wanted to keep them.

The Chinese labour incident apart, the Liberal election campaign was remarkably harmonious. The party had the smell of victory in its nostrils, and that did more than anything else to keep it together. There were differences of stress in the election addresses of the leaders— Asquith's for instance, concentrated almost entirely upon a close-knit argument of the case against tariff reform—but no contradictions.

Polling was spread over nearly three weeks, beginning on January 12th. The first day brought only one Liberal gain at Ipswich, but the second brought a spate of successes in Lancashire, including the defeat of Balfour at East Manchester, and from then right through to the end the story was the same. Supposedly safe Conservative seats crumbled, and Government victories in the most unlikely places brought into the House of Commons a flood of new Liberals who had been fighting almost without hope. There were in all 377 Liberal members. With them, in some ways an even greater sensation, came 53 Labour members, 24 of them closely allied to the Liberal Party, and the other 29 elected under the independent auspices of the Labour Representation Committee; even these 29 had in most cases escaped Liberal opposition

---

The daybreak on the failing force,
The final sabres drawn:
Tall Goltman, silent on his horse,
Superb against the dawn.

The little mound where Eckstein stood
And gallant Albu fell,
· *And Oppenheim, half-blind with blood*
Went fording through the rising flood—
My Lord, we know them well.

in the constituencies. The Irish produced their usual contingent of 83, which gave a total of 513 members who in a straight clash with the Tories might be expected to support the Government. The Opposition had only 157 members—132 Conservatives and 25 Liberal Unionists. The Government's normal majority was 356—a preponderance unequalled since the Parliament of 1832—and the Liberal Party's majority over all others was 132.

Asquith's own result was not out until almost the end, and he chafed at being kept in Scotland long after most ministers (although not Campbell-Bannerman) were able to return to London. " Here I still am, delayed by an increasingly meaningless contest," he wrote on January 27th. The complete and somewhat impatient confidence implied by this statement was not misplaced. But his majority did not soar. East Fife was always a steady rather than a mercurial constituency, and having done adequately for him in the difficult years of 1895 and 1900 it refused to give him a sensational victory in the easy year of 1906. He polled 4723 against his opponent's 3279, and lost the relative edge over Campbell-Bannerman's Stirling performance which he had gained in 1900.

The first post-election Cabinet was on January 31st and the new Parliament met on February 19th. Liberal supporters both in the country and in the House of Commons looked confidently for a great unleashing of radical purpose. The King's speech at least did not disappoint them. It forecast 22 bills, of which three, dealing with education, trades union law and plural voting, were clearly to be of major and controversial importance. In addition, a decision in principle to grant full self-government to the Transvaal had already been taken and announced. It looked a vigorous beginning, but achievement seemed likely to turn on the meaning behind the most pregnant remark of the election campaign. It was the duty of everyone, Balfour had said at Nottingham on January 15th, to see that " the great Unionist Party should still control, whether in power or whether in opposition, the destinies of this great Empire." Asquith, not alone, saw clearly that what lay behind these words was the looming shape of the vast Conservative majority in the House of Lords.

CHAPTER XII

CROWN PRINCE

1906-8

Asquith introduced three budgets—two of them during his time at the Exchequer and the third several weeks after his accession to the premiership; as he had prepared these last proposals it was thought appropriate that he should present them, although the new Chancellor was left to conduct the Finance Bill. Of these three budgets, the first (as Asquith himself recognised, and thought inevitable because of the short time available for preparation) was uninteresting, the second made an important break of new fiscal ground, and the third laid the first brick of the welfare state. They were all presented in a form suitable to a Chancellor " supposed . . . to be a financier of a respectable and more or less conservative type " (as Asquith could later describe himself[a]), but they were highly successful in achieving the maximum of radical result while arousing the minimum of conservative opposition.

The fiscal adventurousness of the second budget lay in the introduction, for the first time, of a differentiation between the rates of tax on earned and unearned income. Asquith records that he had wished to do this in his first budget, but was prevented by Treasury opposition. " I was at once met with the objection, which was considered fatal, that Gladstone had always declared that any such scheme was impracticable."[b] He decided to try and outflank this opposition by the appointment of an all-party Select Committee, and chose Sir Charles Dilke, the erudite and determinedly radical member for the Forest of Dean, as a chairman likely to produce a favourable report. Ironically Dilke, who had become old and arid with disappointment, opposed the recommendation,[1] but was unable to make his views prevail against the rest of the Committee.

[1] He wanted an entirely separate system of property taxation, as in Prussia and Holland.

Fortified by this report (which also contained a super-tax recommendation which Lloyd George was to implement in 1909) Asquith then felt able to defy the mandarins of the Treasury, and to make differentiation the centre-piece of his budget of 1907. The rate of tax was then 1/- in the £. For earned incomes up to £2,000, provided also that the taxpayer's total income, earned and unearned, did not exceed this sum, the rate was reduced to 9d. Although the form in which it is expressed has changed, the taxation system has never since been without this differentiation.

The speech in which this and other changes were proposed took just over two hours and was accounted a masterly performance. Haldane thought it ranked with " the great performances of the great Chancellors," and Sir George Murray said that it rose " in some places to levels which nobody in our time except Mr. Gladstone has ever reached." Mrs. Asquith made a more original and illuminating comment. " No one speaks quite like Henry," she wrote in her diary. " He seems to run rather a bigger show; he can keep to the ground, cut into it or leave it without ever being ridiculous, boring, or wanting in taste, and he is never too long. He gives a feeling of power more than of grace or charm . . ."[c] One of the most notable passages in the speech was a classical statement of the case that the taxable capacity of a man with an income from property is necessarily greater than that of a man with the same income from work.

The budget of 1907 also paved the way for the principal social reform of 1908—the cautious beginning of old age pensions. Asquith put aside part of his modest surplus of £4m. to help provide for this, and announced firmly what he was doing. The idea of making some national provision for the old was one which occupied his mind throughout the period of his Chancellorship. The fact that, even by his own austere financial standards, it was possible to do this in 1908 was probably the main reason why, as Prime Minister, he exercised the prerogative of introducing the budget of that year. The terms in which he did so were typically non-emotional. There were no references to the secure and contented evening of life which he was promoting for an indefinite series of idealised old couples. His approach was severely practical. There was to be a non-contributory pension of 5s. a week at seventy for those whose total income did not exceed 10s. a week, and who had not disqualified themselves by being criminals or lunatics or (within the previous year) paupers; married couples were to receive 8s. 9d.

To modern ears the scheme sounds cautious and meagre. But it was violently criticised at the time for showing a reckless generosity. Rosebery, any trace of radicalism now far behind him, thought the plan " so prodigal of expenditure as likely to undermine the whole fabric of the Empire "; and another peer described it as " destructive of all thrift." Equally, some of Asquith's own supporters expressed disappointment with the extent of the advance. £13 a year for a rigidly circumscribed half million of the aged poor was hardly the beginning of a social millenium. But it was the most important piece of social legislation for several decades past, and it brought England more or less into line with Germany, Denmark and New Zealand, the countries which had hitherto led the way in this field.

Asquith's other principal Treasury task was the scrutiny of the estimates of the other departments. Although he was a careful financier—and succeeded in 1907-8 in making an unprecedently large provision for the redemption of debt—he was not a fanatical economist. Sometimes, in accordance with the custom of the time, he concerned himself with incredibly small items of expenditure, but he did not do so in a particularly cheeseparing way. " I think we might well arrange to provide Bryce with an extra allowance for outfit," he wrote to the Prime Minister at the time of the former Chief Secretary's appointment to the Washington Embassy, " and to make up the month's loss of salary."[d]

The crucial expenditure questions, as usual, related to the armed services. Here Asquith was greatly helped by Haldane, whose War Office administration was as economical as it was efficient. His estimates for the year 1907-8 showed an unrequested saving of £2m. But the demands of the Admiralty, a constantly recurring source of dissension within this pre-1914 Liberal Government, were already causing trouble.

Asquith's position on this issue was a little ambiguous. On the one hand he was a Liberal Chancellor of the Exchequer, the inheritor of the retrenchment traditions of Gladstone and Harcourt. On the other, he was the leader, within the Government, of the group which believed in a strong Britain. Sometimes he sought to compromise his two responsibilities by seeing proposed expenditure as militarily unnecessary. Thus, on December 30th 1906, he wrote to Campbell-

Bannerman: "I am much disquieted by Tweedmouth's memorandum on Navy Estimates. . . . The enclosed article from today's *Spectator*—which is not in any sense pre-disposed to economy in these matters—suggests that we are going ahead in the matter of construction far beyond any real necessity."*e* The irony of an "Imperialist" Chancellor writing in these terms to a "Little Englander" Prime Minister cannot be escaped; but Asquith never pushed his opposition to the estimates to the extent which Gladstone and Harcourt would have considered necessary, and which Lloyd George was to attempt in the future. As a result questions of naval construction led only to a growling dispute under his Chancellorship and not to open crisis as was later the case.

Another of Asquith's responsibilities—semi-departmental this time perhaps—was to be the chief keeper of the free trade shrine. For a time after the crushing victory of 1906 there was little attempt to invade it. But in the spring of 1907 a conference of dominion Prime Ministers assembled in London and the majority of those who came used public as well as private pressure to urge imperial preference on the British Government. Deakin and Lyne of Australia, and Jameson and Smartt of Cape Colony were particularly active, not only in argument with Asquith and with Churchill (his chief assistant on this matter) at the sessions of the Conference, but also at meetings and banquets outside, many of them organised under opposition auspices. These activities had no effect on the Government's policy—Churchill had declared at an early stage and in characteristic terms that the door to a preferential system had been "banged, bolted, and barred" by the election result—but they naturally produced some resentment amongst ministers. Campbell-Bannerman, tactfully purporting to blame the "imperialists" at home rather than the dominion Prime Ministers, delivered a sharp retort on May 10th: "They hold us up to obloquy as indifferent to the cause of the Empire when all we do is to claim for ourselves the same freedom which these self-governing Colonies and communities enjoy, and which nothing on earth can tempt them to forgo."*f*

It was noticeable that Sir Wilfrid Laurier of Canada, the most experienced of the dominion leaders, and General Botha of the Transvaal, perhaps the wisest amongst them, held themselves aloof from the pressure of their colleagues. Laurier was as interested in imperial preference as anyone, but both he and Botha subordinated it to the absolute right of any member of the British family of nations, including the mother country, to be mistress of her own trading policies. To balance their stubbornness on the fiscal issue the Liberal Government had the great advantage, in the eyes of most of the colonial leaders, of the rapid advance towards full self-determination which they were making in South Africa.

The dominant issue in the life of the Government was not of direct Treasury concern: it was the lack of progress of the general legislative programme. When the new Parliament met, the huge Liberal majority in the House of Commons was confronted by an almost equally large Unionist one in the House of Lords. It quickly became clear that the opposition leaders in both Houses were prepared to accord no real primacy to the elected chamber. Occasionally Balfour and Lansdowne instructed the peers to make a tactical show of restraint. More frequently they suppressed their delicate susceptibilities and encouraged a slaughter of Liberal bills on a scale from which their more robust predecessors, the Duke of Wellington or Sir Robert Peel, would have recoiled in horror.

The first victim was the Education Bill. This bill was designed to remedy some of the more keenly-felt grievances of the Nonconformists, while leaving intact the 1902 administrative structure. It was introduced into the House of Commons by Augustine Birrell on April 9th, 1906, and immediately produced a storm of controversy. This came not only from the Unionist Party, but also from the Roman and Anglican churches. It was controversy along well-worn lines. The liturgists had had their way in 1902. The free churches had responded by rallying to the Liberal Party and ensuring that education was one of the two or three central issues of the electoral battle. This rallying of Nonconformists had helped to produce the great radical majority, and they could lay a strong claim to priority of relief. But the peers completely declined to recognise the force and freshness of the mandate behind the measure. When the bill reached them in the autumn, after a strenuous passage through the House of Commons, they treated it exactly in accordance with the instructions they were given by Balfour. They let it through on second reading, and then proceeded so to amend it in committee as not merely to destroy but to reverse its original purpose. In the form in which it returned to the Commons, the bill would have given the upholders of denominational teaching a still more favourable position than they enjoyed under the 1902 Act.

There followed a period of skirmishing between the two Houses. The King tried unsuccessfully to promote a compromise and achieved only an abortive conference between three representatives of the Government, headed by Asquith, three of the opposition, and the Archbishop of Canterbury. By the middle of December it was obvious that complete deadlock had been reached. The Government, full of growls against the enormity of the peers' behaviour, had no option but to abandon the bill.

The other principal bills of the session received mixed treatment from the Lords. The Plural Voting Bill was handled with even less respect than the Education Bill; it was simply rejected on second reading. But the Trades Disputes Bill, in reality the most controversial of the three, was made the occasion for a display of tactical restraint. There were two reasons for this. The first was that the peers preferred for the moment to attack the " political " reforms of the Liberal Government than to run head on into a clash with organised labour. The second was that the place where this bill had aroused most controversy had been within the Cabinet itself; the Unionists strategists no doubt thought that this dissension might be more effectively promoted by keeping the bill alive than by treating it like the Plural Voting Bill.

Asquith was in the centre of the Cabinet controversy over the Trades Disputes Bill. There was no division about the need to give a greater protection to Trade Union funds than that which existed after the Taff Vale and *Quinn v. Leatham* decisions. The dispute arose out of how this was to be done. Asquith and other lawyers wished to proceed by the indirect method of restricting the law of agency. This method had the advantage of appearing to give no favouritism to the unions, and the disadvantage of being so circumlocutory that it aroused no Labour enthusiasm. At first the lawyers carried the day, and a bill along these lines was introduced by the Attorney-General. It was coldly received by the powerful new Labour group, and one of its members, Walter Hudson, countered by introducing a private member's bill based on the alternative method of approach—that of giving a direct exemption from actions for damages to trades union funds. The Prime Minister listened to the arguments deployed in favour of this bill, and proceeded, with a sudden swoop, to accept its principles on behalf of the Government.

The coldness then passed to the lawyers in the Cabinet, and it was not until August that the matter was resolved by amending the principal clause in the Government bill so as to incorporate the substance of Hudson's proposals. Asquith accepted the position reluctantly. He had a determined hostility to giving a specially privileged legal position to any group, but he never contemplated resignation on the issue. He had no wish to magnify the difference with the Prime Minister. His relations with Campbell-Bannerman had become steadily closer and warmer since the formation of the Government, and this, as his official biographers point out, " was his sole difference of any importance with Campbell-Bannerman in the period in which he served with him as his principal lieutenant."[9] Instead he decided to face the issue in the House of Commons. Unnecessarily in view of his lack of departmental responsibility, he intervened at the committee stage and made it clear how reluctant a convert he was to the clause, but attempted to justify it on the ground that it gave an equally direct exemption to unions of masters as to those of men. It was a courageous if unhappy intervention.

The history of this bill shows how indefensible on principle was the attitude of the peers to different pieces of Government legislation. If the object was to delay ill-considered measures upon which the electorate had not pronounced, the constitutional argument for rejecting the Trades Disputes Bill was far stronger than for so treating the Education and Plural Voting Bills. But the Lords were not greatly concerned with building up a constitutional case for themselves. They simply wanted to inflict as much damage as possible upon the Liberal Government.

How could the Government resist this damage? After the withdrawal of the Education Bill in December, 1906, Campbell-Bannerman played with the idea of an immediate dissolution, with a campaign on the straight issue of the supremacy of the Commons. Cabinet opinion was firmly against such a course. The electorate, it was felt, would judge the Lords not by constitutional propriety, but by the popularity of the measures they had destroyed; and the Education Bill did not have a wide enough appeal to be a firm basis for victory. A further consideration was the comparative poverty of many Liberal members. A second election within twelve months would put a heavy financial burden upon them. And there was always the risk, despite the favourable evidence of the by-elections which had so far taken place, of destroying the great majority for which the Liberal Party had waited for so long.

When these arguments were forcibly put by Asquith and others, the Prime Minister did not resist. He swung into agreement. But in subsequent months, as the Government embedded itself still more deeply in the morass prepared by Balfour and Lansdowne, he sometimes expressed regret that the bolder course had not been taken.[h] The true argument against this course was, not that it was too bold, but that it would have accomplished little. In 1910, when the Government had a specific plan for dealing with the Lords, two elections and immense travail were necessary before it could be carried through. In 1906–7 the Liberals would, almost without doubt, have secured a bigger majority than in 1910. But would this consideration alone have enabled them to achieve a quick solution without the starting advantage of clear, agreed proposals?

The alternative to dissolution, in the language of the day, was held to be the policy of " filling the cup "—of giving the Lords so many measures to wreck that, in the process, they would both demonstrate beyond doubt their own iniquity and offend every interest from which the Liberal Party could hope for support. But this was too supine a policy for any Government to pursue wholeheartedly. The price in terms of prestige and of the morale of its supporters, both in the country and in the House of Commons, was too great. During the 1907 session, therefore, the Government havered between this policy, a second one of threatening an immediate attack on the Lords, and a third one of attempting to formulate compromise measures which might produce some sort of legislative harvest.

Thus the King's Speech, in February, gave pride of place to a major Licensing Bill—a measure as certain to be slaughtered by the Lords as any which could be thought of. But it also referred to " unfortunate differences between the two Houses," and announced that " His Majesty's Ministers have this important subject under consideration with a view to a solution of the difficulty." Then the Licensing Bill was postponed, and replaced as the main legislative business of the early part of the session by compromise measures on education and Ireland. The latter was described by the Chief Secretary as a " little, modest, shy, humble effort to give administrative powers to the Irish people." Both these bills suffered from the disadvantages of making some enemies but no friends, and had to be withdrawn for lack of support.

In the meantime the Government had been trying to formulate

detailed proposals for dealing with the Lords. A Cabinet committee was instructed to deal with this, and reported in May. It recommended that where differences between the two Houses arose they should be settled at joint sittings, attended by all the Commons and a delegation of 100 peers. In other words a Liberal Government with a majority of more than 80 to 85[1] would be given immunity from the depredations of the peers, but one with a smaller majority would be left entirely at their mercy. Campbell-Bannerman greatly disliked this scheme, which he thought would actually make matters worse for a Liberal Government with a " normal " majority, and he circulated a memorandum stating both his objections and his alternative proposals. These were for a revival of John Bright's old scheme of a suspensory veto, restricting the peers' right of delay to two sessions. If in the third session the bill were again sent up from the Commons it could then become law independently of any action which the House of Lords might take.

The Prime Minister's memorandum effectively killed the joint session plan of the Cabinet committee, but it did not automatically secure the acceptance of his own proposals. An alternative plan for submitting bills held up by the Lords to a referendum was exhaustively discussed. This would have involved a far sharper break with the established practices of parliamentary government than any diminution of the powers of the Lords. Nevertheless Asquith subsequently confessed that he had " coquetted " with the idea. But he did not do more. And towards the end of a long series of Cabinets he helped to secure a solidifying of opinion behind the Campbell-Bannerman proposals. These were then presented to the House of Commons in the form of a resolution on June 24th. A three day debate, opened by the Prime Minister and wound up by Asquith, led to a vote of 432 to 147 in favour of the resolution.

It was a resounding demonstration, but its only immediate result was to give the Liberal Party a policy for dealing with the Upper House. This was an advance; but until it was put in a form less innocuous than a Commons' resolution it had no effect on the powers of the peers. They rounded off the session by wrecking two Scottish land bills and substantially amending and weakening an Irish bill on the same subject.

With the end of this session, on August 26th, 1907, came the effec-

[1] It was proposed that all peers holding ministerial office should be members of the delegation.

tive close of Campbell-Bannerman's parliamentary career. He appeared in the House of Commons only for another ten days, at the beginning of the following February. Even during his two full sessions as Prime Minister he had been a notably intermittent performer, leaving many of the details and difficulties of leadership to Asquith. This was the period when " send for the sledge-hammer "—a tribute more to the force and reliability than to the elegance of the Chancellor of the Exchequer's debating—was one of his favourite cries. It was not that Campbell-Bannerman was unable to deal with the House of Commons. From the moment of his successful rebuke to Balfour[1] in March, 1906, he achieved a sureness of touch which had always eluded him as leader of the opposition. But his wife's ill-health combined with his own to keep him away a great deal.

Lady Campbell-Bannerman's protracted illness took a turn for the worse in the early spring of 1906, and between then and her death at Marienbad six months later her husband gave a clear priority to looking after her. He performed his duties as Prime Minister (with remarkable skill in the circumstances) during the time which was left spare. Then, within five weeks of her death, he suffered a first heart seizure of his own; and this attack was twice repeated during the next fifteen months. But he was more active during this later period than he had been while his wife was ill.

During these early years of the Liberal Government a crop of physical misfortunes befell the wives of leading ministers. Only a few weeks after the general election of 1906 Edward Grey's wife was thrown from a dog-cart while out driving, and died three days later. For a short time all his old doubts about office revived, but they did not persist. Then, in February 1907, Margot Asquith, after her usual wearing pregnancy, suffered her fifth and last confinement. The result was as disappointing as on the first and third occasions: the child died within

---

[1] This was on the occasion of Balfour's first speech after his by-election return to the House. He had put a series of dialectically ingenious questions to the Prime Minister on the well-worn free trade issue. Campbell-Bannerman concluded his two-minute reply: " They (the questions) are utterly futile, nonsensical and misleading. They were invented by the right hon. Gentleman for the purpose of occupying time in this debate. I say, enough of this foolery! It might have answered very well in the last Parliament, but it is altogether out of place in this Parliament. . . . Move your amendments and let us get to business." (*Hansard*, 4th Series, vol:153. c. 992).

two days of its birth. And there followed a repetition of the desperate sleeplessness and sustained ill-health which had afflicted her ten years earlier.

This major vicissitude apart, Asquith's non-official life during his period as Chancellor proceeded smoothly and agreeably. Office imposed no great strain on him. He was always quick in the despatch of business, and he was somewhat less busy than in his last years at the bar, when he had been trying to combine an exacting practice with the leadership of the free trade campaign. Long holidays (or, at least long periods of relaxed work away from London) were still thought perfectly compatible with ministerial responsibility. In 1906 the family again went to Glen of Rothes for August and September, and in 1907 they took a house near Dingwall on the Moray Firth for the same months. Asquith himself also fitted in a fortnight's February holiday in Rome before the beginning of the 1907 session.

Then, in the autumn of that year the pattern of life changed somewhat, for he and his wife acquired effective possession of Archerfield, a substantial (but now ruined) Adam house on the Firth of Forth near North Berwick, which belonged to Margot's brother Frank Tennant. This they kept for five or six years and normally occupied from mid-August to the end of the Christmas holidays. Asquith was not of course there for the whole of these prolonged autumns, but his periods of residence often amounted to several months a year. The house had the advantage of being near his constituency, although it was a good deal better placed for looking at it—the southern shore of the Kingdom of Fife was often visible across fifteen miles of sea—than for visiting it, which involved a tedious journey through Edinburgh. Still nearer to Archerfield than East Fife was Arthur Balfour's house. Whittinghame was only a few miles away, and Asquith when there sometimes had the pleasure of sharing the same golf links with the leader of the opposition. They both played frequently, but the choice of courses in the area was so wide that they did not necessarily meet often—Archerfield had its own private nine-hole course, and Balfour was frequently immersed in the rival attractions of philosophy and lawn tennis neither of which drew Asquith. Private relations between the two men were always cordial, and they had many mutual friends.

1907 also saw the marriage of Asquith's eldest son Raymond to Katherine Horner, the daughter of his and Haldane's old friend and confidante from Mells Park. Asquith's first family were nearly all grown up. Raymond was well-established at the bar. " Beb " and " Oc " were both at Oxford. Violet was " out." And Cyril, at Winchester, was on the brink of his Balliol scholarship. His second family was clearly not now going to increase beyond two. Elizabeth, the older of these, was ten, and Puffin (or Anthony) was five. Politically, there was little doubt that within a year or two he would take a further and final step forward; but from a private and family point of view it looked as though his life was already settled into a firm and lasting mould.

CHAPTER XIII

AN ASSURED SUCCESSION

1908

Campbell-Bannerman, like Asquith, spent much of the autumn of 1907 in Scotland. Then, on the night of November 13th, less than two weeks after his return south, he suffered a severe heart attack in Bristol, where he had gone to address the annual Colston Banquet. It was not until January 20th, when he returned from a protracted convalescence at Biarritz, that he was again able to devote much attention to official business. But he then enjoyed a final three weeks of full activity. "(He) seemed to have recovered all his old buoyancy and energy," Spender wrote.*a* During this period he presided over the Cabinets leading up to the King's Speech at the opening of the 1908 session.

The chronology of these weeks is important, because it has sometimes been suggested[1] that Campbell-Bannerman's illness and consequent replacement by Asquith was responsible for a crucial two years' delay in the mounting of the Liberal attack on the House of Lords. This theory must rest upon the belief that Campbell-Bannerman wished to follow up his resolutions of 1907 with a Parliament Bill for 1908. Yet there was no hint of this in the Address. Instead, the Licensing Bill was once more given first place, and another attempt was to be made to get the Lords to accept the two Scottish land bills which had fared so badly at the end of the last session. The evidence seems clear that Campbell-Bannerman was not at this stage contemplating immediate constitutional legislation.

The Prime Minister's final burst of vigour lasted only a fortnight into the new session. On February 12th he made his last speech in the House of Commons. That night he had another heart attack, and never again left his room in 10, Downing Street. For two or three weeks

[1] Notably by Professor Emily Allyn, of Wilson College, Pennsylvania, in her *Lords versus Commons*. (New York, 1931)

177

there seemed a reasonable prospect that he might once more recover. On March 2nd he wrote an optimistic letter to Asquith (for transmission to the Cabinet), and on March 4th he received a call from the King, who, on the following day, left for a six weeks visit to Biarritz, hoping that a change could be avoided while he was away. This hope proved ill-founded. As March wore on Campbell-Bannerman deteriorated steadily. Both inside and outside the Cabinet there was mounting pressure for a new Prime Minister. Since the beginning of the year the Government had been losing heavily at by-elections. These setbacks strengthened the demand for a leader who could take effective command. By the last week in March only two men were opposed to an immediate change, but they were both in crucial positions. The first was Campbell-Bannerman's doctor, who wrote to Asquith warning him that any suggestion of resignation would be bad for his patient, and the second was the King, who was opposed to any course which might interrupt his holiday. The *impasse* seemed complete, particularly as Campbell-Bannerman himself, when his hopes of recovery disappeared, showed signs of wanting to die in office. On March 27th he sent for Asquith, and after thanking him for being a " wonderful colleague, so loyal, so disinterested, so able," took farewell of him in a manner at once gruff and effusive: " You are the greatest gentleman I ever met," Campbell-Bannerman is recorded as saying. " This is not the last of me; we will meet again, Asquith."[b] But he did not say when he was going to resign.

A few days later the doctors completely changed their minds and pronounced an immediate resignation to have become imperative. Campbell-Bannerman accordingly wrote to the King on April 1st informing him that his wish for postponement could no longer be acceded to. The resignation was formally submitted two days later, and the King wrote to Asquith on April 4th, calling upon him to form a Government and summoning him to Biarritz. Throughout the period of speculation about the date of resignation there had been no doubt about the succession. Asquith was without a challenger in the Liberal Party. He had acted as leader throughout Campbell-Bannerman's frequent absences; his general parliamentary ability was unequalled; and, although only 55 years old, his Cabinet seniority was exceeded only by that of Morley. The King had made the position explicit on March 3rd when, in preparation for his Biarritz visit, he had seen Asquith and told him that, although he hoped to avoid a change for as long as possible, it would be for him that he would send when one became necessary.

The King also warned Asquith on this occasion that if Campbell-Bannerman resigned before Easter the new Prime Minister would be asked to go out to Biarritz to kiss hands. Asquith appears to have offered no remonstrance against this suggestion (it would, no doubt, have been ungracious to have done so), although when the time came it proved a highly inconvenient arrangement, and one which provoked widespread eyebrow-raising. Buckle of *The Times* wrote incredulously to Asquith on April 5th about the rumour of his visit to Biarritz. He could not believe that it was true. It was " so unlike His Majesty's usual consideration for his Ministers and for public business."[c] In fact something much worse was nearly true. A few days before the King had been proposing a plan by which, after Asquith's own visit to Biarritz, the new Cabinet should go over to Paris *en masse* in order to meet the King and receive their seals of office in the Hôtel Crillon. Lord Knollys, the King's private secretary, wrote to Asquith on March 30th full of dismay at this suggestion. Would Asquith add his protest to the very strong one which Knollys himself had already made? But two days later Knollys was writing again, full of relief this time, to say that the King had agreed to come home for the seals of office ceremony.[d]

The Biarritz part of the plan still stood, however, and on the night of Monday, April 6th, having that afternoon moved the adjournment of the House of Commons until April 14th, Asquith left Cavendish Square after an early dinner. He drove to Charing Cross and took the nine o'clock continental boat train for Paris. There were no crowds for he kept his plans secret. He travelled alone, without even a private secretary. But his secretaries were on the platform to see him off, as were Edwin Montagu and Reginald McKenna. " Mr. Asquith," *The Times* recorded, " wore a thick overcoat and a travelling cap pulled well down over his eyes." Margot could not go to Charing Cross. " Not feeling well enough to go to the station we parted on the door-step and he waved to me out of the motor as it disappeared round the corner of the Square," she wrote. What happened subsequently is best related in a letter which he wrote her on the Wednesday afternoon:

Hôtel du Palais,
Biarritz,
(Direction Pattard)
8 Ap. 08

Darling—only time for a line. I saw Reggie Lister for a few minutes in Paris and then came on here by a train which got in about ¼ past 10 last night. Fritz Ponsonby met me at the station and I am comfortably lodged in the King's Hotel.

This morning I put on a frock coat, and escorted by Fritz and old Stanley Clarke went to the King who was similarly attired. I presented him with a written resignation of the office of Chr. of the Exr; & he then said 'I appoint you P.M. & First Lord of the Treasury' whereupon I knelt down and kissed his hand. *Voilà tout!*

He then asked me to come into the next room and breakfast[1] with him. We were quite alone for an hour & I went over all the appointments with him. He made no objection to any of them and discussed the various men very freely & with a good deal of shrewdness.

I am going to dine in his company at Mrs. Cassel's villa tonight. The weather here is vile beyond description, pouring rain & plenty of wind. I leave at 12 noon to-morrow (Thursday) and arrive Charing Cross 5.12 Friday afternoon. You will no doubt arrange about dinner that evening[2]—Love,

Ever yours*e*

Asquith reached Paris at 10.20 on the Thursday night. At the Gare d'Orsay he was greeted by a crowd of journalists, but he did not do much to make their visit worthwhile. "I have only one thing to say to you: good evening," he announced. "Mr. Asquith then entered a carriage and drove to the Hôtel Ritz," it was reported.

---

[1] Unless the kissing of hands was treated as a sacramental ceremony before which food could not be taken, Asquith appears here to have used the word " breakfast " as a translation of " *déjeuner* " in a way that was quite common in the nineteenth century. In 1881, for example, Sir Charles Dilke gave a " breakfast " at the *Moulin Rouge* restaurant in Paris for the Prince of Wales and Gambetta, but the meal lasted well into the afternoon. According to *The Times*, Asquith's Biarritz audience was at 10 o'clock, and was followed, after an interval, by his lunching with the King.

[2] He had telegraphed earlier asking that Grey should be invited.

The next evening he was back in London, although not at 5.12, admirers of the old London, Chatham and Dover Railway may care to note. It was five to six when the train steamed into Charing Cross· The arrival was less clandestine than the departure had been. There was a large welcoming party on the platform, including Margot, his son Raymond, his daughter Violet and his sister Mrs. Wooding. Outside the station, despite the fact that it was a cold, dull evening, there was a large enough crowd to raise a sizeable cheer most of the way to Downing Street, where Asquith went briefly to enquire after Campbell-Bannerman. He then drove home to Cavendish Square, accompanied by Margot, Haldane and Vaughan Nash, the private secretary whom he inherited from the old Prime Minister.

The long railway journeys, inconvenient though they had been from many points of view, at least gave Asquith ample time for thinking about the distribution of government offices on the way out, and for writing letters of invitation on the way back. Some anticipatory correspondence had taken place earlier. On March 14th, Winston Churchill, whose claims for promotion to the Cabinet were not in dispute,[1] had written to Asquith outlining his order of preference— amongst the possibilities which Asquith had discussed with him. First he put the Colonial Office, second the Admiralty, and a bad third the Local Government Board. As he had little training in the details of domestic politics and no experience of piloting a major bill through the House of Commons he thought that he would find the work of the Local Government Board anxious, thankless and exhausting. " Dimly across gulfs of ignorance " he could see the shape of a policy which he called the Minimum Standard. But he feared that an attempt to carry it out would bring him into collision with men like John Morley, who, after years of thought, had decided that nothing could, or should, be done.*f*

These difficulties Churchill did not have to face. In fact he was offered the Board of Trade, and accepted it with alacrity on April 10th.

The other new appointment which aroused still greater interest was that of Lloyd George as Chancellor of the Exchequer. Asquith's

[1] Despite his age (he was only 33) and the fact that it was less than four years since he had crossed the floor of the House of Commons. There had indeed been an earlier suggestion that he might be admitted to the Cabinet while remaining under-secretary for the Colonies, but the King had vetoed this, saying that he must wait for " a real vacancy."

earlier intention had been to continue to fill this office himself, at least until the end of the session, as Gladstone had done in 1873-4 and again in 1880-2. He told the King of this at his audience on March 4th, and the latter, after being assured that there were precedents, said he thought it much the best arrangement.[g] But Asquith later changed his mind, partly because the Gladstonian precedents were not very encouraging, and partly because he was persuaded that the promotion of a ' man of the left ' was necessary to adjust for the shift of balance following from his own replacement of Campbell-Bannerman. Once he had decided to divide the two jobs he was in no doubt that Lloyd George should be the new Chancellor. He made the formal offer to him immediately on his return from France, and received an enthusiastic acceptance on the Saturday. " I thank you for the flattering proposal contained in your letter," Lloyd George wrote, " and even more for the generous terms in which it is conveyed to me. . . . I shall be proud to serve under your Premiership and no member of the Government will render more loyal service and support to his chief."[h]

Even so, the letter ended on a somewhat rancid note. The Cabinet list had been prematurely published in the *Daily Chronicle*, and it was suggested, from within the Cabinet, that Lloyd George was responsible. Churchill was asked by Asquith to raise the matter with the new Chancellor. He did so and reported at midnight on the Friday that Lloyd George " denied it utterly." In his letter to Asquith of the following day Lloyd George repeated the denial angrily and demanded to know which of his colleagues had made this " amiable suggestion." " Men whose promotion is not sustained by birth or other favouring conditions," he continued, " are always liable to be assailed with unkind suspicions of this sort. I would ask it therefore as a favour that you should not entertain them without satisfying yourself that they have some basis of truth."[i]

Some of the other changes were grudgingly accepted by those involved. Elgin retired reluctantly from the Colonial Office and refused to become a Marquess. He was replaced by Crewe, who took on the leadership of the House of Lords from Ripon, but gave up the Presidency of the Council. Tweedmouth was offered this in place of the Admiralty, and at first wrote a sulky refusal, complaining that Asquith did not trust him and that he ought to have resigned long before rather than allow his estimates to be cut; but he eventually accepted. Reginald McKenna became First Lord of the Admiralty, the King stipulating that, this being so, Fisher should remain First Sea Lord. He apparently suspected, quite falsely, that McKenna would show himself an excessive naval economist.

Morley remained as Secretary of State for India but removed to the House of Lords with a viscounty. " I suppose . . . I have a claim from seniority of service for your place at the Exchequer," he had rather disturbingly opened to Asquith a short time before; " but I don't know that I have any special aptitude for it under present prospects," he had more encouragingly continued.*j* Some of the junior candidates for office created more difficulties. The most importunate of all was Asquith's former pupil from the summer of 1874, when he had acted as a tutor in Lord Portsmouth's household. This boy had now become Lord Portsmouth himself and had served as under-secretary for war in the previous Government. He first wrote asking for Cabinet rank, and when Asquith, who had enjoyed exceptional opportunities of judging his mental capacity, responded by dropping him from the Government altogether, Portsmouth began a series of protests which continued throughout the summer. He did not move the Prime Minister but he succeeded in getting his successor (H. T. Baker, later Warden of Winchester) blackballed at Brooks's.

The parliamentary secretary to the Admiralty wrote asking to remain in office with a peerage, but he too disappeared from the Government. And Charles Trevelyan, whose father, G. O. Trevelyan protested in terms which were rather blatantly nepotic for the head of such a radical family,[1] never got into it. Nor was there any advancement for J. A. Pease, who begged to be promoted after " eleven years' work as a whip," and pronounced himself ready, in an almost classical phrase for a suppliant, to respond to a telegram " in about six hours at any time to talk things over with you." Almost the only man who got anything by asking for it was Charles Masterman, who stipulated that he would not be parliamentary secretary to the Local Government

---

[1] " Since our party came in," he wrote to Asquith on April 15th, " full recognition has been given to the past services of those who in old days served the country and the cause, by the employment of their sons and relatives who are worthy of a chance in the career of administration. Now that several younger men have been placed in office, while my son is left out, I must protest, once for all, that I feel the exception made in our case very deeply." (*Asquith Papers*, XI, ff. 100-1).

Board unless the department was substantially reorganised; and Asquith agreed that this should be done.

Amongst the spate of requests which Asquith received at this time, Augustine Birrell's acceptance of an invitation to stay in the same job, written from the Irish Office on April 11th, stands out as a solitary example of a letter built round a joke (even if not a very good one) rather than a demand: "I am sorry you have overlooked my claims upon the Chancellorship of the ——— Duchy! But am content to remain on here—where at all events you are are never dull."[k]

In spite of these difficulties the lists were all complete by the date of the King's return to England—April 16th,—and the exchange of seals of office proceeded in the normal way—at Buckingham Palace not at the Crillon. Easter came a few days later and Asquith went to Easton Grey, near Malmesbury, a most attractive house belonging to one of his wife's sisters, for more than a week. While he was there Campbell-Bannerman died. Asquith's first House of Commons duties as Prime Minister were therefore those of paying tribute to his former leader, which he did in notably warm and felicitous terms, and of moving yet another adjournment of the House.

The transitional ceremonies were still not complete. On Wednesday, April 29th a Liberal Party meeting assembled in the Reform Club in order to endorse Asquith's leadership. This was a purely formal proceeding. Those present included not only the Liberal peers and M.P.s, but also some representatives of the party organisation outside. The resolution which was put took the form of welcoming his premiership rather than of electing him leader. The way in which it was drafted, by the sometimes querulous but on this occasion perceptively generous hand of John Morley, gave particular pleasure to Asquith. It referred to "his strong sense in council, power in debate, and consummate mastery of all the habit and practice of public business." It was of course carried unanimously.

The same day also saw the first Cabinet meeting over which the new Prime Minister presided in his own right. A week later, the Asquiths moved from Cavendish Square to Downing Street. No. 10 was substantially larger than No. 11, but even so it did not arouse Margot's enthusiasm. "It is an inconvenient house with three poor staircases," she wrote, "and after living there a few weeks I made up my mind that owing to the impossibility of circulation I could only entertain my Liberal friends[1] at dinner or at garden parties."[1] The outside of the house she described as " liver-coloured and squalid." One of its disadvantages, she found, was that no taxi-driver ever knew where it was; they were more likely to go to Down Street, Piccadilly, than to Downing Street, Whitehall. Yet during the eight and a half years for which the Asquiths were tenants of No. 10 they identified themselves more closely with the house and gave it a more distinct social character than had been the case with any Prime Ministerial family for several decades past. Campbell-Bannerman's life there had been dominated by his own and his wife's illnesses. Balfour was a bachelor, Rosebery was a widower, and Salisbury never moved from Arlington House. At least since the days of Gladstone's first two Governments 10 Downing Street had not been occupied as it was by the Asquiths. And even then, the G.O.M's preference for being entertained, rather than himself entertaining, had been well to the fore. But, throughout the Asquith régime and in spite of her ill-health, Margot filled the house with a series of bizarrely assorted luncheon and dinner parties. Her husband looked on, apparently with a detached tolerance, but in fact with a good deal of placid enjoyment.

During that summer of 1908, a relatively calm one politically, Asquith settled down to a Prime Minister's routine. He held Cabinets once a week, usually on a Wednesday morning, and after each meeting he wrote to the King, in his own hand, two or three page accounts of what had occurred. The copies of these letters, made by his principal private secretary, also in his own hand, constituted the only records available to the Government of the business transacted; there was neither a Cabinet secretariat nor Cabinet minutes. But the copy was not circulated to other members of the Cabinet. Nor were the records entirely satisfactory in other respects. In the first place they were biased, not to mislead the King, but to interest him. Foreign and military discussions were described at greater length than questions of domestic social policy. And any matters of specifically royal concern were given extra stress. A quarter of the letter on one occasion was taken up by an account of the Cabinet's decision against increasing the reward offered for some missing Crown jewels. It is difficult to believe that the subject took an equal proportion of the time of the Cabinet meeting. The letters also suffer, as records, from Asquith's bland economy of style and from his natural desire to give the King

[1] Why this did not apply to her non-Liberal friends is not clear.

185

an impression of a united and decisive Cabinet. "After much discussion the Estimates were in substance approved,"[m] he wrote at the end of the year, after a particularly difficult and indecisive meeting on the naval building programme.

Most other interchanges between Buckingham Palace and Downing Street took the form of correspondence between Lord Knollys and Vaughan Nash, the respective private secretaries. But this did not make them anodyne. The subject of honours was a fairly constant and accepted battleground between Sovereign and Prime Minister. Even in this field, however, the fact that real power lay in Downing Street was accepted without much question. The Palace mostly confined itself to peripheral sniping: to complaints about the length of the lists, particularly for knighthoods; to perhaps contradictory (and by no means always successful) attempts to insert a few royal nominees into them; and to open displays of innocent pleasure whenever something could be discovered against one of the Downing Street nominees. "My dear Mr. Nash," Knollys wrote on July 4th, 1908, "the King desires me to say he hears that Mr. ———, one of those recommended for a Knighthood but whose name was he believes withdrawn, is a Bankrupt hatter."[n]

There were also frequent royal complaints about the tone of the speeches of some ministers. Lloyd George and Churchill were by far the most regular offenders. And occasionally the King went so far as to rebuke the Prime Minister. "The King deplores the attitude taken up by Mr. Asquith on the Woman's Suffrage question," Knollys wrote in an undated note. It can only have been the tactics of the Prime Minister which were here considered to be at fault, because his views on the issue differed little from those of the King.

It would be a mistake to assume from these occasional sharp exchanges that relations between Asquith and the King were often strained. They were mostly smooth enough, although never very close. King Edward respected some of Asquith's talents, but he did not feel greatly at ease in his company. He had found Campbell-Bannerman more to his taste. In part this was due to a simple question of compatibility of character. In part, too, it was because the King, as Sir Sidney Lee has pointed out, thought of Asquith as much more of a "new man" than Campbell-Bannerman. Neither of these Liberal leaders had been born into a ruling group. But Campbell-Bannerman had wealth, and this, in the King's view, was the best substitute for lineage. Asquith's polished intellectual equipment did not strike him as in any way a comparable attribute. Paradoxically, therefore, the man who is today often thought of as the "last of the Romans," the final example of the classical tradition in British statesmanship, was regarded by his sovereign as something of a political *parvenu*. This view helped to make King Edward's relations with the Prime Minister stop well short of friendship, but it did not make them hostile. And if, for some other reason, friction occasionally rose, Lord Knollys, liberal, intelligent and warmly friendly towards Asquith, was deftly assiduous in smoothing it away. The unadorned, pungent way in which he could put the King's views to the Prime Minister was a function of the fact that he did not, himself, always take them too seriously.

Another aspect of Prime Ministerial routine with which Asquith concerned himself closely was that of ecclesiastical appointments. As a natural "Athenaeum figure" he would in any event have enjoyed following the careers of the upper clergy. And when he himself achieved the power largely to determine them he exercised it with interest and care, often exchanging two or more long letters a week with Randall Davidson, the Archbishop of Canterbury, upon the subject. They discussed in detail not merely bishoprics, but deaneries and canonries, when these fell vacant and were Crown appointments. Davidson usually put his own order of preference firmly before Asquith, but he never assumed that his first choice would necessarily get the job, and he mostly submitted several names. He expected (even if he did not encourage) the Prime Minister to have some regard, at least if there was equality in other qualifications, for politics in his appointments. Ecclesiastics who were firm Liberals (the Bishops of Hereford and Birmingham and the Dean of Norwich, for example) did not hesitate to point this out to the Prime Minister when writing him patronage letters. Nevertheless, Asquith's first major appointment was firmly non-political. In the autumn of 1908 the Archbishopric of York fell vacant. He nominated Cosmo Lang, 43 years of age and at that time only suffragan Bishop of Stepney. By way of apology Asquith wrote to Dr. Percival of Hereford, the only bishop who had voted with the Government in the 1906 Education Bill controversy, and explained that he had passed him over solely on grounds of age. Percival, who was 74, wrote back in a friendly way, but expressing great disappointment that he was not to be translated after "my 13 years in this Tory backwater."

The relative political calm which marked Asquith's first summer as Prime Minister was not something which most Liberal supporters wished to last. They looked to the Government for a political initiative bold enough to reverse the disastrous flow of the by-election tide. The losses were of no significance from the point of view of the Government current majority, but were on a scale (seven seats changed hands during the year) to suggest that the Unionists might well win a general election. The session, up to the summer holidays, had not been entirely barren. The Old Age Pensions Bill was through, although not without a great deal of grumbling from the peers, and there seemed some prospect of obtaining an educational compromise in the autumn.[1] But the Licensing Bill, after a weary passage through the House of Commons, seemed a certain candidate for slaughter when Parliament resumed in November. A controversial Liberal bill of limited popularity which was anathema to the brewers, was hardly likely to get much mercy from the peers. The legislative impotence of the Government would again be displayed. But the experience of the Old Age Pensions Bill suggested the possibility of the Government regaining its authority by means of financial initiative. The majority of the peers had made no attempt to conceal their hostility to this bill. They had carried a destructive amendment to it, but when the Commons firmly announced that a Lords' amendment to a money bill was inadmissible, they had accepted this as sound if unwelcome constitutional doctrine. Social advance by means of money bills became the obvious course for the Liberal Government.

Haldane was one of the first to see this. He wrote to Asquith from Cloan on August 9th and succeeded in combining in about equal proportions the sweeping and the trivial:

" We should boldly take our stand on the facts and proclaim a policy of taking, mainly by direct taxation, such toll from the increase and growth of this (national) wealth as will enable us to provide for (1) the increasing cost of Social reform; (2) National Defence; and also (3) to have a margin in aid of the Sinking Fund ". . . .

" The import and manufacture of mineral waters," he con-

[1] In fact, this hope proved baseless. Asquith came very near to a provisional agreement with the Archbishop of Canterbury during the first three weeks of November, but Davidson had to draw back at the last moment because it became clear that he could not carry the other bishops with him.

tinued, "supply a luxury. I do not see why, as alcohol ceases to be fashionable and these are increasingly consumed, they should not bear a tax which, in one shape or another, would give £2m.... Look at the consumption of Apollinaris on the one hand and of Soda Water on the other....

"If there is anything in (my scheme)," he concluded, "the condition of success is that you should direct operations yourself. No one else is competent to do it." [o]

The last sentence probably owed as much to Haldane's deep-seated distrust of Lloyd George as to his faith in the Prime Minister, real though that was. But in fact the Chancellor of the Exchequer's mind was already beginning to turn in the same direction (towards more direct taxation, if not towards mineral waters) and it was he who, in the following spring, was to take the fiscal initiative which determined the course of politics for the next two years.

Before that could happen the session of 1908 had to run its course, and the Licensing Bill, the last non-financial furrow in the barren legislative sand which the Government had ploughed since 1906, show itself as firmly blocked by the House of Lords as the others had been. In the meantime, during the recess, a sudden political squall, minor but violent, had blown up out of the temporarily calm atmosphere. As is sometimes the case with these unexpected storms it was an isolated incident having little to do with the general current of politics. But it involved the resignation of one minister and the diversion of the career of another; it touched on the relations between the King and his Cabinet; it provided the first test of how Asquith would deal with such a situation; and the events from which it arose have a certain curious interest of their own. For all these reasons it is worth some detail of treatment.

During the latter part of August and early September a Eucharistic Congress took place in London. It was proposed by the Roman Catholic hierarchy that the conclusion of this, on Sunday, September 13th, should be marked by a ceremonial public procession over an extended route. The Host was to be carried, and a great body of Roman Catholic dignitaries in full vestments were to attend it. Such an arrangement was undoubtedly contrary to the letter of the law. The Catholic Emancipation Act of 1829 contained a prohibition of public observance of the ceremonies of the Church of Rome. But there was ground for believing that this part of the Act was in desuetude.

In 1898 and in 1901 similar although smaller processions had taken place without official interference. The practical position appeared to be that the law was only enforced if a breach was likely to give rise to public disorder. Acting on this assumption, Cardinal Bourne, the Archbishop of Westminster, had approached Sir Edward Henry, the Commissioner of Metropolitan Police (himself a Roman Catholic) at the end of July, had informed him of the proposed procession, and obtained his sanction.

Almost everyone who was to become concerned in the matter, except for the Roman Catholics prelates, then went on their holidays. By early September they were scattered over the remoter parts of the British Isles. Herbert Gladstone, the Home Secretary, was in the south of Scotland. Asquith was at Slains Castle in Aberdeenshire. Lord Ripon, the only Roman Catholic member of the Cabinet, was at Ripon Abbey in Yorkshire. The King was at Rufford Abbey in Nottinghamshire, where Lord Crewe was a fellow-guest. Sir Edward Henry was fishing in Ireland. The only man of relevant authority in London was Sir Edward Troup, permanent secretary to the Home Office. But this did not prevent the squall from developing.

The procession, the scale of which may not have been fully disclosed to Henry in July, was widely advertised in the few weeks before it took place. Militant Protestants began a vigorous campaign of complaint. Some of them wrote to Asquith, and more of them wrote to King Edward. The King reacted strongly and urged the Home Secretary to ban the whole procession. Gladstone was uncertain whether he could do this and dilatory in his replies. As a result the King began telegraphing to Asquith, complaining about the Home Secretary and asking the Prime Minister either to get Ripon to intervene with the Cardinal Archbishop or to put pressure on the Home Office. The royal state of mind was described in a letter which Crewe wrote to Asquith on September 12th: "The King has taken this d.......d procession greatly to heart, and asked me to say that he was 'greatly cut up about it'—a rather curious phrase.... He has received dozens of letters from enraged Protestants, who compare him disadvantageously with his revered mother, now with God, and hint that his ultimate destination may be directed elsewhere."[p]

Asquith's position was difficult, both on the merits of the issue and on the means by which it was proper for him to proceed. His own natural tolerance was fortified by no particular respect for the rites of the Roman church. "... there is a good deal of quite respectable Protestant sentiment which is offended by this gang of foreign cardinals taking advantage of our hospitality to parade their idolatries through the streets of London: a thing without precedent since the days of Bloody Mary," he wrote to Crewe on September 10th.[q] But he had no particular interest in offending the Catholics, most of whom were working class Irish immigrants and Liberal voters. On the other hand Nonconformists were still more important to the Liberal Party than were Catholics, and some of their leaders were already disaffected by the Government's inability to give them educational relief. "You know the way (the Free Churchmen) have fought for Liberal principles for the last six years," Dr. John Clifford wrote to Asquith only a few days later; "but I fear many of them are losing heart."[r]

Then there was the Prime Minister's friendship with Herbert Gladstone, who had been his under-secretary in the government of 1892. He was one of the very few men who wrote to Asquith as "My dear Henry." Gladstone handled the crisis with a mixture of carelessness and indecision. He never went to London to consult with his own officials and the police. He failed to provide either Asquith or the King with a clear statement of the exact legal position. And he gave bewilderingly conflicting advice about the likelihood of the procession leading to public disorder. "Police confident they can preserve order," he telegraphed to Asquith on September 9th. "Difficult to say we anticipate breach of the peace. ·Procession not in main thoroughfares. Troup against interference and on the whole I agree with him." On the following day he telegraphed again: "Further information this morning shows gravity of feelings. Nothing but overwhelming force of police will prevent serious disorder." And on September 12th he was back on his first line of advice. "Troup reports that police find no reason to fear riot," he wrote, "and thinks himself that the chance of serious disturbance is very small."[s]

In the circumstances it was not surprising that Asquith decided to act independently of the Home Office through Ripon. He asked the old Catholic marquess to get the Cardinal Archbishop to abandon the liturgical aspects of the procession. Ripon agreed, but with deep reluctance. "I feel it a great humiliation I have had to make such a communication at the last moment," he wrote to Asquith. Cardinal Bourne, in turn, responded equally reluctantly to Ripon's appeal

"Having considered your communication," he telegraphed to the Prime Minister on September 11th, "have decided to abandon ceremonial of which you questioned legality provided that you authorize me to state publicly that I do so at your request."*t*

The procession therefore passed off without trouble. But it left a legacy of difficulty for the Government. Ripon decided that, torn as he had been between his religious and his political loyalties, he must resign. He refrained from making public the reason for his withdrawal. He allowed it to be attributed to ill-health, and his final letter to Asquith was in notably friendly terms. "And so my public life closes," he wrote on October 7th, "and my last word in it is to wish you and your Government every possible success."*u*

Gladstone created a different difficulty. Most of the other ministers who had been involved (particularly Crewe and Ripon) blamed him for the trouble, and the King was anxious for blood. "You will find H.M. very bitter about Herbert," Crewe wrote to Asquith on September 16th, "and longing to get rid of him."*v* When Asquith went to Balmoral, a week later, he found no improvement in the King's mood towards Gladstone, but, he reported to Crewe, "I succeeded in diverting some of his wrath in the direction of Henry, who (Knollys tells me) is said to be a bigoted Papist. If this is true, it may throw some light on his otherwise inexplicable inaction."*w*

Gladstone himself showed no enthusiasm for resignation. Eventually, on September 24th after receiving a most wounding letter from the King, he wrote saying that perhaps he ought to go. But when Asquith responded by offering him the sinecure of the Lord Presidency of the Council, he refused the change. He thought this would be too obvious a demotion. The Prime Minister therefore let him stay for another year. Then, against the wishes of the King,[1] he went to South Africa as first governor-general of the new dominion, and was created

[1] "If the Prime Minister cannot find a better Governor-General he supposes he must approve of the appointment but that he thinks it a very bad one," was the comment that the King asked Knollys to pass on. (*Asquith Papers*, Box 1, f. 206). At this stage, however, the King was concerned not so much with his dislike of Gladstone, as with the belief that his name would carry unfortunate associations with the "Majuba Hill Policy." Asquith countered by pointing out that Joseph Chamberlain, as a member of the Cabinet in 1882, was a good deal more responsible for that policy than was Herbert Gladstone.

a viscount. Asquith's faith in Gladstone's administrative competence was gravely shaken by the affair of the procession, but he did not rebuke the Home Secretary—he merely replied rather coolly to his apologies—and he had him to stay at Archerfield during the following Christmas holidays.

As 1908 drew to a close, and the Liberal Government looked increasingly becalmed in the lee of the House of Lords, Asquith received vigorous if not wholly accurate letters of information and advice from the new President of the Board of Trade. " I learn that Lansdowne in private utterly scouts the suggestion that the Lords will reject the Budget Bill," Churchill wrote on December 26th. He followed this up with an expression of his own desire to use the new session both to construct a system of Labour Exchanges and to introduce " a big railway bill," which would " devise some form of state control of these amalgamations which will secure the interest of the trading public." Three days later Churchill broadened the canvas. We should follow the example of Germany, he urged: " She is organised not only for war, but for peace. We are organised for nothing except party politics. . . . I say thrust a big slice of Bismarckianism over the whole underside of our industrial system, and await the consequences whatever they may be with a good conscience." *x* In fact it was not the new President of the Board of Trade, but his close associate, the new Chancellor of the Exchequer, who set the tone of the forthcoming session. And it was to be a tone which made organisation for party politics a matter of primary importance.

CHAPTER XIV

A TRIAL OF STATESMANSHIP I

1909-10

The life of the Government, in the early months of 1909, was dominated by a fresh outbreak of the naval controversy and by preparations for the Budget. The Admiralty, acting in response to the acceleration of German building, put forward a programme of six capital ships for the financial year 1909–10. This was strongly resisted by the so-called " economists "[1] in the Cabinet, who thought that four were quite enough. This group was composed of Lloyd George, Churchill, Harcourt, Burns and Morley, although the last three, Asquith recorded, were somewhat disinclined on personal grounds to make common cause with the first two. But on the merits they were all agreed.

On February 2nd, Churchill circulated a printed Cabinet paper expressing his scepticism about the danger of the German challenge. On the same day Lloyd George, who was never a natural letter-writer, took the unusual course of sending the Prime Minister thirteen pages in his own hand. " The discussion of Naval Estimates threatens to re-open all the old controversies which rent the party for years and brought it to impotence and contempt," he began. " You alone can save us from this prospect of sterile and squalid disruption." A little later he stressed the depressing effect which the larger programme would have on " millions of earnest Liberals in the country." It would cause them to " break into open sedition " and bring " the usefulness of this Parliament to an end."[a] The letter also contained a hint, but not more than a hint, of resignation. However it offered something more than blank opposition to the Admiralty demands. Indeed it attacked them not so much for being excessive as for being stupid. If, as he thought likely, the fears about German construction were exaggerated, the Admiralty was asking for too much. But if, as was

[1] So-called because they were reluctant to spend money on armaments and not because of their knowledge of the " dismal science."

194

possible, the fear proved well-founded, they were not asking for enough. The answer was a flexible long-term British building programme, the speed of which could be varied according to what the Germans did. It was a typical Lloyd George argument, ingenious and persuasive.

But it did not settle the Cabinet crisis. This was partly because of the stubborn departmentalism of McKenna, the First Lord, who clung rigidly to the original Admiralty proposal. There were a series of wrangling and inconclusive Cabinets. After the February 15th meeting Asquith took the unusual step of reporting the line-up to the King. Churchill, Harcourt, Burns and Morley, he said were on one side and Grey, Runciman, Crewe and Buxton on the other. The Chancellor of the Exchequer was reported as putting forward his compromise, which was then favourably received by Asquith, Crewe and Grey. A Cabinet committee was set up to go into it. But this did not make much progress, and on February 20th Asquith wrote to his wife complaining, without undue agitation, about Lloyd George and Churchill, who " by their combined machinations have got the bulk of the Liberal press into (their) camp." " There are moments," he said, " when I am disposed summarily to cashier them both. E. Grey is a great stand-by, always, sound, temperate, and strong."[b]

Then, at the Cabinet of February 24th, Asquith himself, having previously allowed others to make the running, felt able to take the lead and propound an acceptable solution. " A sudden curve developed itself of which I took immediate advantage," he characteristically put it, " with the result that strangely enough we came to a conclusion which satisfied McKenna and Grey and also LL.G. and Winston."[c] Four ships should be laid down immediately, and another four if and when the need was proved. It was a variant of the original Lloyd George proposal, but it was more acceptable because of the quarter from which it came. By the summer, as Asquith had confidently expected at the time of the " compromise," the need was considered to have been proved, and at the Cabinet of July 24th the additional four were accepted without much further demur. The " economists " had waged an extraordinarily ineffective battle.

The decision to undertake this unpopular expenditure made it even more necessary, from a party point of view, that the Budget should be strongly radical. Much earlier, however, it had been decided that this was to be a year for the breaking of new financial ground. Old age pensions, even without the additional naval expenditure, meant that more revenue had to be raised. And there was a settled Cabinet view that this should be done in such a way as to strike back at the House of Lords and regain the initiative for the Liberal Government. Asquith's first Cabinet letter of the year, on January 26th, warned the King that "the main business of the year must . . . be of necessity the Budget," although he also informed him of the Cabinet's hope, utterly misplaced as matters turned out, of avoiding an autumn session.[d] But what form was the strike against the peers to take? Was it to be an outflanking move, based on the assumption that the Lords would never touch a money bill? In this case a controversial Budget would be an alternative to a "battle of the veto." Or was it the intention that the Budget should provoke the peers to the rash step of rejection, and thus serve as a favourable prelude to the battle"?

Some commentators, including at least one of Lloyd George's numerous biographers,[1] have suggested that the Chancellor, with the approval of the Prime Minister, deliberately framed his Budget so as to court a peers' rejection. The evidence in favour of this view is unconvincing.[2] What is much more likely is that it never seriously occurred to the leaders of the Government that the Lords would dare to attack a Finance Bill. They would therefore use it as the one legislative means open to them of achieving some radical objectives.

Unfortunately the Cabinet was far from unanimous about what were legitimate radical objectives, particularly in the social and fiscal fields. As a result the budget proposals involved a great deal of internal discussion and controversy. Between mid-March and Budget Day (which was April 29th) fourteen Cabinet meetings were in large part devoted to discussions of the Chancellor's proposals. In each of two weeks (those beginning March 14th and April 4th) no less than three meetings were held. A single meeting was rarely sufficient to produce agreement on a particular point, and the almost invariable practice was to adjourn until the following day. The proposals were considered in groups: the controversial land taxes in mid-March; the liquor and stamp duties at the end of the month; the income tax and estate duties in the first days of April; and the indirect taxes immediately following. Then, after the Easter recess, the general position was discussed and the earlier proposals reviewed in the light of it.

[1] Mr. Malcolm Thompson.
[2] See the present author's *Mr. Balfour's Poodle*, pp. 40–2.

Lloyd George always maintained that he had a most difficult struggle to force his proposals through the Cabinet against the nearly unanimous opposition of his colleagues.[1] Only the Prime Minister, he allowed, gave him decisive help, and that took the form more of the deft turning of difficult corners than of argumentative assistance. Nevertheless the proposals almost all survived. In his Cabinet letters to the King Asquith records only one occasion when the Chancellor was overruled, together with another when he may have been forced to present a proposal in a more conciliatory form than he might himself have wished. Both were concerned with the famous land taxes.[2] The first was on March 19th. "The Cabinet rejected a proposal submitted by the Chancellor of the Exchequer to tax the ground rents of land built upon on the ground that it would involve an interference with existing contracts." And on March 24th the Prime Minister reported: "The provisions for the additional taxation of land values were carefully revised with the object of minimising cases of possible hardship and safeguarding existing contracts."[e] The lawyers, always a powerful body in that Cabinet, were keenly watchful of the Chancellor on anything to do with the sanctity of contracts.

Nevertheless it would be easily possible to exaggerate the dissension

---

[1] He probably had some difficulty in the Treasury as well. On April 7th, Sir George Murray, the Permanent Secretary, wrote to Asquith: "I think the Budget is fairly ship-shape now. The two largest blots on it are (1) the *reversion duty*—which is iniquitous in principle, but will not otherwise do very much harm; and (2) the *Petrol Tax*, which I believe to be quite unworkable...." (*Asquith Papers*, box 22, f. 123).

[2] These were by far the most controversial part of a controversial Budget. As introduced, they provided for (i) a tax of 20% on the unearned increment in land values, payable either when the land was sold or when it passed at death; (ii) a capital tax of ½d. in the £ on the value of undeveloped land and minerals; and (iii) a 10% reversion duty on any benefit which came to a lessor at the end of a lease. The first two provisions were modified, with the Chancellor's consent, during the Committee Stage of the Finance Bill. The yield, and consequently the social effect, of all these taxes proved disappointing. After 1918 they were repealed, ironically enough, by a Government over which Lloyd George was presiding. In reality much the most important part of the 1909 Budget, for future social change, passed with comparatively little notice. This was the introduction of surtax (or super-tax as it was then called). Lloyd George levied it at the rate of 6d. in the £ on the amount by which incomes of £5,000 or more exceeded £3,000.

within the Cabinet. Lloyd George had his enemies—notably Haldane and McKenna—who were always critical of his methods and style. There were others, notably Harcourt (despite his radicalism on other issues), Runciman, and, more silently, Crewe, who disliked the substance of some of his proposals. And there was Grey, who was instinctively hostile to any raising of party controversy. But none of them carried their opposition or hostility into the open. Throughout the long and bitter struggle to get the Budget through there were no obvious attempts on the part of ministers to dissociate themselves from the Chancellor and to suggest that they were above the battle. Still less were there any hints of resignation. Haldane and Burns (another of Lloyd George's enemies) contented themselves with making malicious comments about the Chancellor's Budget Day performance —but then it was a strangely bad speech.

During the late spring and summer and early autumn the battle went on without respite. It was most intense in the House of Commons. Forty-two parliamentary days were required to get the Finance Bill through its committee stage, and a good half of these involved parliamentary nights as well as days. The process was not complete until October 6th—without any summer recess—and even then report and third reading, which between them occupied twelve days, had still to be taken. The bill did not complete its passage through the Commons until November 4th. In these proceedings the Prime Minister, as was natural, left the lead to the Chancellor. He was not over-assiduous in his attendance, and he voted in only 202 of the mammoth total of 554 divisions which took place on the bill. But when he was there he occasionally intervened (as a Prime Minister would be unlikely to do today) with a supporting speech; he several times came across from Downing Street at the end of an all-night sitting and took over for the last hour or so before breakfast; and he moved the minor but permanent procedural changes which, at the end of July, the Government decided were essential if the bill were ever to get through.

Outside the House the battle was equally bitter but more sporadic. At first the opponents of the Budget made most of the running. City opinion was particularly quick to mobilise itself. On May 14th Lord Rothschild (who was a Liberal) sent the Prime Minister a letter of protest which was signed by the principals of most of the leading financial houses. A month later he presided over a crowded meeting of agitated financiers, most of them nominally Liberals. By this time Lord Rosebery had also entered the fray, and had denounced the Budget as "inquisitorial, tyrannical, and Socialistic." The Budget Protest League had been established under more regular opposition auspices.

Asquith showed no sign of weakening under this pressure, and he was equally unyielding when a deputation of thirty rather Whiggish Liberal members waited upon him later in the summer and expressed apprehension about the land taxes. Altogether his behaviour throughout this period fully merited Lloyd George's tribute that he was "firm as a rock." He did not speak much in the country in support of the Budget. But nor for that matter did the Chancellor. Lloyd George's famous Limehouse oration of July 30th, in which he goaded the dukes into some extremely injudicious replies, was an exceptional foray. Asquith never sought to compete with this provocative oratory, but the few speeches which he made gave powerful support to the Budget at crucial times and in crucial places. In July he addressed a meeting of the City Liberals at the Cannon Street Hotel, the scene of Lord Rothschild's protest. And on September 17th he spoke with great force to 13,000 people at Birmingham. By this time attention had moved from the merits of the Budget to the still more important question of whether the Lords dare to break a 250-year-old rule and reject it. And as the constitutional issue replaced the financial one so the Prime Minister replaced the Chancellor of the Exchequer as the Liberal protagonist.

The possibility of a peers' rejection first began to be considered seriously after a speech of Lansdowne's on July 16th, in which the Unionist leader somewhat ambiguously announced that the House of Lords "would not swallow the Finance Bill whole without wincing." Churchill replied to this in a speech at Edinburgh on the following day and stated, apparently without consultation, that a rejection would be followed by a dissolution of Parliament. The Palace immediately complained to Asquith, Knollys's letter rather wearily beginning: "The King desires me to say it is painful to him to be continually obliged to complain of certain of your colleagues."ƒ But on this occasion the Prime Minister treated the indiscretion as seriously as did the Sovereign, and the Cabinet, at its meeting of July 21st, took the most unusual step of formally rebuking Churchill for "purporting to speak on behalf of the Government" in a way that was "quite indefensible and altogether inconsistent with Cabinet responsibility and Ministerial cohesion."

The reason for this sharp reaction was that Churchill's statement ran directly counter to Asquith's tactic, which he continued into the autumn, of treating a peers' rejection as quite unthinkable. " Amendment by the House of Lords," he said at Birmingham, " is out of the question. Rejection by the House of Lords is equally out of the question. . . . That way revolution lies." This did not mean that he was burying his head in the sand. He knew perfectly well that rejection was already more likely than not. Nevertheless, he thought that the best way to bring the constitutional enormity home to the country was for the Government publicly to stress its impossibility. Privately, ministers were more realistic. On September 8th the Cabinet held a preliminary discussion about the consequences of rejection, and the Lord Chancellor and the Law Officers were instructed to go into the legal aspects. The Prime Minister reported to the King that in the opinion of the majority of the Cabinet " such action on the part of the House of Lords ought to be followed by an acceleration of the Register, so as to secure at the earliest possible moment an appeal to the country."[g] Churchill's reaction had been no more than premature.

On October 5th there was a further Cabinet discussion on the subject, but on this occasion the approach was cautious. " It was agreed that until the course of events shapes itself more clearly it would be premature to decide upon any definite course of action," was Asquith's report.[h] This may have been because he was to see the King at Balmoral on the following day, and was reluctant to limit his room for manoeuvre. At this audience he found the King, as he wrote to Crewe, " in the most amiable and forthcoming mood." His Majesty wanted to see the Unionist leaders and put pressure on them not to reject—a course to which Asquith gladly agreed. The King also wanted to know what he could offer them in return and suggested a January general election. Asquith disliked the idea and searched around for arguments against it. It would not, he thought, be of much attraction to Balfour and Lansdowne. They would have to fight at rather a flat moment. Furthermore, an election in the depths of winter was always inconvenient for both parties. There was the added consideration that the most likely result would be a close one, with the Irish holding the balance—" a very undesirable state of things." These were all arguments designed to appeal to the King, and it may well have been with the same thought in his mind that Asquith refrained from using the real one—that to allow the Lords to force a dissolution would be to grant them more than half their case. In any event, he succeeded in turning the King's thoughts away from the idea.

The meeting with Balfour and Lansdowne took place on October 12th. It served little purpose. The King had no influence on them, and they were less than frank with him. They told him no decision had been taken, which was formally correct, but in fact both the leaders had already decided in favour of rejection. On November 3rd the Cabinet held its first discussion based on the definite assumption that a rejection would take place. The preparation of a short Finance (No. 2) Bill dealing with the relatively non-controversial taxes was ordered. This was to be rushed through so as to legalise the collections which had already taken place and to reduce the financial dislocation. This bill was ready by November 5th. But it was never proceeded with. The policy upon which it was based was destroyed in a powerful memorandum which Sir Courtney Ilbert, clerk to the House of Commons, submitted to the Prime Minister on November 16th. To introduce a second bill, with some taxes cut out, would be to concede to the House of Lords the right to determine what financial legislation the House of Commons could and could not pass. It would also, Ilbert shrewdly added, going perhaps a little outside his clerkly functions, give Mr. Balfour great dialectical opportunities. It would be much better to continue to collect taxes on the strength of the Commons' resolutions and to hope for subsequent legalisation. " There are occasions," he concluded, " when respect for the constitution must override respect for the law. This may be one of them."[i]

Asquith responded immediately to the force of this argument. At the Cabinet of November 17th the previous policy was reversed. When the Lords' rejection took place there was to be no bill but an immediate dissolution of Parliament. But the policy on collection was to be more cautious than Ilbert recommended. Payment of the disputed taxes (including the whole of the income tax, which requires annual re-enactment) was to be purely voluntary until the new Parliament passed the Finance Bill, although the liability was then to be retrospective. The gap was to be filled by borrowing.

At the next meeting of the Cabinet a week later the details of the dissolution were fixed. As an immediate response to the action of the Lords the House of Commons was to be asked to carry the following resolution: " That the action of the House of Lords in refusing to pass into law the financial provision made by the House for the service of the year is a breach of the constitution and a usurpation of the rights of the Commons." This done, there was to be an adjournment on the next day. Prorogation was to be on January 8th, and polling was to begin on January 15th and be over by the end of the month. This programme was meticulously followed.

A dissolution was of course inevitable once the Lords had performed the act of rejection. There was no dispute in the Cabinet about this. The legislature had refused Supply, and in these circumstances no government could carry on. This fact gave the full measure of what the Lords had done. They had not merely confronted the Government with the choice between an immediate election and acceptance of the loss of a particular measure, as they had frequently done before. They had left ministers with no choice, and had taken upon themselves the right of deciding when a Government could carry on and when it could not, when a Parliament should end and when it should not. It was a claim which, if allowed, would have made the Government as much a creature of the hereditary assembly as of the elective assembly.

Yet what was the dissolution to achieve? No doubt it would force the Lords, provided the new House of Commons produced a majority in its favour, to accept the disputed Finance Bill. This in itself would hardly be a great victory. Even in their most arrogant moments the peers had never claimed a right beyond that of forcing a general election on a measure which they disliked. But would it enable a new and satisfactory balance between the two Houses to be struck? Would it open the way towards the legislative implementation of the Campbell-Bannerman resolution of 1907? Many enthusiastic Liberals assumed without question that it would. But their assumption was too optimistic. On November 28th Knollys, who was himself a Liberal even if not an enthusiastic one, had written to Asquith saying that " . . . to create 570 new Peers, which I am told is the number required, (to coerce the House of Lords) would practically be almost an impossibility, and if asked for would place the King in an awkward position."[j] And on December 15th, after the campaign had begun, he sent for Asquith's secretary, Vaughan Nash, and was still more explicit.

" He began by saying," Nash recorded, " that the King had come to the conclusion that he would not be justified in creating new

Peers (say 300[1]) until after a second general election and that he, Lord K., thought you should know of this now, though, for the present he would suggest that what he was telling me should be for your ear only. The King regards the policy of the Government as tantamount to the destruction of the House of Lords and he thinks that before a large creation of Peers is embarked upon or threatened the country should be acquainted with the particular project for accomplishing such destruction as well as with the general line of action as to which the country will be consulted at the forthcoming Elections."[k]

Asquith had therefore to fight the campaign burdened by the knowledge that it could only be the beginning and not the end of the struggle, yet unable to share this knowledge at all widely. The burden was made greater by the fact that, in his opening speech at the Albert Hall, five days before Nash's interview with Knollys, although after Knollys's letter, he had made a statement which was generally assumed to mean that he had a far more satisfactory understanding with the King. " We shall not assume office and we shall not hold office," he said, " unless we can secure the safeguards which experience shows us to be necessary for the legislative utility and honour of the party of progress. . . . "[l]

In the circumstances it was not surprising that he sometimes showed a lack of zest during this campaign. It was not always so. His opening speech, before an enthusiastic Albert Hall audience of 10,000 was a great success.[2] And at Liverpool just before Christmas he indulged in some brilliant sustained raillery at the expense of Curzon, who had been particularly orotund at Oldham a few days before. But towards the end he flagged somewhat. Churchill, writing a year later to congratulate him on his handling of the second 1910 election, ventured then to speak of his being " far more effectively master of the situation and argument than at the January election."

As soon as the January campaign was over Asquith retired to Cannes, forgetting in his hurry to get away (what were his secretaries doing?) that he had an engagement to dine and sleep at Windsor. This solecism led both to the King's displeasure and to some publicity, and

---

[1] The number seemed to be rather volatile at this stage.

[2] Its most notable passage was that in which he expressly freed the new Parliament from the " self-denying ordinance " not to raise Home Rule which the Liberals had imposed upon themselves in 1906.

could only be smoothed away by Asquith allowing the King to accept the excuse that he was " completely knocked up by the election." This statement was an exaggeration, but the very fact that it had to be made may have edged the truth a little nearer to it. For several weeks after his return to London on February 9th he exhibited less sureness of touch than at any other stage in the long constitutional struggle.

The election result was not so bad as to be a debilitating shock to the Prime Minister. The Liberal losses were heavy—somewhat more so than the party organisers expected—and the great independent majority of 1906 had melted away. The Unionists gained 116 seats and became the majority party in England. Scotland and Wales redressed the balance. The shape of the new Parliament was:

Liberals	275
Labour	40
Irish Nationalists	70
	385
Unionists	273
Independent Nationalists[1]	12

This gave the Government a normal majority of 112, which as Asquith himself pointed out " compared favourably with the majorities which such statesmen as Lords John Russell and Palmerston considered adequate." It was in fact the largest left-wing majority, with the solitary exception of 1906, since 1832. But it was not of course an independent majority. If the Irish chose to oppose the Government they could put them out. This was exactly the situation which Asquith had foreseen in his conversation with the King on October 6th. It may have been an unwelcome development, but it was not a surprising one to the Prime Minister.

How cohesive was the new majority? Redmond was held to have made a threatening speech at Dublin on February 10th, and the Labour Party, at its Newport conference two days earlier, had spoken in an independent tone. The difficulty with the Irish was that

[1] Independent in the sense that they had broken with Redmond over what they regarded as his excessive subservience to the Liberal leadership. Their whole *raison d'etre* was therefore to be totally unreliable as supporters of the Government.

they did not like one aspect of the Budget. They regarded the £1,200,000 increase in the spirit duty as a blow at the Irish whiskey trade, and they were even more dependent upon liquor interests than were the Tories. But in the previous Parliament, while they had voted against the second reading of the Finance Bill, the shadow of the House of Lords had caused them to abstain on third reading. The two great issues of the day were the curbing of the veto and Home Rule. On both of these the Irish (and the Labour Party) were at one with the Liberals. This being so they had no basis of alliance with the Unionists and were most unlikely to wish to put the Government out. Provided it did not waver on these main issues and kept its nerve, the Cabinet could afford to be tough with its allies on matters of detail or precedence.

In the early days of the new Parliament, however, the nerve of the Cabinet was far from good, and there was a real danger that it would be diverted from the clear issue of the veto on to the shifting sands of reforming the composition of the Lords. Asquith received a welter of conflicting advice from his colleagues. Harcourt was at this stage the most pertinacious in urging concentration upon the veto rather than reform. " We must stick tight to principles and not go a'whoreing after false constitutions," he wrote on February 7th.[m] This was only one of a series of letters along the same lines which he wrote to Asquith at the time. Although, as was seen, Harcourt had not liked the Budget,[1] on this issue he spoke for most advanced opinion in the party. Dilke led a deputation of thirty M.P.'s to the Prime Minister to urge concentration upon the veto; Sir Henry Dalziel, a prominent Scottish radical, threatened to put down a motion in the same sense; and the Irish and the Labour Party were even more restively of this way of thinking. But from within the Government most of the written advice leaned the other way. John Simon wrote to support Harcourt, but he did not become Solicitor-General until a few months later. On the side of reform were Samuel, Haldane, Churchill, and, most powerfully, Grey. Churchill's view was largely based on tactical considerations. " I would not myself be frightened by having only one

[1] Nor had he become any more favourable to its author in the interval. " I found all over the country," another of his post-election letters to Asquith ran, " that all Ll.G.'s speeches and Winston's earlier ones (not the Lancs. campaign) had done us much harm, even with the advanced men of the *lower* middle class." (*Asquith Papers*, box XII, ff. 79–80).

(chamber) ... " he wrote on February 14th, " But I recognise the convenience and utility of a properly constituted and duly subordinated second chamber. . . . The C-B plan will not by itself command intellectual assent nor excite enthusiasm. But even if by a dead-lift effort we succeeded in carrying it—which I gravely doubt—the work would remain unfinished. On the first return of the Conservative Party to power, the Lords would be reformed in the Conservative interest and their veto restored to them."[n]

Grey's view turned more on the merits of the matter. " It is the constitution of the House of Lords, and not its powers, which is an anomaly,"[o] he wrote on February 7th. Five weeks later he strengthened and publicised this view by telling a Liberal banquet that the country would not tolerate single-chamber government, and that to leave reform to the Unionists would mean " disaster, death and damnation " to the Liberals.[p] A week or so after this, he wrote to Asquith saying that he thought he ought to resign. On receipt of this the Prime Minister for once showed signs of impatience with the Foreign Secretary, whom he normally regarded as almost beyond criticism, and wrote to Crewe: " I have had a tiresome letter from E. Grey."[1q] But the matter sorted itself out. No sooner had it done so, however, than Morley was threatening to leave the Government, on grounds which were most surprising for such a determined old Gladstonian. " You all really mean the creation of 500 peers," he wrote on April 14th, " and have only wrapped it up out of friendly consideration for me. *You had far better let me go.*"[r] But Morley by this stage of his career—perhaps this was not the least part of his Gladstonian inheritance—rarely let a month go by without offering or threatening resignation.

Altogether it was a difficult early spring. The Cabinet was in confusion. The Irish were saying that they would not pass the Budget without a firm promise of a veto bill in the same session. And the Liberals were excessively sensitive to Unionist charges that they were buying office at the expense of corrupt concessions to Redmond.[2]

[1] He found many of his colleagues irritating at this stage, and twelve days earlier he had written, also to Crewe, about a letter of Churchill's, " Yes—this is very characteristic, begotten by froth out of foam." (*Asquith Papers*, box XLVI, f. 183.)

[2] Had this not been so it might have been possible to settle the matter by promising the Irish that the increased spirit duty would be dropped in the

Immediately after Asquith's return from the South of France the Cabinet tried to resolve its difficulties and prepare for the opening of Parliament with a long series of meetings. They met on Thursday and Friday, February 10th and 11th, and again on Monday, Tuesday, Wednesday, Thursday and Saturday, February, 14th, 15th, 16th, 17th and 19th. Then on the following Monday Asquith made his first, inevitably disappointing statement to the new House of Commons. " I tell the House quite frankly," he said, " that I have received no such guarantee" —as to the creation of peers—" and that I have asked for no such guarantee. . . . "

The Master of Elibank whom Asquith had just promoted to be Chief Whip[1] described this speech as " the very worst I have ever heard him make," and added: " In a week the Prime Minister's prestige fell to so low an ebb that at one moment I despaired of his ever recovering it."[s] On the day following the speech Asquith had his first post-election meeting with Redmond and found him " cold and critical." " He is not altogether his own master," Asquith reported to the King, " as the Budget is extremely unpopular in Ireland, and the O'Brien party[2] are on his flank."[t] The Labour Party, however, Asquith found to be more friendly than he had expected.

The result of all this was that when the Cabinet met on the Friday of that week ministerial morale was so low that some members thought immediate resignation to be " the wisest and most dignified course." But this was not Asquith's view. He thought at this stage that the end might well be near but that the Government could not voluntarily go out until it had tabled its House of Lords proposals and received the verdict of the new House of Commons upon both these and the Budget. He had no difficulty in rallying the majority to this view. Indeed at this meeting the Cabinet began to recover both its nerve and its power of decision. The Master of Elibank, " was instructed . . . to inform Mr. Redmond that they were not prepared to give any

following year, a step which had in any event been made necessary by checked consumption and diminished revenue; but the Cabinet was against such a bargain.

[1] He had been appointed immediately after the election in spite of the view of his predecessor, J. A. Pease, that he was " a bit too scheming."

[2] Independent Nationalists.

such assurances (about a veto bill being enacted that year), and that he must act on his responsibility as they would on theirs."[u] On the following day the Prime Minister was able to report that it had then become " the universal opinion that there could be no question of immediate or voluntary resignation." The Cabinet even felt able to give up its bad recent habit of over-frequent meetings. It appointed a committee to draft resolutions which would expound its House of Lords policy and adjourned for eleven days.

In the meantime Asquith had to parry a whole series of House of Commons questions about the intentions of the Government both in regard to the resolutions and to the re-introduction of the Budget. In reply to these he used the phrase which was later to be most closely associated with his name. " We had better wait and see," he said in reply to Lord Helmsley on March 3rd. He used the phrase in no apologetic or hesitant way, but rather as a threat; and he obviously liked it, for he repeated it at least three times, in similar contexts, between then and April 4th. It was a use for which he was to pay dearly in the last years of his premiership when the phrase came to be erected by his enemies as a symbol of his alleged inactivity.

The Cabinet committee reported back in favour of resolutions which embodied the Campbell-Bannerman plan subject only to minor amendments.[1] The problem of Grey's threatened resignation then became acute. It was overcome by an agreement that the Parliament Bill, which was to follow immediately in the wake of the resolutions and to give legislative force to them, should have a preamble (which has remained a dead letter from that day to this) declaring that it was " intended to substitute for the House of Lords as it at

[1] The amendments were (1) that the provision for conferences between the two Houses was dropped, and (2) that it was laid down that the three successive sessions in which a bill must pass the House of Commons if it was to become law against the opposition of the House of Lords need not be in the same Parliament. There were three resolutions. The first said that the Lords could neither amend nor reject a money bill, and that the Speaker of the House of Commons should determine, subject to certain rules, what was and what was not a money bill. The second outlined the three session arrangement by which ordinary legislation could pass over the heads of the Lords, provided that not less than two years had elapsed between the first introduction of the bill into the House of Commons and its final third reading there. And the third declared that the maximum duration of Parliaments should be reduced from seven years to five.

present exists a Second Chamber constituted on a popular instead of hereditary basis."

The problem of the Irish still remained. Lloyd George and Birrell saw Redmond and Dillon on March 21st, and the possibility of a modification of the Budget was discussed between the two sides. But the Cabinet later stiffened against such a course. It was considered at a series of meetings on April 11th, 12th and 13th. After the last of these Asquith wrote to the King, who was again at Biarritz, announcing the stiffening: " After full consideration ... your Majesty's advisors are strongly and unanimously of opinion that to purchase the Irish vote by such a concession would be a discreditable transaction, which they could not defend."*v* The King was further informed that it was " possible and not improbable " that this might involve the defeat of the Government.

At the same meeting, however, the Cabinet took a further decision which made such a development highly unlikely. They agreed that if the Lords rejected the veto resolutions the Government would immediately launch the strongest possible constitutional counter-attack. And this, because it would open the way to Home Rule, was of far more importance to the Irish than any possible budgetary concessions, whether on liquor duties or anything else. There were other people in Ireland, as Joseph Devlin, a leading "Redmondite," was a few days later to remind the leading Independent Nationalist, William O'Brien, besides distillers and landlords. The form of the counter-attack was outlined in a later section of Asquith's letter to Biarritz:

" (Ministers) came to the conclusion that, (in the event of a Lords' rejection of the resolutions), it would be their duty at once to tender advice to the Crown as to the necessary steps—whether by the exercise of the prerogative, or by a *referendum ad hoc*, or otherwise—to be taken to ensure that the policy, approved by the House of Commons by large majorities, shall be given statutory effect in this Parliament. If they found that they were not in a position to accomplish that object, they would then either resign office or advise a dissolution of Parliament, but in no case would they feel able to advise a dissolution, except under such conditions as would secure that in the new Parliament the judgment of the people as expressed at the election, would be carried into law."*w*

The form of this declaration was a little elliptical but the meaning was reasonably clear. Either the King would have to agree to a dissolution with guarantees that if the Government were again successful he would create sufficient peers to swamp the House of Lords; or he would have to accept the resignation of his ministers and let Balfour (if he would) try to govern against the wishes of the majority of the House of Commons—with all the hazards to the royal position which would be involved in such a course. The only possible escape from this difficult choice lay in Asquith's suggestion that the issue between the two Houses might be settled by a referendum. There is an element of mystery about this. The Cabinet took the suggestion sufficiently seriously to order the preparation of a Referendum Bill. But when Asquith made a public statement of the Government's intention on the day following his communication to the King, and used language in most respects identical with that of his letter, he omitted any reference to the referendum solution.

The note which he struck was therefore still firmer. The Government Chief Whip was as impressed on this occasion as he had been depressed in February:

"Thursday night," he wrote, "saw a grand Parliamentary triumph for the Prime Minister. All his lost prestige has been recovered. He played a great part on a great occasion, and he announced the decision of the Cabinet in that wonderful language of his, and with a dignity that abashed some of the ruder spirits opposite who tried to interrupt. It was a stirring scene, not likely to leave the memories of those who witnessed it, nor (*sic*) the enthusiasm with which the crowded Liberal, Nationalist and Labour benches cheered the Prime Minister. . . . I accompanied him to his room, and we were shortly afterwards joined by Churchill and Lloyd George, who came to offer him their congratulations. Under that modest, unassuming, almost shy nature —so often mistaken for coldness—the Prime Minister has a softness of character which attaches men to him humanly as firmly as his great intellectual gifts compel their admiration."[x]

After this speech the difficulties with the Irish evaporated. It remains difficult to see quite why they had ever looked so formidable. The Government was able to re-introduce the Budget and to get it through the House of Commons by April 27th. The vote on third reading was 324 to 231, 62 of the Irish voting with the Government. On the following day the Lords passed it through all its stages, without divisions, in the course of a few hours. Lansdowne and his followers were prepared to recognise that the January election had settled the issue of the Budget, even if not the wider constitutional question. Parliament, having missed any real Easter holiday, then adjourned for a ten-day spring recess.

That evening, after Parliament had risen, Asquith went to Buckingham Palace. " I had a good talk with the King this evening and found him most reasonable,"ᵞ he wrote to his wife. Then he attended a dinner at the Savoy Hotel, given by Lloyd George to celebrate the passing of the Budget. Asquith left early in order to motor to Portsmouth with the McKennas. There he embarked on the Admiralty yacht, *Enchantress*, and set off, with the First Lord and his very young, recently acquired wife for companions, on a ten-day cruise to Portugal and Spain. The political outlook was still far from reassuring. But at least it looked a little better than at any time since the January election. The form of the battle seemed reliably predictable. If the Lords remained intransigent another election would have to be faced. If the Government won the King must be forced to create peers, or at least to use the threat of creating them. No doubt that would involve some distasteful audiences, for the Sovereign was clearly distrustful of the whole constitutional policy of the Government. Guided by the urbane and moderate Liberalism of Lord Knollys, he was however unlikely to resist in the last resort. There was one hazard for which neither Asquith nor anyone else made allowance. It did not occur to the Prime Minister that on his visit to Buckingham Palace before leaving London he had seen King Edward for the last time.

CHAPTER XV

A TRIAL OF STATESMANSHIP II

1910-11

By May 6th Asquith and his party had completed their visit to Lisbon, where they had been fêted by the Portuguese royal family ("The Queen ... is still handsome, and like all the Orleans family, quite good company," the Prime Minister recorded), and were steaming towards Gibraltar. A few hours before they arrived a wireless message was received from Lord Knollys with the information that the King had become gravely ill and was in a critical condition. On arrival at Gibraltar Asquith discovered that the 72 hours in which *Enchantress* could return to Plymouth was, surprisingly, less than the journey would take by train. He therefore ordered an immediate turn-round. A short time after they had left, in the early hours of Saturday, May 7th, he received a further message, this time from the new King George V, informing him that King Edward was dead. Later he recorded—for publication—his thoughts on that night:

I went up on deck, and I remember well that the first sight that met my eyes in the twilight before dawn was Halley's comet blazing in the sky. . . . I felt bewildered and indeed stunned. At a most anxious moment in the fortunes of the State, we had lost, without warning or preparation, the Sovereign whose ripe experience, trained sagacity, equitable judgment, and unvarying consideration, counted for so much. For two years I had been his Chief Minister, and I am thankful to remember that from first to last I never concealed anything from him. He soon got to know this, and in return he treated me with a gracious frankness which made our relationship in very trying and exacting times one, not always of complete agreement, but of unbroken confidence. It was this that lightened a load which I should otherwise have found almost intolerably oppressive: the prospect that, in the near future,

212

I might find it my duty to give him advice which I knew would be in a high degree unpalatable.

Now he had gone. His successor with all his fine and engaging qualities, was without political experience. We were nearing the verge of a crisis almost without example in our constitutional history. What was the right thing to do? This was the question which absorbed my thoughts as we made our way, with two fast escorting cruisers, through the Bay of Biscay, until we landed at Plymouth on the evening of Monday, May 9.[a]

On the following Tuesday Asquith held a Cabinet and also had his first audience with the new King. On the Wednesday he moved a vote of condolence in the House of Commons and delivered a notable *éloge* of King Edward. On the Thursday he held another Cabinet, but these meetings were not concerned with the major constitutional issue. They were occupied with arrangements for the change of reign, and in particular with a proposed alteration in the Royal Declaration (of faith) so as to make it less offensive to Roman Catholics. But the constitutional issue simmered under the surface. What was to be done in the new circumstances? Were immediate " guarantees " and an early dissolution to be demanded from King George as they would have been from King Edward? All Asquith's instincts recoiled from this. He had been in no hurry to tender unpalatable advice to the old King, and he was doubly reluctant to do so to the new one. Although King George V was a man of forty-five when he succeeded, and had seen far more of State papers during his period as Heir Apparent than ever his father had done, Asquith was greatly struck by the contrast between the worldly experience of King Edward and the unsophisticated mind and tastes of his son. This made him feel that it would be unfair to confront King George with a most delicate decision at the very outset of his reign. He was not alone in feeling this. Harcourt, the most determinedly radical member of the Cabinet on the constitutional issue, had written to him on the day of his return from Gibraltar urging, on the ground of public feeling about the King's death, the postponement of the conflict until the autumn, with no election until January 1911.[b] Others may well have spoken to him in the same sense.

In any event, despite the lack of Cabinet discussion, Asquith felt justified in telling King George when he saw him again on May 18th, that he would explore the possibility of compromise. " We had a long talk," the King recorded. " He said he would endeavour to come to some understanding with the Opposition to prevent a general election and he would not pay attention to what Redmond said."*c* This interview over, Asquith attended the royal funeral on May 20th and then rejoined *Enchantress* for the remainder of his cruise. This time he went up the West coast to Skye, and occupied himself mainly by reading and preparing a long constitutional memorandum for the new King.

At the first Cabinet after his return, on June 6th, a general political discussion led to " a practically unanimous desire " to try the method of a constitutional conference with the opposition leaders. Balfour and Lansdowne, when approached, responded eagerly to the suggestion, and the conference was able to hold its first meeting (in Asquith's room at the House of Commons) on June 17th. The participants were the Prime Minister, Lloyd George, Crewe and Birrell from the Government side, and Balfour, Lansdowne, Austen Chamberlain and Cawdor from the opposition. Twelve meetings were held before the end of July and some progress appeared to have been made. There was then an interval until early October, Lansdowne having stood out against a proposal for holiday meetings at Crewe's country house on the ground that he did not wish to be thought " softened by the excellence of Crewe's champagne." After this came two brief but intensive series of meetings, separated by another fortnight's adjournment, until November 10th.

The King, not unnaturally, was throughout an enthusiast for the idea of the conference. Militant Liberals, the Irish and the Labour Party, equally naturally, were a good deal less enthusiastic. They saw it as a device for removing the cutting edge from the Government's constitutional policy. But they need not have worried. The conference never came close to success. A Unionist memorandum, presented at one of the early meetings, proposed that legislation should be divided into three categories: financial, ordinary and constitutional. In respect of each of these three categories unresolved difficulties arose. So far as the first category was concerned it was proposed that the Lords should explicitly abandon any right to reject or amend money bills, provided that measures with " social or political consequences which go far beyond the mere raising of revenue " should be excluded from this category. But although there is some conflict of evidence it is doubtful whether the Government representatives ever accepted such a sweeping exclusion. Had they done so, hardly a single Budget from that day to this would have been statutorily protected against the interference of the peers. In regard to " ordinary " legislation it was agreed that when a bill within this category had been twice rejected by the Lords its fate should be determined by a joint sitting of the two Houses. But what was to be the composition of such a joint session? The key to this, as Lansdowne pointed out, was agreement on a scheme for a reformed House of Lords; and this was never near.

Constitutional or " organic " legislation raised still greater difficulties. The Unionists wanted such measures, if they were twice rejected by the Lords, to be submitted to a referendum. The Liberals, Asquith's mind having turned increasingly against such an innovation, preferred totally to exempt a closely limited list of such measures from the operation of the Parliament Act. But what should be on such a list? The Unionists were determined that it should include Home Rule, and the Liberals were equally determined that it should not.[1] This was the nub of the disagreement on which the conference broke down. The man who was primarily responsible for the failure was Lansdowne. Of the other principal participants, Asquith, Balfour and Lloyd George were all anxious for a settlement. But Lansdowne was a Southern Irish landlord who had never forgotten the Land League. He was determined to do nothing to assist the passage of Home Rule, and he pursued his determination with stubborn resource.

Asquith's reasons for wanting a settlement are obvious. The alternative was to coerce the King and to face another hazardous election. Compared with this prospect the difficulties of securing the approval of the Liberal rank and file for a possible agreement were likely to be small. Moreover there was no danger that in these circumstances Lloyd George might lead a radical attack on his left flank. Throughout the conference the Chancellor was even more anxious for a solution than was the Prime Minister. Asquith was bland, optimistic and reasonably accommodating. But Lloyd George gave the impression of searching almost feverishly for compromise. And in August, during a respite at Criccieth, his restless mind turned towards the still bolder solution of a coalition government, with an agreed programme on all

[1] Although Lloyd George, constantly fertile, produced a compromise proposal by which Home Rule could not be proceeded with as " ordinary " legislation until the Government had fought yet another general election on the issue.

the main issues of the day. On August 17th he dictated a long memorandum arguing the case for such a government and listing a twelve-point programme.

Exactly what he did with this memorandum remains in dispute. Lloyd George himself says that it was submitted in the first instance to Asquith, who showed it to four Liberal ministers—Grey, Crewe, Haldane and Churchill—before giving permission to its author to open discussions with Balfour.[d] Elsewhere, however, notably in the present Lord Birkenhead's life of his father and in *The Times* obituary of Balfour, published on March 20th, 1930, it is stated that Lloyd George operated independently of Asquith; and this view is borne out by a suggestion in Mrs. Dugdale's *Balfour* that the scheme involved Asquith's relegation to the House of Lords. He was hardly likely to have been made privy to a plan which would have forced upon him the same fate that the Relugas Compact tried to force upon Campbell-Bannerman. There is no record in the Asquith papers of Lloyd George having sent him the memorandum in the weeks following August 17th. The collection is, however, by no means sufficiently complete for this to be firm evidence of its non-arrival. By late October it was clearly in Asquith's possession. He then sounded out some of the other ministers mentioned by Lloyd George, and showed no resentment at the existence of the document, although he was sceptical about the result that it might produce.

There is no doubt, therefore, that Lloyd George eventually showed his memorandum to Asquith. The mystery lies in what he did with it between mid-August and mid-October. What seems likely is that during this period he operated on a different front, and made informal approaches to the Unionists through Churchill and F. E. Smith, who were close friends and both of whom were enthusiasts for coalition. The memorandum was addressed to Asquith, but it may well have been shown to others before it reached him. This would make it possible to reconcile Lord Birkenhead's account of the matter with Lloyd George's own statement. And it is quite likely that, during these preliminary soundings, Lloyd George's flexible mind may have ranged over the idea of Asquith being forced to accept a nominal premiership in the House of Lords, or even being superseded altogether. When it was later suggested by Balfour that Lloyd George's own membership of a coalition ministry might be an obstacle to its acceptance by the Tory Party, the Chancellor, perhaps a little rhetorically, at once offered to stand down. In these circumstances it is hardly probable that he excluded from discussion the solution of Asquith being asked to make an equivalent, or lesser, sacrifice.

The Prime Minister did not think of the project in these terms. There was no obvious reason for him to do so, for his own position was strong at the time. And his most trusted colleagues in the Government, who would not have contemplated his supersession, were rather favourable to Lloyd George's plan. Crewe wrote on October 22nd saying that the memorandum was " a clever document." He meant this as a favourable comment and added that " we have got not far from the end of our tether as regards the carrying of large reforms."[e] This he saw as a substantial point in Lloyd George's favour.

Four days later Grey, instinctively hostile though he was to the Chancellor of the Exchequer, wrote in still more favourable terms:

> I had a long talk with Lloyd George last night about the big scheme of a coalition for constructive legislation including the settlement of Home Rule. I am favourable to it, though there are many " difficulties." If the Conference breaks up without agreement I foresee the break-up of the Liberal Party and a time of political instability, perhaps of chaos, to the great detriment of the country. The other party of course is paralysed and useless, but behind us there are explosive and violent forces which will split our party, and I do not believe we can resume the old fight against the Lords by ourselves without division.[f]

Asquith received this letter in Scotland, and on the following day he wrote to Crewe in unmistakably detached terms: " I have a letter from E. Grey from which it appears that L.G. has been extending his missionary operations into that quarter, and apparently not without producing an impression."[g] But it was Balfour's caution and not Asquith's scepticism which wrecked the plan. The Unionist leader was personally rather favourable to Lloyd George's scheme, but he was determined not to be another Peel, and when his former Chief Whip, Akers-Douglas, informed him that he could make no response to Lloyd George without producing a major split in the party, he accepted this advice as decisive. By the end of the first week in November both the formal constitutional conference and the informal talks on the Lloyd George coalition proposals had ended in failure. However dangerous

Grey might think the course, there was no alternative for the Government but to resume " the old fight against the Lords."

The Cabinet met on November 10th and decided in favour of an immediate dissolution. Before the decision could be implemented, however, the Prime Minister, unless he was to retreat humiliatingly from his brave words of April 14th, had to obtain " guarantees " from the King about the use of the prerogative. This was likely to be a most difficult operation, and Asquith approached it with considerable distaste and almost excessive delicacy. The day after the Cabinet meeting he went to Sandringham for an audience. But he used it only for a preliminary and general constitutional discussion and not for the purpose of asking for the guarantees. This was a mistake, for the King, noting with relief that he was asked for nothing on this occasion (other than his agreement to the dissolution) assumed that he was to be left free from commitment until after the election. When, four days later, he discovered his mistake, the chagrin of disappointment was added to the repugnance which he would in any event have felt for the course he was asked to pursue. He received the bad news *via* Knollys, who had gone from Sandringham to Downing Street for an interview with Asquith and who reported in the following words: " What he *now* advocates is that you should give guarantees *at once* for the next Parliament." Upon receipt of this letter the King ordered his other private secretary, Sir Arthur Bigge, who had remained with him at Sandringham, to telegraph at once to Asquith's secretary in unyielding terms: " His Majesty regrets that it would be impossible for him to give contingent guarantees and he reminds Mr. Asquith of his promise not to seek for any during the present Parliament."[h]

The latter part of the message was based on a confusion between asking for guarantees *for* the present Parliament and asking for them *during* it; Asquith had certainly never given a promise that he would not do the latter[1]. Confusion or no confusion here, the import of the first part of the message was perfectly clear. The King and his ministers had moved into a position of direct conflict. Asquith at this stage did not envisage the possibility of retreat. It was in any event politically

---

[1] King George, however, was not very adept at appreciating fine verbal distinctions. " Unaccustomed as he was to ambiguous phraseology," Sir Harold Nicolson has written, " he was totally unable to interpret Mr. Asquith's enigmas." (*King George V*, p. 130). In consequence the Prime Minister's over-delicate approach sometimes defeated itself.

out of the question for him.[1] What he did was to formalise the Government's position. On the day of the King's telegram he held another Cabinet at which a minute, setting out their collective advice, was drawn up and unanimously approved. This minute suggested for the first time that, while the King's promise to create peers, should this become necessary, must be given before the dissolution, it need not be made public until the actual occasion arose.

This provision greatly impressed Knollys, to whom the minute was given later that day. As a result he sent it on to the King with a strong recommendation that the advice should be accepted. A battle of private secretaries then developed. Sir Arthur Bigge was as strongly (and more passionately) in favour of the King rejecting the advice as Lord Knollys was in favour of his accepting it; and over the next twenty-four hours they engaged in a sharp and even bitter struggle for the possession of the King's mind. Bigge had the advantage of being with the King throughout and of being better known to him. He had been his own private secretary for ten years and was not merely an inheritance from King Edward as was the case with Knollys. Knollys, on the other hand, had the advantage of greater political experience, and of advising a course which while less palatable was more cautious than that recommended by Bigge; and the natural tendency of constitutional monarchs is always to prefer caution to adventure.

Even so, Knollys only got his way by keeping a vital piece of information from the King. Had the Cabinet's advice not been accepted, Asquith would of course have resigned. The King would then have had to send for Balfour and ask him if he would form a government and endeavour to carry the country at a general election. This would in any event have been a hazardous course for the King, and one which would have laid him wide open to a charge of political favouritism. He would have changed his Government solely because the advice of the incoming Prime Minister was more congenial to him personally than was that of the outgoing one. The ensuing general

[1] The Master of Elibank wrote as Chief Whip a rather curious letter to Knollys at this stage urging the importance of " safeguarding " the Prime Minister's relations with his own party. (Arthur Murray, *Master and Brother*, pp. 60–1). Knollys, doubtfully wisely, sent the letter on to the King, and Bigge (who was a friend of the Master's) returned a sharp reply.

election would inevitably have taken the form of a vote of confidence or censure on his action. Nothing could have pushed the King more firmly into the centre of the political battle. It was because he saw the folly of this course so clearly that Knollys was prepared to go to almost any length to prevent his master from following it.

Nevertheless it was the course towards which the King's mind was turned as he travelled up to London with Bigge on the morning of Wednesday, November 16th. But would Balfour accept such a commission? The answer to this question was vital to the King's decision. If it was " yes " the course remained hazardous but it became possible. If it was " no " the course made no sense at all. The King, with a great loss of face, would have found himself back where he started—with Asquith, and with no possible alternative. The answer to the vital question was supplied by Knollys. In Sir Harold Nicolson's words, he " assured him that Mr. Balfour would in any event decline to form an administration."[i]

This was a strange assurance for Knollys to give, for he had himself attended a meeting with Balfour, arranged by the Archbishop of Canterbury, on April 29th and had written a minute for King Edward which said: " Mr. Balfour made it quite clear that he would be prepared to form a government to prevent the King being put in the position contemplated by the demand for the creation of peers."[j] And there was no evidence that Balfour had changed his mind in the meantime. This minute remained in the archives, but it was not shown to King George. The latter came across it by chance in 1913 after Knollys had given up his appointment and immediately dictated a note saying that, had he known about it at the time, it might have changed his attitude to the guarantees. The responsibility for suppressing the document, which Knollys took upon himself, was a heavy one, but it almost certainly saved the King from an act of constitutional folly which might well have affected not only his personal position but the whole future of the British monarchy.[1]

At 3.30 on the afternoon of that same Wednesday the King saw Asquith and Crewe. Asquith described the meeting as " the most important political occasion of his life," but on his way to the Palace he characteristically kept an engagement to attend the wedding of a

---

[1] A somewhat fuller account of this incident is to be found in the present author's *Mr. Balfour's Poodle*, pp. 118–25.

Conservative M.P.[1] From the point of view of the Government the audience was a great success.

" After a long talk," the King wrote in his diary that evening, " I agreed most reluctantly to give the Cabinet a secret understanding that in the event of the Government being returned with a majority at the General Election, I should use my Prerogative to make Peers if asked for. I disliked having to do this very much, but agreed that this was the only alternative to the Cabinet resigning, which at this moment would be disastrous. Francis (Lord Knollys) strongly urged me to take this course and I think his advice is generally very sound. I only trust and pray he is right this time."[k]

" I have never seen the King to better advantage," was Asquith's relieved judgment on the same evening; " he argued well and showed no obstinacy."[l] But afterwards the King's mind obstinately refused to leave the subject and, Sir Harold Nicolson tells us, he " remained convinced ... that in this, the first political crisis of his reign, he had not been accorded either the confidence or the consideration to which he was entitled." But what was the basis of his resentment? Sir Harold says that what he most disliked was the secrecy of the undertaking. This, however, was a most surprising aspect of the matter to which to take objection. It was only proposed with the object of safeguarding the King. It would have suited the Government much better to have been able to announce the pledge the moment it was given. And Knollys at least attached great value to the secrecy provision, and credited the King with doing so too. He wrote to Vaughan Nash on December 11th: " The King hopes that all the members of the Cabinet clearly understand that he relies on their not divulging in the future or at any time anything whatever regarding the guarantee question any more than at present."[m]

The picture is therefore a little confused, and is not made less so by Sir Harold also assuring us that:

Against the Prime Minister personally he (the King) retained no rancour whatsoever. He realised that Mr. Asquith's hand had also been forced. He was fully aware of the qualities of mind and heart possessed by that shy but greatly gifted man.[n]

By whom then, unless it were only Knollys, whom he kept in his most confidential service for another two years and to whom he gave

[1] L. S. Amery.

221

a step in the peerage in 1911, did the King believe that he had not been accorded " confidence or consideration "? Perhaps Sir Harold Nicolson deliberately introduced a little confusion at this stage, for only thus could he represent what seems to have been the King's feeling—a generalised dislike of the whole incident, accompanied by a reluctant acceptance that nobody (except perhaps for Knollys) could reasonably have been expected to behave differently.

The King's acceptance of the Government's advice cleared the way for the general election. Dissolution took place on November 28th, and the campaign was over before Christmas. There was general agreement that, to a much greater extent than in the previous January, it was dominated by the Prime Minister. Perhaps because the settling of the guarantees had given him an easier conscience, he displayed a far greater measure of confidence, force, and wit. At Hull and Reading, amongst other places, he delivered speeches before huge audiences which were as notable for their trenchancy as for their range of constitutional knowledge. In Churchill's phrase they " stood out in massive pre-eminence whether in relation to colleagues or opponents."

The other point about this election upon which there was also general agreement was that it was for the most part a dull one. Public interest was low. The voters were bored with being asked to go to the polls for the second time within a year and weary of the long drawn-out constitutional struggle. They wanted the matter settled, and they indicated this by producing a result which, in its way, was as decisive as any which could easily be imagined. It was almost an exact replica of the previous result. Over fifty seats changed hands but he net effect was that the Unionists lost one seat and the Liberals three, while the Irish Nationalists and the Labour Party each gained two. For practical purposes the Government majority went up from 124 to 126. The Liberals had performed the feat, unprecedented since 1832, of winning three successive general elections, and by so doing had brought the Unionists to the end of the road so far as appeals to the country were concerned. The Liberal preponderance amongst the voters was not a great one, but for the time being it was solid and unchanging. Thereafter the constitutional battle had to be fought to a finish within the parliamentary arena.

After this election the Government had no decisions of difficulty to face comparable with those which had confronted it eleven months before. The lines upon which it must proceed were clearly defined.

Perhaps for this reason Asquith did not receive the same spate of advisory post-election letters from his colleagues. But there was at least one member of the Cabinet who did not let the occasion pass without setting down on paper his view of the future. In the re-shuffle following the previous election, Winston Churchill had been promoted from the Board of Trade to the Home Office. On January 3rd, 1911, he composed a long hand-written letter to Asquith. In the middle of this task he left for Sydney Street in the East End to carry out his famous direction of operations against the murder gang who had there barricaded themselves. The siege over, he returned to Whitehall to complete his letter, which lost nothing in verve as a result of the interruption. The political world was divided between those who did and those who did not believe that the Liberals were entitled to use the threat of creating peers. But Churchill was almost alone in wanting to carry out the threat:

> We ought as early as possible to make it clear that we are not a bit afraid of creating 500 Peers if necessary. . . . Such a creation would be in fact for the interest of the Liberal Party and a disaster to the Conservatives. . . . We should at a stroke gain a great addition of influence in the country. The wealth and importance of British society could easily maintain 1,000 notables—much more easily than 300 a century ago.

The Parliament Bill, Churchill went on to argue, ought to be pushed through before the Coronation, which was fixed for June 22nd. And if it did not make proper progress " we should clink the coronets in their scabbards." But once it was through the Government should pursue " *une politique d'apaisement.*"

" Privy Councillorships to Bonar Law and F.E. (Smith); the order of merit for Joe; a proportion of Tory peers and Baronets; something for the Tory Press; and if you could find a little place for Neil (Primrose) it would please Rosebery in spite of himself. . . . We ought to pursue a national not a sectional policy; and to try to make our prolonged tenure of power as agreeable as possible to the other half of our fellow-countrymen." [0] [1]

Asquith was by no means inclined to reject all these suggestions.

[1] Another point of interest in this remarkable letter was Churchill's suggestion that he would like to see " a provision enabling Peers to stand for the House of Commons on renunciation of their privilege, and its counterpoise, ministers to be allowed to speak in both Houses."

He gave both Bonar Law and Smith their privy councillorships in the Coronation honours (although not without a good deal of trouble with Balfour so far as Smith was concerned);[1] he made two Tory " press lords " into real barons;[2] and, although not until a few years later, he even found " a little place " for Primrose. But his attitude to the creation of 500 peers was quite different from Churchill's. He both hoped and believed that it would be unnecessary. Indeed, immediately after the December election, he thought it quite likely that it would not even be necessary to make further use of the threat of creation. The Lords might accept the verdict of the electorate to the extent of offering little further resistance to the Parliament Bill. This hope proved unfounded, and it became impossible to achieve Churchill's aim of getting the bill through before the Coronation. Balfour, in January, was already prepared to accept the inevitable. But Lansdowne took a

[1] Balfour wanted an undistinguished but hard-working Unionist parliamentarian, Hayes Fisher, to have the honour instead. After a good deal of argument both Smith and Fisher became Privy Councillors. Smith wrote to Asquith: " I can only say that it is a paradoxical and singular circumstance that those against whom I have been fighting for fifteen years have paid me the greatest compliment I have ever had in my life; while those on whose behalf I have been fighting did their best to prevent it. You will I think believe me when I say that there is no one at present in political life from whom I would have valued this recommendation so highly as from yourself." (*Asquith Papers*, box 13, ff. 24–5). This did not prevent Smith from playing a leading part in shouting down Asquith in a House of Commons scene six weeks later.

[2] Asquith had difficulty in getting any peerages through that year, for the King, who had said the same thing more mildly in 1910, protested strongly against any new creations while the issue of the 500 was still undecided. But he probably objected less to the Tory peerages than to the Liberal nominations. " The King says he does not pretend to understand the logic of those people who while vilifying the House of Lords on every convenient occasion are yet apparently anxious to become members of that Body," Knollys wrote to Asquith. (*Asquith Papers*, box 2, f. 151). But the King's objection did not extend to " steps " for members of the Government. In the Coronation list Crewe became a marquess and Loreburn an earl, both at the suggestion of the Palace.

Another point of dispute between King and Prime Minister that year was whether Sargent should be made an O.M. The King successfully resisted the proposal. He admired Sargent neither as a painter nor as a man. (*Asquith Papers*, box 2, f. 211).

less clear-sighted view. He neither dug in for resistance à *outrance* nor prepared himself for retreat. He merely decided to stay where he was for as long as he could in the hope that delay might shift the dispute on to slightly different ground and enable the powers of the Lords still to be preserved. He started on a course which six months later was to lead both himself and the less blameworthy Balfour into a position of humiliating weakness; but in the meantime his tactic effectively prevented the Government making rapid progress with its bill.

It took until May 15th to get the bill through the Commons, the Government having to pick its way between more than 900 amendments tabled for the committee stage. The Lords, during this period, had been occupied with a Referendum Bill, introduced by Balfour of Burleigh, and with Unionist schemes for their own reform. They turned distastefully to the Parliament Bill in the last week of May, and proceeded after a three-day debate to give it a second reading without a division. But it was made clear that this emollient attitude was only a prelude to severe amendment in committee. Knowledge of the exact severity of these amendments, however, was not available until after a Whitsun recess lengthened to include the Coronation.

This festivity therefore occurred at a moment of high party tension. Feeling at the time was much higher amongst politicians than amongst the general public. Lloyd George was booed on his way to the Abbey —but only by some of those in the stands reserved for members of Parliament and their families and friends. And when Asquith himself, a few weeks later, was involved in a formidable scene and shouted down for nearly an hour with cries of " traitor," it was in the House of Commons that this occurred. Even so, it is easily possible to exaggerate the degree of social ill-feeling which surrounded Asquith at this time— although the position became a little worse during the Home Rule quarrel two or three years later. Throughout the constitutional struggle the Prime Minister retained easy personal relations with the leader of the opposition, and close ones with other members of his family. Lady Frances Balfour drove over from Whittinghame to Archerfield for Asquith's small birthday luncheon party in September 1910. And in May 1911, the Prime Minister did not hesitate to attend (although wearing nothing more exotic than a tail coat) a lavish fancy dress ball which F. E. Smith and Lord Winterton gave at Claridge's and which was one of the most flamboyant events of that hot and fevered Coronation summer.

The Lords returned to the Parliament Bill on June 28th and proceeded in six committee days to make a massacre of the Government's intentions. On July 6th Asquith drafted a minute for the King saying the contingency envisaged in November was about to arise, that ministers would advise the exercise of the prerogative of creation, and that they could not doubt that in the circumstances " the Sovereign would feel it to be his Constitutional duty to accept their advice." This minute was shown to Knollys for the King's information before it was approved by the Cabinet on July 14th and formally submitted to His Majesty. The King made no substantial difficulty about accepting the minute, merely asking that the peers should not be created until the Lords, having seen their amendments rejected by the Commons, had been given an opportunity to reconsider their intransigence. Asquith agreed.

From this point onwards the battle became an internal one within the Unionist Party. The "hedgers" fought the "ditchers," the former advocating a retreat under pressure which would at least prevent the dilution of the peerage by a swarm of new Liberal creations, the latter demanding resistance at all costs. The roles both of the King and of the Government became rather like that of the German armies surrounding Paris at the time of the Commune. Their presence had precipitated the civil quarrel, but once it had started they became little more than onlookers holding their ground and waiting for the outcome. Occasionally however they were appealed to by the more moderate of the contestants and asked to strengthen their hand by some pronouncement of intention. Thus on July 20th Lansdowne wrote to Asquith asking if he could have by return a written statement of exactly what the Prime Minister proposed to do, as he had a meeting of Unionist peers fixed for the following day and wished to disillusion those who still believed that the Government was bluffing. There was no difficulty at this stage about secrecy, for a week earlier Bigge had telegraphed on behalf of the King urging a public disclosure of the position to Balfour and Lansdowne. He was now eager to make the threat as real as possible in order to avoid having to carry it out. Accordingly, Asquith on July 20th wrote identical letters to Balfour and Lansdowne:

" I think it courteous and right," they ran, " before any public decisions are announced, to let you know how we regard the political situation.

" When the Parliament Bill in the form which it has now

assumed returns to the House of Commons, we shall be compelled to ask the House to disagree with the Lords' amendments.

" In the circumstances, should the necessity arise, the Government will advise the King to exercise his Prerogative to secure the passing into Law of the Bill in substantially the same form in which it left the House of Commons; and His Majesty has been pleased to signify that he will consider it his duty to accept, and act on, that advice."

That seemed clear enough; and the fact that Asquith's next appearance in the House of Commons provoked the famous scene of July 24th[1] could be regarded merely as the yelping in defeat of some sections

[1] The following description of the scene is taken from the author's *Mr. Balfour's Poodle:*

" (Asquith) was cheered by crowds in the streets as he drove with his wife in an open motor car from Downing Street, and he was cheered by his own back-benchers as he walked up the floor of the House of Commons. But as soon as he rose to speak he was greeted by a roar of interruption. ' Divide, divide,' was the dominant shout, but interspersed with it were cries of ' Traitor,' ' Let Redmond speak,' ' American dollars ' and ' Who Killed the King ? ' For half an hour the Prime Minister stood at the box, unable to make any full sentence heard to the House, and unable to fill more than a staccato, half-column of Hansard. F. E. Smith and Lord Hugh Cecil were manifestly the leaders (Will Crooks, the Labour Member for Woolwich, proclaimed that ' many a man has been certified insane for less than the noble Lord has done this afternoon '), but there were many others who took a full part . . . . Balfour sat unruffled in his place throughout these proceedings. He took no part in the scene, but he did not make any attempt to restrain his followers.

" At last Asquith gave up. With a remark about ' declining to degrade himself further,' he sat down. Balfour followed and was heard in silence throughout his speech. . . . Then Sir Edward Grey rose. He had been subjected to a perhaps understandably hysterical note passed down from the Ladies' Gallery by Mrs. Asquith, but it was not clear whether or not this was the decisive cause of his intervention. ' They will listen to you,' the note had run, ' so for God's sake defend him from the cats and the cads.' This Grey made some attempt to do. . . . When Grey had finished F. E. Smith rose and attempted to carry on the debate. . . . Uproar again developed, and after five minutes the Speaker suspended the sitting on the ground that a state of ' grave disorder ' had arisen. Standing Order 21, under which he did this, had not previously been invoked since 1893, and a precedent for the refusal of a hearing to a Prime Minister could not be found without a

of the Unionist Party. But a fresh point of doubt quickly arose. Was the creation, if it became necessary, to be on such a scale as to give the Liberals a permanent majority in the House of Lords or was it merely to be sufficient to close the gap between the number who persisted in voting against the Parliament Bill and the number who voted in its favour? In the latter case, assuming that the Unionist " moderates " abstained, fifty or at most a hundred new peers were all that would be necessary; and there were many, including Balfour, who were not prepared to regard creation on this limited scale as a disaster.

There is no evidence that the Government, or the King, ever contemplated such a limited operation. Indeed, once Asquith had acceded to the King's request that the prerogative should not be exercised until the bill had been to the Lords for the second time, it became an impracticable course. Had the Lords then insisted on their amendments, the bill would have been lost for that session. The Government would have had to start again in the autumn. In these circumstances they would never have been willing to embark on another circuit of the parliamentary course with a majority so insecure that it could be destroyed by a change of mind on the part of a few abstaining Unionists.

Furthermore, Asquith already had in his possession a list of 249 men of Liberal conviction whom he proposed to ennoble should the need arise.[1] This number, while insufficient for the larger operation, was far greater than was necessary for the smaller one. And the calibre of most of the names on this list did not suggest that he had scraped the barrel of possible Liberal nominees or that he would have difficulty in preparing a suitable supplement. This point about the size of the threatened creation was not finally cleared up until August 10th, the last day of the final debate in the House of Lords, when Morley, at the instigation of the King, read out a statement saying that " His Majesty would assent . . . to a creation of Peers sufficient in number to guard against any possible combination of the different parties in opposition

---

much longer research. . . . ' The 'ugliest feature,' Mr. Churchill. . . . accurately reported to the King, ' was the absence of any real passion or spontaneous feeling. It was a squalid, frigid, organised attempt to insult the Prime Minister '." (pp. 158–60).

[1] The list, with certain annotations, is printed in appendix A.

by which the Parliament Bill might be exposed a second time to defeat."

In the meantime the disunion of the Unionists had proceeded apace. The " ditchers " or " die-hards " organised hard under the leadership of Halsbury, Selborne and Salisbury in the Lords and Austen Chamberlain, Carson, F. E. Smith and George Wyndham in the Commons. All the other leading Unionists were in varying degrees " hedgers," but almost the only one who organised energetically for retreat was Curzon. Apart from the great bulk of the Unionist peers, who in the final division abstained with Lansdowne, Curzon persuaded a decisive 37 to follow him in voting for the Government. The bitterness to which these internal divisions led was at least as great as that between the two parties.

While this civil strife developed, relations between the King and the Prime Minister, the two generals of the investing army, showed some signs of strain. As the issue moved towards its conclusion the King could not emulate Asquith's calm passivity. " The King has at present a rage for seeing people about the crisis," Knollys wrote to the Prime Minister on July 23rd, " Lord Salisbury yesterday, the Archbishop of Canterbury today and he also wanted to see Lord St. Aldwyn, but he is out of Town. . . . These appointments are generally told me after they have been settled as my opinion about them is known."*p* At the beginning of August the King left London, first for Cowes and then for Sandringham. There could be no more political audiences for the moment, but (through his private secretaries) he bombarded ministers with letters. First there was a request that Crewe, who had been ill for several months, should speak in the Lords debate on August 8th and stress the reluctance with which the King had given the November pledge. This debate was to be on a Unionist motion of censure, similar to one which had been taken in the Commons on the previous day. Asquith, on this earlier occasion, had delivered a notable reply to the accusations which were levelled against him, but it had been insufficiently apologetic in tone to give much comfort to the King:

I am accustomed, as Lord Grey in his day was accustomed, to be accused of breach of the Constitution and even of treachery to the Crown. I confess, as I have said before, that I am not in the least sensitive to this cheap and ill-informed vituperation. It has been my privilege, almost now I think unique, to serve in close and confidential relations three successive British Sovereigns. My conscience tells me that in that capacity, many and great as have been my failures and shortcomings, I have consistently striven to uphold the dignity and just privileges of the Crown. But I hold my office, not only by favour of the Crown, but by the confidence of the people, and I should be guilty indeed of treason if in this supreme moment of a great struggle I were to betray their trust.*q*

Crewe did better from the King's point of view and talked of the latter's "natural, and if I may be permitted to use the phrase, in my opinion . . . legitimate reluctance." But this was not enough for the King. He made Knollys write to Asquith on the following day asking if his " reluctance " could not be made still clearer. On the same day he made him write a letter to Churchill protesting against part of his speech in the censure debate, and send a copy to Asquith. Churchill replied softly, although it was difficult to tell what he intended to be the effect of his assurance, that " before making (the speech) I consulted . . . the Chancellor of the Exchequer."*r* But Asquith for once reacted with some irascibility. After the censure debate he travelled down to Wallingford to stay with friends and nurse the laryngitis which had attacked him, and Knollys's letter was sent on to him there. It may be that this unaccustomed ill-health, occurring unpropitiously in the hottest weather for seventy years, with the shade temperatures over most of England exceeding 95°, gave an unusual edge to his reaction. Or it may be that he would in any event have regarded this further request of the King's as entirely unreasonable. As it was, he covered the letter with a series of controversial annotations and sent back a strong reply to Knollys: " I cannot give any countenance," he wrote " to the ' pathetic story ' (in Lansdowne's phrase) that last November the King was ' browbeaten ' and ' blackmailed.' Nothing of the kind happened. . . . "*s*

The crisis could not have continued for much longer without an all-round deterioration of relations. Fortunately, it was all over within twelve hours of Asquith drafting this reply to Knollys. The final division in the House of Lords was taken at 10.30 on the night of August 10th. By a vote of 131 (81 Liberals, 13 bishops and 37 of Curzon's Unionists) to 114 diehards the House decided not to insist on its amendments. The Parliament Bill was law; the need for creation had disappeared; the session was effectively over. The King's complaints were dissolved in his sense of relief. " So the Halsburyites were

thank God beaten. . . . and I am spared any further humiliation. . . . "[t]
he wrote. The next day he left London to join the Duke of Devonshire's shooting party at Bolton Abbey.

Asquith had written a laconic note to his secretary and sent it up
with his reply to Knollys:

> If the vote goes wrong in the H. of L. to-night the Cabinet should
> be summoned for 11.30 Downing St. tomorrow morning, and
> the King asked to postpone his journey till the afternoon. . . .
> If I have satisfactory news this evening I will come up for Cabinet
> 12.30; if otherwise by 11.30. My voice is on the mend but
> still croaky.[u]

Accordingly he returned to London at about the same time as the
King's departure. The fact that the long constitutional struggle had
ended without the upheaval of a mass creation was as important to him
as to the King; Asquith always preferred to achieve his radical purposes
within a conservative framework. Still more vital was the fact that
it had ended successfully. The struggle had consumed the best part
of two years of parliamentary time. It had involved two general
elections and the sacrifice of the vast independent Liberal majority of
1906. Not only the future legislative utility of the Government but its
prestige and authority had become inextricably bound up with a
successful outcome. And what was true of the Government as a whole
was doubly true of the Prime Minister. From the time that the merits
of the 1909 Budget had been subsumed in the wider question of the
peers' right to reject, the responsibility for the conduct of the battle
had been overwhelmingly his. His generalship had not been without
fault. In particular, his hesitancy between January and April 1910 had
wasted much more than three months, for it prevented the issue being
pushed near to a conclusion during the lifetime of King Edward. But
on the whole Asquith's slow moulding of events had amounted to a
masterly display of political nerve and patient determination. Compared either with Lansdowne's sullen lack of foresight or with
Balfour's casual indecisiveness, his leadership was outstanding.

The battle had been fought on ground particularly suitable to a
display of Asquith's skill. It had almost all taken place on the parliamentary stage and according to the classical rules of nineteenth century
politics. Important new ground had been broken, but in a direction
which would have been perfectly familiar to Lord Grey or Russell or
Gladstone. Beneath that stage, however, and while the battle was

proceeding, new and potentially violent forces had been simmering away. One of them, symbolically, erupted as the issue of the Parliament Bill was being settled. The Cabinet for which Asquith returned to London on August 11th could not be a calm gathering of mutual congratulation. It had to address itself to a menacing dock strike and a still more threatening railway dispute.

CHAPTER XVI

STRANGE AILMENTS OF LIBERAL ENGLAND

1911-13

The industrial eruption which agitated the Cabinet at its meeting cn August 11th was only one part of the troubled prospect which then confronted the Government. Since early July, when the Germans had sent a gunboat to Agadir, the Moroccan dispute between France and Germany had been critical. No settlement was reached until the beginning of October, and there were several periods during the three months when ministers feared that Europe was on the brink of a general war. From September 8th to 22nd the threat was taken sufficiently seriously for the tunnels and bridges of the South Eastern Railway to be patrolled day and night.

Nor were the industrial difficulties isolated ones. During the previous autumn there had been a series of local disputes in a wide range of industries, one of them culminating in the long remembered riots at Tonypandy. 1911 had begun more quietly, but the calm did not persist. A widespread seamen's strike had accompanied the Coronation, and at the end of July there came the trouble in the London docks. There was some violence there, and worse violence in Liverpool, after the dispute had spread north. Then came the news that the four railway unions were proposing, at 30 hours' notice, to call all their men out. This was an industrial threat on a scale without precedent in Britain. The railways were then at the peak of their importance as the sinews of the national life. They were the key not only to the functioning of the economy but almost to the authority of the Government itself—and certainly to its ability to deploy any worthwhile military force. In the previous year when a French railway strike had paralysed two of their five regional systems, a government headed by three men of the left (Briand, Millerand and Viviani) had responded by arresting the leaders and issuing a mobilisation order for the other participants. That dispute, unlike the British one, had not occurred during an international crisis. Nor had it occurred at the height of a summer of febrile heat. During the first three weeks of August, 1911, there were ten days with a shade temperature of above 90°. This torrid weather brought violence closer to the surface and gave an added menace, in the eyes of the official classes, to any threat which emerged from the foetid and overcrowded quarters of the industrial towns.

A sharp Government reaction to the proposed railway strike might therefore have been expected. Asquith held another Cabinet on August 16th and reported to the King: " There is no doubt that the men have real grievances. . . . " On the next day he met the union leaders at the Board of Trade. On the merits of the dispute he believed they had a good case, and he offered an immediate Royal Commission to investigate the grievances. But towards the strike threat he adopted an attitude which, to repeat the word which John Morley had used about him eighteen years earlier, was perhaps unduly *cassant*. He was determined to keep the railways open (as any Prime Minister must have been in the circumstances) and he magisterially informed the leaders that he would not hesitate to " employ all the forces of the Crown " to this end. He did not suggest (as was probably the case) that his sternness sprang to some extent from the dangers of the international situation.

This was an unwise tactic. The union leaders returned in anger and the men came out at midnight. The strike was partial in the South, but the North and Midlands were paralysed. Lloyd George was then given the job of trying to get the men back to work. He employed all the cajolery, all the psychological insight, all the appeals to patriotism which Asquith had disdained to use. And in 48 hours he succeeded. He worked on the union leaders and on the employers; and he succeeded in convincing both sides that he had a real understanding of their difficulties. Asquith had merely succeeded in disguising from the men his sympathy for their case. He had lectured the employers too, but it did not occur to him that it was important to let the unions know this.

Lloyd George's exercise of gifts so totally different from his own commanded Asquith's full respect and even gratitude. " It is the latest, but by no means the least, of the loyal and invaluable services which you have rendered. . . . " he wrote to him.[a]

234

The King was equally warm in his congratulations to the Chancellor of the Exchequer. His concern with the strike, however, was almost too close for the Government's liking. While it was in progress he wanted to return to London and be available for consultation. But Knollys quashed that. " I don't see what good he could have done there," he wrote to Vaughan Nash, " and in fact I should say he might even have been in the way."[b] Then, a fortnight later, Knollys was instructed to send Asquith some longer term reflections. The King, he said, was afraid that " political elements " were being introduced into industrial conflicts which might affect " not the existence, but the position of the Crown, independent of other evils." Knollys continued:

" He desires me therefore to urge most strongly on the Government the importance (and it is also their duty) of their taking advantage of the lull, and of Parliament not meeting until the end of October, to devise a scheme, which although not entirely preventing strikes (perhaps that is not possible) would to a large extent prevent a threatened strike from coming to a head, and might be the means of preventing " sympathetic " strikes from taking place. Under any circumstances he hopes that, what is called " peaceful picketing " which most people now condemn, will be put an end to by legislation."[c1]

[1] There 's no doubt that in the first years of his reign King George V thought of any individual or movement tinged with " socialism " as inimical to the throne. In February, 1911 Knollys was ordered to write to Asquith protesting against a letter which the Home Secretary had written and published. " The King thinks that W. Churchill's views, as contained in the enclosed, are very socialistic," the protest began. " What he advocates is nothing more than workshops which have been tried in France and have turned out a complete failure". (*Asquith Papers*, II, f. 125). And again, in March, 1912, he expressed surprise that a possessor of the Order of Merit should avow himself to be a socialist. He added that he did not care whether a man was a Tory, a Liberal or a Radical. But the King's acceptance of radicalism was a little less than whole-hearted. Three months later he strongly (but unsuccessfully) opposed the bestowal of a privy councillorship upon Sir Henry Dalziel, rather curiously urging that, as he was uncongenial to the King, he should be made a baronet instead. " In the eyes of the Master of Elibank," Knollys wrote, " it may perhaps be a claim that Sir Henry is leader of the ' advanced Radical Party,' but he can hardly expect other people to look upon it in the same light." (*Asquith Papers*, III, f. 99).

The introduction of anti-trades union legislation was the last thing which the Government wanted to do at the time. The triple alliance between the Liberals, the Irish and the Labour Party gave them their majority. And the Labour Party was still smarting under the Osborne judgment, declaring political levies by trades union to be illegal. The effect of this had been realised during 1910. It had destroyed the basis of Labour Party finance. One aspect of this destruction was quickly remedied by the Government in the Budget of 1911, when a salary of £400 for members of Parliament had been introduced. But the Labour Party looked for more than this, and as early as November, 1910 the Cabinet had decided to restore by legislation the position which had been presumed to exist before the decision in the Osborne case, subject to the right of individual trades unionists to contract out of political payments.[1] The payment of M.P.s had formed the basis of a bargain between the Master of Elibank and Ramsay MacDonald. In return the Labour Party, apart from two or three members who could not be controlled, agreed to support the Health Insurance Bill, which Lloyd George had introduced in May, 1911, but which had then been delayed by the constitutional struggle. By the autumn it was obvious that this great measure ("more comprehensive in its scope and more provident and statesmanlike in its machinery than anything that has hitherto been attempted or proposed,"[d] as Asquith described it to the King) was not popular with the electorate. The duchesses and the doctors were united but not alone in disliking its provisions. In these circumstances it became doubly important to prevent the Labour Party swinging into opposition. Any suggestion that the Government was proposing restrictive rather than liberalising trades union legislation, would have run directly counter to this aim.

The King's views were therefore an embarrassment to Asquith, as misguided, he thought, as they were politically inexpedient. He dealt with them by a typical display of patient statesmanship. He did not return a sharp answer. Instead he circulated Knollys's letter to the Cabinet, waited for the unfavourable replies which he knew he would mostly receive, and then buried the proposal under the cloying earth of Cabinet disagreement.

The industrial problem itself was not so easily buried. In January, 1912 the Miners' Federation decided by ballot to call a national strike in favour of minimum wage rates. Here, as with the railways, the

[1] A bill to this effect was eventually carried in the session of 1913.

236

industry involved was more crucial to the national life than is the case today. Coal was almost the only available source of energy. Again, therefore, the Government was forced to take an active part in the dispute. The notices were due to expire on February 29th, and on the 20th of the month the Cabinet authorised four of their number, Asquith, Grey, Lloyd George and Buxton, to meet both the owners and the men, and try to effect a settlement. This move did not succeed, and at the end of the month the strike began.

The Cabinet negotiating team remained in being, and tried hard to bring the two sides together. For three days from March 12th they sat in conference with the representatives of both sides, without avail. Like other ministers, both before and after him, Asquith found that he could not break through the stubbornness of the coalowners. He urged them to pay the minimum of 5s. a shift (and 3s. for boys) which was demanded by the Miners' Federation, but when they refused he would not accede to the demands of the men to the extent of enforcing such wages by legislation. The Cabinet did however decide (despite the doubts of Morley and Churchill) to introduce an emergency bill setting up compulsory machinery, on a district basis, for settling minimum rates, but without stipulating what these rates should be. Despite the hostility of the owners, the dissatisfaction of the miners, and the opposition of the Conservatives, the bill was pushed through both Houses within a week.

At this stage, however, a settlement could not be effected without a definite figure, and on March 25th the Government representatives made another effort to get the owners to accept 5s. On the following day Asquith reported failure to the Cabinet. His account to the King continued:

Sir E. Grey (then) brought forward a proposal that with a view to facilitating such an agreement the Government should intimate to the owners that if, after trying the experiment for a year, it resulted in loss they should be indemnified by the Exchequer— up to a maximum amount of (say) £250,000. This suggestion gave rise to a long debate which manifested acute differences of opinion. It was pointed out by the Prime Minister—who was prepared, if *force majeure* compelled, to consent to some such proposal—that it would be difficult to justify to the country a subvention, at the cost of the general taxpayer, to one of the most prosperous industries in the country. Mr. Burns, Mr. McKinnon Wood and Mr.

Runciman were very adverse to Sir E. Grey's proposal as was also Lord Morley.[e]

This more than usually explicit account of Cabinet divisions[1] shows clearly where in the Government the *laissez faire* strength lay. It was amongst some of the new men, supported by Morley as heir to Gladstonian individualism, rather than amongst either the few old Whigs who remained or the traditional Right of Liberal Imperialism. Grey's paternalism—he was described by Balfour as " a curious combination of the old-fashioned Whig and the Socialist "—made him indifferent to the mythology of market forces. Haldane's position was similar. A few months later he was (unsuccessfully) urging the Cabinet to make the rate of wages negotiated by the dockers' trades union binding on all employers in the Port of London, or, alternatively, to give the Port Authority the power to fix the rates. Asquith, never so stubbornly non-partisan as were Grey and Haldane on purely political issues, was also somewhat less adventurous than were they on social or economic ones. He opposed the Haldane proposal on dockers' wages, for instance. But he was by no means a businessman's Liberal of the type of Walter Runciman.[2] Nor did his economic caution ever rival that of John Burns.

[1] The only more explicit account which Asquith gave the King was after the meeting on April 5th, 1911, when he took a vote on a proposal of Haldane's to move a section of the Natural History Museum in order to make room for an extension to the College of Science. Morley and Grey, who were both British Museum trustees, opposed. " In the end the Prime Minister decided on the unusual course of taking a division in the Cabinet— with the result (there being several abstentions) that 5 voted with Lord Morley and 9 or 10 with Lord Haldane." (*Asquith Papers*, box 6 ff. 24–5). Asquith was following a Gladstonian precedent by taking a vote on building works in London. In 1883 the G.O.M. made the Cabinet vote three times on whether or not the Duke of Wellington's statue should be removed from Hyde Park Corner. But in that government he also allowed votes on several matters of real importance—which Asquith never did—and sometimes got himself defeated.

[2] Asquith's detachment from the business outlook, combined with his acceptance of some of its doctrines, is well illustrated by a story of C.F.G. Masterman's, relating to the period after the outbreak of war: The question of large speculative profits being made out of shipping cargoes of food or munitions to England arose: " Disgusting," said Asquith:

" A minister at once protested. He declared that this was the normal

The miners had returned to work by mid-April. The Government's wage machinery bill, unwelcome though it had been to the owners and inadequate though it had seemed to the men, destroyed the force behind the strike. The next threat came from the Transport Federation —with the trouble again centred on the London docks. This time the Government, at Asquith's instigation, tried to act in advance and established a Cabinet committee composed of Lloyd George, Haldane, Beauchamp, Buxton and McKinnon Wood to watch the situation and attempt mediation. It was unsuccessful, as was a further attempt by Asquith himself after the strike had started. The employers under Lord Devonport, who as H. E. Kearley, M.P. had been Lloyd George's parliamentary secretary in the early days of the Government, were determined to hold out for a clear victory. They secured it, and the men trickled back to work at the end of July, 1912. That was effectively the end of the great pre-1914 strike wave.

The threat of European war, which in the summer of 1911 had closely matched the dangers of violent industrial upheaval, subsided more quickly but less permanently. The year between the Moroccan settlement of October, 1911, and the outbreak of the first Balkan War —the fourth of the five great crises which led up to August, 1914— was a period of relative calm. But after Agadir, and the fears which that incident engendered, opinion amongst the members of the Liberal Government and the officials who served them was never quite the same again. Hitherto, only a few clear-sighted fanatics like Sir Henry Wilson, the Director of Military Operations at the War Office, had acted on the assumption that a major war was likely. The great majority of those in positions of power passed through occasional moments of nervousness, but in general they averted their eyes from the prospect of a holocaust, dismissing it as unlikely as well as distasteful. The change during the Moroccan crisis was symbolised by Lloyd George and Churchill. Earlier in the life of the Government, as has

---

operation of trade. He declared that if their men had not done it other men would have done the same. He declared that if they had chosen not to bring the stuff to England they could probably have attained as much or greater profit by taking it to neutral or allied countries. 'I can see nothing disgraceful,' he said ' about the whole transaction.' 'I did not say disgraceful ' said Mr. Asquith with a characteristic shrug of the shoulders. ' I said disgusting.' " (Masterman: *England After War*. p. 143).

been seen, they were the leading "economists," sceptical of the German danger and instinctively hostile to any increase in the service estimates. Behind Lloyd George, moreover, there still trailed his Boer War past. If Haldane and Grey were the most "imperialist" members of the Government, so it was assumed, almost without question, that he was the firmest of the "Little Englanders." But on July 21st, at the height of the Moroccan dispute, he went out of his way at the Lord Mayor's annual dinner to the bankers to deliver a sharp warning to Germany and to proclaim that peace at the price of our exclusion from European influence "would be a humiliation intolerable for a great country like ours to endure." And in August he wrote to Churchill: "The thunderclouds are gathering. I am not at all satisfied that we are prepared, or that we are preparing."*f*

As for Churchill himself, Grey has described how he reacted to the events of that summer and to the tension which continued without respite as the hot days grew shorter:

> One other colleague, not tied to London by official work, kept me company for love of the crisis. . . . He insisted on taking me once to see (Sir Henry) Wilson, and their talk was keen and apparently not the first that they had had. Let me not be supposed to imply that Churchill was working for war, or desired it. . . . It was only that his high-mettled spirit was exhilarated by the air of crisis and high events. His companionship was a great refreshment, and late in the afternoon he would call for me and take me to the Automobile Club, which was but thinly populated, like other clubs, at that season. There, after what had been to me a weary, perhaps an anxious, day he would cool his ardour and I revive my spirits in the swimming bath.*g*

Henceforward a large part of Churchill's interest was concentrated on the field of national preparedness; and he saw an early opportunity to involve himself much more closely with these matters. On August 27th Asquith had convened a special meeting of the Committee of Imperial Defence. Of those who normally attended Balfour was away —nursing his Parliament Bill grievances (against his own colleagues much more than against the Government) at Bad Gastein. Lloyd George and Churchill were specially summoned. At this meeting it transpired that there was a wide divergence between the war plans of the Admiralty and those of the War Office. The naval plan was to attack the German fleet and then to land packets of troops at different points along the Baltic coast. The army wanted six divisions transported to France immediately. Furthermore, the organisation of the two departments was utterly different. The army had the Imperial General Staff. The navy had nothing analogous. They merely had Admiral Sir Arthur Wilson as First Sea Lord, and at this highly disputatious meeting he was badly worsted by the generals. Asquith, his own inclinations reinforced by a threat of resignation from Haldane, decided that the Admiralty must be made to accept both the War Office plan and sweeping changes in its own organisation. " The present position, in which everything is locked up in the brain of a single taciturn Admiral, is both ridiculous and dangerous," he wrote to Crewe a few weeks later.[h]

This could not be done without a political change at the Admiralty. McKenna was too loyal a servant of his department to be an effective instrument for imposing changes upon it. At the meeting on August 27th a new First Lord of the Admiralty emerged as an urgent requirement. Churchill saw this, and greatly coveted the post. So did Haldane, who was senior, closer to the Prime Minister, and far more experienced in service matters. That same night Asquith left for his autumn holiday in Scotland, taking the problem away with him. But he did not escape from the two suppliants. Haldane motored over from Cloan to Archerfield to press his claim upon the Prime Minister. On arrival he was met by a surprising and not entirely agreeable sight. " As I entered the approach," he wrote, " I saw Winston Churchill standing at the door."[i] Churchill had had much farther to come, but he had got there first. He had the added advantage of having established himself as a house guest. Haldane had to motor back to Cloan that evening, although he returned for further consultations on the next day. On this occasion Asquith characteristically shut his two ministers up in a room together and allowed them to argue with each other. Haldane tried hard, but he got the worst of the argument. " Churchill would not be moved," he rather sadly recorded, " and Asquith yielded to him."[j]

In giving the appointment to Churchill, however, Asquith was influenced by considerations beyond the younger man's greater pertinacity. The reason he gave to Haldane was that, with naval affairs likely to be a centre of controversy, certainly within the Liberal Party and perhaps between the two parties, he wanted a First Lord in the Commons.[1] The still more compelling reason, was that, although he had given the victory to the generals in the clash of August 27th, he did not wish to rub the noses of the admirals too deeply in the dirt; and this meant he could not ask the Secretary of State for War to step in and clean up their mess. In addition, there may have been yet a third reason at the back of his mind. If, by appointing Churchill to the Admiralty he could permanently detach him (and perhaps Lloyd George as well) from the " economist " wing of the party, the cohesion of the Government would be considerably increased. This proved to be the case. Haldane, who took his defeat without bitterness, wrote to his mother a few weeks later:

Winston and L.G. dined with me last night and we had a very useful talk. This is now a very harmonious Cabinet. It is odd to think that three years ago I had to fight those two for every penny for my army reforms. Winston is full of enthusiasm about the Admiralty and just as keen as I am on the War Staff. It is delightful to work with him. L.G. too has quite changed his attitude and is now very friendly to your " bear ", whom he used to call " the Minister for Slaughter."[k]

Churchill's first task at the Admiralty was to get rid of Wilson. It had been assumed that this could not be done until the following April, when the Admiral was due to retire, but the new First Lord accomplished it by the end of November.

The other principal consequence of the Moroccan crisis, for the Liberal Government, was that it brought somewhat more into the open the military conversations which had taken place with the French. During the election of 1906 a previous Moroccan crisis—leading up to the Algeciras Conference—had been in progress. The French ambassador had asked Grey what help France could expect in the event of a German attack. Grey, without putting the matter before the Cabinet, had replied that he could enter into no commitment, but that his personal view was that in this event we would not stand aside. The French then asked for military conversations. Grey decided that to

[1] Haldane had been created a viscount in April, 1911. Crewe's illness made it necessary to strengthen the Government front bench in the Lords. Grey was suggested but refused to go. Haldane was more amenable. His principal ambition was still centred on the Woolsack (to which he was to succeed on Loreburn's retirement a little over a year later), so that he lost little by leaving the Commons.

refuse these would be to pre-judge the issue—against intervention. Without such conversations we would have no ability to render effective help, even if we desired to do this when the time came. Accordingly, after consultation with Haldane, he told the ambassador that talks might proceed. The Cabinet remained unaware of these developments until 1911.

Grey himself subsequently admitted that he had made a mistake in not asking for Cabinet sanction in 1906. But the view, widely propagated after 1914, that he failed to do this because of a Liberal Imperialist plot to mislead the more pacifist members of the Government, is untenable. Not only Haldane, who might have been part of the plot, but Campbell-Bannerman and Ripon (as leader of the House of Lords), who could not have been part of it, were fully consulted and informed. Campbell-Bannerman, had he so wished, could have brought the matter before the Cabinet at any time. And Asquith, ironically, was kept far more in the dark than his " Little Englander " predecessor. He was not informed in 1906, and there is no evidence that he was told of the position even when he succeeded to the premiership. In April, 1911, when it seemed likely that the French would ask for further conversations, Grey wrote Asquith an informal account of what had occurred in 1906, and did so in terms which suggested that he was telling him for the first time. And he specifically asked that Morley, who was as pacifist as any member of the Cabinet, should be brought into the discussion.

Perhaps because he was told so late, Asquith was always a little cool towards the military interchanges. Later in the year, when the second round was in progress, he wrote from Archerfield:

September 5, 1911

" My dear Grey,

Conversations such as that between Gen. Joffre and Col. Fairholme seem to me rather dangerous; especially the part which refers to possible British assistance. The French ought not to be encouraged, in present circumstances, to make their plans on any assumptions of this kind.

Yours always,

H.H.A.[1]

Grey replied unyieldingly: " It would create consternation if we forbade our military experts to converse with the French. No doubt these conversations and our speeches have given an expectation of support. I do not see how that can be helped."*m* For the moment he had his way.

Later in the autumn, when ministers had returned to London, Morley raised the whole matter in full Cabinet. The best part of two meetings was devoted to the discussion. After the first, on November 1st, Asquith reported to the King:

Lord Morley raised the question of the inexpediency of communications being held or allowed between the General Staff of the War Office and the General Staff of foreign States, such as France, in regard to possible military co-operation, without the previous knowledge and directions of the Cabinet. Lord Haldane explained what had actually been done, the communications in question having been initiated as far back as 1906 with Sir H. Campbell-Bannerman's sanction, and resumed in more detail during the spring and summer of the present year The Prime Minister pointed out that all questions of policy have been and must be reserved for the decision of the Cabinet, and that it is quite outside the function of military or naval officers to prejudge such questions. . . . Considerable discussion ensued, and no conclusion was come to, the matter being adjourned for further consideration later on.*n*

This further consideration took place on November 15th, and Asquith wrote of " a prolonged and animated discussion ":

Sir E. Grey made it clear that at no stage of our intercourse with France since January 1906 had we either by diplomatic or military engagements compromised our freedom of decision and action in the event of war between France and Germany. On the other hand there was a prevailing feeling in the Cabinet that there was a danger that communications of the kind referred to might give rise to expectations, and that they should not, if they related to the possibility of concerted action, be entered into or carried on without the sanction of the Cabinet.

In the result, at the suggestion of the Prime Minister, unanimous approval was given to the two following propositions:

(1) That no communications should take place between the General Staff here and the Staffs of other countries which can, directly or indirectly, commit this country to military or naval intervention.

(2) That such communications, if they relate to concerted action by land or sea, should not be entered into without the previous approval of the Cabinet. *

This outcome cannot have been welcome to Grey. First, he regarded at least one of the propositions as unduly restrictive, although he did not press his opposition. Upon their original draft (which was in Asquith's hand), Grey wrote, " I think the last paragraph is a little tight "; but he subsequently crossed out this comment. Secondly, it is difficult to believe that the form taken by the Cabinet discussions did not amount to a mild rebuke for what the Foreign Secretary had done. But reluctant minister although Grey always claimed to be, this produced no suggestion of resignation. Nor did it lead to any diminution of Asquith's confidence in him. A fortnight later the Prime Minister was writing to Crewe in unusually effusive terms about a speech of the Foreign Secretary's. He spoke of " a tremendous day," " a great performance," and "the effect which (Grey) alone is capable of producing in the House of Commons."

The Cabinet may have been unrealistic in pretending that there ever could be staff conversations without some indirect commitment. But if there was deceit, it was self-deceit. From November, 1911 onwards the basic facts of what was taking place were in the possession of every minister. In the spring of 1912 there were further requests from the French for naval co-operation. These were reported to the Cabinet and led to an exhaustive discussion, spread over four meetings, on the whole disposition of the British fleet. And in November of that year, when the Anglo-French understanding was committed to writing in the form of an exchange of letters between Grey and Cambon, the draft of Grey's letter was submitted to, and amended by, the Cabinet. Morley in particular, who after 1914 complained that he had been kept in ignorance throughout, was fully informed, both as the instigator of the vital Cabinet discussions in 1911, and as a member of the Committee of Imperial Defence.

The third threat of violence which hung over England in 1911 came from the suffragettes. " Militancy " had begun as long before as October, 1905, when Christabel Pankhurst and Annie Kenney succeeded in wrecking a meeting which Grey was addressing in Manchester.[1]

[1] The occasion on which this first attack took place was curiously symbolic of the irrational choice of targets which was to become a growing characteristic of the movement. Grey was in opposition at the time; he

In the early years of the Liberal Government it grew gradually, and the methods employed became progressively more violent. In September, 1909 the permanent secretary to the Home Office sent Herbert Gladstone a Metropolitan Police report that women were practising pistol shooting at an address in Tottenham Court Road, " The annexed report," he commented, " seems to me to show that there is now definite ground for fearing the possibility of the P.M's being fired at by one of the pickets at the entrance of the House (of Commons)."[p] He added, however, that he was against the pickets being removed as the police were confident that they could get a woman before she " damaged " the Prime Minister. Gladstone was nervous, but Asquith unhesitatingly pronounced against removal.

In fact the Prime Minister was never shot at, but numerous other assaults upon him were attempted. He emerged unharmed from them all, although others sometimes suffered on his behalf. Lord Weardale, when mistaken for him, was whipped at Euston. Augustine Birrell, when accompanying him in Whitehall, had his knee-cap damaged. And Redmond, sitting in the same carriage in Dublin, was wounded in the ear by a hatchet. At other times the intimidation was less vicarious. The Downing Street windows were occasionally smashed; and Asquith himself was often hectored and sometimes hustled by militant women. What he particularly disliked about the hectoring was that it tended to occur at evening parties and contrasted sharply with the form which he believed conversation between the sexes should take on such occasions.[1] The hustling took a still more disagreeable form. On the golf links at Lossiemouth some militants tried to tear off his clothes, and were frustrated only by the presence and intervention of his daughter Violet. Thereafter a repetition of this form of attack was one of his principal fears, even when something more vicious was attempted. In November, 1913 when motoring to Stirling to unveil the Campbell-Bannerman memorial he was held up by women lying across the road. As the car slowed down others emerged from behind

---

was a determined supporter of female suffrage; and a victory for the party whose case he was endeavouring to advocate would result in a House of Commons far more favourable to the women's cause than that which then existed.

[1] On one of them, an India Office reception in June, 1912, Margot is reputed to have boxed the ears of an importunate lady in a pink dress.

the hedgerows on either side of the road, jumping on the running-boards, and proceeded to belabour him over the head with dog whips. His top hat provided a surprisingly adequate degree of protection.

All this and the other dramatic manifestations of the time—the slashing of the Rokeby Venus, Miss Wilding Davison's death fall in front of the King's horse at the 1913 Derby, the burning of pillar boxes, the destruction by acid of golf course greens—had no favourable effect upon Asquith. He found the whole performance both distasteful and mystifying. As Mr. Roger Fulford has written:

The idea of converting a human being's reason by parades, marches and fighting the police was incomprehensible to him. The more the women marched, the less his reason marched with them. Therefore the work of the militants strengthened his opposition to the vote. The women pursued him with much shrill invective—some of which was not without its effect in damaging his standing in the country—but he remained like a rock, which by reason of its natural formation, repels the froth and fury swirling round it.*q*

In part Asquith's attitude to the suffrage question was due to a failure of imagination. He simply could not understand why anyone, man or woman, should get so excited about the matter. It should be settled, not on the basis of abstract right, but by the practical test of whether or not a change would be likely to improve the system of government. He therefore always wanted to play the issue down. He was an effective controversialist on the subject, but, unlike some of the other anti-suffragists—Lewis Harcourt amongst the Liberals or F. E. Smith amongst the Tories—not a happy one. He would much rather that the subject had never been raised, and like other leaders confronted with a subject on which they did not wish to lead, he tried unsuccessfully to take the passion out of an essentially passionate controversy.

" There are very few issues in politics," he told the House of Commons in May, 1913, "upon which more exaggerated language is used both upon the one side and upon the other. I am sometimes tempted to think, as one listens to the arguments of supporters of woman suffrage, that there is nothing to be said for it, and I sometimes am tempted to think, when I listen to the arguments of the opponents of woman suffrage, that there is nothing to be said against it."*r*

Asquith's position on the suffrage question even if not happy, was both pivotal and bizarre. It was pivotal because there were only two effective obstacles to female enfranchisement before 1914. The first was the excesses of militancy; and the second was the person of the Prime Minister, stubbornly unconvinced and occupying a commanding position in the House of Commons. It was bizarre because it placed him in opposition to a majority of his own Cabinet, to a majority of the Liberal parliamentary party, and to Balfour, whose own attitude placed him in turn in opposition to the majority of the Unionist party. Asquith was not alone in the Cabinet, however. Apart from Harcourt, already mentioned, John Burns and Herbert Samuel were strongly opposed to the women's case. But on the other side, although varying greatly in the degree of their enthusiasm, was a formidable array which included Grey, Lloyd George, Haldane, Churchill, Birrell, Runciman and McKenna.

In these circumstances there was naturally some pressure from within the Cabinet for Government time to be given for private members' women's suffrage bills. But these bills, partly to win Conservative support and partly to give a general impression of moderation, almost all proposed a strictly limited female enfranchisement. Both from an age and a property point of view the women's vote would be more restricted than the men's. Lloyd George and Churchill were quick to see that measures along these lines would merely result in adding a substantial preponderance of Tory voters to the registers. They both went into the division lobby against the so-called Conciliation Bill in the summer of 1910. The suffragist forces in the Cabinet (like those outside) were therefore far from united on questions of tactics, and Asquith had at first little difficulty in holding the position. By May, 1911, the pressure had grown stronger, and Asquith had to report to the King that a clear majority of the Cabinet was in favour of giving facilities to a bill. Eventually it was agreed that in the following (1912) session a week of Government time should be made available for a committee stage; but in that year the bill, which had been successful at this stage in both 1910 and 1911, failed by a narrow margin to secure a second reading.

The Cabinet then proposed that the women's claim should be dealt with by the offer of a place in a major Reform Bill which the Government was about to promote. This bill was designed to abolish plural voting and extend the male franchise from $7\frac{1}{2}$ to 10 million voters. The Cabinet offer, announced by the Prime Minister in July, 1912, was that the House of Commons should have the opportunity, on a free vote, to amend the bill so as to put women on the same new voting basis as men. For symbolic reasons the offer was unattractive to the leaders of the women's movement. They wanted a bill of their own, a specific recognition of their claim to equality. But from a practical point of view the offer had great advantages. It disposed of the doubts of Lloyd George and many other Liberals. It meant that the amendment, if accepted, would be incorporated in the body of a bill which would have the full force of the Government behind it. There need be no fear that it would founder at a later stage for want of parliamentary time; and if the House of Lords proved recalcitrant, as was more than likely, it could expect the protection of the Parliament Act.

The amendment was to come up for discussion in late January, 1913, towards the end of a session which started in February, 1912 and continued for more than thirteen months. On January 22nd the Cabinet prepared for the debate by making an " agreement to differ " and deciding that, whatever the result, no question of ministerial resignations would arise.

The Cabinet met again two days later—in very different circumstances. Speaker Lowther had in the meantime destroyed the assumption on which the Government—and the public—had been acting for the previous six months. He had decided that if the women's suffrage amendment were to be carried it would so change the bill as to make it necessary for it to be withdrawn and re-introduced. In other words it could not be carried that session. This was an almost unprecedented parliamentary *dégringolade*.

" This is a totally new view of the matter," Asquith wrote to the King, " which appears to have occurred for the first time to the Speaker himself only two or three days ago, and is in flat contradiction of the assumptions upon which all parties in the House hitherto treated the bill. In Mr. Asquith's opinion, which is shared by some of the best authorities on procedure, the Speaker's judgment is entirely wrong and impossible to reconcile with what took place in the case of previous Franchise Bills in 1867 and 1884."[8]

Complaints against the Speaker, however well justified they might be, were of little use. There was no possibility of an effective appeal against his ruling, and the only thing the Cabinet could do was to agree, unanimously, that it would be a breach of faith to the suffragists to proceed with the Government bill without the women's amendment being voted upon and that they must therefore drop it. Facilities would be given, early in the next session, for a private member's bill dealing with female enfranchisement. The whole incident was a bad blow to the Government's intentions and prestige. But Asquith was a sufficiently committed anti-suffragist to find consolation in the new situation. "The Speaker's *coup d'état* has bowled over the Women for this session—a great relief,"*t* he wrote in a private letter on January 27th.

The private member's bill came up for second reading on May 6th, and the House was presented with the diverting spectacle of the principal speaker in its favour being the Foreign Secretary and the principal speaker in opposition the Prime Minister. The one spoke immediately after the other. Asquith, assisted by the mounting tide of feminist illegality, was more persuasive than Grey. The bill was lost by 268 to 221, and that, parliamentarily, was the end of the matter for a time. Outside the law-breaking and the arson continued, but against growing public hostility and at the price of increasing dissension within the suffragette movement itself.

During 1912 and 1913 the troubles of the Government were increased, and its authority for dealing with them temporarily diminished, by the eruption of the Marconi scandal. Four ministers were in some form involved: Lloyd George; Rufus Isaacs, the Attorney-General; Herbert Samuel, the Postmaster-General; and the Master of Elibank, the Chief Whip. The Master had left the Government, the House of Commons, and the country (for the improbable destination of Bogota) before the scandal boiled over, but the share transactions which involved him had been made while he was still Patronage Secretary. Some of them, indeed, were not on his own account but for Liberal Party funds. Samuel, on the other hand, had dealt in no shares. The suggestion against him was that, as head of the Post Office, he had given the Marconi Company an improperly favourable contract (concluded in March, 1912) for the erection of a chain of wireless telegraphy stations throughout the Empire because its managing director was the brother of the Attorney-General. There was never the semblance of a case against Samuel, and the pretence of one was only sustained in order that the anti-Semitic overtones of the affair might be exploited to the full. To bring together one Samuel and a couple of Isaacs in a skein of transactions bordering on the world of high finance was an irresistible attraction for Belloc and Cecil Chesterton.

The real case was against Lloyd George and Rufus Isaacs. They both indulged in share transactions which, while not remotely dishonest, were certainly unwise for men in their positions, the one with his special financial responsibility, the other with his special legal responsibility. In April, 1912, Isaacs bought 10,000 shares in the American Marconi Company from a third brother who had himself obtained them from the brother who was managing director of the English company. One thousand of these he immediately sold to Lloyd George (and another thousand to the Master of Elibank). There followed a complicated series of sales and re-purchases. Eventually all three ministers lost money on their speculations, although at certain stages they realised substantial capital profits. What was more important than the net outcome, however, was the fact that they dealt in these volatile shares with the purpose (even if incompetently exercised) of making short-term Stock Exchange profits.

There was no trace of corruption in their behaviour. The contract had been concluded (although not approved by the House of Commons) before they entered the field. They used no special knowledge; they exercised no improper influence. And the American company, in which alone they dealt, stood to make no gain from any contract entered into by the English company. The English company was a shareholder in its sister, but not *vice versa*. Nevertheless there was a certain irrational sympathy of movement between the prices of the shares of the two concerns. This apart, however, the American shares, as those concerned quickly realised, were most unsuitable material for ministerial dealings.

During the summer of 1912 there were a spate of rumours and libellous statements about ministers and their relationship to the contract. As a result it was decided, in October, to set up a House of Commons select committee to investigate. Lloyd George and Isaacs in the course of the debate on the appointment of the committee intervened to deny in precise terms that they had ever had any interest, direct or indirect, in the English Marconi Company. They did not inform the House of their dealings in the American shares. This fact only came to light in the Law Courts months later when Isaacs and Samuel took a libel action against the French newspaper *Le Matin* and the Attorney-General empowered his counsel (Sir Edward Carson, strangely enough; F. E. Smith was appearing for Samuel) to make the disclosure. The belated nature of this disclosure was one of the main counts against Lloyd George and Isaacs when the report of the select committee (which divided on strict party lines) was debated in June, 1913. If they believed in the innocence of their own behaviour, why had they not been more frank with the House in the previous October?

Asquith was not closely involved in these matters. None of the ministers involved were his intimate friends (Isaacs was the closest to being one). But as head of the Government his advice was occasionally sought by his colleagues, and it fell to him, at the end of the affair, both to decide whether any resignations were called for, and to lay down a guide to ministers, in the conduct of their private financial affairs, which has kept its validity until the present day.

Asquith was at once unsympathetic and tolerant towards the peccant ministers. Without a trace of hypocrisy, he could not for a moment have imagined himself behaving as they had done. Although on the whole an economic as well as a political liberal, he felt an instinctive distaste for the process of money-making. At the same time he was never harsh towards human frailty. Few Prime Ministers have had less ambition to be a Savonarola within their cabinets. He greatly disliked the whole business and regarded it as "the most difficult and painful personal incident" of his public life. But he regarded much of the clamour as malicious and uncalled for and he refused to do anything which might fortify it. As one result he advised Isaacs (possibly unwisely) against taking an earlier libel action. This was in August, 1912, and the paper then complained of was Cecil Chesterton's *Eye-Witness*. Asquith gave his advice from Scotland in characteristically unruffled terms:

"I suspect (it) . . . has a very meagre circulation. I notice only one page of advertisements and that occupied by books of Belloc's publishers. Prosecution would secure it notoriety, which might yield subscribers. We have broken weather, and but for Winston there would be nothing in the newspapers."[u]

Another result of this attitude was that Asquith firmly repulsed the tentative offers of resignation which Lloyd George and Isaacs made in the following January. He later told the King that this was immediately after they had told him of their dealings in the American shares, conduct which he described as "lamentable" and "so difficult to defend."*v* Nevertheless, once he had refused the resignations, he was committed to this intractable defence and he discharged it in the June debate with great force and considerable success:

"Their honour, both their private and their public honour," he told the House, "is at this moment absolutely unstained. They have, as this Committee has shown by its unanimous verdict, abused no public trust. They retain, I can say with full assurance, the complete confidence of their colleagues and of their political associates."

In private he was, not unnaturally, a little more critical. "I think the idol's wings are a bit clipped," he said to Masterman one day on the front bench, when they were listening to Lloyd George addressing the House. "A bit clipped," he repeated with a typical shrug of his shoulders. But in public he gave Lloyd George, already thrusting hard behind him, a support as complete as it was necessary.

Mrs. Donaldson's recent penetrating study of the case,[1] however, suggests that Asquith, while undoubtedly firm and loyal, was also a little disingenuous in pretending that he was kept in ignorance of the American transactions for much longer than was in fact the case. To the King, as has been seen, he fixed January, 1913, as the time when Lloyd George and Isaacs "confessed" to him. And writing many years later in *Memories and Reflections*, he implied (although he did not state) that he was unaware of the American transactions at least until after the debate of 11th October, 1912. Samuel's *Memoirs*, however, state that the author informed the Prime Minister about the American purchases in or soon after June, 1912, and that Asquith showed that he had assimilated the information to the extent of commenting that "our colleagues could not have done a more foolish thing."*w* If this was so, it is suggested, Asquith must bear some part of the blame for not forcing Lloyd George and Isaacs to make a full disclosure on 11th October.

Was it so? Samuel, despite attributing to Asquith such an uncharacteristic phrase as "our colleagues" was a reliable witness, and

[1] *The Marconi Scandal* by Frances Donaldson (1962).

his testimony is to some extent supported by the Master of Elibank. On the other hand, the only reference to the Marconi case in a voluminous private correspondence which Asquith was conducting at the time[1] is in a letter dated 7th January, 1913. In this correspondence there was no question of Asquith writing "for the record." He recounted events as they occurred, and this January letter fits in with the date which he gave to the King three months later, and is more consistent than not with his having just heard for the first time of the American transactions. "I am bothered with various things," he wrote, "——the latest being certain follies wh. Rufus Isaacs and Ll. George have committed in regard to Marconi shares."

There can now be no certainty on the point one way or another. But had Asquith known the full facts it seems unlikely (although not impossible; he always allowed his ministers a wide latitude of judgment) that he would not have remonstrated strongly against the narrowly accurate but misleading denials of 11th October. He might not have been in time to prevent them, for he was ill at the time, and he might have preserved the public front, for this was always his instinct when ministers made mistakes, but it is difficult to believe that he would not have commented sharply in private correspondence. And why, if the Prime Minister had been fully informed all along, should the issue of resignation have arisen at all in January?

Six weeks after the final Marconi debate in the House of Commons, Isaacs wrote to Asquith again suggesting resignation. This time it was because publicity was being given to his having falsified his age, thirty-four years earlier, in order to secure membership (most unfortunately for himself as it turned out) of the London Stock Exchange. Asquith's reply was clear, succinct, and perhaps a little weary. "Certainly not," he wrote. Two months after this he appointed Isaacs Lord Chief Justice, and by so doing provoked Kipling's poem *Gehazi*, one of the most vitriolic in the English language. It would have been much easier both for the Prime Minister and for Isaacs if the appointment could have been postponed. But Alverstone, the incumbent Chief Justice, was determined to resign. Once he had done so, Asquith did not hesitate about appointing Isaacs. The Attorney-General traditionally enjoyed the reversion to this office. Isaacs was an Attorney of outstanding legal quality. To have denied him the job in these circumstances would have undermined his position almost as much

[1] see pp 257-58 *infra*.

as allowing the House of Commons to carry the Conservative motion which had been proposed against him and Lloyd George in the previous June. Asquith had used his authority to defeat this, and he did not weaken in the autumn. Lloyd George and Isaacs were both lucky in the Prime Minister under whom they made their errors of judgment.

CHAPTER XVII

A PRIME MINISTER'S ROUTINE

1912-14

Apart from the ill-fated Franchise Bill, the long session of 1912–13 was occupied with the Government's two remaining major legislative commitments. The third Home Rule Bill was introduced by Asquith on April 11th, 1912, and completed a laborious passage through the Commons on January 16th, 1913. A fortnight later it was summarily rejected in the House of Lords by a vote of 326 to 69. The Welsh Church Disestablishment Bill moved along a roughly parallel course. Clearly neither measure could pass into law without the protection of the Parliament Act and the three laps of the parliamentary circuit which this involved.

The Home Rule Bill was eventually to produce a crisis still more acute than the battle with the peers, and a threat of violence still more menacing than anything the suffragettes could command or industrial unrest might unleash. The positions which made this crisis inevitable were taken up by the Unionist leaders (and by their Ulster supporters) between July and September, 1912. Nevertheless, the period in the middle of the Home Rule Bill's slow progress towards the statute book was one of relative political calm. This was particularly true of the short session of 1913, which lasted only from March to August, and which was almost entirely occupied with a second passage of the two rejected bills. The Commons had discussed them before. They knew they would have to discuss them again. However threatening the prospect, the intermediate stage of the process was inevitably one of *longueur*. The Cabinet, as Asquith's letters to the King clearly show, was more than usually concerned with routine matters during these months. If, during the whole of his long premiership there was any period of lull, it lay in this short session and the months on either side of it: from December, 1912 to January or February, 1914.

Asquith's capacity for the swift and almost effortless transaction of business was always such that he never worked excessively long hours, although he was often subjected to the strain of constantly recurring crises and restricted to short snatches of holiday. But during these thirteen or fourteen months, his life took on a somewhat more leisurely pattern. It was a pattern, moreover, which can be reconstructed in unusual detail.

Throughout his last three or four decades Asquith's personal life was unusually dominated by two characteristics. The first was an ability to express intimate thoughts more easily on paper than in conversation. His published works do not show him as a master of English prose. His speeches, mostly underprepared, have a far greater claim to distinction than his books, some of which were equally underprepared, but which suffered in addition from his repugnance to the true role of the autobiographer. He had no desire to tell the world what really happened. and he was insufficiently interested in himself. As a result his four volumes of memoirs are less revealing than those of almost any other major politician. But in private letters, provided the recipient aroused his interest, he was entirely different. He wrote easily, casually, economically, and as a relaxation. If he had a spare half-hour between important meetings, or even during one of them, it was no effort for him to write a quick five-hundred-word comment on his recent doings.

The second characteristic was that he preferred writing to women rather than to men. (To a slightly lesser extent—he was a great dining-club attender—this was also his conversational preference.) His business letters were generally brief. Except for occasional congratulatory or commemorative notes, he carried on no social correspondence with male friends. Even in the 'nineties he rarely wrote to Grey, or Haldane, or Rosebery, unless there was some pressing issue to be discussed. But to a few women he wrote—and wrote copiously—without immediate cause. In the early 'nineties he did so to Lady Horner, with whom he was not in love; a little later he did so to Margot, with whom he was; and in the last decade of his life he wrote to Mrs. Harrisson, a series of letters which were later to be edited by Desmond MacCarthy into two volumes of published correspondence. Lady Scott, the widow of the explorer and Miss Lillian Tennant, one of his wife's nieces, were others who received his epistolary attention.

In 1910, he began the first faint trickle of what was later to become a flood of letters to Venetia Stanley. Miss Stanley was the youngest

daughter of Lord Sheffield (or, as members of his family have sometimes chosen to be known, Lord Stanley of Alderley), who was the
possessor both of an old barony and of firm Liberal views. Asquith had
known her for several years before the correspondence began. Miss
Stanley was an exact contemporary and close friend of his daughter
Violet. As such she was a constant visitor to Downing Street. At first
there was no indication that she aroused Asquith's particular interest.
Even when the letters began they were of no great significance.
But then, in February 1912, Miss Stanley accompanied Asquith, his
daughter, and Edwin Montagu on a Sicilian holiday. Thereafter
the letters became much more frequent. During the remainder
of that year Asquith wrote her seventeen substantial letters and nine
notes.[1]

At this stage Miss Stanley was 25—a young woman of high
intelligence and strong personality. She remained unmarried for another
three years, and then, with a sudden swoop, married one of the most
intimate of Asquith's political associates. During this period she was
the recipient of a mounting spate of letters. In 1913 Asquith sent her
about fifty letters. Then, during the early months of 1914 and on into
the early part of the war, the interchange became still more intensive.
From July of that year he rarely wrote less than once a day and
sometimes more often. This vast epistolary output, as it had become
by 1914, would for most men with anything like Asquith's responsibilities have been an impossible additional burden. For him this was
not so. The writing of the letters was both a solace and a relaxation,
interfering with his duties no more than did Lloyd George's hymn-
singing or Churchill's late-night conversation.

In addition, of course, he often saw Miss Stanley. On most Friday
afternoons, when they were both in London, he used to find time to
go for a motor drive with her—a fairly stately progress, seated behind
a chauffeur in his recently-acquired Napier, to Richmond or Roe-
hampton or Hampstead. They would sometimes meet at luncheon or
dinner or evening parties, and occasionally Asquith would pay an
early evening call on her at her parents' house in Mansfield Street.
Then Asquith would stay once or twice a year at one of Lord Sheffield's

[1] There are no records of letters from Miss Stanley to Asquith. No doubt
they were victims of his belief that most papers are better destroyed. But
the evidence suggests that she wrote almost, but not quite, as frequently as he
did.

country houses, Penrhôs, near Holyhead in Anglesey, or Alderley in Cheshire. And there would perhaps be another three or four week-ends when Miss Stanley would stay with the Asquiths. It was in the letters, however, that the relationship found its most regular and perhaps its most important expression. As a result their existence provides a remarkably close picture of his daily movements, of his immediate reaction to events, and of his uncensored opinion of those with whom he had to deal. For the three years beginning in mid-1912 they are far more informative about Asquith's life than any other source.

First, they show the geographical distribution of his time, how often he was able to be away from London, and where he went on these occasions. This is what happened between December, 1912 and the outbreak of the war. For Christmas of that year he went to Easton Grey, near Malmesbury, the house of his wife's sister, Mrs. Graham Smith. He left there on Boxing Day and motored, with his daughter Elizabeth—" an endless motor drive . . . in pouring rain "[1] to Lympne Castle, near Folkestone, to stay with another Tennant relation. After a few days at Lympne, Margot Asquith, who was not well, left for the South of France, and Asquith, with a day in London on the way, went to his own newly-acquired house at Sutton Courtney for the New Year. This house, the Wharf, a rambling and unpretentious collection of buildings on the river near Oxford, was to play a great part in the remainder of Asquith's life. Archerfield, the East Lothian house, had been given up after the long recess of 1911; and during that summer and the early part of the next one the Asquiths had spent a number of week-ends at Frank Lawson's house Ewelme Down, near Wallingford, and from there they had decided to acquier a North

---

[1] Although he complained on this occasion, Asquith was in general a most enthusiastic motorist—although always as a passenger. He usually preferred to do journeys of 100 miles or so by road, and he made no effort to avoid them—frequently going this distance for a 24-hour stay. Even when in the country he often liked to motor somewhere else, particularly if the weather was bad, and female companions were available. "It poured continuously for 48 hours, and we were reduced to motoring to Sir Sympne's (a private description of Sir John Simon) at Fritwell," he wrote after a wet week-end in early 1914. And three weeks later, after having the Churchills to stay, he wrote: " The weather was vile and we could not golf—only trundle about at a snail's pace (in deference to Clemmie's fears) in a shut-up motor."

Berkshire house of their own. They moved into the Wharf in July, 1912.

After his New Year visit there in 1913 Asquith went on to Alderley on January 3rd for a three-day week-end as the guest of Lord Sheffield. From January 6th onwards he was back in London, but he went away for each Saturday and Sunday during that month, twice to Easton Grey and once to Sandwich—where he golfed with two of his sons. Margot did not return from France until January 26th. Then, on the 28th, accompanied by his daughter Violet and his son Cyril, he went to his constituency and addressed " a really fine meeting at Leven without a single incident." Next day he spoke again at Dundee, and then, with Churchill, boarded the Admiralty yacht in the Tay and spent four days (including a storm-bound 24 hours) cruising south to Chatham. The next Saturday and Sunday he was at Sandwich again, and after that he spent almost every week-end up to and beyond Easter at the Wharf. His normal routine on these occasions was to leave London a little after noon on the Saturday, lunch at Skindles' hotel at Maidenhead, golf at Huntercombe, and motor on to Sutton Courtney in the early evening. On the Sunday he sometimes played golf again, but a more regular commitment was the entertainment of a large party of luncheon guests. Early on the Monday morning he would motor back to London.

On Friday, May 11th, the Whitsun holiday being early that year, he left for Venice by train. The next evening he again joined the Admiralty yacht, and with a larger party—both the Churchills, Margot, Violet, Edward Marsh and Masterton-Smith (another member of Churchill's staff)—set off on a three-week cruise to Dalmatia, Greece and Malta. It was an almost ideal holiday for Asquith. It enabled him to play bridge at night, to read a great deal at all hours, and to indulge his taste for minute classical scholarship.

" As you can imagine," he wrote off the coast of Albania, " it is a journey which affords endless opportunities for the conscientious student of Baedeker, and after nearly a week's experience I can assure you that you need not fear the rivalry of any of my present trip-fellows. Eddie and Masterton are both good at the Classical side, but neither of them has any notion of the unimportant things which it is right and fruitful to remember. Winston is, of course, quite hopeless: his most salient remark as we wandered thro' Diocletian's Palace at Spolato was: ' I should like to bombard the swine.'[1] Margot and Violet, as you know, do not excel in this branch of research, & Clemmie is very patchy."

Throughout the voyage the Prime Minister viewed Churchill with a mixture of amusement, admiration and mild apprehension. In the same letter from Albania he wrote: " It was with great difficulty that I prevented Winston from going himself to Scutari "—where an international naval action was forcing the Montenegrins to withdraw from their conquest—" to witness (if not preside over) the surrender of the town. I did not want another Sidney Street in Albania." And then from Malta he reported: " Winston never set foot on shore at Syracuse, but dictated in his cabin a treatise (which I am about to read) on the world's supplies of oil."

Asquith returned to London on May 31st. During June, July and the early part of August he spent most week-ends at the Wharf. On August 19th, he went north to Morayshire, where the family had rented a house called Hopeman Lodge. "I am agreeably surprised with this place," he wrote. "It is small and has practically no garden, but the house is quite comfortable, possessing no less than 4 bathrooms, and we look almost straight down into the sea, and across the Firth to the Caithness mountains, and have no neighbours. The sunset view is really very fine." He stayed there until September 26th. Lossiemouth was only a few miles away, and on this holiday he was able to substitute Ramsay MacDonald for Arthur Balfour as an occasional golfing companion. " Violet rather lost her heart to the brindle-haired Labour leader," he recorded after one of these encounters.

From Hopeman Asquith went to Arran to stay for three days with Percy Illingworth, who had replaced the Master of Elibank as Liberal Chief Whip. There he was collected by Churchill with the Admiralty yacht, and spent the inside of a week cruising round the north of Scotland. The party on board included the Secretary of State for War (Seely), Mrs. Churchill, and the wife of Winston's younger brother, Lady Gwendoline Churchill. One evening when they were anchored off Cromarty Sir Archibald Sinclair came to dinner on board and Asquith was unusually captivated by the charm of " one of the ' nicest ' young men I have met for a long time." " He is only 23," he added, " owns 100,000 acres or thereabouts, is in the 2nd Life Guards, and when in London flies every morning before breakfast. In addition he has good looks and manners, a slight but attractive

[1] But who were " the swine? "

stammer, and wears a kilt of a sober but striking pattern." The very model of a future Liberal leader, he might have added.

After leaving the yacht Asquith stayed the week-end of October 4th-5th with Jack Tennant at Edenglassie in Aberdeenshire, and then went to Balmoral for three days of duty. From October 10th to 20th he was back in London, although he escaped to the Wharf for one of the intervening Sundays. He then went to Scotland again, first for a brief renewal of the Hopeman holiday, where the party included Miss Stanley as well as his daughter Violet and his new private secretary, Maurice Bonham Carter,[1] and then for a one-day constituency visit and speech. The Hopeman party moved complete to East Fife.

Before the end of the month Asquith was back in Downing Street, and from then until a few days before Christmas he left London only for short but regular week-ends at the Wharf. On Saturday, December 20th, he went with Margot and several children to Easton Grey, and remained there, apart from a Tuesday visit to London, until the morning of Boxing Day. That night " the whole family " went to see *Charley's Aunt*, and on the following morning they separated. Margot took their son Puffin to Antibes, and Asquith motored with their daughter Elizabeth for another visit to Lympne Castle. After three days there he went to Alderley and stayed with the Stanleys over the New Year of 1914. On Friday, January 2nd, he returned to London with Edwin Montagu, " perched," as he put it, for a few hours writing letters at Montagu's house in Queen Anne's Gate, and then motored once more " in twilight and silence " to Lympne, where he remained for another week-end.

The week beginning January 5th he spent in London and the Saturday and Sunday at the end of it at Easton Grey. Then on Tuesday, January 13th, with his niece Laura Lovat as a travelling companion, he set off to visit Margot at Antibes. He found Lady Lovat " an agreeable and amusing partner" in what "was (technically) a very bad journey: a peculiarly ' dirty ' Channel crossing, the train held up by snow between Lyons and Marseilles (an unheard of thing), arrival here three hours late, and not a ray of sun to illuminate the Riviera in its unwonted garment of white." In this weather the four-day visit hardly justified the two twenty-four hour journeys. It was too wet for golf,

[1] 1880–1960. Asquith's secretary from 1910 to 1916. In December, 1915 he married Violet Asquith.

but the family went to the cinema in Cannes and there were some remarkable evening activities in the Hôtel du Cap:

At the small hotel soirée after dinner last night (Puffin[1]) " obliged " with a short discourse on Musical Composers, in which he passed in review Bach, Mozart, Scarlatti, Beethoven, Wagner, Grieg and some others, much to the delight and amazement of some 20 or 30 matrons and spinsters with a sprinkling of clergy and old gentlemen—all subjects of King George, as we acknowledged by a few bars of the National Anthem at the close of the proceedings.

After his return from Antibes Asquith settled down to a regular London régime for the remainder of the winter and the early spring of 1914. He had another week-end at Alderley at the end of January. In February he went to dine and sleep at Windsor. In March he spent a Saturday and Sunday at Easton Grey. And in April he paid a special two-day visit to his constituency.[2] For the rest he was at Downing Street, apart from short but fairly regular week-ends at the Wharf. Easter that year was in the middle of April, and he was then able to go to Sutton Courtney from Thursday to Tuesday.

From Easter until Whitsun the pattern continued as before. Only two week-ends were spent away from the Wharf, one in Sussex as the guest of Lord De La Warr, and the other with the King at Aldershot, in a Royal Pavilion which had been specially erected for a granu military review. For Whitsun Asquith went to Penrhôs, Lord Sheffield's house in Anglesey, and remained there until the following Saturday, when he motored by way of Shrewsbury and Stratford[3] to Nuneham Park, near Oxford, and stayed there, with " Lulu " Harcourt and a large party, until the Monday morning.

Thereafter there were seven remaining week-ends before the crisis one of August 2nd-3rd. Asquith spent five of them at the Wharf, one in London, and one on board the royal yacht, off Portsmouth, again with the King, but this time for a naval review. The last pre-war

---

[1] Then aged ten.

[2] See pp. 314-15, *infra*.

[3] At Stratford he recorded: " I got out of the motor and revisited the church with the Shakespeare bust and other relics. A typical Dickens verger came up and said " Have I the honour of addressing our distinguished Prime Minister? " I tried to shake him off with a gruff and uninviting affirmative, but he at once produced an autograph book. . . . "

week-end at the Wharf was typical enough, except for its rather abrupt end.

"I motored with Oc to Skindles where we met the McKennae," Asquith wrote of the Saturday, "and proceeded with them to Huntercombe to engage in a family foursome. I am glad to say that we beat them by 2 & 1: Pamela has certainly improved wonderfully, and did 2 or 3 quite excellent drives.

"There is no guest here so far except Montagu and Bongie (Bonham Carter) who arrived just in time for dinner—the former after playing tennis with Maxine Elliott, the latter after driving Violet to the Curries' in Wiltshire. The Somersets and Ottoline (Morrell) arrive some time today—just for the night. Elizabeth has gone to Holland for a week to stay with the Keppels at their place near The Hague. Between now & Tues. I have to think out something to say about the Amending Bill. . . . "

On the following day Asquith reported: "We had a fine Sunday and I played golf with Lady Kitty[1] (who is pretty good) in the afternoon." The Serbian crisis overhung the week-end, and Asquith already regarded it as " the most dangerous situation of the last 40 years." But when he hurriedly left the bridge table at eleven on the Sunday night and motored back to London with Bonham Carter, it was Ireland and not the Balkans which was the cause of his sudden decision; there had been shooting that afternoon at Howth. Asquith was back in Downing Street by 1.0 a.m. on the morning of July 27th. His peacetime pattern of life was effectively over. The following week-end there could be no question of leaving London.

This account of Asquith's movements during the eighteen months or so before August, 1914, can only give the barest impression of the content of his life. What was within the framework? His political duties apart, for they belong to other chapters, what occupied his time, whether in London, or at the Wharf, or as a guest in someone else's house? A large part of the answer is reading: the rapid, rather unplanned assimilation of the contents of a highly heterogeneous collection of books. He read for pleasure, particularly novels, but he also read in order to acquire information. He liked " useless knowledge," and he was a great setter of literary conundrums. At first, indeed, these figured prominently in his letters to Miss Stanley:

[1] Somerset.

> *Witty as Horatius Flaccus,*
> *Short, but not as fat, as Bacchus,*
> *As great a Jacobin as Gracchus,*
> *Riding on a little jackass,*

he wrote on April 20th, 1912. " Who of whom ? "

Perhaps Miss Stanley was not as good at solving them as he was at setting them, for they soon dropped out. But he retained a strong taste for conversation which was erudite without being ideological. " There was a nice old Papist don from Oxford staying in the house," he wrote after an Easton Grey week-end in the spring of 1914, "and I had good talks with him about the texts of Cicero and the Western mss. of the Gospels, and such like succulent topics." His literary conversation quite often took a simple competitive form. One of the attractions for him of men's dining clubs was that they provided partners (or victims) for the indulgence of this taste. " I was near Gosse," he wrote after a Grillion's evening much later in his life, " and had what I thought were two quite good scores off him. He didn't know the lines about the four Georges (Landor's) or Moore's about Lord Castlereagh."[a] And after another evening at the same club: " We had an unusually good company at Grillion's where I went to dinner last night—Baldwin, Archbishop of York, Austen Chamberlain, Fisher, Gosse, etc.—and had quite an excellent talk about books. I challenged them to produce a better twenty years of literary output in England than 1740 to 1760 in the despised eighteenth century."[b]

Asquith's pattern of reading, which helped to preserve his skill at these contests, was prompted by an eclectic and continuing intellectual curiosity. During a Lympne visit at the beginning of 1914 he " foraged " in the library and read Gosse's *Ibsen*, Fabre on spiders, and Dean Stanley's *Annals of Westminster Abbey*. A few weeks later he recorded: " I have been trying for some strange reason to read at nights a History of the Wars of the Roses . . . " On a Tuesday in March he spent " a quiet solitary afternoon reading a book by a Jew called Hirsch about the fortunes of his race in the Middle Ages." In July, a month which possessed not only the hidden quality of being the edge of the European precipice but also the overt one of continuing Irish crisis, he undertook some sustained philosophical reading including T. H. Green's *Prolegomena to Ethics* and two volumes of " Chamberlain's (the German) Kant, translated by old Redesdale who gave it

A.   265   12 to me the other day." He also read *Our Mutual Friend* as one of a number of Dickens novels which he had re-discovered that summer.

Occasionally Asquith's general reading occupied a whole evening after a quiet dinner in Downing Street, but more often it was fitted into an hour in the early evening, or a train journey or a late session in his bedroom. Whatever the time, he always read for at least an hour before going to bed, His social life was active, although not quite so *mondain* as Margot's reputation might lead one to suppose. Her great field was the luncheon party. Several days a week in London and most Sundays at the Wharf she would assemble a heterogeneous group for this meal. Particularly in London, Asquith took little part in the selection of guests. He often did not know who they were to be until he emerged from the Cabinet room to greet them. He regarded these parties as very much Margot's affair, but he usually participated, presiding over the table with a detached benignity which sometimes concealed boredom, but more often interest and amusement.

" We had the usual menagerie at lunch . . . " was his comment on March 11th, 1914. " We had a huge party . . . today," he wrote on April 22nd, " including Anne Islington,[1] Ottoline,[2] Crewe, John Burns & c—as incongruous a lot as even we have ever got together, since Pierpont Morgan sat between Frau[3] and Elizth." Strangely, perhaps, he did not come to take the incongruity for granted. " We had a curious lunch party even for us," he wrote on July 22nd, " —Cambon, Comte d'Haussonville, Chaliapine, Diana Manners, Lady Paget, Raymond, Mrs. Lyall, Count Kessler—were a few of the figures that I found seated at the table. I was rather pre-occupied and did not get much out of this rarely mixed lot." But July 22nd was a peculiarly worrying Irish day. Asquith's pre-occupation was not normally such that he could not give his mind to other things.

Nor did he regard a luncheon party as something which worked against the transaction of the day's business. When Margot was away he often went to some trouble to find guests of his own—although the result was usually a smaller and less variegated collection than she would have been likely to provide. " Are you coming to lunch

[1] Wife of Lord Islington, formerly Sir John Dickson Poynder, Governor of New Zealand, 1910-12.

[2] Lady Ottoline Morrell.

[3] The German governess.

tomorrow? " he wrote to Miss Stanley on January 16th, 1913. " You *must*. We have at any rate 3 poets—Yeats, De la Mare, and " AE " (Russell), and possibly another. Also the great impresario—E. M.[1]— & Birrell. It might be amusing." And on another occasion: " My luncheon party (improvised) was very *chic*: The Assyrian[2] (fresh from Seville) and my two fav. nieces Dinah and Kathleen."[3]

There were also occasional Downing Street dinner parties, but these were less frequent than the luncheon ones. Sometimes they were fairly large formal gatherings. " The guests have slowly disappeared from a regular Downing St. dinner," he wrote on December 8th, 1913. " No Masefields, but Sir E. Cassel, Mrs. Keppel, Murrays, Harcourts, Aubrey Herbert, & c. & c. Thank God, they are all now in their taxis, and I am alone." But more often they were small gatherings of close friends and relations, assembled at short notice and without much regard to even numbers or a balance of the sexes. Dinners of this sort were quite frequently the prelude to some other activity—a play (he would see perhaps six or eight a year) or an evening party at some other house.

Official dinners were mercifully rare in Asquith's life, and when one arose he usually greeted it with mild complaint, and escaped as soon as he could. " The Speaker's dinner was like such things generally are: neither better nor worse," he wrote on February 21st, 1914. " I sat between the host and Illingworth, and after dinner talked shop with Birrell and the Impeccable.[4] There was a *levée* later, but we got away by 10.30, and I went on with a party of gay and giddy youths[5] to the Silken Tent[6], where we played 2 or 3 rubbers of Bridge." A month later he wrote: " I have got to dine at 7 with the Chambers of Commerce: a foolish bit of good nature wh. has come home to roost." And a fortnight after that: " I am in for a rather dreary function tonight—a dinner here at the House of Scotch members given by McK. Wood."[7]

Apart from occasional special engagements like this last Asquith

[1] Edward Marsh.
[2] Edwin Montagu.
[3] Daughters of Margot's brother Frank Tennant.
[4] Asquith's name for Sir John Simon, then Attorney-General.
[5] In fact they were all members of the Government.
[6] Asquith's name for Edwin Montagu's house in Queen Anne's Gate.
[7] The Secretary of State for Scotland.

dined only rarely at the House of Commons. On one occasion indeed he expressed a forlorn surprise at finding himself there. " I find I have nowhere else to go...." he wrote. His speeches were mostly delivered at the beginning rather than the end of debates, and his votes (about which he was not in any event over-meticulous) could easily be delivered after dinner at Downing Street or some almost equally convenient address. In general he dined out, during the session, about five times a fortnight. One of these engagements would probably be at a dining club, and one of the others might be a men's dinner with some other minister or ministers; Grey, who did no mixed entertaining after his wife's death, quite often secured Asquith to dine with some visiting foreign dignitary. But the others would be ordinary social dinners. For the most part, however, they would be " scratch " gatherings of close friends rather than elaborately organised parties with a wide selection of guests. When Asquith was present on such a " grand " occasion, he usually commented with a mixture of surprise and mild distaste:

(11 January 1913) I dined last night at Mrs. Cavendish Bentinck's & played Bridge with Mrs. Ford and Mrs. Keppel: quite a worldly evening. I sat at dinner next Lady Ponsonby (Mrs. Fritz) who snubbed me most persistently: all out of temper, because her husband hadn't been made Govr. of Bombay. Aren't women wonderful?

(20 December 1913) I went to a large dull would-be fashionable dinner at Lady Paget's on Thursday night—Grand Duke Boris, Countess Torby, & the like. I didn't enjoy it, and can't conceive why I went. Yesterday by way of contrast Puffin and I spent the evening together *à deux* at the *Great Adventure*.

(27 February 1914) The Crewes' dinner last night was a big affair, and there were some beautiful ladies there, such as Lady Curzon. I did not fare badly in my partner as I took in Lady Pembroke, whom I had not met for 2 years. I rather like her refined slightly expressionless face, and she is not at all stupid. She is a strong Tory and lives among the worst types, but was kept from being too aggressive by a faint sense of humour to which I ministered all I could. My main energies however were taken up with the Queen who sat on my other side. There was not a subject under Heaven—dress, the Opera, sea-sickness, the suffragettes & c & c—which I didn't drag in by the scruff of its neck, & by the

end of dinner I was more exhausted than after a debate in the House. I played Bridge of a mild kind afterwards with Lady Kerry and Lady Selborne.

Much more usually he dined out (as he dined in Downing Street) with small parties of chosen political friends. To a remarkable extent his social life was organised around a few of the younger members of his Government. Montagu, treated in the correspondence as a figure of fun, but one to whom an almost obsessive attention was paid, was the most central. He was constantly staying at the Wharf and in and out of Downing Street; and Asquith would dine in " the silken tent "— or " the tents of Shem " in a variant of the same joke—twenty or more times a year. Then came the Churchills and the McKennas, with one or two minor figures, like Lord Lucas, the under-secretary for the Colonies and Harold Baker, the under-secretary for War, supporting the fringes. The Churchills were a frequent source of informal hospitality:

(18 June 1912) I am going to lunch on Friday with Winston and Clementine (at Eccn Sq.) *en petit comité*—for she is, as you know, out of action. Winston said he would ask you, which I thought an excellent idea. . . .

(13 December 1913) I dined last night at the Admiralty with the Winstons who keep curious company. . . . We had some Bridge, and Mrs. Keppel and I lightened the pockets of our host and hostess.

(5 February 1914) I dined at the Churchills' last night. Winston slept placidly in his armchair while I played Bridge with Clemmie, Goonie[1] and the Lord Chief Justice (Isaacs) being our antagonists. With some feeling of compunction I went home with £3 of Goonie's money in my pocket.

The McKennas also organised occasional small dinner parties for the Prime Minister, but not as often as the Churchills, although they were probably more frequently at Downing Street. Asquith sometimes testified to his social energy by summoning them at short notice when he found he had no other engagement:

(25 July 1914) As Margot was tired and in bed, I improvised a little dinner here, consisting of the 2 McKennae, Masterton Smith and myself. We played some really amusing Bridge. . . . Afterwards I went on with Pamela (McKenna) to supper at the

[1] Lady Gwendoline Churchill.

Assyrian's who had been doing an evening with his constituents in the company of Birrell. Their respective accounts of one another's speeches were quite entertaining. Violet and Bongie came in, but we did not stay late.

Another member of the Government who figured prominently in Asquith's social life at the time was Sir John Simon, Solicitor-General until the autumn of 1913, and then Attorney-General. But Asquith was always a little cynical about Simon. He was not so much a friend as a very frequently encountered acquaintance; and on one occasion after a series of such meetings Asquith concluded his list of those present at a club dinner with a slightly weary " and of course the Impeccable, who for these social purposes might almost be described as the Inevitable."

Of his near contemporaries in the Government, even those who were politically very close to him, Asquith saw much less. Grey and Crewe were the two members of the Cabinet upon whom he most depended. The Foreign Secretary was an old friend, of course, but although their relations were always perfectly agreeable they never visited each other's houses in the country during this period and their encounters in London were mostly semi-official. The same was true of Crewe. His wife (Rosebery's daughter), and less frequently he, sometimes lunched at Downing Street, but the Asquiths rarely dined with them, or *vice versa*, and then only upon the rather grand basis which Asquith described after his encounter with the Queen and Lady Pembroke in February 1914. Morley, Birrell and John Burns were all fairly regular Downing Street luncheon guests, and were all considerable favourites of Margot's. But they rarely appeared in the evenings and never themselves entertained the Asquiths. Their wives, for a variety of reasons, were hidden from public view, and would not have been likely, even had this not been the case, to make a particular appeal to the Prime Minister.

Asquith's other contemporary in the Cabinet—and his oldest friend of the lot—was Haldane. But during these immediate pre-war years social relations with him were slight. Throughout 1913 and the first seven months of 1914 there is no record of Haldane visiting the Wharf, or attending any meal in Downing Street, or securing (or even attempting to secure) Asquith for a meal at his own house in Queen Anne's Gate—only four doors away from the much visited Montagu residence. And on May 13, 1914, Asquith wrote: " Tonight we are giving a wedding dinner (20th anniversary) mostly to old *habitués* of Cavendish Square in its earliest days. Haldane excused himself on account of the death of a step-brother who had just passed away in the Shetlands at the ripe age of 80!"

There was one other Cabinet colleague of great note—Lloyd George. By virtue of his official residence at 11, Downing Street, he was the Prime Minister's nearest neighbour. But their social relations were not as close as their houses. They never met casually at one of the Liberal houses where Asquith was a frequent guest. In part this was because they had a different circle of friends. This was particularly so outside politics. Lloyd George had no knowledge of, or interest in, the smart cultivated world of Margot's luncheons and of the *jeunesse doré* whom the Asquith children (particularly Raymond) brought into their father's life. The Parsons, the Horners, the Listers, Diana Manners, would all have been very shadowy figures to him.

Even in politics the circles did not much overlap. Lloyd George was never on remotely intimate terms with Grey or Crewe or Haldane, and there was a deep mutual antipathy between him and McKenna. But he knew Churchill well,[1] and Montagu too, at least after February 1914, when "the Assyrian" became Financial Secretary to the Treasury. Yet he was never invited to Admiralty House or Queen Anne's Gate when Asquith was to be present.

Asquith himself assumed there was a certain restraint over their social relations. "I am going to dine with Lloyd George (a very unusual adventure)," he wrote to Miss Stanley on March 2, 1914, "to talk 'shop' with one or two choice colleagues (none I fear of your particular favourites)." Yet it was not in fact a particularly unusual adventure. He dined with Lloyd George on two other occasions in the next ten weeks, and the Chancellor lunched at No. 10 (with Edward Marsh and Lady Crewe) between the first and the second of these dinners. The restraint seems to have been more imaginary than real, with Asquith exchanging meals with Lloyd George more frequently

[1] Asquith wrote in March, 1914 of an evening when Morley, Birrell, Lloyd George and Churchill dined together, and "Winston in a rather maudlin mood said to Ll.G: 'A wonderful thing our friendship! For 10 years there has hardly been a day when we haven't had half an hour's talk together'." Birrell commented that they must both be awfully bored by that time.

than with either Crewe or Haldane; and in the whole of this part of his voluminous correspondence with Miss Stanley the Chancellor (frequently if distantly mentioned) attracted less than his fair share of astringent remarks.[1]

One social divide between Asquith and Lloyd George was that the Chancellor did not play bridge. Asquith's comments on his enjoyment, or otherwise, of various evening engagements show how fond he was of this game.[2] If there was no bridge he was a little inclined to sulk. It was one of his complaints about royal evenings. " We didn't play Bridge and I left fairly early this morning," he somewhat inconsequently wrote after his Windsor evening in February, 1914. And three months later, during his stay with the Court at the Aldershot Royal Pavilion, he recorded: " We had a lot of generals to dinner, but the evening was dull—no Bridge—& everybody went early to bed."

Yet to say he was an addict would be to use too strong a word. He rarely allowed one pursuit to interfere with his enjoyment of another. The chief impression of his private life which emerges from these years is of his extraordinary ability to fit in the widest possible range of activities. He even went to the opera, which he considerably disliked, two or three times a year. " I spent about 2 hours at the Opera . . . and tried to get some pleasure out of Boris, not with any very successful result I fear," he wrote on July 16th, 1914.[3] " There was a crowded house of fashionable people and others who seemed to be of a contrary opinion," he added.

Mostly, however, his time was more sensibly spent. He transacted his official business with great speed, but without any suggestion of neglect, and he left himself plenty of time for his family and his

[1] Nor were Lloyd George's occasional letters to Asquith in any way unfriendly. On December 28th, 1912 he wrote on the subject of a possible dissolution of Parliament, and after suggesting June, 1913, as a favourable month, concluded: " Wishing you as brilliant a New Year as the present has proved itself to be." (*Asquith Papers*, box XIII, ff. 110 1).

[2] Although, even in peace-time, strictly as an after-dinner pursuit (except perhaps for an occasional wet Sunday afternoon at the Wharf), readers of Mr. Robert Blake's *The Unknown Prime Minister* may care to note.

[3] Three years later he wrote of the Gilbert and Sullivan operas as being " almost the only form of music that has ever given me real pleasure." (*Letters from Lord Oxford to a Friend*, I, p. 19).

friends, for a wider but by no means undiscriminating social life, for golf and bridge, for general reading, and for private letter writing. As Prime Minister he probably lived a more agreeable life than he had ever done before, but his satisfactions were by no means exclusively those of power.

CHAPTER XVIII

THE IRISH IMBROGLIO I

1912-13

When drafting the third Home Rule Bill the Cabinet had one question of great difficulty to settle. Was the precedent of the two Gladstonian bills to be followed, and the whole of Ireland to be treated as a single unit? Or was Ulster, or at least a part of Ulster, to be excluded? Anything short of the first solution would be most unwelcome to the Nationalists. The degree of devolution they were offered was in itself mild enough. The Dublin parliament was to be so circumscribed in its powers as to be closer to a " glorified county council " than to a sovereign assembly.

Nevertheless its prospective powers were sufficient to provoke the Ulster Protestants to a paroxysm of hostility. In February, 1910, Sir Edward Carson, a Southern Irishman of Italian origin who sat for Dublin University and combined great personal charm, hypochondriacal neurasthenia, a huge law practice, and a strong taste for melodrama, had become leader of the Ulster Unionists. His choice as chief of the narrow, charmless, dour bigots of Belfast was almost as bizarre as that of Parnell, a generation before, as head of the Nationalists. And he was almost equally effective. In September, 1911, he responded to the new Home Rule prospect which had been opened up by the passage of the Parliament Act with the most extreme threat of resistance. " We must be prepared . . . the morning Home Rule is passed," he told a large audience at Craigavon, " ourselves to become responsible for the government of the Protestant Province of Ulster."

There were prominent members of the Cabinet who could not be insensitive to the Ulster problem. Churchill, never lacking in filial piety, was unlikely to forget that his father had responded to the first Home Rule Bill by announcing that " Ulster will fight and Ulster will be right."[1] And Lloyd George, closely in touch with the leaders of the

[1] The moral force, but not the electoral effectiveness, of Lord Randolph's

Free Churches, knew the political dangers of forcing unwilling Protestants under Catholic rule. The fact that Home Rule could be presented as "Rome Rule" was a much greater liability to the pre-1914 Liberals than it would be to any party in the Britain of today.

There was no likelihood of the Conservatives failing to exploit this—or any other promising line of attack. To many of them (although Bonar Law was a notable exception) the plight of the northern Protestants made little instinctive appeal. Balfour, and the whole Cecil connection, found the Ulstermen deeply antipathetic. Lord Hugh Cecil's one attempt to address an Orange rally was a dismal failure. Balfour himself avoided all such distasteful enterprises. His knowledge of Ireland was greater than that of any other Prime Minister of the last hundred years, but his interest was in trying to preserve the Union as a whole and not in salvaging an Ulster corner from the wreck. Lansdowne held the same views in a still more accentuated form. He was a Kerry landlord, and no concessions for Antrim or Armagh could ever have changed his attitude towards Home Rule. But they all quickly recognised that "the Orange Card" was the one to play. And they were prepared to play it with the utmost ruthlessness. The Conservatives of those days were sick with office hunger. Three successive electoral defeats had severely shaken their self-confidence. The lesser men amongst them became consumed by a mixture of hatred and jealousy for the long-lived Liberal Government. The intellectual blandness which was a characteristic of Asquith's leadership—and one copied from him by some of the other ministers—they found peculiarly irritating. The Liberals had established themselves as the natural mandarins of Whitehall, and the Conservatives had become the lesser-known, inexperienced men. When would it end? From the perspective of today it is easy to look back on the last pre-Great War years as the obvious swan song of the old Liberal Party. At the time it was much less obvious that the swan was going to die.

The epoch-barrier of August, 1914 could not be foreseen. If the next general election could be taken in the Liberals' own time, per-

---

slogan was however somewhat reduced when it became known (on the publication of his son's biography in 1906) that he had written a contemporary letter to James Fitzgibbon saying: "I decided some time ago that if the G.O.M. went for Home Rule the Orange Card would be the one to play. Please God it may turn out the ace of trumps and not the two."

haps in the spring of 1915, with a successful Irish settlement behind
them, who could be sure that they would not win again? Then the
Unionists would assume the appearance of a permanent opposition.
This was an eventuality which had to be prevented at all costs. Bonar
Law's leadership between 1912 and 1914 was in part an expression of an
almost " poor white " sense of inferiority,[1] and in part based upon
a deliberate tactic of using the Ulster issue to force the Government out
of office. " I am afraid I shall have to show myself very vicious, Mr.
Asquith, this session," Law said as they walked together in procession
to the House of Lords to listen to the King's Speech in February, 1912.
" I hope you will understand," he added, with the simplicity which
was one of his few engaging characteristics.

" I had no hesitation in reassuring him on that point," Asquith
recorded,[a] and by so doing gave a good example of his bland style.
But did he really understand just how " vicious " Bonar Law and the
other Unionists were prepared to be, not only in 1912, but in 1913 and
1914 as well? Did he realise the extent to which the Ulster struggle,
unlike that over the veto of the Lords, was to be carried on outside the
parliamentary arena?

In one sense it might seem that the Government had prepared
themselves well for trouble. They decided to present the Home Rule
Bill in a form which would be acceptable to the Nationalists, but to
leave a line of retreat if Ulster proved adamant. After a crucial
Cabinet meeting on February 6th, Asquith reported to the King that a
discussion had taken place as to whether the Ulster counties with large
Protestant majorities should be allowed to contract out of the Bill:

The subject was debated at great length and from a number of
diverse points of view. In the end the Cabinet acquiesced in the

---

[1] After 1910 the Conservatives also had a sense of being cheated by the
alliance between the Liberals and Redmond. The alliance was based on
Asquith's new commitment to carry Home Rule, and would have foundered
without it. This the Unionists persisted in regarding as a corrupt arrangement, although as the Liberals had for a generation regarded Home Rule as
part of their creed (if not always of their programme) it is difficult to see
where the corruption lay. The Unionists had worked themselves into a
peculiarly illogical position *vis-à-vis* the Irish. They were dedicated to
keeping them in the Imperial Parliament, while resentful that their votes
should count for anything there. But illogicality is rarely a bar to deep
feeling.

conclusions suggested by Lord Crewe and strongly recommended by the Prime Minister, *viz:*

(*a*) that the Bill as introduced should apply to the whole of Ireland;

(*b*) that the Irish leaders should from the first be given clearly to understand that the Government held themselves free to make such changes in the Bill as fresh evidence of facts, or the pressure of British opinion, may render expedient;

(*c*) that if, in the light of such evidence or indication of public opinion, it becomes clear as the Bill proceeds that some special treatment must be provided for the Ulster counties, the Government will be ready to recognise the necessity either by amendment of the Bill, or by not pressing it on under the provisions of the Parliament Act. In the meantime, careful and confidential inquiry is to be made as to the real extent and character of the Ulster resistance.[b]

The nature of the Government's " confidential inquiry " in Ulster has never been revealed, but all the public evidence which emerged from that province (or at least the north-east corner of it) pointed to a highly-organised but deep-rooted resistance. The English Unionists stoked up the agitation and made unprecedented offers of illegal support. F. E. Smith, who had been quite willing to throw over Ulster in the 1910 coalition negotiations, suddenly discovered that a birthday on the anniversary of the Battle of the Boyne, combined with his affiliations in Liverpool politics, made him an honorary Orangeman. He became Carson's principal henchman in Belfast. In September, 1912, he watched him, as the first of 471,444, so it was claimed, sign the " Solemn Covenant " in which the signatories individually pledged themselves never to recognise the authority of a Dublin Parliament; and in the following year he acted as his " galloper " at a review of 7,000 Ulster Volunteers. Throughout the agitation these two leaders of the English bar, both of whom were later to be Law Officers under Asquith, vied with each other in the calculated extremity of their language.

They could not go too far for the Orangemen. There was never any sign that the merchants, manufacturers and ministers of religion of Belfast and the surrounding counties, or their followers, ever found these English lawyers too extreme and irresponsible for their taste. Ulster may have been " a business community, desiring rest," as Carson once put it to Asquith. But the Orangemen were fanatics before they were businessmen. Nor were Carson and Smith ever in much danger of going too far for Bonar Law. The new leader's golden rule was to be as unlike Balfour as possible. He never attempted to steer a course inside that of his more extreme followers. He looked always, at this stage, to his reputation *inside* and not *outside* the Unionist Party. As a result he fully kept his promise to be " very vicious " that session. He denounced the Government for being as corrupt as it was revolutionary. He talked of its Irish policy as being ' a conspiracy as treacherous as ever has been formed against the life of a great nation." He accused Asquith, across the table of the House of Commons, of not even having any convictions to sell, and at Edinburgh of a crime against the Crown greater " than has ever been committed by any minister who had ever held power."

From behind the sad eyes of Bonar Law the tide of quiet violence poured out. Its first high-water mark came at Blenheim on July 29th, 1912. There, before a gathering of 15,000 Unionist stalwarts, who were also addressed by Carson and Smith, he announced:

I can imagine no length of resistance to which Ulster can go in which I should not be prepared to support them, and in which, in my belief, they would not be supported by the overwhelming majority of the British people.[c]

Nor was there any length to which Bonar Law was not prepared to go to get the Government out. One night in May, after dinner at Buckingham Palace, he told the King:

Your only chance is that they (the Government) should resign within two years. If they don't, you must either accept the Home Rule Bill, or dismiss your Ministers and choose others who will support you in vetoing it: and in either case, half your subjects will think you have acted against them. . . . They may say that your Assent is a purely formal act and the prerogative of veto is dead. That was true as long as there was a buffer[1] between you and the House of Commons, but they have destroyed this buffer and it is true no longer.[d]

During the first parliamentary circuit[2] of the Home Rule Bill,

[1] By this he meant the pre-Parliament Act House of Lords.

[2] This lasted from April 11th, 1912 to January 30th, 1913. A laborious committee stage occupied much of the summer and autumn. Then, on January 16th, the House of Commons gave the bill a third reading by a majority of 109. A fortnight later it was thrown out on second reading by

therefore, Asquith was not without warning that a crisis of unprecedented difficulty was building up over Ulster. But neither during that circuit nor during the second, much shorter one[1] did he make a firm move for a negotiated settlement along the lines of the Cabinet letter of February 6th, 1912. The fact that he neither did this, nor deployed the full force of the criminal law against those who sent seditious threats echoing from Belfast to Blenheim and back again has often been made the chief count against his peace-time leadership.

Yet it is easy to see why he took no precipitate action. In politics he was never a restless man. The whole technique of his statesmanship was to watch events calmly until he saw an opportunity for effective intervention. " A sudden curve developed of which I took immediate advantage," was his typical description, previously quoted,[2] of how he solved the Cabinet naval crisis of 1909. In Irish affairs, no such curve showed itself during 1912 and 1913. It was unlikely to do so. The Parliament Act procedure put a premium on delay. The first two circuits were dummy runs. Why should anyone settle until they saw what the disposition of the forces was likely to be when it came to the final confrontation?

Independently of Asquith's character, this was the position of both sides at this stage in the dispute. The Nationalists and many of the Liberal back-benchers would not countenance the division of Ireland until they were convinced that this was the only way to avoid civil war. There was no reason why they should. There was a great case, economic, administrative and mystical, for a united Ireland. Asquith himself felt the force of it. " . . . Ireland is a nation, not two nations, but one nation," he said in Dublin in July, 1912. But even had he not done so, and even if he could have persuaded all the Liberal back-benchers

---

the Lords by a vote of 326 to 69. In this and in the two subsequent sessions the Welsh Church Disestablishment Bill followed an almost exactly parallel course.

[1] This lasted only from March to July, 1913. This time there were no committee stages for either the Home Rule or the Welsh Church Bills. As a result they went through the House of Commons, to use one of Asquith's favourite phrases, " on oiled castors." But this did nothing to reduce the force with which they again hit the wall of House of Lords opposition. The Irish Bill was rejected by 302 to 64 on July 15th, and the Welsh one by 243 to 48 on July 22nd.

[2] See p. 195, *supra*.

to fall easily into line, there would still have remained the problem of the Nationalists. For them to have abandoned any part of the country at the first whiff of braggadocio from Craigavon would have been political suicide. And with Redmond against him Asquith had no parliamentary majority. There was nothing discreditable in recognising this fact. So long as the Irish were in the Imperial Parliament their votes were as good as anybody else's and they were fully entitled to every scrap of influence which they could extract from them.

Of course Redmond in the last resort was most unlikely to put Asquith out. This would have meant a Unionist Government and the end of Home Rule of any sort for another decade. The real danger was not what Redmond might do, but the support which he would lose in Ireland as a result of the accommodations forced upon him. Throughout the Ulster crisis the Unionists and (less excusably) the King constantly spoke of Redmond as a rock of unreasonable recalcitrance. But the perspective of history leaves no room for doubt that, on the contrary, this agreeable and slightly weary parliamentarian was far too amenable to Asquith to be a true representative of feeling in his country.

Even within his parliamentary group there were several tougher spirits, notably Devlin, who as an Ulsterman himself was particularly strong against exclusion. Still more important were the new forces in Ireland which were beginning to arise under the Irish Parliamentary party and which eventually cut it off from any real contact with its constituency. Arthur Griffith's Sinn Fein, Patric Pearse's Irish Republican Brotherhood and James Larkin's Irish Citizen Army were all equally inimical, in the long run, to the constitutional leadership of Irish Nationalism and the acceptance of limited Home Rule. Asquith, in 1913 and 1914, saw their significance even less clearly than did Redmond. He continued to regard the Irish parliamentary leader as possessing a Parnell-like hold on the country. But can it possibly be held that Asquith would have shown greater statesmanship had he further undermined Redmond's position by a more brutal and rapid extraction of concessions?

The " Agar-Robartes amendment " is often regarded as a great missed opportunity. This was proposed in June, 1912, by the Liberal member for the St. Austell division of Cornwall and provided for the complete exclusion from the bill of the four clearly Protestant counties of Antrim, Armagh, Londonderry and Down. It involved permanent partition, and as such could not possibly have been accepted by the Nationalists. It was also opposed by the Government spokesmen. But had it been supported by them, it would not have satisfied the opposition. At all stages the Unionists insisted on the exclusion of the mixed counties of Tyrone and Fermanagh. At that stage they were demanding the exclusion of the whole of Ulster, including the Catholic counties of Cavan, Monaghan and Donegal.

Still more important is the fact that no arrangement for exclusion, however extensive it had been, would in 1912 have destroyed the opposition to Home Rule. Half of the English Unionists were in reality much more interested in Dublin than in Belfast. They were merely " playing the Orange card." Even the other half, represented by Bonar Law, although genuinely concerned with Ulster, were still more concerned with smashing the Liberal Government. A victory without a fight would not have satisfied them. They would have swallowed the concession as though it were nothing and looked for a fresh battleground. The Nationalists would have been disaffected without the conciliation of the Unionists. There was no sign of a favourable " curve " developing, a prior condition for which had to be such a concentration of Unionist opposition upon the Ulster issue that, if it were removed, there could be no effective re-grouping of forces against other aspects of the bill. This did not occur until sometime in the course of 1913.

It is therefore unlikely that Asquith would have achieved more by an earlier attempt at an Ulster settlement. Ought he then to have moved in the other direction and arrested those who were openly preaching sedition in Belfast? One difficulty here, not perhaps inspiring in principle but real in practice, was the position of the men involved. The Government could not move against any local firebrand without moving against Carson and Smith. And it would have been almost equally difficult to draw a line between them and Bonar Law; the Unionist leader never allowed himself to be outbid in sedition.

To lock up the leaders of the opposition would have been a bold stroke for any government. For Asquith it would have been a fatal one. It would have undermined the whole position he was trying to maintain. The House of Commons was the one battleground on which the Liberals always won. It was therefore in their interests to pretend that it was the only one which counted. " I tell you quite frankly that I do not believe in the prospect of civil war " Asquith said at Dublin.

When it came to the issue, he argued, British subjects would not stand against " the supreme authority of the Imperial Parliament." But the Unionists were tired of an arena in which they always lost. They were only too anxious to appeal to some other authority—to the Lords, to the King, to the streets of Belfast. During 1913 Bonar Law played with alternative ideas of a mass Unionist withdrawal from Parliament and of provoking such constant disorder as to bring its proceedings to a standstill. The arrest of himself or any other Unionist leaders would have given him the perfect excuse for one or other of these courses. Furthermore the effect upon the King and the army, both a little wobbly in any event, would have been catastrophic. Asquith's stand was on the inviolability of the parliamentary system. To maintain this stand he had to pretend that the system was working normally, even if it was not—and this meant that, whatever they did, he could ot lock up his principal opponents.

Asquith's relative inactivity on Ireland during the sessions of 1912 and 1913 therefore had more to commend it than is commonly allowed. Additional action beyond the trundling of the Bill round its first two parliamentary circuits might easily have made matters worse. Furthermore, for a Government which appeared to be beset on all sides—Ireland, strikes, the Marconi scandal, the threatening international situation, the suffragettes—and which faced a constant series of parliamentary crises, a certain massive calmness on the part of its head was by no means a negligible asset. At one time the Speaker was threatening to resign; at another the air was thick with rumours that the King wanted to abdicate; and at most times Augustine Birrell the Chief Secretary, thought that he had better vacate the Irish Office. Had Asquith been a restless political genius he might have struck out at the problem, with a faint chance of solving it; but had he been a lesser man than he was he might easily have lost his nerve and begun himself to indulge in petulant and self-pitying resignation talk. Instead he remained calm, detached and mildly optimistic. When confronted with apparently insoluble crises he consoled himself with his " fixed belief," as he wrote to Miss Stanley, " that in politics the expected rarely happens."

The King was less phlegmatic than Asquith. Throughout the spring and summer months of 1913 he received a spate of constitutional complaint and advice from Unionist leaders, elder statesmen and anonymous correspondents. " The one man," Sir Harold Nicolson comments, " who . . . had never even alluded to the subject was the Prime Minister himself."*e* All this made the King extremely agitated. On July 24th he saw Birrell and pointed out " that apparently the Government were " drifting " and that with this " drift " his own position was becoming more and more difficult."*f1* He then asked Stamford-ham[2] to find out the views of the opposition leaders. As a result he received on July 31st a memorandum jointly composed by Bonar Law and Lansdowne. Armed with this, he retired to the royal yacht off Cowes, and wrote in his own hand a 400 word document for the Prime Minister. This he handed to Asquith at a specially arranged audience on August 11th. It outlined all his fears about the effect of the Ulster situation upon the Crown and showed that Bonar Law's harsh words of the previous summer had fixed themselves in his mind:

Whatever I do I shall offend half the population.

One alternative would certainly result in alienating the Ulster Protestants from me, and whatever happens the result must be detrimental to me personally and to the Crown in general.

No Sovereign has ever been in such a position . . . .*g*

The King suggested an all-party conference to see whether a settlement by consent might be possible. Asquith took the memorandum away with him, having been asked to compose a considered reply. This he did during his Morayshire holiday, which started a few days later. It was in two parts. The first dealt with the general constitutional position of the Sovereign, and was a document of exceptional clarity and force.[3] The right of the Crown to withhold its assent from a bill which had received parliamentary sanction had died early in the reign of Queen Anne, he stated. " We have had, since that date, Sovereigns of marked individuality, of great authority, and of strong ideas (often,

---

[1] Birrell's own account of this interview, written for Asquith, contained the following sentence: " He (the King) left on my mind the clear impression that he was being pressed to entertain the idea, though not able quite to see how it could safely be done, of forcing a dissolution next year. He has been told that the Home Rule feeling (outside Ulster) is not really strong—that it is dying out and that all the people really want is more money and continued prosperity." (*Asquith Papers*, Box 38, 109–13).

[2] The title taken by Sir Arthur Bigge in 1911.

[3] Both parts of Asquith's paper are reproduced in full in Spender and Asquith, II, pp. 29–34. For that reason they are only summarised in this chapter, but are reprinted in appendix B (see p. 541 *infra*).

from time to time, opposed to the policy of the Ministry of the day) but none of them—not even George III, Queen Victoria or King Edward VII—have ever dreamt of reviving the ancient veto of the Crown."

As for the right of the sovereign to dismiss his ministers, that perhaps still existed, but it was worth recalling what happened when it was last exercised.

This was in 1834, when William IV (one of the least wise of British monarchs) called upon Lord Melbourne to resign. He took advantage (as we now know) of a hint improvidentially given by Lord Melbourne himself, but the proceedings were neither well-advised nor fortunate. The dissolution which followed left Sir R. Peel in a minority, and Lord Melbourne and his friends in a few months returned to power, which they held for the next six years. The authority of the Crown was disparaged, and Queen Victoria, during her long reign, was careful never to repeat the mistake of her predecessor.

The Parliament Act had in no way changed the position. It dealt only with the relations between the two Houses. The only way for the Crown to keep clear of politics, Asquith sternly concluded, was for it to follow the constitutional precedents. Otherwise it would become " the football of contending factions."

Asquith's second memorandum dealt with his view of the Irish situation. When the Home Rule Bill became law there was " the certainty of tumult and riot, and more than the possibility of bloodshed " in Ulster. But to speak " of what is likely to happen as Civil War," was, in his opinion, " a misuse of terms." If, on the other hand, the Bill failed to become law, the prospect " was much more grave." " It is not too much to say that Ireland would become ungovernable— unless by the application of forces and methods which would offend the conscience of Great Britain, and arouse the deepest resentment of all the self-governing Dominions of the Crown." A general election before the Bill became law would settle nothing. If the Government won, the Ulster trouble would persist. If it lost, the problem of governing Ireland as a whole would become no easier. Furthermore, the acquiescence in the demand for an election at that stage would make a mockery of the purpose of the Parliament Act.

Was there a prospect of settlement by conference? Only, Asquith thought, if there was " some definite basis upon and from which its deliberations can proceed." This basis must be the acceptance by the Unionists of the principle of Irish Home Rule. Once that was done he was ready to consider "any reasonable suggestion" for the problem of Ulster. But until it was done there was "a chasm of principle" which no conference could bridge. "I fear that at present (it may be different nearer the time)," he added, "no such basis can be found."

The King received these papers at Balmoral in two instalments, one in the second and one in the third week of September. He replied on the 22nd of the month with a 1500 word typewritten letter, which one may guess was a joint product of himself and Stamfordham. The tone was courteous, painstaking and worried. But the substance was highly argumentative. He set himself to contest most of Asquith's points. He quoted both Bagehot and Erskine May to suggest that the Sovereign did have some residual right to dismiss his advisers or to dissolve Parliament on his own initiative. He suggested strongly that the Parliament Act did make a difference. He argued in favour of a general election before the Bill became law. And he showed clearly how deeply he was influenced by the Tory case against Home Rule as such:

But is the demand for Home Rule for Ireland as earnest and as National today as it was, for instance, in the days of Parnell?

Has not the Land Purchase Policy settled the agrarian trouble, which was the chief motive of the Home Rule agitation?

I am assured by resident Landowners in the South and West of Ireland that their tenants, while ostensibly favourable to Home Rule, are no longer enthusiastic about it, and are, comparatively speaking, content and well-to-do.

The hierarchy of the Church of Rome is indifferent and probably at heart would be glad not to come under the power of an Irish Parliament.[h]

Worse still, he raised a new point not touched upon in Asquith's memoranda. What would happen when there occurred the "tumult and riot" which Asquith himself had predicted?

Do you propose to employ the Army to suppress such disorders? This is, to my mind, one of the most serious questions which the Government will have to decide. In doing so you will, I am sure, bear in mind that ours is a voluntary Army; and Soldiers are none the less Citizens; by birth, religion and environment they may have strong feelings on the Irish question. . . . Will it be wise, will it be fair to the Sovereign as head of the Army, to subject the discipline, and indeed the loyalty of his troops, to such a strain?*i*

Altogether this was a formidable letter for a Prime Minister, at a time of mounting crisis, to receive from the Sovereign. Asquith replied on October 1st. He reiterated one or two of his constitutional statements and commented rather sharply on the King's point about the army: " There is, in my opinion, no sufficient ground for the fears—or hopes—expressed in some quarters, that the troops would fail to do their duty."*j* Within a week he was due to go to Balmoral and he was holding some of his fire.

Asquith's three days at Balmoral was one of a series of political visits which the King had organised for that autumn. As Crewe, who was one of the first guests, put it to Asquith: " He is ... haunted ... by the feeling that if he does not take off his coat and work for a settlement of some kind, and there is serious loss of life after the Bill passes, he will not only be held responsible by Opposition partisans, but will actually be so to some extent."*k*[1] Later in the month Crewe was succeeded by Churchill as minister in attendance, and this visit overlapped with one by Bonar Law. The two visitors had a long talk together, which was reported by Churchill to Asquith and by Bonar Law to Lansdowne and Carson. There was no direct contradiction between these accounts, but Churchill's implied a less cautious conversation than did Bonar Law's. Law summed up his attitude by writing to Carson: " The whole question as to the exclusion of Ulster really turns upon this—whether or not it would be regarded as a betrayal by the solid body of Unionists in the South and West."*l* But Churchill spoke of " the spirit of courage and goodwill " with which Bonar Law had expressed his desire for a settlement; of his desire first for secret meetings between one or two on each side and then for a regular conference; and of the possibility that this might even lead to a revival of the old 1910 coalition scheme. As a result of this " remarkable conversation " Churchill was swept along by a wave of enthusiasm for a conference and for compromise. He reminded Asquith how he and Lloyd George had originally pressed the exclusion of Ulster upon the

[1] Crewe also wrote that " the King was sedulous, even in talking to me very intimately, to express no opinion against Home Rule; ' it might be a very good thing ' and anyhow ' some form of it is evidently now necessary, as a majority in Parliament favours it '." (*Asquith Papers*, box 38, ff. 126–7).

Cabinet and how "Loreburn (had) repulsed us in the most blood-thirsty manner."[1]

For the moment Churchill could see moderation in everyone, and four days later he wrote again to Asquith:

I have been agreeably surprised by the character of my talks with the King. He is of course all for a conference and for a settlement on the basis of excluding Ulster for a time. But I found him more reasonable and able to see both sides on the Irish question than on others I have sometimes discussed with him: and nothing in his conversation gives the slightest countenance to an unconstitutional intervention by the Crown.[m]

The next report which Asquith received from Balmoral came from Birrell on October 3rd:

There is a considerable change ... in the constitutional atmos-phere, so I think your efforts have had a bracing effect and got rid of some dangerous matter. . . . When I first came it was all conference. . . .[n]

Even so, it was obvious to Asquith that the time had come when he should try to talk to the Unionist leaders. Even if agreement proved impossible (and he was much less sanguine than Churchill) it was important to show the King, and even some members of the Cabinet, that he had at least tried. Accordingly, he wrote from Balmoral on October 8th:

Dear Mr. Bonar Law,

Churchill has reported to me the substance of a conversation he had with you here last month.

You will probably agree with me that anything in the nature of a " Conference " (as proposed for instance by Lord Loreburn) between the leaders of parties is under existing conditions out of the question, whatever may be the case hereafter.

I understand, however, the suggestion thrown out by you to

[1] This was a thrust calculated to win Asquith's sympathy. Loreburn (formerly Sir Robert Reid) had been Lord Chancellor when the Bill was being drafted. He had left the Government in June, 1912, and fifteen months later, with a typical elder statesman's show of non-partisan wisdom, he had embarrassed and irritated his former colleagues by writing to *The Times* to propound exactly the solution which he had so strongly opposed from inside.

Churchill to be that an informal conversation of a strictly confidential character between yourself and myself—with perhaps another colleague on either side—might be useful as a first step towards the possible avoidance of danger to the State, which all responsible statesmen must be equally anxious to avert.

I write, therefore, to say that (if you are still in the same mind) I should be happy to take part without delay in a conversation so conditioned.

I shall be back in London on Friday night and shall remain there for the best part of a week. Perhaps you would kindly address your reply to Downing Street.

Yours very truly,

H. H. Asquith[o]

The coolness of tone was accounted for by the fact that Asquith hardly knew Bonar Law, and had no great liking for what he knew. The caution of the proposal (combined with a determination to pin upon Law the responsibility for the initiative) arose from Asquith's conviction that any compromise plan must be suggested by the opposition and not by himself. The Government's bill, supported by a majority in the House of Commons, was on the table. It was not for him to tell the opposition what he would give them for threatening to break the law—particularly as he thought they would always ask for more. But if the opposition chose to state what provisions, within a general Home Rule framework, would meet the Ulster problem, that was a different matter. This fencing to avoid the initiative was an important factor in the negotiations of the next few months.

Bonar Law, after consulting Lansdowne, agreed to the meeting and suggested Cherkley Court, " the house of a friend of mine, Sir Max Aitken " as an appropriate rendezvous. " It is about an hour by motor from London," he added, " it is quite isolated and the only risk of publicity would be through the servants which in this case would not be great."[p] Asquith agreed to the arrangement, and after luncheon on Wednesday, October 14th, he drove out to meet the leader of the opposition. " He arrived," so Mr. Robert Blake informs us, " to find Bonar Law, characteristically, engaged in a game of double dummy with his host—the need for secrecy precluding a four."[q]

Unlike Bonar Law himself on a later and equally famous (but probably more apocryphal) occasion Asquith showed neither surprise nor annoyance at this frivolous exhibition.[1] Instead, motivated by a mixture of shyness and good manners, he plunged into almost anecdotal talk. " I had a conversation with Mr. Asquith which lasted for about an hour," Bonar Law severely recorded. " The conversation was very frank, but the larger part of it quite irrelevant, dealing, for instance, with personalities in the House of Commons and general subjects of that kind. . . . "[r]

The substance of the interview was recorded by Asquith in some pencilled notes written on the following day. They do not differ greatly from Bonar Law's account, except that this included a long discussion about a general election which did not figure at all in the Prime Minister's document. Asquith found Bonar Law more sympathetic in private than he had done in public. The Unionist leader was obviously frank: he admitted to doubts about his extreme commitment to Carson; he said that most of the English Conservatives cared more about preserving the Welsh Establishment than about the Home Rule issue; and he made no attempt to conceal the electoral importance to him of " the Orange card "—without it he thought the Unionists would lose again. He stressed his trouble with the " ex-diehards " on the one hand, and his difficulties with Lansdowne on the other. Law's sadly pessimistic outlook rather cheered Asquith. He felt a new magnanimity towards him. The difficulties of the Unionist leader were so enormous that Asquith became relatively encouraged about his own position. According to Law's account, he even indulged in some comforting reflections about his strength *vis-à-vis* the Irish Nationalists.

Nothing very concrete emerged from this meeting. Asquith understood (for the first time) that Bonar Law would accept Home

---

[1] On June 12th, 1916, again according to Mr. Blake, Bonar Law went to see Asquith at the Wharf and found him " engaged in a rubber of bridge with three ladies." Law was " considerably annoyed " and " the episode left a lasting impression upon his mind." Lady Violet Bonham Carter has deployed formidable arguments against this incident ever taking place. But even in the unlikely event that it did, it is not clear why Bonar Law should have been so shocked. If it was " characteristic " for a leader of the opposition to play cards on the afternoon of a working Wednesday in October, in the midst of a ferocious Irish crisis, why should a Prime Minister not do so on a Whitsun Monday morning (for that is what June 12th was), even in wartime? But perhaps the difference lay in the choice of fellow-players. Lord Beaverbrook was all right, but not " three ladies."

Rule with an Ulster exclusion provided that Lansdowne as the spokesman of the "loyalists" of the South and West did not protest too
strongly. But "Ulster" was not defined, although the difficulties of
definition were touched upon and recognised by both sides. There was
no discussion about the permanency or otherwise of exclusion. "We
had a good deal of more general and informal conversation," Asquith
concluded, "and in the end I said that after reflection and consideration
I would communicate with him again."[8]

Asquith's next meeting with Bonar Law was on November 6th,
again at Cherkley. As on the previous occasion, he afterwards made a
pencilled note. The impression given is that, so far from there being a
steady move towards agreement, the previous meeting might never
have taken place; both leaders spent much of the time traversing
familiar ground, often repeating themselves, occasionally contradicting
themselves, but never showing much awareness that they had been
there before:

I saw and talked with B.L. for best part of an hour.

We agreed that on both sides—his and mine—opinion was
stiffening among the rank and file, and that the idea of compromise
and even conference, was regarded with growing disfavour and
suspicion.

We discussed (without prejudice) the suggestion of a general
election before the next session of Parliament opens. I gave my
reasons for holding that—if an agreed settlement of the Irish
question was to be desired—such a procedure was the most dangerous expedient that could be risked.... He said ... that unless
(of which he saw no prospect) there was a sweeping swing of the
electoral pendulum in favour of his side, the best that could be
hoped ... would be such a comparatively balanced state of
parties as would make compromise inevitable. I rejoined that ...
it would (in such an event), after all the bad blood of an embittered
election, be more difficult than now.

I said that I was no more a plenipotentiary than he was; that
I was not even a bearer of proposals: that I might, probably,
be able to carry my own Cabinet and Party with me, in any form
of settlement that in the end I deliberately pressed upon them;
but that I could not (in their present and prospective temper)
answer even for that, and still less for the Irish Nationalists, whose
leaders, of the old guard, had hanging on their flank and rear the

new and bolder spirits of which Devlin is the type. I added that I had no doubt he was in similar difficulties. He replied frankly that he was not sure that his were not even greater; he had to reckon not only with Carsonism (not Carson himself), but with a probable revival of a " diehard " movement among the English Unionists.

These reservations having been duly made, I said we might proceed on the hypothetical basis that a Home Rule Parliament and Executive was to be set up in Dublin for Ireland, *minus* an area to be at least temporarily excluded which might provisionally be called " Ulster "—the actual definition of Ulster for this purpose being for the moment postponed.

How was it suggested that this area should be dealt with? (1) As regards legislation. (2) As regards administration and finance. He dismissed as unacceptable all schemes for giving it a local legislature and executive of its own.

(1) As regards Legislation. This, he said, must remain with the Imperial Parliament. The Ulster men could not (without sacrificing their root principle) recognise any other *law-making* power. At this point we discussed the question of the conditions of exclusion. His view was that the excluded area should have the option (*as a whole*) of voting by plebiscite, after the expiration of a prescribed time, for inclusion. (He repudiated immediate inclusion with an option of exemption.)

(2) As regards Administration and Finance. I pointed out that in respect of Land and Police there was no difficulty, as under the Home Rule Bill these are reserved services which remain, at any rate for a time, in the hands of the Imperial Executive. . . . He said that the dropping of the proposed Irish Post Office (which under the plan of exclusion would be something of an absurdity) would give great satisfaction to Unionists. I said I had never attached the least importance to the postal provisions in the Bill.

We then came to the question of the geographical definition of the excluded area. He said that Carson would stand out in the first instance for the whole province of Ulster. I urged that this was quite out of the question: in three counties, (Donegal, Monaghan and Cavan) the Nationalists were in an overwhelming preponderance, and in two more (Tyrone and Fermanagh) there was a fairly even balance—Protestants being to Catholics in the proportion of about 6 to 5. As to the three first-mentioned he agreed that they could not be separated from the rest of Ireland. But he was disposed to insist on Tyrone and Fermanagh. . . .

We agreed that any settlement come to must be acquiesced in by both parties in the State at least until it had had a fair trial. . . .

In the end I said that I would report the substance of our conversation to my colleagues in the Cabinet next Tuesday, and if they approved of the matter going on, confidential steps might be taken by Mr. Birrell to sound the Nationalists leaders. We parted in good will but in no very sanguine spirit.

H.H.A.[t]

The extracts from Bonar Law's account of this second conversation which are quoted by Mr. Robert Blake are in fairly close harmony with this record of Asquith's. But there was an important divergence on one point. Bonar Law thought that Asquith had entered into a definite commitment to urge upon the Cabinet, and then upon the Nationalists, an exclusion scheme with the conditions that he (Bonar Law) had outlined. Asquith thought much more in terms of reporting the bargaining possibilities to the Cabinet, and taking their advice on the next step. As a result of this misunderstanding, according to Mr. Blake, Bonar Law believed henceforward that Asquith " had broken his word to him."[u] Unless he wanted an excuse for distrusting Asquith, it is difficult to see why he should have felt so affronted. On November 7th he wrote to Walter Long, and his letter made clear both that his desires were mixed and that he regarded his own course as determined, not by a Cherkley commitment, but by objective considerations.

" From a party point of view," he wrote, " I hope the Nationalists will not agree, for, if they do, I am afraid that our best card for the Election will have been lost. On the other hand if he (Asquith) makes us a definite proposal on these lines I don't see that we could possibly take the responsibility for refusing."[v]

If Bonar Law was free after Cherkley, surely Asquith was too? There seems no reason to think that he let down Bonar Law; yet it cannot be denied that he made little attempt to drive on towards a settlement. The Cabinet met on Tuesday, November 12th, to hear the Prime Minister's report, and again on the Wednesday to consider what should be done. After the second meeting Asquith reported to the King:

All the Cabinet were agreed that the temper of the party outside was strongly and growingly opposed to any form of compromise, largely, no doubt, because the rank and file wholly disbelieve in the reality of the Ulster threats. Apart from this, the difficulties of the situation were well illustrated by two observations of Ministers who are specially well acquainted with the Irish problem: The one (Mr. Birrell's) that the exclusion of Ulster, in whole or in part, is universally opposed by all sections of Irish opinion as a bad and unworkable expedient: the other (Lord Morley's) that to start Home Rule with a baptism of bloodshed would be fatal to its prospects.

Mr. Samuel suggested a plan. . . . which would give to the Ulster members in the Irish Parliament, for a time at any rate, a veto on legislation (including taxation) affecting Ulster. This was rejected by the Cabinet with practical unanimity: it would give satisfaction to neither party and would create the maximum of friction.

The Chancellor of the Exchequer proposed, as a basis of possible compromise, but still more as the best means of avoiding armed resistance, the exclusion of Ulster (i.e. of the Protestant counties) for a definite term of five or six years, with a provision for its automatic inclusion at the expiration of that time. This, he pointed out, would have two distinct advantages: (1) no one could support or sympathise with the violent resistance of Ulster to a change which would in no way affect her for years to come; (2) before the automatic inclusion of Ulster took place, there would be two General Elections which would give the British electorate—with experience of the actual working of Home Rule in the rest of Ireland—the opportunity—if so minded—of continuing the exclusion of Ulster.

This suggestion met with a good deal of support and it was agreed that the Prime Minister should discuss it with Mr. Redmond whom he is to see privately on Monday.[w]

Asquith's meeting with Redmond took place at Edwin Montagu's house in Queen Anne's Gate. He told the Irish leader that he was increasingly worried about " a baptism of blood " for Home Rule. This could only be avoided by an agreement or by " the prevention, or at any rate the indefinite postponement, of the bloody prologue." His conversations with Bonar Law, of which Redmond was informed, combined with the temper of the rank and file of both parties, made him pessimistic about an agreement. The alternative was Lloyd George's scheme for a postponement of the trouble. Redmond reacted strongly against this. " He could conceive of no proposal which would create against it a more compact and united body of sentiment in Ireland, both Nationalist and Unionist. If put forward at the last moment by B. Law as the price of an agreed settlement he might look at it. Otherwise he could not entertain it for a moment."^x Asquith then asked Redmond what concessions he was prepared to accept, and the latter replied with an offer of what came to be known as " Home Rule within Home Rule "—a large degree of Ulster autonomy under a united Irish Parliament.

Redmond followed up this interview by a long letter to Asquith dated November 24th. He argued strongly and cogently against the Government putting forward any proposals for a compromise. It was much better to wait and let them come from Bonar Law. Redmond, " writing with a full knowledge of my country and its conditions," also expressed scepticism about the seriousness of the Ulster threat: " I do not think that anything like a widespread rebellious movement can ever take place; and all our friends in Ulster, who would be the first victims of any rebellious movement, have never ceased to inform me that all such apprehensions are without any real foundation."^y

The Cabinet considered this letter on November 25th. After considerable discussion it was agreed that Redmond should be told there was no question of an immediate " offer " to Bonar Law, but that the Government must be free " when the critical stage of the Bill is ultimately reached " to do what it thought best. Grey, traditionally the coolest towards Home Rule of the senior ministers, then proposed that " if and when the conversation with Mr. Bonar Law was resumed, he should be told that our party could not be brought to agree to . . . the permanent or indefinite exclusion of Ulster, but that we were prepared to discuss plans for its temporary exclusion or separate administrative treatment."^z

This satisfied Redmond for a time, but it did not satisfy the King, who wrote from Sandringham on November 30th, asking when Asquith was next going to see Bonar Law. Prompted by this letter Asquith arranged a third Cherkley meeting for December 10th.[1] This

---

[1] Mr. Robert Blake gives the date as December 9th, but there seems no doubt from the Asquith papers that Wednesday, December 10th was the

was completely abortive. Asquith wrote: "I found B.L. less hopeful of a settlement by consent than when I last met him. He took a gloomy view of the temper and attitude not only of the extremists but of the rank and file of both parties . . ." But so, presumably, did Asquith. He told Bonar Law that there could be no settlement on the basis of indefinite exclusion, and Bonar Law rejected without detailed consideration the Lloyd George proposals for temporary exclusion. After some further rather weary re-traversing of old ground they parted.

Asquith made one further attempt at negotiation before Christmas. On December 16th he saw Carson, again using Montagu's house as a meeting place. The Prime Minister knew Carson somewhat better than Bonar Law—he was an old colleague at the bar—and, notwithstanding his seditious activities, was much more instinctively friendly towards him. Despite his own lack of dramatic sense, Asquith was often rather drawn to figures who cut something of a dash. He persuaded himself that there was a possibility of making progress with Carson where there had been none with Law.

As a result he took the trouble to draw up highly tentative proposals for a fresh compromise and to send them to Carson, accompanied by a notably friendly letter, on December 23rd. The suggestion was that a "statutory" Ulster (the boundaries of which remained to be defined) should have special powers of veto in the Irish Parliament. If a majority of the members from this area so wished, no Irish legislation on fiscal, religious, educational, industrial or land tenure matters would apply to Ulster. On December 27th Carson dismissed the proposal out of hand. Asquith persisted and on January 2nd he got Carson to come to another meeting at Queen Anne's Gate. On this occasion he reproached him for dismissing "carefully considered" proposals without putting forward any counter-suggestion, and tried hard to make Carson commit some scheme of his own to paper. But Carson—as was to be proved during the war—was always a negative man. One of his strengths was that he recognised this. He rarely allowed himself to be manoeuvred on to ground which called for constructive action. He was much too fly to be caught in this way by Asquith. When asked to put forward a detailed plan for the exclusion

correct day. Asquith says so in his memorandum of the talk and he also wrote to Miss Stanley that afternoon: "I paid a rather interesting call in the country this morning, of wh. I will tell you some day. Tonight to dine with Gosse & the Poets—at any rate the Laureate & Housman."

of Ulster he replied firmly that if the principle could be agreed the details could best be filled in by the parliamentary draughtsmen. And that, on January 7th, 1914, was the end of another attempt at negotiation.

On January 9th, Bonar Law wrote to Asquith asking permission to say in a public speech that conversations had taken place between the two leaders. Asquith agreed, and at Cardiff on January 15th Law announced not only that negotiations had taken place but that they had failed and were finished. His next step was to suggest, through Stamfordham, that the time had come for the King to write an official letter to his ministers, which he would reserve the right to make public later, telling them that it was their duty to hold a general election before the Home Rule Bill became law. The King had informed Bonar Law at Balmoral in the autumn that this was his intention. But by the end of January, although still anxious for an election, he had become doubtful about the wisdom of putting this form of pressure upon Asquith. Furthermore, he was displeased with the Unionist leader for slamming the door so firmly on any further negotiations. Law accordingly received a snubbing reply from Stamfordham: " As to any special communications to his Ministers, His Majesty's action will be guided by time and circumstances."[aa]

The King's constant desire for a general election was based upon no wish to get rid of Asquith, " for whom," Sir Harold Nicolson informs us, " he had acquired (and for ever retained) feelings of warm affection."[bb] There is no evidence that he ever entertained such feelings for Bonar Law, and at this stage he thought him likely to be an uncomfortable and even disagreeable minister. In addition the King believed that the departure of Grey from the Foreign Office would be " a European misfortune." At the same time the shelving of Home Rule which would follow from a Unionist victory would be a great personal relief. The King was more sensitive to trouble from the " loyalists " of Ulster than from the " disloyalists " of the South. What, no doubt, he would most have liked was a combination of " Whig men and Tory measures "—perhaps always the ideal solution from a royal point of view. But if he could not get this, a general election offered the prospect of removing some of the weight which he felt resting on his shoulders. If the opposition won, it would be a new situation. If the Government won, the election would at least " clear the air," as he put it.

Asquith persisted in believing that an election would settle nothing —except the ineffectiveness of the Parliament Act. But, his negotiations with Bonar Law and Carson having failed, and the critical date when the bill would become law being now only six months off, Asquith clearly had to proceed on some alternative course. This was the situation which confronted him when he returned from Antibes on January 19th, 1914. Three days later the Cabinet met. He reported on the failure of negotiations with Law and the new proposal that he had made to Carson. It was agreed, with some opposition from Morley (who thought Asquith was giving away too much) and enthusiastic support from Lloyd George and Churchill, that this last proposal, which had failed as a basis for negotiation, should be made public, but that Redmond should first be informed.

CHAPTER XIX

THE IRISH IMBROGLIO II

1914

At the beginning of 1914 Ireland was briefly superseded by the Naval Estimates as the most critical issue confronting Asquith. It was the old battle of 1909 over again, except for some piquant changes of personal position. As before, the First Lord of the Admiralty, supported with modified enthusiasm by the Prime Minister, the Foreign Secretary, and one or two others, was fighting for more generous provision against most of the rest of the Cabinet. But Churchill, instead of being with Lloyd George the leader of the " economists," had become the extravagant, demanding First Lord; and McKenna, relieved of his naval responsibilities, felt free to be one of Churchill's best-informed and most determined critics. Behind the struggle, on this as on the previous occasion, lay the conviction of the " economists " that they had the Liberal rank and file firmly on their side.

The first obtrusion of this phase of the dispute on to Asquith's correspondence came on December 8th, 1913, when he wrote: " We had a Cabinet which lasted nearly 3 hours, 2¾ of wh. was occupied by Winston." Then, on January 1st, Lloyd George gave what Asquith described as " a heedless interview " to the *Daily Chronicle*. This was in one sense a charitable judgment. In fact Lloyd George was making a calculated move to take the issue before the Liberal public. He spoke of the " overwhelming extravagance of our expenditure on armaments," expressed particular scepticism about the need for a stronger navy, and pointedly reminded his readers of Lord Randolph Churchill's 1887 resignation from the Exchequer. The clash was at this stage a long-distance one, for Churchill was in France when the interview was published, and Lloyd George left for Algeria immediately after he had given it. Asquith saw Churchill on January 9th, and became more apprehensive about the outlook. He was writing to Miss Stanley about the possibility of an expedition in the Admiralty yacht and continued rather gloomily:

That assumes that the good ship is likely to be at our disposal, which after the hour's talk I have just had with Winston seems to me to be by no means certain. He has been hunting the boar in Les Landes and has come back with his own tusks well whetted, and all his bristles in good order. There will be wigs on the green before his tussle with Ll.G. is over.

Asquith's Antibes visit then intervened, and it was January 20th before he could see Lloyd George and Churchill together. He remained gloomy after this meeting. His own view was in favour of the Admiralty case on the main points at issue, but he thought Churchill's methods were needlessly provocative. "There is no doubt that Winston tries them rather high," he wrote a little later; "to use his own phrase today he 'gyrates around the facts'."[a] The opposition which Churchill had aroused in the Cabinet was formidable. Lloyd George was in fact one of the most moderate of his opponents, his attitude untinged by personal antipathy. This was not the case with many of the others. John Simon ("the Impeccable is the real and only Irreconcilable," Asquith commented) was the most extreme. He was full of anti-Churchill arguments:

"The loss of W.C., though regrettable, is *not* by any means a splitting of the party," he wrote to Asquith, "—indeed large Admiralty estimates may be capable of being carried *only* because W.C. has gone. The party would feel itself strengthened in its Radical element and among the Economists; the feeling that the Cabinet *fights for economy* but preserves Home Rule unflinchingly is just what is wanted. A majority of the Cabinet certainly take this view."[b]

Whether or not he was right about the majority, Simon had a substantial group organised. A few days later he wrote again to the Prime Minister, and this time the letter was signed by McKenna, Runciman, Beauchamp, and Charles Hobhouse, as well as himself. In addition, not only Lloyd George but also Herbert Samuel were strongly critical of the Admiralty proposals without going the whole way with Simon.

Asquith's method of dealing with this situation was, first, to let it be known that if the issue were forced by either side to the point of resignation he proposed to have a general election rather than carry on with a weakened Cabinet;[1] and, secondly, to play the argument along fairly slowly in the hope that the passage of time or the intervention of other events might cause passions to weaken. On January 27th he recorded:

And now as I am writing we are in the full stress of Cabinet discussion. Happily Huck[2] is not present, but the bigger breed have their ears well laid back, & from time to time give tongue. (Some considerable time, say $\frac{1}{2}$ or $\frac{3}{4}$ of an hour, has elapsed since I wrote the last sentence, full of animated sound, including a few mellow and melodious *glapissements* from ' Sweetheart '.[3]) We shan't decide anything today & shall meet again tomorrow. But the air is more than a trifle thunderous.

Detached and dilatory though he sounded, Asquith's methods were highly effective. He acted throughout on the assumption that it was crucial to promote a movement towards accommodation between Lloyd George and Churchill. Simon and the others could then be treated cursorily. As soon as the Prime Minister saw signs of such a movement developing, during the last week of January, he began to breathe freely and to regard the crisis as past its worst. He still did not force an early settlement. He was happy to wait for this until the Cabinet of February 11th. An arrangement was then reached which avoided not only resignations but any legacy of bitterness. It also gave the Admiralty most of what they wanted and what Asquith had throughout believed they should have. This result, Churchill recorded, was largely due " to the unswerving patience of the Prime Minister, and to his solid, silent support."[c]

Ireland was less easily settled. As soon as the King received news of the Cabinet's decision of January 22nd to propose an Ulster veto upon any act of the Dublin legislature which affected the Protestant counties, he wrote to Asquith to say that in his view this was not enough: " I have always given you as my opinion, that Ulster will never agree to send representatives to an Irish Parliament in Dublin, no matter what safeguards or guarantees you may provide. For this reason I would point out to you the danger of laying before Parliament

[1] How this would have resolved the problem is not wholly clear. He presumably thought the threat could be an effective deterrent against both sets of extremists.

[2] Miss Stanley's dog.

[3] Lord Beauchamp.

and the Country, your proposed concessions (as) if they are to be your last word."[d] This did not make it easier for Asquith to deal with Redmond. He could hardly speak to him with decision and finality when he knew that he would probably have to come back later and ask for a further concession. Moreover, by the time that his interview with the Irish leader took place, on February 2nd, Asquith knew that the Conservative leaders were discussing the use of the House of Lords to amend the Army Act. Such a move would be revolutionary both in motive and in consequence. It would cripple the authority of the civil power. Its effect would be either to force a general election or to leave the Government without any military force which it could deploy in Ulster. At the interview he informed Redmond not only about the course of his negotiations with Bonar Law and Carson and of the Cabinet decision, but also of this possibility:

"I had Birrell with me at the Leviathan[1] interview" he wrote. "I developed the situation with such art as I could muster, until the psychological moment arrived for discharging my bomb. My visitor shivered visibly and was a good deal perturbed, but I think the general effect was salutary. He wisely refused to commit himself on the spot, and promises further communication in a day or two."

The next day Birrell had "a rather gloomy second interview with our Leviathan"; and then, on February 5th, "a rather unsatisfactory communication (tho' very well put)" arrived from Redmond. The gist of this was that Asquith in any public statement should say no more than that he would do everything in his power to secure a settlement by consent provided that it was consistent with "an Irish Parliament, an Irish Executive and the integrity of Ireland." "Such a statement by you," Redmond added, "would place me in a position to give it my wholehearted support."[e]

That same day Asquith went to Windsor to see the King. "I spent about an hour and a half with the Sovereign before dinner and we covered a good deal of ground," he wrote to Miss Stanley. "I spoke to him very faithfully, but I am not sure that I produced an abiding impression. Esher (who was at dinner) told me that the King liked me but (how unlike you!) was rather afraid of me! I am sure you will find this impossible to believe and difficult to imagine. We finished up our talk on very friendly terms. . . ."

[1] This was Asquith's private name for Redmond.

Sir Harold Nicolson's account of the audience, while in no way contradicting this view about the friendliness of the exchanges, suggests that the King believed he had dealt with Asquith as " faithfully " as Asquith believed he had dealt with him. The King warned Asquith that, if negotiations failed, many army officers might resign their commissions rather than fight in a civil war.[1] He reiterated his view that Ulster would in no circumstances consent to be placed under a Dublin Parliament. And, while stressing that the Prime Minister had not forfeited his confidence, he refused to commit himself to Asquith's contention that the only tolerable alternatives were either to dismiss the Government at once or to exclude the possibility of doing so at some subsequent stage in the dispute. The King said that " he had no intention of dismissing his Ministers, although his future action must be guided by circumstances."*

This audience helped to force Asquith beyond the solution of " Home Rule within Home Rule," which he had urged upon Redmond on February 2nd, and to make him accept in some form the temporary exclusion of Ulster. For the moment he made no public commitment to this new course, although he endeavoured to use the next parliamentary round—the King's Speech at the opening of the new session and the debate on the Address which followed—to create as conciliatory an atmosphere as possible. As a result the King was pleased not only with his own speech but also with the Prime Minister's. And Asquith himself thought he saw some response from the other side. " The event of this afternoon's debate with us," he wrote on February 11th, " was Carson's speech. He followed a somewhat arid display by the Impeccable, and was really very impressive. I wrote him a line of congratulation. . . . " The following night he found Bonar Law's contribution less worthy of congratulation— " Bonar Lisa was rather spitfire," he wrote—but he was nevertheless " inclined to be satisfied with the debate."

The next step was to persuade Redmond that he must make a further concession. The early stages of this process were entrusted to Lloyd George and Birrell, but Asquith himself had another meeting with the Irish leader on March 2nd. As a result of this Redmond reluctantly agreed " as the price of peace " to acquiesce in a three year exclusion. Each Ulster county could opt, by a simple majority, for such exclusion. At the end of the three years, which would date from

[1] " But whom are they going to fight?" Asquith blandly replied.

the first meeting of the new Irish Parliament, the provision would automatically cease to apply; but as at least one British general election would by then have intervened, the Unionists, if successful, could extend its life. The Nationalists made it clear that they would not vote for this arrangement in the House of Commons. They would merely abstain from voting against it provided that the Unionists did so too.

The Cabinet adopted this plan at its meeting of March 4th. Asquith immediately conveyed the decision to the King, while another minister conveyed it with equal speed to the lobby correspondent of the *Daily News*. Neither action eased the path of the Government. The King wrote back on the same day urging a longer exclusion: " I must confess that I have grave fears that the proposed limit . . . will not be acceptable to Ulster. This will make Sir Edward Carson's position an almost impossible one, but I know he will do all in his power for peace."[g]

The lobby correspondent published his information on the following morning, which was held to be a grave embarrassment both to the Government and to the Irish leaders. Asquith reacted so sharply that he took what he called " the very unusual step of sending round to the Cabinet a rather scorching document " and demanding written answers from all ministers. It was in the following, somewhat magisterial terms, and produced a large number of more or less characteristic replies:

The Prime Minister, with much regret calls the attention of the Cabinet to the disclosure in today's *Daily News* of what was agreed at yesterday's meeting.

Cabinet discussion & action becomes impossible if breaches of confidence of this kind are to continue.

He must, therefore, request that he should be at once informed if any member of the Cabinet has held any communication with Mr. Nicholson (the *Daily News* reporter) on the subject.

5 March 1914

I have not seen Nicholson for many months. *L.H.*[1]
None. *W.R.*[2]
The only communication I have had with Nicholson since he went

[1] Lewis Harcourt.
[2] Walter Runciman.

303

to the D.N. was to tell him (in answer to his request that I should treat him better than I did when he was on *The Times*) that he was the same prying knave *now* as he was *then*. A.B.[1]

I have not spoken to Nicholson since the Cabinet meeting or had any communication with him. *J.Mck.W.*[2]

I have not spoken to Mr. Nicholson since Feb. 12. C.H.[3]

Had no communication with him. *J.B.*[4]

I have not seen or spoken to Mr. Nicholson for nearly a year.
H. of C.[5]

I have not seen or had communication with him for several months. B.[6]

Before Wednesday I had never heard the suggestion of polling by counties, and I have not seen Nicholson since. About a week ago I saw him in the Lobby, he asked me if I had any news—I said, " Yes, I am going to Germany to study German educational methods on Saturday." He referred to it in the Press next day, but *nothing more was said by me on any other subject* nor was the Irish topic ever mentioned by him to me. *J.A.P.*[7]

I saw Nicholson the day before the Cabinet. He asked me what the Prime Minister was going to say on Monday. I said that if I knew I shd. not tell him. I have not seen him since the Cabinet.
W.S.C.[8]

I have not seen Mr. Nicholson. C.[9] 6:iii:14.

I have not seen him, nor had any sort of communication with him. M.[10] 6.3.14.

Not seen Nicholson for weeks. D.Ll.G.[11]

As far as I can recollect I haven't seen Nicholson for more than a year. I haven't yet seen the disclosure in the *Daily News.* E.G.[12]
6.3.14.

---

[1] Augustine Birrell.   [2] J. McKinnon Wood.   [3] Charles Hobhouse.
[4] John Burns.   [5] Haldane of Cloan.   [6] Beauchamp.   [7] J. A. Pease.
[8] W. S. Churchill.   [9] Crewe.   [10] Morley.   [11] D. Lloyd George.
[12] Edward Grey.

I have been in bed or away at Ramsgate since the proposals were told to me by J.A.P. after the Cabinet which I was unable to attend. *J.S.*[1] 10.3.14.

Five members of the Cabinet apparently failed to submit a written certificate of innocence, but one of these (McKenna) delivered a somewhat elaborate verbal exculpation to the Prime Minister. Asquith wrote at first that he knew whom he suspected, but two days later he sounded less certain: " The mystery of the leakage is still unpenetrated: I can see that Ll.G. suspects Winston. . . . "

The King's reaction presented a more serious problem for the Government than did the disclosure of the *Daily News.* If he regarded a three-year exclusion as much too short and thought that Carson would do so too, the chance of securing Unionist agreement seemed small. Accordingly, on the morning of March 6th, Birrell was deputed to see Redmond and tell him that the three years must be extended to six. Redmond wrote to Asquith that afternoon, reluctantly accepting the change. The way was then clear for the concession to be publicly announced when Asquith moved the second reading of the Home Rule Bill—in its third parliamentary circuit—on Monday, March 9th. " There was a huge crowd," he wrote, " but I did not count to excite them: so I adopted rather a funereal tone. Bonar Law was really at his worst." But it was Carson and not Law who most decisively threw the concession back in the face of the Government. " We do not want," he said in one of the more memorable phrases of the controversy, " sentence of death with a stay of execution for six years."

Nevertheless Asquith thought " the *general* effect of (the) proceedings not too bad, tho' it is too soon yet to say whether there is a real chance of rapprochement"; and he went off to dine at Grillion's, where he sat next to the Bishop of Winchester and opposite Sir Edmund Gosse, in a reasonably good humour. There were several weeks in which the Unionists could decide whether they would come round to accepting an Amending Bill embodying the Government's concession, or some variant of it.

The immediate menace lay not in the political situation in London, but in some move by the Ulster Volunteers against the arms depots in the province. At the Cabinet on March 11th a committee was set

[1] John Simon.

up, composed of Churchill, Birrell, Seely and Simon, with Crewe in the chair,[1] to consider this danger. Asquith did not appear to take the threat too seriously. He commented that this Cabinet, " after recent excitements and agitations . . . was a rather tame affair."

The committee reported on March 17th. The guard on the depots was to be reinforced, and this was to be achieved by moving troops in from the South and from England. The constabulary in Ulster was to be concentrated in five or six centres. The First Lord of the Admiralty told the Council that " the forthcoming practice " of the 3rd Battle Squadron would take place off the Isle of Arran. Two or three destroyers were being ordered to the South of Ireland. In the meantime Churchill had been to Bradford, on March 14th, and had delivered his powerful speech of warning to those who sought to challenge parliamentary institutions by force. If that was to be done, he concluded, " let us go forward together and put these grave matters to the proof." His warships, Unionists subsequently noted, he had already ordered forward to Lamlash.

These developments provoked a sharp parliamentary reaction. Already on Monday, March 16th there was what Asquith called " a regular rough and tumble " at question time. The tension was still higher on the Thursday when Bonar Law proposed a vote of censure. The Government's military moves were turning Ulster into " a new Poland " he claimed. Asquith replied with his voice in such " bad condition that I had difficulty in keeping it up." Carson, as usual, provided the real drama. He launched a great attack on Churchill. He announced in a threatening way that his own real place was not in the arid debates of Westminster but at the head of his movement in Ulster. Then, twenty-five minutes before the departure of the Belfast mail from Euston, he accused Devlin of telling " an infamous lie." When ordered by the Speaker to withdraw he went no further than to substitute the words " wilful falsehood " and stalked from his place. When he got to the far end of the front opposition bench he turned and raised his hand in a gesture of departure. The Tories gave him a standing and tumultuous farewell. He left to catch his train. Had he gone to proclaim the provisional government of Ulster? Or had he merely given a classic example of how to frustrate parliamentary discipline? No one was certain, which was no doubt his intention.

[1] On the following evening Crewe was taken ill in the Savoy Hotel, and took no part in the work of the committee.

Carson proclaimed no provisional government. Despite the drama of his departure, the boat trains to Ireland that night contained another passenger whose journey was of great significance in the history of the Ulster dispute. Soon after Carson left for Belfast, General Paget,[1] the Commander-in-Chief in Ireland, left for Dublin. He had been in London for two days of War Office consultation about the troop movements into Ulster and the consequent strain which might be imposed upon the loyalties of some officers. As with all the military events and consultations of those and subsequent days, there were varying versions of what was said and what was contemplated. The report of the Secretary of State for War to Asquith, dated the day after Paget's departure, was in the following terms:

I discussed the question of officers' resignations with C.I.G.S.,[2] A(djutant) G(eneral)[3] and Sir A. Paget yesterday. Sir A. Paget strongly urged that in the few exceptional cases where officers have direct family connection with the disturbed area in Ulster, so that in the event of serious trouble arising their future private relations might be irretrievably compromised if they were engaged with our troops, they should be permitted to remain behind either on leave or with details. Sir John French and Sir Spencer Ewart having expressed their concurrence with this view it was decided that this course should be followed.

In all other cases Sir A. Paget wished to be able to say that any officer hesitating to comply with orders or threatening to resign should be removed. Sir John French was of opinion that such officers should be court-martialled, a view which he had urged upon me a year ago. Upon Sir Spencer Ewart pointing out the technical difficulties and delay that might be involved, Sir John French agreed for the present that removal should be the course followed. Sir John French and Sir Spencer Ewart agree to this memorandum.

J.S. 20.3.14.[h]

[1] General Sir Arthur Paget (1851–1928), a grandson of " One-leg," 1st Marquess of Anglesey, a close friend of King Edward VII, and a gallant rather than a clear-headed or notably diligent officer.

[2] General Sir John French (1852–1925), later 1st Earl of Ypres.

[3] General Sir Spencer Ewart (1861–1930).

This document strongly suggests that the discussions had not been wisely handled by the Secretary of State and his principal military advisers. But their lack of wisdom was as nothing compared with the crass foolishness of Paget's behaviour when he returned to Ireland. There is no suspicion that Paget, like Sir Henry Wilson at the War Office, was engaged in a calculated plot against the Government. No doubt he subscribed to sound anti-Liberal views and found it natural at a meeting of officers under his command to speak of " those swines of politicians." But these opinions were subordinate, as he later put it to Asquith, to " my way of thinking, viz. that duty came before all other considerations."

The trouble was that his method of carrying out his duty was so inept. Within a few hours of landing at Kingstown on the morning of Friday, March 20th, he held a conference of seven senior officers in the Royal Hospital, Dublin. He briefed them about the precautionary moves he had been instructed to carry out, but did so in such alarmist terms that he spoke of the whole country being " ablaze " within twenty-four hours. He told of the concession he had obtained for officers living in Ulster, but said that this must be very strictly interpreted. For the rest, he wished to know what were the officers' intentions. Were they prepared to do their duty or would they rather accept dismissal? Paget himself did not dispute that he put this hypothetical question to his senior officers. Those who were not prepared to accept the former course were to absent themselves from the second part of the conference at two o'clock that afternoon. But he denied that he intended the question to be put in the same form to subordinate officers. Two of those present—Major-General Fergusson, commanding the 5th Division and Brigadier-General Hubert Gough, commanding the Cavalry Brigade within that division—got a different impression. Fergusson recorded that brigadiers were told to go at once and put the alternatives before their officers; and he was a clear-headed general who expressed himself well on paper and was resolved throughout " to do his duty."

Gough may have been less cool and he was certainly more partisan. He was an Ulsterman, but as he had no house there he was excluded from the protection of the concession. He absented himself from Paget's afternoon conference, and spent the remainder of the day with his three regiments, mostly at the Curragh, thirty miles south-west of Dublin. That evening he reported that five of the officers under his command could claim Ulster domicile. Of the remainder, twelve were prepared to obey whatever orders were given, but sixty,[1] including himself and the commanding officers of the 4th Hussars and the 5th and 16th Lancers, preferred to accept dismissal than be involved in " the *initiation* of active military operations against Ulster."[2] This was the so-called Mutiny at the Curragh. Other, less fashionable regiments in the area showed signs of restiveness but were restrained by Paget or Fergusson or Pulteney, the commander of the 6th Division. The news of the cavalry revolt was telephoned to London that Friday night.

Asquith was dining with Lord and Lady Sheffield in Mansfield Street. He made a hurried departure from the bridge table to Downing Street. The letter which he wrote to Miss Stanley (who had been at her parents' party) on the Saturday evening described both what he found when he got there and his immediate view of the trouble:

I found there Winston, the Arch-Colonel,[3] Sir John French and Gen. Ewart with some pretty alarming news. The Brigadier and about 57 officers of the Cavalry Brigade at the Curragh had sent in their resignations sooner than be employed in " coercing " Ulster. The Brigadier—Gough—is a distinguished Cavalry officer, an Irishman, and the hottest of Ulsterians, and there can be little doubt that he has been using his influence with his subordinates to make them combine for a strike. We sent orders for him and the 3 Colonels to come here at once and they will arrive this evening. Meanwhile, from what one hears today it seems likely that there was a misunderstanding. They seem to have thought, from what Paget said, that they were about to be ordered off at once to shed the blood of the Covenanters, and they say they never meant to object to do duty like the other troops in protecting depots & keeping order. This will be cleared up in a few hours: but there have been all sorts of agitations & alarums in high quarters, and I

---

[1] The number has usually been given as 57, probably excluding Gough himself, but the itemisation given in A. P. Ryan's highly informative *Mutiny at the Curragh* adds up to 60, with ambiguity as to whether or not Gough was included.

[2] The form in which the decision was announced is a striking illustration of the foolish way in which Paget posed his questions, even assuming that he had to pose them at all.

[3] Seely.

had a visit this morning from Stamfordham[1] who wore a very long face. I took the opportuntiy of saying that the main responsibility for all this mutinous talk rested with Lord Roberts, who is in a dangerous condition of senile frenzy.

The King not only sent Lord Stamfordham. He also wrote saying that he was " grieved beyond words at this disastrous and irreparable catastrophe which has befallen my Army " and complained bitterly at the lack of information with which he had been provided.[i] Altogether Asquith soon began to think that his initial view had been too optimistic. After a Sunday which included an hour with the King, a call from the Archbishop of Canterbury, and a letter from Bonar Law giving notice of House of Commons trouble on the following day,[2] he wrote:

The military situation has developed . . . and there is no doubt if we were to order a march upon Ulster that about half the officers in the Army—the Navy is more uncertain—would strike. The immediate difficulty in the Curragh can, I think, be arranged, but that is the permanent situation, and it is not a pleasant one. Winston is all for creating a temporary Army ad hoc—but that of course is nonsense . . . This will be the third successive Monday that we have a " crisis " in the House.

As the parliamentary situation developed, Asquith began to feel a little easier. On the Monday he wrote:

What with Paget's tactless blundering and Seely's clumsy phrases, and the general Army position, I had rather a tough job to handle. A.J.B., who is the only quick mind in that ill-bred crowd, hit the right nail, or rather touched the sore spot.[3]

By the Wednesday he thought the opposition were winning his battle for him:

Never in the whole of my experience at the bar and in Parliament have I seen a really strong and formidable case . . . so miserably presented and so coldly backed up. It is quite clear the Tories

[1] The King's Secretary.

[2] Also, Asquith recorded, "(contrary to my settled practice) I saw Geoffrey Robinson of the Times, & gave him a few hints of a quieting kind."

[3] The inexcusable foolishness of the way in which Paget, apparently acting on the direct instructions of the Secretary of State for War, put the issue at his conference of senior officers.

are thoroughly cowed over this army business; they think it is going to do them harm in the country. Our people on the other hand are really hot and excited—more than they have been for a long time, and I am beginning to believe that we are going to score out of what seemed an almost impossible situation.

Unfortunately, if the Liberals were that week winning the battle in the House of Commons, they were losing it in the War Office. Gough, with his three colonels, was in London for Sunday and Monday. In his discussions at the War Office he showed an inflexible determination to get his own way. It was as though he were disciplining the Secretary of State and the General Staff. When it was suggested, in view of the misunderstanding, that he should go back and carry on as though nothing had happened, he declined absolutely—unless he were given a written assurance that the army would never be used to impose Home Rule on Ulster. After some havering Seely allowed Ewart to produce a draft of such an assurance. This came before the Cabinet on the Monday morning, March 23rd, and Asquith, after a short discussion, wrote out an amended and unexceptionable version in his own hand:

" You are authorized by the Army Council," it ran, " to inform the Officers of the 3rd Cavalry Brigade that the Army Council are satisfied that the incident which has arisen in regard to their resignations has been due to a misunderstanding.

It is the duty of all soldiers to obey lawful commands given to them through the proper channel by the Army Council, either for the protection of public property and the support of the civil power in the event of disturbance, or for the protection of the lives and property of the inhabitants.

This is the only point it was intended to put to the officers in the questions of the General Officer Commanding, and the Army Council have been glad to learn from you that there never has been and never will be any question of disobeying such lawful orders."

Seley was absent—he had been summoned to the King—when this was discussed. He returned to Downing Street just as the Cabinet was breaking up. The Prime Minister, according to a letter which Margot Asquith subsequently wrote to Lady Islington, gave him the document and he stuffed it in his pocket, and remained in the Cabinet room talking to John Morley. While these two were still talking, but after Asquith had left the room, a messenger arrived from the War Office to ask if Gough could have his reply. Seely and Morley—the one a notably incautious and relatively new minister but the other the most experienced member of the Cabinet—then proceeded to add two paragraphs of their own. One paragraph added nothing of substance; the other gave Gough far too much. They were as follows:

His Majesty's Government must retain their right to use all the forces of the Crown in Ireland, or elsewhere, to maintain law and order and to support the civil power in the ordinary execution of its duty.

But they have no intention whatever of taking advantage of the right to crush political opposition to the policy or principles of the Home Rule Bill.

How Morley ever came to take part in this totally unwarranted re-drafting is incomprehensible. Margot's explanation, given in the same letter, was that "J. Morley is quite deaf and *much* too vain poor dear to own up that he did not know what was going on (in the Cabinet);" and this seems as good as any other.

The document was then given to Gough. The brigadier was as insatiable as he was intrepid. He told French and Ewart that it was not good enough. He asked for a further written assurance that the correct interpretation of the last paragraph was that the army in Ireland would not be used to enforce the Home Rule Bill upon Ulster. After a little hesitation, French wrote " That is how I read it. J.F. " beside this interpretation. With this in his pocket Gough set off as soon as he could for Dublin. He was able to return in triumph. It was not surprising that Sir Henry Wilson, the arch Unionist intriguer in the War Office, wrote in his diary: " So long as we hold the paper we got on Monday, we can afford to sit tight."[j]

Asquith was not so fortunately placed. As soon as he saw the offending paragraphs—on the Monday evening—he realised that they could not be allowed to stand without giving away the entire position on civilian control over the army. Officers would have been persuaded back to duty at the price of extracting a policy concession from the Government. He immediately sent for Seely and told him that the additions must be struck out. It was too late. Gough had already taken the document to Ireland. Asquith's only course was therefore that of public repudiation, although this would clearly make it difficult for Seely and the two generals to remain in office. How much he cared about losing Seely is doubtful. He liked him, but had by this stage lost all confidence in his judgment and sense—"the greatest fool of all after Paget," was Margot's description of him. But Asquith was most reluctant to see French go. "French offered his resignation but has withdrawn it for the moment at any rate," Asquith wrote. "His position is a very difficult one, but he has been so loyal and has behaved so well that I would stretch a great many points to keep him."[1] This was written on the Thursday, although Asquith had already repudiated by inference both Seely's added paragraphs and French's special assurance.

On the Friday Asquith made a statement in the House of Commons promulgating a new Army Order, which was intended to clear up the whole position. He had hoped to do this at noon, after a morning Cabinet with French and Ewart in attendance. He then planned to take an afternoon motor drive with Miss Stanley. But the meeting was more protracted than he had anticipated, and he was forced to delay his statement until five, taking his motor drive first. The new order conveyed in different words the substance of the three original paragraphs.

Asquith went to the Wharf for the Saturday and Sunday, where he had the Churchills and "Bluey" Baker, the under-secretary at the War Office, as guests. While there he contemplated the problem of how to fill Seely's place—although there was still some doubt as to whether the resignations would take place—and decided that the most steadying solution would be to take the job himself.

"I started the idea of the two offices at once," he wrote to Miss Stanley when he had returned to London on the Monday (March 30th), "and I need not tell you that Winston's eyes blazed and his polysyllables rolled, and his gestures were those of a man possessed. Even Bluey's wary deep-set gaze lighted up. On Sunday Bongie (Bonham Carter) arrived with a long hazy diplomatic document which Haldane had drawn up, & over persuaded the wretched 2 Generals to accept, as a *pièce justificative* for not

[1] Margot Asquith (still in the same letter to Lady Islington) added an intriguing—but certainly unauthorised and probably inaccurate—gloss to this by writing: "French put his name to what he thought was a Cabinet document so he said he had better go—he is a hot Liberal & of course comes back to a high place in a very short time."

resigning. I saw at once that from their point of view it was a sophistical evasion, and from ours a surrender of the whole position. Winston and Bluey quite agreed, & Bongie took back a discouraging negative."

Soon after Asquith got back to London on the Monday morning it was settled that the resignations were to take place:

The Generals (i.e. French and Ewart) had come back to the position that as a matter of personal honour they must go. Poor Seely, who was there, of course was bound to follow suit. French behaved admirably, & when I told him privately that I thought of going to the W(ar) O(ffice), he was delighted and promised all his help. So then I proceeded to the King and put my scheme before him. He remarked—naïvely, as Bonar Law wd. say—that the idea had never occurred to him! But he was quite taken with it and gave it his emphatic approval. So after questions—as you will see by the papers—I threw two bombshells on the floor of the House, and I think the effect was all that one cd. have hoped. On the advice of the Impeccable I cleared out at once, not wishing to incur a penalty of £500 for sitting after my seat was legally vacant.[1] So I am no longer an M.P.

At the end of that week, accompanied by his wife and elder daughter, Asquith went to Fife. " Such a journey ! ! " Margot wrote. " I thought I shd. have died—I've never known the Tories so vile, so rude and so futile as now." Asquith himself found the experience more encouraging:

" Wherever we stopped we had a cheering crowd, with a deputation, address & c," he wrote to Miss Stanley, " and the climax was at Edinburgh where the Waverley Station was simply packed. They cheered and roared & sang " jolly good fellow " and " Scots wha hae," and I only protected Violet from loud demands for a speech by asking them to sing " Auld Lang Syne," of which they proceeded to give us 2 or 3 verses, ending up with " Will ye noe

---

[1] Until 1918 the acceptance of any Cabinet office made it necessary for a member to seek re-election. In fact Simon's subsequent advice was that Asquith had probably committed a technical offence by appearing to announce his own appointment, and that a bill of indemnity was necessary. If this was blocked by the opposition, Simon's suggestion was that " 250,000 working men " should be asked to subscribe ½d. each.

come home again." We arrived at last just before 8 at Cupar where there was a final demonstration."

On the Saturday afternoon he addressed a "wonderfully enthusiastic" meeting at Ladybank. "The Army," he said, "will hear nothing of politics from me, and in return I expect to hear nothing of politics from the Army." He returned to London after two days, but he was still out of the House of Commons. It was another four days before he heard that no candidate had been nominated against him, and another five after that before, on Easter Tuesday, April 14th, he was able to take his seat.

The Prime Minister's decision to take over the War Office proved a successful and steadying move. "The soldiers trusted Asquith," was Mr. A. P. Ryan's summing up; "his massive common sense and refusal to be stampeded into the excitement of the moment proved invaluable."[k] Nevertheless the Curragh incident and its repercussions left a legacy of bitterness and unrest in the army—particularly that part of it stationed in Ireland—which could not quickly be eradicated. This feeling was expressed with great forthrightness in a report written by Major-General Fergusson about April 20th. One of the troubles, he said, was the common belief that the General Staff would resign when the crisis came, accompanied by a conviction that "certain Officers holding high appointments, in and out of the War Office, are in the confidence of the Ulster Party, and are practically working against the Government and the constituted authority of the army." Nor had the soft treatment of Gough and his three colonels helped. "These Officers returned covered with glory, while those who had taken the other line had had to put up with misrepresentations and reproach from their relations and friends. It is not surprising that many of them, especially the younger, are resentful, and inclined to think that they 'backed the wrong horse'."[l] This document was at once an encouragement to firm civilian control of the army and an indication of how much damage had been done by Seely and Paget.

The state of the army apart, Asquith's Irish worries during that April would have been crushing to a man of less equable temperament. The King was pressing him hard to make further concessions to Ulster. In the week before Easter he had received what he described as "a rather hysterical letter from G.R." This communication was an extreme example of royal pressure in favour of a particular policy.

The King wanted the six counties to be allowed to contract out without a plebiscite and for an indefinite period.

" Surely you could persuade Mr. Redmond and his friends ' to go to this length ' for the sake of peace, which the whole country is longing for," he wrote. " I trust that you will lose no time to renew your conversations with Mr. Bonar Law and Sir E. Carson as you promised me. I repeat what I said to you last week, that I have every confidence in you. I have also absolute confidence in your ability to bring about a peaceful solution, whenever you put in force the great powers you possess. You appreciate I know the terrible position in which I shall be placed if that solution is not found. My duty will be to leave nothing undone which lies within my power to save Ireland from what you have yourself described as civil strife."[m]

But Asquith believed that he had already forced Redmond to the limit of what was reasonable. In addition, before any further meeting with Law or Carson could be arranged, there occurred the highly provocative illegality of the Ulster gun-running at Larne. This took place on the night of Friday, April 24th, and was reported to Birrell in the following telegram sent *via* Dublin Castle on the morning of the 25th:

About 8 p.m. last night a large body of Ulster Volunteers Force armed with truncheons numbering about 800 mobilised at Larne under Sir William Adair and Major McCalmont, M.P. They drew a cordon round the harbour and vicinity and allowed no one to pass except a few on business; police and Customs officers particularly excluded; signals from sea had been observed and large numbers of motor cars arrived. Two steamers believed " Mountjoy " and " Millswater " discharged cargoes of what appeared to be arms and ammunition which were conveyed away by motor cars. Reporting fully today. Telegraph and telephone communication interrupted.[n]

Aberdeen, the Viceroy, followed up this message with a telegram to Asquith urging the immediate arrest of McCalmont and Adair, and asking for authority to proceed even though he judged that " the persons named and other leaders will be prepared to resist." This request—and other possible courses of action—were considered by the Cabinet on the Monday morning. Three methods of procedure suggested by the Irish Law Officers were rejected. Instead it was decided, on the advice of Simon, that the proper course was to prosecute by what sounded the somewhat ineffective method of "exhibiting an information" in Dublin. Eventually, after Cabinets on four successive mornings, even this method of proceeding was abandoned. "Please do not sign informations until further notice," Asquith telegraphed to Birrell in Dublin as soon as the Thursday Cabinet broke up; and that was the end of the matter.

The pressures which pushed the Cabinet towards this retreat were typical of those which always destroyed the possibility of resolute action against Ulster illegality. The King was firmly against prosecution, of course. But so was Birrell, the member of the Cabinet with direct responsibility, and so too was Redmond. The latter wrote insistently to Asquith on April 27th. He did not believe that any Irish problem could be solved by the application of the criminal law. Most insidious of all the influences, however, was the line taken by the Unionist leaders in the House of Commons debate on the Tuesday and Wednesday. Carson, in particular, let drop a few hints of moderation. Perhaps these were an invitation to a settlement. The Government, at any rate, was only too prepared to hope that they were and to abandon the possibly exacerbating prosecutions.

Partly in genuine pursuit of this hope, and partly to satisfy the King, Asquith took part in further secret conversations on May 5th. Edwin Montagu's house was once again the meeting place, but on this occasion the Prime Minister was confronted by both Bonar Law and Carson. Law did not depart from his usual mood of dogged pessimism, and the meeting was not fruitful. His party, he announced, were " growingly averse to any kind of settlement." Nevertheless a little procedural progress was made. It was agreed that a committee stage for the Home Rule Bill would serve no purpose, and that it was better that any changes should be incorporated in a separate amending bill which would receive the Royal Assent on the same day as the Home Rule Bill itself. But it was not agreed what should be in this amending bill, and such agreement was of course a necessary prelude to its running a quick parliamentary course over the twin hurdles of the Liberal and Nationalist majority in the House of Commons and the Unionist majority in the House of Lords. Law and Carson insisted that the Home Rule Bill ought not to leave the Commons for the last time until the terms of a settlement were agreed.

Asquith was unable to accept this last demand, if only for the obvious reason that it would have given the opposition complete control over the whole Home Rule parliamentary timetable. He was determined to get rid of the major bill before Whitsun, and this, at the price of another day of almost unprecedented disorder in the House of Commons, was satisfactorily accomplished. In the meantime, the Cabinet, to the accompaniment of insistent royal requests that the Ulster case should be met as completely as possible, was engaged in drafting the amending bill.

The terms were announced after Whitsun[1] and the bill was introduced into the Upper House by Lord Crewe on June 23rd. It was obviously sensible to see what the peers would do to this measure before wasting the time of the House of Commons upon it. There was no need to wait long for an answer. Within little more than a week the Lords had re-fashioned the amending bill so as to make it accord with the most extreme Unionist demands. All the nine counties of Ulster were to be excluded, without plebiscites and without a time limit. For the first time Asquith was brought up against a complete *impasse*. Within a month the Home Rule Bill, protected by the Parliament Act, would at last be ready for the Royal Assent. Trouble with the King would no doubt have to be faced, but even assuming that this was overcome, how was the measure to be implemented? It would have been difficult enough to enforce it upon parts of Ulster in any event, but once the Government had publicly declared in favour of some form of exclusion, this became simply impossible. Yet the Lords would only allow the bill to be amended in a form that was unacceptable to the majority in the House of Commons. A settlement by negotiation had therefore become an urgent necessity for the Government. Asquith could only hope that the opposition, as the critical moment approached, had become equally worried by the dangers of continued deadlock.

The time had clearly arrived to put into practice his theory that negotiations were most likely to succeed when the pressure for settlement had become urgent upon both sides. On May 3rd Speaker Lowther had written to Asquith suggesting that an all-party conference on the Irish problem might be held in his library. Asquith wrote a stalling reply, and later returned similar answers to the King, who, on

[1] They were almost identical with those which Asquith had offered in March. Each Ulster country could opt out by plebiscite for a period of six years.

May 17th and 23rd, and again on June 19th and 29th, had pressed hard for a meeting between Redmond and Carson, under the aegis either of the Speaker or of himself. The Prime Minister thought that May and June were too early for serious negotiations of any sort, and even in the first half of July he believed that they should be kept as informal as possible in order to avoid what he regarded as the disaster of a formal failure. But during these July weeks he used a variety of go-betweens and created an almost over-complicated private net. Lloyd George saw Redmond and Dillon together; J. A. Spender, on Asquith's behalf, saw Dillon alone; and the Master of Elibank (by then Lord Murray) was brought in for a series of negotiations with Lord Rothermere[1] and later with Carson.

Asquith's object in these discussions was to try to narrow the difference to a simple and limited question of geography. By mid-July he thought that he had succeeded. Everything was still tentative, but if acceptable partitions of Tyrone or Fermanagh could be agreed or imposed, both sides seemed likely to acquiesce in the exclusion, without a time limit, of the resultant five or five-and-a-half county *bloc*.

On July 16th, accordingly, Asquith told the King that the moment for a conference had at last arrived, and proposed that it should be held at Buckingham Palace. He broached the matter at a State Ball:

I found the royal person in a tent in the garden and had nearly half an hour with him. He was full of interest and excitement about the Conference—and made one really good suggestion—namely that the Speaker should preside.

We arranged that I should write a memorandum for the

---

[1] Lord Northcliffe, Rothermere's brother, spent a week in Ulster at this time, and Murray, perhaps because he thought it would ease his negotiations with Rothermere, was anxious that Asquith should see Northcliffe. Asquith was reluctant. " I hate and distrust the fellow and all his works," he wrote, " and will never make any overture to him ; so I merely said that if he chose to ask me directly to see him, and had anything really new to communicate, I would not refuse. I know of few men in this world who are responsible for more mischief, and deserve a longer punishment in the next: but it doesn't do to say this to Winston."

Murray persevered, and the meeting took place three days later in his flat in Ennismore Gardens. Whether or not it served any other purpose, Asquith remarked that he used it " to impress upon (Northcliffe) the importance of making *The Times* a responsible newspaper."

King, advising a Conference and that the King should send a cordial reply amounting to an invitation. He was anxious that Arthur Balfour shd. come in, but I objected to this strongly, as A.J.B. is in this matter a real wrecker. As between Crewe and Ll.G.—the K. was (with me) in favour of the latter.

Asquith got his way about both Balfour and Lloyd George, although the choice of the latter involved a delicate and excusably disingenuous letter to Crewe. " I find that our Irish friends are very insistent that Lloyd George should be our second man," Asquith wrote, " believing as they do (perhaps partly from the experience of victims) that his peculiar gifts of blandishment and negotiation would be invaluable."*o* Crewe made no difficulty about the change,[1] and the conference was quickly constituted. Asquith, Lloyd George, Redmond and Dillon confronted Bonar Law, Lansdowne, Carson and Captain Craig.[2] The first meeting was held on July 21st and the last on July 24th. Despite all Asquith's careful preparation of the ground, Lloyd George's " blandishments," and the choice of meeting place, with the atmosphere of national unity it was intended to convey, the conference was a complete failure. Mr. Robert Blake, in his biography of Bonar Law, states forthrightly that the Unionists never expected success and " only attended in deference to the King's wishes."*p* Their expectations were not disappointed. Two subjects were marked out for discussion—area and time limit. After some initial scuffling, it was agreed that area should be discussed first. As a result the second subject was never reached. The conference, in Churchill's phrase, lost itself in " the muddy by-ways of Fermanagh and Tyrone." After the second meeting, on July 22nd, Asquith wrote Miss Stanley an account of how this happened:

We sat again this morning for an hour and a half, discussing maps and figures, and always getting back to that most damnable creation of the perverted ingenuity of man—the County of Tyrone. The extraordinary feature of the discussion was the complete agreement (in principle) of Redmond & Carson.

[1] " I have never known either of the two Nationalist members at all well," he wrote in reply, " and have no great liking for them—for Dillon indeed rather the opposite, so that George is far more likely to be able to cajole or frighten them, or both, than I could be. . . ." (*Asquith Papers*, box 46, f. 213).

[2] Later Lord Craigavon and first Prime Minister of Northern Ireland.

The Prime Minister: Asquith in Whitehall, about 1910

Venetia Stanley, later Mrs. Edwin Montagu

Each said ' I must have the whole of Tyrone, or die; but I quite understand why you say the same.' The Speaker who incarnates bluff unimaginative English sense, of course cut in: ' When each of two people say they must have the whole, why not cut it in half? ' They wd. neither of them look at such a suggestion. L.G. and I worked hard to get rid of the county areas altogether and proceed on Poor Law Unions wh. afford a good basis of give and take. But again both Irish lots would have none of it. Nothing could have been more amicable in tone or more desperately fruitless in result. We agreed to meet again tomorrow, when we shall make a final—tho' I fear futile—effort to carve out a ' block '. I have rarely felt more hopeless in any practical affair: an impasse, with unspeakable consequences, upon a matter which to English eyes seems inconceivably small, & to Irish eyes immeasurably big. Isn't it a real tragedy ?

Two days later—"a black letter day in my Calendar "—he announced the failure of the conference to the House of Commons. He also described the closing stages to Miss Stanley:

The last meeting this morning was in some ways dramatic, tho' the actual business consisted merely in " settling the words to be publicly used." At the end the King came in, rather *émotionné*, & said in two sentences (thank God! there was not another speech) farewell, I am sorry, and I thank you. He then very wisely had the different members brought to him privately, and saw each in turn. Redmond was a good deal impressed by his interview, especially as the King told him that he was convinced of the necessity of Home Rule.

We then had a meeting at Downing Street—Redmond & Dillon, Ll. George, Birrell & I. I told them that I must go on with the Amending Bill—*without* the time limit: to which after a good deal of demur they reluctantly agreed to try & persuade their party to assent. It will come on on Tuesday . . .

Asquith then permitted himself a few thoughts about the mysteries of the Celtic mind:

Redmond assured us that when he said good-bye to Carson the latter was in tears, and that Captain Craig who had never spoken to Dillon in his life came up to him and said: ' Mr. Dillon, will you shake my hand? I should be glad to think that I had been able to give as many years to Ulster as you have to the service of

A.   321   L

Ireland.' Aren't they a remarkable people? And the folly of thinking that we can ever understand, let alone govern them!

When the following Tuesday came, however, the Amending Bill was not proceeded with. During the intervening week-end the Nationalist Volunteers followed the example of Ulster with a gun-running exercise of their own at Howth. This led to a mild street scene in Dublin on the Sunday afternoon. A foolish Assistant Commissioner of Police sent for the military—" a most improper proceeding," in Asquith's view—and a minor incident was turned into a massacre. Three Nationalists were killed and thirty-eight were wounded. Asquith, as was described in chapter XVII, was hurriedly summoned back from the Wharf to London to deal with this " malignity of fortune." One effect of the incident was to disillusion Asquith, perhaps none too soon, with the quality of the administration in Dublin Castle and even with the agreeable and easy-going Chief Secretary. " I am tempted to regret," he wrote, " that I didn't make the ' clean cut ' 6 months ago, and insist upon the booting out of Aberdeen, . . . & the whole crew. A weaker and more incompetent lot were never in charge of a leaky ship in stormy weather; the poor old Birrell's occasional & fitful appearances at the wheel do not greatly improve matters."

The second effect was a hardening of opinion amongst the Nationalist M.P.s. The Amending Bill had obviously to be postponed for at least a day or so in order to allow their mood to steady. The Government Chief Whip pressed hard for a delay until the following week, but Asquith reacted with surprising violence against what he described as this " idiotic proposal which would have made everyone say we were drifting on." He announced on the Monday that the bill would definitely be taken on Thursday.

But Thursday brought another postponement, although for a different reason. Throughout these last stages of the Irish crisis the international situation provided increasingly loud off-stage noises. The Sarajevo murders occurred while the House of Lords was busy re-fashioning the Amending Bill. The Austrian ultimatum to Serbia became known as the Buckingham Palace conference was breaking up. But, at least until the Tuesday of the following week (July 28th), Ireland was the central worry in the Prime Minister's mind, and the " Eastern problem," as he called it, a peripheral one. After Tuesday the balance shifted. On the Wednesday he wrote that " the Amending Bill & the whole Irish business are of course put into the shade by the coming war." Then, on the Thursday morning, as he described it to Miss Stanley:

I was sitting in the Cabinet room with a map of Ulster, & a lot of statistics about populations & religions, and some choice extracts from Hansard (with occasional glances at this morning's letter from Penrhôs), endeavouring to get into something like shape my speech on the Amending Bill, when a telephone message came from (of all people in the world) Bonar Law, to ask me to come & see him & Carson at his Kensington abode—Pembroke Lodge. He had sent his motor, which I boarded, and in due time arrived at my destination: a rather suburban looking detached villa in a Bayswater street,[1] with a small garden, and furnished and decorated itself after the familiar fashion of Glasgow or Bradford or Altrincham. It was quite an adventure, for I might easily have been kidnapped by a section of Ulster Volunteers.

I found the two gentlemen there, & B. Law proceeded to propose, in the interest of the international situation, that we should postpone for the time being the 2nd reading of the Amending Bill. He said that to advertise our domestic dissensions at this moment wd. weaken our influence in the world for peace & c.... I of course welcomed this attitude, but I said I wd. consult some colleagues before giving a definite answer.

The colleagues consulted were Lloyd George and Grey, who both agreed that the offer should be accepted. So did Redmond, whom Asquith saw at the House of Commons immediately after luncheon. The intention was that the Home Rule Bill itself should become law, but that its operation should be suspended until a new amending bill could be passed. On this basis Asquith announced a further and indefinite postponement on the Thursday afternoon. That was the end of the pre-war phase of the Irish dispute. The unsolved problem was bundled into cold storage. But it took a little more effort, after the outbreak of war, to get the door of the storage room closed upon it. And when the issue was next exposed to view, at Easter, 1916, the freezing plant was shown to be disappointingly ineffective. The maggots had been hard at work.

[1] A curious topographical inaccuracy for Asquith; Pembroke Lodge was not within a mile of Bayswater.

CHAPTER XX

THE PLUNGE TO WAR

1914

From 1911 onwards the European scene was menacing, and in a general way was recognised as such by Asquith and his leading ministers. But there was no especial menace in the first half of 1914. The Balkan wars were over, and no fresh crisis had developed. It was a period of relative calm. There was no slow, inevitable edging towards war as in 1939.

Even after the murders at Sarajevo, the mood did not change. When the Cabinet could take time off from the Irish crisis it was more concerned with planning for the end of the Parliament than with the international scene. After a meeting on July 8th Asquith informed the King that the intention was to prorogue in August, and then to have one more short session beginning in December and leading on to a general election in the summer of 1915.

On July 24th, when the Austrian ultimatum to Serbia had been delivered, Grey made a report to the Cabinet. It was the first foreign affairs discussion that month. But it riveted attention. Asquith's Cabinet letter spoke of the Austrian ultimatum as " the gravest event for many years past in European politics " and a possible " prelude to a war in which at least four of the great powers may be involved." At that stage he nevertheless believed that we should have little difficulty in remaining outside the conflict. " Happily there seems to be no reason why we should be anything more than spectators," he wrote later that day.

During the week-end of July 25th-26th he remained of the same mind. Indeed he was somewhat divided on the merits of the issue. " The curious thing is," he wrote on the Sunday, " that on many, if not most, of the points Austria has a good and Servia a very bad case. But the Austrians are quite the stupidest people in Europe (as the

Italians are the most perfidious), and there is a brutality about their mode of procedure which will make many people think that it is a case of a big Power wantonly bullying a little one." On the Monday he was heavily occupied with Ireland. On the Tuesday he noted with sadness the collapse of Grey's attempts to organise a 4-power conference, and assumed that " nothing but a miracle " could now avert a war. But he did not necessarily mean a British war. That night, after entertaining at dinner the Churchills, Benckendorffs (Russian ambassador) and Edward Marsh, he walked across Downing Street and sat in the Foreign Office with Grey and Haldane until 1 a.m.

In Cabinet the next morning two " decisions " were taken. The first was a real one. It was to send warning telegrams to all the naval, military and colonial stations and to initiate a " precautionary period ", which was short of the German *Kriegsgefahr*, but which nevertheless involved a considerable state of readiness. Surprisingly, in view of the traditions of the War Office and the national taste for improvisation, British plans for the entry into hostilities had been meticulously prepared. Much of the credit for this belonged to Haldane. A " War Book " had been in existence for several years past; at 2.0 p.m. on the Wednesday (July 29th) the order was given for the turning of its pages to begin.

The second " decision " was less decisive. It concerned the British attitude in the event of a German violation of Belgian neutrality. Asquith reported it to the King in the following words:

The Cabinet consider that this matter, if it arises, will be rather one of policy than of legal obligation. . . . After much discussion it was agreed that Sir E. Grey should be authorised to inform the German and French Ambassadors that at this stage we were unable to pledge ourselves in advance, either under all conditions to stand aside or in any conditions to join in.

It sounded a little pusillanimous, but so it was bound to be unless the Cabinet was to be split wide open. There was a potential " peace party " comprising no less than ten ministers[1]—of a total of twenty. As in the naval estimates dispute six months earlier, Lloyd George was the most powerful but by no means the most extreme of this group. He had however made an " economy " speech in the House of Com-

[1] Nine of them (Morley, Lloyd George, Beauchamp, Simon, Harcourt, Pease, Samuel, McKinnon Wood and Runciman) even met together at Beauchamp's house on one occasion; John Burns was the tenth.

mons as late as July 23rd—the day before the Austrian ultimatum to
Serbia—and had delivered himself then of a statement of epic mis-
timing. Relations with Germany, he said, were better than for years
past. Asquith, unless he wished to proceed without half his Government and with the Liberal Party split down the middle, had to allow a
little time for Lloyd George to recover from this extravagance and for
other ministers to move with the pressure of events. Margot Asquith,
always at least as extreme as Lloyd George, might be tempted, as she
confided to her *Autobiography*, by thoughts that her husband could
respond by forming a coalition and isolating the whole " peace
party "; but Asquith himself had no wish to enter the war a prisoner
of the " ill-bred " Unionist party with his own support rent in two.
He wanted to keep the Cabinet as united as possible, and he had no
doubt that Lloyd George was the key to this objective.

No bridges were therefore to be crossed until they had to be. Nor,
at this stage, independently of Cabinet opinion and contrary to what
has sometimes been assumed, did either Asquith or Grey believe that a
clear British commitment would necessarily assist the cause of peace.
It might encourage France, and still more Russia, to a greater intransigence. It would destroy any mediatory influence which we might
have with Germany and Austria. An apprehensive uncertainty
about the British attitude might be the best hope. " Of course we
want to keep out of it," Asquith wrote on the Wednesday evening,
" but the worst thing we could do would be to announce to the
world at the present time that in *no circumstances* would we intervene."

On the Thursday (July 30th) he found the situation " at least one
degree worse than it was yesterday " and was struck by " the terrible
state of depression and paralysis" of opinion in the City, combined with
a desire to keep out at almost any cost. The " pacifists " were not
all in the Liberal Party. By the Friday (July 31st) a further decline
of hope had taken place. The French, on the verge of mobilisation,
were beginning to apply heavy pressure in London. Cambon, their
ambassador, was resolutely using every form of moral blackmail at
the Foreign Office. " E. Grey had an interview with him this afternoon
wh. he told me was rather painful," Asquith wrote.

Yet throughout these days of mounting crises and declining hope,
Asquith still believed that he might be able to fulfil a Chester engagement on the Saturday (August 1st) and go on to Anglesey for the

weekend. " If I come, it will be by the train wh. gets to Holyhead at
6.45 p.m.", he wrote on the Friday afternoon. But, of course, it was
not to be. Asquith never neglected his duty, although he sometimes
wished that he could. That night he made a dramatic visit to Buckingham Palace and on the Saturday morning he presided over the first
really difficult Cabinet meeting. After dinner on the Friday he was
sitting in Downing Street with Grey and Churchill when Sir William
Tyrrell arrived from the Foreign Office with a message from the
embassy in Berlin suggesting that, if Russian mobilisation could be
held up, the Kaiser might be willing to restrain Austria:

> We all set to work. . . . to draft a direct personal appeal from the
> King to the Czar, and when it was settled I called a taxi and . . .
> drove to Buckingham Palace at about 1.30 a.m. The poor King
> was hauled out of bed, & one of my strangest experiences . . .
> was sitting with him—he in a brown dressing gown over his night
> shirt & with copious signs of having been aroused from his first
> " beauty sleep "—while I read the message and the proposed
> answer. All he did was to suggest that it should be more personal
> and direct—by the insertion of the words " My dear Nicky " and
> the addition at the end of the signature " Georgie " ! I got home
> again about 2 a.m. and tossed about for a little on my couch (as
> the novelists say)—but really I didn't sleep badly . . .

Next morning the Cabinet met at 11.0 and sat for 2½ hours.
Resignations began to loom.

" It is no exaggeration," Asquith wrote, " to say that Winston
occupied at least half of the time. We came, every now and again,
near to the parting of the ways: Morley and I think the Impeccable (Simon) are on what may be called the *Manchester
Guardian* tack—that we shd. declare now and at once that *in no
circumstances* will we take a hand. This no doubt is the view for the
moment of the bulk of the party. Lloyd George—all for peace—
is more sensible and statesmanlike, for keeping the position still
open. Grey, of course, declares that if an out and out uncompromising policy of non-intervention at all costs is adopted he will
go. Winston very bellicose and demanding immediate mobilisation. Haldane diffuse . . . and nebulous. The main controversy
pivots upon Belgium and its neutrality. We parted in a fairly
amicable mood, & are to sit again at 11 tomorrow (Sunday) an
almost unprecedented event.

" I am still *not quite* hopeless about peace, tho' far from hopeful. But if it comes to war I feel sure (this is entirely between you and me) that we shall have *some* split in the Cabinet. Of course, if Grey went I should go and the whole thing would break up. On the other hand, we may have to contemplate with such equanimity as we can command the loss of Morley, and possibly (tho' I don't think it) of the Impeccable."

Asquith was right about Simon's ultimate decision but wrong in thinking that would leave Morley alone. At the Cabinet the following morning (Sunday, August 2nd) when it was " agreed at last (with much difficulty) that Grey should be authorised to tell Cambon that our fleet would not allow the German fleet to make the Channel the base of hostile operations," John Burns at once resigned, and was persuaded only with difficulty to stay on until the evening. Lloyd George, Asquith recorded, was still against " any kind of intervention in any event," and was supported by Harcourt as well as by Morley. Crewe, McKenna and Samuel he spoke of as " a moderating intermediate body."

This Cabinet lasted from 11.0 until 2.0. The next meeting was from 6.30 until 8.0 that same Sunday evening. It brought no lightening of either the international or the domestic prospect. Burns remained unalterably determined to go. Several others were threatening to follow him. Lloyd George still inclined in that direction. When the meeting broke up Asquith went with three of his children (Violet, Cyril, and Margot's daughter Elizabeth) to dine with the McKennas. Edwin Montagu was the only other guest. It was exactly the sort of " scratch dinner party " (his own phrase) which he liked most, and which, however tense the crisis, was his natural way of preparing for the next phase. On his way back to Downing Street he noted with distaste the beginnings of war hysteria:

> There were large crowds perambulating the streets and cheering the King at Buckingham Palace, & one could hear the distant roaring as late as 1 or 1.30 in the morning. War or anything that seems likely to lead to war is always popular with the London mob. You remember Sir R. Walpole's remark: " Now they are ringing their bells; in a few weeks they'll be wringing their hands." How one loathes such levity.

Next morning Asquith received resignation letters from both Morley and Simon. When the Cabinet met at 11.0 Beauchamp added

his *nunc dimittis*. " That is 4 gone! " Asquith wrote. But there was a
more important change the other way. The Belgians had rejected the
German ultimatum early that morning, and with that development
Lloyd George began to move in favour of intervention. He made a
strong appeal to the four not to go, or at least to delay their resignations;
and they all responded to the extent of sitting on the Government
front bench that afternoon.

It was a crucial occasion. Asquith described how he and Margot
and their luncheon guests all went across to the House of Commons
and then:

> Grey made a most remarkable speech—about an hour long—
> for the most part almost conversational in tone & with some of
> his usual ragged ends; but extraordinarily well reasoned &
> tactful & really *cogent*—so much so that our extreme peace-lovers
> were for the moment reduced to silence; tho' they will soon find
> their tongues again.

After that England was effectively in the war. That night Grey
sat in his room at the Foreign Office and coined his famous phrase—
the only memorable one of his life—about the lamps of Europe.
Asquith, after another scratch dinner party,[1] received a surprise visit
from Bonar Law. He had to reassure him and his nervous followers
that there would be no "jiggery-pokery" about the Home Rule and
Welsh Church Bills. He also wrote a letter of strong personal appeal
to Simon.

This appeal worked, and after the Cabinet the next morning
(Tuesday, August 4th) Asquith was able to write of " a slump in
resignations." Simon and Beauchamp both decided to stay, but
Morley remained " obdurate " and neither he nor Burns attended.
Neither at the time nor subsequently did Asquith show the slightest
sign of bitterness about these resignations. He noted that Morley
wrote him " a particularly nice letter," and to Margot he spoke of
him " as one of the most distinguished men living." Both Morley
and Burns continued to be occasional Downing Street luncheon
guests.[2]

This Tuesday Cabinet, which Asquith rather oddly described as,

[1] " Jack Pease, Mrs. Keppel & girl, Anne Islington & Pauline (Cotton)
Harry Wilson & Barbara &c &c."

[2] " I had a nice talk John Morley," Asquith wrote three months later:
" He and Birrell are the best of all company."

"interesting," received the news that German troops had entered Belgium, and responded by issuing an ultimatum, to expire at midnight, for their withdrawal. A British declaration of war became virtually certain.

In the afternoon Asquith went across to announce the news to the House of Commons. "It is curious how, going to and from the House, we are now always surrounded and escorted by cheering crowds of loafers & holiday makers," he wrote. And a day or two later he added: "I have never before been a popular character with the 'man in the street,' and in all this dark and dangerous business it gives me scant pleasure." The House, he found, took the news "very calmly & with a good deal of dignity and we got through all the business by ½ past 4." Asquith then went for an hour's solitary motor drive. It was not perhaps the way that many men of power would have chosen to spend their time at this watershed of history. But it gave him a good opportunity to survey his feelings and collect his thoughts. He was clear that the decisions towards which he and Grey had coaxed the Cabinet were right. He felt no enthusiasm for the outcome. "The whole prospect fills me with sadness," he wrote. "... We are on the eve of horrible things." Yet he did not doubt that he could deal with the tasks ahead. He was very well, he said, though at times rather tired, and he contrasted himself with Grey who "like Winston and others ... is much overstrained." He believed that he had a broad back for problems of policy and administration, and his nerve was in no way impaired. He would continue, no doubt under greater pressure, to apply his well-tried methods of government and his civilised standards of behaviour. His six-year premiership had already presented so many problems that no new one seemed likely to be insuperable.

His drive over, Asquith returned to Downing Street to wait, without hope, for the expiration of the ultimatum. Margot described some of the events of the evening:

I looked at the children asleep after dinner before joining Henry in the Cabinet room. Lord Crewe and Sir Edward Grey were already there and we sat smoking cigarettes in silence; some went out; others came in; nothing was said.

The clock on the mantelpiece hammered out the hour, and when the last beat of midnight struck[1] it was as silent as dawn.

[1] The ultimatum in fact expired at 11.0 p.m. (midnight in Berlin), but arithmetical accuracy was never Margot's strongest characteristic.

We were at War.

I left to go to bed, and, as I was pausing at the foot of the stair-case, I saw Winston Churchill with a happy face striding towards the double doors of the Cabinet room.[a]

The group that he found within was less happy.

CHAPTER XXI

A PRIME MINISTER AND
HIS COLLEAGUES

1914-15

When the war started Asquith was nearly sixty-two. He had been Prime Minister for six and a quarter years, which was already a longer period of office than all but two of his predecessors of the previous century. He had become the "natural" head of the Government, with his own well-established routine of authority, and it required an effort of imagination on the part of his colleagues, his opponents, the electorate, and even himself, to visualise anyone else in his place.

He did not make the mistake of regarding himself as indispensable. Indeed, one more than usually adventurous motor journey, a few months later, set his mind contemplating how short-lived would be the reaction to his sudden removal.

" As we drove up this morning in the motor (it is about 80 miles)," he wrote, " we had two or three very narrow shaves of collision & disaster. And after each, I said to myself—suppose it had gone wrong, and I had (as Browning says) ' ended my cares,' what would have been the consequence?

Lots of stuff in the Press—a ' nine days ' wonder in the country: violent speculation as to who was to succeed me—E. Grey, Ll. George, Crewe & co; many obituary notices; and after a week or 10 days (at the outside) the world going on as tho' nothing had happened: ... a few ripples, even, if you like, a bit of a splash in the pool—but little or nothing more.

Of the men with whom I have been most closely associated, I think that those who wd. (for a time) feel it most are, oddly enough Haldane, McKenna & the Assyrian (Montagu): a strange trinity; of my own family Violet, Oc & perhaps Puffin; and

among women I am inclined to think Viola[1] (tho' I am not at all
sure about this)."[2]

Although Asquith was never vain or foolish enough to think that
the world, or even a small part of it, would stop without him, he rarely
doubted his authority over his colleagues or the permanence of his
command.[3] When Montagu on one occasion (in March, 1915)
assured him that if there were any question of his resigning " the *whole*
Cabinet, including Ll.G. and Winston, would go with (him), & make
any alternative impossible," Asquith implicitly believed the assurance.
And when, later in the same month, he had to compose a bitter quarrel
between Lloyd George and McKenna, he thought (and rightly, it
appeared at the time) that the best way to do so was to remind them
that he had been Prime Minister for nearly seven years but that if
" anyone among you has even the faintest doubt or suspicion about
me, I will gladly (for what have I to gain or lose?) abandon this chair,
& never sit in it again." " Their mutual anger dissolved like a frost
under a sudden thaw," Asquith recorded; " and they both with a
united voice exclaimed: ' The day you leave that chair, the rest of us
disappear, never to return.' And I am sure they meant it."

This, however, was an uncharacteristic incident, for there can
rarely have been a Prime Minister who talked, or thought, less about
resigning than did Asquith. There was no sulkiness in his character,
and unlike Gladstone, he did not take easily to the weapon of the false
resignation. Nor did he ever seriously look forward to a life of ease
and retirement. He sometimes found his duties burdensome. He
longed for the war to be over, and for the unfamiliar and distasteful
problems which it brought with it to be removed from his agenda.
But his wish then was to return to a life of normal government and not
one of well-earned rest. In all the vast outpouring of letters which he
sent to Miss Stanley during the first nine months of the war, in his
seventh year of supreme responsibility, there were hardly more than

---

[1] Parsons, born Tree.

[2] This was all written " after midnight." Next morning Asquith added
the comment " a stupid letter!" but he did not refrain from sending it.

[3] Nevertheless he recorded on November 3rd, 1914: "My dreams
continue .... There was another, of which I have only a dim memory,
in which (with the concurrence of all my colleagues) I was supplanted by
Herbert Samuel—as Prince Hal says ' a Jew, an Ebrew Jew .' Do you think
that is going to be my fate?"

three or four references to the possibility of retirement. He was full of vague romantic yearnings for a more satisfying inner life, but so far as the outer framework was concerned he did not pretend to discontent. He was happier as Prime Minister than he had ever been before. He suspected that anything afterwards was likely to be anticlimax; and he was too honest to suggest otherwise.

This was not because he had an exaggerated view of his own political talents. At one stage during these months, exercising his extraordinary taste for relaxation with pen and paper, he constructed, in a moment of *ennui* with the world around him and in a typically classical mould, a little play about his own qualities and limitations.[1] The picture which emerged, he hastened defensively to add, was not himself as he really was, but as " a fairly intelligent observer " might see him:

> *Scene*—THE INFERNAL TRIBUNAL
> *On the Bench*—RHADAMANTHUS
> *At the Bar*—SELF-RELEASED SHADE

Rhad. (*loquitur*): So here you are, my friend—before your time. I am rarely surprised, but your premature appearance gives me a slight & welcome shock of something approaching to astonishment.

You, of all people! *Que Diable!*

Let me (in self-justification) dwell for a moment on the improbabilities of the case—which is nearly unique, even in my infernal experience.

You were, in the world above, almost a classical example of *Luck.* You were endowed at birth with brains above the average. You had, further, some qualities of temperament which are exceptionally useful for mundane success—energy under the guise of lethargy; a faculty for working quickly, which is more effective in the long run than plodding perseverance; patience (which is one of the rarest of human qualities); a temperate but persistent ambition; a clear mind, a certain quality and lucidity of speech; intellectual, but not moral, irritability; a natural tendency to understand & appreciate the opponent's point of view: and, as time went on, & your nature matured, a growing sense of proportion, which had its effect both upon friends and foes, and

[1] The date was March, 1915.

which, coupled with detachment from any temptation to intrigue, and, in regard to material interests & profits, an unaffected indifference, secured for you the substantial advantage of personality and authority.

The really great men of the world are the geniuses & the saints. You belonged to neither category. Your intellectual equipment (well cultivated and trained) still left you far short of the one; your spiritual limitations, and your endowment of the " Old Adam," left you still shorter of the other.

Nevertheless, with all these curtailments & shortcomings, you were what is called in the slang vocabulary of your time a " good get out."

The same *Luck* helped you in external things—in unforeseen opportunities, in the disappearance of possible competitors, in the special political conditions of your time: above all (at a most critical & fateful moment in your career) in the sudden outbreak of the Great War.

Everything was going well for you; the Fates, often malignant, or at least perverse, seemed to be conspiring to help you. I had almost given up hope, for years to come, of seeing you here at my bar: and yet, by your own choice, *here you are.*

The Shade (interrupting): There is a modicum of truth, and a good deal of plausibility, in your rather prolix allocution. But, so far, you have not got near the essential and dominating fact.

Rhad: You mean, I suppose, that I have omitted any reference to the softer and more emotional side of your not very complex nature. Very well. I agree that, in this respect, you rather took in your contemporaries. The world in which you lived regarded you as hard, calculating, insensitive. In almost all the popular " appreciations " which as a conspicuous personage, you provoked, you were depicted as shy, reserved, unforthcoming, coldblooded. Even those who saw more clearly did not credit you with more than a certain capacity for the enjoyment of comfort and luxury, with a moderate fondness for social pleasures, and (perhaps) a slight weakness for the companionship of clever and attractive women. As I am the embodiment & Minister of strict Justice, I will go a step further. You hated and eschewed domestic dissension, and your sons & daughters were genuinely fond of you. So, in a sense, were your colleagues and political followers. At first they looked rather askance at your leadership, with wistful retrospective glances at the much-lamented shade of the defunct C.B. It is odd, but true, that in the course of time—apart from old friends like Haldane, E. Grey, & Crewe—you gained the loyal attachment of men so diverse as Lloyd George & Winston Churchill, as Illingworth, McKenna & Montagu. Some people, sadly wanting in perspective, went so far as to call you "chivalrous"; it would be nearer the truth to say that you had, or acquired, a rather specialised faculty of insight & manipulation in dealing with diversities of character and temperament. But the conclusion, by whatever road it is reached, is the same: that you ought not to have left them in the lurch.

The Shade: "Tired with all these, for restful Death I cried."

Rhad: Pooh! You know very well that that was not the reason for your precipitate appearance here. You had excellent health, a good digestion, an adequate capacity for sleep, unabated authority in your Cabinet, big events to confront & provide for. No man ever had less temptation to violate the "canon fixed by the Everlasting against self-slaughter."

The Shade: Not bad! I could have made the same speech, without preparation, in the House of Commons. Its only defect is that it ignores the central reality of my life.

Rhad: What was that?

The Shade: It is something beyond the ken of your damned tribunal. Give me my sentence, and call up the next Ghost.

(*Curtain*)

A few days later Asquith completed his joke by constructing an imaginary sentence which was passed upon him by the infernal judge. It was an interesting revelation of the fate which he would have regarded as worse than death:

The sentence of the Court upon you is that you go back to the World whence you came. . . . There you are to be born again in a new body, with the bare average of faculties and brains, and are to live up to the allotted span a toilsome monotonous existence—an inconsidered item in the dim millions of mankind. You will not even be a madman or a criminal. You will have no big moments, no exceptional chances, no "roses & raptures." You and your environment will be equally homespun and humdrum.

Poetry, art, politics, the living interests and ideals of your country and your age, will be to you a sealed book. You will not even have the curiosity to try & break the seal. From birth to death you will be surrounded by, imprisoned in, contented with, the commonplace.

Thus does Infernal Justice redress the balance of the Upper World, and secure an equal lot for the Sons of Men.

It was dull obscurity, therefore, rather than excessive burdens which Asquith feared. There rarely can have been a man who had less desire to return to the life of his childhood. " You shall go back to Morley and shall live there the rest of your days without contact with the great world outside " would not be an unfair parody of the worst fate which he could envisage. If, in occasional moments of depression, he thought of release, he did so in terms of sudden death rather than of calm retirement. In spite of his " guise of lethargy " he rather despised those who liked living at half-pressure. " Anything would be better than to *rust*," he wrote in October, 1914.

This outlook to some extent affected his attitude towards his various colleagues. There were two members of his Cabinet—Lloyd George and Churchill—who could, under no circumstances, have been accused of living at half-pressure. For both he had a curious semi-admiration, modified by a lack of faith in their consistency and judgment. In Lloyd George's case the admiration was further modified by an assumed lack of social compatibility and by a belief that he lacked " the best sort of courage."

" McKenna and I had a walk & talk," Asquith wrote on November 28th, 1914, " about persons & particularly about courage (of which, with all his limitations, he is a shining example). I found that we didn't differ much, both marking Ll. George rather low in this respect, & E. Grey too *nervy* to put really high."

On another occasion Asquith commented that Lloyd George " was kept at Walton Heath by one of those psychological chills which always precede his budgets when he does not feel altogether sure of his ground. . . . (He) would like to see me take his budget for him. . . . I'll see him a long way off first."

At the same time Asquith's letters were studded with constant (if faintly surprised) tributes to Lloyd George's skill in committee and the penetration of his contributions. Much less frequently he would deliver himself of a strongly disparaging comment: " . . . Lloyd

337

George, who almost got down to the level of a petty police court advocate," he wrote after one Cabinet row.[1] But he never referred to him as George, a form of address particularly disliked by the Chancellor, and one which, no doubt for this reason, was constantly employed, not only by most of the Tories, but by Crewe, and one or two other Cabinet members as well. Furthermore, on the one occasion during the first year of the war when Lloyd George was a guest at the Wharf,[2] Asquith found the week-end unusually agreeable.

At the root of Asquith's attitude to Lloyd George there lay a puzzled conflict of emotions. He admired the energy of the Chancellor's mind, but disliked what he regarded as its uncontrolled indiscipline. Some part of the conflict emerges from this passage of a letter written " after midnight " on March 3rd, 1915. It was, however, a moment when Asquith felt more than usually exasperated by Lloyd George's darting unpredictability:

No sooner had I settled the row between Ll.G. and McK(enna) . . . and all but settled the earlier row between Ll.G. and K(itchener), than this versatile and volatile personage goes off at score on the question of drink, about wh. he has completely lost his head. His mind apparently oscillates from hour to hour between the two poles of absurdity: cutting off all drink from the working man, which wd. lead to something like a universal strike; and buying out (at this moment of all others) the whole liquor trade of the country, and replacing it by a huge State monopoly, which wd. ruin our finances and create a vast engine of possible corruption. He is a wonderful person in some ways, but is totally devoid of either perspective or judgment: and on the whole during these 7 years he has given me more worry than any other colleague.

But Asquith never understood the Celts, particularly their Cambrian variety. "As you know I am not *passionately* fond of the Welsh," he wrote before a Cardiff visit.

From Churchill he was separated by no similar barrier. On the contrary, his half-admiration was in this case fortified by a bond of strong, if occasionally exasperated, affection. " I can't help being fond of him," Asquith wrote on October 27th, 1914, "—he is so resourceful

[1] But he thought McKenna, a much closer friend, had behaved at least equally badly on this occasion.

[2] During this period Lloyd George also stayed a very brief week-end with the Asquiths at Walmer Castle.

and undismayed: two of the qualities I like best." He carried his
fondness to the extent, during the autumn of 1914, of spending more
time in Churchill's company, despite the twenty year gap between
their ages, than in that of any other member of his Cabinet. There
were innumerable small dinner parties at 10, Downing Street or
Admiralty House as well as frequent country Sundays. Yet Asquith
could sometimes be strongly critical of Churchill's social qualities—
in particular his addiction to monologues and his indifference to the
views or reactions of his neighbours. " He never gets fairly alongside
the person he is talking to," Asquith wrote on one occasion, " because
he is always so much more interested in himself and his own pre-
occupations and his own topics. . . . "

About Churchill's command of the Admiralty, Asquith was usually
enthusiastic, but about his general political prospects he was uncertain.

" It is not easy to see what W(inston)'s career is going to be here,"
he wrote on February 9th, 1915: " he is to some extent blanketed
by E. Grey and Ll. George, & has no personal following: he is
always hankering after coalitions and odd regroupings, mainly
designed (as one thinks) to bring in F. E. Smith & perhaps the
Duke of Marlborough. I think his future one of the most puzzling
enigmas in politics. . . . "

At that stage Asquith was playing with the idea that, after the war,
he might make him Viceroy of India.

Six weeks later he wrote in similar but more critical terms. He had
been told that Churchill was intriguing to push Grey out of the Foreign
Office and have Balfour brought in to replace him, and he thought
Churchill was to blame at least to the extent that his temporary but
excessive friendliness towards Balfour laid him open to such a charge:
" He has him at the Admiralty night and day, and I am afraid tells him
a lot of things which he ought to keep to himself, or at any rate to his
colleagues."[1]

" It is a pity," Asquith continued, " that Winston hasn't a better
sense of proportion, and also a larger endowment of the instinct of
loyalty . . . . I am really fond of him, but I regard his future with
many misgivings. . . . He will never get to the top in English
politics, with all his wonderful gifts; to speak with the tongue of

[1] Ironically enough, when Balfour was brought into the Government, by
Asquith, only two months later, it was Churchill at the Admiralty and not
Grey at the Foreign Office whom he replaced.

men and angels, and to spend laborious days and nights in administration, is no good if a man does not inspire trust."

Yet on another occasion, only a few months previously, Asquith could write of Churchill as " certainly one of the people one would choose to go tiger-hunting with." And he could be fascinated by the extravagance of his personality even when he was treating him as a figure of fun.

" His mouth waters at the sight and thought of K(itchener)'s new armies," Asquith wrote on October 7th, 1914. " Are these ' glittering commands ' to be entrusted to ' dug-out trash,' bred on the obsolete tactics of 25 years ago—' mediocrities, who have led a sheltered life mouldering in military routine ' & c & c. For about ¼ of an hour he poured forth a ceaseless cataract of invective and appeal, & I much regretted that there was no shorthand writer within hearing—as some of his unpremeditated phrases were quite priceless. He was, however, quite three parts serious, and declared that a political career was nothing to him in comparison with military glory. He has now left to have a talk with Arthur Balfour, but will be back here at dinner. He is a wonderful creature, with a curious dash of schoolboy simplicity (quite unlike Edward Grey's), and what someone said of genius—'a zigzag streak of lightning in the brain '."

Amongst the members of his Cabinet, Asquith placed both Lloyd George and Churchill high and equal—but not at the top. His precise views on this subject—at least as they stood on February 26th, 1915— he conveyed to Miss Stanley:

I will give you what I think (if it were an examination, & you had to classify the candidates—like a Tripos at Cambridge) is the order in which I would put them: I leave out myself and (Montagu) as a newcomer— & our dear Birrell, who is in a class by himself.

1. Crewe
2. Grey
3. McKenna
4. (bracketed)   Ll. George
                 Winston
                 Kitchener (he ought
                     perhaps to be put in
                     a separate class)

340

7. Harcourt
   Simon (again a bracket)
9. Haldane   bracketed
   Runciman
11. Samuel
12. Pease
    Beauchamp
    Emmott
    Lucas
    Wood

Crewe owed his eminence to never irritating Asquith, except by the extreme slowness with which he played golf, and to the unobtrusive steadiness of his judgment. He did not offer opinions on a wide range of topics, but when appealed to, he was firm, moderate, and generally, but not automatically, on the side of the Prime Minister. Furthermore, as a legatee of the Whig tradition, he gave the impression of representing a wide body of uncommitted outside opinion; and he was useful in relations with the King. He made little impact on the public, and he could never have run a government. But, partly perhaps for this reason, he was an almost ideal colleague to a Prime Minister. Thirty years later, Lord Attlee found a similar solace in Lord Addison.

Grey was different. He made a considerable public impact, and, despite their old and close political friendship, he often irritated Asquith, mainly by his lack of buoyancy. " E. Grey (as usual) was most dolorous and despondent," was a typical Asquith comment on one of the Foreign Secretary's Cabinet appearances. Fortified himself by unusually good health, Asquith found it difficult to comprehend Grey's physical infirmity. Then he was constantly struck (and a little puzzled) by how different Grey's mental processes and modes of relaxation were from his own. Nevertheless, he had the greatest respect for the integrity and determination of the Foreign Secretary, as well as for the general direction of his views. It has already been seen how sharply the Prime Minister reacted to the rumour of a Churchill " plot " to get rid of him and bring in Balfour.

The other notable features of Asquith's list were provided by McKenna, because his position was so high, Haldane, because his position was so low, and Kitchener, because he was such a strange addition to an otherwise wholly Liberal and wholly civilian Cabinet.

As soon as the war broke out it was obvious that Asquith himself could not continue as Secretary of State for War. On August 3rd Kitchener, on his way to Egypt, was summoned back from Dover and asked to hold himself available for consultation. On August 5th, believing that none of his colleagues were suitable for the post, Asquith decided on the " hazardous experiment " of appointing Kitchener as Secretary of State. The latter reluctantly accepted. His appointment was to be for the emergency only. It was recognised that he had no politics—not Liberal ones at any rate—and his special status, as Sir Philip Magnus has informed us, was symbolised not only by his sitting on the right hand of the Prime Minister in Cabinet, but also by his drawing three salaries.[a]

Asquith's early impressions of Kitchener as a Cabinet colleague were mostly favourable. " My own opinion of K's capacity increases daily," he wrote on November 3rd, 1914. " I think he is a really fine soldier, and he keeps his head and temper, and above all his equability wonderfully, considering how all three are tried." But he often found him slow to grasp a new point (" K. who generally finds things out sooner or later—as a rule rather later," was an October comment), and inclined to provoke Cabinet disputes by an unnecessary inflexibility. The first, but by no means the last of these disputes was with Lloyd George and the subject was Welsh recruiting. Kitchener's view was that no purely Welsh regiment was to be trusted and Asquith thought his handling of the argument " clumsy and noisy."[1]

In addition, there was the constant ill-feeling between Kitchener and Sir John French.[2] At first Asquith, who had been very well-disposed towards French at least since the days of the Curragh, put this down to a simple incompatibility, and rationalised the position by saying that there was much to be said for having an optimist at the front balanced by a pessimist in the rear. In November, 1914 he sent French a confidence-giving letter expressing in the most unqualified terms the trust of the Government in his leadership in the field; and in the following January he noted sadly that the King, " a strong

[1] Even unusual delicacy and quietness might have left it an unappealing one to Lloyd George.

[2] After French resigned as C.I.G.S. after the Curragh incident he was reappointed to the post of Inspector-General of the Forces, which he had previously held from 1907–11. Then in August he was given command of the Expeditionary Force.

Kitchenerite," underestimated French. But as the winter and early spring of 1915 wore on Asquith became more inclined to accept Kitchener's view of the Commander-in-Chief. The optimism did not appear to be as well-founded as the pessimism. In February he was surprised by the inadequacy and lack of order of an important despatch of French's, and on March 18th, he passed on, without adverse comment, Kitchener's damning summing up of the qualities and limitations of French:

> K. spoke to me *very confidentially* about French. He says he is not a really scientific soldier: a good and capable leader in the field; but without adequate equipment of expert knowledge for the huge task of commanding 450,000 men. K. is going out there at the end of the week to confer with Joffre, and to put things on a solid basis.

Throughout this first period of the war, therefore, Kitchener—the only politically alien element within the Cabinet—held the substantial confidence of the Prime Minister. Asquith saw him, not as an infallible demi-god, but as a most valuable addition to the Government. At this stage he would not have subscribed to Margot's view that Kitchener was more of a great poster than a great man.[1]

The pattern of Asquith's life during these first nine months of the war did not undergo any great change. He had a new range of problems with which to deal, of course, as well as some of the old ones which continued, with inconsiderate persistence, to create political bitterness at home. Ireland, despite the show of all-round goodwill in the first days of August, took six weeks to put into cold storage. During this time Asquith was subjected to all the old pressures. Bonar Law and Lansdowne were constantly accusing him of breaches of faith; the King was appealing for more concessions from the Irish; and Redmond was complaining that Nationalist goodwill was already strained beyond the bonds of endurance. The bitterness

---

[1] Margot Asquith, although she most uncharacteristically concealed this in her *Autobiography*, had a deep-seated anti-Kitchener prejudice. As long ago as May 18th, 1910, she had written to Lord Crewe: " I wanted so much to talk to you about Kitchener last night. Just one word—I know him very *well*. He is a natural cad, tho' he is remarkably clever. I know if you and Henry . . . send him to India you will regret it all your days. Hardinge is the man to send and he is younger and straight and a great gentleman. Never have dealings with a liar however clever." (*Asquith Papers*, box 46, f. 126).

could not be kept under the political carpet. On September 15th, (with the Battle of the Aisne in full progress), after a violent attack upon the Prime Minister by Law, the Unionist Party staged a mass exodus of the House of Commons " by way of washing their hands of responsibility for our wicked ways." " Bonar Law never sunk so low in his gutter as today," Asquith wrote later that evening.

The Welsh Disestablishment Bill, with the Archbishop of Canterbury stirring up as much trouble as possible, provided an even longer wartime hangover. As late as March, 1915 Asquith was complaining that " McKenna (of all people) has let us in for a terrible mess in this Welsh Church business."[1] Nevertheless, it was exceptional, at least after the first six weeks of the war, for such traditional controversies to obtrude on to Asquith's agenda. Parliamentary business as a whole occupied substantially less of his time. The House of Commons, when in session, continued to sit at normal hours and to meet five days a week. But there was rarely need for the Prime Minister to be there late in the evening, and there were frequent and long recesses. In addition, nearly all outside political activity had come to a stop. In late September and early October Asquith addressed four meetings organised by the Lord Mayors of each of the capital cities—London, Edinburgh, Dublin and Cardiff. Apart from an appeal for more munitions, delivered at Newcastle in April, 1915, these were the only speeches of any importance which he made outside the House of Commons during the first nine months of the war. He did not visit his constituency during this period.

The time so released was more than taken up with Cabinet, War Council and other committee meetings. At first the Cabinet met almost daily. There were sixteen meetings between August 10th, 1914 and the end of that month. This degree of frequency continued almost unabated throughout September and October.[2] There were also occasional meetings of the Committee of Imperial Defence as well as

[1] By then it was the Welsh M.P.s, " *moutons enragés*," as Asquith described them, " . . . (who) baa-ed and bleated and tossed their crinkled horns as if they were in a gale on one of their native mountainsides," who were after the blood of the Government. The Archbishop, never Asquith's favourite prelate, had done his worst in the autumn.

[2] These meetings were often concerned with surprisingly detailed questions of troop movements. Another " war " subject, which caused acute controversy and occupied two full meetings was the amount of pension for childless army widows. The King had written before the first meeting

more frequent informal gatherings, sometimes late at night, of the ministers intimately concerned with the progress of the war.

During November the pattern changed. A War Council (the term had sometimes been used before to describe meetings of the Committee of Imperial Defence) was set up. It was formally a committee of the Cabinet, with the Prime Minister in the chair and Kitchener, Grey, Crewe, Lloyd George and Churchill as the representatives of the parent body. Balfour was a permanent member from outside, and Haldane was added in January. In addition, the Chiefs of Staff attended regularly and other service experts were called in as required. Colonel Hankey was secretary. This body normally met several times a week. With its formation the Committee of Imperial Defence ceased to function as such, and the Cabinet reverted nearer to a peacetime pattern of meetings. For the remainder of 1914 twice weekly meetings were the rule. In the first months of 1915, more than one meeting a week was unusual. There were also occasional *ad hoc* Cabinet committees, although the Prime Minister did not habitually participate in these. In early 1915 he made an exception and acted as chairman of one on food prices—of which the secretary was " a clever young Cambridge don called Keynes."

These changes, and the circumstances from which they sprang, meant that Asquith could no longer be away from Downing Street for more than a few days at a time. The long autumn holidays and the

---

urging greater generosity, and somewhat unexpectedly praying in aid the views of George Bernard Shaw. Eventually Asquith took a vote on the matter (some members wanted a secret ballot but he overruled that). The date was October 13th and the result was as follows:

For 7/6	For 6/6	For 5/-
Churchill	Asquith	Lloyd George
	Harcourt	Lucas
	Simon	Wood
	Emmott	Runciman
	Haldane	McKenna
	Pease	Runciman
	Masterman	Grey
	Kitchener	Beauchamp
	Crewe	Hobhouse
	Samuel	

substantial Christmas, Easter and Whitsun breaks of pre-war days became impossible. But during any single week of normal activity the demands on his time were not vastly greater than they had been before. He continued with his habit of frequent informal dinner parties followed by a few rubbers of bridge. He continued to read voluminously and developed a new practice of retreating, in the late afternoons when the House of Commons was not sitting, to the Athenaeum library. He found it the only place where he could avoid constant interruption. Thus, on January 21st, 1915, he wrote to Miss Stanley:

> After writing to you, and writing my Cabinet letter, and disposing of a lot of smaller things, I walked across after 6 to the Athenaeum, & took up a novel, " Sir Perryworm's Wife " (a good title), wh. with judicious skipping I read from cover to cover. . . . I found it readable & *rather* soothing.

His reading (often more serious than this) did not interfere with the vast flow of his correspondence. He was quick and meticulous in replying to his official letters, as he was in dealing with all papers, and he had a wide range of private correspondents as well. But to Miss Stanley the tide continued to mount. By the outbreak of the war he was already writing an average of almost a letter a day to her. For August, 1914 the total was twenty-six. And they were very substantial letters. Few were under 500 words in length; many ran to a thousand.

This volume of communication continued until the end of 1914, and then became even greater. Miss Stanley, who had spent most of the autumn in Cheshire, came to London to undergo a course of training as a nurse at the London Hospital in Whitechapel. Her proximity, aided by the extraordinarily good posts of those days, was an incentive to still more frequent letters. During the first three months of 1915 Asquith wrote to her on 141 separate occasions. On one day— Tuesday, March 30th—he wrote her four letters of a combined length of just over 3000 words. The convenience of Sunday deliveries (for payment of an extra ½d.) avoided any large gaps in the flow, and the speed of the week-day ones (letters posted in Whitehall at about 6 p.m. arrived at the hospital the same evening) kept it almost even throughout the twenty-four hours.

During this period Asquith saw Miss Stanley only about once a week. On Friday afternoons he often took a rather time-restricted motor drive with her. When it was over he would drop her back at the

London Hospital and then endeavour, for he had again taken to going to the country for week-ends, to get through the City and Embankment traffic in time to catch the 5 o'clock train from Victoria Station. Sometimes he succeeded, but sometimes, despite the station master waiting hopefully outside to escort him hurriedly in, he missed it. The journey then took several hours longer.

His destination on these occasions was Walmer Castle, beyond Dover. This battlemented residence, commanding a fine view of the Straits and, on a clear day, of the occupied coast of Belgium and the Pas-de-Calais, was (as it is today) the perquisite of the Lord Warden of the Cinque Ports. When that office had fallen vacant in the autumn of 1913, Asquith had been tempted to take it for himself. It was an appropriate enough office for a Prime Minister, particularly for a war-time one as he was soon to become. He would have followed Pitt and Palmerston and preceded Churchill. But the King wrote discouragingly, suggesting that he might find the expense excessive. The result of Asquith's own enquiries pointed in the same direction. He found that the gardens alone would cost £800 a year to maintain. His mind then turned away from the plan, and he appointed Lord Beauchamp in his place.

With the outbreak of war he was again drawn to the south-eastern corner of Kent. His first war-time week-end away from London was at Lympne on August 30th and 31st. " I always think the view here across the Marsh when there is a real play of light and shade one of the most fascinating in England," he wrote. On the Sunday he motored to Folkestone and Dover and visited the Belgian refugees and some of the first of the British wounded. That autumn he went very little to the Wharf. It was open and available, but he seemed to think it was in the wrong direction, and in December he persuaded Beauchamp to let him have Walmer for three or four months. It was a convenient half-way house to the front. French and his staff officers could easily be brought there for consultation; Kitchener was available from Broome; and Churchill, either using his own destroyers to make mostly unauthorised visits to the B.E.F. or arranging for others to be transported by them, was frequently passing through. Several notable conferences were organised in the library of the house which was at once the most and the least insular in England. Its position gave Asquith a sense—almost entirely appropriate—of detached participation in the war which he was called upon to direct.

347

" Mr. Asquith, do you take an interest in the War? " Lady Tree asked him after one drive from Walmer. And he passed the remark on, commenting that she had " a good tho' often disguised sense of humour." To Northcliffe and other critics the question would have seemed a shrewd thrust. To Asquith it was a joke, and not even a dangerous one. Of course his life was dominated by the fighting and his letters were full both of the sweep of events and of the personal tragedies which they brought in their train. The battles had to be fought and the suffering had to be endured, but he was too eclectic to fill his mind with any single subject and too fastidious to pretend to an enthusiasm which he did not feel.

CHAPTER XXII

FROM LIBERALISM TO COALITION

1915

By the end of 1914 there was widespread discontent with the conduct of the war. The public was disappointed by the absence of quick victories. The generals, the Press and the politicians were on terms of mutual irritation. Within the Cabinet, the most questing minds were looking for some alternative to the bloody stalemate in France which had settled in with the Battle of the Aisne.

On December 29th Churchill wrote to Asquith transmitting Lord Fisher's scheme for forcing open the Baltic and landing on the flat shore 90 miles north of Berlin. This was certainly preferable, he commented, to sending more armies " to chew barbed wire in Flanders." Two days later he wrote again, raising the possibility of an attack on Gallipoli as well as the Baltic landing, and urging a series of daily meetings of the War Council for a thorough review of the whole range of strategic possibilities. " No topic can be pressed to any fruitful result at weekly intervals,"[a] he concluded.

Lloyd George also sent a New Year's Eve letter. He, too, wanted more frequent War Council meetings and the opening up of a new theatre—preferably from Salonika; but he was also full of criticism of the military leaders (including Kitchener) for their incompetence about the supply of ammunition: " Had I not been a witness of their deplorable lack of provision I should not have thought it possible that men so responsibly placed could have displayed so little foresight."[b]

Asquith did not treat these communications defensively. " I have also received today two long memoranda—one from Winston, the other from Lloyd George (quite good, the latter) as to the public conduct of the war," he wrote to Miss Stanley. . . . " I am summoning our little ' War Council ' for Thursday and Friday to review the whole situation. . . . " At these meetings (on January 7th and 8th) and at a subsequent one on January 13th a more comprehensive piece of forward planning than anything hitherto known was attempted. Unfortunately for our knowledge of Asquith's state of mind on these occasions, he saw Miss Stanley very quickly after two of them. As a result he communicated most of his impressions verbally instead of by letter. On January 13th, he wrote: "A most interesting discussion, but so confidential and secret that I won't put anything down on paper, but I will talk fully to you tomorrow. . . . " He did however record some comments about personalities:

I maintained an almost unbroken silence until the end, when I intervened with my (four) conclusions. . . . French sat next to me on one side and A.J.B. on the other; next to French, K(itchener), then old Jacky Fisher, Winston and Sir A. Wilson (the Naval Trinity); and beyond them Crewe, Grey and Ll. George. You won't often see a stranger collection of men at one table. Of the lay disputants the best were A.J.B. and Ll. George. French and K. were polite and almost mealy-mouthed to one another. Happily the great question upon which they are nearly at daggers-drawn (how the new ' K ' armies are to be organised—as separate entities, or intermingled with the old units) tho' broached, was tacitly postponed to a later and more convenient date. Winston (if such a phrase is possible) showed a good deal of rugged fluency.

Asquith's four conclusions were sensibly worked out compromises between conflicting views. But these compromises contained the seeds of destruction of the Liberal Government. The great conflict was between " Easterners " and " Westerners," those on the one hand who were constantly seeking an escape from the Flanders *impasse*, and those on the other who thought that the decisive battles must inevitably be fought in the West and who were consequently hostile to any deflection of resources from the vital theatre. Asquith stood between the two schools, but appreciably nearer to the " Westerners." In consequence, while he did not resist the demands of Churchill and Lloyd George for some diversion which would help both ourselves and the Russians, he did not force the military leaders to disgorge from France the men and materials which might have given it a high chance of success.

This was not only because Asquith was torn in his own mind. It was also because he never thought it his duty to impose strategic decisions upon the service chiefs. They were the experts. When they disagreed his duty was to coax them towards agreement. But he would no more have thought it right to issue a directive which ran counter to their united voices than to tell the Lord Chief Justice what judgments he should deliver.

As a result, the caution of the military leaders—and of Kitchener in particular—led to a somewhat half-hearted mounting of the Dardanelles expedition. The original plan was to force the Narrows and to capture both the Gallipoli Peninsula and Constantinople by a purely naval force composed of a large number of semi-obsolete battleships. This plan commanded the support of Kitchener, because it might help Russia without the employment of any British troops, and of Churchill (although he would have liked a more complete commitment), because it offered the prospect of a world-shaking naval victory. It did not command the support of Fisher. The First Sea Lord was never much attracted by the idea of a foray in the Eastern Mediterranean. If any amphibious move was to be attempted he preferred his own plan for a Baltic landing. Still more was he influenced by a naval version of the extreme " Western " theory. The great task of the Royal Navy was to defeat the German Grand Fleet in pitched battle. Until that had been accomplished any diversion was dangerous. But if, in spite of the risks, a diversion was to be attempted, it was essential that the army should be involved in the enterprise. Fisher, like the Dardanelles Commission when it came to report in 1917, did not believe that a fleet could capture a peninsula; and his views here were fortified by a growing jealousy of Kitchener's position.

In all military matters the Secretary of State for War was supreme. He had a politician (H. J. Tennant, Margot Asquith's brother) under him, who was useful for dealing with the House of Commons, but there was no question of one being over him. Not only was he impregnable in his own department, but he had enough spare prestige to exert considerable influence over naval dispositions. His voice was an important one in favour of the Dardanelles plan, but he gave his blessing to the naval part of the expedition while retaining complete freedom as to whether or not to commit any troops.

Fisher enjoyed no such power in his own department, let alone the right to interfere in others. Above him he had a highly political, determined and argumentative First Lord, who was 34 years his junior. In peacetime and during the early months of the war Churchill and Fisher worked together well enough. The admiral was grateful to the politician for having brought him back into active service; they warmed each other with mutual congratulations on the Navy's readiness for the conflict; and the fondness of the one for working from the early hours of the morning and of the other for continuing far into the night meant that the high command of the Admiralty was virtually on a shift system and that these two dominant personalities did not see too much of each other. At the close of 1914 Fisher was still concluding letters to Churchill with assurances that he was " yours till hell freezes." But alas, as Churchill pointed out in *The World Crisis*, the moment soon came when this improbable event had apparently occurred. As the plans for the Dardanelles were driven forward by the force of Churchill's eloquence, Fisher became increasingly apprehensive and sulky. On January 28th Asquith wrote:

Another personal matter which rather worries me is the growing friction between Winston and Fisher. They came to see me this morning, before the War Council, and gave tongue to their mutual grievances. I tried to compose their differences by a compromise, under which Winston was to give up for the present his bombardment of Zeebrugge, Fisher withdrawing his opposition to the operation against the Dardanelles. When at the Council we came to discuss the latter—wh. is warmly supported by Kitchener and Grey and enthusiastically by A.J.B.[1]—old " Jacky " maintained an obstinate and ominous silence. He is always threatening to resign & writes an almost daily letter to Winston, expressing his desire to return to the cultivation of his " roses at Richmond." K. has now taken on the role of conciliator, for wh. you might think that he was not naturally cut out!

Here then was the rift at the Admiralty, which despite the efforts of Asquith, Kitchener and other would-be conciliators was never again to be fully healed. This departmental quarrel eventually brought down a government which over $8\frac{1}{4}$ years had suffered and survived almost every known political vicissitude. Before that could happen, however, the quarrel had to be exacerbated and Conservative distrust of Churchill increased by failure to achieve a quick success in the Dardanelles. These two conditions were abundantly fulfilled by the middle of May. The naval action started reasonably well at the end

---

[1] What peculiar manifestation of " enthusiasm " by Balfour, one wonders, can have caused Asquith, so rarely loose with language, to differentiate between this and the " warmth " of Kitchener and Grey?

Reginald McKenna addresses a meeting

A visit to Ireland, 1912:
Left to right, standing: Sir H. Verney, Mr. Arthur Asquith, Master of
Elibank, Miss Elizabeth Asquith, Mr. Cyril Asquith, Mr. Bonham Carter
Sitting: Lady Verney, Mr. Asquith, Mrs. Asquith,
Mr. Birrell, Miss Violet Asquith

Chained together at the Admiralty: Fisher and Churchill

of February and reached its first climax on March 18th, when the fleet carried out a major bombardment and advanced to within a few miles of the Narrows. Had there been troops available for a large-scale landing at this stage, or had the navy pressed on relentlessly on its own, a quick break-through to Constantinople might well have been achieved. But the troops were not available. It was not until March 10th that Kitchener agreed to the despatch from England of the 29th Division, the employment of which had been at issue throughout February; and it was not until March 12th that he gave command of the expeditionary force to Sir Ian Hamilton.

Asquith allowed himself, perhaps against his better judgment, to accept Kitchener's procrastination. The movement of his mind on the issue is clearly shown by two letters to Miss Stanley. In the first, dated 23rd February, he wrote:

We are all agreed (except K.) that the naval adventure in the Dardanelles shd. be backed up by a strong military force. I say " except K.," but he quite agrees in principle. Only he is very sticky about sending out there the 29th Division, which is the best one we have left at home. . . . One must take a lot of risks in war, and I am strongly of opinion that the chance of forcing the Dardanelles, & occupying Constantinople, and cutting Turkey in half, and arousing on our side the whole Balkan peninsula, presents such a unique opportunity that we ought to hazard elsewhere rather than forgo it. If he can be convinced, well & good: but to discard his advice and overrule his judgment on a military question is to take a great responsibility. So I am rather anxious.

Kitchener was not convinced. And on February 26th Asquith wrote:

Our War Council lasted nearly 2½ hours. Winston was in some ways at his worst—having quite a presentable case. He was noisy, rhetorical, tactless & temperless—or full. K., I think on the whole rightly, insisted on keeping his 29th Division at home, free to go either to the Dardanelles or to France. . . .

Close on the heels of this military delay there followed an even more damaging piece of naval delay. Paradoxically, it appears to have arisen directly out of Kitchener's eventual decision to commit a large force to the theatre. After the partially successful bombardment of March 18th the Turks waited with apprehension for an early renewal of an attack which they were in poor condition to withstand. Such a renewal was the original intention of de Robeck, the British admiral in command. But on March 22nd he conferred with Hamilton, who had just arrived in the Aegean, and who persuaded him, perhaps without too much difficulty, to wait until the expeditionary force was assembled for a simultaneous thrust.

This news was received by Churchill with incredulity and by Asquith with disappointment.

" Winston came to see me about the Dardanelles," the Prime Minister wrote late at night on March 24th. " The weather is infamous there, and the Naval experts seem to be suffering from a fit of nerves. They are now disposed to wait until the troops can assist them in force, which ought to be not later than about April 10th. Winston thinks, and I agree with him, that the ships, as soon as the weather clears, & the aeroplanes can detect the condition of the forts & the position of the concealed guns, ought to make another push; & I hope this will be done."

But it was not done. Fisher stood out against Churchill's attempt to overrule de Robeck; and, once again, Asquith subordinated his own better (if tentative) judgment to the opinion of the professional experts. The delay which then followed was considerably longer than had been feared. It was April 25th before the combined attack could be mounted. The Turks, under their German commander, used the interval to great advantage. The Gallipoli landings, which took place on a coast which a month before had been deserted and unfortified, met with the stiffest resistance. Casualties were fearful and only the most constricted beachheads could be established. Within a few days the concept of a great war of movement in the Eastern Mediterranean had lost itself in a confrontation as immobile as that which prevailed on the Western Front.

Meanwhile the fleet could do little but hang ineffectively about. At the end of the first week in May de Robeck proposed a further attempt at a naval forcing of the Narrows, but this was vetoed from London. Even Churchill was doubtful about a full-scale attack at this stage— mainly because he was trying to encourage the Italians into the war by offering to put some of the Dardanelles ships under their command. He and Fisher nevertheless managed to quarrel about the exact form in which the veto should be applied. Then, on May 12th, at the price of great bitterness from Kitchener, it was decided that the threat from man U-boats made it necessary to withdraw *Queen Elizabeth* from the Dardanelles. She was the flagship of the expedition and the only great modern vessel which had been committed. Her withdrawal was a heavy blow to morale and as near to a confession of failure as can easily be imagined. In these circumstances the tension within the Admiralty increased to breaking point, and Churchill's reputation outside (and particularly with the Tories) plunged downwards.

This situation at the Admiralty and not the shell crisis, as French, Northcliffe, and, for different reasons, Churchill, wished to believe, was the real cause of the fall of the Liberal Government. " Churchill did not know it," Lord Beaverbrook wrote, " but he was like a man chained to an enemy—so that both must live or die together. If you throw your chained enemy into the sea he pulls you after him."[c] But the position was worse than that. Immersion did not depend upon Churchill's volition. If Fisher chose to throw himself into the sea (which metaphorically is precisely what he did, early on the morning of May 14th) the First Lord had to go in too. And, for the moment, the Government was chained to Churchill just as tightly as Churchill was chained to Fisher.

This is not to say that the trouble about ammunition supply was without its effect on the Government's standing, and on its internal cohesion. Shell shortage was perennial throughout the First World War. This was partly due to lack of energy and imagination in organising supply to meet the incredible rate of consumption involved in repeated assaults upon heavily fortified positions. It may also have owed something, as Mr. Alan Moorehead has suggested, to the fact that when the generals set themselves an impossible objective, and failed to achieve it, they had to blame something. As they would not question the rules by which they fought, they blamed the lack of ammunition: " If only they had had more shells to fire all would have been well. Just a few more rounds, another few guns, and the miracle would have happened."[d] But the miracles did not happen, and the generals blamed the politicians. The trouble was accentuated by the fact that Kitchener, who counted almost as a politician for this purpose, was congenitally mean about the expenditure of ammunition—as well as about some other things. He had won his reputation in a campaign fought on a shoestring, and he hated to see his juniors squandering money and material in France.

The issue began to come to a head after the battle of Neuve Chapelle on March 10th. Nearly as many shells were expended in that doubtful success as in the whole 2¾ years of the Boer War. When it was over French began secretly to use the British Press for complaints against Asquith and Kitchener. Critical articles appeared in *The Times*, *The Observer* and the *Morning Post*. These in turn led to accusations of intrigue and mutual recriminations amongst ministers. Massingham (the editor of the *Daily News*) told Asquith on March 24th that Churchill was intriguing to get Grey replaced by Balfour at the Foreign Office, and Lloyd George, who came across to 10, Downing Street on the following day for " his favourite morning indulgence (it corresponds to the dram drinking of the Clyde workmen)—a 10 minute discursive discussion of things in general," gave Asquith his view that the story was substantially true. Then, on March 29th, McKenna told Asquith that Northcliffe was engineering a campaign to supplant him as Prime Minister and that both Lloyd George (the chosen successor) and Churchill were parties to the scheme. But Edwin Montagu, whom Asquith consulted at luncheon, said that McKenna and Balfour were the real mischief-makers, and this view, at least so far as it concerned McKenna, was reinforced with passion by Lloyd George, to whom Asquith put the story direct that evening. He denied his own part in it with such emotion that " his eyes were wet with tears " and Asquith was " sure that, (for) all his Celtic capacity for impulsive and momentary fervour, he was quite sincere."

The next move was for Asquith to summon Lloyd George and McKenna to a tripartite meeting, by the end of which he thought that he had established a better feeling between them, but not before Lloyd George had accused McKenna of having inspired an article in the *Daily Chronicle*, which implicated the Chancellor in a plot against the Prime Minister. Asquith, in the midst of this spate of rumour and counter-rumour, plot and counter-plot, showed little sign of bad nerves. This may have owed something to complacency about his own position; but to a much greater extent it was due to a natural generosity of temperament which made it almost impossible for him to believe that others were not as contemptuous of intrigue as he was himself.

Nevertheless, the poisoned atmosphere made it more difficult to set up a new Munitions Committee. Lloyd George was the obvious chairman, but he would not serve unless Kitchener were excluded from membership, and Kitchener threatened that if the body were constituted over his head he would resign. Eventually Lloyd George got his way, but only at the price of a blinding Cabinet row, during which Kitchener strode towards the door (which was fortunately blocked by J. A. Pease) and Churchill and McKenna gleefully joined in at the heels of the protagonists. Asquith eventually restored some semblance of unity and good humour, but the incident left him with a lasting sense of resigned distaste.

"Not for years," he wrote, after talking it over with Crewe, " ... have I on reflection been more disillusioned and from the personal point of view depressed. The man who came out of it best is Kitchener, clumsy and tactless in expression as he often is.... On the other hand the people who ought to have known better showed themselves at their worst. Winston was pretty bad, but he is impulsive and borne along on the flood of his too copious tongue.... The two who came out really worst were Ll.G., who almost got down to the level of a petty police court advocate, and McKenna, who played the part of a wrecker, pure and simple. It will take me a long time to forget and forgive their attitude and you know well that I am not prone to be censorious or resentful.... I *hate* this side of politics, when it compels one to revise for the worse one's estimate of men whom one likes ...."

Four days after this incident Asquith went to Newcastle-upon-Tyne to make his " munitions " speech to employers and workmen. Before going he received a written assurance from Kitchener that French had told him that " with the present supply of ammunition he will have as much as his troops will be able to use on the next forward movement." On the basis of this assurance, Asquith, while urging great efforts in the future, congratulated the armament workers on what had already been done, and refuted any charge that they had let the country down. French subsequently recorded[1] that, with this speech, he " lost any hope that (he) had entertained of receiving help from the Government as then constituted." Three weeks later, as the Commander-in-Chief watched the early stages of the battle of Festubert from a ruined church tower, this lost hope, so he later said, drove him to a sacrifice which he knew meant his certain recall from France: " I could see that the absence of sufficient artillery support was doubling and trebling our losses in men. I therefore determined on taking the most drastic measures to destroy the apathy of a Government which had brought the Empire to the brink of disaster."[e] These measures

[1] He dealt with this 1915 incident in his somewhat loosely entitled book, *1914*, published in 1919.

involved handing his carefully if partially documented case against the Government to the military correspondent of *The Times* and sending his politically agile A.D.C., Captain Guest, M.P., to England with instructions to lay it before Lloyd George, Balfour and Bonar Law. The direct result, French believed, was the fall of the Liberal Government and its replacement by the first Coalition.

Whatever the exact merits of the shell dispute between the Commander-in-Chief and the Government, it is clear that this account by French is on several counts far too self-heroic. It is possible that Kitchener's mid-April letter to Asquith was based on a misinterpretation of what French had said to him. But French was well capable of saying to different people what he thought they most wanted to hear. On May 20th, ten days after his " drastic " decision at Festubert, he wrote to Asquith in the following terms:

For two days I have been hesitating to add an iota to the troubles and anxieties which must weigh upon you just now. You have, however, shown me so much true, generous kindness throughout this trying campaign that I venture at this critical juncture to convey to you what is in my inmost thoughts. I am sure in the whole history of war no General in the field has ever been helped in a difficult task by the head of his Government as I have been supported and strengthened by your unfailing sympathy and encouragement. I am sure therefore I may address you privately and informally as a friend.*

French then went on to complain bitterly about the treatment he received from Kitchener. But whatever the purpose of his letter, its tone was wholly incompatible with his view that he was fighting a resolute, reckless, selfless campaign against the lethargic head of a complacent Government. Nor, in reality, did he in any way sacrifice his own position by his actions that May. His removal from France did not take place until seven months and hundreds of thousands of casualties later; and it had nothing to do with the part he had or had not played in the fall of the Liberal Government. Nor even, as has been already suggested, was that part in fact decisive. This was largely accidental. The campaign in England which French mounted after his return from the Festubert church tower might well have been more effective than those which he was directing in France. But it was forestalled. Colonel Repington of *The Times* made use of his information in the edition of Friday, May 14th. But soon after five o'clock that morning Fisher had stalked out of the Admiralty intent on resignation. Before *The Times* article could be digested news of his departure was beginning to seep out. Guest had given French's memorandum to Lloyd George and Bonar Law two days before, but when they together saw Asquith on the following Monday morning it was the problem of the Admiralty rather than of the shell shortage which filled their minds. And by the middle of the next week, when other newspapers were taking up and embroidering the disclosures of *The Times*, the formation of a Coalition Government had been already announced.

For a few days Asquith tried hard to dissuade Fisher from resignation. First, he had to track him down—his early morning resignation letter to Churchill announced that he was leaving immediately for Scotland—but in fact he had locked himself in a room in the Charing Cross Hotel. There Asquith had delivered to him a sharp letter ordering him, in the King's name, to return at once to duty. This at least had the effect of bringing Fisher to Downing Street, and the Prime Minister tried upon him a combination of his own magisterial manner, Lloyd George's cajolery and McKenna's appeal to old friendship. None of these were of much effect, although Fisher did go back to the Admiralty for a few days. While there he composed various ultimata against Churchill, including a remarkable statement of the conditions on which he would stay and " guarantee the successful termination of the war." He would serve under neither Churchill nor Balfour nor indeed under any other First Lord unless the powers of the civilian were so restricted that he occupied " the same position towards me as Mr. Tennant, M.P., does to Lord Kitchener (and very well he does it)." Fisher also demanded the dismissal of the rest of the Board of Admiralty.

This document convinced Asquith that he was dealing with a megalomaniac, and he let him go without further remonstrance. By the time that he received it (May 19th) Fisher's presence in office had ceased to be important. On the 17th, confronted with the threat of a vicious Tory attack in the House of Commons upon the whole administration of the Admiralty, which would have been most damaging both to the Government and to its hopes of enticing a wavering Italy into the war,[1] Asquith had quickly agreed that a coalition was

[1] Grey was away ill, and Asquith, in temporary charge of the Foreign Office, was closely engaged in these delicate negotiations.

the only way out. He laconically conveyed his decision to Stamfordham (for the King) that evening:

After much reflection, & consultation today with Lloyd George
and Bonar Law, I have come decidedly to the conclusion that, for
the successful prosecution of the war, the Govt. must be re-
constructed on a broad and non-party basis.[g]

On the 19th Bonar Law formally signified his agreement. Such an
arrangement meant that Churchill would have to leave the Admiralty.
This was a clearly understood Tory condition for joining. Fisher could
therefore be allowed to throw himself overboard.

Asquith's next task was the delicate one of the allocation of offices.
It was one which he approached with distaste. Although he had
always been a moderate in politics he hated, in a way that would have
been incomprehensible to Lloyd George or Churchill, the idea of
bringing Tories into his Cabinet. It was not so much the policies as
the political manners of the opposition which he disliked. It was
his old Liberal mandarin spirit coming out again. "To seem to
welcome into the intimacy of the political household, strange alien,
hitherto hostile figures," he wrote, was "a most intolerable task."

So was the sacrifice of old friends. The two most difficult acts of
political butchery which he had to perform were the removal of
Churchill from the Admiralty and the complete exclusion of Haldane.
Both were laid down by the Conservatives, with an almost equal lack
of justice and prescience, as *conditiones sine qua non*. Asquith reluctantly
accepted them both. With Churchill he had a great deal of trouble.
Between May 17th and 21st he received six letters from the First Lord,
pointing between them to violent alternations of mood. In the first of
these letters Churchill appeared to accept the inevitability of his
removal from the Admiralty, and asked for "another military department"—he was probably including Colonies in this category—
but if that was not convenient, he asked for employment in the field.
In the second letter (18th May) he said that he would accept Colonies
if offered but pleaded to be allowed to stay on at the Admiralty. In the
third (20th May) he told Asquith that Sir Arthur Wilson (whom he had
quickly retired in 1911) would serve as First Sea Lord under him and
under no-one else. "This is the greatest compliment I have ever been
paid,"[h] he added.

Asquith replied firmly and at once to this letter. "I have your
letter," he wrote. "You must take it as settled you are not to remain

at the Admiralty. I am sure you will try to take a large view of an unexampled situation. Everyone has to make sacrifices. . . . "[i] He hoped to offer him another post, but he could not for the moment say what.

Churchill came back with a highly-charged six-page epistle on the following day (May 21st): " It is not clinging to office or to this particular office or my own interest and advancement which moves me. I am clinging to my *task* and to my *duty*. . . . I did not believe it was possible to endure such anxiety. . . . I can only look to you. . . . You alone can do me justice and do justice to the military need."[j]

It was of no avail. The Tory leaders, to whom he also appealed, were inflexible, and Asquith had no room for manoeuvre on the issue. Perhaps because of a hard little note from Bonar Law, Churchill came, later that day, to accept the inevitable. He wrote again to Asquith with contrition and resignation: And then, still on the same day, he sent the sixth and last of this series of letters. He had tried hard to persuade Sir Arthur Wilson to serve under Balfour, but in vain.

Wilson's importance lay more in Churchill's mind than in that of anyone else. Balfour became First Lord, Sir Henry Jackson became First Sea Lord, and Churchill, a seven-year phase of brilliant Cabinet success firmly behind him, retired into the semi-shadows with the sinecure post of Chancellor of the Duchy of Lancaster. He had gone down fighting, although much the best letter on his behalf had been written, not by himself, but by his wife.

" Winston may in your eyes and in those with whom he has to work have faults," Clementine Churchill told Asquith, " but he has the supreme quality which I venture to say very few of your present or future Cabinet possess—the power, the imagination, the deadliness, to fight Germany."[k]

Haldane put up no similar struggle. He went quietly, but he went with some bitterness against Asquith. The bitterness was more easily understandable than were Asquith's actions. The Conservatives' veto on Haldane was even firmer than that on Churchill; they would not serve in a Cabinet with him, and Grey, when he tried to intervene, found them quite unshakable on the point. It was a veto of pure prejudice. In Churchill's case the Tories genuinely believed that he had failed at the Admiralty and that the progress of the war would be assisted by his replacement by one of their own men. There was no question of Haldane having failed as Lord Chancellor,[1] or of its being of much importance to the war if he had. Nor did the Conservatives particularly want the post for themselves—it was in fact filled by the Liberal Solicitor-General, Stanley Buckmaster. They were against Haldane for reasons which the more intelligent of them must have known in their own minds were absolute nonsense—that he spoke German well, had visited the country many times, and had once said, in a purely philosophical sense, that it was his spiritual home; and the Harmsworth Press, on the basis of these straws, had mounted a vicious " McCarthyite " campaign against him. The force of this campaign and the difficulty of Asquith's decision should not be under-estimated. Had he insisted upon the retention of Haldane the whole coalition scheme might have collapsed and the country, at a most critical stage, been left in political confusion. Even so it was exactly the sort of issue on which Asquith might have been expected to be at his best, where his disdain of clamour, intolerance and prejudice should have given him a rock-like firmness. But he was not. He capitulated, sadly and self-critically, but relatively easily.

Still more surprisingly, he failed to express to Haldane the deep regret which he undoubtedly felt. He wrote to Grey in the warmest terms about Haldane. He wrote to Crewe (who remained in the Government) to thank him for his help in the chapter which was closing. But to Haldane he neither wrote nor spoke. The intimacy between the two men, as was seen in chapter XVII, had foundered on the jagged edge of divergent tastes, but Haldane remained Asquith's oldest political ally, as the Prime Minister did not fail to point out to Grey. They had stood together in every battle for 30 years. Henceforward, as a result of the Prime Minister's silence, they stood a little apart. It was the most uncharacteristic fault of Asquith's whole career.

[1] Although Asquith thought that Haldane's taking of the " King's Pledge " (total abstinence for the duration of the war) in early April led to a notable diminution in his energy and buoyancy. As soon as he ceased to be a minister Haldane reverted to more normal habits. " When you come to London let us meet as of yore one evening," he wrote to Rosebery on June 9th. " As I am no longer a servant of the Crown I have ceased to confine myself to soda-water." (Heuston; *Lives of the Lord Chancellors*, 1885–1940, p. 225). Asquith himself never made the mistake of following the example which Lloyd George had persuaded the King to set.

How can it be explained? How, indeed, can his whole attitude throughout these crisis days be explained? The unusual factor was not his passivity; that had long been a characteristic, and one which was sometimes a considerable source of strength. What was unusual was the speed with which he permitted solutions which were not his own to be pressed upon him. Churchill subsequently criticised him for not allowing a few days' delay, accompanied by Italy's entry into the war (which took place on May 23rd) to strengthen his own position. It was most unlike Asquith not to give this a chance to happen.

What was still more unlike him was the note of self-pity, rendering him insensitive to the wounds of others, which crept into his correspondence. In conversation with Samuel, in letters to Churchill and to Redmond he stressed his own troubles, trials and sacrifices. He spoke as though having to reconstruct a government was the worst burden that could ever be imposed upon a man. But this was not the only trouble that lay upon him at this time. Throughout the crisis he was preoccupied with private suffering.

Towards the end of April and at the beginning of May there had been signs that his relationship with Miss Stanley was breaking up. The spate of correspondence continued unabated, but an uneven note of anxiety entered into it. On the 22nd he wrote: " You will tell me, won't you, the real truth at once? However hard it may be to me." Then, immediately on top of that " wave of distress and uncertainty " came the news of Rupert Brooke's death on Lemnos, which, he said, caused him " more pain than any (previous) loss in the war." But on April 26th he clutched at a straw and his spirits revived: " To see you again, & be with you, & hear your voice, and above all to feel everything is unchanged, has made a new creature of me. You are the best and richest of life-givers."

The respite was short-lived. For the week-end at the beginning of May he went to stay with Miss Stanley and her family at Alderley. While still there he wrote: " I thought once or twice yesterday, for the first time in our intercourse, that I rather bored you."

Before he left there was another glint in the clouds, and he returned to London with better hope. But by midnight two days later (May 4th) he was again completely cast down and full of general self-doubt: " I walked almost the whole way back to Downing Street[1]

[1] From Mansfield Street, near Oxford Circus.

(nearly run over) ruminating over these things. I sometimes think
that Northcliffe and his obscure crew may perhaps be right. . . ."
For the next few days he oscillated violently between deep
gloom and short bursts of optimism. His letters, to a far greater
extent than ever before, were concerned not with events but with
states of mind and feeling. Miss Stanley was due to go as a nurse to a
military hospital at Wimereux on Monday, May 10th, and this may
have been one reason for the heightened atmosphere. But she did not
go. She was struck down by a fever and took to her bed instead.
Asquith visited her for ten minutes on the Monday evening and
returned to Downing Street with another of her callers. He was in
better spirits than on the occasion of his return six days before:
"I walked back with the Assyrian [Edwin Montagu] from Mansfield Street," he wrote later that night, "and we had (as always)
good conversation. I don't honestly believe that, at this moment,
there are two persons in the world (of opposite sexes) from whom
I cd. more confidently count, whatever troubles or trials I had to
encounter, for whole-hearted love and devotion than you and he:
of course, in quite different ways & senses."
On the Tuesday Asquith wrote her two calm " pattern of events "
letters and paid a brief call at Mansfield Street, but (not greatly to his
surprise) was not allowed to see her. On the Wednesday (May
12th) she wrote and told him that she had decided to marry Edwin
Montagu.
The blow to Asquith was severe. He had long thought of
her marriage as something which must one day occur. They had
discussed it together and he had stressed that he must not be allowed to
stand in its way, and had comforted himself with the wishful thought
that her acquisition of a husband need make little difference to the
intimacy with which they discussed events and individuals. But all
this was very abstract. She had no active suitors, except for Montagu
himself, who had proposed to her two years before and whom,
as was well-known within the Asquith circle, she had then rejected
with some horror. Apart from anything else, she would, unless
Montagu was to lose his fortune, have had to change her religion and
become a Jewess.[1] Asquith subsequently had never thought seriously
of him—the frequent object of their mocking but affectionate joint
laughter, his former parliamentary private secretary and most loyal

[1] In 1915 she took this obstacle in her stride.

supporter, the man whom only two days before he had described as his most devoted male friend—in this context. Probably he had never thought seriously of anyone, for once the news was broken to him all wishful thinking about continuing intimacy quickly went out of his mind. He never reproached Miss Stanley, not even for the suddenness of her action. He never reproached Montagu. " I have just had a most characteristically noble and generous letter from E.S.M.", he wrote on May 21st. " I love him." But he made no attempt to conceal from either of them or from himself what a heavy blow he had received, and how great a change it must make.

He wrote a three-line note to Miss Stanley on the Wednesday, and another on the Friday night, a few hours after Fisher's resignation. Then, at the end of the following Monday morning, and just after his crucial interview with Bonar Law and Lloyd George, a " most revealing and heart-rending reply " came from her. Asquith wrote back at once: she alone in all the world could have helped him in the " most hellish days " that had just gone by. The question now was whether he should see her before she went away on the Thursday. He was excessively self-abnegatory about it. He was determined not to " add to (her) perplexities or increase (her) suffering." Over the next few days of his crisis with Churchill, his crisis with Haldane, he tormented himself with this problem. It was made worse by the postponement of her departure from London.

Then, at last, a week later, he saw her for a brief half-hour and she was away.

He next wrote to her from G.H.Q. in France, where he had gone for a short visit to the battlefront on June 3rd. He had recovered somewhat:

I have made up my mind to try (with whatever I have left) to push this war through. Apart from that, " *tout passe, tout casse, tout lasse.*"
I have only one prayer—night & day, day & night—that you may be truly & perfectly happy.

On July 24th the marriage took place. Asquith sent Miss Stanley two little silver boxes " with all my love, and more wishes than words can frame for your complete and unbroken happiness." During that autumn he wrote to her three or four times, but it was noticeable that all these letters were in reply to initiatives of hers. The last, before a gap of several years, was a note of thanks for a Christmas present.

So this great epistolary friendship came to an end. Miss Stanley, the evidence suggests, deeply fond of Asquith and excited by his confidence though she was, had begun to find it a crushing and frightening emotional burden. This was probably one of her motives for escaping into a *mariage de raison*. It was a pity that she chose the moment that she did. Her sustenance of Asquith collapsed at a time when he was in peculiar need of it.

CHAPTER XXIII

A TROUBLED GOVERNMENT

1915

The agreement of the party leaders to the formation of a Coalition Government was announced on Wednesday, May 19th, but it was not until a week later that the Cabinet list was ready for publication. During the latter part of this interval Asquith's grip on events tightened considerably. He began to exert himself to achieve what he regarded as the most able and cohesive Cabinet for the carrying on of the war. This did not mean that he wanted it to be narrowly based. Once the relative intimacy of a Liberal Government had gone, he was in favour of the widest possible representation. He brought in Henderson from the Labour Party, and he tried hard, but unsuccessfully, to secure the adhesion of Redmond. But it did mean that he was reluctant to give high posts to Conservatives simply because of their position in that party's hierarchy. In particular, he was loath to offer a crucial post to Bonar Law.

This was for two reasons. First, he had no respect for either the ability or the character of Law. (A few months before he had come across Bolingbroke's remark about Bishop Warburton: " Sir, I never wrestle with a chimney-sweep "; and had commented: " A good saying, which I sometimes call to mind when I am confronting Bonar Law.") Second, his whole instinct was against allowing the new Government to become a two-headed monster. Unlike Lloyd George after him he did not wish to turn the leader of the Unionist Party into a specially trusted (and specially burdened) lieutenant. A Coalition there had to be, but it was to be as much like a normal party Government as possible, with no unusual position for the leader of the minority party. All ministers should have their direct lines to the head of the Government, which would in practice function with varying frequency and clarity according to his view of their position and abilities, but there should be no subsidiary exchange. This system, which Asquith operated for the next nineteen months, did not turn out to be a recipe for political stability.

In accordance with it, Asquith pushed up those Conservatives whom he liked or trusted, and pushed down Law. He was happy to give Balfour (who, as a member first of the Committee of Imperial Defence and then of the War Council, had been almost in the Government since the outbreak of war) the key post at the Admiralty, although this was not an appointment which particularly commended itself to the new First Lord's Unionist colleagues. He gave Curzon high precedence if not much work as Lord Privy Seal, and he was generous about admitting Carson, as Attorney-General, to the Cabinet, despite complaints from Redmond. He was determined to keep Grey at the Foreign Office, and, after a momentary hesitation on May 17th, Kitchener at the War Office. This left two posts of first-rate importance, the one—the Exchequer—carrying great traditional prestige—and the other—the new Ministry of Munitions—offering the greatest challenge. Lloyd George obviously had to have one of them. Asquith believed it right to prevent Bonar Law having the other; and in this blocking aim he was surprisingly successful.

Lloyd George accepted Munitions. This in itself was a relief to Asquith, and he wrote in glowing terms to the new minister to thank him for his " self-forgetfulness." But it made the exclusion of Bonar Law still more difficult. The Exchequer was a more obviously suitable post for him than the Ministry of Munitions. Asquith then toyed (as in 1908) with a plan for reverting to Gladstone's 1880 arrangement (but how different were the circumstances) and doubling the Treasury with the Premiership. This was coldly received on all sides.[1] Asquith therefore decided on a simple show of strength against Law. But, as he and the Unionist leader were always uncomfortable in each other's company, he used Lloyd George as an intermediary.

" On the morning of Tuesday, 25 May," Asquith recorded in a pencilled memorandum, " I commissioned Ll. George to see B. Law, & to point out

[1] It was a strangely perverse idea. Apart from the impossible burden which would have been thrown upon Asquith himself, it would have exacerbated rather than eased the political problem with which he was trying to deal. The difficulty in forming a Coalition is to find jobs for men rather than *vice versa*.

(*1*) the resentment of our party at the exclusion of Haldane
(*2*) their resentment at the inclusion of Carson
(*3*) the impossibility from a party point of view of both Admiralty and War Office being in Tory hands[1]
(*4*) the impossibility of having a Tariff Reformer at the Exchequer.
This was intended to prevent B. Law taking either the office of Munitions or the Ex[er].
Later in the day the Tory leaders in substance accepted the position, Ll.G. going to Munitions and McKenna to Exchequer."[a]

This was a remarkable capitulation on Law's part. McKenna had no particular claim on the Exchequer—his wife wrote Asquith a letter of almost amazed gratitude—and, after Haldane and Churchill, he was the Liberal whom the Conservatives would most like to have excluded completely. Instead they accepted his promotion without even the compensation of securing his former place at the Home Office for one of their own men. Walter Long, who wrote to Asquith asking in precise and pressing terms for this post, was given the Presidency of the Local Government Board. Simon was promoted to be Home Secretary. And Law himself became Colonial Secretary, by no means a convenient position from which to co-ordinate the Unionist forces in the Government.

Why did he allow this to happen? Part of the reason probably lay in the criminal prosecution which was pending against William Jacks and Company. This was the firm in which Bonar Law had pursued an active business career until 1901. His brother was still a fully participating partner. He himself habitually lent the company any loose money which he had available. The charge against the business was that, in the early days of the war, it had traded with the enemy. During May it looked as though John Law would be one of the accused. In fact, when the case came on in Edinburgh in June, he was left out. But two other partners were found guilty and sentenced to brief terms of imprisonment.

No one seriously thought that Bonar Law had himself behaved improperly. But in view of the attitude which both he and his party had taken, first about the Marconi affair and then towards Haldane,

---

[1] The point of this argument was that Asquith regarded the Ministry of Munitions as part of the War Office, the department which initially provided the whole of its staff.

he could hardly expect to escape all of the backwash.[1] Asquith's comment when he heard of the matter in February was fairly typical of Liberal feeling: " It will be one of the ironies of fortune (after what we innocently suffered over Marconi) if B.L. (equally innocent) were to encounter a like injustice." Innocent though he might be, the incident hardly made mid-May the ideal time for Law to demand either the Exchequer, with its Inland Revenue function, or the Ministry of Munitions, with its intimate supervisory functions over a large number of industrial firms.

The final shape of the Cabinet gave twelve posts to Liberals, eight to Unionists, one to Labour, and one to Kitchener. The real preponderance of the Liberals was greater than this; only Balfour and Kitchener impaired their monopoly of key positions. Apart from Haldane, Asquith had to drop from the Cabinet seven previous members: Samuel, Pease, Emmott, Lucas, Hobhouse, Beauchamp and Montagu. He found lesser jobs for five of them, and re-promoted Montagu in a little over a year.

The new Cabinet came together for the first time on May 27th, and settled down to a routine of much more frequent meetings than had been the recent habit of the old. Until the beginning of August at least two and sometimes three meetings a week was the pattern. The old War Council had disappeared, but was to some extent replaced by a new Dardanelles Committee of eleven members. Five of them were Unionists. As the summer wore on this Committee, under the guidance of its secretary, Colonel Hankey, began increasingly to concern itself with general military matters. In August Carson was added to the list of members. Kitchener, after the change of Government, had suggested a new War Council, to be composed only of the Prime Minister, Balfour and himself, with Hankey as secretary. But this was impracticable. The Unionists would never have agreed to delegate real authority to a body on which their only representative was Balfour, whom they regarded as implicated in the mistakes of the previous Government.

In June the uneasy Coalition began to face a new problem—that of compulsory military service—which was to be with it, often in an acute form, for much of the remainder of its life. At this stage all that was proposed and agreed to was a Registration Bill, but some mem-

[1] What, it may fairly be asked, would the Unionists have said had some family firm of Haldane's been involved in this way?

bers of the Cabinet—notably Lloyd George, Curzon, Austen Chamberlain and Churchill—saw it as paving the way to conscription. So, probably, did the King, who wrote somewhat disingenuously to Asquith on the 23rd of the month:

> I fear recruiting for the Army is by no means as brisk as it was a fortnight ago. I earnestly trust that the Cabinet will agree without delay to registration being carried out as no one could object to that. I trust we shall not be obliged to come to compulsion; but I am interested to see it has been advocated in the H. of C. this evening by one of your late whips who has been at the front for ten months! ! ![b]

This was clear notice of the direction in which the King would endeavour to push the Government. But his influence was minor compared with the appalling rate at which men were consumed in France. So long as the Government permitted the generals to engage in frontal attacks on heavily fortified positions, with the frightful losses which were inevitably involved, they left themselves no ultimate alternative to conscription. Asquith saw this, but, supported by Kitchener, he wished to approach the decision in the most gradual way possible. Kitchener's reasons were associated with the traditions of War Office administration and his own prestige as " a great poster." Asquith's were largely political. Despite the cross currents within the Cabinet, back-bench opinion on the issue divided sharply on party lines; and the Liberals' allies, the Labour Party and the Irish Nationalists, found compulsory service even more repugnant than they did themselves. Early in August Runciman, the President of the Board of Trade, told Asquith that all the trades union leaders were " hotly against compulsion in any form and will use the whole force of their organisation to fight it inch by inch." Later the same month Asquith recorded what his own Chief Whip had told him:

> Gulland, whom I saw this morning for the first time for weeks, tells me that he gets letters from Liberal chairmen, etc., all over the country denouncing Lloyd George as a lost soul, and some of them predicting that conscription would bring us to the verge, or over the verge of revolution. I have had several interviews with colleagues—Harcourt, Simon, etc.,—all strong in the same sense.[c]

Whatever Asquith's supporters at home might say, military developments during August tilted the argument still further in favour of compulsion. At the end of the first week came the failure of the landings at Suvla Bay on the Gallipoli Peninsula. A third precarious bridgehead was established, but contrary to the most confident expectations, General Hamilton, badly served by an elderly but inexperienced corps commander, failed to break through to the high ground which dominated the Narrows. Asquith described this as the worst disappointment of the war. It destroyed the hope of victory by strategic adventure rather than by stubborn slaughter.

Then, on August 20th, after a four-day conference with Joffre and French, Kitchener told the Cabinet that he had been forced to agree to a new Allied offensive in the west. Asquith wrote to the King:

General Joffre is quite determined both on political and military grounds (the main element in the former being the situation in Russia) to take the offensive without delay and on a considerable scale. Sir J. French has agreed with him as to the urgency of such a step from a military point of view. Lord Kitchener while far from sanguine that any substantial military advantage will be achieved is strongly of the opinion that we cannot, without serious and perhaps fatal injury to the alliance, refuse the co-operation which General Joffre invites and expects. The drawbacks and even dangers of the proposed operation were pointed out with great force by Mr. Churchill and other members of the Cabinet, including the Prime Minister and Lord Lansdowne, and Lord Kitchener himself expressed his concurrence in some at any rate of their apprehensions. But after much consideration the Cabinet adopted Lord Kitchener's view and the necessary steps will be taken.[d]

The " necessary steps " led, for the British, to the Battle of Loos and for the French to the great offensives at Souchez towards Vimy Ridge, and in Champagne. All the assaults were launched on September 25th, and they were effectively over by the early days of October. The gains were negligible, but the casualties were immense. The British lost 60,000 and the French 150,000. Although the Champagne offensive was kept going in some form until November 8th, the campaigns of 1915 were substantially at an end. Throughout the whole year the front had nowhere moved by more than three miles and the gains, such as they were, were mainly in the Germans' favour. But their casualties were barely two-fifths of those of the Allies.

All this was at least half foreseen by the Cabinet at its gloomy, resigned meeting on August 20th. Certainly the likely manpower consequences of the proposed offensive were in Asquith's mind. He faced them only because he saw no other way of avoiding a fatal rupture with the French. But he was perfectly aware that, apart from the appalling human loss, the offensive would force forward the conscription issue in a way that might well lead to the destruction of the Government. It was to be another nine months before the problem was finally disposed of—by the adoption of general compulsion from the age of 18 to 41—and during this period Asquith, advancing slowly and patiently towards the almost inevitable conclusion, managed the component parts of his pre-1915 majority with consummate skill. He lost Sir John Simon from the Government in January, 1916, but he circumnavigated the threatened resignations of Grey, Runciman and McKenna; and, against all the likely odds, he retained the services of Henderson and the Labour junior ministers. He never put himself in the position of being dependent upon Tory votes to carry the policies of the Government through Parliament.

The reverse side of the coin was that he managed his relations with the Unionists on the issue a great deal less skilfully. His old fault of underestimating Bonar Law and overestimating Balfour and Curzon was well to the fore. On August 11th it was decided to set up a special Cabinet Committee on manpower. Bonar Law was absent from that meeting of the Cabinet, but he wrote to Asquith on the following day to express great surprise that "as the leader of our Party in the House of Commons" he had been excluded without consultation. Asquith returned a bland reply which made matters a good deal worse. Law's name had been on the original list, he explained, but when he had discussed this with Curzon they had both thought it rather too long, and had agreed that Law and Simon should be struck off.

Asquith would however now be delighted if Law would serve. But at this stage Law would not. He returned a sulky answer and persisted in his refusal when Asquith tried again.[e]

The barrier which separated the two men is neatly illustrated by the fact that in this, as in other exchanges between them, all Law's letters began with a stiff "Dear Mr. Asquith," and all Asquith's with a gracious "My dear Bonar Law." It was as much Law's fault as it was Asquith's. If he had behaved like an equal the Prime Minister would have been more likely to treat him as one. Instead, despite his supposed tenacity of character, Law showed every sign at this stage of being frightened of Asquith. He avoided interviews with him whenever he could, and when they did occur he often agreed to something which

373

he had subsequently to retract by letter. He gave little enough cause for respect but Asquith might have been a wiser Coalition Prime Minister if he had responded to the barrier of incomprehension by deliberately according a special consideration to the leader of the Unionist Party.

He did the reverse of this. Having snubbed Law in August, he proceeded in September to attempt an elaborate bridge-building exercise with Balfour. On the 18th of that month Asquith wrote a long and " most secret " letter about compulsory service to the First Lord of the Admiralty:

> My mind has been inclining to the view that a joint interven-
> tion on your part and mine may be necessary, or at any rate
> highly expedient. . . .
> It is now indisputable that any attempt at the moment to estab-
> lish compulsion, either military or industrial, would encounter
> the practically united and passionately vehement opposition of
> organised Labour. The speech of J. H. Thomas, who is the ablest
> man and one of the most successful peace-makers among the
> Trade Union leaders, is very significant. . . . I need say nothing
> about the Irish, except that the whole Nationalist party, including
> the O'Brienites, would fight against the change with all their
> resources. I come lastly (for I purposely say nothing about the
> Unionists) to my own, the Liberal Party. I have received during
> the last few days from the most trusted and representative men of
> the rank and file a number of apparently spontaneous communica-
> tions, and all in the sense of resolute and dogged opposition. It is
> no exaggeration to say that, at this moment, the two most un-
> popular and distrusted men in the party are Ll. George and W.
> Churchill. . . . I sincerely believe that, great as is my personal
> authority (I can say so without undue vanity) if I were to announce
> myself tomorrow a reluctant but whole-hearted convert to Com-
> pulsion, I should still have to face the hostility of some of the best,
> and in the country some of the most powerful elements of the
> Liberal Party. . . . I should be glad to know how far these (general
> considerations) commend them to your judgment. I have come to
> think that it is only by our joint efforts that a bridge can be con-
> structed over a yawning and perilous chasm.*f*

This curiously inconclusive letter—what solution was the joint intervention to propound?—was sent to the wrong man. Balfour had neither the authority to impose a policy upon the Unionist Party nor the desire to embroil himself in a problem which was not his own. He was never a man for courageous interference, and there is no record that he returned any substantial answer to the Prime Minister.

By the middle of October Asquith's personal and political fortunes appeared to have reached a nadir—but it was in fact a false bottom. The offensive in France had subsided into obvious failure. Sir John French had clearly outlived his usefulness as a commander. The memory of the Suvla Bay disappointment was still fresh, and Gallipoli faced the Government with the problem of large forces clinging almost without hope to three precarious beachheads. From there it was unlikely that they could be evacuated without heavy casualties, a serious loss of prestige throughout the East, and bitter quarrels at home. The French who at one moment in September had surprised everyone by offering large reinforcements for this theatre, had subsequently insisted on an expedition to Salonika, in which Asquith had no faith at all. They were supported in this plan, and in subsequent demands for a strengthening of the Salonika force, by important members of the British Cabinet, notably Lloyd George and Carson. On October 12th Carson announced that, in view of the inadequacy of our support for Serbia and his general dissatisfaction with the conduct of the war, he proposed to resign. On October 19th, with the need for immediate conscription brought in as an additional reason, his resignation was made public.

The machinery of government at home was creaking badly, but Asquith's attempt in late September to set up a new, smaller, and more effective War Council was coldly received by his colleagues. Balfour, always adept at pointing out difficulties, had propounded the simple doctrine of despair that it was the personalities that were the trouble and that unless the leading ministers changed their characters, no administrative change would improve matters. Lloyd George brought this view into sharper focus by saying that nothing would work so long as Kitchener remained at the War Office. As a result the only change that was made was to give the Dardanelles Committee, with its membership of twelve, the name of War Council.

Kitchener's own abilities, always exaggerated as most members of the Cabinet now believed, were obviously flagging. The system which he had created, by which he acted not only as Secretary of State but also as a generalissimo without a general staff, was clearly a failure. But his reputation with the public still persisted. He remained the greatest of all recruiting sergeants. If he were to go, all lingering hopes of raising enough men by voluntary service would go with him. The Prime Minister's biggest political problem would become much more acute.

To all these troubles Asquith suddenly found that the most unusual one of ill-health had been added. On October 19th he became seriously unwell during the night. " I have not spent a day in bed for almost untold years," he wrote on the 19th, " nor do I quite know what is the matter with me." But Margot thought she did. " I have had an agonising time," she wrote to Lady Islington on October 26th. " I never got such a fright in my life. I thought Henry was *absolutely done.* I think he thought so too." The doctor's diagnosis, she added, was that " overwork, hot rooms and no sort of exercise had gripped his liver and driven bad blood all over him." After the first attack he slept for thirty-six hours. A week later he was substantially well, and by the beginning of November he was back in full harness.

His convalescence was not a restful one. On October 19th came Carson's resignation and a letter of general complaint from Walter Long. Feeling both amongst the public and in the House of Commons was bad, Long said: " I have had many representations from quiet loyal men who only want to help to win the war. . . . They say they do not know how things stand or what we are doing."*g* On the following day Selborne wrote an equally critical letter, and Lord Robert Cecil, who had joined the Cabinet in July as second Foreign Office Minister, wrote to demand a War Council of three. " If Queen Victoria was still alive I should suggest that the Crown be asked to nominate this Triumvirate, but as things are I think they would have to be elected by Parliament, or perhaps a H. of C. vote by ballot. I am perfectly certain that unless some step of this kind can be taken, the Ministry will be turned out. . . . "*h*

More serious than this was the view which the Cabinet took at its meeting of October 21st. Crewe reported thus to the King (and in similar terms to Asquith):

> This conversation (a criticism of Grey for offering Cyprus to Greece after consultation only with the Prime Minister and Kitchener[1]) led on without any pre-arranged scheme to a dis-

[1] This sounds a very drastic step to have been taken in such a way, but Grey may have been influenced (although the Unionist ministers would

cussion of the conduct of war business and the working of the War Council. Most of the Ministers took part in this and it was the unanimous view of the Cabinet that the present system is the opposite of effective only owing to the undue size of the Council.[1] Lord Crewe who stated that it had been his personal intention in any case to press the necessity for change on the Prime Minister was instructed to convey to him the unanimous conviction of the Cabinet that a drastic change is imperatively necessary. He was asked not to name a particular number as representing the view of the Cabinet as on this detail opinion somewhat differed; but all were agreed that the body should be quite small and, as far as can be, non-departmental. Lord Crewe feels sure that after what Your Majesty stated in his audience on Wednesday that action of Your Majesty's Ministers will be approved.[i]

This report, from one of Asquith's most loyal colleagues, sounds remarkably as though the Cabinet, with the King privy to the arrangement, had seized the opportunity of the Prime Minister's absence to hold a generally critical session and to present him with something near to a united ultimatum. It was most unfair, in view of the action Asquith had endeavoured to take in September and of the opposition he had then encountered, but the incident was nevertheless symptomatic of general discontent within the Government; and Crewe's report cannot have made pleasant reading for a bed-ridden Prime Minister.

There were few compensating factors for him to contemplate. Politically, he was gravely worried that Kitchener might pronounce for conscription. If he did, the Derby scheme (a complicated com-

---

hardly have been mollified by this) by the exhaustive discussion of the issue which had taken place under the former Government in January, 1915. Lord Stamfordham, students of the 1957–9 crisis may care to note, had then written: " The King desires me to express the earnest hope that the Government will, on further consideration, decide to support Sir E. Grey's proposal and offer Cyprus to Greece on condition of her joining the Allies. . . . Financially Cyprus is I suppose a loss to this country. Strategically, H.M. understands that it has proved a failure: the harbours impracticable and ships obliged to lie off six miles from the coast." (*Asquith Papers*, box IV, f. 78).

[1] This seems a direct contradiction of the views which Balfour and Lloyd George had expressed in September, but precision in the use of words was never Crewe's most notable characteristic.

promise under which both married and unmarried men were encouraged to attest by a Government pledge that, unless all but a
negligible quantity of single men came forward, either the married
men would be released from their engagement or compulsion would
be introduced for the single men) would be dead before it was under
way.[1] Bonar Law was threatening resignation unless a clean cut were
made in the Dardanelles, and Lloyd George, his relations with the
Prime Minister less close than at the formation of the Coalition, had
become a centre of general discontent.

Privately, Asquith was still suffering from the loss of Mrs. Montagu
as a confidante. In addition, so far from being personally immune from
the horrors of the war, as many people chose to assume, he was deeply
exposed through the sons of his first marriage. They were all four in
the army by this time, and only Cys, the youngest, relegated by ill-
health to a home defence battalion, was in a position approaching
permanent safety. Oc, an outstanding soldier, had been in Gallipoli
since the beginning and had by then received one of his four wounds.
Beb, an artillery officer, was already in France. Raymond, who had just
transferred to the Grenadiers, was preparing for whatever specially
hazardous role might be assigned to his battalion. There were few
strategic decisions which did not involve Asquith in the possibility of
family grief.

Then, half-way between politics and private affairs, there was the
stream of personal vilification and misrepresentation to which he and
his wife were at this time subjected. A left-wing Prime Minister,

[1] In an attempt to avoid this danger Asquith wrote Kitchener a most
uncharacteristic letter of urgent appeal on October 17th. It was so utterly
different both in style and substance from his normal measured periods and
calm content that, were it not for knowledge of his illness and for Sir Philip
Magnus's testimony (*Kitchener*, pp. 352–3) it would be difficult to believe
that it came from his pen. " I should like you to know," one passage ran,
" that what is now going on is being engineered by men (Curzon and Lloyd
George, and some others) whose real object is to oust you. They know well
that I give no countenance to their projects, and consequently they have
conceived the idea of using you against me. God knows that we should both
of us be glad to be set free. But we cannot and ought not. So long as you
and I stand together, we carry the whole country with us. Otherwise, the
Deluge! Cannot you say that, while you aim at, and would like to obtain
70 divisions, the thing should be done gradually and with general
consent. . . . ."

perhaps because Conservatives so resent his being there at all, is always
more exposed than one of the right in this respect, but Asquith was
peculiarly unlucky. Margot gave some examples in her *Autobiography:*

> The D......ss of W.......... and others continue spreading
> amazing lies about me and mine: they would be grotesque if they
> were not so vile. Elizabeth is in turn engaged to a German
> Admiral or a German General; Henry has shares in Krupps; I
> " feed Prussian prisoners with every dainty and comestible," and
> play lawn tennis with them at Donnington Hall—a place whose
> very whereabouts is unknown to me.
>
> These private fabrications are not only circulated but believed,
> and, had it not been for my receiving £1,000 for a libel action
> which I took in the Law Courts against the Globe Newspaper, the
> whole of our thoughtful Press would have published them. . . .
> I am told by John Morley and other students of History that
> no greater campaign of calumny was ever conducted against
> one man than that which has been, and is being, conducted
> against my husband today. . . . Henry is as indifferent to the
> Press as St. Paul's Cathedral is to midges, but I confess that I am
> not!^j

In addition to this generalised slander there was a specialized
campaign which Lord Alfred Douglas conducted against the Asquiths
during this period. It arose mainly out of the Asquiths' (and in particular Margot's) friendship with Robert Ross, Oscar Wilde's literary
executor. Douglas published such an extreme attack on Ross, accusing
him of the most depraved homosexual practices, that he was prosecuted
for criminal libel. In the course of the trial, which ended in a jury
disagreement, it emerged that Ross was a frequent visitor at 10,
Downing Street. After his discharge—there was no second trial—
Douglas, assisted by T. W. H. Crosland, made continual public demands that Asquith should denounce Ross. Instead, the Prime Minister
joined a mixed and distinguished group, including Shaw, Garvin,
Wells, Lady Ottoline Morrell and Bishop Gore of Birmingham, to
organise a testimonial to Ross. This drove Douglas to a paroxysm of
anger.[1] He wrote fearful letters of denunciation to Asquith; he wrote

---

[1] Later, in 1916, Douglas's fury was further increased when Algernon
Methuen, who was Wilde's publisher and had recently been fined £10 at
Bow Street for issuing D. H. Lawrence's *The Rainbow*, was given a
baronetcy on Asquith's recommendation.

to the King urging him to act against the Prime Minister; and he wrote to Churchill saying that he must take over the leadership of the Liberal Party. More tiresomely he published the most vicious satirical poems. The worst was entitled " All's Well With England," the quality and tone of which can be judged from the following stanza:
> Out there in Flanders all the trampled ground,
> Is red with English blood. Our children pass
> Through fire to Moloch. Who will count the loss,
> Since here ' at home ' sits Merry Margot, bound
> With Lesbian fillets, while with front of brass,
> ' Old Squiffy ' hands the purse to Robert Ross.[k]

Asquith's façade might be like St. Paul's Cathedral, but he would have been less than human had he not reacted with some displeasure to these and other, less hysterical but equally malevolent pieces of calumny. They all added to his depression during that October illness.

Many men of sixty-three might in these circumstances have thrown in their hands, or at least gone into a permanent decline, shuffling off as much responsibility as possible. Asquith reacted in exactly the opposite way. On October 31st Lloyd George had written to him threatening to resign if Kitchener was not replaced at the War Office. On November 1st, almost the first day of his return to full activity, Asquith suggested to Bonar Law that this problem might be solved by his becoming his own Secretary of State for War and combining it with the premiership as he had in the days after the incident at the Curragh. Law, overawed as usual in the presence of the Prime Minister, responded with some enthusiasm to the idea. He quickly changed his mind. On the following day he sent a letter to say that he could not possibly give his agreement, and covered his confusion by writing in bleakly ungracious terms: " The criticism which is directed against the govt. and against yourself is chiefly based on this—that as Prime Minister you have not devoted yourself absolutely to co-ordinating all the moves of the war because so much of your time and energy has been devoted to control of the political machine."[l] He ended, typically, with an excuse for not seeing Asquith to tell him this.

Asquith had to accept this veto, and his way seemed blocked. But he was determined to get his hands on the War Office for at least a period. He believed that he could quickly effect certain necessary changes and make a lasting improvement in its administrative machinery. Accordingly he persuaded Kitchener to go out to Gallipoli and report on the desirability of evacuation. The visit was to last at least a month and the Prime Minister was to deputise for him while he was away. " We avoid by this method of procedure the immediate supersession of K. as War Minister, while attaining the same result," Asquith wrote to Lloyd George. " And I suppose even B.L. would hardly object to such a plan."[m] Kitchener left on the evening of November 4th, taking with him, with a suspicious peasant's misplaced sense of cunning, his seals of office.

Asquith was wrong in one respect. Bonar Law did object, not to the War Office arrangements, but to the scheme which made them possible, to a decision on the evacuation of Gallipoli being postponed until Kitchener could present a report. At the Cabinet on November 4th he accepted the plan, but, once again, a night's reflection changed his mind, and he wrote to Asquith on the following morning hinting at resignation and demanding another Cabinet to take an immediate decision on Gallipoli. Asquith was unusually irritated by this further sudden switch, and he replied sharply and firmly on the same day:

My dear Bonar Law,
Your letter of today is in effect a request that the Cabinet should at once reverse its unanimous decision of yesterday. There is, as far as I know, no ground for your statement that the whole Cabinet realise now that we must withdraw from the Dardanelles, or that we are seeking to " postpone a disagreeable but inevitable decision."
I will call a Cabinet for tomorrow morning so that you may have full opportunity for stating your view.
Yours sincerely,
H. H. Asquith[n]

At this special Saturday Cabinet Bonar Law found himself alone. There followed a perturbed week-end, during which, Lord Beaverbrook stated, Law believed that he had obtained a verbal promise from Asquith to support his demand for evacuation forthwith, independently of anything that Kitchener might say.[o] There is no confirmation of this amongst any of Asquith's papers, and the letter which Law wrote on the Monday was one of withdrawal rather than of victory: " In view of the discussion at the Cabinet on Saturday and of the general appeal made to me by yourself and supported by our colleagues I have determined to postpone the consideration of my position in relation to the Gallipoli policy until Lord Kitchener's report has been received."*p*

This difficulty overcome, Asquith was able to proceed to the construction of the new, small War Council, which had been demanded by the Cabinet on October 21st, and to which he had given his formal agreement a week later. The new body was set up at the Cabinet of November 11th. The members were Asquith, Balfour, Lloyd George, Bonar Law and McKenna. No mention was made of Kitchener. The agreement of the Cabinet to this list led to the resignation of Churchill, who would have been left with no duties other than the administration of the Duchy of Lancaster. He declined this opportunity of " well-paid inactivity " and departed, after a moderately friendly exchange of letters, to command a battalion at the Front.

Asquith's next major step, after settling several matters of long-standing dispute between the War Office and the Ministry of Munitions, was to change the Commander-in-Chief in France. Few of those whose opinion counted were in much doubt that the time had come for French to go. The King thought so; Lloyd George thought so; Bonar Law thought so; Sir William Robertson (French's own Chief of Staff) thought so; and Kitchener, cf course, had long been distrustful of his military competence. But the War Minister had been strangely reluctant to make a change. Asquith, although far more favourably disposed to French as a man than Kitchener had ever been—he still did not know about the part which the Field-Marshal had attempted to play in the events of May, 1915—was prepared to cut the knot.

He deliberately acted before Kitchener's return. He did not discuss the issue widely, but took the full responsibility himself. On November 23rd he entertained Sir Douglas Haig, the commander of the First Army, under French, to luncheon at Downing Street. On the following day he asked Lord Esher, who recommended himself for the task both as an old friend of French's and as a professional go-between of several decades' standing, to proceed to St. Omer, and put the decision to the Field Marshal as delicately as he could. At this stage French took the news reasonably well. He immediately came to London and wrote Asquith a letter full of good feeling.

A few days later new problems arose. French made difficulties about accepting an appointment as Commander-in-Chief of the Home

Forces. Asquith, at a stage when his own mind was already fixed upon Haig, courteously but mistakenly asked French's view about his successor. French recommended Robertson, and when this advice was ignored he became more resentful. However, he overcame his hesitations about his new post. On December 8th a formal offer was made to a far from surprised Haig. On December 18th he took over at St. Omer.

In the meantime Asquith had made progress with another piece of military re-organisation. For the first year of the war, Kitchener had operated without a General Staff. He had attempted to do everything himself: to inspire the war effort of the Empire; to run the administrative machinery of the War Office; and to be the sole adviser to the War Council and the Cabinet on all matters of military strategy. By the early autumn of 1915 the other ministers had lost faith in his ability to discharge this last task, and Kitchener himself was sufficiently on the defensive to agree to the re-creation of an Imperial General Staff. How big a change this was likely to mean would depend principally on whether the new C.I.G.S. was to be a man who could get his way against Kitchener. The appointment was unsettled when the Secretary of State for War departed for the Eastern Mediterranean.

There were two possible candidates of strength, two men of utterly contrasting character and ability. The first was the subtle and serpentine Sir Henry Wilson, who had been liaison officer with the French High Command. He might have got his way by the ingenuity of his intelligence and the determination of his intrigue. But he was the one officer whom Asquith never forgave for his part in the Curragh trouble. " That poisonous tho' clever ruffian Wilson," he had written of him a few months before. The other was Sir William Robertson—dour, unimaginative, but highly competent and resolute. He was a man of humble origin, the one " ranker " general in a caste-ridden army. But he allowed no feelings of inferiority to weaken his force. He rarely made the mistake of talking too much. His favourite reply to an argument with which he did not agree was " I've 'eard different "—a singularly difficult one to controvert if delivered with sufficient authority.

Robertson was Asquith's choice for C.I.G.S. It was known that he would not accept unless his powers were clearly and extensively defined in a written agreement with the Secretary of State. But this made him no less attractive a candidate. By November 30th, the date of Kitchener's somewhat unwelcome return from Gallipoli, Asquith had Robertson available in London, willing to be nominated on these terms.

Kitchener drove straight from the railway station to Downing Street. Suspicious of what had happened to his powers in his absence he immediately told Asquith that he wanted to resign. The Prime Minister, in return, told Kitchener that he had changed the Commander-in-Chief, that he had transferred some of the functions of the War Office to the Ministry of Munitions, that he wanted Robertson to be C.I.G.S. with very wide powers, but that it was nevertheless Kitchener's duty to remain in office as " the symbol of the nation's will to victory."�q Kitchener accepted everything that had been done and withdrew his resignation. He even invited Robertson to dine with him at York House that same evening in order to begin negotiations.[1] It was one of Asquith's most successfully persuasive interviews, and it was the culmination of four weeks' determined and effective work at the War Office. The department which he handed back to Kitchener was substantially different from the one which he had taken over from him. Several festering boils had been lanced.

Unfortunately, Asquith's plans for a more effective general political direction of the war ran up against greater difficulties. The Gallipoli decision was the first test of the new War Council. Kitchener had telegraphed on November 22nd recommending the immediate evacuation of Suvla and Anzac, but the retention for the present of the bridgehead at Helles. The War Council met on the following morning and unanimously endorsed the first part of the recommendation, although it thought it wise to evacuate Helles as well. So far, so good. The decision was reported to the full Cabinet on November 24th, but the report was not accepted. Curzon launched the full force of his rhetoric against the course recommended, and Crewe and Lansdowne supported him to the extent of asking for a short delay. The Cabinet

[1] These negotiations, on the basis of Robertson's tough conditions, giving him complete control over strategy, lasted until December 10th. Kitchener then accepted the substance of Robertson's demands. " He is tired and sore," Esher wrote to Asquith from Paris (where the other two both were) on that day. " He will find it a relief to get the substantial backing of Robertson's knowledge and character." Esher went on to say in effect that the French Government at this stage wanted both Kitchener and Joffre kept in their posts, not because they were competent but because they were *points fixes* in a dangerously fluid situation. (*Asquith Papers*, box xv, ff. 192–5).

adjourned the matter until two days later. By this time Curzon had circulated what Hankey described as " one of the most able papers I have ever read." The result was further disagreement, and a further postponement of decision until Admiral de Robeck got back to London on December 1st.

On December 3rd the Cabinet met again, with the benefit of an anti-withdrawal paper from Hankey and a further expostulation from Curzon. Influenced by these the " no evacuation " party appeared to be gaining strength—F. E. Smith (who had replaced Carson), Balfour, even Kitchener, were attracted by the new arguments. These arguments were based on the assumption that Salonika would be evacuated instead. But by December 6th it became clear that the French would not agree to this, and that too much pressure could not be put upon them without endangering the life of the Briand Government. For this reason, the Cabinet, at its meeting of December 7th, at last came round to endorsing the War Council recommendation on Suvla and Anzac (but not Helles).

The delay, as it happened, was not serious. The evacuations were carried out, with great efficiency and without loss, on the nights of December 18th-19th and 20th-21st.[1] Asquith wrote of " the intense relief of knowing the almost incredible, and indeed miraculous, methods and results of the evacuation at Suvla and Anzac." " It is the most wonderful retirement in war history," he continued, " far surpassing even Sir John Moore's at Corunna."[r] Had a half the military skill been applied to the landings, he might have added, Constantinople would long since have been in the hands of the Allies.

But it was a close run thing; less than sixteen hours after the last boat pulled away, a fearful storm broke. Even had the margin not been close, the method of decision-making which had been followed obviously made nonsense of the idea of a small, effectively functioning War Council. The Cabinet's willingness to delegate authority was purely theoretical. Part of the trouble lay in the Prime Minister's respect for the traditional power of " the plenum of the Cabinet " as he called it. And another part lay in the composition of the War Council. It was largely made up of departmental ministers—Balfour, Lloyd George, Bonar Law, McKenna—while the non-departmental ones—Curzon, Crewe, Lansdowne—were outside. In these circum-

---

[1] The evacuation of Helles, decided on by the Cabinet on December 27th, was equally successfully carried out on the night of January 8th-9th.

stances the latter category, if only to find employment for themselves, were almost bound to interfere. It was a mistake which both Lloyd George in 1917 and 1918 and Churchill, in the Second War, were to try hard to avoid.

Even this sad and early decline of the new War Council did not neutralise the effect of Asquith's dynamic month at the War Office. As the turn of the year approached, his reputation stood much higher than had seemed possible at the end of October. It needed to be so, for the problems of 1916 cast daunting shadows ahead. The first was that of conscription, which could no longer be postponed, as the Derby scheme had obviously proved a failure. The Cabinet took cognisance of this at its meeting of December 22nd. " The impression left upon me is profoundly disquieting," Asquith wrote, " . . . we seem to be on the brink of a precipice. The practical question is "—a familiar one for him to ask himself—" shall I be able . . . to devise and build a bridge?"[8]

CHAPTER XXIV

COMPULSION IN ENGLAND AND REBELLION IN IRELAND

1916

The salient fact about British military prospects at the end of the year 1915 was that the Army had passed into the firm control of determined " Westerners." Both Haig and Robertson were unswerving in their belief that the war could only be won by killing Germans in Flanders. And they were both prepared to accept without flinching the British share of the casualties which this must involve. At its meeting of December 28th the War Cabinet, under Robertson's new guidance, gave general approval to a vast Allied offensive in the early spring of 1916. As it happened, this never took place. It was forestalled by the German offensive which began at Verdun on February 21st and continued until the first days of July, when Haig began his counter-offensive on the Somme. But it did not make a vast difference which side was attacking. In either event the gains were negligible but the killing was immense. The war of attrition was in full swing.

In these circumstances the job of the politicians ceased to be that of looking for strategic alternatives and became concentrated upon supplying men and munitions for the slaughter. Appropriately, December 28th was not only the day on which the War Council made formal obeisance to the supremacy of the Western Front, but also that on which the Cabinet first came to real grips with the problem of conscription. Once it was clear that the Derby scheme had failed— 650,000 single men remained unattested—Asquith knew that compulsion for them could no longer be avoided. " I do not need to tell you," Austen Chamberlain wrote to his stepmother, " that . . . the Prime Minister never hesitated."[a] But several other Liberal ministers did.

By December 29th four of them—Simon, McKenna, Runciman and Grey—had submitted their resignations, and a fifth, Birrell, had written to say that while he could accept compulsion as " a disagreeable necessity," he did not think that he could remain in a Government from which the others had resigned. If these were all to go, Asquith himself would be left in a singularly isolated position. Then, indeed, he would find himself " surrounded and cut off," as he had rather exaggeratedly described his situation to Redmond eight months earlier.

All these resignations were not of equal authenticity. Simon's was the most determined. He stuck firmly to the narrow point that it was wrong to compel men to be soldiers, and he attended no further Cabinet after that of December 28th. His letters to Asquith were full of regret and good feeling, and the latter felt no resentment against him. " Poor Simon, I am so sorry for him in his self-righteousness," was the harshest remark that he made.

Grey, on the other hand, did not feel particularly strongly about the principle of conscription. " . . . . On the point of compulsion for unmarried men," he wrote, " I am prepared to support you and the decision of the majority at the last Cabinet."[b] But he agreed with McKenna and Runciman " on general questions of economic and financial policy." If they went there was no hope of these policies triumphing in the Cabinet. It was a tenuous reason for resignation; coupled with his telling Asquith that he felt increasingly uneasy about not having gone with Haldane in May, it suggested that he was looking for an excuse to leave a political scene which had become distasteful to him. Dissuaded by Asquith on this occasion, he tried again at least twice during the next six months, and during one of these attempts Asquith sharply reminded him that the two of them were more responsible than any other Englishmen for Britain being in the war, and that they had better both be prepared to see it out.

McKenna and Runciman, on account both of their reasons for resigning and of the firmness of their determination to do so, occupied an intermediate position between Grey and Simon. As almost the last representatives of a highly individualistic, nineteenth century businessman's Liberalism, they were instinctively hostile to any form of State interference with private decision making. But they were not prepared to go to the stake on the narrow point of whether or not unmarried men should be compulsorily enrolled. They wanted, very sensibly, to fight their battle on the wider issue of the shape of the British war effort. Kitchener said that to fulfil her commitments Britain must have 70 divisions and a rate of enrolment of 30,000 men a week. McKenna and Runciman said that these were mistaken targets which, if hit, would destroy our capacity to act as the arsenal of the Alliance.[1]

Asquith's " bridge-building " in this situation took several forms. First, the anti-conscriptionists had to accept an immediate but limited measure of compulsion for single men. Anyone, like Simon, who stood out against this would have to go. Second, a very skilfully chosen Cabinet committee—the members were Asquith, McKenna and Austen Chamberlain—was appointed to investigate, over a period of a month, the competing military and economic claims. Third, Briand and Galliéni, under the guise of advice-seeking, were to have the central issue put bluntly before them. Which did they prefer: more men or more money? They must be made to see that they could not have both without limit.

On the basis of these arrangements Asquith got through the first reading debate and division on January 6th without any resignation other than that of Simon. The majority was highly satisfactory. Simon had only a handful of Liberals with him. The Labour members split almost equally. Only the Irish Nationalists provided a solid phalanx of opposition. Then trouble came from a new quarter. The National Executive Committee of the Labour Party came out flatly against the bill, and the parliamentary party took a majority decision to follow the Executive's lead. Henderson, whose lack of self-regard made him always see himself as a purely representative figure, felt that he must resign. On January 10th he wrote a sad but clear-cut letter to Asquith:

In consequence of the decision of Organised Labour to oppose the Military Service Bill I have no alternative but to tender you my resignation. . . . I supported the . . . Bill in the Cabinet; I

[1] McKenna presented this argument in too intelligent a way. He was asked whether it meant that, as Chancellor, he could not afford to pay for 70 divisions. Had he returned a firm *ex cathedra* affirmative, both Kitchener and Austen Chamberlain (a strange couple of Gladstonians) might have bowed to the mystique of the Treasury. But when he patiently explained that it was not so much money as the physical allocation of resources, or the " depletion of industry " as it was then called, which was the trouble, they became mystified and unconvinced.

shall continue to do so in the House as the representative of my constituents on the ground of military necessity.[c]

Roberts and Brace, the two Labour junior ministers, followed Henderson's lead. The Cabinet, that same day, could think of no remedy other than that Asquith should himself meet the parliamentary Labour Party and endeavour to set their fears at rest. This he did on January 11th—and was triumphantly persuasive. He did not convert them all to conscription, but he did get them to agree that Henderson and the others should stay in the Government. Another hurdle was past.

The next day, McKenna began to have fresh doubts. Asquith's irritation with him was not lessened by the fact that he thought he had a very good case. On the evening of January 13th Asquith went to see Lady Scott, the widow of the Antarctic explorer, who at this time was one of his confidantes, and she wrote in her diary for that day:

P.M. came at 6.30. I hadn't seen him for a week. . . . he has been so worried. Said McKenna changes ground so often. Three days ago he (Asquith) would have said they were practically out of the wood, yesterday he would have said things could scarcely be worse. McKenna isn't insisting on the pecuniary impossibility of the compulsion bill, but adopting the Runciman depletion of industry attitude, and, added the P.M., " the Dickens is that I so agree with him."

A month later, on the basis of mutual compromise by the War Office and the Board of Trade, the tripartite Military-Finance Committee (as Hankey, the secretary, called it) had succeeded, after daily meetings, in reaching agreement. But the process did not improve Asquith's feeling about McKenna. Lady Scott is again the witness. " The P.M. told me," she wrote on February 13th, " that the man who had disappointed him most for many a long year was McKenna. Said he proved himself unstable mentally and morally —moreover he hadn't the excuse of a stupid man, nor the excuse of artistic temperament or any such thing—it saddened him."

But here again Asquith may have been influenced by a sneaking respect for McKenna's views. Perhaps the best way for a minister to irritate his chief is stubbornly to advocate a policy which the Prime Minister would half like to follow, but knows he cannot, and to do it by always threatening resignation, while never carrying the threat into effect. By this time, however, Asquith had got his bill safely through the House of Commons. And this achievement, even if it did not make him more tolerant of McKenna, at least gave him a short stretch of substantially calmer water.

He used it to make his longest wartime trip abroad. He left London on March 25th and was away for ten days. After a conference with the French ministers in Paris, and a visit with Hankey to the Marne battlefield, he travelled on to Italy. A letter which he wrote to Margot from the train shows that, for important passengers, the French did not allow the agony of Verdun to interfere with the amenities of their railway service:

> We started from the Gare de Lyon at eleven in the forenoon and I have never travelled in such luxury—large saloons, eating car, wonderfully appointed bedrooms, etc; no stoppages except now and then to take in water. Apart from servants and attendants there were only four of us aboard—Bongie (Bonham Carter), O'Beirne (a diplomat), Hankey and self.[d][1]

In Rome, according to Hankey, Asquith created an excellent impression on the Italian ministers, and the visit was " a gigantic success," contributing substantially to Italy's decision, later that year, to declare war against Germany—at first she was only at war with Austria. Asquith made a number of excellent speeches, some in French and some in English, as well as impressing Hankey with his " vast store of knowledge on all classical and historical matters." " However can he remember it all amid his tremendous burden of State affairs? " the latter wrote. He was received in audience by Pope Benedict XV, and when His Holiness hinted at the desirability of an early peace " pursed up his mouth and said words to the effect that we should continue to the end."[e] At the station he was seen off by an enthusiastic crowd and some shouts of " *Viva Asquitti!* " The Prime Minister then paid a two-day visit to King Victor Emmanuel at his farmhouse headquarters near Udine. He arrived back in London at 4.0 a.m. on April 7th and was almost immediately confronted with two major crises.

The first was a renewal of the old compulsion trouble. Recruiting under the January system did not go as well during the early months of 1916 as had been hoped. There was mounting pressure for general

---

[1] Hankey's comment on the journey was: " Never before or since have I so much regretted my ignorance of ' bridge,' which compelled the others to play ' dummy ' until we were joined in Italy by the Military Attaché." (*The Supreme Command*, 1914–18, II, p. 482).

conscription from the Press, from the Unionist back-benchers, organised under Carson, and from Lloyd George. The " Military-Finance
Committee," meeting again with the addition of Lansdowne, recommended a further compromise, but half the Cabinet were unwilling
to accept this. By April 17th and 18th London was thick with rumours
that Asquith was on the point of resignation. They were not far from
the truth. In the words of his official biographers, he was buffeted and
mortified. And all, he believed, for a controversy which had been
unnecessarily forced upon the Government at that particular stage.
" The argument has become purely academic," he told Lady Scott
on April 18th. " Why could they not have waited till the June attack[1]
has shown us more clearly what to expect for the future."[2] The chief
blame he put on Lloyd George, with whom his relations had deteriorated drastically. " Of course Lloyd George is the villain of the piece,"
he said, " you know what I think of him." But his feelings towards
Grey, who was once again " reconsidering his position " were also
fairly sharp.

The next morning Asquith was so near to resignation that he
wrote of " preparing to order my frock-coat to visit the Sovereign this
afternoon." But a three-hour Cabinet improved the atmosphere. It
was agreed that the House of Commons should meet in secret session
on the following Tuesday and Wednesday, and that Asquith should
open the debate with a disclosure of new facts and further suggestions
for a compromise. Even so, when announcing this parliamentary plan
that afternoon, he told the House that the Cabinet was divided and that
unless the difference could be settled by agreement the Government
must break up. It was an unusual disclosure. The only comfort he
could offer to members was that the Cabinet was at least united in
thinking that such a break-up would be " a national disaster."

That evening (April 19th) a hundred Liberal members, including
Simon, met at the House of Commons and unanimously passed a
resolution assuring the Prime Minister of their conviction that " his
continuance as the head of the Government is a national necessity."
On the following day, the King, believing a little prematurely that
the difficulty was over, wrote a letter of warm congratulation to
Asquith:

During the last six years you and I have passed through some

---

[1] The Somme, which was in fact postponed until early July.

[2] In the way of casualties and military demands.

strenuous and critical times and once again, thank God, we have " weathered the storm " .... In expressing my relief at the termination of the crisis, I wish again to assure you of my complete confidence in my Prime Minister.*f*

With such crumbs to comfort him he departed for an Easter week-end at the Wharf. He read Quiller-Couch's lectures on *The Art of Writing* and recorded that, although the house was " almost over-guested (not in quality but in number)," he was " spending a more placid Easter than I could have hoped for."*g* On the Monday afternoon Hankey arrived to help Asquith prepare his speech for the following day. Hankey's diary entry was as follows:

I arrived at 4 p.m. and spent three hours with the P.M. ... There was a conclave to decide whether it would be best for him to spend the night at ' The Wharf' or to motor to Town that night. Finally it was left to me to decide—in fact the whole party treated me as though I were a " trainer " charged with the duty of bringing " the Bantam " into the ring in the pink of condition. I decided, knowing his habits, to go up that night, so he and I started at 10.30 p.m. to motor to Town. He was very chatty and jolly and I thoroughly enjoyed the ride. ... On arrival (at 12.30 a.m.) we got the first news of the Dublin outbreak. Asquith merely said " well, that's something " and went off to bed.*h*

In spite of these preparations the secret session speech was not a success. The House was disappointed with the Asquith proposals, of which the essence was that unattested married men were to be given a further opportunity to come forward voluntarily. Unless 50,000 of them did so by May 27th, and 15,000 a week thereafter, general conscription would be introduced. There were subsidiary proposals involving immediate legislation, and Walter Long introduced this bill " very badly " on Thursday, April 27th. The House reacted violently against it. Asquith, deeply embroiled at Downing Street with the problem of Ireland, was hurriedly sent for. He sized up the atmosphere in the chamber and decided that the bill must be withdrawn and a more drastic solution propounded. " It was very difficult, for it wanted a light touch to do such a humiliating thing," was his curious comment to Lady Scott.

The Cabinet met on the Saturday morning to face the new situation. Asquith opened by saying that the House of Commons had left the

Government with no alternative but to proceed immediately with legislation for general compulsion.

" This view," he wrote to the King, " met with the assent of the whole Cabinet. Mr. Henderson referred to the difficulties of his own position and, while agreeing with the Prime Minister's proposals, warned his colleagues of the possibilities of serious labour trouble, especially in South Wales. Mr. Runciman also expressed apprehension as to the attitude of the railwaymen. Mr. Lloyd George believed that all these fears and forebodings were exaggerated. Lord Curzon and Mr. Chamberlain thought the Government ought to show more vigour and self-defence in debate and on the platform. Lord R. Cecil believed that the right course was for the Government to resign or be re-constructed,[1] but yielded to the Prime Minister's objection that, in view of the troubles, actual or threatened in Ireland, Mesopotamia and elsewhere, " this was not the moment for such a change."[i]

Asquith himself introduced the new measure on May 2nd. Hankey witnessed the scene and wrote:

He did not much like the job and was not at his best. The House was astonishingly cold. The fact was that the people who wanted compulsory service did not want Asquith, and those who wanted Asquith did not want compulsory service. Nevertheless Asquith faced the situation with his usual courage.[j]

He could console himself with the thought that the issue was at last out of the way. The bill met with little opposition and was through all its stages by May 25th. On third reading only twenty-seven Liberals and ten Labour members voted against. Fourteen Labour members voted for, and the Irish Nationalists (the bill did not apply to Ireland) abstained.

Throughout the controversy Asquith was at fault in over-estimating the feeling in the country against the final solution. The verdict of history is also firmly against voluntary recruitment as an efficient method of deploying the manpower resources of a nation engaged in

[1] On the previous day he had sent Asquith a memorandum urging this course. If Asquith resigned the King would have to send for Sir Edward Carson. Carson would fail to form a government, and Asquith could then come back in a much stronger position, at the head of a " National Government " rather than a Coalition of party representatives. (*Asquith Papers*, box xxx, ff. 78–81).

total war. There was no question of depending upon it in the Second World War. But on the other aspect of the anti-conscriptionists' case—their scepticism about the wisdom of Britain concentrating her resources upon a mass army to be used for offensive operations against heavily defended positions in France—there is more room for argument. From the decision to do that, a distinguished American military commentator has recently written, stemmed " the beginning of the end of Britain's long preponderance as a world power."[k]

The second major crisis which followed Asquith's return from Italy was the Dublin Easter Rebellion. The first news of this, as Hankey mentioned, reached the Prime Minister when he returned to London late on the Monday night. That afternoon James Connolly's Citizens' Army had risen in Dublin. St. Stephen's Green and the General Post Office were occupied. A provisional republican government, with Patric Pearse as president, was proclaimed. There was sporadic rioting elsewhere in Ireland, but this was easily suppressed. The German ship which was supposed to supply ammunition had been sunk off the coast of Kerry three days before, and Sir Roger Casement, landed by a U-boat, had been immediately arrested.

In Dublin the rising was more serious. The Government in London immediately sent over General Sir John Maxwell and moderate military reinforcements (Asquith would have liked to have sent more). Augustine Birrell, the Chief Secretary, also made a hurried crossing of St. George's Channel. Even so it was six days before British control could be re-established in the Irish capital. Eventually the insurgents were forced into surrender, but before this happened there was bitter fighting and heavy killing. Much of Sackville Street and several important public buildings went up in flames. Flames were also lit in the hearts of many Irish patriots who were tired of Redmond's ineffective constitutionalism. And these took longer to extinguish.

The revolt left the Cabinet with two problems. First there was the question of the future government of Ireland. The existing system depended upon a colonial type administration in Dublin Castle, a Viceroy in Phoenix Park, and a Chief Secretary, nominally the Viceroy's chief of staff but in fact the real source of power, who spent most of his time in London. It was not only unpopular but ineffective. The Royal Commission on the rebellion, which reported in July, described the system as " anomalous in quiet times, and almost unworkable in times of crisis."

Resignations were inevitable. Birrell, who had received plenty of warnings about the dangers of a Sinn Fein outbreak but had chosen to discount them, was insistent that he must go. No doubt he wished that he had slipped out quickly before, as he had several times offered to do. On this occasion he was more determined. He pressed his resignation upon Asquith in a series of letters written from Dublin on April 28th, 29th and 30th. The Prime Minister accepted it by telegram " with infinite regret " on May 1st. The following day he saw Birrell in Downing Street, and was greatly distressed at the parting. " I don't remember what he *said*," Birrell wrote, " but I know he *wept* and stood staring out of the window jingling some half-crowns in his pocket."[1] Apart from a deep personal attachment Birrell was one of the few Cabinet colleagues left from the first days of Asquith's government. There were only three others and one of them was Lloyd George.

On May 3rd, Sir Matthew Nathan, the permanent under-secretary, also resigned, but a good deal more reluctantly. Asquith thought that Lord Wimborne, the Viceroy, should go too, and sent Pease, the Postmaster-General, over to Dublin, partly to look into the disruption of the postal services, but also to tell him this. Wimborne argued hard,[1] and although a grudging letter of resignation was obtained from him on May 9th, he was recalled to England for only a short time and was back in Dublin by August.

Resignations were not enough. It was the whole system of government, and not merely the competence of individuals, which had been found wanting. Asquith himself became quickly convinced that the Lord Lieutenant and the Dublin Castle system must be swept away. Much of the summer was occupied in an unsuccessful search for something to put in its place.

The second problem was that of suppressing the revolt sufficiently firmly to ensure that it did not recur, while not acting so harshly as either to drive the bulk of Irish Nationalist opinion into the arms of Sinn Fein or to alienate opinion abroad—particularly in America. Birrell before he went gave the Government some good advice in this direction, but it would be an exaggeration to say that they profited greatly from it or avoided the dangers of harshness. Part of the

[1] Asquith always had difficulty in removing Lords Lieutenant of Ireland. Wimborne's predecessor, Lord Aberdeen, had clung like a limpet over the winter of 1914–15.

trouble was that, with martial law proclaimed throughout the country and the civil administration in practical dissolution, the military were given an almost free hand in the week or so after the surrender of the rebels. During this period fifteen executions were carried out after summary trials by courts martial. James Connolly, the labour leader, too badly wounded to stand, was carried on a stretcher to the execution point and shot sitting in a chair. Patric Pearse, the Gaelic romantic, went to his death with immortal words of revolt upon his lips, and his grave soon became a national shrine. They both found prominent places in the list of Irish martyrs.

Lord Wimborne thought the policy of retribution by execution was carried too far, but he hardly knew what was happening until it was over. The Cabinet was also a little nervous, but decided, on May 6th, that General Maxwell must be given discretion in individual cases, subject to general instructions that no woman should be shot, that "death should not be inflicted except on ringleaders and proved murderers," and that the executions should be brought to an end as soon as possible.

On the night of May 11th Asquith himself crossed to Dublin. After the resignations of Birrell and Nathan, he had sent over the permanent secretary to the Treasury, Sir Robert Chalmers, to try to pull together the civil administration, and this official wrote to him on May 9th begging for a new political head of the Irish Office as quickly as possible. Asquith's difficulty was that he did not know whom to appoint. He had played with the names of Montagu, Runciman and McKinnon Wood, and rejected them all. He had staved off a Unionist demand for Walter Long. He had thought of Crewe as Lord Lieutenant (in the Cabinet) with " some underling " as Chief Secretary, but Redmond would not have that. " I am in despair for a Chief Secretary," he wrote. " If only Simon were available."*m*

In these circumstances Asquith fell back upon a characteristic solution. Whenever a department was in difficulties he was always willing temporarily to add its burdens to his own and to try, for a time, to pull its administration together. This is what he did in Dublin. He could not find a Chief Secretary to send, so he sent himself. Loath though he would have been to admit it, his visit was also an exercise in public relations, designed to reassure the Irish parliamentary party. But it was by no means only this. He spent long hours sitting in Dublin

Castle with Sir Robert Chalmers and performing, with his usual expedition, the work of a Chief Secretary.

He was particularly concerned to investigate the administration of justice, relating both to the executions and to the large numbers of imprisonments. He went in detail through a list of cases which had been submitted to him by Dillon. He was not too dissatisfied with what he found. Maxwell assured him as soon as he arrived that, after the two that morning, there need be no further executions. " On the whole," he wrote, "—except the Skeffington case[1]—there have been fewer bad blunders than one might have expected with the soldiery for a whole week in exclusive charge."[n] But there were a lot of men in jail who ought not to have been. He visited 300 to 400 " Sinn Fein (or so-called) prisoners" in Richmond Barracks and found them " very good-looking fellows with such lovely eyes." He ordered a drastic comb-out before they were transferred to England.

From his headquarters at Viceregal Lodge Asquith also made expeditions about the country, to Cork, where there was some fear of further trouble, and to Belfast, where he met eight or ten of " the most hard-bitten Carsonite leaders." He was rather impressed by them, as by the whole Orange capital, which had so heavily scarred his political life but which he had never before visited. " Certainly Belfast, which is to look at a very superior Manchester," he wrote to his wife, " is a wonderful creation of its kind—in marvellous contrast to the ' out of repair ' look which everything (including the scenery) wears in the greater part of Ireland."[o] He noted with more curiosity than distaste the implacable hatred and contempt of the Orange leaders for the Catholics of the South, but he thought they might accept an immediate Home Rule settlement for a partitioned Ireland.

Back in London, on May 19th, he told Lady Scott that he " was inclined to put much of the Rebellion down to economic conditions. Some 12,000 families in Dublin live in single rooms." But the solution he was looking for was a political one. The " Home Rule in cold storage " arrangement which the Unionists had forced upon him at the outbreak of war would clearly no longer work. A fresh attempt at a

---

[1] Sheehy Skeffington, a Dublin journalist who was in no way implicated in the rising, had been shot without the knowledge of Maxwell. The officer responsible was subsequently court-martialled and found guilty but insane. But the incident was a frightening example of the casualness with which judicial bullets had been discharged.

deal between Redmond and Carson, which would enable the Irish parliamentary party to regain its power by taking over the government of the South, was his strategy. To carry this through he needed a strong and resourceful Chief Secretary. His mind turned towards Lloyd George. Lady Scott wrote on May 24th:

P.M. came about 6, very stimulated by Ireland. He has suggested Ll.G. going there as Chief Secretary. Bonar Law upheld suggestion. Ll.G. consulted Irish leaders who agreed, but thought it should only be until the situation was settled. He would keep on his present position. The P.M. said in response to my many protests that he (Lloyd George) was an ambitious man, he'd stand or fall by the success he made. Couldn't grind any axe, etc.

The invitation to Lloyd George was conveyed in slightly more flattering terms. " It is a *unique* opportunity," Asquith wrote, " and there is no-one else who could do so much to bring about a permanent solution."[p] Lloyd George, who wanted to go on a mission to Russia with Kitchener, hesitated for a short time. He was not prepared to contemplate a permanent assignment such as might be implied in his taking the Chief Secretaryship. Nor would he accept responsibility for the Irish administration. But he agreed to attempt a settlement. By so doing he probably saved his own life.

With Redmond and Carson, Lloyd George was completely and quickly successful. By mid-June he had secured the agreement not only of the negotiators, but of their followers as well, to a settlement on the basis of immediate Home Rule, with the whole of the Six Counties excluded for the period of the war. The ultimate solution for this area, and, indeed, the long-term future of Irish government as a whole was to be determined after the war by an Imperial Conference; in the meantime all the 80 Irish members were to continue to sit at Westminster.

The publication of these terms provoked a Unionist revolt. It was not the Ulstermen, but the bulk of the English Conservatives, particularly the peers with Southern Irish connections, who made the trouble. Back-benchers and members of the Cabinet were equally involved. Once again the Coalition seemed on the brink of breaking up. June 28th was a day of Cabinet crisis—there were meetings from 11.0 until 2.0 and again from 7.0 until 9.0, but Lord Selborne had already resigned without waiting for these deliberations. Asquith's account to the King, the longest he ever wrote,[1] described the course of the argument. The scheme, he said, was strongly opposed by Lansdowne and Long, with Lord Robert Cecil in their camp but a little less firm. Bonar Law differed sharply from these colleagues and said that he would recommend the plans to a meeting of Conservative M.P.s, but that his own subsequent actions must depend upon their decision. Curzon spoke rather tentatively against the proposals, mainly on the ground that it would be impossible to get them through the House of Lords.

In the evening " Sir E. Grey strongly supported an arrangement on the lines proposed and dwelt with great force on the effect of its rejection and a divided Ministry in the situation in America." Then: Mr. Balfour delivered the most effective pronouncement in this prolonged conclave. As a veteran Unionist he dissociated himself entirely from the position taken up by Lord Lansdowne and Mr. Long. . . . (He) laid stress on the importance of not alienating American opinion at this juncture and declared himself a whole-hearted supporter of the policy of Sir E. Carson and Mr. B. Law. Mr. Lloyd George intervened to point out that if the resignations of Unionist members of the Cabinet could be averted by a further consideration of possible safeguards for the maintenance of imperial naval and military control during the war, he would do his best to secure such an arrangement, and he suggested that a small Committee of the Cabinet. . . . should be at once appointed to discuss its terms. Lord Curzon and Mr. Chamberlain intimated that they were ready to fall in with this suggestion, as was also Lord Lansdowne. Mr. Long was still recalcitrant. . . .

Thereupon the P.M. intervened. He told his colleagues frankly that in his opinion at this critical conjunction in the War[2] a series of resignations and a consequent possible dissolution of the Government would be not only a national calamity but a national crime. He appealed with much emphasis to all his colleagues to avert such a catastrophe. The proposed settlement would in his opinion have been accepted on all sides before the War and would be accepted with equal unanimity after the War. He therefore proposed (and the Cabinet with the exception of Mr. Long unanimously agreed) that a Committee consisting of the P.M., Mr.

[1] He was still doing so in his own hand, as he continued until the end.

[2] The British offensive on the Somme was just about to begin.

Lloyd George, Lord R. Cecil and the Attorney-General (F. E. Smith) should at once proceed to consider and to formulate such additions as seemed to them to be necessary . . . between now and next Monday. On this footing all the Ministers who had threatened resignation (including with much personal reluctance Mr. Long) agreed to retain in the meantime their offices.[q]

The division in the Unionist Party was a strange one. The " new men " who had made the running over Ulster in 1913 and 1914— Bonar Law, Smith and Carson—were all moderates on this occasion. So was Balfour, whom Asquith had described at the time of the Buckingham Palace Conference as " a real wrecker " on the Irish issue. It was the old Tories who made the trouble, men who had never cared much for the Orange cause, but who were wedded to Imperial supremacy throughout Ireland. They had the bulk of Conservative opinion with them. The combined efforts of Bonar Law and Balfour made little impression upon a Carlton Club meeting.

The Cabinet met on July 5th to receive the report of its committee of five. The opening of Asquith's account of this occasion is as succinct a commentary on the relationship of the Cabinet at this time to military affairs, on its pre-occupation with other matters, and on the character of the Chief of the Imperial General Staff, as could reasonably be wished for:

Sir W. Robertson attended and with the aid of a large map described and explained to the Cabinet the operations in France so far as they had proceeded. His account was of a very reassuring character and gave general satisfaction. The Prime Minister then invited the attention of the Cabinet to the latest development in the Irish negotiations.[r]

The meeting went more easily than had been expected. The committee proposed that when the plan became a bill there should be a special provision safeguarding imperial naval and military rights for the duration of the war. Asquith thought this unnecessary, but was prepared to agree to its insertion as the price of agreement with the Unionists. So was Redmond. Long and Lansdowne did not pretend to be pleased with the proposals, but they reluctantly agreed to accept them and to abandon the idea of resignation. Asquith thanked them for their " patriotism and public spirit " and wrote with relief to the King: " The result, Mr. Asquith humbly submits to your Majesty, is very satisfactory. . . . "

This time it was the Prime Minister and not the Sovereign who was prematurely optimistic. On July 11th, Lansdowne, a moderate on many issues but always a cold and determined extremist on anything touching his position as a Kerry landlord, placed a dagger firmly into the back of the agreement. Speaking for the Government in the House of Lords, he stressed that the exclusion of Ulster must be permanent and that Southern Ireland would in effect be governed by a strengthened Defence of the Realm Act, with which the Dublin Parliament would have no right to interfere. Asquith wrote sadly to Crewe: "Lansdowne's speech has given the greatest offence to the Irish, and it was with difficulty that they were dissuaded from asking me today whether it represented the policy of the Government. It is, of course, the general tone and temper which especially irritates them."[8]

The practical significance of Lansdowne's speech was that it created a new atmosphere of suspicion amongst the Nationalists. This strengthened the position of Dillon, who, Lloyd George said, was the difficult man throughout the negotiations, and weakened that of Redmond and Devlin. Such a change might not have been decisive without Bonar Law's decision that he could continue to support the agreement only with a further substantial concession. The Irish members at Westminster must either be drastically reduced or confined to voting on issues which directly concerned them. Whether Redmond could in any circumstances have agreed to this is not known. Asquith believed that he did not really object. But after Lansdowne's speech he would ask for no more from his followers. It was even possible that he, like Bonar Law, had by this time become anxious to escape from any arrangement. On July 24th Asquith told Lady Scott that he thought Redmond was now "trying to kill the whole thing." "In fact it's dead," he added; and when asked what alternative was proposed, he replied hopelessly: "They have nothing to suggest but despair."

At the Cabinet of July 27th arrangements were made for burying the agreement, and putting into operation this policy of despair. Wimborne was to be sent back as Lord Lieutenant. A Unionist lawyer (H. E. Duke), the least distinguished holder of the office since 1880, was appointed Chief Secretary. The old Dublin Castle system went on, and the troubles of 1921 and 1922 became inevitable. Asquith had again tried hard to solve the Irish problem, but the prejudices of some of his Unionist colleagues were too great, and his authority over them too small, for this last opportunity to be seized.

Before Ireland could be entirely tucked back under the carpet, there remained one further matter for the Cabinet to settle. This was the question of Casement's execution. After his arrest on the coast of Kerry, Casement had been brought to London for trial. On June 29th, with F. E. Smith prosecuting, he was convicted of high treason and sentenced to death. The case was taken to the Court of Criminal Appeal on July 17th and 18th, but his appeal was there rejected by a panel of five judges. Smith declined to give his fiat for a further appeal to the House of Lords. All that remained, therefore, was for the Home Secretary[1] to decide whether or not he should exercise the prerogative of mercy. Exceptionally, he did not attempt to decide this for himself. Casement's execution was a Cabinet matter even before the Court of Appeal had given its decision. At the end of the meeting of July 5th it was decided to submit his now famous homosexual diaries to an " alienist," as the word then was. " Several members of the Cabinet (including Sir E. Grey and Lord Lansdowne)," Asquith wrote, " were strongly of opinion that it would be better (if possible) that he should be kept in confinement as a criminal lunatic than that he should be executed without any smirch on his character[2] and then canonized as a martyr both in Ireland and America."[t]

On July 12th the Cabinet received the alienist's report and noted that it declared him " to be abnormal but not certifiably insane." On July 19th, the day after the Court of Appeal decision, Asquith told the King that " it was the unanimous decision of the Cabinet that (Casement) should be hanged." On July 27th it was decided that the Foreign and Home Offices should co-operate in drawing up a statement of the Government's reasons for proceeding with the execution. Since the previous meeting Asquith had received strong representations for a reprieve from Bryce (who had been both Chief Secretary and Ambassador to Washington), Dillon and Devlin. On August 2nd:

The greater part of the sitting was occupied in a further and final discussion of the Casement case, in view of some further material and the urgent appeals for mercy from authoritative and friendly quarters of the U.S. The Cabinet was of the opinion that no ground existed for a reprieve, and Lord Grey[3] drew up a state-

[1] Herbert Samuel, who had succeeded Simon in January.

[2] A curious phrase in the context.

[3] Grey had become a peer at the beginning of July. Asquith had wanted to make him an earl, but Earl Grey (the third successor of the Reform Bill

ment of reasons to be shown by Sir C. Spring-Rice[1] to Senator Lodge and others.[u]

On August 3rd Casement was hanged. There can be few other examples of a Cabinet devoting large parts of four separate meetings to considering an individual sentence—and then arriving at the wrong decision. The effect in the United States was as bad as it could have been. In Ireland, Casement became a martyr. And even in England the effects of the case reverberated on for forty years or more. Asquith himself would have preferred a reprieve based on medical evidence, but in the absence of this he did not feel it right to treat Casement more leniently than his supposed followers had been treated by Maxwell.

Prime Minister) objected, in these circumstances, to his retaining his name in his title. The Foreign Secretary then said that he cared much more for his name than his rank and became Viscount Grey of Fallodon.

[1] The British Ambassador in Washington.

CHAPTER XXV

A DECLINING AUTHORITY

1916

In the middle of May, when Asquith was in Dublin, Kitchener received an invitation from the Czar to visit Russia. For a month or so the Government had been considering sending a mission to help with the military and supply situation there. Kitchener, although he had worked much better with Robertson than might have been expected, was restless with his lack of power and eager to get away for a time. Once again, although less urgently on this occasion, his colleagues were anxious to see him go. A plan for Lloyd George to accompany Kitchener and deal with the munitions side of the problem was abandoned when he accepted the Irish assignment. Except for a small staff Kitchener went alone. He left London on the night of June 4th. On the following evening he was drowned off the Orkneys. The news was published at noon on June 6th.

On May 30th Asquith had called on Lady Scott for one of his regular conversational exchanges. She recorded in her diary:

The Prime Minister came in the evening. He was wonderful. Talked a great deal about Kitchener. I asked him why he was going to Russia. First he said " to occupy his leisure, incidentally to talk about munitions, finance, etc." Later he said " He's abdicated. He's going to be abused in the House tomorrow," & the P.M. said " I suppose I must defend him, I can't leave it to little Tennant, but upon my word I don't know what I shall say, he's *such* a liar ! "

" In South Africa . . . they thought they'd got a plain bluff soldier in Kitchener and a subtle diplomat in Milner. They were wonderfully wrong. If K. can put a thing in a tortuous fashion he always prefers to—& then he repeats himself so horribly; he came to me this morning to say a thing which could be said in 2 minutes—& he said it in 2 minutes, & then began again, & then *again*."

Yet there remains considerable doubt as to whether these disillusioned, harsh words represented Asquith's final view of Kitchener. Lady Scott's diary never catches the exact turn of Asquith's phraseology. His cynicism was softer, more tolerant, less brittle, than she allows. Hankey, who knew Asquith very well at this time, supplies an element of confirmation for Lady Scott by saying that, when he first told him that Kitchener wanted to go to Russia, " Asquith . . . was rather amused." But Hankey also wrote, admittedly as part of a posthumous justification of Kitchener, that the latter never lost the confidence of those who knew him best and about whose opinion he cared most, the King and the Prime Minister.[a] And Asquith wrote in his own memoirs of the importance which he attached to Kitchener's mission to Petrograd: " I have always thought, and still think, that his arrival there might have deflected the subsequent course of history."[b]

No doubt the truth, allowing for all the changing moods of human feeling, lies somewhere between Lady Scott and this. But whatever opinions he left behind him, Kitchener was dead. Twice in five days the country had been rocked by news of great events. On May 31st and June 1st Admiral Jellicoe had engaged the German High Seas Fleet in the drawn battle of Jutland, and the first communiqué had presented a picture still less encouraging than the reality. Now Kitchener, who was still such a public legend that rumours denying his death persisted for years, had gone. Greatly though his power had been pared, he left vacant, at a critical stage in the struggle, one of the offices most vital to its prosecution. Asquith's next problem was whom to make Secretary of State for War.

It was three weeks before a decision was made and another week after that before the new Minister—Lloyd George—took over the department. The currently accepted view of what took place during this interval is that Asquith found himself confronted by two almost equally unwelcome candidates for the post—Lloyd George and Bonar Law; that he decided to procrastinate in the hope that time would enable him to slip Lord Derby in between the two as a more accommodating occupant of the office; but that Law and Lloyd George frustrated this plan by getting together at Lord Beaverbrook's Leatherhead house on Sunday, June 11th and agreeing that Lloyd George should have the job. On the following morning—Whit Monday—

Law drove from Leatherhead to the Wharf to see Asquith[1] and present him with a joint ultimatum. Asquith countered by offering the job to Law himself, as the lesser of the two evils. But when Law told him it was too late for that, he capitulated and agreed to accept Lloyd George.[c]

Such an account is not wholly convincing, although it contains substantial elements of truth. Asquith did delay over the appointment. He wrote to the King on June 8th to say that he did not intend to rush into a precipitate solution. He did make a tentative offer to Bonar Law on the Monday, and a firmer one to Lloyd George on the Tuesday evening. But there is no indication that he regarded his hands as tied after the Law interview, or that this was decisive in securing the appointment for Lloyd George. The latter, in his *War Memoirs*, writes as though he assumed from the beginning that the office was available to him, provided he was prepared to take it on the terms which Robertson had imposed upon Kitchener.[d] Mr. Robert Blake says that the forcing of a modification of this agreement was an essential part of the Bonar Law-Lloyd George compact. But was this even raised, let alone agreed, during Law's brief discussion at the Wharf? It may have come up during the Prime Minister's interview with Lloyd George on the Tuesday; but it may not have emerged until another interview two days later. On the Thursday evening (June 16th) Asquith told Lady Scott, with apparent surprise, that "Lloyd George was behaving absurdly, & suggesting tremendous powers for himself at the W.O.— much more than K. had had. Also he was suggesting leaving the Cabinet altogether, saying he could be more useful outside it."

On the Friday Lloyd George followed up the interview by writing a perhaps purposely obscure letter :

My dear Prime Minister,
I have given a good deal of consideration to your kind offer of the War Secretaryship and I have come to the conclusion that I should be rendering a greater service to the country in this emergency by not accepting it. As I told you at our interview I thought then I should be of greater use in another sphere. I am still of that opinion. There is another—an insuperable—difficulty. I have taken a strong

[1] This is the occasion on which Bonar Law, *via* Lord Beaverbrook and Mr. Robert Blake, claimed to have found Asquith " engaged in a rubber of bridge with three ladies." (see p. 289*n, supra*).

line in the Cabinet on the question of enfranchisement of our soldiers. I feel they have a right to a voice in choosing the Government that sends them to face peril and death. Were I now to accept a new office in the Government it would fetter up my action when the Cabinet comes to decide that great issue, as they must soon. It is better therefore from your point of view as well as mine that you should give no further thought to my appointment as War Minister. I thank you all the same for the offer.

Yours sincerely,

D. *Lloyd George* [e]

Obviously Lloyd George was playing hard to get. He could hardly have expected his " insuperable difficulty " of soldiers' votes at some hypothetical general election to be taken seriously. But how hard was he prepared to play? On the same day he wrote another, much longer letter to Asquith. This was also a letter of resignation, but it gave his real reasons for wanting to go. There was no mention in it of soldiers' enfranchisement. Instead there were strong attacks on the generals, a demand for much greater powers for a civilian Secretary of State for War, and general criticism of the whole direction of the war " which we are undoubtedly losing." Only the importance of his munitions task, which was now discharged, had prevented him from " long ago (joining) Carson with whom I have been in the main in complete sympathy in his criticisms of the conduct of the war."[f]

There was another difference between this letter and the first one. This one was never sent. Lloyd George, influenced by Reading, Law and Carson, thought better of it. What effect it would have had on Asquith it is difficult to say. At this stage, contrary to the view of the " Beaverbrook historians," he was probably genuinely in favour of Lloyd George having the War Office. Right through from 1908 he had never hesitated to give him big, difficult, worth-while assignments. That same Friday evening he argued strongly to Stamfordham that Lloyd George was one of the only three remaining " Englishmen "[1] with a reputation abroad (the others were Grey and himself). With Kitchener gone, Lloyd George's presence at the War Office would have a good effect upon the Allies. But Asquith did not believe that tearing up the Robertson agreement was remotely practicable—or indeed

[1] Lloyd George might not have liked the word.

desirable. Even without this he was finding enough difficulty in persuading the generals (backed by the Palace) to look with grudging favour upon Lloyd George.

Their view, and that of the King, was that much the best solution was for Asquith to take the job himself. Lord French had been to see him on the Thursday and " on behalf of the whole Army . . . begged him " to do this. Stamfordham wrote that the whole Army Council wanted it. This solution had its attractions for Asquith. He always enjoyed exercising his deft quality of effortless administration upon a department, and he was particularly fond of the War Office, of which he had again been in charge since Kitchener's death. But he realised that there might be political objections.

On the Monday (June 20th) he became aware of a new difficulty. Not more than four Secretaries of State could, by law, be in the House of Commons. Grey, Samuel, Bonar Law and Austen Chamberlain already made up the complement. " So that rules out the Gnat (Lloyd George) and the P.M.," was the assumption of Lady Scott, with whom he discussed the matter. This set him to work upon the political jig-saw, another activity which he always enjoyed. Perhaps Law could be asked to give up Colonies—it does not sound as though Asquith was very intimidated by him at the time, although a non-departmental office was no doubt to be offered in exchange—and Harcourt moved there with a peerage. Perhaps " a figurehead, say Derby " could be brought in, and " the work (left) to carry on as it does very well at present."*g*

This is the first Asquith mention of Derby in this connection, and not a very flattering one. But that peer, whose public reputation, largely without foundation, was so great that he was sometimes spoken of as a possible Prime Minister, was singularly accommodating. He wanted very much to be Secretary of State,[1] but he was prepared to serve as under-secretary, preferably in support of Asquith or Bonar Law, but of Lloyd George if need be.

This made it easier for Asquith to get the generals to accept Lloyd

[1] " I should like the office—like it very much—but I can't bring myself to ask for it," he wrote to his brother-in-law on June 23rd. " If however you could do anything to get my claim considered, the P.M. need have no fear of my loyalty. . . ." (Randolph Churchill: *Lord Derby*, p. 212). This letter is completely incompatible with the view that he was throughout " Asquith's candidate " for the job.

George. Derby would give them confidence and act as a commodious cushion between them and the new Secretary of State. Two further changes eased Lloyd George's appointment. The first was Asquith's discovery that Grey would be glad to lessen his burdens by becoming a peer. The second was that Lloyd George himself tacitly withdrew his conditions about the amendment of the Robertson agreement. It was he and not Asquith who capitulated on this point. Between June 24th and 26th he exchanged inconclusive but barbed letters with the C.I.G.S. They were an inauspicious augury for the future, but they changed little for the present. Lloyd George accepted the office on virtually the same terms that Kitchener had latterly held it. It was all settled by June 28th.

When Margot Asquith heard of the new appointment, she wrote in her diary: " We are out: it can only be a question of time now when we shall have to leave Downing Street."[h] Her husband did not take an equally dramatic view. He saw the outcome rather as a more or less satisfactory solution which he had managed to find for another wearisome problem.

After this War Office arrangement the remainder of the summer of 1916 unfolded itself without much encouragement. There was some light but also a great deal of heavy, lowering cloud. The Russians made sweeping progress in their offensive against the Austrians north of the Roumanian frontier. It was their outstanding success of the war. But on the Somme the British casualties mounted to unprecedented heights, without any corresponding gains. In the first twenty-four hours of this offensive there were 20,000 dead and 40,000 wounded. Within three weeks the casualties had risen to 120,000. At this stage there came the disappointment of the Irish failure. And in the shadow of it, in Hankey's view, Asquith committed his greatest parliamentary blunder of the war. He agreed to Commissions of Inquiry into the Dardanelles expedition and the Mesopotamian failure which had culminated in the surrender of Kut in April. The trouble had started on June 14th, when Bonar Law had promised, with little consultation, to lay the Gallipoli papers before the House of Commons. The departments concerned protested violently. Such publication, they held, would have disastrous military and diplomatic consequences. As a result, after six weeks' disputation by the War Council and the Cabinet, it was decided that the promise must be rescinded. Asquith announced this to the House on July 18th. His statement was badly received on all sides, and he and the

Cabinet felt forced, two days later, to offer the sop of secret Commissions of Inquiry with published reports.

"Certain it is," Hankey wrote, "that the Coalition never recovered from (this) decision. For the last five months of its existence the function of the Supreme Command was carried out under the shadow of these inquests . . . . A good deal of mutual suspicion was engendered. Such homogeneity as the Government had possessed gradually weakened. . . . Before long . . . the power of decision in difficult questions was affected."[1]

The consequences of this "blunder" took time to make themselves felt. August was a calm month politically, although the Battle of the Somme ground on. Plans for the Speaker's Conference on electoral reform were put in hand. There were financial difficulties with the French, and Asquith had to pay a hurried visit to Calais on the 23rd.

[1] Hankey was perhaps a little jaundiced by the fact that, between July 24th and September 27th, he had to spend 174 hours of his "free" time preparing the Government case for the Dardanelles Commission. He lost his August holiday (which would have been his first since 1913) but felt partially compensated by Asquith's assurance that the result of his work was "the greatest State paper he had ever read"; Curzon's letter of congratulation, accompanied by the offer of a week-end party to meet the Queen of the Belgians, he found less of a recompense. (*The Supreme Command*, II, p. 523).

On the other hand, Hankey, before this diversion, was a considerable partisan of the British system of Supreme Command as it had evolved under Asquith. His retrospective judgment was that it was certainly superior to the German system. The November, 1915, arrangements were a great advance on anything which had gone before: "The machinery of the War Committee was at this time (the first eight months of 1916) working smoothly. An Agenda paper was issued before each meeting. Full records were as before kept in manuscript. The conclusions after being approved and initialled by the Prime Minister—in this matter Asquith was prompt and punctilious—were circulated to the Cabinet whose members were thus kept fully abreast of what was going on."

Hankey's conclusion was that, "with a loyal and united team," this system might have been adapted to meet the requirements of the latter part of the war. "But, with a Government composed of members of opposite political parties who had never been able entirely to forget their differences and in an atmosphere poisoned by the Dardanelles and Mesopotamia Commissions, this proved impossible even under so patient and experienced a leader as Asquith." (*ibid.*, II, pp. 543–4).

Early in the month the Italians gained an expensive but real victory and occupied Gorizia. Late in the month the Roumanians entered the War on the Allied side, and there were false hopes that this might change the whole Balkan balance; within three months they were smashed and the Germans were outside Bucharest. The French went over to the offensive before Verdun, but continued to bleed themselves white.

In the last week of August Asquith escaped for a few days to the Wharf. Then, at the beginning of September, he went with Hankey, whom he described at about this time as "the most useful man in Europe—he has never been wrong," on a visit to the front. They were both greatly interested in the plans for the first employment of the tanks or "caterpillars," which, stemming from Churchill's original directive of March, 1915, were now ready for service in small numbers. Hankey pressed the two principal staff officers at G.H.Q. not to fritter away the shock of their first use in limited attacks over the unfavourable (because heavily shell-scarred) terrain of the Somme. They should be kept for a new offensive over less weary ground. Asquith, he said, urged the same point of view upon Haig.[1]

The visit was also notable for a meeting between Asquith and his

[1] "Asquith stayed at a G.H.Q. house during this visit. After dinner the first evening Haig wrote in his diary: "Mr. A. and I had a long talk after dinner. . . . . He seems fully determined to fight on till Germany is vanquished". After the second evening he wrote to his wife: "You would have been amused at the Prime Minister last night. He did himself fairly well—not more than most gentlemen used to drink when I was a boy, but in this abstemious age it is noticeable if an extra glass or two is taken by anyone! The P.M. seemed to like our old brandy. He had a couple of glasses (big sherry glass size) before I left the table at 9.30, and apparently he had several more before I saw him again. By that time his legs were unsteady, but his head was quite clear, and he was able to read a map and discuss the situation with me. Indeed he was most charming and quite alert in mind." (*The Private Papers of Douglas Haig*, p. 164)

Haig's picture fits in well with other accounts of Asquith's dining habits. For the last ten or fifteen years of his life, at least, he was a fairly heavy drinker. Occasionally this made him look a little unsteady (even in the House of Commons) late at night. But no one ever suggested that his mind lost its precision or that there was any faltering in his command over what he did or did not want to say.

eldest son, and for the close experience of the Somme battlefield which it gave to the Prime Minister. Hankey described how, on September 6th, a " glorious hot day," they motored up from G.H.Q., through the ruined town of Albert, to the three-storied dug-out headquarters of the 7th Division, which was in action at the time:

Near Fricourt we met Raymond Asquith, the Prime Minister's eldest son, who was waiting at a cross-roads, having ridden over on horseback to meet us. As we jolted up the broken shell-smitten road . . . I heard the curious whizz of a large howitzer shell. . . . As we came through the " street " at Fricourt—as a matter of fact there was literally not one stone left on another—another shell came and burst not more than a hundred yards away. We got out of our cars and hurried to a " dug-out." Just as we arrived a third shell greeted us and landed not fifty yards away—but I am not sure that it burst. We had to wait some considerable time in the " dug-out " until the shell shower had passed over. . . . . The Prime Minister was as usual quite composed, but I thought his hand was trembling rather, and no wonder.ⁱ

Asquith's comment on his meeting with his son was that he found him looking " so radiantly strong and confident that I came away from France with an easier mind."ᵏ On the next day he and Hankey motored to Crecy, where they had a chance encounter with Edwin Montagu, who had succeeded Lloyd George as Minister of Munitions; and Asquith derived considerable and typical amusement from Montagu's ignorance of the fact that they were on ground which had seen an earlier battle.

The next big push on the Somme came on September 15th. The advice which Asquith and Hankey had given to Haig and his staff officers was then ignored. The tanks were frittered away. " This priceless conception," as Churchill wrote, " . . . was revealed to the Germans for the mere petty purpose of taking a few ruined villages." But that day brought far worse news for Asquith than that. In the first wave of the attack Raymond Asquith was killed.

The news reached London two days later. Margot Asquith has described how it arrived at the Wharf:

On Sunday, September the 17th, we were entertaining a week-end party. . . . While we were playing tennis in the afternoon my husband went for a drive with my cousin, Nan Tennant. He looked well, and had been delighted with his visit to the front. . . .

413

As it was my little son's last Sunday before going back to Winchester I told him he might run across from the Barn in his pyjamas after dinner and sit with us while the men were in the dining-room.

While we were playing games, Clouder, our servant . . . came in to say that I was wanted.

I left the room, and the moment I took up the telephone I said to myself, "Raymond is killed."

With the receiver in my hand, I asked what it was, and if the news was bad.

Our secretary, Davies, answered, "Terrible, terrible news. Raymond was shot dead on the 15th. Haig writes full of sympathy, but no details. The Guards were in and he was shot leading his men the moment he had gone over the parapet."

I put back the receiver and sat down. I heard Elizabeth's delicious laugh, and a hum of talk and smell of cigars came down the passage from the dining-room.

I went back into the sitting-room.

"Raymond is dead," I said, "he was shot leading his men over the top on Friday."

Puffin got up from his game and hanging his head took my hand; Elizabeth burst into tears. . . . Maud Tree and Florry Bridges suggested I should put off telling Henry the terrible news as he was happy. I walked away with the two children and rang the bell: "Tell the Prime Minister to come and speak to me," I said to the servant.

Leaving the children, I paused at the end of the dining-room passage; Henry opened the door and we stood facing each other. He saw my thin wet face, and while he put his arm round me I said:

"Terrible, terrible news."

At this he stopped me and said:

"I know . . . I've known it . . . Raymond is dead."

He put his hands over his face and we walked into an empty room and sat down in silence.[1]

The blow to Asquith was a heavy one. Of the four sons of his first marriage Raymond was not the closest to him. Nor was he academically pre-eminent. But he was the most generally gifted. He had immense gaiety; he was a symbol of the talent of a generation;

and he was most like what Asquith himself, in his occasional moods of romantic impatience with what he sometimes regarded as his own pedestrian qualities and success, would have liked to be. " Whatever pride I had in the past," he wrote on September 20th, " and whatever hope I had for the far future—by much the largest part of both was invested in him. Now all that is gone. It will take me a few days more to get back to my bearings."[m]

.In fact it took him much longer. Throughout the autumn he remained, for most people, withdrawn and difficult to approach. He missed several Cabinets, and on October 11th he was writing:

This has been a great blow to me and I am much shaken by it— there is or ought to be every kind of consolation and I have numberless letters from all parts of the world and all sorts and conditions of people. But I don't know that it all helps one very much. . . . Today I braced myself up to propose a vote of credit in the House of Commons; a trying and difficult speech, especially the latter part of it. I got on better than I expected as everyone was very kind and sympathetic.[n]

This special public kindness was inevitably short-lived. *The Times* and the *Daily Mail*, Lord Northcliffe's twin scourges for the mortification of the Prime Minister, continued their attacks almost without respite. Asquith preserved his equanimity by taking little notice of what they said. He was never much of a newspaper reader, preferring always to have hard covers between his hands, and it is doubtful if he even looked at them at all regularly. But much of the rest of the country did. In an age of mass-literacy, before broadcasting, and with a House of Commons disorganised by coalition and too far removed from election to be effectively representative, Northcliffe exercised an influence greater than that of any newspaper proprietor before or since. Between them his two organs gave him a dominant grip on both ends of the London newspaper market. And their constant, unanswered denunciations of Asquith, while they may have provoked him less than they would have provoked most other men, did much to undermine his position.

Within the Government new quarrels had erupted after the August lull. In late September Lloyd George had given his so-called " knock-out blow " interview to an American newspaperman. In this interview he discounted entirely any possibility of a negotiated settlement. Britain would fight on to " a decisive finish," however long the time, however great the sacrifice. His purpose was to warn off President Wilson who was thought to be contemplating a peace initiative. Several members of the Cabinet, including the Foreign Secretary, believed the interview to be ill-judged and unnecessarily intransigent. Grey wrote a letter of remonstrance, but Lloyd George replied jauntily: " You will find that it will work out all right. I know that American politician. He has no international conscience. He thinks of nothing but the ticket. . . ." [o1] This was the beginning of a dispute which was to boil up again in November.

Lloyd George was a principal participant in most quarrels at this time. He allowed a bitter argument between Balfour and Curzon about the use of aeroplanes to pass over his head, but he was central to every other major dispute. In mid-October he exchanged wounding letters with Robertson over the C.I.G.S's refusal to divert troops from the Western Front to Salonika. In the same week he was in the thick of an argument about the working of the Military Service Act. Carson, an increasingly effective leader of the dissidents in the House of Commons, was waging a campaign, with wide newspaper support, to press more men into service. Lloyd George echoed this point of view in a speech on October 12th. Bonar Law commented a few weeks later that the Secretary of State for War was " at the same time the right hand man to the Prime Minister and to the leader of the Opposition."[p] But from where were the extra men to be pressed? Montagu threatened to resign if more were taken away from munitions. The Cabinet (for once) was nearly unanimous that conscription could not be applied to Ireland, although it noted sadly that recruiting there, and amongst the Irish in Australia, had come to an almost complete standstill. This was one price of the failure of the June and July negotiations. But neither the Press nor Carson accepted the facts which circumscribed the Government.

Eventually a sop was found. Asquith wrote to the King on November 6th: " The Cabinet resolved (the Prime Minister dissenting) to introduce a Bill to compel the enlistment of unnaturalised aliens of allied countries (mostly Russian Jews) giving them at the same time an option to emigrate to some other country."[q]

By this time the situation had been exacerbated by the final collapse, after 400,000 British casualties and very small territorial

---

[1] This passage was expurgated from Lloyd George's *War Memoirs*, although he published the rest of the correspondence.

gains, of the Somme offensive; by the imminent surrender of Roumania; and by the increasing menace of shipping losses to U-boats.

The War Council attempted to deal with these and other lesser problems by meetings of mounting frequency. It had swollen to a membership of nine regular members—Asquith, McKenna, Lloyd George, Bonar Law, Balfour, Grey, Crewe, Curzon and Austen Chamberlain—with Runciman and Montagu as additional frequent participants, and Robertson, Henry Jackson and Hankey always present in their professional capacities. Day after day, in the early part of November, it would meet at 11.30 and adjourn at 1.15 or 1.30 with many of the agenda issues unresolved. "These have been really dreadful War Committees," Hankey wrote.

It was not that the chairmanship was bad. It was rather that the lack of trust between members was so great, and the external pressures so demoralising, that agreement had become impossible. On November 1st Asquith spoke almost casually of there being "some six resignations looming." On November 8th a further element of instability was introduced into the Unionist side of the Coalition by the humiliation of Bonar Law in the House of Commons. In a debate on the somewhat peripheral issue of the disposal of enemy property in Nigeria, for which as Colonial Secretary Law was departmentally responsible, Carson had attacked him with the utmost ferocity. In the division which followed the Government was sustained mainly by Liberal votes. 65 Unionists voted with Carson, 73 with Bonar Law, and 148 were either absent or abstained. The minority was made up not only of Unionists, and not only of those who felt strongly about the pattern of ownership in Lagos, but of a general alliance of malcontents.[1] Churchill, who, against Asquith's advice, had returned from the front to politics in the spring of 1916, was with them; and Lloyd George, who had been dining with Carson that same evening, did not vote.

Into this atmosphere of mutual mistrust and recrimination there was inserted the naked light of the Lansdowne memorandum. It was ironical that such an explosive document should have been provided by such an unflamboyant character. He wrote it in response to a

[1] One of Carson's supporters met F. E. Smith in the lobby and told him that Law had been saved by the votes of " the paid members." " We will cross off the votes of the members who are paid," Smith said, " if you cross off those who want to be paid." (Blake: *The Unknown Prime Minister*, p. 299).

general invitation from Asquith that members of the Cabinet should circulate their views about the prospects for the next phase of the war and the terms upon which the country might be willing to conclude peace. It was an eminently sensible time for general stocktaking and Lansdowne discharged his part of the task faithfully. His document was long, cogent, and extremely pessimistic. With his usual quiet ruthlessness he refused to leave any question unasked:

> We are slowly but surely killing off the best of the male population of these islands. . . . The financial burden which we have already accumulated is almost incalculable. . . . All this it is no doubt our duty to bear, but only if it can be shown that the sacrifice will have its reward. If it is to be made in vain, if the additional year or two years or three years finds us still unable to dictate terms, the war with its nameless horrors will have been needlessly prolonged, and the responsibility of those who needlessly prolong such a war is not less than that of those who needlessly provoke it. . . . Many of us must of late have asked ourselves how the war is ever to be brought to an end. . . . it seems as if the prospect of a " knock-out " was, to say the least of it remote. . . . Is it not true that unless the apprehensions which I have sketched can be shown . . . to be groundless, we ought at any rate not to discourage any movement, no matter where originating, in favour of an interchange of views as to the possibility of a settlement?[r]

This memorandum was circulated on November 13th. Its conclusions did not represent Asquith's view. He believed, and had expressed in a speech at the Guildhall four days before, that the moment for peace overtures had not come and that the war must be fought on, probably for a long time to come. But he also thought, as did Grey and most of the other Liberals in the Cabinet, that Lansdowne was perfectly within his rights, and might indeed be performing a public service by raising the questions which he did. This view was not taken by Lloyd George or Bonar Law within the Government, or by Carson or Northcliffe outside. The memorandum almost immediately became public property. Cabinet security at this time was appallingly bad. A few months before action had been threatened against any newspaper which published the details of Cabinet disputes. But no one thought it worthwhile to try and stop the leaks at source —a different situation from that of two and a half years earlier when Asquith had circulated his magisterial rebuke to his colleagues.

Hostile critics outside used the memorandum as a stick with which to beat most of the Government, and Asquith in particular. The Cabinet, it was suggested, was hopelessly divided, not merely about the conduct of the war, but about whether it should continue to be fought at all. Lansdowne's views were fathered upon Asquith and Grey. Clearly he was acting as their stalking horse. The whole incident, coming at a time of dissension and dismay, was made into a further piece of evidence of the Prime Minister's lukewarmness about the national effort which he was trying to direct.

On the day after the memorandum was circulated Asquith went to Paris for a major Allied conference. The end of the 1916 Western offensives, accompanied by the crushing defeat of Roumania and growing signs of Russian exhaustion, made high-level re-appraisal urgently necessary. Asquith was accompanied by Lloyd George, Hankey and Bonham Carter, as well as by Robertson and General Sir Frederick Maurice, who with Haig, were to attend a parallel but separate military conference at Chantilly. Before their departure there had been dispute (but not of an acrimonious nature) about a Lloyd George draft for the Prime Minister's opening speech at the conference. This was in many ways a curiously similar document to Lansdowne's memorandum. The analysis was almost equally pessimistic and largely parallel, but the conclusions were different. Asquith insisted on toning it down. He cut out some of the pessimism and most of the offensive references to the Allied generals. In spite of this, and of all the other tensions within the curiously assorted group of travelling companions, it was, Hankey noted, " an extraordinarily harmonious and almost hilarious party which travelled that day to Paris." A shadow, he thought, came over them all as the train passed the " great war cemetery at Étaples, already terribly full," and Asquith's thoughts turned to Raymond. But within a few minutes a bad joke of Robertson's had restored the atmosphere.[8]

In Paris the proceedings were not equally cheerful. Briand, harried by Clemenceau (then in opposition) was in an unreceptive mood, and the real decisions (in favour of making 1917 a repeat performance of 1916) were made by the generals at Chantilly. Lloyd George became increasingly discontented. On the evening of the third and last day he recorded that when the British delegates had returned to the Hôtel Crillon and the Prime Minister had " retired to his usual rest before dinner,"[1] he and Hankey went for a walk together. Lloyd George said he wanted to resign, but his companion argued against this course. Then, as they were passing the Vendôme Column, Hankey paused and said:

You ought to insist on a small War Committee being set up for the day-to-day conduct of the War, with full powers. It must be independent of the Cabinet. It must keep in close touch with the P.M., but the Committee ought to be in continuous session, and the P.M., as Head of the Government, could not manage that. . . . The Chairman must be a man of unimpaired energy and great driving power.[t]

Lloyd George was greatly attracted by the idea, even though they both agreed that it was important that Asquith should continue as Prime Minister. He tells us that he immediately telegraphed to Sir Max Aitken (later Lord Beaverbrook), asking him to arrange a meeting with Bonar Law for the following evening, so that the proposition might be put before the Unionist leader.

The next day they all travelled back to London. At Boulogne the Prime Minister, Hankey noted, " was recognised on the quayside . . . by a number of British soldiers and given quite an ovation. This looked as if the attacks on him by the halfpenny Press had had less effect than might have been expected, at any rate so far as the Army was concerned."[u]

But soldiers on the quayside at Boulogne did not choose British governments—nor would Asquith have wished them to do so. He never went abroad again as a minister.

---

[1] This was typical of Lloyd George's desire to see Asquith as a tired old man, and in sharp contrast with Hankey's description, three evenings previously, of his late-night work being interrupted by " the Prime Minister coming in from the Embassy at about midnight in a very talkative and communicative mood, and telling us a lot of interesting information he had picked up from Briand." In fact, Asquith never rested before dinner. He merely liked, in a way that was incomprehensible to Lloyd George, to get away from conversation and to devote himself to private reading and writing.

CHAPTER XXVI

A PALACE REVOLUTION I

1916

The idea of a small War Committee with himself as chairman was not in fact implanted in Lloyd George's mind by Hankey during their walk through the Place Vendôme. The colonel's views merely gave useful support to a plan which he had already formulated, and on behalf of which, before leaving London, he had commissioned Sir Max Aitken to enlist the support of Bonar Law. In this task Aitken had, at that stage, achieved only a very limited success. He had talked at length to Law on the night of Tuesday, November 14th, but he had found him " desperately ' sticky '." " The root cause of the trouble," Aitken wrote, " was that Bonar Law had formed the opinion that in matters of office and power Lloyd George was a self-seeker and a man who considered no interests except his own."[a]

There was another consideration in Law's mind. He had become obsessed by Carson's increasing hold upon the Unionist Party. This was the significance of the Nigerian debate. It had convinced Law that, unless drastic changes were made, he could not long continue to control his own party. This, for him, would have been a disaster. His modesty and his sense of limited loyalty made him see himself as essentially a representative figure. In this respect he was like Henderson, and unlike Balfour and Curzon, who were quite content to operate as independent "statesmen," believing that their views required attention without regard to whether they were held by anyone else. Law did not therefore feel able to dismiss Lloyd George's overtures out of hand, particularly when he was told that the Secretary of State for War was operating in close alliance with the dreaded Carson.

At any rate Aitken made sufficient progress for him to feel justified in sending Lloyd George a telegram telling him that he should come home quickly and see Law. Lloyd George's own telegram from Paris appears to have been a reply to this, rather than an initiative of his own.

When he got back to London, however, Lloyd George discovered that Bonar Law would not dine with him alone on the Friday night. Law merely sent him an invitation to make a third at a party with Sir Henry Wilson. This invitation, on Aitken's advice, Lloyd George refused. He retired to Walton Heath, and dined with his family. Law was clearly not rushing into an alliance.

On the next day Law saw Asquith and informed him, contrary to the expectations of Aitken and their author, of Lloyd George's plans. Asquith reacted calmly to this information, which was probably not new to him, but expressed scepticism as to whether Lloyd George would regard the chairmanship of such a War Committee as more than a stage on his road to complete power. He also queried the value of bringing in Carson as one of its members, on the ground that when the latter was in the Government he had not formed a very high opinion of his " constructive abilities "—a view with which, within six months, both Bonar Law and Lloyd George were more than ready to agree.

As had often been the case in the past, Bonar Law found it difficult to disagree with Asquith in his presence, or for a little time afterwards. But he allowed Aitken to arrange, for the Monday evening (November 20th) the first meeting of " the Triumvirate "—Lloyd George, Carson and himself. This took place at the Hyde Park Hotel, and Aitken, the catalyst and the chronicler of this alliance, was also present.[1] It was not

[1] Lord Beaverbrook (as Sir Max Aitken became within a month) was very close to Bonar Law at the time, and was present at almost all his meetings with Lloyd George and Carson, although not at those with the other Unionist ministers or with Asquith. His account of what went on (given in Volume Two of *Politicians and the War*, first published in 1932) is detailed, dramatic, and invaluable to any study of the period. But it is self-confessedly partisan. It is a view of the battle seen, not from a hovering aeroplane, but by a deeply committed man operating in the far from calm atmosphere of one of the combatant headquarters. Nevertheless Lord Beaverbrook, for the sake of completing his picture, also tried to describe what went on in the other camps—in 10, Downing Street and amongst the Unionist ministers, notably Curzon, Chamberlain and Cecil, who were operating independently of Bonar Law. Inevitably his information was less authoritative here than when he was dealing with what he himself saw. Yet, so completely has his account come to dominate the field, that his views of when and why Asquith or Curzon or Chamberlain acted as they did are now widely accepted as indisputable facts. Innumerable books on the subject,

an easy start. Bonar Law remained suspicious of Lloyd George and at the end of the discussion arrived at the blinding conclusion that his " plans boiled down to one simple proposal—to put Asquith out and to put himself in."[b] Yet there was one substantial ray of light. Law had assumed before that Carson would never again agree to serve in a government of which Asquith remained even the titular head. Now he seemed disposed to join Lloyd George's War Committee. If that could be brought about it would be an immense relief to Law.

From this stage onwards the negotiations gathered momentum. The next day Bonar Law saw Carson at the House of Commons, first alone and then with Lloyd George. That evening he had a further meeting with Lloyd George at the Hyde Park Hotel. At luncheon on the Wednesday Lloyd George told Hankey of the proposed composition of his committee—himself, Carson, Bonar Law and Henderson—and pressed him, unsuccessfully, to join the first three of them at dinner that night.[c] On the Thursday there was a further " protracted and fruitful " session of the Triumvirate. Bonar Law was moving slowly, unhappily, but steadily along the road to full co-operation. At first he had not understood that Asquith was to be completely excluded from the new committee, but he swallowed this new knowledge without too much difficulty during the week. By the Saturday (November 25th), when there was yet another meeting, this time at his own house, Pembroke Lodge, he was ready to accept a written agreement and to put it before the Prime Minister. This document, drafted by Aitken,

---

including almost all of those published within the last ten years, lean heavily, with or without attribution, upon Lord Beaverbrook's version. Even J. A. Spender, in the relevant chapter of Asquith's official biography, used a great number of Beaverbrook's facts, (mis-transmitting at least one of them), while controverting many of his opinions. It is therefore often the case that, at first sight, a statement appears to be overwhelmingly confirmed from about six different sources; but on closer examination the six " sources " all turn out to be subsidiaries of the central Beaverbrook fount. This does not matter so long as the original " fact " was within Lord Beaverbrook's field of highly reliable knowledge. It matters greatly if it began life only as a surmise. Unfortunately there is no source on the Asquith side of the battle which is remotely as clear or gushing as the Beaverbrook one. There we have to gather together a few drops from a variety of sporadic trickles, checking them carefully against each other.

was in the form of a statement of re-organisation to be issued by Asquith himself. The operative portion of it ran as follows:

I have decided, therefore, to create what I regard as a civilian General Staff. This staff will consist of myself as President and of three other members of the Cabinet who have no portfolio and who will devote their whole time to the consideration day by day of the problems which arise in connection with the prosecution of the war.

The three members who have undertaken to fulfil these duties are:
[Here was left a blank space for the filling in of names but it was an understood part of the scheme that, apart from Lloyd George, they were to be Carson and Bonar Law.[1]]
and I have invited Mr. Lloyd George, and he has consented to act as chairman and to preside at any meeting which, owing to the pressure of other duties, I find it impossible to attend.

I propose that the body should have executive authority subject to this—that it shall rest with me to refer any questions to the decision of the Cabinet which I think should be brought before them.[d]

This was a compromise document. It sought to reconcile Carson, who openly wanted Asquith out, Law, who wanted Carson in but also wanted Asquith to retain both his position and some power, and Lloyd George, who wanted to transfer as much power as possible to himself without seeming so self-seeking as to frighten off Law. It was skilfully drafted so as to offer to all three the possibility of achieving their objectives. It was not the last of the ambiguous communications of the next few weeks.

Bonar Law took the document to Asquith on the Saturday afternoon. During the preceding week the Prime Minister had been less preoccupied with the battle for position than his principal colleagues. His concern had been more with the search for a Food Controller (Speaker Lowther, the third man to be offered the job, declined on November 23rd); with the composition of another mission to Russia; with a joint *démarche* from the unlikely combination of Arthur Henderson and Lord Robert Cecil saying that they could not agree to a franchise reform to give votes to soldiers without women's suffrage being dealt with as well; with trouble in the South Wales coalfield; and Henderson appeared to have been dropped.

424

with the growing menace of the exhaustion of British credits in the United States. Until the Thursday he was hardly aware that a crisis was brewing. On that morning, however, he was to some extent alerted. The *Morning Post*, one of the papers which Asquith read, came out strongly for a Lloyd George premiership. Gwynne, the editor, was a close associate of Carson's, but he had not hitherto been well-disposed towards the man whom he now proclaimed as the necessary "saviour of society." As recently as October 11th he had written to Asquith complaining bitterly about an anti-Haig intrigue, in which he said Lloyd George was joined by Churchill, F. E. Smith and Lord French.[1] Asquith did not fail to note the significance of his change of front.

Nevertheless he did not react sharply to Bonar Law's visit. He reiterated his suspicions that this was not the last of Lloyd George's territorial demands and his lack of confidence in Carson as a minister, but left on Law's mind the impression that he was not "altogether opposed to the idea" (of the small War Committee), to which he undertook to send a considered reply from the Wharf, where he was going that same afternoon. Bonar Law, his willingness to perform a Cassius-like role once again weakened by contact with Caesar, retired to the War Office to report to his more resolute allies. The probability seems to be that he had failed to inform Asquith of the full significance of the demand he was presenting. At any rate the Prime Minister's considered answer, written on the Sunday, and given to Bonar Law in an interview on the Monday morning, contained the following paragraph:

But the essence of your scheme is that the War Committee should disappear, and its place be taken by a body of four—myself, yourself, Carson and Lloyd George.*

Even without appreciating how completely and immediately he was to be excluded, Asquith returned a firm but friendly negative to the scheme which Bonar Law had outlined. He argued against it on three grounds. First, while he by no means ruled out changes in the composition or procedure of the War Committee, he did not believe that

---

[1] "You know, of course, of the visit of Mr. Lloyd George to General Foch, where, with the Lord Chief Justice as interpreter, he ventured on criticism of the British Generals and the British armies in France. This has aroused considerable indignation among our officers of all ranks out there. . . . It will need your personal intervention to put matters straight." (*Asquith Papers*, box xxx, ff. 261–4).

the body could work effectively unless it had the heads of the War Office and the Admiralty amongst its members. Second, he would not promote Carson over the heads of Balfour, Curzon or McKenna, all of whom, in his view, had better claims to be a member of a small War Committee. To do so would cause great resentment amongst both Liberal and Unionist ministers. " It would be universally believed to be the price paid for shutting the mouth of our most formidable parliamentary critic—a manifest sign of weakness and cowardice." Third, there was the question of Lloyd George:

He has many qualities that would fit him for the first place, but he lacks the one thing needful—he does not inspire trust. . . . Here, again, there is one construction, and one only, that could be put on the new arrangement, that it has been engineered by him with the purpose, not perhaps at the moment, but as soon as a fitting pretext could be found, of his displacing me. In short, the plan could not, in my opinion, be carried out without fatally impairing the confidence of loyal and valued colleagues, and undermining my own authority.*f*

Bonar Law took this reply back to a meeting with Lloyd George and Carson in his room at the Colonial Office. It threw " the Triumvirate " into a state of considerable confusion. No consensus of view emerged as to what they should do next. Carson wanted to declare full-scale war against Asquith, but Bonar Law was still hesitant, and Lloyd George was somewhat inhibited, perhaps by his desires, certainly by his position. During the ensuing week the three seem to have acted more independently than had been the case in the immediately preceding period.

Carson, supplemented more effectively by Aitken, tried to increase the newspaper pressure upon Asquith. On the Wednesday (November 29th) the *Daily Chronicle*, an important Liberal paper, came out with a strong criticism of the direction of the war. The editor, Sir Robert Donald, had been in close touch with Aitken and Law. He was a man either of extraordinary naiveté or of considerable disingenuousness for he wrote later: " The article had precisely the opposite effect intended. It was intended to be helpful to the Government, but it was most useful to Mr. Lloyd George in pushing his scheme for the reform of the War Committee."*g*

By the end of the week the *Daily Express* (not then owned by Aitken but greatly influenced by him) and the *Daily Chronicle* had published main news stories which took the crisis before the public in a form highly favourable to Lloyd George. The *Daily Mail*, at this stage, was a little less well-informed about the detailed moves behind the scenes, but on the Saturday it published a leader headed " The Limpets: A National Danger."[1] *The Times* was of course in line with its stablemate, and the *Morning Post*, uninformed by Carson that Law had moved over to Lloyd George—perhaps he thought a little further harrying fire would do his leader no harm—continued to denounce the Prime Minister's conduct of affairs and Law for supporting him.

In the meantime Bonar Law had decided that he had better consult tne other Unionist ministers. It is an extraordinary fact, explicable only by the extent to which he was influenced by Aitken and frightened by Carson, that he had not done this before. He called them together for the afternoon of Thursday, November 30th. Lansdowne, Curzon, Austen Chamberlain, Walter Long, Robert Cecil and F. E. Smith all attended. Did Balfour? Nearly all accounts, following Beaverbrook. say that he did not, owing to illness. But Balfour himself says that he did, and that his influenza did not strike him until later that evening.[h] This discrepancy apart, there is substantial agreement about what took place at this meeting—which was by no means the case with subsequent Unionist gatherings during the crisis. The essence of the agreement lies in the fact that Aitken's description obtained from Law immediately after the meeting, is confirmed by Austen Chamberlain, who has supplied much the best account of these events to be written by any ministerial participant. But he was not a central participant.

Chamberlain (in a letter to the Indian Viceroy, Lord Chelmsford, dated December 8th) described how Law told the meeting of the proposals that he had made to Asquith, with the agreement of Carson and Lloyd George. The Unionist ministers were affronted both by their leader having proceeded so far without consulting them, and with the nature of the proposals themselves. There was no dispute about the need for some considerable change in the machinery of government. But no-one except Bonar Law wanted to do it in such a way as to give Lloyd George complete power. Perhaps not even Bonar Law wanted to do this. He gave Chamberlain the impression that he still wanted Asquith as Prime Minister. But nearly all his colleagues thought

[1] Northcliffe was only dissuaded at the last moment from advertising this with a placard of " Asquith: A National Danger." (Tom Clarke: *My Northcliffe Diary*, p. 105).

that, whatever his intentions, he was playing directly into the hands of the War Minister. It was at this meeting that Cecil accused him of " dragging the Conservative Party at the coat-tails of Lloyd George."

The Unionist ministers, Chamberlain says, " made certain alternative proposals " to Bonar Law. These, however, " did not commend themselves to (him) who had, it was evident, committed himself too deeply to Carson and Lloyd George."[i] The proposals were similar to a scheme which had been put forward by Cecil and provisionally adopted at the Cabinet—the last over which Asquith was ever to preside—on the previous morning. This provided for two small committees instead of one, the first to look after military and foreign affairs and the second to concern itself with the home front. Even if Lloyd George was to secure the chairmanship of the first—and there was no suggestion of this; Hankey, indeed, believed that he might be offered that of the second—he would certainly have to bring in the Prime Minister on matters which overlapped both committees. Bonar Law firmly rejected these proposals, and the Unionist meeting broke up in disagreement.

Ironically, the preceding 48 hours may have seen Asquith moving a little way towards the Lloyd George/Bonar Law proposals. On the Tuesday he had summoned Hankey to luncheon and told him that he was inclined to support the scheme, provided that matters of personnel could be satisfactorily arranged. But this may not have meant much more than that Asquith was in favour of a small War Committee under his own chairmanship. At any rate, when Lloyd George made his next definite move, on the Friday morning, this was reported, again by Hankey, as having reduced Asquith to a state of mild gloom.

" War Committee at 12.45," his diary entry for December 1st ran. " I noticed that the Prime Minister was rather piano and I learned afterwards that Lloyd George had delivered his ultimatum, practically threatening to resign unless the War Committee was reconstituted with himself as Chairman, and demanding that Carson should have a place in the Government and Balfour leave the Admiralty. It is all an intolerable nuisance. . . . "[j]

Whether or not Hankey correctly observed Asquith's mood he gave a moderately accurate summary of what Lloyd George had put to the Prime Minister, in an interview, at noon that day. Lloyd George had accompanied his words with a brief written memorandum. The essence of this was conveyed in the first three clauses:

(1) That the War Committee consist of three members, two of whom must be the First Lord of the Admiralty and the Secretary of State for War, who should have in their offices deputies capable of attending to and deciding all departmental business, and a third Minister without a portfolio. One of the three to be Chairman.

(2) That the War Committee should have full powers, subject to the supreme control of the Prime Minister to direct all questions connected with the war.

(3) The Prime Minister in his discretion to have power to refer any question to the Cabinet.[k]

This was the first definite proposal for his own exclusion from the War Committee which was put to Asquith. On the other hand the new scheme was in one respect nearer to his own view than the one which had been put to him by Bonar Law on the previous Saturday; the Committee was not to be largely non-departmental, but was to include the two Service ministers. Perhaps for this reason the answer which he returned to Lloyd George, in a letter written that same Friday afternoon (December 1st), was somewhat more conciliatory than the one which he had given to Bonar Law:

My dear Lloyd George,

I have now had time to reflect on our conversation this morning and to study your memorandum.

Though I do not altogether share your dark estimate and forecast of the situation, actual and prospective, I am in complete agreement that we have reached a critical situation in the War, and that our methods of procedure, with the experience that we have gained during the last three months, call for reconsideration and revision.

The two main defects of the War Committee, which has done excellent work, are (1) that its numbers are too large, and (2) that there is delay, evasion, and often obstruction on the part of the Departments in giving effect to its decisions.

I might with good reason add (3) that it is often kept in ignorance by the Departments of information, essential and even vital, of a technical kind, upon the problems that come before it; and (4) that it is overcharged with duties, many of which might well be delegated to subordinate bodies.

429

The result is that I am clearly of opinion that the War Committee should be reconstituted, and its relations to and authority over the Departments be more clearly defined and more effectively asserted. I come now to your specific proposals.

In my opinion, whatever changes are made in the composition or functions of the War Committee the Prime Minister must be its Chairman. He cannot be relegated to the position of an arbiter in the background or a referee to the Cabinet.

In regard to its composition, I agree that the War Secretary and the First Lord of the Admiralty are necessary members. I am inclined to add to the same category the Minister of Munitions. There should be another member, either with or without portfolio, or charged only with comparatively light departmental duties. One of the members should be appointed Vice-Chairman.

I purposely in this letter do not discuss the delicate and difficult question of personnel.

The Committee should, as far as possible, sit *de die in diem*, and have full power to see that its decisions (subject to appeal to the Cabinet) are carried out promptly and effectively by the Departments.

The reconstruction of the War Committee should be accompanied by the setting up of a Committee of National Organisation, to deal with the purely domestic side of our problems. It should have executive power within its own domain.

The Cabinet would in all cases have ultimate authority.

Yours always sincerely,

H. H. Asquith[1]

The difference between these proposals and Lloyd George's was real but by no means limitless. The small War Committee was common ground, but Asquith was insisting on his own chairmanship, although his suggestions that meetings should be daily and that a vice-chairman should be appointed contained at least a hint that Lloyd George might be allowed to do much of the work on his own. The only other substantial difference about membership lay in the fact that, while they were both agreed that the First Lord of the Admiralty should be included, Asquith wanted Balfour to continue in this office, and Lloyd George wanted him replaced by Carson. Asquith also wanted the parallel " Home Front " committee, which Lloyd George did not, but this point only had major significance if, with the Prime Minister firmly excluded, the chairman of the other body were seeking effective Prime Ministerial powers without the name. It was therefore subordinate to the first disagreement.

Lloyd George found Asquith's reply "entirely unsatisfactory." He was in no doubt that he would fight on the issue. What was less certain was whether Bonar Law would fight with him. Lord Beaverbrook said that this question was in doubt until late on the Friday, but not after that. But it is not clear, either from Beaverbrook's detailed account of events and conversations or from Mr. Robert Blake's biography, what factors finally swung Bonar Law over to a completely committed position. During the earlier part of the day the pressures had been the other way. He had the disturbing memories of his isolation at the Unionist meeting the previous afternoon, which were fortified by a letter from Lansdowne complaining that these proceedings had left "a nasty taste" in his mouth. Then, at the end of the morning, Lloyd George showed Law his memorandum and reported on his interview with Asquith. Law was disturbed both at the extent to which Asquith was to be excluded and at the demand; which Lloyd George told him he had put forward, for the removal of Balfour from the Admiralty.

That evening Aitken dined alone with Law at the Hyde Park Hotel and exercised all his powers of persuasion in favour of Lloyd George. He was sufficiently successful for Law, towards the end of the meal, to say that he wanted to see Lloyd George at once. "I had the means of finding Lloyd George at that time at any hour of the day or night," Aitken wrote; and he set off in a taxi, accompanied by Law, to exploit his knowledge.

Lloyd George was the guest of Lord Cunliffe, Governor of the Bank of England, in the public restaurant of the Berkeley Hotel. The other members of the party were Edwin and Venetia Montagu. Lord Reading joined them after dinner. Montagu's position throughout the crisis was openly equivocal. His personal attachment to Asquith was extreme. A year or so before he had written to him:

In all the things that matter, in all the issues that frighten, in all the apprehensions that disturb, you show yourself clear-sighted and self-possessed, ready to help, to elucidate, to respond, to formulate, to lead, to inspire. That's why loving you and following you is so easy and so profitable; it's worth while all the time.[m]

Montagu also had a high regard for Lloyd George. He saw the crisis as the tragedy of " two great men of England . . . being slowly but surely pushed apart." This result he attributed to the evil geniuses of Carson and Northcliffe operating upon the one, and of McKenna upon the other. His own endeavour throughout was to assist a solution which would marry the " fertile, ever-working imagination and constructive power " of Lloyd George with Asquith's " incomparable capacity for mastering a particular case at once, detecting the vital considerations, discarding the bad arguments, and giving a clear and right decision." He and Reading were the only Liberals who kept open their lines of communication with both camps. Montagu, in particular, was indefatigable (although ineffective) in trying to arrange a compromise.

On the occasion of this Berkeley Hotel dinner he was able to do little in this direction. He found Lloyd George " very disturbed and distrait, very little conversation occurred between us and he was called away."[n]

It was Aitken who did the calling. He beckoned from the corner of the restaurant and Lloyd George responded immediately. He knew that Law was the crucial man to influence. They joined the Unionist leader in the waiting taxi and drove back together to the Hyde Park Hotel. Lloyd George had already received Asquith's reply to his memorandum, but it seems likely that he did not show it to Law that night; perhaps he did not have it with him. With or without it, he made the most delicate use of his persuasive powers. Aitken records that he " exercised consummate tact." By the following morning he felt certain enough of his man to send Law the following note:

> War Office,
> Whitehall, S.W.
> December 2nd, 1916

My dear Bonar,
I enclose copy of P.M.'s letter.
The life of the country depends on resolute action by you now.

Yours ever,
D. Lloyd George [o]

Asquith in the meantime was behaving with his usual aplomb. He had made plans to go to Walmer for the Saturday night and Sunday, and he intended to stick to them. Reading endeavoured to dissuade him, and received the curious reply that "he (Asquith) was told that Carson was in the neighbourhood of Walmer and was very anxious to see him and discuss the matter."[1] Before going the Prime Minister again summoned Hankey to lunch at Downing Street. The latter wrote in his diary for that day:

I suggested a solution to the Prime Minister, but it was not well received. . . . Very shortly after lunch the Prime Minister left by motor for Walmer Castle. It was very typical of him that in the middle of this tremendous crisis he should go away for the week-end! Typical both of his qualities and of his defects; of his extraordinary composure and of his easy-going habits. After lunch, at Mrs. Asquith's request, I saw Bonar Law, and learned from him that he had called a party meeting of Unionist Cabinet members for the following day, and that he would probably "send a letter" (*viz.* of resignation) after it. He explained that he must do this in order not to appear in the eyes of his party to be dragged at the heels of Lloyd George. . . . Bonar Law told me that he might put off his party meeting if he was sure that Lloyd George would not resign first. . . . So I went after Reading. . . . Reading, however, had only been able to persuade Lloyd George to post-pone action until tomorrow. I went back to Bonar Law, but this was not good enough for him and he decided to go on with his party meeting. So back to Downing Street where we arranged that Bonham Carter should follow the Prime Minister to Walmer and bring him back tomorrow morning. I walked home with Reading. We both agreed that the whole crisis is intolerable. There is really very little between them. Everyone agrees that the methods of the War Committee call for reform. Everyone agrees that the Prime Minister possesses the best judgment. The only thing is that Lloyd George and Bonar Law insist that the former and not the Prime Minister must be the man to run the war. . . . The obvious compromise is for the Prime Minister to retain the Presidency of the War Committee with Lloyd George as Chairman, and to give Lloyd George a fairly free run for his money. This is my solution.[p]

[1] The fact that he was misinformed about Carson's whereabouts makes his reason still stranger. Reading told Montagu, with whom he breakfasted on the Saturday morning, about the interchange, and the latter recorded it.

It sounded a tangled situation, and so indeed it was. Montagu, and not only Reading, tried to intervene with Lloyd George that afternoon. The three of them had an hour's talk at the War Office. " We could not shake (Lloyd George's) determination. He insists upon the Chairmanship of the War Committee and upon removing Balfour from the Admiralty," Montagu noted.*q* Montagu also wrote a long letter to Asquith and sent it down to Walmer with Bonham Carter. It was a letter of near despair:

Audacious as I am of advice, I am at a loss to give any. I receive very bitter letters from Margot, but I have not had time or courage to answer them. She, like McKenna, attributes everything that has happened in the Press to L.G., notwithstanding the fact that the views of the Press are nearly all inconsistent with L.G's scheme. I remain of opinion, based not only on affection but on conviction, that there is no conceivable Prime Minister but you. I remain of opinion that Lloyd George is an invaluable asset to any war government. . . . I would most earnestly suggest that you should come to London to discuss this matter. You may entertain your own opinion, as I have expressed mine, of the vital mistake Lloyd George is making in plunging the country into this condition. But it is for you as Prime Minister, I assume, to try and prevent this wherever the fault. I cannot believe that this can be done by the mere exchange of two formal letters. . . . It is all a nightmare to me.*r*

Influenced by this letter, by Bonham Carter's verbal persuasion, and perhaps by his inability to find Carson (who had not left London), Asquith agreed to return on the Sunday morning (December 3rd). He reached Downing Street at 2.0 p.m., was greeted by Montagu, and immediately sent for Crewe, who joined them at the end of a late luncheon.

While Asquith had been motoring through Kent the Unionist ministers had met at Bonar Law's house in Kensington. On this occasion there is no doubt that there were two absentees. Balfour was in bed, and Lansdowne, who had retreated to Bowood on the Friday evening, taking Grey with him, was pleased to discover, when he received the summons, that there were no trains which would get him to the meeting in time. Several other aspects of this meeting remain shrouded in mystery. A resolution, which ran as follows, was carried for transmission to Asquith:

We share the view expressed to you by Mr. Bonar Law some time ago that the Government cannot continue as it is.

It is evident that a change must be made, and, in our opinion, the publicity given to the intention of Mr. Lloyd George makes reconstruction from within no longer possible.

We therefore urge the Prime Minister to tender the resignation of the Government.

If he feels unable to take that step, we authorise Mr. Bonar Law to tender our resignation.

The reference to " the publicity given to the intention of Mr. Lloyd George " was provoked by an article which had appeared in *Reynolds'* newspaper that morning, and which Beaverbrook subsequently described as " like an interview with Lloyd George written in the third person." It gave the readers of that newspaper, who apparently included all the Conservative ministers, a full inside picture of the game at that stage from Lloyd George's point of view, including the information that if his terms were not accepted he intended to resign and appeal to public opinion.

These revelations gave great offence to the assembling ministers. They were already aggrieved by Bonar Law's tardiness in telling them what was happening. It was intolerable that they should be better informed as readers of *Reynolds'* than as colleagues of the Unionist leader. Furthermore they regarded Lloyd George's fault as completely in character. They were eager to give him a sharp rap over the knuckles. But what else did they intend to achieve with the remainder of their resolution?

This remains the greatest mystery of the whole crisis. It was not a mystery to everyone. Lord Beaverbrook gave a perfectly clear explanation of what they had in view. " . . . the tone of the meeting," he wrote, " had changed since Thursday from one of passive hostility to Lloyd George's plan to an active determination to force an issue and compel Lloyd George to accept the domination of the Prime Minister or retire from the Government." When Asquith resigned, Lloyd George would be forced to try to form an administration. " On his failure, which was thought certain, Asquith would return stronger than ever, and Lloyd George and his few friends would be thrown out of the Government on its re-formation."[8] But is this a convincing explanation?

First, it must be said that if the intention of the Conservative

435

ministers was to strengthen Asquith and destroy Lloyd George, they behaved with an almost unbelievable ineptitude. Their resolution, which was to be transmitted by the one man amongst them who had gone over to Lloyd George, breathed no word of confidence in Asquith. On the contrary, the instruction that if he would not resign himself, he must accept their resignations struck a distinctly hostile note. How was this likely to strengthen his hand against Lloyd George?

This particular instruction apart, the whole resignation gambit, which they urged upon Asquith, was a most hazardous one. Lord Beaverbrook, and other commentators following him, have written as though this was a weapon frequently and successfully employed by Prime Ministers. They assume that a short visit to Buckingham Palace is a time-honoured way of dealing with a recalcitrant colleague or a confused Cabinet situation: the resigning Prime Minister can confidently expect to be recalled within a day or so. In fact there is not a single post-1832 example of a Prime Minister behaving in this way and strengthening his position. Gladstone in 1873 tried to force Disraeli to form a minority administration, but that was because he wished to escape from office before the forthcoming election; he failed in his objective and led his party to a heavy defeat. In 1885 he tried the same tactic on Salisbury, who took office for six months, and then made an unexpectedly good electoral showing.

On both these occasions the party situation was relatively stable. There was no question of another Liberal stepping into the place which Gladstone had vacated. A more fluid situation existed in 1931 which was a precedent for Beaverbrook and the other commentators, although not of course for Asquith or the Tory ministers. On this occasion MacDonald did from some points of view strengthen his position by going to Buckingham Palace to resign—but only because he was careful not to leave again until he had secured a commission to form a new Government. He did not make the mistake of allowing anyone else to try first.

For the Unionist ministers to have assumed—if they did—that the best way to help Asquith was to demand his resignation was therefore extraordinarily foolish. But was this the way their minds worked? There is contrary evidence, from both Curzon and Austen Chamberlain. Curzon wrote to Lansdowne a few hours after the Unionist meeting. There is such a difference between the beginning and the end of his letter that it is possible almost to sense the mind of that patrician but flexible character adjusting himself to a new situation as he rapidly added one spidery sentence to another. He began with strong criticism of Lloyd George. Then he defended the tactic of the Unionist resolution. It was designed, he said, to bring Lloyd George face to face with the facts of political responsibility. " His Government will be dictated to him by others, not shaped exclusively by himself." The assumption was that Lloyd George would form a government, not that he would fail to do so. Curzon concluded with some harsh remarks about Asquith:

> Had one felt that reconstruction by and under the present Prime Minister was possible, we should all have preferred to try it. But we know that with him as Chairman, either of the Cabinet or War Committee, it is absolutely impossible to win the War, and it will be for himself and Lloyd George to determine whether he goes out altogether or becomes Lord Chancellor or Chancellor of the Exchequer in a new Government, a nominal Premiership being a protean compromise which, in our view, could have no endurance.[t]

Curzon behaved in a double-faced way throughout the crisis. A day later he wrote to Asquith to assure him that " my resignation yesterday was far from having the sinister purport which I believe you were inclined to attribute to it."[u] ; and there is a widely believed story that he followed this up by a verbal assurance to the Prime Minister that he would never serve under Lloyd George. Even so, he can have had no motive for dissimulating in Lloyd George's favour when writing to Lansdowne. Curzon's letter is strong evidence that the feeling at the Unionist meeting was much more confused than Beaverbrook allowed.

Curzon's evidence is supported by Austen Chamberlain. Chamberlain was more straightforward, less clever, and much less ambitious than Curzon. He was at least as suspicious of Lloyd George,[1] although at a later stage he was to be much more loyal to him. In his already quoted letter to the Indian Viceroy, Chamberlain described the situation with which, as he saw it, the Unionist ministers were confronted on the Sunday morning:

> Lloyd George was in revolt and the controversy on his side was being carried on in the Press by partial and inaccurate revelations. Asquith, Grey and Balfour were being openly denounced and told

[1] He had strong family reasons for disliking him, and these were always powerful with Chamberlain.

437

they must go. No Government could continue to exist on such terms, and since the Prime Minister had failed to assert his authority and to reorganize his administration in time, we thought that the ordinary constitutional practice should be followed and the man who had made the Government impossible should be faced with his responsibilities. If he could form a Government, well and good. If not, he must take his place again as a Member of an Asquith Administration, having learned the limits of his power and deprived thenceforward of the opportunity for intrigue. In any case, power and responsibility must go together and the man who was Prime Minister in name must also be Prime Minister in fact. It seemed to us at that time that the only hope of a stable Government still lay in combining somehow or another in one administration the separate forces represented by both Lloyd George and Asquith. It was not for us to say which of the rival Liberals could secure the greatest amount of support in the Liberal Party and the Parties which habitually worked with it.[v]

If the hope of these Conservative ministers was to combine the forces of Asquith and Lloyd George, it was singularly foolish of them to stand indifferently aside and leave the Liberal battle to be fought out—particularly as they knew that their own leader was pursuing no such policy of neutrality. But this was typical of the ineffectiveness of the " three C's " (and of Long) throughout the crisis. Not knowing quite what they wanted, and without close contact with Asquith, Lloyd George, or even Bonar Law, they never managed to exert much influence on events.

Nevertheless the clause in the Conservative resolution rebuking Lloyd George for his press disclosures might well weaken Bonar Law's hand when he showed it to the Prime Minister. So at least Aitken thought. He spent the whole of Sunday luncheon trying to persuade Law to delete it. " But he did not take my persistency in good part," Aitken wrote. Eventually Law fled from the table, but Aitken quickly followed him upstairs to his study and renewed the pressure. It was then agreed that F. E. Smith, who maintained a fairly detached position throughout the battle, should be brought in to give a third opinion. He gave it unequivocally against deleting the disputed clause. To do this would be to pervert the intentions of the Unionist ministers.

Bonar Law then drove to Downing Street to see Asquith. He went with the resolution in his pocket, and there it remained throughout

438

the interview. About this there is no dispute. It is stated by Asquith,[w] and confirmed by Law, who says that although he communicated the contents, "I forgot to hand him the actual document."[x] But how completely and how accurately did his verbal explanations convey the contents? About this there can never now be certainty. Asquith took the meaning to be that all the Unionist ministers had swung into a position of complete hostility to him. Aitken, to whom Law returned immediately after the interview, confirms this, although he claims that this misapprehension was Asquith's own fault: "(He) seized on nothing in the Tory resolution except the demand that he should resign. This single word RESIGNATION frightened him. . . . The point that caught his sole attention was not therefore the motives which induced the three C's and Walter Long and others to urge him on to resignation—but the mere fact that they demanded that he should resign."[y]

This passage is part of a long refutation of the possibility that Law could have acted dishonestly. Such behaviour, Aitken argued (and so later did Mr. Robert Blake), would have been so out of keeping with his character as to be inconceivable. The much more likely explanation, Mr. Blake suggests, is that Asquith lost his head—about as uncharacteristic a piece of behaviour, it might be thought, as any temporary fall on the part of Law from his normal high standards of probity. Furthermore, it is clear from what is known that Law was behaving most oddly that afternoon. Had the morning's resolution been in the terms he wanted, and had he therefore given it little further thought before going to see Asquith, his failure to produce it, while careless, might have been comprehensible. But as nearly the whole of the three hours between the end of the morning meeting and the beginning of the interview had been occupied with a wearing dispute as to whether part of the resolution could be deleted (the starting point being fear about the effect on Asquith of reading this part) his "forgetfulness" becomes simply incomprehensible. Nor can any faith be placed in his ability to have given Asquith an equally satisfactory verbal explanation. In the first place Bonar Law himself did not know exactly what the resolution meant. (Nor probably did anybody; but this was an additional reason for allowing Asquith to make his own interpretation.) Secondly, Law was notoriously ineffective, as there were many previous examples to show, in exposition to Asquith.

The onus for misunderstanding at the Downing Street meeting

must therefore rest squarely upon Law. To say that Asquith must have lost his head, because this is the only way in which Law's honesty can be defended, is not good enough. One or other of the two men clearly acted out of character, and we cannot now be certain which it was. In either event Law plainly neglected his duty—which was to show Asquith the resolution and let him decide for himself what it meant.

Did this omission make any difference to the outcome of the crisis? On Beaverbrook's showing it did. It led Asquith to under-estimate (and, indeed, to alienate) his Unionist support by seeking an unnecessary accommodation with Lloyd George. On Mr. Blake's showing, however, it did not. The Unionist support was not really there. They would all have agreed to serve under Lloyd George at any moment at which the pistol was put to their heads. These assumptions of Mr. Blake are probably correct, but he does not allow for the fact that the Conservative ministers might have been confronted with a different pistol. Had Asquith been shown the resolution, and had he, like everyone else, found it confusing, and discovered from Bonar Law that it was the product of a confused meeting, a natural reaction on his part would have been a demand to see the other Unionist ministers, who were still serving under him.

A meeting later that afternoon between Asquith and the " three C's " might have had considerable effect. To begin with, he would no doubt have found them wavering. But he was not without influence over them. In the course of the discussion their doubts about Lloyd George would have come to the surface, and the conclusion might have been that they would have stiffened Asquith, and he would have stiffened them. The only obstacle to such a meeting would have been Asquith's reluctance, due to a mixture of inertia and distaste for promoting his own interests, to take the decisive step of summoning it.

The possibility did not arise, however. Law left Asquith with the impression that the Unionists were almost solid against him. In these circumstances the Prime Minister saw his next caller—Lloyd George. Lloyd George had been summoned from Walton Heath by a telephone call from Bonham Carter. Before going to Downing Street he had called in at the War Office and had smoked a preparatory cigar with the ubiquitous Aitken. Then he walked across to see the Prime Minister. Aitken thought that he " had never seen any man exhibit so much moral courage in the face of such great events." [z] For the moment it was unnecessary. The interview with Asquith, in the words of Montagu, who was present in an adjoining room and had almost assumed the role of a Liberal Aitken, was "long and very friendly." Asquith gave way to a substantial part of Lloyd George's previous demands. He agreed that there should be a small War Committee under Lloyd George's chairmanship, operating with certain safeguards, which he subsequently defined as follows:

The Prime Minister to have supreme and effective control of War policy.

The agenda of the War Committee will be submitted to him; its Chairman will report to him daily; he can direct it to consider particular topics or proposals; and all its conclusions will be subject to his approval or veto. He can, of course, at his own discretion, attend meetings of the Committee.*aa*

Lloyd George accepted this, and an amicable but inconclusive discussion about personalities appears to have followed. The main difficulty was still Balfour *versus* Carson as First Lord of the Admiralty. Asquith, in an earlier conversation with Montagu, had thought that this might be a breaking-point, but it did not prove so at this stage. Asquith also wanted a Committee of four (including Henderson), not of three, and Lloyd George agreed readily to this, although he had been playing with the idea of Montagu as an alternative additional member.

After the Asquith-Lloyd George meeting had made some progress, Bonar Law came back and joined them for the last half-hour. It was agreed that all ministers other than the Prime Minister should resign, and that Asquith should reconstruct on the basis of the new War Committee. Bonar Law then left for another meeting of the Unionist ministers at F. E. Smith's house in Grosvenor Crescent. Lloyd George went back to the War Office, pausing on the way out of 10, Downing Street to tell Hankey "that the Unionists had insisted that he should become Prime Minister, but he had flatly declined, and had insisted that he would only serve with Asquith."*bb* Thus is history quickly confused by even the most intimate participants—or misreported by even the most reliable witnesses.

Lloyd George was closely followed to the War Office by Montagu.[1] Six days later Montagu recorded his mixed impressions of that visit:

I joined George at the War Office, where he expressed his great

[1] It is surprising that he and Beaverbrook did not frequently collide with each other, like characters in a stage farce, as they scurried from one focus of power to another.

gratification at the fact that he was going to work with Asquith . . . and see (him) every day. He recognised my share in this happy issue and urged me to persuade Asquith to put the agreement in writing that night, in order that there might be no watering down or alterations, and in order that it might not be misconstrued. I told him that I would do my best.

As I came away I saw, with fear and foreboding in my heart, Northcliffe waiting in his Private Secretary's room. This secret has been locked in my knowledge ever since; I have told nobody but Primrose that I know George did see Northcliffe that night.[cc]

For the moment, therefore, the apparition of Northcliffe made no wider impact. That night Asquith dined with Montagu in the familiar ambience of Queen Anne's Gate. Mrs. Montagu was in the country, but Crewe and Reading came in after dinner. Montagu, as he had promised, urged Asquith to enshrine the afternoon's agreement in a late-night letter to Lloyd George; but that was not done. Instead a brief Press statement was sent out at 11.45 p.m. This merely said that " the Prime Minister, with a view to the most active prosecution of the war, has decided to advise his Majesty the King to consent to a recon-struction of the Government."

Beaverbrook thought that from Asquith's point of view this was a " disastrous statement "—because it alerted both the unconsulted Liberals and the unconsulted Unionists—and he attributed the mistake to Montagu's insistence. For once Beaverbrook was imperfectly informed about developments within the Bonar Law camp. Law had written to Asquith earlier that evening (presumably during his visit to F. E. Smith's house, for the letter was on Attorney-General's writing paper), demanding just such a statement:

My dear Prime Minister,

I think it is almost certain that it will be stated in the papers to-morrow that the Unionists Ministers have sent in their resigna-tions. The only way to prevent the danger resulting from this is, in my opinion, that it should be formally stated tonight that you have decided to reconstruct the government.

Yours sincerely,

A. Bonar Law.[dd]

That night, however, Asquith worried neither about the state-ments nor about the possible machinations of Lord Northcliffe. He believed that another very disagreeable crisis was nearly over, and expressed his thoughts in a private letter:

I drove down to Walmer yesterday afternoon hoping to find sunshine and peace. It was bitterly drab and cold, and for my sins (or other people's) I had to drive back soon after 11 this morning.

I was forced back by Bongie & Montagu and Rufus to grapple with a " Crisis "—this time with a very big C. The result is that I have spent much of the afternoon in colloguing with Messrs. Ll. George & Bonar Law, & one or two minor worthies. The " Crisis " shows every sign of following its many predecessors to an early and unhonoured grave. But there were many wigs very nearly on the green. *ee*

On this occasion Asquith's calm was misplaced. The situation changed sharply the next morning, and the Government reached its grave earlier than did the crisis.

CHAPTER XXVII

A PALACE REVOLUTION II

1916

The next morning (Monday, December 4th) *The Times* published a leading article which grew to a fame unmatched by any similar emission until 1938. This article was written throughout in a tone that was hostile and insulting to Asquith. From the Northcliffe Press the Prime Minister was used to this. Such a fact alone would not even have caused him to show much interest, let alone to react strongly. What was more significant was that the article (and the despatch from the Parliamentary Correspondent which appeared alongside it) had obviously been written or inspired by someone who was privy to Sunday afternoon's Downing Street discussions, and who was interpreting them to mean that Asquith, persuaded even by "his closest supporters" that he was ineffective as a war leader, had made a complete surrender of power to Lloyd George.

Asquith had not been told of Northcliffe's visit to the War Office on the previous day. But even without this enormous piece of circumstantial evidence he assumed that Lloyd George was the source of the leak, and that it was due, not to carelessness, but to a deliberate policy of using the Press to make the Sunday arrangements unworkable except on the basis of a complete Lloyd George hegemony.

In a narrow sense his suspicions were probably unfounded. The article does not appear to have stemmed directly from Lloyd George. Northcliffe left Tom Clarke of the *Daily Mail*, who was close to him at the time, with the impression that he had written the leader himself.[1] But there is strong evidence that Dawson, the editor, was in fact the

---

[1] " Then he (Northcliffe) came to town, saw L.G., and then wrote a two-column article on the political crisis," Clarke wrote on the Monday. (*My Northcliffe Diary*, p. 106).

author, and that he acted independently of Northcliffe. Hankey wrote:

Long after I learned the true history of this episode. It was at dinner at Reading's house on Sunday, December 15th, 1920, on which I wrote in my diary:

... Perhaps the most interesting item was contributed by Lloyd George, who said that on the previous week-end he had learned the true history of *The Times* article, which four years ago, wrecked Asquith's government. Geoffrey Dawson had told him that he wrote the article himself at Cliveden (the Astors' place on the Thames) without prompting from anyone, and without communication of any sort or kind with Northcliffe, and because he disliked the arrangement agreed between Asquith and Lloyd George. The particulars of the proposed arrangement had been given him by Carson.[a]

But Carson could hardly have supplied this information before Dawson left for Cliveden, for it was not then available. Beaverbrook avoided this contradiction by explaining that Dawson wrote the first half of the article in the country on the Saturday, but completed it in London on the Sunday after talking to Carson. This is confirmed in Sir Evelyn Wrench's life of Dawson.

It still leaves two points for explanation. First, if there was no collusion between Lloyd George and Northcliffe, why was the latter paying such frequent visits to the quarters of the Secretary of State at the War Office? Northcliffe was not the man to waste his time in pointless errands. Yet he was there on the Friday morning (December 1st), the Saturday morning (December 2nd) and the Sunday evening (December 3rd). No politician, at a moment of acute crisis, should expect to hold such a series of private interviews with a partisan and editorially active newspaper proprietor, who is the sworn enemy of his own governmental chief, without accepting that some of the responsibility for what then appears in the proprietor's political columns will be pinned upon him.

Secondly, where else except from Lloyd George did Carson get his detailed knowledge of the Downing Street arrangement to pass on to Dawson? And if he received facts was it not likely that he received views as well? It is not, after all, in dispute that he and Lloyd George were working in the closest association. The introduction of Carson as an intermediary does not therefore, as Hankey for instance assumes, dispose of the view that *The Times* article gave Lloyd George's interpretation of his agreement with Asquith.

In any event this is what Asquith thought—and not without considerable justification. Beaverbrook stated that Asquith's beliefs were fortified by a visit which a group of Liberal Ministers paid him early on the Monday morning. McKenna, Harcourt, Runciman and Grey were all there, according to this account: " Their note was one of surprise, dismay and protest. When they heard Lloyd George's terms they objected to them altogether."*b* As a result of these objections (and of expressions of determined loyalty), Beaverbrook suggested, Asquith decided to go back on his Sunday agreement with Lloyd George and to use *The Times* leader as an excuse for doing so. The meeting was the direct cause of his writing to Lloyd George in the following terms:

Dec. 4th, 1916

My dear Lloyd George,

Such productions as the first leading article in today's *Times*, showing the infinite possibilities for misunderstanding and misrepresentation of such an arrangement as we considered yesterday, make me at least doubtful as to its feasibility. Unless the impression is at once corrected that I am being relegated to the position of an irresponsible spectator of the War, I cannot possibly go on.

The suggested arrangement was to the following effect:

The Prime Minister to have supreme and effective control of War policy.

The agenda of the War Committee will be submitted to him; its Chairman will report to him daily; he can direct it to consider particular topics or proposals; and all its conclusions will be subject to his approval or veto. He can, of course, at his own discretion, attend meetings of the Committee.

Yours sincerely.

H. H. Asquith *c*

Did this meeting take place at the time stated? There is no corroboration in the lives or memoirs of any of the supposed participants. Nor is it referred to in the memoranda which Crewe and Montagu wrote within a few days of these events, although Montagu wrote of a different meeting at a different time. On the Monday afternoon, he wrote,

Asquith met McKenna, Grey, Runciman and Henderson. Furthermore it is improbable that Grey, whether in the morning or the afternoon, would have contributed to the stiffening of the Prime Minister. He was thoroughly office-weary; with Haldane already jettisoned and himself eager to go, his instinctive view was that the bell, harsh and discordant though its note might be, was tolling for Asquith too. "His attitude towards Mr. Lloyd George's aspirations was not quite the same as that of the closer bodyguard of Asquith," Grey's biographer, G. M. Trevelyan, subsequently wrote. "As between the two men (Grey) greatly preferred his old friend the outgoing Prime Minister, but he had a suspicion that the country desired a change and that the fulfilment of its desire might perhaps help on the war."[d]

Beaverbrook also noted that a group of Conservative ministers visited Asquith on that morning. They were Curzon, Robert Cecil and Austen Chamberlain, and they spoke for Walter Long as well as for themselves. They assured the Prime Minister, the account continued, that they were behind him and against Lloyd George and Bonar Law. Crewe, without specifying the day or time, appeared to confirm this visit. But Chamberlain, who was a very clear witness of the small segment of these events in which he himself participated, denied that any such Monday meeting took place. The only time on which the three of them saw Asquith was on the Tuesday afternoon, and they then had quite a different purpose in view.[e]

If these meetings did not take place on the Monday morning then they were clearly not responsible for Asquith's letter of protest to Lloyd George about *The Times* article. This must have been based upon spontaneous reaction and not upon any new estimate of his own strength.

Lloyd George replied (perhaps a little disengenuously) within an hour or so:

Dec. 4th, 1916

My dear Prime Minister,

I have not seen *The Times* article.[1] But I hope you will not attach undue importance to these effusions. I have had these mis-

---

[1] He was usually an eager newspaper reader—much more so than Asquith—and, even if he had himself overlooked *The Times* article, it seems most unlikely that Carson and Derby, with whom he breakfasted, would not have drawn his attention to it.

representations to put up with for months. Northcliffe frankly wants a smash. Derby and I do not. Northcliffe would like to make this and any other arrangement under your Premiership impossible. Derby and I attach great importance to your retaining your present position—effectively. I cannot restrain nor I fear influence Northcliffe.

I fully accept in letter and in spirit your summary of the suggested arrangement—subject of course to personnel.

Ever sincerely,

D. Lloyd George.*

Disingenuous or not, this reply was clearly conciliatory. There was no possible reason for it not being so. Lloyd George wanted to consolidate the favourable position which he believed he had secured in the previous day's discussions, and to avoid any upset until the new arrangements had been firmly made. Nor had Asquith's letter said that they would not be made. He had merely expressed his displeasure and warned of reconsideration. Indeed the latter part of Asquith's letter was purposeless unless his mind was still open. This was the view of Montagu, who continued to perform his intermediary role.

" I left George and went to Downing Street," he wrote, " where I found Asquith very angry about the Northcliffe article. He said that Henderson's name[1] was known only to George and himself. I reminded him that Bonar Law also knew it and had communicated it to his friends. He said he was just about to see the King. I urged him not to be put off by the Northcliffe article; he had never paid any attention to newspapers, why should he give up now because of Northcliffe? He said it was because the Northcliffe article showed quite clearly the spirit in which the arrangement was going to be worked by its authors. I told him I felt certain he was wrong, and that Lloyd George meant to work it honestly and in the spirit as well as in the letter. He promised to write to Lloyd George before he went to see the King, as in fact he did.

I do not understand why he should have gone to see the King if

[1] As a member of the War Committee; the despatch of the Parliamentary Correspondent, but not the leading article, had mentioned it in this context.

448

The Exit of Haldane

A Moment of Indecision: Lord Kitchener and Sir Edward Grey in Paris

The Last Period of Power: Asquith at the War Office in 1915

he had not at that moment, about mid-day on Monday, still (been) determined to carry the matter through."*g*

Asquith's audience with the King was at 12.30. He submitted the resignations of all his colleagues but not of himself—a normal procedure when a general reconstruction is envisaged—and received authority to form a new government. He returned to Downing Street for luncheon and then went to the House of Commons where he was to move an adjournment for three days. Bonar Law came to see him in his room there and asked whether he was still in favour of the Sunday arrangement. Beaverbrook supplied the following account of what ensued:

> Asquith replied that he was not so keen on the War Council plan as he had been. When pressed he gave as reasons that all his colleagues, Liberal and Conservative, seemed to be against it, and that Lloyd George was trafficking with the Press. . . . Before the discussion could proceed further, Asquith was suddenly called to the Front Bench to answer questions. . . . After question time Asquith attempted to avoid Bonar Law and so dodge a continuation of the argument. He left the House of Commons and went to Downing Street. Bonar Law, however, was not to be put off on such a vital occasion, and with his quiet pertinacity pursued Asquith to Downing Street. When he got there he found Grey, Harcourt, and Runciman, waiting outside the Cabinet Room with the Premier inside. . . . He was duly admitted, but found McKenna closeted with Asquith. He then urged on the Prime Minister very strongly the necessity of standing by Sunday's agreement on the War Council. . . . Failing to receive any satisfactory reply, Bonar Law made it clear beyond all possibility of doubt that if the War Council scheme was not adopted he would break with Asquith. He then left the Prime Minister, who still sat in sulky silence.*h*

This was of course a partial account. The interchanges were seen through Bonar Law's eyes, and the arguments used fitted with Beaverbrook's theory of Asquith's motivation. But the description of events seems as accurate as it is dramatic. These Downing Street discussions were taking place at a most decisive moment, and McKenna's position of apparent privilege was not without significance. Soon after they were over Asquith declined Lloyd George's request for an interview, but wrote to him again in the following terms:

Dec. 4, 1916

My dear Lloyd George,

Thank you for your letter of this morning. The King gave me today authority to ask and accept the resignation of all my colleagues, and to form a new Government on such lines as I should submit to him.

I start therefore with a clean slate.

The first question I have to consider is the constitution of the new War Committee.

After full consideration of this matter in all its aspects, I have come decidedly to the conclusion that it is not possible that such a Committee could be made workable and effective without the Prime Minister as its Chairman. I quite agree that it will be necessary for him, in view of the other calls upon his time and energy, to delegate from time to time the chairmanship to another Minister as his representative and *locum tenens*; but (if he is to retain the authority which corresponds to his responsibility as Prime Minister) he must continue to be, as he has always been, its permanent President. I am satisfied on reflection that any other arrangement (such for instance as the one I indicated to you in my letter of today) would be in experience impracticable and incompatible with the Prime Minister's final and supreme control. The other question which you have raised relates to the personnel of the Committee. Here again after deliberate consideration I find myself unable to agree with some of your suggestions.

I think we both agree that the First Lord of the Admiralty must, of necessity, be a member of the Committee.

I cannot (as I told you yesterday) be a party to any suggestion that Mr. Balfour should be displaced. The technical side of the Admiralty has been re-constituted with Sir John Jellicoe as First Sea Lord. I believe Mr. Balfour to be, under existing conditions, the necessary head of the Board.

I must add that Sir E. Carson (for whom personally and in every other way I have the greatest regard) is not, from the only point of view which is significant to me (namely the most effective prosecution of the War) the man best qualified among my colleagues, present and past, to be a member of the War Committee. I have only to say, in conclusion, that I am strongly of opinion that the War Committee (without any disparagement of the existing

Committee, which in my judgment is a most efficient body and has done, and is doing, invaluable work) ought to be reduced in number, so that it can sit more frequently and overtake more easily the daily problems with which it has to deal. But in any reconstruction of the Committee, such as I have, and have for some time past had in view, the governing consideration to my mind is the special capacity of the men who are to sit on it for the work which it has to do.

That is a question which I must reserve for myself to decide.

Yours very sincerely,

H. H. Asquith.[i]

The meaning of this letter was clear. If Asquith was to remain Prime Minister he was going to reconstruct the Government as he wished, and not as Lloyd George wished. Balfour rather than Carson as First Lord of the Admiralty was to be the symbol of the difference between their two approaches. The letter also bore several marks of being written " for the record." Many of the parentheses sound as though they were inserted, not to give Lloyd George information, but with subsequent publication in mind.

It is therefore fair to assume that Asquith anticipated a sharp reaction from Lloyd George. He was more likely to resign than to accept the terms of the letter. But it by no means follows from this, as Beaverbrook assumed, that Asquith sent the letter off in the confident expectation that it would enable him to vindicate his own power. He had just received Bonar Law's ultimatum. Even on the assumption that Balfour would remain with him, and perhaps the " three C's " also, the formation of a new Government against the combined opposition of Lloyd George, Bonar Law and Carson, would have been a most formidable undertaking; and Asquith cannot have thought otherwise. He must have known that he was taking a heavy risk by offering this direct challenge to Lloyd George, but preferred to do so rather than to sell more and more of the substance of his power as continuing ransom for the shadow of his place. " Il faut en finir " was at last his reaction to a mounting series of exasperations. But it was not a complacent reaction. Asquith's premiership was just as likely to be finished as Lloyd George's indiscipline. Any leader of self-respect would have felt that one or the other had to go.

After sending off his letter, Asquith dined, as on the preceding evening, with Edwin Montagu in Queen Anne's Gate. There he " refused to discuss the situation at all," and Montagu " feared the worst." Nevertheless the fact that he chose to go there is supporting evidence for the view that he was resigned rather than falsely confident. He knew that Montagu would not approve of the letter, but he knew too that he could keep him off the subject. Had he wanted congratulation on a master-stroke he could easily have found it at McKenna's house in Lord North Street.

Lloyd George did not receive Asquith's letter until the following morning—Tuesday, December 5th. He replied at length and almost at once. There was no question of his accepting the new situation. He intended to fight; and, to a much greater extent than Asquith had done, he wrote a manifesto and not a letter:

As all delay is fatal in war, I place my office without further parley at your disposal.

It is with great personal regret that I have come to this conclusion. In spite of mean and unworthy insinuations to the contrary—insinuations which I fear are always inevitable in the case of men who hold prominent but not primary positions in any administration—I have felt a strong personal attachment to you as my chief. As you yourself said, on Sunday, we have acted together for ten years and never had a quarrel, although we have had many a grave difference on questions of policy. You have treated me with great courtesy and kindness; for all that I thank you. Nothing would have induced me to part now except an overwhelming sense that the course of action which has been pursued has put the country—and not merely the country, but throughout the world, the principles for which you and I have always stood throughout our political lives—in the greatest peril that has ever overtaken them.

As I am fully conscious of the importance of preserving national unity, I propose to give your Government complete support in the vigorous prosecution of the War; but unity without action is nothing but futile carnage, and I cannot be responsible for that. Vigour and vision are the supreme need at this hour.[j]

This letter of strong but not unexpected challenge reached Asquith soon after noon. So did one from Balfour, written from a sick-bed in Carlton Gardens. This announced, quietly but determinedly, that Balfour did not want Asquith's backing for the Admiralty:

I am well aware that you do not personally share Lloyd George's view in this connection. But I am quite clear that the new system should have a trial under the most favourable possible circumstances; and the mere fact that the new Chairman of the War Council *did* prefer, and, as far as I know, *still* prefers, a different arrangement is, to my mind, quite conclusive, and leaves me in no doubt as to the manner in which I can best assist the Government which I desire to support.[k]

It is doubtful whether Asquith fully assimilated the shift of allegiance which this letter quietly announced. He saw Balfour and Lloyd George in such different lights that, the issue of the Admiralty apart, the idea of an alliance between them hardly entered his head. In any event he had little time to give careful immediate consideration to the letter; he merely wrote a short reply pressing Balfour to reconsider his position. At 12.30 Crewe arrived at Downing Street. He had been to Buckingham Palace for a Privy Council, and he was able to inform Asquith that the King still hoped for a solution without a change of Prime Minister. Then, at one o'clock, all the Liberal ministers with the exception of the Secretary of State for War assembled. Lloyd George was resentful at the absence of a summons, but as he had chosen to work almost exclusively with Unionists during the preceding weeks this resentment was hardly justified. The business of the meeting was to consider the situation created by Lloyd George's letter of resignation. Montagu apart, there was unanimous agreement that his challenge must be resisted, and that Asquith could best do this by resigning. The outcome, it was believed, would then turn on the attitude of the Unionist ministers. Montagu's alternative proposal was that the King should be asked to convene a conference of Asquith, Lloyd George, Bonar Law and Henderson. " My suggestion was derided," he recorded, " and McKenna most helpfully asked me if I wanted four Prime Ministers, or, if not, which one I wanted."[l]

The attitude of the Unionist ministers was made clear during the afternoon. At 11 o'clock in the morning they had met—Curzon, Cecil, Long and Chamberlain—in the Secretary of State's room at the India Office. At three o'clock the " three C's " were summoned to Downing Street. Asquith asked them two questions. Were they prepared to continue in a Government from which both Lloyd George and Bonar Law had resigned; and what would be their attitude towards Lloyd George if he attempted to form an administration? To the first question, in Austen Chamberlain's words, " we replied that our only object was to secure a Government on such lines and with such a prospect of stability that it might reasonably be expected to be capable of carrying on the war; that in our opinion his Government, weakened by the resignations of Lloyd George and Bonar Law and by all that had gone on during the past weeks, offered no such prospect, and we answered the question therefore with a perfectly definite negative." " This was evidently a great blow to him," Chamberlain added. " Had we replied in the affirmative, he would clearly have been prepared to make the attempt. . . . "*m*

To the second question their reply was equally discouraging. In effect they said that if Lloyd George looked like succeeding, they would join him. Cecil urged Asquith to do the same, but, Chamberlain said, Asquith " would not allow (him) to develop this idea, which he rejected with indignation and even with scorn." The three Unionists then crossed Downing Street for a meeting with Bonar Law. From this meeting they sent back Curzon with a formal resolution, urging Asquith's immediate resignation, and saying that he must in any event accept and publish theirs. In the meantime Asquith had received Balfour's second letter, written at 4.0 p.m. Once again the style was casual but the intention was firm. Balfour would offer no opposition to Lloyd George.

In these circumstances immediate resignation was the only course open to Asquith. He announced this to the Liberal ministers who had once again congregated in 10, Downing Street. Perhaps one or two of them were so blinded by hatred of Lloyd George as to believe that the move would still show up his impotence. But this was not the general view. Montagu testified that they never seriously doubted Lloyd George's ability to form a Government. And it was certainly not Asquith's view. He decided to resign, not as a tactical manoeuvre, but because he did not have sufficient support to carry on.

He gave effect to his decision at seven o'clock that evening. He had been Prime Minister for eight years and 241 days.

" The Prime Minister came to see me," the King recorded in his diary, " & placed his resignation in my hands, which I accepted with great regret. He said that he had tried to arrange matters with Lloyd George about the War Committee all day, but was unable to. All his colleagues both Liberal and Unionist, urged him to resign as it was the only solution to the difficulty. I fear that it will cause great panic in the City & in America & do harm to the Allies. It is a great blow to me & will I fear buck up the Germans."n

Back in Downing Street, Asquith dined with Crewe. The King in the meantime had asked for a constitutional memorandum, dealing with a new Prime Minister's right to a dissolution, from Haldane, and had summoned Bonar Law. His interview with Law went as badly as it is easily possible to imagine. They argued about a dissolution, about the course of the war, about the relations between politicians and the military. Having established this happy basis of almost universal disagreement, the King performed his constitutional duty by asking Law to form a Government.

The Unionist leader then went immediately to see Lloyd George, with whom he had conferred before his visit to the Palace. Afterwards he went to Downing Street where he called Asquith out from dinner and asked him if he would serve under him.[1] Asquith demurred, and also responded discouragingly to a suggestion that they might all serve under Balfour. He did not believe that any such combinations would work, but he did not close his mind on continuing consultation.

Later that evening Bonar Law again saw Lloyd George, this time at Carson's house. The following morning (Wednesday, December 6th) they went together to see Balfour, still in his sick-room. It was probably this occasion which prompted Lloyd George to write of Balfour: " I confess that I underrated the passionate attachment to his country which burnt under that calm, indifferent, and apparently frigid exterior "o; upon which Balfour's latest biographer has somewhat severely commented: " By ' passionate attachment to his country,' Lloyd George presumably meant Balfour's backing for him as Prime Minister . . . "p But this may be a little hard. Such a firm commitment was not sought at this stage.

A Buckingham Palace conference was to take place that afternoon. There is doubt as to where this idea originated. Beaverbrook said

[1] Austen Chamberlain (*Down the Years*, pp. 125-6) thought that the order of the visits should have been reversed, and that it was characteristic of Bonar Law who " is an amateur and will always remain one " not to do so. There is no evidence that such a reversal would have made any difference.

that it came from Henderson; Balfour said that it came from Bonar Law; Law's biographer said that it came from Balfour; and Crewe said that it came from Montagu and Derby. Whoever sowed the seed, the conference was due to meet within a few hours. Balfour's role was likely to be crucial. He had kept himself the most aloof from the crisis so far. The main concern of Bonar Law and Lloyd George was that he should give no support for an Asquith restoration. Law that morning, according to Montagu, "had objected to any Conference to put Asquith back." They went away reassured.

Balfour saw the King for half an hour before the others came. He gave his opinion that no one man could be effectively Prime Minister, leader of the House of Commons, and chairman of the War Committee. It was arranged that he should open the discussion with a statement of this and other views. Then the other participants—Asquith, Lloyd George, Bonar Law and Henderson arrived. Beaverbrook, presumably informed by Law, wrote that Asquith's mood differed from that of the other members of " this grave assembly." " His manner in fact was fairly like that of a schoolboy who has got an unexpected half-holiday. He was jocular with everybody."*q*

This is to some extent contradicted by Lloyd George, who subsequently wrote:

It is now a matter of history how we expressed our readiness to serve under Mr. Balfour—all of us except Mr. Asquith, who asked indignantly, " What is the proposal? That I who have held first place for eight years should be asked to take a secondary position." This broke up the conference.*r*

Whatever else this interchange may be, it is not a matter of history. There is no hint in the contemporary accounts of either Balfour or Stamfordham that such a conversation ever occurred; indeed it seems unlikely that the premiss of a Balfour premiership was ever before the conference. Lord Stamfordham's memorandum describes how Asquith was urged by all the other participants to serve under Bonar Law, and then continues:

Mr. Asquith maintained that the Prime Minister and nobody else could preside over the War Committee, otherwise decisions might be arrived at which he could not agree to, which would result in friction and delay. . . . Mr. Asquith continued by denouncing in serious terms the action of the Press. The Prime Minister's work was sufficiently heavy and responsible without

456

being subjected to daily vindictive, merciless attacks in the columns of the newspapers, and he urged that whatever government might come into office, measures should be taken to prevent the continuance of this Press tyranny. He had been accused of clinging to Office, but he appealed to all those present to say whether such a charge was justifiable. He could honestly say that on waking this morning he was thankful to feel he was a free man. Mr. Asquith referred in touching terms to the unquestioning confidence the King had invariably placed in him, of which he had received His Majesty's assurance only two days ago. He deeply valued it, and only hoped that his successor might enjoy the same generous trust and support which His Majesty had graciously reposed in him.[s]

This may not have been very constructive, but, except towards the newspaper proprietors, it did not sound particularly bitter. Furthermore, it is an account almost exactly borne out by Balfour. But what next? The King, after Asquith had spoken, pointed out that no decision had been reached. Balfour attempted to sum up:

(He) said that he considered it was impossible for Mr. Asquith to form a Government after what Mr. Bonar Law had said about his party. A Government without Mr. Lloyd George was impossible. Apparently Mr. Bonar Law was ready to form a Government if Mr. Asquith would agree to accept a subordinate place, but, failing this, he would propose that Mr. Lloyd George should form an Administration.

The result of the meeting was an agreement that Mr. Asquith should consider the proposals made to him, and let Mr. Bonar Law know as soon as possible whether he would join the Government under him. If the answer was in the negative, Mr. Bonar Law would not form a Government, but Mr. Lloyd George would endeavour to do so.[t]

Again Balfour's account is in substantial agreement, although he adds the gloss that when, at one stage in his summing up he referred to his assumption that Asquith would not serve under either Law or Lloyd George, Asquith intervened to say that he had not gone quite so far as that; he must consult his friends before giving a final answer.

The conference broke up at 4.30. Asquith returned to Downing Street and immediately began this consultation. There was a full turn up of Liberal ministers, with the exception of Lloyd George. Henderson was also present. Decisions were taken in two stages. First it was agreed (the meeting in this respect giving the impression of being a little behind events) that Asquith should make no attempt to form a Government without Lloyd George and the Unionists. Then came the question of whether he would serve in a subordinate post. Crewe, Grey, McKenna, Runciman, Buckmaster and McKinnon Wood all urged him not to. Three others (Harcourt, Samuel and Tennant) apparently indicated silent agreement with this view. Montagu and Henderson were alone in dissenting, not only from the advice tendered but also from the implied assumption that if Asquith did not serve, none of the others present would either.

" Mr. Asquith," Crewe recorded, " entirely concurred with our statements . . . " He did so, the account continued, not out of " personal dignity or *amour propre*." What, then, were his reasons? First, he could hope to exercise no real influence in the new Government. Its tone would be set by those who were most distrustful of his leadership. It was doubtful whether he would even be a member of the War Committee. He saw no prospect of avoiding for long a head-on collision. It was better to stand out at the beginning than to go in with the expectation that he would soon have to provoke a further crisis by resignation.

Secondly, if on the other hand he were completely to subordinate himself to the new Government his influence in Parliament and the country would quickly be eroded. This was not a selfish consideration. Politicians exist to exercise influence. Unless they believe that they can do so beneficially they have no *raison d'être*. Asquith thought that the erosion of his would lead to the growth of an irresponsible opposition, undermining the near unanimity of support for the war effort. This may have been something of a rationalisation of his instinctive desires, but it was a perfectly defensible attitude. While not the most encouraging offer which a Prime Minister can receive, support from outside is a time-honoured formula and one which has frequently been used with much less excuse than Asquith had on this occasion. Furthermore he interpreted it in such a way that " support " was not an empty word. He did not cause Lloyd George a tenth of the trouble that Lloyd George, outside, would have caused him.

There was a third consideration, not mentioned by Crewe, in Asquith's mind. He believed that so long as he remained in the

Government the Press attacks would continue and that his supposedly malevolent influence would be blamed for every failure. This would further undermine his position both with his colleagues and with the public. It would be an extreme form of responsibility without power.

By six o'clock Asquith had conveyed his decision, in a letter, to Bonar Law. The importance of the communication was symbolised by Lord Curzon, who had come across to 10, Downing Street to hear the news, acting as messenger boy. At seven Law went to Buckingham Palace and declined the King's commission. At 7.30 the commission was passed on to Lloyd George. Within 24 hours he had succeeded in discharging it. " Mr. Lloyd George came . . . and informed me that he is able to form an administration & told me the proposed names of his colleagues," the King wrote in his diary. " He will have a strong Government. I then appointed him Prime Minister & First Lord of the Treasury."*u*

The new Government was principally but not exclusively a Unionist one. The War Cabinet was composed of Lloyd George, Curzon, Milner, Bonar Law and Henderson. Carson, although not after all included in this body, became First Lord of the Admiralty. Balfour, directed by the pistol's point,[1] moved with speed but dignity from the Admiralty to the Foreign Office. No Liberal member of the late Cabinet (except for Lloyd George himself), not even Montagu,[2] joined the new Government. None was formally invited, except for a late and not very attractive offer to Montagu, but Lloyd George would probably have been glad to have two or three of them had he believed that they would accept. A few lesser-known Liberals were brought in, and there were two Labour heads of departments, apart from Henderson.

Asquith, as has been stated, believed that the end had come on the Tuesday, when he saw the Unionist leaders and gave his resignation to the King. On the Wednesday, after the Buckingham Palace Conference and his letter of refusal to Bonar Law, he was certain of it. Suggestions that, buoyed up by a false complacency about Lloyd

[1] When offered the Foreign Secretaryship, Lord Beaverbrook wrote, Balfour " jumped up " and said: " Well, you hold a pistol to my head— I must accept." (*Politicians and the War*, p. 502).

[2] He was badly torn by a conflict of loyalties, and in fact joined six months later.

George's inability to form a Government, he was playing a tactical game, are unfounded. They are without support, either from Asquith's character or from the course of events. Late on the Wednesday night he wrote a private letter from Downing Street:

You see I am using up my stock of official paper. . . .

I have been through the hell of a time for the best part of a month, and almost for the first time I begin to feel older.

In the end there was nothing else to be done, though it is hateful to give even the semblance of a score to our blackguardly Press. I have very nice letters from all manner of people. . . .

The colleagues today were unanimous in thinking—what seems obvious to me—that it is not my duty to join this new Government in a subordinate capacity. Apart from the personal aspect of the matter, it would never work in practice.

So we are all likely to be out in the cold next week. We think of living under Violet's roof on Cys's salary, wh. he has just begun to earn at the Ministry of Munitions. *v*

The humour of this letter was wry, and the sadness was pervasive, although by no means uncontrolled. But there was no hint of fighting back from a prepared position. There was a feeling of having been badly treated—but what Prime Minister, forced out and replaced by a lieutenant of eight years' standing, would not have felt this? Bitterness, however, was reserved principally for the Press, about which, after years of being, in Margot's phrase, "like St. Paul's Cathedral," Asquith was beginning to show signs of a mild obsession.

The actions of most of the politicians he had discounted in advance. For this reason he showed no great resentment at Lloyd George, and even less at Bonar Law. What did surprise him was the amount of Cabinet support which they acquired. Here Asquith was misled, partly by Curzon's falseness, but more importantly by his own mis-appraisal of Balfour. Although he had often been critical of Balfour in the past, Asquith instinctively regarded him as a man of much the same values as himself. He liked dealing with him, he persisted in treating him as the real leader of the Unionist Party, and he saw him as a fellow-member, perhaps the vice-captain, of the team of gentlemen in politics. But Balfour never thought as much of this team as did Asquith. Asquith thought they were far superior to the players. Balfour's disdain and arrogance was greater: he did not think there was much to choose between the two sides. In addition, he had an unusually strong although carefully concealed love of office, and a complete faith in his own ability to look fastidious in any company.[1] He was more attracted by opposites than was Asquith. One of his family referred jokingly to his having fallen in love with Lloyd George at the Buckingham Palace conference.[w] For all these reasons he found no difficulty in changing his allegiance to the new team. But for Asquith the shock of seeing Balfour stroll nonchalantly out of the pavilion, as happy as ever under the captain of the players, was profound. He should perhaps have remembered that others —GeorgeWyndham and Austen Chamberlain, for instance—with more claim upon Balfour than Asquith had, had previously found themselves let down. If Asquith was wrong about Balfour's character, he was right about the importance of his switch of allegiance. It was the most decisive single event of the crisis.

Before leaving Downing Street Asquith had one important engagement to fulfil: to attend a full party meeting at the National Liberal Club—a similar one had not been summoned since his election to the leadership nearly nine years earlier—and place before the audience an account of his actions in the preceding week. This took place on the Friday (December 8th). The result was an overwhelming vote of confidence in his leadership. Montagu wrote of being " deeply moved " by " Asquith's firm hold on the affections of the whole Liberal Party." That event over, he slept his last night in Downing Street, and then motored down the familiar Kent roads to Walmer. From there he wrote a characteristic letter to Mrs. Harrisson, a friend of a year or so's standing, who was to be the recipient of many of his confidences for the remainder of his life:

Sunday, 10 Dec. 16

Dearest Hilda,

I have two sweet letters from you still unanswered: I have been a shocking correspondent lately, but you will make excuses for me. If you want to understand something of the inner history

[1] Sir Winston Churchill (*Great Contemporaries*, p. 249) has described how Balfour passed from one Cabinet to another, from the Prime Minister who was his champion to the Prime Minister who had been his most most severe critic, " like a powerful graceful cat walking delicately and unsoiled across a rather muddy street."

of recent events you should look at the article called " A Leap in the Dark " in this week's *Nation*. When I fully realised what a position had been created, I saw that I could not go on without dishonour or impotence, or both; and nothing could have been worse for the country and the war. Curiously enough, almost exactly the same thing has been going on in France, where the same forces have been at work producing nearly if not quite, the same result.[1]

You cannot imagine what a relief it is not to have the daily stream of boxes and telegrams: not to mention Cabinets & Committees & colleagues & co. We are spending Sunday here by the sea: unluckily it is a gloomy day, but the vast crowd of shipping is a wonderful sight. I am writing in the little room where two years ago one Sunday Kitchener and French visited me and had a battle royal which I had to compose. Violet is here and the Crewes and Jimmy Rothschilds.

The King offered me the Garter, but of course I refused. I am glad you are reading the Book of Job: I think I must refresh my memory of it.

Bless you, dearest,

Ever your loving,

H.H.A.[x]

Asquith's long premiership, still unequalled in duration since Lord Liverpool's, was over. He was 64, and was never again to return to office. No brief summing up can do justice to his achievements and his failures, his qualities and his weaknesses; the balance of these should have emerged from the unfolding of events. But perhaps an appraisal by Edward Grey, always a notably cool (and even flat) writer on men and events, may serve as an epitome of his concept of leadership:

Asquith took no trouble to secure his own position or to add to his personal reputation. When things were going well with his Government he would be careful to see that any colleague got credit, if he (the colleague) were entitled to it, without regard to whether any credit were given or left for himself. On the other

---

[1] Briand was under heavy fire at this time, but in fact survived as Prime Minister until March, 1917, when he was replaced by Ribot (then aged 75). Clemenceau did not come in until November, 1917.

hand, if things were going badly he was ready to stand in front and accept all responsibility: a colleague who got into trouble was sure that the Prime Minister would stand by him.[y]

"These qualities," Grey added, "are happily not unique. . . ." They are sufficiently rare to explain why, at least until 1915, Asquith was above all a great head of a Cabinet.

CHAPTER XXVIII

THE LAST OF THE ROMANS

1917-19

Asquith spent his first Christmas out of office in the Isle of Wight, at a house lent by his former War Minister, Seely, and then saw in the New Year of 1917 at the Wharf, with Margot and " a few intimates." This was close to the pattern of any of the preceding six years, but there was no familiar press of events as soon as the holidays were over. " It is a novel sensation for me to be master of my own time all day long,"[a] he wrote on January 2nd.

He was neither bored nor unoccupied. His intellectual resources were too manifold for that. He had been reading " *Shakespeare's England* and Stow's *Survey of London* with some dips into Heraldry and browsing in *The Ship of Fooles*—written by an old monk called Barclay just on the eve of the Reformation."[b] But, more than most Prime Ministers who have just ceased to hold office, he had no clear political role. He had not retired: he did not feel ready for this, and he was still head of the Liberal Party. As such he was nominally leader of the opposition. When the House of Commons met again, he sat opposite the left-hand despatch box, asked the business questions, and spoke second on ceremonial occasions. But who comprised the opposition, and where did Asquith want to lead them?

There was no doubt about the former Liberal ministers who sat alongside him on the front bench. Some of them were much more aggressively disposed to the new Government than he was himself. The attitude of the Liberal back-benchers was less clear. Although they had given Asquith his unanimous vote of confidence at the National Liberal Club meeting, at least 126 of them, according to Christopher Addison, one of Lloyd George's few Liberal ministers, had agreed to support the new Coalition. Asquith himself did not intend to oppose it. It never for a moment occurred to him that Lloyd George, having obtained power, could or should be overturned without the opportunity to give his new system of government a run for its money. The country was in the midst of a desperate struggle. Political activity in the constituencies, largely by Asquith's own wish, was at a standstill. In these circumstances any normal opposition role would have been both dangerous and ineffective. It would also have been distasteful to Asquith. He interpreted his commitment to help keep opinion steady and frustrate the spread of opposition to the war in much more than a purely formal way. He felt a heavy, continuing responsibility for the decision of August 4th, 1914, and he was genuinely nervous of damaging national unity.

Even had he felt otherwise, he would at this stage have found little room for manoeuvre. His motives would have been too open to misinterpretation. The charge of personal jealousy would have been raised against him, with the newspapers ensuring that it echoed around the country with the utmost shrillness. The Press lords remained curiously unappeased by his fall. They showed no magnanimity in victory, and continued to lay the blame for anything that went wrong at his door. As a result, the danger was, not that Asquith might be tempted to be too hostile to the new Government, but that his utility as even a gently probing critic was seriously undermined. Ironically, the only other Prime Minister of the century who, leaving office with his physical powers unimpaired, was to find himself equally bereft of a role, was Lloyd George. The process of Liberal self-destruction had begun.

For the moment, however, the sound of the blows was muffled. At the beginning of February Asquith paid a post-resignation visit to his constituency—his first for a very long time. His speech there, at Ladybank on February 2nd, was more restrained than illuminating. Its keynote was the need for " wise and united concentration of all resources on the war," and he gave no new information about the events which had led to the fall of his Government. Nor did he express any views about its successor.

This Scottish visit over, he settled down to a new and leisurely régime. In mid-February he was writing: " ... this week I have been two days at the House of Commons, and attended a funeral service and wedding, finishing up this morning by a visit to McEvoy's studio."[c1] At this stage the Asquiths, without a London house of their

[1] Ambrose McEvoy (1878–1927) was currently painting Asquith's daughter Elizabeth.

own, were temporarily living at Forbes House, Belgravia. By March they had succeeded in dislodging the tenants from 20, Cavendish Square and re-installed themselves there. Asquith was then able to begin a relatively happy period of getting his books " into something like decent order." He went no more to Walmer, but the Wharf continued (and in due course expanded, for one or two adjacent houses had been acquired), and became increasingly the centre of his life. Travel was sometimes a problem, as wartime restrictions increased, but in November 1917 he obtained a special white badge from Walter Long,[1] and was able to motor freely wherever he liked.

It was not therefore a question, as Asquith had suggested in his mock-serious letter of December 6th, of living " under Violet's roof." Nor were they quite reduced to " Cys's salary." Nevertheless the Asquiths were, and remained for the rest of their lives, a good deal better off for roofs than for salaries—or any other form of income. They were far from penniless, of course. But Margot's extravagance required substantial under-pinning. " I hope you will get a lovely London house and spend *all* the money you can as life is short," she wrote to a friend a few years later. " People who worry about money are never worth much. *I* shall certainly die beyond my means ... " And Asquith himself liked a generous establishment. There was the large motor car with its chauffeur. There was Clouder, the familiar butler, who admittedly doubled between London and the country, but who was supported by a full complement of indoor servants. There was the constant flow of hospitality. And there was the retinue of secretaries and relations with which he habitually did his political travelling.

Asquith could therefore have done very well with some additional income. Later he wrote hard in an attempt to fill part of the need, but this phase did not really begin until the 'twenties. All that he worked on during the last years of the war was a small volume of *Occasional Addresses*—non-political speeches which he had delivered over the previous quarter century—and this neither took much time nor produced much money.

The temptations of an official salary were acute. In May of 1917 soundings were made to see whether he might accept the Lord

[1]Why Long, who was then Colonial Secretary, should have been approached for this purpose is by no means clear. Perhaps Asquith found him the least distasteful member of the new Government with whom to deal.

Chancellorship, which then carried the highest of all—£10,000 a year and a pension of £5,000. His former Chief Whip, Murray of Elibank, and the Lord Chief Justice, Reading, were used by Lloyd George as intermediaries. Asquith never really thought that he could accept, but he went so far as to consult Crewe. The latter wrote, on May 31st, that in his view Asquith was quite right to refuse: " You are in fact invited to turn yourself into Bonar Law, which is absurd."[d] Asquith was glad to concur. He never felt that he would be at home in a Lloyd George Government, and he would have been loath to enter any Cabinet without the Liberal ministers who had resigned with him. Furthermore, he believed it his duty to preserve his independence for the peace settlement and for the sake of the Liberal Party. It did not then occur to him that a general election before the time of that settlement would smash the party almost beyond recognition.

During the remainder of 1917 and early 1918 Asquith kept up a moderate level of political activity. He paid a visit to the Western Front as the guest of Haig. He maintained contact with the leaders of the Irish party. He spoke quite often in the House of Commons. He declared his support, fatalistically for women's suffrage, far-sightedly for proportional representation, and enthusiastically for President Wilson's idea of a League of Nations. He made occasional speeches in the country, at Liverpool in October, 1917, at Birmingham two months later, and at Manchester in September, 1918.[1] He delivered a carefully-prepared and widely circulated Romanes lecture at Oxford entitled *On the Victorian Age*. But, until the late spring of 1918, he delivered no challenge to the Government. His speeches were cautious, and he never entered the division lobby against Lloyd George.

Then came the Maurice debate. On May 7th, Major-General Sir Frederick Maurice wrote a letter to several newspapers. Maurice, the son of Charles Kingsley's Christian Socialist friend and the father of the economist Joan Robinson, was not a typical soldier. His letter contained a series of challenges to the accuracy of ministerial statements. The most important of these was directed at the Prime Minister. The military background to the challenge was that the Germans, during

---

[1] The Birmingham speech, at a large meeting in the Town Hall, with an overflow to follow, was the most notable of these. He demanded a " clean peace " and gave his own gloss and modified approval to the famous (or notorious) Lansdowne letter, which had appeared in the *Daily Telegraph* a few days before.

March and April, had launched two sledgehammer blows—the first instalments of their all-out drive for victory before the Americans arrived—against the British sector of the Western Front. Both the attacks were eventually contained, but not before the biggest advances since 1914 had been made, Amiens and Hazebrouck had been threatened, and morale at home had been badly shaken. In addition, another staggering wave of casualties had been suffered, and Haig had been driven to the limit of his reserves. But why were his reserves so low? Why were some of his divisions " skeletonised " even before the attacks began?

The suspicion was that Lloyd George, as a counter to Haig's fondness for bloody offensives (Passchendaele had been the culmination of the previous autumn's slaughter) deliberately kept him short of troops. The Commander-in-Chief, according to the Prime Minister's plan, would have to save casualties by remaining on the defensive throughout 1918. In the outcome, however, the plan had greatly increased them, and nearly lost the war as well. This was the result of Lloyd George's upstart conviction that he knew better than the soldiers. So, at least, some of the criticism ran. Lloyd George replied by denying the premiss. " Notwithstanding the heavy casualties in 1917," he told the House of Commons on April 9th, " the army in France was considerably stronger on 1st January, 1918, than on 1st January, 1917."

General Maurice, who was Director of Military Operations at the War Office until late April (when he was removed by the C.I.G.S. Sir Henry Wilson), wrote to denounce this statement. " (It) implies," he said, " that Sir Douglas Haig's fighting strength on the eve of the great battle which began on 21st March had not been diminished. That is not correct." He also denied the accuracy of a statement by Bonar Law about the circumstances in which a recent extension of the British line had been agreed upon, and of another by the Prime Minister relating to troop strength in the Middle East. He referred to Law's statement as " the latest of a series of mis-statements which have been made recently in the House of Commons by the present Government." He used the phrase " that is not correct " as a reiterative chorus after each of Lloyd George's claims. He passed to a justification of his own action. The falseness of these statements was appreciated by a large number of soldiers and " this knowledge is breeding such distrust of the Government as can only end by impairing the splendid morale of our troops."

" I have therefore decided," he ended, " fully realising the consequences to myself, that my duty as a citizen must over-ride my
duty as a soldier, and I ask you to publish this letter, in the hope that
Parliament may see fit to order an investigation into the statements
I have made."*e*

The letter was a heavy challenge to the Government. It was also
a clear breach of military discipline, as Maurice himself admitted by
implication. But was it in addition, as Lloyd George insisted in his
War Memoirs, part of a general Asquithian plot " to blow up the
Government "? The evidence is against this. Maurice was well-
known to Asquith, who held him in high regard, and the general no
doubt looked to the former Prime Minister to press the matter in
Parliament. But he had not consulted him beforehand, although he
had very nearly done so. The first that Asquith heard was when he
received the following letter from Maurice on the morning of publication:

20, Kensington Park Gardens,
6. 5. 1918

Dear Mr. Asquith,

I have today sent to the press a letter which will, I hope, appear
in tomorrow's papers. When I asked you to see me last Thursday, I had intended to consult you about this letter, but on
second thoughts I came to the conclusion that, if I consulted you,
it would be tantamount to asking you to take responsibility for
the letter, and that I alone must take that responsibility. I ask you
to believe that in writing the letter I have been guided solely by
what I hold to be the public interest.

Believe me,
Yours sincerely,
*F. Maurice*ᶠ

Even without prior consultation, Asquith acted rapidly. That
afternoon he asked a private notice question of Bonar Law (as leader
of the House). Law replied that the Government proposed to ask two
judges to act as " a court of honour " and to enquire into the alleged
mis-statements. During supplementary questions the idea of a judicial
enquiry came under heavy fire, and not only from Asquith. Another
Liberal, George Lambert, first put forward the alternative demand
for a select committee of the House of Commons. Carson, who had

once again resigned from the Government, made several menacing interventions about the need for Cabinet and (perhaps more significantly) ex-Cabinet ministers to be absolved from their oaths of secrecy when appearing before the enquiry. Asquith demanded a debate before a decision. Law countered by offering to let Asquith nominate the two judges. Asquith refused to be mollified by this and persisted in his demand that the issue must be debated before the court of enquiry was set up.

As soon as he left the chamber Bonar Law found that his offer was as ill-received by some of his colleagues in the Government as by the Asquithians and Carson. Churchill[1] argued vehemently against a judicial enquiry on grounds of high principle, and carried the Prime Minister with him. A minister, he said, should never ask judges to enquire into his own integrity.[9] In view of this sudden movement of opinion it was fortunate for the Government that Asquith had not immediately accepted Law's offer.

The debate came on two days later. Asquith moved that a select committee of the House of Commons be set up. His speech was brief and restrained, but uncertain and therefore unconvincing in tone. He disclaimed any desire to censure the Government. He had believed that they might accept his motion. Drawing with some effect upon his experience of the Parnell Commission, he pronounced against the method of judicial enquiry. But when an interrupter suggested that the Marconi select committee provided an equally unsatisfactory precedent for this method, he returned no adequate answer. He was also put out when he asked the rhetorical question: "What is the alternative (to the select committee)?" and received from a somewhat jingoistic miners' member, the reply of "Get on with the war."[2]

At the conclusion of his speech Asquith drew from Bonar Law the typically stark argument that a select committee could never be impartial because there was no member of the House who was not "either friendly (to) or opposed to the Government." After expressing his dismay at hearing such unparliamentary statements from the leader

[1] He had joined Lloyd George's Government as Minister of Munitions in July 1917.

[2] The member was Charles Stanton (Keir Hardie's incongruous successor at Merthyr Tydfil), and Lloyd George, no doubt a partial witness, said that the interjection was received with one of the biggest cheers he had ever heard in the House of Commons.

of the House, but without any attempt to weave his own points into a final crescendo of argument, Asquith sat down. There was no sense of a great parliamentary occasion about his speech. He had chosen a minor key, and had played it without his usual sureness of touch.

Lloyd George, who followed, struck a different note. He spoke for $1\frac{1}{4}$ hours, nearly twice as long as Asquith, but the pace of his speech was much faster. He was determined to escape from the judicial enquiry offer, to force the issue there and then, to refute and discredit Maurice, to accuse Asquith of having been party to a fractious plot to bring down the Government, and to secure an overwhelming vote of vindication from the House of Commons. He succeeded in all these objectives. He not only destroyed the demand for a select committee. He also laid down the principle, which prevailed for the rest of the war, that House of Commons criticism of the Government's military leadership was equivalent to disloyal sabotage of the national effort. His speech was a great parliamentary *tour de force*.

Asquith felt the force of the storm, but did not bow before it. Wisely or unwisely, he had committed himself to put down his motion and, if necessary, to vote for it. He had argued the case on purely procedural grounds, whereas Lloyd George had insisted, with daring persuasiveness, in bringing the substance of the matter before the House. This unbalanced the debate from the beginning, and the critics of the Government never recovered their equilibrium. But Asquith did not feel that he could be driven into withdrawal by Lloyd George's aggressive tactics. He watched passively the unsatisfactory unfolding of the debate. It lasted less than three hours after the Prime Minister sat down. Carson turned about and gave almost whole-hearted support to Lloyd George. Three Conservatives—General Croft, Colonel Archer-Shee and Lord Hugh Cecil—delivered damaging criticisms of the Government, Croft in particular applying himself to the substance of the dispute, and said they would abstain. Joynson-Hicks and two others, one a Liberal and one a Conservative, said that they had come with open minds, but had been convinced by the Prime Minister that there was no case for an enquiry. Colonel Josiah Wedgwood said that he had three times changed his mind as to how to vote,[1] and appealed despairingly for some further guidance from the front opposition bench.

He appealed in vain. McKenna was there, Runciman was there,

[1] In fact he too abstained.

Samuel was there. But none of them rose to wind up. The debate petered out, with brief inconclusive speeches and increasingly impatient shouts of " divide, divide." Asquith mustered a vote of 108 (including the two tellers), made up of 100 Liberals and a minority of the Labour members. The Government had 295, including 71 Liberals. Asquith and his followers went gloomily home. They could not have been pleased with themselves. They had been badly out-manoeuvred. But they had no idea that they had participated in one of the great divisive debates of history, in an event from which Lloyd George would never allow the Liberal Party to recover.

What were the merits of the argument? Did Asquith eagerly seize upon the false accusations of a sour and neurotic general (as Lloyd George insisted on regarding Maurice[1]) or did the Prime Minister tear up the truth in order to discomfort his critics and gain a spurious House of Commons victory? Lloyd George, in his speech, rested upon two sets of alternative defences. The first was that his statements were correct, but that, even if they were not, the responsibility was Maurice's who, as Director of Military Operations, had supplied him with the figures. The second was that, in making his comparison between January, 1917 and January, 1918 he had not included the non-combatant troops (labour battalions etc.), which had grown greatly in strength in the interval, but that he would in fact have been justified in doing so, as the distinction was an unreal one.

The last point would have been a difficult one to sustain in detailed argument, and in any event it had been discounted in a parliamentary answer by the under-secretary for War on April 18th. So far as combatant troops were concerned, however, the final War Office

[1] The index entry for Maurice in Lloyd George's *War Memoirs* is a remarkable example of importing invective into a section of a book which is normally neutral:

" *Maurice, Sir Frederick* . . . comfortably placed as any politician, 1675; usbservient and unbalanced, 1685; . . . his astonishing arithmetical calculations, 1763–4; the instrument by which the Government was to be thrown out, 1778; . . . his astounding *volte face* of 22/4/18, 1780–1 . . . intrigues against the Government, his mind being apparently unhinged, 1784; false allegations against Lloyd George and Bonar Law published by, 1784–6; the tool of astuter men, 1786 . . . his double-dealing denounced by Lloyd George, 1787–8 . . . his grave breach of discipline condoned by Asquith, 1791; dismissed, 1791."

(pre-debate) figures did not bear out Lloyd George's contention. Those prepared on May 7th gave a total of 1,198,032 in January, 1918, as compared with 1,283,696 in January, 1917.[h] Yet Lloyd George had acted in good faith and on War Office authority when he made his statement on April 9th; and Maurice was directly involved in providing that authority.

How, then, did the discrepancy arise? Part of the explanation was provided four years later. General Maurice, seeking to vindicate himself, and after a careful review of the facts, wrote to Lloyd George in July, 1922. The War Office document upon which Lloyd George's first statements was based, he said, had been prepared in a hurry. By mistake the strength of the armies in Italy had been included in those in France. This mistake was quickly discovered, however (so one would hope, for the sake of General Maurice's reputation as head of the Military Operations department), and a correction was sent to Lloyd George within a few days. When the Prime Minister made his May 9th statement, therefore, he did so on the basis of information which he knew had since been amended.

But did he? In 1922 he brushed Maurice's letter aside. He was never a man for the careful unravelling of past mysteries, particularly if the process might be embarrassing to him. He preferred the events of the moment, and he wanted no dealings with Maurice. At this stage, therefore, the matter remained unresolved. But in 1934 Lady Lloyd George (then Miss Frances Stevenson and still, as she had been for many years, one of Lloyd George's most trusted secretaries) made an entry in her diary. And in 1956 Lord Beaverbrook, making use of his vast store of early twentieth century political papers, revealed this entry. It ran as follows:

Have been reading up the events connected with the Maurice Debate in order to help Ll.G. with this chapter in volume v (of the *War Memoirs*), and am uneasy in my mind about an incident which occurred at the time and is known only to J. T. Davies[1] and myself. Ll.G. obtained from the W.O. the figures which he used in his statement on April 9th in the House of Commons on the subject of manpower. These figures were afterwards stated by Gen. Maurice to be incorrect.

[1] Sir J. T. Davies, 1881–1938, Lloyd George's principal private secretary from 1912 until the end of his premiership. Subsequently a director of the Suez Canal Company and a trustee of the Lloyd George Fund.

I was in J. T. Davies' room a few days after the statement, and J.T. was sorting out red despatch boxes to be returned to the Departments. As was his wont he looked in them before locking them up and sending them out to the Messengers. Pulling out a W.O. box, he found in it, to his great astonishment, a paper from the D.M.O. containing modifications and corrections of the first figures they had sent, and by some mischance this box had remained unopened. J.T. and I examined it in dismay, and then J.T. put it in the fire, remarking, " Only you and I, Frances, know of the existence of this paper."

There is no doubt that this is what Maurice had in mind when he accused Ll.G. of mis-statement. But the amazing thing was that *the document was never fixed upon.* . . . I was waiting for the matter to be raised, and for the question to be asked: Why did L.G. not receive these supplementary figures? Or did he? But the questions never came and I could not voluntarily break faith with J.T., perhaps put L.G. in a fix, and who knows, have brought down the Government!

I suppose it is too late for the matter to be cleared up and I had better keep silent. But I will talk it over with J.T. In any event, no good could come of any revelation made now. . . .[i]

So, with this interesting sidelight on Downing Street life under the Lloyd George régime, the mystery appears to be cleared up. So far at least as his main charge was concerned, Maurice was right. Asquith knew that he was right, and acted from a high sense of duty, although with less than his usual parliamentary skill. But Lloyd George may genuinely have believed that Maurice, saying one thing in the War Office and another as soon as he was outside, was a conspirator against the Government rather than a performer of public duty. Nor did the Prime Minister understand how he had been misled on April 9th. He can therefore be acquitted of the heaviest charges which are laid against his conduct of the Maurice debate. The use which he subsequently made of it is a different matter.

This use occurred seven months later. During the first half of 1918 the end of the war seemed almost infinitely remote. The generals and the politicians were thinking in terms of the campaigns of 1919 and 1920. And the public, which in 1914–15 had found it so difficult to adjust to the idea of a long war, now found it almost equally difficult to comprehend that peace might be near at hand. By the early autumn, however, the mood had changed. Asquith, who had spent a quiet summer, golfing at North Berwick and (a most uncharacteristic activity) climbing " on about the hottest afternoon of the year " to the highest of the Clumps behind Sutton Courtney, was deeply embroiled, by early October, in talks about the peace prospect and the possible terms. " I came up here yesterday morning," he wrote from Cavendish Square on October 8th, " a day sooner than I intended, as I wanted to be in touch with people about this German Peace Note ... Lansdowne and Gilbert Murray are coming to lunch: E. Grey after lunch: and Lord Reading about tea-time: so I am not wanting for counsellors."*j*

Asquith believed at this stage that he might have a great part to play in the peace negotiations, and in the subsequent reconstruction of Europe. He had a good deal of traditional English scepticism about the intentions and capacity of the Americans, but he was most anxious to meet Woodrow Wilson and to co-operate closely with him. When he heard that the President was coming to London he wrote:

I confess he is one of the few people in the world that I want to see and talk to: not quite in the spirit of Monckton Milnes, of whom it was said that if Christ came again he would at once send him an invitation card for one of his breakfasts; but because I am really curious to judge for myself what manner of man he is. Gilbert Murray, who was here this morning and knows him, thinks that I should like him.*k*

Asquith's assumption was still that the Liberal Party would retain a dominant position in post-war politics. The process of disillusionment began, mildly at first, in early November. Lloyd George, following up a series of October talks, had written a formal but for the moment secret letter to Bonar Law on November 2nd, proposing that there should be a quick election and a Coalition ticket. Ten days later this proposal was accepted at a Unionist meeting. Before that Asquith had gathered what was intended. " I suppose that tomorrow we shall be told the final decision about this accursed General Election," he wrote on November 6th. " If, as seems more than likely, it is to be upon us soon after the end of the month, it will be difficult to make any plans, as one may find oneself roaming about like the Wandering Jew."*l* A strong deputation from Liberals in the constituencies waited upon Lloyd George during this week and urged him to fight in alliance, not with Bonar Law, but with Asquith. They received a discouraging answer. Asquith was of course informed of what occurred at this meeting.

Then came the Armistice. Asquith had only a peripheral part to play in that dramatic and emotion-charged day of brilliant autumn sunlight. His main duty during the morning was to motor to Golders Green and attend the cremation service of a distant relation. When he returned he found a telegram from the King (in reply to one which Margot had sent earlier in their joint names). "I look back with gratitude," it said, "to your wise counsel and calm resolve in the days when great issues had to be decided resulting in our entry into the war." After luncheon he drove with Margot to the House of Commons, and listened to Lloyd George reading the terms of the Armistice. He contributed a few brief but appropriate remarks. The House then adjourned and moved in procession to St. Margaret's for a service of thanksgiving. At Cavendish Square Margot had ordered all available flags to be put out, and Asquith found a Welsh harp " fluttering greenly " from his library window. The next day the Asquiths attended the national thanksgiving service at St. Paul's, and lunched afterwards with the King and Queen at Buckingham Palace.

Sometime in the next few days Asquith had an important interview with Lloyd George. Although at least three accounts of this survive, none of them fixes the day, but it seems likely to have been in the week following the Armistice. None of these accounts is in serious conflict with another, so perhaps Margot's version (always the most graphic) may be given:

. . . Henry was asked to go to the Prime Minister's room in the House of Commons.

Upon his return he told me what had occurred. He had been received with a friendliness which amounted to enthusiasm and asked where he stood. Mr. Lloyd George then said:

" I understand you don't wish to take a post under the Government."[1]

To which my husband answered that that was so; and added that the only service he thought he could render the Government would be if he were to go to Versailles, as from what he

[1] The account of Vivian Phillipps, Asquith's secretary from 1918 onwards, says that the question was asked directly, without assuming a negative. Lloyd George's own account says that he offered Asquith the Lord Chancellorship, " and the opportunity of attending the Peace Conference."

knew both of President Wilson and M. Clemenceau he was pretty sure they knew little of International Law or finance, and that these two problems would be found all-important in view of fixing future frontiers and the havoc the war was likely to create in all the Foreign Exchanges.

At this Mr. Lloyd George looked a little confused. He was walking up and down the room, and in knocking up against a chair a pile of loose books were thrown upon the ground. Hastily looking at his watch and stooping down to pick up the books, he said he would consider my husband's proposal. Nothing more was said; the interview was over, and my husband never heard another word upon the matter.[m]

Neither of the two was willing to accept the other's terms. Asquith was loath either to compromise his position as the head of an independent Liberal Party, or to desert his old friends, by entering the Coalition Government. Lloyd George was determined that, if Asquith wanted to go to Paris, he should first pay the price of subordinating himself in the Government. The *impasse* was complete, although Asquith continued to hope, even when the election had left its legacy of additional bitterness, that he might still be allowed his independent delegate status.

The election campaign was as disagreeable for the independent Liberals as it was discreditable for the leaders of the Coalition. Lloyd George unaccountably claimed that he did not allude to the Maurice debate " during the whole contest,"[n] but in fact he raised it at length (although without mentioning the name " Maurice ") at one of the first meetings—Wolverhampton on November 23rd—and made it clear that performance the previous May was to be the principal test of whether or not a sitting Liberal M.P. was to receive the endorsement of Bonar Law and himself. Nearly all who had voted for the select committee were provided with Coalition opponents—mostly Unionists. In this way " the coupon," as Asquith described it, was born.

Asquith fought a campaign of integrity, but a slightly weary and dispirited one. " I doubt whether so far there is much interest in the elections," he wrote on November 25th, " despite the efforts of the newspapers to keep the pot boiling. The whole thing is a wicked fraud, which will settle nothing."[o] And on another occasion: " I am rather in need of something to read on my journeys: I loathe all this knocking about, but it has to be done."[p]

477

He had some good meetings and found the Liberals on occasion "breast-high against all this coalitioneering." But it would be an exaggeration to say that he was optimistic about the general result. The best that he could hope for was to maintain a bastion of a hundred or so independent Liberal seats against the Coalition flood. Most of these, he believed, would hold. In particular, he felt no doubts about East Fife. "I confess that I felt so little apprehension for my seat that I spent most of my time ... in visiting and addressing other constituencies," he wrote.[q] He was there for polling day, however, and was edified by posters somewhat clumsily proclaiming: "Asquith nearly lost you the War. Are you going to let him spoil the Peace?"

The results were delayed for a fortnight to allow the soldiers' votes to come in. This interval included Christmas, and Asquith spent most of it at the Wharf. He did not return to Scotland for the counting. That day (December 28th) he began by leading a deputation of Grey and Gilbert Murray to tell President Wilson of their support for the idea of the League of Nations. Later in the morning he went to see the Freedom of the City of London conferred upon the President. The freedom ceremony over, the company adjourned to the Mansion House for a Lord Mayor's luncheon. Asquith sat at the high table, only a few places away from Lloyd George. As the meal drew to an end whispers of the election returns began to circulate amongst the guests. On their way out the air was heavy with fact and rumour. It was clear that the Coalition had won a crushing victory. Margot described the scene:

> ... I heard a man say: "Herbert Samuel, McKinnon Wood and Runciman are out."
>
> We left the dining-room and made our way down to the crowded front door. People waiting for their motors were standing in groups discussing the Election returns.
>
> "McKenna is beat: Montagu is in by over 9,000" was whispered from mouth to mouth, while the men thrust their arms into their coat sleeves, changing their cigars from hand to hand in the process, and asking for their motors.
>
> The news spread; man after man of ours was out.
>
> Where we all *beaten*? .... Who *could* I ask? Who would tell me? Henry crushed up against me and said calmly:
>
> "I see our footman" ...
>
> Among the crush in the large open doorway ... I perceived

Rufus Reading, looking snow-white. Did he or did he not know if Henry was beaten? . . . perhaps they all knew.

I was jammed up against my husband and had no idea what he had heard.

I looked at him out of the corner of my eyelids; he was standing a little in front of me, but not a sign of any kind could be seen on his face. . . .

I saw as if in a trance the cheering crowds, eager faces, mounted police, and swaying people, while we shot down the streets with our minds set and stunned. Not one word did we say till we got near home; then Henry broke the silence:

"I only hope," he said, "that *I* have not got in; with all the others out this would be the last straw."

. . . The motor slowed down; we had arrived. I jumped out and ran through the open door in front of Henry; I found the odd man labelling our luggage piled up in the hall. Not a note or a message of any kind was to be seen.

Henry went into his library, and I rang up 21 Abingdon Street (the Liberal headquarters) on the telephone in my boudoir.

"Not got all the returns? . . . Yes? . . . East Fife. Yes? . . . Asquith beat? . . . Thank God . . . "

Henry came in . . .

"I'm out, am I?" he said; "ask by how much; tell them to give us the figures, will you?"

"Give me the East Fife figures," I said, and taking a pencil wrote:

Asquith 6994—Sprott 8996.*r*

The blow was of course a crippling one. However much both he and Margot might bravely protest that, with nearly all the others out,[1] it was better for Asquith to be beaten too, this was not so. It spared him the early years of a harsh and hostile Parliament, but at the price of a personal humiliation which destroyed his hope of exercising any influence on the peace settlement. He was the rejected man, whose constituency of thirty-two years' standing had not even needed the spur of the coupon (Lloyd George and Bonar Law, with self-conscious generosity, had withheld it from the Conservative Sprott) to vote him out. The wheel of political fortune had indeed turned full circle for

[1] The Asquithian Liberals in fact won 26 seats, as against 59 for the Labour Party and 474 (338 Unionists and 136 Liberals) for the Coalition.

him. After three decades of mounting success almost all power had crumbled away in two years. He was left with only a remnant of a party, and no forum from which to lead it. Yet he remained one of the two or three most famous Englishmen, and there were many, not necessarily amongst his supporters, who felt a sense of shock and re-pugnance that his years of distinguished service had been repaid in this way, and his high standards of controversy thrown back so violently in his face. A flood of letters poured in upon him in his defeat—greater in quantity and more intense in dismay than those which he had received when he was forced out of Downing Street.

A sense of shame that it should have occurred was a frequent note " I did not expect it of my countrymen,"[s] Haldane wrote in a calming but affectionate letter. " I feel humiliated as an Englishman at such a result,"[t] the Bishop of Chelmsford said. His colleague of Southwark added: " I am left today wondering whether this is really England, and I am a British citizen. . . . We have disgraced ourselves, I mean we ordinary people."[u] And the Master of Balliol (A. L. Smith) wrote to express " what I find to be a feeling universal, even amongst those who would politically be far from your party—a feeling of deep regret and shame that such a thing could possibly happen to *you*."[v]

The politicians divided into those, like Bryce (" There has not been a time, even when Mr. Gladstone lost his two seats, when so much turned on one man's presence.") who were dismayed at Asquith's absence from the House of Commons; and those like Birrell, always one for graceful withdrawal, who could see advantages for Asquith in being away from the squalid scene: " You surely are better out of it for the time, than watching Ll.G. lead apes to Hell."[w1]

Some correspondents thought more of the past than of the future. Hankey wrote: " When times are less breathless and the public per-spective is restored, the people will learn what those who were with you at the time know well—the tremendous burden you carried through the first half of the War, and that it was you who saved the Empire from absolute disaster."[x] Sir William Robertson, after refer-

[1] He also said, a characteristic touch from a former member for Fife, " Now that it is over I don't mind telling you that *I never did like East Fife*, although I imagine the blunder is attributable to the absorption in the County of those plaguey boroughs with that fishing population which has broken the hearts of so many good (and bad) Liberals ere now. But they won't break yours." (*Asquith Papers*, box XXXIII, f. 25).

The Coalition at Work: Lloyd George and Lord Derby

Evening Honours: Asquith goes to Buckingham Palace for
Investiture as Earl of Oxford, 1925

ring to his experience of " *the greatest kindness, consideration and straight-forwardness* from you in the troublous time we have together been through," went on to say: " Perhaps this is a permissible occasion for me to tell you that poor K(itchener) had a great admiration and affection for you and *often* told me that you were a great help to him in the early and critical days of the war, and then displayed far and away more courage than most others in the Cabinet, especially than some who would have us believe they are so very courageous."*y*

Other letters sought to explain away the result. The best informed of these came from James Scott, Asquith's chairman in East Fife. He wrote:

For a week before the election we had a swarm of women going from door to door indulging in a slander for which they had not a shadow of proof. This was used to such purpose as to influence the female vote very much against you. When the man was a weak subject, if not swayed, he was induced to abstain from voting, which latter course was followed in not a few cases. With others who had been employed on munitions, and in receipt of good wages, their pocket outweighed their principles. Again we had those who made a point of your absence from the constituency and did not hesitate to say that we never see him and are not going to work.*z*

Whatever the explanation, and however great the sympathy, Asquith was out, and politically down. Politics, even had he wished them to do so, offered no employment for more than a fraction of his time. During the first six months of 1919 not a single invitation to speak reached him from any Liberal Association in the country. He was the proscribed man. His platform activities were confined to two or three non-party meetings in support of the League of Nations and other progressive causes. He travelled, he read, and he wrote. Occasionally he attended official ceremonies and banquets—the King, a loyal friend at this stage, would have seen to that, even had no-one else; and at them he retained his edge of sharp, sensible and tolerant comment:

" We went yesterday to the Luncheon in honour of Foch," he wrote on July 31st, 1919. " I had a little conversation with him, and I thought he talked a lot of nonsense about Germany sinking never to rise again, etc. " *Quel dommage* (as Talleyrand said of Napoleon, not as soldier but as Emperor) *que les soldats soient si mal élevés!* " Haig, who sat next to us, also has his limitations, but he got through his little speech without any flaring *gaffes.*"[aa]

No one could have been less unbalanced by setback than was Asquith. He lived amongst his relations and friends and books, and he lived agreeably. But he lived without power, or public honour, or real occupation.

CHAPTER XXIX

THE OLD CHIEF RETURNS

1920-24

The later months of 1919 saw a slight easing of Asquith's isolation. In August he was asked to preside over a Royal Commission on the Universities of Oxford and Cambridge, and accepted. It was hardly a substitute for membership of the Peace Conference delegation, but it was something to do, and it took him to familiar old haunts at Oxford and agreeable new ones at Cambridge. He discharged his duties with some enthusiasm.[1] Then, at the end of the year, together with Lloyd George, he received a special award of military medals—the 1914 War Star, the 1914-18 War Medal, and the 1918 Victory Medal—from the Army Council. At first the intention of the War Office (under Churchill) had been to give these to Lloyd George alone, but the King had demurred, and withdrew his opposition only when both of the war Prime Ministers were included.

Social life, both at the Wharf and in Cavendish Square, became more expansive. It had never been unduly restricted, but now there was a return almost to the pre-1914 pattern:

" We drove up in good time to receive our ' young visitor ' (the Prince of Wales)," he wrote on January 20th, 1920, " the fellow guests with whom we provided him being the two Bibescae, Soveral, Birrell, Sir D. and Lady Maclean, and my niece Kakoo Granby,[2] who was in wonderful looks. The Prince has excellent

---

[1] But it was, in fact, a bad appointment. As Gladstone had been before him, and Lord Attlee was to be after him, Asquith was a natural conservative on most subjects outside politics. This was particularly so on anything touching both scholarship and his early life, and he led the Commission into producing an unadventurous report.

[2] The " Bibescae " were Elizabeth Asquith and her new Roumanian diplomat husband, Prince Antoine Bibesco; Soveral was the Portuguese Minister and a great Edwardian social figure; Birrell was Birrell; Sir

manners and has come on immensely in ease and *savoir faire*.
He talked quite amusingly of his experience in America, and I
think is not sorry to be off again in March, even to so dismal a goal
as Australia. I fancy the evenings at the fireside of Sandringham
Cottage pass with somewhat leaden feet. Both Soveral and
Birrell were in excellent form, and Lady Maclean, who is still
young and quite good-looking, surveyed the scene with glowing
cheeks and glittering eyes . . . the meal was a great success."[a]

Much more important for Asquith than either the small signs of
public recognition, or the revival to full pressure of his and Margot's
social life, was the growing public disillusion with the Coalition. The
post-war honeymoon was over. Some of the ill-considered cries and
extravagant promises of the Coupon election were already coming
home to roost. For an independent Liberal the political climate was
still chilly, but no longer so frigid that it was suicide for him to venture
out of doors. Over the turn of the year Sir John Simon was the first
of the old front benchers to make a foray. He was narrowly defeated
at Spen Valley. If Asquith himself was to come back the attempt
could not be too long delayed. Inevitably, his desires were mixed.
After thirty-two years of dominant membership, he missed the House
of Commons. But he knew that the 1918 Parliament could never be
one in which he would enjoy sitting. Its atmosphere was too alien to
his views and style. A hazardous contest was also unattractive. He
never much enjoyed electioneering, even at the best of times, and least
of all was he likely to do so after the disaster of the previous year at
East Fife. Another failure would be almost a final blow. Transcending
all these considerations, however, was his massive disapproval of both
the policy and methods of the Coalition, and his obligation to give the
most effective possible expression to this view. This he could not do
from the sidelines.

The glimmering of an opportunity came early in the New Year
of 1920. The death of one of the small band of independent Liberals
created a vacancy at Paisley, a Lanarkshire industrial town on the edge
of the Glasgow conurbation. There, in 1918, with strong local ties

Donald Maclean was leader, in Asquith's absence, of the Liberal remnant
in the House of Commons; and the Marchioness of Granby, who later
became Duchess of Rutland, was the daughter of Margot's brother Frank
Tennant.

behind him, the dead member had been returned by the bare majority of 106. It was not clear how transferable was his support. Nor was it clear that the local Liberal association wanted Asquith. At that time the position within local Liberal associations was rather like that in Berlin in the early days of the cold war. No one doubted the enmity of Lloyd George and Asquith, but the adherents of both attempted to co-exist within the same associations, running them as single units upon the basis of two (rather than four) power control. The introduction of Asquith as a candidate was obviously likely to have a fissiparous effect, and those members who inclined in a Lloyd George direction were, to say the least, cool towards the idea.

The question of an invitation remained in doubt for several weeks after it was first mooted. But on January 21st a favourable decision was taken by a majority of 25 or so in a meeting of several hundreds.

"As you would see by today's paper," Asquith wrote to Mrs. Harrisson on the 22nd, "the Paisley people have at last got down on the right side of the fence. I don't look forward with much pleasure to the adventure, which however has to be faced. For one thing I am not very fond of going back to Scotland, for another the issue is extremely doubtful, notwithstanding that the press is practically all with us. My present plan is to leave here by the night train on Monday."[b]

On arrival in Glasgow on the Tuesday morning his first task was to install himself, Margot, his daughter Violet, and his secretary Vivian Phillipps in the Central Station Hotel there. His second was to proceed to Paisley and to turn a tepid and divided Liberal association into a compact body of enthusiastic supporters. That night he met 600 members at the Liberal Club, and in a short, thirty-minute speech achieved a remarkable success. From then until polling day, sixteen days ahead, his campaign never looked back.

He even showed signs of enjoying it himself, despite the strain of four and five meetings a day and the unfamiliar experience of soliciting women's votes.

"We are having a wonderful time here," he wrote on January 30th, "and if outward enthusiasm were a reliable index we should not have much doubt as to the result. But street crowds and photographers and meetings are most untrustworthy guides. There are about fifteen thousand women on the Register—a dim, impenetrable, for the most part ungettable element—of

485

whom all that one knows is that they are for the most part hopelessly ignorant of politics, credulous to the last degree, and flickering with gusts of sentiment like a candle in the wind. Then there are some thousands of Irish, who have been ordered by their bosses to vote Labour—as if Labour had ever done or was ever likely to do anything for them. It is on the whole an incalculable problem. The only certain fact is that the Coalition man—a foul-mouthed Tory—will be well at the bottom of the poll. The meetings are wonderful: always a lot of opponents there, but when I speak they never interrupt and you could hear a pin drop. They are among the most intelligent audiences I have ever had, but the heckling is of very poor quality. Violet is a marvellous success as a speaker."[c]

The Labour candidate was J. M. Biggar, who had fought the seat in 1918 and come within an ace of victory. He had the advantage on this occasion, so strangely does time alter political alliances, of a message of support from Lord Haldane. If Asquith was to be beaten it would be by him, and not by the "foul-mouthed Tory," J. A. D. MacKean. Yet Asquith directed the main effort of his campaign against the Coalition. Partly this was because it corresponded with his feelings; partly because it was a sound electoral tactic. The Labour vote was big and solid, but not a majority. Asquith's task was to defeat it by securing every available Liberal vote and some moderate Tory ones as well.

He did not attempt to do this by a soft approach. He roundly attacked the whole policy of trying to grind Germany into the dust by the exaction of impossible reparations. He was equally forthright —and far-sighted—on Ireland. Nothing short of immediate dominion status, a proposal which was at the time denounced by the Government as "insanity," could avoid a future of violence, bloodshed and bitterness. Less controversially, he upheld the future of the League of Nations, and warned of the danger of the new states—and the old ones—engaging in damaging tariff wars.

He was supported in the campaign, apart from local workers, by those two eminent Liberal lawyers, Sir John Simon and Lord Buckmaster, both outstanding platform orators. But his daughter Violet was better than either of them. Using a peculiar combination of highly-charged emotional phraseology and polished political wit, she was the great success of the contest. "Her father," as Churchill was later to write, " . . . found in his daughter a champion redoubtable even in the first rank of Party orators."[d] Each night Asquith retired to the Central Station Hotel in Glasgow to read *Dr. Thorne* and *Framley Parsonage* and to contemplate with quiet satisfaction this new addition to his strength and a more generally favourable development of events than anything he had known for several years.

Polling day was on February 12th, but there was once again a delay of two weeks before the counting. As in 1918 Asquith went south as soon as the voting was over, but this time he did not stay there for the result. Nor did he waste much time on this second " Paisley excursion," as he called it. The whole family travelled up by sleeper one night and back by sleeper the next.

"I was present during most of the counting," he wrote the following day, " and it was clear after the first half-hour that we had won, but the majority steadily increased as fresh ballot boxes were opened till it mounted to close upon 3,000.[1] Perhaps the most satisfactory feature of the whole business was the sorry figure cut by the wretched Coalitionist MacKean: he fought dirtily and deserves the penalty he has to suffer of losing his deposit.

We had a gigantic farewell meeting—nearer 5,000 than 4,000—in the early evening, at which Violet made one of her best speeches, and when we took the night train (at) Glasgow we were nearly done to death by the demonstrative attentions of the University students.[2] However, we got through and after another tumultuous greeting at Euston this morning, arrived here (Cavendish Square) for a late breakfast. We found a magnificent wreath

[1] The figures were: Asquith   14,736
                               Biggar   11,902
                               MacKean   3,795
The poll was up by over 8,000 on the 1918 total.
[2] Margot gave a more dramatic account of this event. " . . . we had to have police protection after the declaration of the poll, and I was knocked on to the railway line at St. Enoch's Station by the rush of my husband's admirers seeing him off by the night train that took us to London. But it is surprising how excitement and happiness protect one, as after being pulled on to the platform by the willing porters I found instead of the bruises I had expected to see I had not received a single scratch." (*More Memories*, pp. 246–7).

over the front door, a characteristic gift from Lady Tree: and more letters and telegrams than it is possible to count.

It is Elizabeth's birthday, and Puffin is up from Winchester for the day. We are all going this afternoon to a matinée of B. Shaw's *Pygmalion* with Mrs. Campbell and Marion Terry in the chief parts."*e*

Amidst all the letters and telegrams which flowed in there was none from any leading supporter of the Coalition. No personal note came from Churchill or Montagu, from Balfour or Curzon, from Austen Chamberlain or Walter Long, let alone from Bonar Law or Lloyd George.[1] Less surprisingly, the public welcome which Asquith received from the Government benches (then five-sixths of the total) in the House of Commons was equally chilly. But it was counterbalanced by extraordinary scenes of enthusiasm outside.

On the following Monday, when Asquith took his seat, there was a great crowd all the way from Cavendish Square to Westminster, and they gave him " a tumultuous but most enthusiastic procession." A band of medical students in Parliament Square added their own tribute by annexing his new top hat and doing one hundred pounds' worth of damage to his motor car. But he found this much more agreeable than the " stony silence " with which the unfamiliar occupants of the familiar benches greeted him within.

A few days later, when his daughter Violet, guest of honour at a National Liberal Club luncheon, delivered what still reads as one of the best speeches of its sort ever made, she painted the contrast:

One last scene—the closing scene of the drama of Paisley. Let us remember it together, for you have shared it with me—the sight of those great cheering crowds that thronged Whitehall and Parliament Square the day he took his seat. When I went in out of the noise, into the silence of the House—the House in which I had seen him lead great armies to great triumphs; when I saw that little gallant handful of men which is all his following now, and heard their thin cheer raised, for a moment I felt—is this all, are these all he has behind him? But then I remembered the great voice of the crowd—it rang in my ears; and I knew that this,

[1] The nearest approach to an exception was a warm letter from Lord Cave, who had been Home Secretary from 1916–19. This was ironical, for later, in 1925 (see page 511 *infra*) Cave was to be the agent for the delivery of one of the last and most severely felt blows against Asquith.

this was the voice of England—not the drilled cheers of those conscript ranks on the Coalition benches. And I knew that our small force that day was like the little gallant garrison of a beleaguered city that hears for the first time the great shout of the relieving forces—" Hold on, hold out; we are coming." *And they are.*[f]

But they never did. Paisley was a false dawn, both for Asquith and the Liberal Party. At best it was the equivalent of some late winter daybreak on the fringes of the Arctic Circle. For a time the light grew gradually a little stronger. After a few years the Coalition crumbled. In the period of political confusion which followed the Liberal Party achieved an uncomfortable reunion and gained a little in influence. Asquith won two more elections at Paisley and even had something approaching a worth-while party to lead. But, compared with the " great armies " and " great triumphs " of pre-war days, it was very small stuff. The post-war Liberal day never achieved more than a grey and short-lived light. By 1924 it was dusk again. By 1926, for Asquith at least, it was political night.

Fortunately, on that exhilarating March afternoon in 1920, he could not foresee all this. Otherwise, even his massive reserves of self-assured fortitude would hardly have been enough to enable him to begin the long and unrewarding parliamentary battle against the Coalition. Unrewarding it certainly was. " You have given the best proof since the G.O.M. took up Home Rule in 1886 that courage has not vanished from political life,"[g] Bryce wrote to him. Asquith in 1920 was ten years younger than Gladstone at this turning-point, but the ground was still less promising and he fell further short of success.

It was not for want of trying. After his election for Paisley he spoke in the House of Commons far more frequently than ever previously when not a minister. He did the same in the country, stumping up and down from Portsmouth to Manchester and Cardiff to Newcastle in a way that he had never done before. As a result, when the Chief Whip delivered a report in June, 1921 on speaking activity, Asquith came out top of the list—" a complete refutation," as he rather defensively noted, " of the silly legend that I have lost ' grip and keenness '."

Until the settlement of 1921 it was mainly Ireland which engaged his attention. He kept up a constant pressure against the Government. But he felt that it was an ineffective pressure. The House was deaf **to** his appeals. "I took some pains with my speech," he wrote after his first major effort on this subject, "and said all that I intended. Five years ago it would have been rapturously applauded, but this House is the most impossible place, and though they crowd in and listen attentively there is practically no response."[h]

He did not mind the isolation. His inner resources were proof against that. "Now that Ll.G. calls me a lunatic and Carson calls me a traitor I begin to feel sure that I must be on the right lines,"[i] he wrote in October, 1920. But he hated the waste of ineffective action. He had no taste for speech-making for its own sake. "Squandering himself like a fountain spraying into desert sand," was his description of Coleridge, than whom "there is no more tragic figure in literature"[j]; and free from self-pity though he was, he might have thought that the words had some application to himself.

Even his own supporters were sometimes hesitant. "And if one tries to strike a bold true note," he wrote on October 24th 1920, "half one's friends shiver and cower, and implore one not to get in front of the band: in other words, to renounce both the duties and the risks of leadership."[k]

Asquith represented a strand of distinguished opinion in the country. "You have stood for what is fine in the soul of this country in the greatest months of her history," John Masefield wrote to him after the Paisley election, "and my wife and I send you our heartiest congratulations that you are now to bring back fineness and sanity to the councils of this heaving time."[l] The weakness of the strand was that it had more distinction than width, and that some of those within it felt more nostalgia than hope. Yet Asquith tried as hard as he could, both to broaden his basis of support and to think of the future as well as the past. Over the summer of 1921 he held a series of "conclaves" designed to promote a new basis for an alternative Government. First he tried to get Grey committed to a return to active politics. On June 29th he wrote:

E. Grey came to see me this morning by appointment. After some preliminaries I said to him that in my opinion the policy of the Coalition brought us both at home and abroad to a dangerous and almost desperate pass: that there was every ground for thinking that this was not only the growing but the dominant feeling of the country: that the success of anti-waste candidates at the by-elections was a crude expression of that feeling; and that everything pointed to a general desire for a strong alternative government to which it could rally. At present there was no such government in sight. In my judgment it could only be provided by the Liberal Party re-inforced by such men as Lord R. Cecil, and perhaps with an infusion of moderate Labour. But (I told him) the first essential was *his avowed and open co-operation*, both in a declaration of general policy and the ultimate responsibilities if and when the country should decide on a change."*m*

Asquith said he had only delayed approaching Grey before because of worries about his health. Grey said this was all right apart from his eyes. He could not read papers or do the work of an office. Asquith said that did not matter: he could be Lord President of the Council, lead the House of Lords, and speak outside. Then they discussed policy. Grey was " particularly strong on Ireland." They agreed that if the current negotiations broke down British troops must be withdrawn, and the Irish left to govern themselves. It was to be the Indian policy of 1947. The League of Nations must be made a " reality instead of a sham on a shelf." Grey said that " he had coquetted before the war with the nationalisation of industries, but experience of government controls had completely converted him." Co-partnership and profit-sharing was therefore to be the policy here. For unemployment (then mounting rapidly) they did not have a remedy (who did?), but agreed (it would have been difficult not to) that it " required close consideration."

So far, so good. A wider " conclave," composed of Asquith, Grey, Cecil, Crewe, Runciman and Maclean met at Asquith's house on July 5th. Then the difficulties began to arise. Cecil made it clear that he would not become a Liberal or join a Government which was merely the Liberal Party in disguise. This meant that he wanted Grey and not Asquith to be Prime Minister, for he considered Asquith more committed in a party sense. Sir Arthur Steel-Maitland, who, at a later stage, became the only other Tory to join in the discussions, took the same view. Cecil wanted the campaign to start with a manifesto signed only by himself and Grey, which Asquith and Crewe, as official Liberal leaders, would subsequently support.

Asquith himself made no difficulty about these suggestions that he should take second place. Perhaps he did not take them very seriously, for, as was apparent from their conversation on June 29th, Grey was in reality quite incapable of carrying the burden of the Premiership.

Asquith was, moreover, desperately anxious to secure the co-operation of Grey, and, to a lesser extent, that of Cecil. There were others in the " conclave," however, who quickly showed ruffled feathers at the proposed supplanting of the Liberal hierarchy. Donald Maclean, according to Asquith's note of the meeting " said that R.C(ecil)'s plan was wholly impracticable. It would take the life and heart out of the Liberal rank and file, who would protest that they were being asked to join another Coalition."[n] Runciman and Crewe spoke in a similar sense.

This basic difficulty was never overcome, although there were various ingenious attempts to circumnavigate it. It was suggested that there should be no initial manifesto, but that Asquith would begin by writing publicly to Grey, who would reply more fully and equally publicly. Then Cecil would declare his support for the exchange. Steel-Maitland, however, would not have this. It would still look too much like " a domestic Liberal affair."

At this stage Grey turned cold. He had always been a difficult bird to catch, and advancing years accentuated the characteristic. He arrived (late) for the fourth meeting of the " conclave," having missed the third because he was " feeding his squirrels . . . in Northumberland," and immediately threw everything into confusion by announcing that " with the state of his eyesight it would be wrong for him to undertake any ' definite political obligations.' Candidates might come forward on the strength of his emergence who would feel that they had been misled in the event of his (probable) return to retirement."

When this scruple was over-ruled by the others he changed his tack. " He then declared that his real motive for coming out was the Irish business—reprisals, etc: this was now in abeyance and perhaps on the road to settlement."[o] It all sounded fairly hopeless; indeed it is difficult not to catch the faint aroma of émigré meetings rising from all these "conclaves." But Asquith would not accept defeat. Eventually it was agreed that, while the exchange of letters should be abandoned, Grey would " open the business " by speaking in his old constituency early in October.

The meeting took place, but nothing very much came of it. Nevertheless the idea of a new centre-left grouping was, with difficulty, kept alive. In January, 1922, Asquith reported that Scott of the Manchester Guardian was strongly in favour of such a plan. It was proving difficult to embrace "moderate Labour," however, and Scott regarded their inclusion as essential. Geoffrey Howard, the Liberal Chief Whip, was deputed to explain to him "the efforts we had made and were making to get an electoral arrangement, and how they were, time after time, frustrated by the inability of the Labour leaders here to exercise authority over their local branches and ' deliver the goods '."ᵖ

By this time the Coalition was nearing its end. It collapsed in October, 1922. Its fall owed almost everything to growing Conservative distrust of Lloyd George, brought to a head by the stubborn adventurousness of his policy in Asia Minor, and almost nothing to the opposition which Asquith had been able to mount against him. Over the summer of that year Asquith's interest in politics was lower than at any time since his return to the House of Commons. He felt that he had done his best, and failed. He was also increasingly worried about money. In the spring of 1920 he had been forced to abandon Cavendish Square and to move to a cheaper but still commodious London house at 44, Bedford Square in Bloomsbury. Cheaper though it was, this was a house of considerable architectural distinction, which had previously belonged to Lady Ottoline Morrell and was used to spectacular if unorthodox entertaining. Then Margot had written the first volume of her *Autobiography*, and this, serialised in the *Sunday Times* and selling well both in England and the United States, had produced some welcome relief—as well as alienating a number of friends.[1] By 1922 the second volume was in an advanced state of preparation, and she followed up the success of the first by an American lecture tour, which it was hoped would be profitable.[2]

[1] Curzon was perhaps the most extreme case. "After reading my *Autobiography*," Margot wrote later, "in spite of meeting him on many occasions, to my unending regret George Curzon never spoke to me, and the day he invited me to dine with him to put an end to our quarrels was the day on which he died." (*More Memories*, p. 205).

[2] In fact the tour produced more vicissitudes than profit. Both the nature of these and the high gearing of the tour can be guessed from some comments of Asquith's written on March 21st: "Some letters of Margot's ... arrived this morning. She had had rather a fiasco at Pittsburgh: thanks to the reporters having published a lying statement that she had said that the ' American female is a painted plaything,' a large Club of women cancelled their seats, and she had an audience of 12,000 instead of 15,000. ... She was going on South and West to places like Cincinnati and St. Louis: terrible

Even so the financial pressure was again heavy upon Asquith. He began to think and write more about literary earnings, his own and those of other people:

Someone said (at a dinner of " The Club ") that the author of *If Winter Comes* had netted here and in America at least £50,000: which I don't believe, but if it was half as much, it is a wonderful achievement for a writer of unsuccessful novels. (June 14th, 1922).

I am rather exhausted, for I have just finished my 1,500 words of the *John Bull* article, and dictated them to a young woman who came from the office. (June 15th, 1922).

I see that Ll.G. is reported to be selling his memoirs for a fabulous sum. (August 13, 1922).

Out of the proceeds of his book he (Churchill) has bought a modest country house and 80 acres of land in Kent. . . . He has sold 10,000 copies of his first volume at 30s. and hopes to reap a second harvest by a cheap edition at 10s. (April 25th, 1923).

I wish I could find a way to make a little money.[1] (June 5th, 1923).

I got back to a late lunch today, am now about to grapple (for a reasonable fee) with Winston's book. (November 6th, 1923).*q*

During the summer recess of 1922 Asquith himself was hard at work on a book—*The Genesis of the War*. This was a serious essay in diplomatic history; he delved deep into the sources and initiated a wide international correspondence, although he was less painstaking with the actual writing. It was far too impersonal a record to compete for sales with Margot, or Churchill, or Lloyd George. Asquith wrote it for money, but he was unwilling and unable to stoop for a lucrative coiquest. "I had a visit this morning from Mr. Flower, the literary entor of Cassells," he wrote on November 21st, "who came to talk about my book. He evidently thinks it is going to be too meticulous and elaborate.   I gave him no encouragement, and said that I must do it in my own way—or not at all. In the end he acquiesced and went courteously away.   I suppose publishers have always been the

---

distances." (*Letters from Lord Oxford to a Friend*, II, p. 1). Asquith was the last English statesman of note never to visit America.

[1] He wrote this, rather incongruously, after recording that he had declined the Aga Khan's invitation to take him to the Oaks but was just about to attend " Col. Faber's Derby dinner."

same. . . . ."*r* Then, on the day after publication, in September, 1923, he noted resignedly: "The reviews, so far as I have seen any, are not unfriendly, tho' they are evidently disappointed that I have been so sparing of the tittle-tattle."*s* However, he immediately started to edit a collection of his earlier writings, some of them going back to the 'seventies, which were published in 1924 under the title of *Studies and Sketches*.

In the autumn of 1922, while Asquith was completing the *Genesis of the War*, the political situation was suddenly transformed. The Carlton Club revolt of October 19th led to the majority of Conservatives withdrawing their support from the Coalition. Lloyd George had no alternative but to resign immediately. Bonar Law, who had retired from the Coalition eighteen months before because of ill-health, became Prime Minister at the head of an undistinguished Conservative Government. In Birkenhead's words "the second eleven" had taken over. He and Balfour and Austen Chamberlain remained in the pavilion. The Cabinet's leading figures were the accommodating Curzon as Foreign Secretary and Baldwin, whom Asquith had described as "the nicest fellow in the (previous) Government" as Chancellor of the Exchequer.[1] "A clever lawyer called Pig," as Derby and Devonshire had reputedly referred to Sir Douglas Hogg, provided the Government with its main debating strength.*t*

Bonar Law at once dissolved Parliament and presented this team to the country under the watch-word of tranquillity. Lloyd George fought with his usual gyratory energy and a very small band of adherents. "We are asked to choose," announced Asquith's daughter, in one of the few remarkable phrases of a rather flat election, "between one man suffering from Sleeping Sickness and another from St. Vitus's Dance."

In Paisley, however, the choice was once again between Asquith and the persevering Biggar. It was made in Asquith's favour, but only by a margin much narrower than in the 1920 by-election. He was in by 316.

"I went to the counting at Paisley shortly before midnight on Wednesday," he wrote two days later (November 17th), "and watched the process until about 1.30 a.m. when the result was

[1] McKenna, out of politics since 1918, was offered the job, but declined it on the ground that, failing an independent Tory majority, he wished to promote a coalition between Bonar Law and Asquith.

495

declared. We had been assured that all was more than safe, so that I was not a little surprised to find when I arrived that it was beginning to look like a neck-and-neck affair. I had quite an exciting hour while the numbers fluctuated up and down, keeping on the whole almost even: indeed it was not until the last quarter of an hour that we forged ahead, and proceeded to win (as the racing people say) 'cleverly.' I polled more votes than I did three years ago, and the drop in the majority was entirely due to the enormous addition to the Labour vote, owing to the 5,000 unemployed in Paisley (of whom there were none in 1920) and the sullen anti-bourgeois feeling which is swelling like a tidal wave over the whole of the West of Scotland . . . . The general result does not greatly surprise me. The suicide of the Coalition before the election took much of the punch out of the fight, and left the country divided between Tranquillity and Socialism."[u1]

What the general result gave was a large Tory phalanx of 344 members, confronted by a Labour Party of 138 (twice its previous strength and enough, for the first time, to enable it to form a real opposition) and 117 Liberals. These last were divided into 60 Asquithians and 57 Lloyd Georgites. In one sense the result was much worse for Lloyd George than for Asquith. Within a short time he had crashed from a great height. "Lloyd George can be Prime Minister for life if he likes," Bonar Law had said less than two years before. But in another sense it was still more depressing for Asquith. He had fought on a much broader front than Lloyd George, putting up 348 candidates to secure his meagre harvest of 60; and although his group was a little bigger than its rival, the difference was so small that he could no longer be regarded as the only guardian of the true Liberal faith. The anti-Pope was almost as strong as the Pope. Furthermore, the country seemed set for a long period of Conservative Government.

The election also produced a notable crop of casualties. In the same letter in which he recounted his own close result at Paisley, Asquith wrote about these: "For the moment the thing that gives me the most satisfaction is to gloat over the corpses which have been left on the battlefield, Winston, Hamar Greenwood, Freddie Guest, Montagu, Kellaway—all of them renegades. . . . I am terribly disappointed at the loss of Donald Maclean and Geoffrey Howard. They are both most difficult to replace."[v] Asquith's grief was more genuine than his

[1] A more accurate but less picturesque description than his daughter's.

" gloating." Had it been otherwise he would hardly have written so openly about the latter. No doubt for the moment he felt it appropriate that the former lieutenants who had sailed so triumphantly (and unconcernedly) past his shipwreck of 1918 should find their own rocks. But this feeling—so alien to Asquith's nature—quickly passed. In particular he recovered something of his old affection for Churchill and Montagu. A few months later he saw Churchill at the wedding of the Duke and Duchess of York (subsequently King George VI and Queen Elizabeth), and wrote about him almost in the old pre-1915 way:

I sat in the stalls with a curious little knot of neighbours: Ramsay MacDonald, and Clynes (who wore black frock-coats), Buckmaster, Simon and Winston Churchill! The ennui of the long waits were relieved for me by being next to Winston, who was in his best form and really amusing. Between two fugues (or whatever they are called) on the organ, he expounded to me his housing policy: " Build the house round the wife and mother: let her always have water on the boil: make her the central factor. The dominating condition of the situation," etc. etc.—in his most rhetorical vein. [w]

And two years after this, when Churchill had found his way into a Conservative Government, Asquith wrote: " At lunch we had amongst others Winston Churchill, who was in his best form: he is a Chimborazo or Everest among the sandhills of the Baldwin Cabinet." [x] Montagu had been re-admitted earlier to Bedford Square. " The Spanish Duke and Duchess of Alba, who were very kind to Margot in Spain," Asquith wrote on October 10th, 1923, " came to lunch: also Edwin Montagu, who had not been at our table for at least four years. . . . He is, as he always was, excellent company." [y]

After the 1922 election the remaining years of Asquith's life were a period for the healing of old quarrels and the forgiving of old wounds. The bitterness of 1916 to 1921, was largely past. The least genuine of the reconciliations was that with Lloyd George. It was the one which was most forced by circumstances. In the new Parliament it was obvious that the two Liberal groups faced a doubtful future in any event—and none at all unless they could come together. The natural tendency of the backbenchers was in this direction. Within a week of the assembly of the House Asquith wrote:

There was a kind of " fraternity " gathering last night in one of the Committee rooms between the rank and file of our lot and the ex-Coalie Liberals. The latter seem prepared to " re-unite " on almost any terms. . . . Meanwhile Ll.G. is evidently dallying with visions of reconciliation. He took Hogge[1] . . . into his room last night and talked to him for an hour and a half in his most mellifluous vein. Amongst other things he declared that he was quite ready to serve with and under me (!), with whom he had never had a quarrel and whom he had never ceased to admire and respect![2]

Asquith gave little active ancouragement to these unity moves. He believed that Lloyd George (who quickly announced that he was " neither a suppliant nor a penitent ") should make the running. The natural tendency was towards a hesitant reunion, but something more than this was needed, and from where was the catalyst to come? Suddenly, in the early autumn of 1923, Baldwin (who had succeeded to the premiership in the spring) provided it. At Plymouth, on October 22nd, he announced that protection was the only remedy for unemployment and that the Government would seek a new mandate for this view.

It was almost 1903 all over again. The only differences were that Asquith was twenty years older, the issue was a little staler, and the Liberal Party was not quite what it had been. But a surge to unity resulted. In mid-November Parliament was again dissolved. A Liberal Free Trade manifesto, signed first by Asquith and then by Lloyd George, was quickly issued. The election which followed resulted in substantial Conservative losses and moderate Labour and Liberal gains. Asquith, by chance, had an easier run in Paisley than in 1922. Biggar's vote was split by the intervention of a semi-Communist candidate. In these circumstances it hardly needed one of the most remarkable political occasions of the ' twenties—a visit of support from Lloyd George—to ensure his return. But it took place:

" At 7 o'clock Sat. evening," Asquith wrote to Mrs. Harrisson, " the rites of Liberal Reunion were celebrated at an enthusiastic meeting in the Town Hall. Ll.G. arrived with his Megan, and I was accompanied by Margot and Violet. I have rarely felt less exhilaration than when we got to the platform amid wild plaudits and a flash-light film was taken, ' featuring ' me and Ll.G. separated only by the chairman—an excellent local Doctor. I spoke for about quarter of an hour, and Ll.G. then plunged into a

[1] Asquith's new whip, not an exotic spelling of the Attorney-General.

characteristic speech—ragged and boisterous, but with quite a good assortment of telling points. He was more than friendly and forthcoming, and the meeting was full of demonstrative fraternity. After it was over, Ll.G. and Megan, and their bodyguard of secretaries and detectives, were swept off by their host, Lord Maclay, to some baronial retreat, and we supped here in peace."[aa]1

For the rest Asquith's campaign was energetic, enthusiastic (he loved the Free Trade cause), and curiously badly planned. " I have been living the life of a dog," he wrote on December 2nd: " much of it wasted in long railway journeys." In one week he spent the whole of Monday travelling from Paisley to Nottingham (although he was compensated by an audience of 10,000 when he got there), the whole of Tuesday travelling back, most of Thursday going to Manchester, Friday in agreeable idleness at Alderley (an echo from the past), and Saturday on his way back once more to Paisley.

Four days before the poll he wrote:

I have been going through the general list of candidates, and I cannot for the life of me see how we are going to come back more than 200 strong, it may be less. Labour is the dark horse. The result which I should welcome would be that we should exceed Labour and Baldwin find himself with a majority of 30 to 40— useless for his purpose, but sufficient to compel him to go on with the Government.[bb]

In fact the Liberals were well short of 200 at 158, and none of Asquith's other wishes were achieved. Baldwin, with 285 seats, lacked even a bare majority over the combination of his opponents; and the Labour Party, with 191 seats, was well ahead of the Liberals. Almost any Government would have been possible in this Parliament,

---

1 As " here " was on this occasion not the Central Hotel, Glasgow, but Ferguslie Park, Paisley, which Asquith had previously described as " a typical millionaire villa with some Corots, a Sir Joshua, and a Hoppner intermixed with family photographs, and some sentimental Victorian mezzotints," his strictures against " some baronial retreat," even though the irony was kindly, was hardly justified. Lady Bonham Carter (as she then was) added to the gaiety of this occasion by making the final speech and proclaiming, in response to obvious jokes about " the lion lying down with the lamb ": " I can only say, for myself, that I have never seen Mr. Lloyd George look less voracious or my father more uneatable." (Memories and Reflections, II, p. 180).

but Asquith, who was clearly the pivotal figure, seems to have decided at an early stage that it had better be a Labour one. He regarded the protection issue as so dominant that there could be no question of his supporting the Conservatives. As the leader of the smallest of the three parties he had no claim himself to independent office; and he recoiled instinctively from a coalition. Furthermore, he was anxious that the Labour Party should not be soured by the opposition of a " bourgeois " alliance. And he was able to comfort the conservative part of his conscience with the reflection that " if a Labour Government is ever to be tried in this country, as it will be sooner or later, it could hardly be tried under safer conditions."

These views he communicated to a Liberal Party meeting on December 18th. They were supported by Lloyd George and accepted by the meeting. From then on it was assumed that the meeting of Parliament in January would be quickly followed by the accession of the first Labour Government in the history of Britain. But there were some who went on appealing to Asquith to save them from this fate. He was by no means displeased to receive these appeals, though he had no intention of responding to them.

" You would be amused if you saw the contents of my daily post-bag," he wrote on December 28th: " appeals, threats, prayers from all parts, and from all sorts and conditions of men, women, and lunatics, to step in and save the country from the horrors of Socialism and Confiscation. . . . One cannot help contrasting the situation with that only exactly five years ago, in December, 1918, when I and all the faithful lost our seats, and were supposed to be sentenced to damnation for the rest of our political lives.

The City is suffering from an acute attack of nerves at the prospect of a Labour Government. One of the leading bankers came to see me this morning with a message from the City Conservatives, that if only I would set up an Asquith-Grey Government, all the *solid* people in the country would support it through thick and thin. Isn't it an amusing whirligig? "cc1

¹ Some financiers were willing to help Asquith even more actively. Sir Alfred Mond (ex-Coalition Liberal, soon to be the first Lord Melchett) wrote from a steamship at Port Said on January 22nd: " I am writing to let you know that if by any chance in my absence you may be called on and decide to form a Government, my services are entirely at your disposal. . . . To be quite frank I would very much like an opportunity of filling the post of

He remained convinced that it was right for him to vote for the Labour amendment to the Conservative Government's address; and he assumed that this would put Baldwin out and MacDonald in. He was less convinced, however, that it was right for either of these leaders to act as he assumed that they would. On January 10th he wrote from a sick-bed (" where I have been for 3 consecutive days for the first time for 40 years ") to W. M. R. Pringle:

It would seem that the immediate future is now settled: that Baldwin is to resign and Ramsay to come in. I doubt whether either of them is right. Baldwin could easily have snapped his fingers at the no confidence amendment and announced that, as leader of much the largest section of the House, he had better moral authority than anyone else to carry on the King's Government until he was absolutely blocked, and Ramsay might well have declined to start the first Labour Government under impossible Parliamentary conditions. . . . I agree of course that we must give the Labour Government a reasonable chance, at the same time being careful not to arouse the suspicion that we are acting in collusion with a new Coalition."*dd*

A week later the vote took place. Five days after that Ramsay MacDonald announced his Cabinet. " The new Labour Government . . . is indeed for the most part a beggarly array," Asquith wrote. " I had a nice and really touching letter from Haldane (the new Lord Chancellor) this morning.[1] He says he is (as well he may be) full of ' misgiving '."*ee* But Asquith never doubted that he had been right to put the Government in. He was on the whole impressed by Mac-Donald's handling of foreign affairs and wrote of " the delight " of the Foreign Office at being " relieved of the incubus of the Archduke Curzon." Few other aspects of the Government's performance earned his approval. His old parliamentary mandarin spirit was much to the

Chancellor of the Exchequer." He did not have a seat, but was sure he could get one. (*Asquith Papers*, box XVIII, ff. 94–7).

[1] Strangely, Asquith's personal relations with Haldane were closer after their definite political separation (which occurred in 1922) than they had been in the preceding decade. They exchanged fairly frequent letters, which were always warm but brief; Haldane read the proof of *The Genesis of the War;* and they enjoyed occasional luncheons or dinners in each other's company.

fore, and the best that he could do was to forgive the Labour ministers their ineptitude.

His followers, however, were often less inclined to be forgiving than he was. One difficulty was a lack of consultation between the Labour and Liberal parties. There was a basic contradiction in the situation. The Government was absolutely dependent on Liberal votes, but many Labour members regarded the possessors of these votes as class enemies, little if any better than the Tories. In these circumstances close co-operation was impossible. By the late summer of 1924 most Liberal M.P.s were tired of supporting the Government. Asquith took a more friendly view of the Russian Treaty than the majority of his followers. Then came the Campbell Case. The Government first initiated and then withdrew a prosecution for sedition against the editor of the *Daily Worker*. It looked as though the Attorney-General had responded to political pressure. A parliamentary storm blew up at the beginning of October. The Tories put down a vote of censure. Asquith sought a middle course by tabling an amendment in favour of investigation by a select committee of the House of Commons. It was a device of which he remained peculiarly fond throughout his political life—despite his experience of the Marconi investigation. In a sense it was the Maurice debate over again. Asquith's speech rehearsed many of the arguments which he had used on that occasion, and MacDonald maintained the pattern by throwing back the amendment as an intolerable attack upon the Government.

But there were at least three differences. The first was that Lloyd George, on this occasion, both spoke and voted in favour of the enquiry. The second was that Asquith's motion now commanded the support of a big majority of the House of Commons. It was carried by 364 to 198, and MacDonald immediately applied for a dissolution of Parliament. The third and consequential difference was that Asquith's speech in favour of this motion was the last that he was ever to make in the House of Commons. The green benches and the battered despatch boxes which he had known for so long he was to know no longer. The first Labour Government and his elected parliamentary career perished together, the one after eight months, the other after 38 years.

CHAPTER XXX

THE LAST PHASE

1924-8

When Asquith held up the knife upon which MacDonald became impaled, he was perfectly aware that he might be doing more harm to himself than to the Labour Party. But he did not see what else he could do. He could not withdraw his amendment because the Prime Minister did not like it. He could not support the Government on the case they had put up. Once again the Maurice analogy was obvious: his sense of political tactics was overcome by his sense of parliamentary propriety.

The outlook which confronted him on the dissolution was dismal enough. At the age of 72, without any hope of a great national triumph, he had to journey to Paisley and fight his fourth campaign there within five years. One " Midlothian " might be stimulating for an old man, but four were another matter. Apart from anything else the personal expense was considerable. And on the wider Liberal financial front there were great difficulties about a 1924 election. Lloyd George had made it clear in August that, without a complete re-casting of the Abingdon Street organisation, he would not make as much money available from his personal fund as he had done in 1923. The honeymoon of Liberal re-union, never ecstatic, was over. This dispute about money was to persist throughout Asquith's remaining period of Liberal leadership.

Asquith faced the Paisley contest with his usual equanimity. Margot thought he was exceptionally oratorically vigorous. " I've never seen H. in such amazing form!" she wrote on October 25th. But his daughter Violet, who was a better judge in this field, thought that the campaign was the hardest of the four to flog into life: " The Campbell case and the Russian Treaty were short commons on which to feed a hungry electorate for three weeks, and Father and I used to fling ourselves on the papers every morning in the wild hope of finding some utterance, by friend or foe, which might form a peg on which to hang one of the many speeches which had to be delivered before nightfall."

The Paisley atmosphere was not pleasant. The "jungle tactics of Glasgow" had spread there. Asquith had to put up with a good deal of noise. But he took it all very calmly. As his daughter recorded in her diary:

His patience was as impersonal as if he had been waiting for a shower of rain to pass. When a musical offensive began he might ask me with a sudden detached curiosity: "What is that melancholy dirge they are crooning now?" On my telling him it was the Red Flag he would evince mild interest, than lean back in his chair again with a sniff and a shrug and resume his own train of thought. When they had sung and shouted themselves hoarse he would rise and deliver with perfect calm the speech he had come there to make, quite untinged by any shade of indignation at the events which had delayed it.[a]

On the other hand the local voting prospect looked encouraging. Asquith was without a Conservative opponent. He had a straight fight with a new Labour candidate, a Glasgow solicitor named Rosslyn Mitchell. Margot, however, was sceptical of the advantage of Conservative withdrawal.

"Here it is of doubtful benefit," she wrote to her old friend Lord Islington, "as the Tories—the stupidest people in the world—are so angry they threaten to vote for our *very* powerful opponent. Mitchell is better dressed than Peter Flower, is highly educated and no more Labour than you, an orator wind-bag and dangerously courteous with a face like the actor John Hare, only handsomer. He may run us very close."

Mitchell did more than that. He beat Asquith by 2,228 votes. When it was over he looked intensely depressed and said "I'm so sorry, so terribly sorry this has happened." Asquith merely grunted and seconded a vote of thanks to the returning officer. The next morning he and his family party had another railway departure from Glasgow, different but in its way no less memorable than that of 1920. Asquith's daughter is again the chronicler:

We had a difficult send-off, at Glasgow, saying good-bye to faithful old supporters there, who came with tears and flowers. As we steamed out of the station, I lay back feeling bruised from head to foot—and recoiling instinctively from the pile of news-papers that lay by my side—their head-lines stinging me like adders. I looked across at Father in an agony of solicitude (for I knew how the good-byes had moved him)—then meeting his calm gaze I realized suddenly that he had already made his peace with events. Groping wildly for a life-line that might draw me into smooth waters by his side, I asked in as steady a voice as possible: " I suppose you haven't by any chance got an old P. G. Wodehouse in your bag that you could lend me? " A smile of instant response, mingled I thought with relief, lit up his face as he replied triumphantly: " Being a provident man I have got in my bag, not one, but *four brand new* ones! " My wounds were healed—for I knew that he was invulnerable.[b]

At Euston there were also cheering crowds of welcome. But they could not disguise the extent of the defeat either for Asquith or for the Liberal Party as a whole. It was reduced to 40 members, with Lloyd George the natural leader in the Commons. What could Asquith do? There could be no question of his going back to Paisley, in spite of the affecting singing of " Will ye no' come back again? " to which he had been subjected in the Liberal Club the night before. Baldwin had a huge majority and was not likely to repeat the mistake of 1923. At seventy-two Asquith could hardly look forward to the next general election. Should he then seek a safe Liberal seat elsewhere? There were not many left, and in any case he was fastidious. " I'd sooner go to hell than to Wales," he told C. F. G. Masterman.

On November 4th, the King wrote and offered him another haven. Asquith's absence from Westminster, the letter said, was " a national loss." On the other hand the King felt strongly that, after his long and eminent career, he should not be subjected to the strain and uncertainty of further electoral contests. " For these reasons it would be a matter of the greatest satisfaction to me to confer upon you a Peerage. . . . If I could persuade you to (accept) this, it would give *me great pleasure*."[c]

The letter was most tactfully timed. It was sent on the day of the change of Prime Minister. The offer was therefore able to come from the King himself, without the intervention of any of Asquith's suc-cessors. This consideration was appreciated by Asquith, and he was from the start greatly tempted by the offer. But there were pulls the other way. It was a wrench finally to abandon the House of Commons after so many years of service there. There were obvious difficulties, too, in trying to lead the Liberal Party from the Lords, while Lloyd George held sway in the Commons. Then there was the consideration that so much of his active life had been spent in battling against the Upper House; was there perhaps an element of bathos in ending up there after all this? The change of name was also a hurdle. To die, as he had so far lived, in the great commoner tradition of Mr. Pitt and Mr. Gladstone was not something to be lightly abandoned. Nor, at a time when high titles were still considered to require the backing of great fortunes, was he financially secure.

Asquith therefore delayed a decision. On November 6th he was due to leave with his son Oc for a tour of the Middle East and the Nile Valley. He asked the King if he could postpone an answer until his return in January. While he was away Asquith had plenty of time for thought. He spent much of the visit alone, including a week in the First Cataract Hotel at Assuan where he wrote 14,000 words of a new book (*Fifty Years of Parliament*). By the time of his return to England his mind was made up in favour of acceptance. On January, 20th, 1925, he wrote to the King:

I have ventured to take full advantage of your Majesty's kind permission that I should delay a definite reply to the gracious offer of a Peerage, conveyed to me in November last, until I should have had time for mature and deliberate consideration.

The consideration involved, as your Majesty will understand, matters both personal and political of perhaps exceptional delicacy and difficulty. As a result, I now have the honour respectfully to submit my grateful acceptance of your Majesty's proposal. . . .

If it should be your Majesty's pleasure, in accordance with precedent, to confer upon me the dignity of an Earl, I should propose to take the title of Oxford, which has fine traditions in our history, and which was given by Queen Anne to her Prime Minister, Robert Harley.[d]

The King replied three days later:

It is with great satisfaction that I have received your letter of the 20th inst., accepting in, if I may say so, such charming terms, the offer of a Peerage. . . Your Peerage will of course be an Earldom, and subject to the necessary references to the College of Arms which will at once be made, I shall be very glad that the historic title of Earl of Oxford should now be restored in your favour. I have informed the Prime Minister.[e]

The title of Oxford was, of course, somewhat " grand." It might almost have been a royal one, in the category of Cambridge or Gloucester or York. Even apart from the University significance, it was a more imposing territorial designation than that chosen by any ennobled Prime Minister, or indeed by any politician, except for Lord Norwich (formerly Duff Cooper), in the past hundred years. Yet Asquith had a very good claim to it. He was the most distinguished Oxonian then alive and he had epitomised the methods and style of his University—or at least of a leading college within it. In addition, he had lived for much of the preceding fifteen years within striking distance of the city, and was a familiar figure in its streets and at its tables.

Many recognised this, and wrote with pleasure of his choice. The Bishop of Durham (Henson) stated: " There is no living statesman who has a better right to have his name thus closely bound to his University." Maurice Baring wrote: " Many congratulations. It is a nice Shakespearean title." The Master of Balliol (Lindsay), announced his pleasure " that the College has at least some share in your title." Lytton Strachey described it as " singularly suitable "; Max Beerbohm wrote to say how glad he was that it had been chosen; and Dean Inge apologised for not having written before " to congratulate you on your accession to the grandest of all English titles." Gilbert Murray mingled congratulation with regret, but at the passing of Asquith's commoner status and not at the new name:

My dear Mr. Asquith: I must write to you once more in the old name that I have learnt to love and honour and which I associate with so much kindness to myself. The new title is splendid; better than one could have expected. I hardly know why the change should make one sad.

The Bishop of Oxford (Burge) was so little worried by having to share his territorial name in the House of Lords that he wrote an enthusiastic letter beginning " My Lord Chieftain "; and Lord Shaw of Dunfermline, a former Scottish law officer, went one better with " My dear and revered Chief."*f*

Elsewhere, however, there were some mutterings and raised eyebrows. Such titles as Oxford, it was suggested, were not for radical leaders, however eminent, particularly if they were of non-patrician origin.

" It is like a suburban villa calling itself Versailles," the present Lady Salisbury, then a very young woman, took it upon herself to inform the new peer. Asquith found her letter funny rather than wounding and himself spread the story around.

Others suggested that the King ought to stop it. But the King, as has been seen, was in favour. The most sustained hostility came from some descendants of the Earls of Oxford of the second creation— Asquith's was the third creation. J. R. H. Harley wrote from Herefordshire to ask Asquith not to take the title, and when he received no reply, wrote again in more offensive terms:

Sir,

I am sorry that you have not thought fit to answer my letter of the 27th ult. In writing to you as head of the Harley family and living at the home of the late Earls of Oxford, I should have thought that my letter would have had some consideration from you. However, I see that you have decided to ignore all requests. Perhaps you consider old traditions and sentiments to be of no account in these days.

Yours faithfully,

J. R. H. Harley [9]

He still got no reply. Perhaps it was the syntax as much as the substance which made Asquith loath to supply one. Then came a similar letter from a Lady Duplin, who was also a Harley connection, but the effect of this was diminished by her cousin writing on the following day and begging Asquith to take no notice of " a lot of rubbish."

The College of Heralds, however, supported the Harley interest to the extent of insisting on the clumsier double title of *Oxford and Asquith*. This would not have been Asquith's own choice, for he disliked complicated names.[1] His peerage was gazetted on February

---

[1] In 1916 he had given a " step " to the Earl of Aberdeen. The new marquess had insisted on changing to the double name of *Aberdeen* and *Temair*, and Asquith had commented rather adversely. In 1925 he recalled this, at least to the extent of talking about it to the King and telling Mrs. Harrisson of an old anecdote which formed part of the conversation: " Lady A. sent to a friend a photograph of herself with a Scotch terrier on her knee signed with the new style. The friend replied with effusive thanks, adding, ' It was so nice, too, to see your little dog Temair.' This, Asquith added, made the King " roar with laughter." (*Letters from Lord Oxford to a Friend*, II, p. 124).

10th and his status was changed " for better or for worse, but at any rate for good and all." Not taking his new rank too seriously, Asquith noted that his butler, Clouder, " did his best to live up to the occasion, and his first ' My Lord ' had an unmistakable tinge of delicate court-liness."[h] On February 17th, sponsored by Balfour and Beauchamp, he took his seat in the House of Lords.

Asquith became a moderately frequent attender and speaker in his new chamber: the demands were not heavy, for it sat only two days a week at the time. But, unlike some more recent political ennoble-ments, he never developed any respect for its deliberative quality. "The standard of speaking there is deplorably low," he wrote on March 26th: " men like —— and —— and —— would hardly be listened to in an average County Council. They mumble away a lot of spine-less and disconnected platitudes."[i] And again on June 30th: " It is an impossible audience: as Lowe said fifty years ago, it is like ' speaking by torchlight to corpses in a charnel-house '."[j] In his first six weeks he thought that he listened to only one good speech, and that was " poor Curzon's last " on March 4th. A fortnight later Curzon was dead, and Asquith made his own maiden speech during an afternoon of tributes. It was appropriate, moving and effective, as might have been expected. Even had bitterness still been there, Asquith would have allowed no trace of it to show on an occasion like this. But in fact it had long since disappeared. Curzon was an old friend, and Asquith, never a man for rancour, felt sadness at his going and a sense of his own increasing isolation.

" Poor George Curzon died quietly at 5 this morning," he wrote, " after a fortnight of pain and constant restlessness. It is exactly a fortnight since I heard him speak in the House of Lords, appar-ently in full vigour, excellent form and high spirits. He was seven years younger than I am, and I have known him ever since I examined him, as a schoolboy at Eton, very nearly fifty years ago. We entered the House of Commons in the same election in 1886. It makes one feel, as Browning says in the *Toccata*, ' chilly and grown old '."[k]

A few months before a much younger and closer friend of previous days had gone. In November, 1924, Edwin Montagu had died at the age of forty-five. A few days later Venetia Montagu wrote to Asquith —the first letter to pass between them for nearly ten years:

My dearest Mr. Asquith,

We found this letter for you amongst Edwin's papers, written, I think, just before he went to India. I know it is not necessary for me to tell you how deeply he loved you and what a real and lasting grief your political separation was. He always used to say that tho' he was still absorbingly interested in his work after he left you, it was no longer any fun.

I feel I am terribly lucky to have had $9\frac{1}{2}$ such happy years and that I was able, owing to my very unimaginative and unapprehensive frame of mind, to help him sometimes to cast off those great fears and glooms which used to torture him. Do you remember how we used to laugh at him in Sicily?

Thank you for all you did for him to make his life happy. He was always grateful to you.

All my love,

Venetia [l]

Then she wrote again, when Asquith was in Egypt:

My darling Mr. Asquith,

Edwin asked me to give you something of his and I finally thought you might like this Hamlet which I'd given him a long time ago. I've never thanked you for your divine letter, you know how dumb and inarticulate I am, but you do realise I hope how glad I was to get it. I hope I may see you sometime when you get back.

Much love always,

Venetia [m]

Thereafter there was an occasional interchange, both of letters and of visits.

The early months of 1925 were a time of accumulating evening honours for Asquith. In May, following his earldom, he accepted the Garter from Baldwin. And in June, with a typical combination of good sense and easy gratitude, he accepted the robes—free:

I have just had a noble offer from Lady Breadalbane—a widow— —who proposes to give me her late husband's (he was a K.G.) Garter robes as a present. I shall jump at this, as it will save me a lot of money. [n]

Then the process faltered. Curzon's death created a vacancy, not only in the Lord Presidency of the Council, which Balfour filled, but in the Chancellorship of the University of Oxford. Asquith was an obviously suitable candidate for this office, and there was immediately a move for his nomination. He would have greatly valued the honour, more than any which had come his way since 1908. He therefore accepted with alacrity, but with no misplaced optimism. " The plot thickens around the Oxford Chancellorship," he wrote at an early stage, " and as it seems more than probable that the Tories will run a candidate . . . we will have an interesting contest, though with our friends the country clergy in full blast, the result is a foregone conclusion."⁰

At first there was a plan, fostered by Blakiston, the President of Trinity, to run Randall Davidson as a clerical candidate against Asquith, but the Archbishop refused and wrote to Asquith expressing the hope that he would be elected without a contest, although not failing to point out that his own support came from a " rather big group." Then Cave, the Lord Chancellor of the day, was enrolled as a substitute candidate. He was at once a friend of Asquith's, the least distinguished occupant of the Woolsack of the first thirty years of this century, and an Oxonian of no great university fame. None of these considerations disqualified him from the support of the bulk of Oxford M.As. They were determined to pay off some party scores against Asquith, and perhaps to make a mild mockery of his title as well.

" Lord Oxford," Birkenhead wrote to The Times, " is the greatest living Oxonian. If he were a Conservative he would be elected by acclamation. To reject him because he is a Liberal is to admit partisan prejudices as narrow as they are discreditable." But the " partisan prejudices" were freely admitted. Asquith got much the more distinguished list of supporters, but, as he noted, " unfortunately it is not the elect who form the big battalions of voters." The " cavemen" also had their published lists of adherents, mostly the lesser known, but including a fair number of Heads of Houses and, " of all people," Lord Robert Cecil. Essentially, however their strength was inarticulate, hidden away in country rectories, and quiet manor houses. It showed itself on the days of the poll. Asquith was defeated by 987 votes to 441.

Although he had expected defeat, he felt it heavily. Desmond MacCarthy, who knew him well, wrote that it affected him " more than any disappointment, save one, in his life after he ceased to be Prime Minister." The successful candidate, Lord Cave, held the Chancellorship for only two years. Edward Grey (who left Balliol without a degree) was then elected without opposition.

Politics provided Asquith with little consolation. The two-headed leadership of the Liberal Party posed impossible problems. Asquith, in the Lords, exercised titular authority over the whole party. Lloyd George, in the Commons, was chairman of the small parliamentary party. The armies to be led, even had there been no question of sharing the command, were hardly adequate to the reputation and experience of either. But the command had to be shared: it was like appointing Field-Marshals Haig and French to the same infantry battalion and expecting the result to be a contented co-operation.

Asquith made some attempt to get back on to reasonable personal terms with Lloyd George. Margot and he even had him to luncheon at Bedford Square—with the Queen of Roumania, Desmond Mac-Carthy and Viola Tree—an event which would have seemed inconceivable five years before. But Asquith's heart was hardly in this *rapprochement;* and Lloyd George's certainly was not. His position had perhaps become the more difficult of the two. His fall from power had been more recent and more precipitate. His international fame was unparalleled, and his energy, at this stage at least, not only appeared to be, but was much greater than Asquith's. Yet he had to occupy the subordinate position.

There was one respect, however, in which his position was far from subordinate. He had the money. The Lloyd George Fund far exceeded any sums which the Liberal Party as such was able to command. Lloyd George was determined to preserve this position, and the power which it gave him. He argued that the terms on which the Fund had been raised made it illegal for him to hand it over to the Liberal Party. At one stage the Liberal Shadow Cabinet proposed that this should be tested before a Chancery lawyer, but it would have required more than counsel's opinion to make Lloyd George hand over these resources to the Chief Whip.

The issue naturally caused great bitterness within the Liberal Party. The separate existence of the Fund was a constant reminder both of the incompleteness of the Liberal re-marriage and of the profitable if doubtfully respectable past of the Liberal Coalitionists. Nor did Lloyd George try to use the Fund in such a way as to assuage the bitterness. At the 1924 election he had not hesitated to force a reduction in the number of Liberal candidates from a projected 500 to 343. The money was there, but he made only a relatively small sum (£60,000) available.

Asquith responded with some impatience and more distaste. He disliked concerning himself with money, most of all political money. He believed that such matters should be left to the Chief Whip and not obtrude upon the party leader. But Lloyd George made the continuation of this old practice impossible. Asquith either had to raise a substantial sum under his own aegis or see his authority drained away by the pull of Lloyd George's money. Accordingly, in January 1925, he launched the so-called Million Fund Appeal. The sponsoring body was the National Liberal Federation, and the purpose was clearly to make Asquith and the party independent of the money which Lloyd George would only grudgingly and conditionally dispense.

The Appeal was not a success. Some money came in, but not nearly enough. Partly, no doubt, this was because of lack of confidence in the future of the Liberal Party generally. But it was also due to the existence of the Lloyd George Fund. This pervasive *cache* was responsible both for the launching and for the failure of the Appeal. Rich Liberal supporters did not see why they should subscribe when the leader of the party in the House of Commons had large sums of money—to which they had probably contributed—already at his disposal.

The failure of the Appeal weakened Asquith *vis-à-vis* Lloyd George. This was pointedly brought home during the autumn of 1925. Lloyd George had presided over a committee of enquiry charged with a review of Liberal land policy. The result was a controversial scheme, which was strongly opposed by a number of leading Liberals, notably Runciman, Charles Hobhouse and Mond. They protested to Asquith against Lloyd George mounting a public campaign in favour of his own proposals before they had been accepted by the party. Asquith asked Lloyd George about his intentions. Lloyd George replied intransigently that he proposed to act in accord with " the whole tradition of independent Liberal initiatives . . . ranging from the anti-Corn Law League, through the Liberation Society to various campaigns for local option and even prohibition." Asquith then wrote one of the few letters of rebuke which he ever sent to Lloyd George. There was to be a conference to thrash the whole matter out. In the meantime he " strongly deprecated a great campaign led by the Liberal leader in the House of Commons on an issue which was not accepted as (party) policy."[p]

The effect of the rebuke upon Lloyd George was negligible. He continued his campaign (supported by his own Fund); the conference broadly endorsed his policy; and Asquith had to come into line with a speech at a joint meeting in February, 1926. This incident did much both to disenchant Asquith with the terms on which he held the Liberal leadership and to weaken his always precarious post-1922 relationship with Lloyd George. It only needed one more incident to provoke a severance. This incident was quickly provided.

The General Strike began on May 3rd, 1926. On that day the Liberal Shadow Cabinet met, and there seemed to be no great difference of opinion amongst those present (including Lloyd George) as to what the party attitude should be. On the following day Asquith spoke in the House of Lords, unreservedly condemning the strike and supporting the Government's efforts to resist it, although adding some words of criticism of their handling of the coal dispute. In addition, he and Grey each sent messages in a similar sense to the emergency paper, the *British Gazette*, and Simon used the House of Commons to condemn the strike as illegal. But Lloyd George spoke, if not in a directly contrary sense, at least in a very different one. He condemned the Government more than he condemned the strike; and he wrote a syndicated article for the American Press (a regular commitment at the time), which was pessimistic about the Government's ability to win the day.

As a result of these differences, Lloyd George did not attend the next meeting of the Shadow Cabinet (on May 10th), and wrote saying that he was refraining from doing so on policy grounds. Asquith at first did not appear to take this defection too seriously:

" When I came up yesterday morning to our ' Shadow Cabinet ' at Abingdon Street," he wrote to Mrs. Harrisson on May 11th, " there was one notable absentee—Ll.G.—who was in the sulks, and had cast in his lot for the moment with the clericals—Archbishops and Deans and the whole company of the various Churches (a hopeless lot)—in the hope of getting a foothold for himself in the Labour camp. He is already, being a creature of uncertain temperament, suffering from cold feet. So much so, that I have a message this morning from Miss Stevenson asking me to arrange for a joint meeting in July at Carnarvon, which he and I are to address!"*q*

A few days later, perhaps because of the representations of colleagues, or because of reflection on previous difficulties, Asquith came to take a more serious view of the matter. On May 20th, he wrote Lloyd George a long and somewhat portentous letter. He rehearsed the events leading up to the meeting of May 10th:

All my colleagues attended with the notable exception of your-self. The reasons for your absence, as set out in a letter dated the same morning, seem to me to be wholly inadequate. . . . It was, in my judgment, the primary duty of all who were responsible for Liberal policy, and certainly not least of the Chairman of the Par-liamentary Party in the House of Commons, at such a time to meet together for free and full discussion, and to contribute their counsels to the common stock. Your refusal to do so I find im-possible to reconcile with my conception of the obligations of political comradeship.[r]

After despatching this letter Asquith retired to Castle Howard in Yorkshire. While there he was pressed by his closest colleagues, including his host, Geoffrey Howard, to announce that he would explain his whole position in an early public speech. But he refused to do more than telegraph a peremptory instruction for the publication of his letter on May 20th. He greatly overestimated the degree of Liberal support which this would win. Nor did he allow for the obvious consideration that Lloyd George would respond by himself publishing a persuasive and subtle reply. This was issued on May 25th. The effect was made more damaging by the non-publication of Lloyd George's original letter of May 10th. It looked as though Asquith had started a largely unprovoked quarrel.

He returned to London to find a situation of unforeseen difficulty. On June 1st, he wrote to the Chief Whip what was in effect a reply to Lloyd George's letter of May 24th; he could no longer bring himself to communicate direct with the leader in the Commons. In this letter to Sir Godfrey Collins Asquith laid great stress on Shadow Cabinet responsibility, equating it with the real thing: "I have sat in many Cabinets under various Prime Ministers, and I have not known one of them who would not have treated such a communication from a colleague, sent at such a time, as equivalent to a resignation." He also raised, for the first time, the question of his own position:

I am this month completing forty years of service to the Liberal Party. For a considerable part of the time I have been its Leader, and I have honestly striven, during the last two years, to recreate

and to revive the broken fabric of Liberal unity. It has been a
burdensome, and in some of its aspects, a thankless task. I will
not continue to hold the leadership for a day unless I am satisfied
that I retain in full measure the confidence of the party.[s]

On the same day twelve of his leading colleagues[1] wrote to him
(and published in *The Times*) a letter of unqualified support. But,
once again, it was "not the elect who form the big battalions of
voters." From outside the inner circle the response was different.
On June 3rd the London Liberal Candidates Association recorded its
"profound dismay (at) any intention to exclude Mr. Lloyd George
from the Councils of the Liberal Party."[t] On June 8th the Liberal
Parliamentary Party voted by twenty to ten to deprecate "the publicity given to the differences between the Liberal leaders" and to urge
the restoration of unity. This was near to a vote of censure upon
Asquith. On June 11th, the Liberal and Radical Candidates Association,
striking a slightly more conciliatory note, appointed a deputation to
convey to him their desire for unity under his leadership.

He never saw that deputation. On June 12th he suffered a slight
stroke and was incapacitated for nearly three months. He was unable
to attend the annual meeting of the National Liberal Federation at
Weston-super-Mare, at which he had intended to fight back. For his
convalescence he went once more to Castle Howard. Slowly, over the
summer, he recovered his health, but not his political position. Back
in London, at the end of September, he faced the end of the road.
He attended a final, sad and hopeless "conclave of the faithful" at
Edward Grey's house. When it was over he wrote to Margot:

The alternatives are to lead a squalid faction fight against Ll.G. in
which he would have all the sinews of war; or to accept his money
and patch up a hollow and humiliating alliance. I am quite resolved
to do neither, so I shall *faire mes paquets*, for which I have ample
justification on other grounds, age, etc.[u]

For private circulation he wrote a long *pièce justificative* beginning
resignedly: "The disintegration of the Liberal Party began with the
Coupon Election of December 1918. It then received a blow from
which it has never recovered." Publicly he announced his resignation
in a short, dignified letter to the heads of the English and Scottish

[1] Lords Grey, Lincolnshire, Buckmaster, Buxton and Cowdray; Sir
John Simon, Sir Donald Maclean, Sir Godfrey Collins; Runciman, Vivian
Phillipps, Geoffrey Howard and W. M. R. Pringle.

Liberal Federations. This was published on October 15th, 1926. For that same night he had arranged a farewell meeting at Greenock. He travelled to Scotland with a large party. Grey, Simon, Runciman, Maclean, members of his family, and many others were present on the platform. His thoughts can hardly fail to have gone back to another October evening, thirty years before, when he had himself sat on the stage of the Empire Theatre in Edinburgh and supported Rosebery's farewell speech.

Asquith's was much shorter and less self-regarding. But the occasion was at least equally moving.

" The meeting at Greenock," he wrote two days later, " . . . was unique in my experience: at moments thrilling in its intensity. There were a lot of my old and trusty friends from Paisley there, as well as good and true men and women from all parts of Scotland. It was sad, however necessary, to have to cause so much pain. But I have not a doubt that I have taken the only wise and honourable course." *v*

The end of Asquith's leadership had been a painful and protracted business. He had stayed too long in an impossible situation, believing, falsely, that the Liberal Party could be revived by its old leaders, and feeling it his duty to hold on for the sake of his small band of faithful followers. But after the harsh death, the Greenock meeting and the response it evoked provided a funeral more appropriate to the great past which lay behind him.

Between Greenock and Asquith's own death there was an interval of only sixteen months. At first his health was quite good again. He was even able to play golf. His interests remained as wide as ever. He was buying books and reading them, and working hard on another publication of his own (*Memories and Reflections*). He saw most of the new plays and films and even musicals of any note. He paid two or three visits a week to galleries and exhibitions, and kept fully alive the strong interest in contemporary painting and sculpture which he had developed since 1918. He made occasional speeches, in the House of Lords and elsewhere, and was constantly motoring to and fro between Sutton Courtney and Bedford Square, and about the countryside. He wrote frequent letters to Mrs. Harrisson, and he presided, benign and detached as he had always seemed, over the variegated and sustained social life of the Wharf. His mind remained balanced, tolerant and eclectic, his private edge of comment assured and sharp.[1] His life was not quite what it had been, but it was neither unoccupied nor dismal.

Early in 1927 he suffered a sudden loss of power in one leg. At first the trouble was only momentary and he was able to spend some of January and most of February in the South of France; in March he spoke in the House of Lords. Then his symptoms returned and he was forced for several months to submit to a wheel-chair. This experience had a deeply lowering effect upon his spirits. He had been used for too long to nearly perfect health to be able to take easily to an invalid's régime. Even his correspondence faltered. But by the later summer there was an improvement. He went for several weeks in September to North Berwick and wrote of his " powers of locomotion " returning. He motored over to Glen and " picnicked in the open." He lunched with Balfour at Whittinghame and was tinged with jealousy to find him " still a keen player at lawn tennis." He even thought of playing golf—although in fact he did not do so. He worked a little at his book most mornings and went for a motor drive most afternoons. Only " the persistence of execrable weather " marred this last Scottish holiday.

In mid-October Asquith moved south to Castle Howard, and went from there to York on the 19th, where he received the freedom of the city and responded with his last public speech. He was at the Wharf for a few weeks and then went with Mrs. Harrisson to see an exhibition of pictures at Norwich and to stay one night with Venetia Montagu at Breccles, which was nearby. It was his last excursion. On his return to Sutton Courtney he found himself unable to get out of his motor car, and never again succeeded in mounting the stairs to his own room.

Thereafter the decline was rapid, although uneven. His illness

---

[1] The following comment on Mrs. Sidney Webb, written a few months earlier, just before he gave up the leadership, is a good example of Asquith's latter-day style and outlook: " I have finished Beatrice Webb's *Apprenticeship* —a remarkable story in its way. To me hers is, *au fond*, a tiresome type of mind, but she has lived, ever since she was eighteen, an independent and industrious and at times adventurous life. And it is to the credit both of her insight and character that, being lapped in bourgeois luxury, and really very good-looking, she finally at the age of thirty married Sidney Webb, a highly-knowledgeable *Saint*. Since then in their partnership they have jointly produced some twenty solid, though for the most part unreadable, books." (*Letters from Lord Oxford to a Friend*, II, p. 159).

was a hardening of the arteries, which at times affected his mind and produced confusion about his surroundings. He suffered the intermittent delusion that he was kept an unwilling prisoner at the Wharf, and responded to this by attempting to make plans for an escape to London. At other times his mind was perfectly clear. He received visitors with pleasure, although he watched them go with apprehension. On January 21st, Vivian Phillipps, his private secretary of the post-war years, went to see him. Phillipps wrote:

When the time came to say good-bye to him, he held my hand and said, " You will come and see me again—right to the end," and then, quickly—as if he had said more than he meant to— " I mean right on to the end of this Parliament."*w*

Asquith died on the evening of February 15th, 1928. He was buried in the village churchyard at Sutton Courtney, between the Thames and the Berkshire Downs. He had started on a bleak Yorkshire hillside, and in politics he had been mostly sustained by Scotland and the North. But a South of England resting-place, within ten miles of Carfax Tower, was nevertheless wholly appropriate. He had always been faithful to liberal, humane ideas, and to civilised, even fastidious, standards of political behaviour. He never trimmed for office. Yet he was essentially a man of Government, a great servant of the State, rather than a tribune of the people. And with him there died the best part of the classical tradition in English politics.

A short time afterwards, by the decision of Parliament, a memorial tablet was placed in Westminster Abbey. As an epitaph, after much thought by his family, the following lines from Milton were chosen:

> *Unmoved*
> *Unshaken, unseduced, unterrified,*
> *His loyalty he kept, his love, his zeal;*
> *Nor number, nor example with him wrought*
> *To swerve from truth, or change his constant mind.*

They were as appropriate as the Sutton Courtney churchyard.

REFERENCES

REFERENCES

CHAPTER I

a. Oxford and Asquith: *Memories and Reflections*, i, p. 2
b. Spender and Asquith: *Life of Lord Oxford & Asquith*, i, p. 16
c. ibid., i, p. 18–19
d. Oxford and Asquith, *op. cit.*, i, p. 8
e. Spender and Asquith, *op. cit.*, i, p. 22
f. ibid., i, p. 23
g. ibid., i, p. 24
h. J. M. Angus in an article which he contributed to the City of London School Magazine after Asquith's death in 1928
i. Spender and Asquith, *op. cit.*, i, p. 28
j. ibid., i, p. 30
k. Stanley letters, 20th February, 1915
l. ibid., 22nd February, 1915
m. Davis: *Balliol College*, p. 193
n. Margot Oxford, *More Memories*, p. 187
o. Letter to Lady Horner, quoted in Spender and Asquith, *op. cit.*, i, p. 37
p. Oxford and Asquith, *op. cit.*, i, p. 19
q. ibid., i, p. 25

CHAPTER II

a. Stanley Letters, 22nd February, 1915
b. Spender and Asquith: *Life of Lord Oxford & Asquith* i, p. 43
c. ibid., i, p. 43
d. Haldane: *Autobiography*, p. 103
e. Letter to Mrs. (later Lady) Horner, September 11th, 1892
f. *Memories and Reflections*, i, p. 68
g. *Studies and Sketches*, 1924
h. *Memories and Reflections*, i, pp. 67–9
i. *The Times*, 30 July, 1956
j. Haldane, *op. cit.*, pp. 103–4

CHAPTER III

a. Spender and Asquith, *Life of Lord Oxford & Asquith*, i, p. 56

b. Haldane: *Autobiography*, p. 104
c. *Parliamentary Debates, Commons*, 3rd Series, Vol. 312, col. 1395
d. Gardiner, *The Life of Sir William Harcourt*, ii, p. 152
e. *Memories and Reflections*, i, p. 112
f. Spender and Asquith, *op. cit.*, i, p. 57
g. Haldane, *op. cit.*, p. 101
h. Gardiner, *op. cit.*, ii, p. 152
i. Crewe: *Lord Rosebery*, i, p. 347
j. Spender and Asquith, *op. cit.*, i, p. 48
k. *Memories and Reflections*, i, pp. 79–80
l. Spender and Asquith, *op. cit.*, p. 49

CHAPTER IV

a. Magnus: *Gladstone*, p. 394
b. Margot Asquith: *Autobiography*, i, pp. 262–3
c. Spender and Asquith: *Life of Lord Oxford & Asquith*, i, p. 98
d. Crewe: *Lord Rosebery*, ii, p. 391
e. *Fifty Years of Parliament*, i, pp. 200–1
f. *The Letters of Queen Victoria*, 3rd Series, vol. ii, p. 156

CHAPTER V

a. Magnus: *Gladstone*, p. 402
b. *Memories and Reflections*, i, pp. 131–2
c. *ibid.*, i, p. 132
d. *ibid.*, i, p. 142
e. *ibid.*, i, p. 130
f. *Strand* magazine, Oct., 1933
g. *Fifty Years of Parliament*, i, p. 215
h. *ibid.*, i, pp. 216–17
i. *Memories and Reflections*, i, p. 143
j. *Fifty Years of Parliament*, i, pp. 221–2

CHAPTER VI

a. Margot Asquith: *Autobiography*, i, pp. 267–8
b. *ibid.*, i, pp. 261–2
c. Spender and Asquith: *Life of Lord Oxford & Asquith*, i, p. 98
d. Margot Asquith, *op. cit.*, i, pp. 192–3
e. Margot Oxford: *More Memories*, p. 44
f. Spender and Asquith, *op. cit.*, i. p. 96
g. Margot Asquith, *op. cit.*, i, pp. 269–70
h. Crewe: *Lord Rosebery*, ii, p. 466

REFERENCES

i. *ibid.*, p. 468
j. Gardiner: *The Life of Sir William Harcourt*, ii, p. 308
k. *Fifty Years of Parliament*, i, p. 224
l. *ibid.*, i, p. 230
m. *Parliamentary Debates, Commons*, 4th Series, Vol. 30, col. 866
n. Gardiner, *op. cit.*, ii, p. 348

CHAPTER VII

a. Margot Asquith: *Autobiography*, i, p. 163
b. *Asquith Papers*, box ix, pp. 169–72
c. Margot Asquith, *op. cit.*, ii, pp. 35–6
d. *ibid.*, ii, p. 36

CHAPTER VIII

a. Gardiner: *The Life of Sir William Harcourt*, ii, p. 376
b. Crewe: *Lord Rosebery*, ii, pp. 522–3
c. Gardiner, *op. cit.*, ii, p. 418
d. *ibid.*, ii, p. 418
e. *ibid.*, ii, p. 421
f. *Fifty Years of Parliament*, i, p. 253
g. Margot Asquith: *Autobiography*, ii, p. 23
h. *ibid.*, ii, p. 25
i. *Fifty Years of Parliament*, i, p. 254
j. *Asquith Papers*, box ix, f. 92
k. *ibid.*, ix, ff. 129–32
l. *ibid.*, ix, ff. 147–52
m. *ibid.*, ix, ff. 109–28
n. *Campbell-Bannerman Papers*, 41210, 155–6
o. *Asquith Papers*, box ix, ff. 139–42
p. *Campbell-Bannerman Papers*, 41210, 159–60
q. *Asquith Papers*, box ix, 167–8
r. *Campbell-Bannerman Papers*, 41210, 163–4
s. *Asquith Papers*, box xlvi, ff. 9–12

CHAPTER IX

a. Garvin: *Life of Joseph Chamberlain*, iii, pp. 414–16
b. Spender and Asquith: *Life of Lord Oxford & Asquith*, i, p. 133
c. Speech at the Liverpool Street Station Hotel, June 17th, 1901
d. Gardiner: *The Life of Sir William Harcourt*, ii, p. 513
e. *Fifty Years of Parliament*, i, p. 270
f. Trevelyan: *Grey of Fallodon*, p. 80
g. Gardiner, *op. cit.*, ii, p. 517

h. Garvin, *op. cit.*, iii, p. 599
i. *ibid.*, iii, p. 603
j. Spender: *The Life of the Rt. Hon. Sir Henry Campbell-Bannerman*, i, p. 297
k. *ibid.*, i, p. 336
l. *Campbell-Bannerman Papers*, 41210, 206–7
m. *Asquith Papers*, box x, ff. 3–4
n. *ibid.*, box x, ff. 13–14
o. *ibid.*, box x, ff. 21–2
p. *Campbell-Bannerman Papers*, 41210, 208–9
q. Spender and Asquith, *op. cit.*, i, p. 141
r. *Asquith Papers*, box x, ff. 23–24
s. *ibid.*, box x, ff. 16–17
t. Spender and Asquith, *op. cit.*, i, p. 141
u. *Asquith Papers*, box x, ff. 25–6
v. Crewe: *Lord Rosebery*, ii, p. 573
w. Spender, *op. cit.*, ii, p. 17

CHAPTER X

a. Holland: *Life of the Duke of Devonshire*, ii, p. 284
b. Margot Asquith: *Autobiography*, ii, p. 53
c. Spender and Asquith: *Life of Lord Oxford & Asquith*, i, p. 154
d. Spender: *The Life of the Rt. Hon. Sir Henry Campbell-Bannerman*, ii, p. 120
e. *Asquith Papers*, box x, ff. 124–9
f. Spender: *op. cit.*, ii, p. 138
g. *Asquith Papers*, box x, ff. 98–9
h. *ibid.*, box x, f. 123
i. *Campbell-Bannerman Papers*, 41210, 227–8
j. *Asquith Papers*, box x, ff. 90–1
k. *ibid.*, box x, ff. 92–3
l. Lee: *King Edward VII*, ii, p. 442
m. Haldane: *Autobiography*, pp. 158–9
n. *Asquith Papers*, box x, ff. 138–40
o. *ibid.*, box x, ff. 148–9
p. Sommer: *Haldane of Cloan*, p. 147
q. *Asquith Papers*, box x, ff. 144–5
r. *ibid.*, ff. 153–4
s. Haldane, *op. cit.*, p. 161
t. Margot Asquith, *op. cit.*, ii, pp. 66–8
u. *Asquith Papers*, box x, f. 165
v. *Campbell-Bannerman Papers*, 41210, 247–252

CHAPTER XI

a. Spender and Asquith: *Life of Lord Oxford & Asquith* i, pp. 174-5
b. *Asquith Papers*, box x, ff. 27-32
c. ibid., box x, ff. 180-1
d. Margot Asquith: *Autobiography*, ii, p. 71
e. ibid., ii, p. 73
f. ibid., ii, p. 74
g. Spender: *The Life of the Rt. Hon. Sir Henry Campbell-Bannerman*, ii, p. 198
h. Margot Asquith, *op. cit.*, ii, p. 75
i. Spender and Asquith, *op. cit.*, pp. 174-5
i. Margot Asquith, *op. cit.*, ii, p. 77

CHAPTER XII

a. *Fifty Years of Parliament*, ii, p. 69
b. *Memories and Reflections*, i, p. 254
c. Spender and Asquith: *Life of Lord Oxford & Asquith*, i, p. 190
d. *Campbell-Bannerman Papers*, 41210, 272-3
e. ibid., 273-6
f. Spender: *The Life of the Rt. Hon. Sir Henry Campbell-Bannerman*, ii, p. 336
g. Spender and Asquith, *op. cit.*, i, p. 184
h. Spender, *op. cit.*, ii, p. 313

CHAPTER XIII

a. Spender: *The Life of the Rt. Hon. Sir Henry Campbell-Bannerman*, ii, p. 377
b. Spender and Asquith: *Life of Lord Oxford & Asquith*, i, p. 196
c. *Asquith Papers*, box xi, ff. 39-40
d. ibid., box xi, ff. 16-19
e. Reproduced in *facsimile* in Margot Asquith's *Autobiography*, ii, p. 102
f. *Asquith Papers*, box xi, ff. 10-15
g. Letter from Asquith to his wife, quoted by Spender and Asquith, i, p. 195
h. *Asquith Papers*, box xi, ff. 77-8
i. ibid.
j. Morley: *Recollections*, ii, p. 251
k. *Asquith Papers*, xi, ff. 69-70
l. Margot Asquith: *Autobiography*, ii, p. 107
m. *Asquith Papers*, box v, ff. 75-6
n. ibid., box i, f. 42
o. ibid., box xi, ff. 162-5
p. ibid., box xx, ff. 153-4
q. ibid., box xlvi, f. 169

r. *ibid.*, box xx, ff. 25–7
s. *ibid.*, box xx, ff. 91–142
t. *ibid.*, box f. 139
u. *ibid.*, box xi, ff. 203–4
v. *ibid.*, box xx, ff. 167–8
w. *ibid.*, box xlvi, f. 171
x. *ibid.*, box xi, ff. 239–54

CHAPTER XIV

a. *Asquith Papers*, box xxi, ff. 61–7
b. Spender and Asquith: *Life of Lord Oxford & Asquith*, i, p. 254
c. *ibid.*
d. *Asquith Papers*, box v, ff. 77–8
e. *ibid.*, box v, ff. 93–6
f. *ibid.*, box i, f. 194
g. *ibid.*, box v, ff. 150–1
h. *ibid.*, box v, ff. 160–1
i. *ibid.*, box xxi, ff. 274–9
j. *ibid.*, box i, ff. 230–1
k. Quoted in Spender and Asquith, *op. cit.*, i, p. 261
l. *ibid.*, i, p. 268
m. *Asquith Papers*, box, xii, ff. 114–15
n. *ibid.*, box xxiii, ff. 70–6
o. *ibid.*, box xxiii, ff. 62–6
p. Annual Register for 1910, p. 56
q. *Asquith Papers*, box xlvi, f. 183
r. *ibid.*, box xxiii, ff. 94–5
s. Murray: *Master and Brother*, p. 39
t. *Asquith Papers*, box v, ff. 190–1
u. *ibid.*, ff. 192–3
v. *ibid.*, box v, ff. 208–11
w. *ibid.*
x. Murray, *op. cit.*, p. 45
y. Margot Asquith: *Autobiography*, ii, p. 135

CHAPTER XV

a. *Fifty Years of Parliament*, ii, pp. 87–8
b. *Asquith Papers*, box xii, ff. 136–8
c. Nicolson: *King George V*, p. 131
d. Lloyd George: *War Memoirs*, p. 22
e. *Asquith Papers*, box xii, f. 198
f. *ibid.*, box xii, ff. 214–15

g. *ibid.*, box xlvi, f. 188

h. Nicolson, *op. cit.*, p. 134

i. *ibid.*, p. 135

j. *ibid.*, p. 129n.

k. *ibid.*, p. 138

l. Spender and Asquith: *Life of Lord Oxford & Asquith*, i, p. 297

m. *Asquith Papers*, box ii, f. 83

n. Nicolson, *op. cit.*, p. 139

o. *Asquith Papers*, box xiii, ff. 1–4

p. *ibid.*, box ii, f. 258

q. *Parliamentary Debates, Commons*, 5th Series, vol. 29, col. 817

r. *Asquith Papers*, box ii, f. 276

s. *ibid.*, box ii, f. 278

t. Nicolson, *op. cit.*, p. 155

u. *Asquith Papers*, box ii, ff. 278–9

CHAPTER XVI

a. Owen: *Tempestuous Journey*, p. 216

b. *Asquith Papers*, box iii, ff. 4–5

c. *ibid.*, box iii, ff. 8–9

d. *ibid.*, box vi, ff. 24–5

e. *ibid.*, box vi, ff. 125–6

f. Owen, *op. cit.*, p. 211

g. Grey of Fallodon: *Twenty-five Years*, i, p. 238

h. *Asquith Papers*, box xlvi, f. 191

i. Haldane: *Autobiography*, p. 230

j. *ibid.*, p. 231

k. Sommer: *Haldane of Cloan*, pp. 248–9

l. Grey of Fallodon: *op. cit.*, i, p. 95

m. *ibid.*

n. *Asquith Papers*, box vi, f. 75

o. *ibid.*, box vi, ff. 79–80

p. *ibid.*, box xxii, ff. 224–6

q. Fulford: *Votes for Women*, p. 184

r. *Speeches of the Earl of Oxford*, p. 183

s. *Asquith Papers*, box vii, ff. 7–8

t. Stanley Letters, f. 46

u. Donaldson: *The Marconi Scandal*, p. 57

v. Nicolson: *King George V*, p. 210

w. Samuel: *Memoirs*, p. 57

CHAPTER XVII

a. *Memories and Reflections,* i, p. 271
b. *ibid.,* p. 273

CHAPTER XVIII

a. *Memories and Reflections,* i, p. 202
b. *Asquith Papers,* box vi, ff. 95–6
c. Blake: *The Unknown Prime Minister,* p. 130
d. Austen Chamberlain: *Politics from Inside,* pp. 486–7
e. Nicolson: *King George V,* p. 221
f. *ibid.,* p. 220
g. *ibid.,* p. 223
h. *ibid.,* pp. 226–7
i. *ibid.,* p. 226
j. *Asquith Papers,* box xxxviii, ff. 216–19
k. *idib.,* box xxxviii, ff. 126–7
l. Blake, *op. cit.,* p. 156
m. *Asquith Papers,* box xxxviii, ff. 198–201
n. *ibid.,* box xxxviii, ff. 220–1
o. *ibid.,* box xxxviii, ff. 222–3
p. *ibid.,* box xxxviii, f. 230
q. Blake, *op. cit.,* p. 161
r. *ibid.,* p. 161
s. *Asquith Papers,* box xxxviii, ff. 231–4
t. *ibid.,* box xxxiv, ff. 1–6
u. Blake, *op. cit.,* p. 165
v. *ibid.,* p. 165
w. *Asquith Papers,* box vii, ff. 71–2
x. *ibid.,* box xxxix, ff. 23–26
y. *ibid.,* box xxxix, ff. 29–35
z. *ibid.,* box vii, ff. 77–8
aa. Blake, *op. cit.,* p. 170
bb. Nicolson, *op. cit.,* p. 222

CHAPTER XIX

a. Spender and Asquith: *Life of Lord Oxford & Asquith,* ii, p. 77
b. *Asquith Papers,* box xxv, ff. 148–9
c. Churchill: *World Crisis,* i, p. 178
d. *Asquith Papers,* box xxxix, ff. 97–8
e. *ibid.,* box xxxix, ff. 111–16

f. Nicolson: *King George V*, p. 234
g. *Asquith Papers*, box xxxix, ff. 143–4
h. ibid., box xl, f. 19.
i. ibid., box xl, ff. 27–8
j. Callwell: *Sir Henry Wilson*, i, p. 143
k. Ryan: *Mutiny at The Curragh*, p. 160
l. *Asquith Papers*, box xl, ff. 118–21
m. ibid., box xxix, ff. 157–8
n. ibid., box xli, f. 5
o. ibid., box xlvi, f. 213
p. Blake: *The Unknown Prime Minister*, p. 215

CHAPTER XX

a. Margot Asquith: *Autobiography*, ii, p. 196

CHAPTER XXI

a. Magnus: *Kitchener*, p. 278

CHAPTER XXII

a. *Asquith Papers*, box xiii, ff. 242–3 and 244–53
b. ibid., box xiii, ff. 254–5
c. Beaverbrook: *Politicians and the War*, p. 101
d. Moorehead: *Gallipoli*, p. 220
e. French: *1914*, pp. 356–7
f. *Asquith Papers*, box xxvi, ff. 226–31
g. ibid., box xxvii, ff. 162–3
h. ibid., box xiv, ff. 43–4
i. ibid., box xiv, ff. 44–6
j. ibid., box xiv, ff. 47–50
k. ibid., box xiv, ff. 172–5

CHAPTER XXIII

a. *Asquith Papers*, box xxvii, ff. 216–7
b. ibid., box iv, ff. 129–30
c. *Memories and Reflections*, ii, pp. 109–10
d. *Asquith Papers*, box viii, ff. 82–3
e. Blake: *The Unknown Prime Minister*, pp. 262–3
f. *Asquith Papers*, box xxviii, ff. 162–7

g. *ibid.*, box xv, ff. 44–5
h. *ibid.*, box, xv, ff. 46–50
i. *ibid.*, box viii, ff. 111–12
j. Margot Asquith: *Autobiography*, ii, pp. 221–2
k. *Asquith Papers*, box xxvi, ff. 125–65
l. Blake, *op. cit.*, p. 269
m. Lloyd George: *War Memoirs*, p. 311
n. *Asquith Papers*, box xv, ff. 95–6
o. Beaverbrook: *Politicians and the War*, pp. 162–3
p. *Asquith Papers*, box xv, ff. 128–9
q. Magnus: *Kitchener*, p. 367
r. *Memories and Reflections*, ii, p. 112
s. *ibid.*, ii, pp. 112–3

CHAPTER XXIV

a. Petrie: *The Life and Letters of the Rt. Hon. Sir Austen Chamberlain*, ii, p. 48
b. *Asquith Papers*, box xxviii, ff. 291–2
c. *ibid.*, box xvi, ff. 8–9
d. Spender and Asquith : *Life of Lord Oxford & Asquith*, ii, p. 176
e. Hankey: *The Supreme Command*, ii, pp. 483–4
f. *Memories and Reflections*, ii, pp. 126–7
g. *Letters from Lord Oxford to a Friend*, pp. 3–5
h. Hankey, *op. cit.*, ii, p. 475
i. *Asquith Papers*, box viii, 159–60
j. Hankey: *op. cit.*, ii, p. 476
k. Hanson Baldwin: *World War I*, p. 73
l. Spender and Asquith, *op. cit.*, ii, p. 214
m. *ibid.*, ii, p. 216
n. *ibid.*, ii, p. 215–16
o. *ibid.*, ii, p. 217
p. Lloyd George: *War Memoirs*, p. 419
q. *Asquith Papers*, box viii, ff. 171–8
r. *ibid.*, box viii, ff. 179–82
s. *ibid.*, box xlvi
t. *ibid.*, box viii, ff. 179–82
u. *ibid.*, box viii, ff. 189–90

CHAPTER XXV

a. Hankey: *The Supreme Command*, ii, p. 509
b. *Memories and Reflections*, ii, p. 84
c. ⎰Blake: *The Unknown Prime Minister*, pp. 288–90
⎱Owen: *Tempestuous Journey*, pp. 319–20

d. Lloyd George: *War Memoirs*, p. 456

e. *Asquith Papers*, box xxx, ff. 163–4

f. Lloyd George: *op. cit.*, pp. 457–9

g. Lady Scott's diary for June 20th, 1916

h. Margot Asquith: *Autobiography*, ii, p. 245

i. Hankey: *op. cit.*, ii, p. 525

j. *ibid.*, ii, pp. 512–13

k. *Memories and Reflections*, ii, p. 158

l. Margot Asquith, *op. cit.*, ii, pp. 242–4

m. *Memories and Reflections*, ii, pp. 158–9

n. *Letters from Lord Oxford to a Friend*, p. 10

o. Cameron: *1916*, p. 192

p. Hankey, *op. ct.*, ii, p. 557

q. *Asquith Papers*, box viii, ff. 209–10

r. Lloyd George, *op. cit.*, pp. 514-20

s. Hankey, *op. cit.*, ii, pp. 558–9

t. Lloyd George, *op. cit.*, pp. 574–5

u. Hankey, *op. cit.*, ii, p. 563

CHAPTER XXVI

a. Beaverbrook: *Politicians and the War*, pp. 329–30

b. *ibid.*, p. 343

c. Hankey: *The Supreme Command*, ii, p. 564

d. Beaverbrook: *op. cit.*, p. 348

e. *ibid.*, p. 356

f. *ibid.*, pp. 355–7

g. *ibid.*, p. 346

h. Dugdale: *Arthur James Balfour*, ii, p. 168

i. Austen Chamberlain: *Down the Years*, p. 117

j. Hankey: *op. cit.*, ii, p. 565

k. Spender and Asquith: *Life of Lord Oxford & Asquith*, ii, pp. 252–3; a very slightly different version is given in Beaverbrook, *op. cit.*, p. 387.

l. *ibid.*, ii, pp. 253–4

m. *Asquith Papers*, box xiv, f. 65

n. A note written by Montagu on December 9th, 1916

o. Lloyd George: *War Memoirs*, p. 589

p. Hankey: *op. cit.*, ii, pp. 565–6

q. Montagu note

r. *Asquith Papers*, box xxxi, ff. 8–12

s. Beaverbrook: *op. cit.*, pp. 411–14

t. Newton: *Lord Lansdowne*, pp. 452–3

u. Spender and Asquith, *op. cit.*, ii, p. 260

v. Austen Chamberlain: *op. cit.*, pp. 117–18

w. *Memories and Reflections,* ii, p. 131n.

x. Blake: *The Unknown Prime Minister,* p. 320

y. Beaverbrook, *op. cit.,* pp. 426–7

z. *ibid.,* p. 430

aa. Spender and Asquith, *op. cit.,* ii, p. 264

bb. Hankey: *op. cit.,* ii, p. 566

cc. Montagu note

dd. *Asquith Papers,* box xxxi, ff. 16–7

ee. Beaverbrook, *op. cit.,* p. 435

CHAPTER XXVII

a. Hankey: *The Supreme Command,* ii, pp. 567–8

b. Beaverbrook: *Politicians and the War,* p. 439

c. Spender and Asquith: *Life of Lord Oxford & Asquith,* ii, p. 26₃

d. Trevelyan: *Grey of Fallodon,* p. 329

e. Austen Chamberlain: *Down the Years,* pp. 123–4

f. Lloyd George: *War Memoirs,* pp. 595–601

g. Montagu note

h. Beaverbrook, *op. cit.,* pp. 450–1

i. Spender and Asquith, *op. cit.,* ii, p. 266

j. Lloyd George: *op. cit.,* i, pp. 593–4

k. Dugdale: *Arthur James Balfour,* ii, p. 126

l. Montagu note

m. Chamberlain, *op. cit.,* p. 124

n. Nicolson: *King George V,* pp. 287–8

o. Lloyd George, *op. cit.,* p. 596

p. Young: *Arthur James Balfour,* p. 368

q. Beaverbrook, *op. cit.,* p. 495

r. Lloyd George, *op. cit.,* 595–6

s. Nicolson, *op. cit.,* pp. 290–1

t. *ibid.,* p. 291

u. *ibid.,* p. 292

v. Quoted in part in Beaverbrook, *op. cit.,* p. 501

w. Dugdale: *op. cit.,* ii, p. 134

x. *Letters from Lord Oxford to a Friend,* pp. 12–13

y. Grey of Fallodon: *Twenty Five Years,* ii, p. 241

CHAPTER XXVIII

a. *Letters from Lord Ofxord to a Friend,* p. 15

b. *ibid.,* p. 15

c. *ibid.,* p. 17

d. *Asquith Papers,* box xviii, ff. 8–9

REFERENCES

e. *The Times*, May 7th, 1918
f. Spender and Asquith: *Life of Lord Oxford & Asquith*, ii, p. 303
g. Beaverbrook: *Men and Power*, pp. 253–4 and 382
h. Spender and Asquith, *op. cit.*, ii, p. 306
i. Beaverbrook, *op. cit.*, pp. 262–3
j. *Letters from Lord Oxford to a Friend*, p. 77
k. *ibid.*, p. 83
l. *ibid.*, pp. 81–2
m. Margot Asquith: *Autobiography*, ii, pp. 302–3
n. Lloyd George: *War Memoirs*, p. 1786
o. *Letters from Lord Oxford to a Friend*, p. 86
p. *ibid.*, p. 90
q. *Memories and Reflections*, ii, p. 171
r. Margot Asquith: *op cit.*, pp. 332–4
s. *Asquith Papers*, box xxxiii, f. 37
t. *ibid.*, box xxxiii, f. 26
u. *ibid.*, box xxxiii, f. 67
v. *ibid.*, box xxxiii, ff. 50–1
w. *ibid.*, box xxxiii, f. 25
x. *ibid.*, box xxxiii, ff. 27–8
y. *ibid.*, box xxxiii, f. 76
z. *ibid.*, box xxxiii, ff. 29–31
aa. *Letters from Lord Oxford to a Friend*, p. 98

CHAPTER XXIX

a. *Letters from Lord Oxford to a Friend*, p. 122
b. *ibid.*, p. 123
c. *ibid.*, pp. 125–6
d. Churchill: *Great Contemporaries*, p. 139
e. *Letters from Lord Oxford to a Friend*, pp. 129–31
f. *Memories and Reflections*, ii, p. 182
g. *ibid.*, ii, p. 183
h. *Letters from Lord Oxford to a Friend*, p. 135
i. *Memories and Reflections*, ii, p. 192
j. *Letters from Lord Oxford to a Friend*, ii, p. 38
k. *Memories and Reflections*, ii, pp. 192–3
l. *ibid.*, ii, p. 183
m. *Asquith Papers*, box xxxiv, ff. 1–6
n. *ibid.*, box xxxiv, ff. 15–18
o. *ibid.*, box xxxiv, ff. 30–1
p. *Letters from Lord Oxford to a Friend*, p. 204
q. *ibid.*, ii, *passim*
r. *ibid.*, ii, p. 38

s. *ibid.*, ii, p. 74
t. Randolph Churchill: *Lord Derby*, p. 461
u. *Letters from Lord Oxford to a Friend*, ii, p. 36
v. *ibid.*, ii, p. 37
w. *ibid.*, ii, p. 53
x. *ibid.*, ii, p. 123
y. *ibid.*, ii, p. 78
z. *ibid.*, ii, pp. 39–40
aa. *ibid.*, ii, pp. 84–5
bb. *ibid.*, ii, pp. 90–1
cc. *Memories and Reflections*, ii, p. 208
dd. *Asquith Papers*, box xlvi, f. 93
ee. *Memories and Reflections*, ii, p. 209

CHAPTER XXX

a. Extract from the diary of Lady Violet Bonham Carter
b. *ibid.*
c. Spender and Asquith: *Life of Lord Oxford & Asquith*, ii, p. 351
d. *ibid.*, ii, p. 354
e. *ibid.*, ii, p. 355
f. *Asquith Papers*, box xxxv, ff. 9–127
g. *ibid.*, box xxxv, f. 159
h. *Letters from Lord Oxford to a Friend*, ii, p. 122
i. *ibid.*, ii, p. 131
j. *ibid.*, ii, p. 139
k. *ibid.*, ii, p. 128
l. *Asquith Papers*, box xviii, ff. 101–2
m. *ibid.*, box xviii, ff. 103–4
n. *Letters from Lord Oxford to a Friend*, ii, p. 135
o. *ibid.*, ii, p. 133
p. *Asquith Papers*, box xxxiv, ff. 277–9
q. *Letters from Lord Oxford to a Friend*, ii, p. 171
r. *Asquith Papers*, box xxxv, ff. 226–9
s. *ibid.*, box xxxv, ff. 241–4
t. *ibid.*, box xviii, ff. 115–16
u. Spender and Asquith, *op. cit.*, ii, p. 369
v. *Letters from Lord Oxford to a Friend*, ii, pp. 182–3
w. *Memories and Reflections*, ii, p. 253

APPENDICES

APPENDIX A

The following is the list of those whom or some of whom it was proposed to approach with a view to the submission of their names to the King in the event of a creation of Peers becoming necessary. It is printed without alteration exactly as found among Asquith's papers.

The Rt. Hon. Sir John T. Brunner, Bart.

The Rt. Hon. James Stuart.

The Rt. Hon. Robert Farquharson, M.D., LL.D.

The Rt. Hon. Sir Algernon West, G.C.B.

The Rt. Hon. Frederick Huth Jackson.

The Rt. Hon. Arnold Morley.

The Rt. Hon. Sir John Rhys.

The Rt. Hon. Sir Edgar Speyer, Bart.

The Rt. Hon. Sir George O. Trevelyan, Bart.

The Rt. Hon. Arthur H. Dyke Acland.

The Rt. Hon. Eugene Wason, M.P.

The Rt. Hon. John W. Mellor, K.C.

The Rt. Hon. Sir William Mather.

The Rt. Hon. Sir Henry E. Roscoe, F.R.S., Ph.D., LL.D.

The Rt. Hon. George W. E. Russell.

The Rt. Hon. Thomas W. Russell.

The Rt. Hon. John F. Cheetham.

The Rt. Hon. Robert G. Glendinning.

The Rt. Hon. James Caldwell.

The Rt. Hon. Arthur Cohen, K.C.

The Rt. Hon. Alfred Emmott, M.P.

The Rt. Hon. Sir T. Vezey Strong (Lord Mayor).

H. J. Tennant, Esq., M.P.

Sir J. Herbert Roberts, Bart., M.P.

Sir Archibald Williamson, Bart., M.P.

Sir John A. Dewar, Bart., M.P.

John S. Ainsworth, Esq., M.P.

William Phipson Beale, Esq., K.C., M.P.

The Earl of Clonmel.

Sir Thomas Courtenay T. Warner, Bart., C.B., M.P.

Sir Edward Strachey, Bart., M.P.

Charles Norris Nicholson, Esq., M.P.

Sir Thomas Borthwick, Bart.

Sir Francis Layland-Barratt, Bart.

David Erskine, Esq.

Sir William H. Lever, Bart.

Sir A. Thomas.

J. Crombie, Esq.
Sir Frederick Pollock, Bart.
Sir James Low, Bart.
Sir George H. Lewis, Bart.
Sir Edward Donner, Bart.
The Hon. Arthur L. Stanley.
Major Gen. J. F. Brocklehurst, C.B., C.V.O.
Col. Arthur Collins.
Col. Sir Arthur Davidson, K.C.B., K.C.V.O.
The Hon. O. S. B. Brett.
Sir Francis D. Blake, Bart.
Sir John Barker, Bart.
R. Farrer, Esq.
The Hon. W. Pember Reeves.
Sir H. Harmsworth, Bart.
Seymour Allen, Esq.
—— Caird, Esq. (Dundee.)
A. Chamberlain, Esq.
Sir K. Muir Mackenzie, G.C.B., K.C.
George Fuller, Esq.
H. Holloway, Esq.
Captain A. F. Luttrell.
Sir Walter Runciman, Bart.
Sir E. Russell.
Sir H. Primrose, K.C.B., C.S.I., I.S.O.
Sir A. R. Simpson.
Professor Henry Jones, LL.D.
Anthony Hope Hawkins, Esq.
Henry Neville Gladstone, Esq.
H. Beaumont, Esq.
J. A. Bright, Esq.
Hugh E. Hoare, Esq.
Sir Edward T. Holden.
Emslie J. Horniman, Esq.
Oswald Partington, Esq.

Sir T. T. Scarisbrick, Bart.
F. Verney, Esq.
Capt. The Hon. Clive Bigham.
The Hon. A. J. Davey.
Sir Murland de Grasse Evans, Bart.
The Lord Haddo.
The Hon. W. J. James.
Sir Harry H. Johnston, G.C.M.G., K.C.B.
Commander the Hon. H. A. Scudamore Stanhope, R.N.
R. C. Phillimore, Esq.
Sir Robert H. Hobart, K.C.V.O., C.B.
The Hon. John Wallop.
Sir Albert E. H. Naylor-Leyland, Bart.
The Hon. H. W. Blyth.
Sir Kenelm E. Digby, G.C.B.
Sir Philip Burne-Jones, Bart.
The Hon. L. U. K. Shuttleworth.
Major A. L. Langman.
The Hon. Sir Edward Chandos Leigh, K.C., K.C.B.
The Hon. Bertrand Russell.
Sir Edgar Vincent, K.C.M.G.
Major Gen. Sir Alfred E. Turner, K.C.B.
Sir T. D. Gibson-Carmichael, Bart., K.C.M.G.
Principal Roberts.
R. Collins, Esq.
G. Freeman Barbour, Esq.
Admiral Sir Cyprian A. G. Bridge, G.C.B.
Sir Fowell Buxton.
The Hon. Geoffrey Coleridge.
Sir W. Dunbar, Bart.

Principal Donaldson.

W. S. Haldane, Esq.

Victor Horsley, Esq.

Sir John F. F. Horner, K.C.V.O.

Gwynne Hughes, Esq.

Sir T. W. Nussey, Bart.

General Sir R. S. S. Baden-Powell, K.C.B., K.C.V.O.

Frank Lloyd, Esq.

Joseph Rowntree, Esq.

F. Thomasson, Esq.

Sir Ernest Soares, LL.D.

Sir Charles E. Tritton, Bart.

Sir James Woodhouse.

Donald Crawford, Esq., K.C.

—— Tangye, Esq.

—— Bowring.

T. H. Amory, Esq.

Lord Ernest St. Maur.

Sir T. Barlow, Bart.

Lord R. Cavendish.

John Cowan, Esq.

A. H. Crosfield, Esq.

Laurence Currie, Esq.

Sir Andrew Fraser, K.C.S.I.

Sir Walter Gilbey, Bart.

G. P. Gooch, Esq.

The Rt. Hon. Sir J. Gorst, LL.D., F.R.S., K.C.

Cecil Grenfell, Esq.

General Sir Ian S. M. Hamilton, G.C.B., D.S.O.

F. Harrison, Esq., or }
R. H. Harrison, Esq. }

Norman Lamont, Esq.

R. C. Lehmann, Esq.

Sir H. S. Leon.

—— McKenna.

I. P. Maclay, Esq.

John Massie, Esq.

Gilbert Murray, Esq.

Sir William Robertson Nicol.

Sir Owen Philipps, K.C.M.G.

The Hon. Rollo Russell.

Arthur Sedgwick, Esq.

Captain C. W. Norton, M.P.

Sir David Brynmor Jones, K.C., M.P.

T. R. Ferens, Esq., M.P.

Sir Edwin Cornwall, M.P.

Sir Leonard Lyell, Bart.

Austin Taylor, Esq.

Sir William L. Younger, Bart.

Sir William J. Crossley, Bart.

Sir William J. Collins.

Sir E. Evans.

J. A. Spender, Esq.

Sir William E. Garstin, G.C.M.G.

Sir Francis A. Channing, Bart.

Major Edward M. Dunne.

The Hon. M. Napier.

Ernest A. Villiers, Esq.

Sir William Wedderburn, Bart.

Sir Henry Ballantyne.

Sir Samuel Chisholm, Bart.

Sir Jeremiah Colman, Bart.

Sir Frank Crisp.

Robert Wallace, Esq., K.C.

Sir T. Roberts.

Sir Abe Bailey.

Sir Alexander D. Kleinwort, Bart.

Alexander Cross, Esq.

Harold Ellis, Esq.

Thomas Hardy, Esq., O.M.

Sir Hubert H. Longman, Bart.

W. H. Dickinson, Esq., M.P.

James Brain, Esq.

John Churchill, Esq.

C. H. Corbett, Esq.
Sir George J. E. Dashwood, Bart.
Alfred Edison Hutton, Esq.
Sir Clarendon Golding Hyde.
Sir Benjamin Sands Johnson.
Algernon Marshall S. Methuen,
  Esq.
Sir Swire Smith.
Sir William James Ingram, Bart.
Harry Sturgis, Esq.
—— Leedam.
Sir Robert Buckle.
The Hon. Charles Lawrence.
Sir Francis Flint Belsey.
Charles Edward Mallet, Esq.
The Hon. Geoffrey R. C. Fiennes.
David Davies, Esq., M.P.
Sir Robert A. Hadfield.   ⎫
Sir William E. Clegg.   ⎬
Sir William Angus.   ⎭
J. M. Barrie, Esq.
Sir Robert Andrew Allison.
Charles R. Buxton, Esq.
Sir Joseph F. Leese, Bart.
William Fuller-Maitland, Esq.
Sir Frank Hillyard Newnes, Bart.
H. J. Glanville, Esq., M.P.
Sir E. J. Boyle, Bart.
J. H. Brodie, Esq.
Col. Henry Platt, C.B.
Percy Barlow, Esq.
Stanley George Barwick, Esq.
—— Nelson.
—— Neumann.
Sir J. Briscoe, Bart.
Sir Charles Cameron, Bart.
Chatfield Clarke, Esq.
Frank Debenham, Esq.

E. O. Fordham, Esq.
Sir John Fleming.
St. George Lane Fox Pitt, Esq.
Capt. The Hon. Fitzroy Hemp-
  hill.
A. Holland, Esq.
Sir Jonathan Hutchinson.
Sir Thomas J. Lipton, Bart.
Wilson Marriage, Esq.
Sir H. Marshall.
Sir Edward L. O'Malley.
Sir C. Parry, Bart.
Sir David Paulin.
Sir George Riddell.
—— Dunean.
Sir William Robertson.
Sir C. Shaw.
J. Seligman, Esq.
Sir George H. Sutherland.
David S. Waterlow, Esq.
Sir Frederick W. Wilson.
Lord Wodehouse.
—— Muspratt.
R. Hunter Craig, Esq.
Sir Charles Gold.
Sir A. P. Gould.
B. F. Hawksley, Esq.
Sir Frank Hollins, Bart.
Sir Alexander Waldemar Law-
  rence, Bart.
Sir Wilfrid Lawson, Bart, M.P.
Sir H. Munro.
Henry Oppenheim, Esq.
F. St. Quintin, Esq.
F. H. Smith, Esq.
J. Weston Stevens, Esq.
Halley Stewart, Esq.
James Thornton, Esq.

APPENDIX B

The Constitutional Position of the Sovereign

I propose to deal in this memorandum with the position of a Constitutional Sovereign in relation to the controversies which are likely to arise with regard to the Government of Ireland Bill. In a subsequent paper I will deal (1) with the actual and prospective situation in Ireland in the event of (*a*) the passing, (*b*) the rejection of that Bill; and (2) with the possibility and expediency of some middle course.

In the old days, before our present Constitution was completely evolved, the Crown was a real and effective, and often a dominating factor in legislation. Its powers were developed to considerable lengths by such kings as Henry VIII, and enforced with much suppleness and reserve by Queen Elizabeth; but the Tudor Sovereigns had a keen eye and a responsive pulse to the general opinion of the nation. The Stuarts, who followed, pushed matters to extremes, with the result that Charles I lost his head, and James II his throne. The Revolution put the title to the Throne and its prerogative on a Parliamentary basis, and since a comparatively early date in the reign of Queen Anne, the Sovereign has never attempted to withhold his assent from a Bill which had received Parliamentary sanction.

We have had, since that date, Soverigns of marked individuality, of great authority, and of strong ideas (often from time to time, opposed to the policy of the Ministry of the day) but none of them—not even George III, Queen Victoria or King Edward VII—have ever dreamt of reviving the ancient veto of the Crown. We have now a well-established tradition of 200 years, that, in the last resort, the occupant of the Throne accepts and acts upon the advice of his Ministers. The Sovereign may have lost something of his personal power and authority, but the Crown has been thereby removed from the storms and vicissitudes of party politics, and the monarchy rests upon a solid foundation which is buttressed both by long tradition and by the general conviction that its personal status is an invaluable safeguard for the continuity of our national life.

It follows that the rights and duties of a constitutional monarch in this country in regard to legislation are confined within determined and strictly circumscribed limits. He is entitled and bound to give his Ministers all relevant information which comes to him; to point out objections which seem to him valid against the course which they advise; to suggest (if he thinks fit) an alternative policy. Such intimations are always received by Ministers with the utmost respect, and considered with more care and deference than if they proceeded from any other quarter. But in the end, the Sovereign always acts upon the advice which Ministers, after full deliberation and (if need be) reconsideration, feel it their duty to offer. They give that advice well knowing that they can, and probably will, be called to account for it by Parliament.

The Sovereign undoubtedly has the power of changing his advisers, but it is relevant to point out that there has been, during the last 130 years, one occasion only on which the King has dismissed the Ministry which still possessed the confidence of the House of Commons. This was in 1834, when William IV (one of the least wise of British monarchs) called upon Lord Melbourne to resign. He took advantage (as we now know) of a hint improvidently given by Lord Melbourne himself, but the proceedings were neither well advised nor fortunate. The dissolution which followed left Sir R. Peel in a minority, and Lord Melbourne and his friends in a few months returned to power, which they held for the next six years. The authority of the Crown was disparaged, and Queen Victoria, during her long reign, was careful never to repeat the mistake of her predecessor.

The Parliament Act was not intended in any way to affect, and it is submitted has not affected, the Constitutional position of the Sovereign. It deals only with differences between the two Houses. When the two Houses are in agreement (as is always the case when there is a Conservative majority in the House of Commons), the Act is a dead letter. When they differ, it provides that, after a considerable interval, the thrice repeated decision of the Commons shall prevail, without the necessity for a dissolution of Parliament. The possibility of abuse is guarded against by the curtailment of the maximum life of any given House of Commons to five years.

Nothing can be more important, in the best interests of the Crown and of the country, than that a practice, so long established and so well justified by experience, should remain unimpaired. It frees the occupant of the Throne from all personal responsibility for the Acts of the

Executive and the legislature. It gives force and meaning to the old maxim that 'the King can do no wrong.' So long as it prevails, however objectionable particular Acts may be to a large section of his subjects, they cannot hold him in any way accountable, and their loyalty is (or ought to be) wholly unaffected. If, on the other hand, the King were to intervene on one side, or in one case—which he could only do by dismissing Ministers in *de facto* possession of a Parliamentary majority—he would be expected to do the same on another occasion, and perhaps for the other side. Every Act of Parliament of the first order of importance, and only passed after acute controversy, would be regarded as bearing the personal *imprimatur* of the Sovereign. He would, whether he wished it or not, be dragged into the arena of party politics; and at a dissolution following such a dismissal of Ministers as has just been referred to, it is no exaggeration to say that the Crown would become the football of contending factions.

This is a Constitutional catastrophe which it is the duty of every wise statesman to do the utmost in his power to avert.

H.H.A.

September 1913.

The Irish Situation;
The Constitutional Position of the Sovereign

I proceed to consider the prospective situation in Ireland in the event of the passing or of the rejection of the Bill.

If the Bill becomes law (whether or not its passing is preceded by another general election) there will undoubtedly be a serious danger of organised disorder in the four north-eastern counties of Ulster. It is, in my opinion, a misuse of terms to speak of what is likely to happen as Civil War. The total population of the area concerned is little over 1,000,000. It is divided between Protestants and Roman Catholics— and in that part of the world political and religious differences roughly coincide—in the proportion of seven to three (Protestants 729,624, Roman Catholics 316,406). In two of the four counties (Armagh and Londonderry) the Protestant preponderance is not greater than six to five. It is not, therefore, the case of a homogeneous people resisting a change to which they are unitedly opposed. On the contrary, there will be a considerable and a militant minority strongly in favour of the new state of things, and ready to render active assistance to the forces of the executive. In the remainder of Ulster, and in the three other provinces of Ireland, there will be an overwhelming majority of the population on that side of the law.

But, while anxious that things should be seen in their true perspective, I have not the least disposition to minimise the gravity of the situation which will probably arise. The importation of rifles has, so far, been on a small scale, and the drilling and training of volunteers, though it is no doubt accustoming numbers of men to act together, to obey orders, and to develop *esprit de corps*, is not likely to produce a body which can stand up against regular troops. But the genuine apprehensions of a large majority of the Protestants, the incitements of responsible leaders, and the hopes of British sympathy and support, are likely to encourage forcible resistance (wherever it can be tried); there is the certainty of tumult and riot, and more than the possibility of bloodshed.

On the other hand, if the Bill is rejected or indefinitely postponed, or some inadequate and disappointing substitute put forward in its place, the prospect is, in my opinion, much more grave. The attainment of Home Rule has for more than 30 years been the political (as distinguished from the agrarian) ideal of four-fifths of the Irish people. Whatever happens in other parts of the United Kingdom, at successive general elections, the Irish representation in Parliament never varies. For the last eight years they have had with them a substantial majority of the elected representatives of Great Britain. The Parliament of 1906 was debarred by election pledges from dealing with the matter legislatively, but during its lifetime, in 1908, the House of Commons affirmed by an overwhelming majority a resolution in favour of the principle. In the present Parliament, the Government of Ireland Bill has passed that House in two successive sessions, with British majorities which showed no sign of diminution from first to last. If it had been taken up by a Conservative Government, it would more than a year ago have been the law of the land. It is the confident expectation of the vast bulk of the Irish people that it will become law next year.

If the ship, after so many stormy voyages, were now to be wrecked in sight of port, it is difficult to overrate the shock, or its consequences. They would extend into every department of political, social, agrarian and domestic life. It is not too much to say that Ireland would become ungovernable—unless by the application of forces and methods which would offend the conscience of Great Britain, and arouse the deepest resentment in all the self-governing Dominions of the Crown.

It follows, from what has been said above, that while in my opinion—from the point of view of social order—the consequences of the passing of the Bill would be unquestionably less serious than those of its rejection, yet no forecast, in either event, can be free from anxiety. Any practicable means of mitigation—still more, of escape—deserves, therefore (whencesoever it is suggested), impartial and mature consideration.

The demand, put forward recently by Mr. Balfour, for a General Election, between now and the beginning of next session, is open to objections of the most formidable character. (1) If such an election resulted in a majority for the Government, and the consequent passing of the Irish Bill next session, the recalcitrance of North-East Ulster would not in any way be affected. Sir E. Carson, and his friends have told the world, with obvious sincerity, that their objections to Home Rule have nothing to do with the question whether it is approved or disapproved by the British electorate. It is true that the Unionist Leaders in Great Britain have intimated that, in such an event, they would not give 'active countenance' (whatever that may mean) to the defiance of the law. But what effect can that have on men who have been encouraged to believe, and many of them do believe, that under Home Rule their liberties and their religion would be in jeopardy? (2) If the election resulted in a Government defeat, the circumstances are such that neither in Ireland nor in Great Britain would it be accepted as a verdict adverse to Home Rule. There may not be much active enthusiasm for Home Rule in the British constituencies, but the evidence afforded, not only by the steady and persistent majorities in the House of Commons, but by the bye-elections, tends to show that (at the lowest) it meets with acquiescence as an inevitable necessity in itself, and as a first step towards further devolution. All the most trustworthy observers agree that, even where the bye-elections have gone against the Government, the attempt (wherever made) to arouse interest and resentment by pushing to the forefront the case against Home Rule and the supposed wrongs of Ulster, has met with no success. The General Election would be fought, as the bye-elections have been, not predominantly on Home Rule, but on the Insurance Act, the Marconi contract, and a score of other 'issues' which happened for the moment to preoccupy public attention. (3) The concession of the demand for a General Election, at this stage, would be in the teeth of the intentions of the Parliament Act. One of the primary and most clearly avowed purposes of that Act was to abrogate the power of the House of Lords to force a dissolution. The assumption which underlies the whole measure is, that a Bill which can survive the ordeal of three sessions, prolonged over two years, in the House of Commons, ought without the need of another election, to pass into law.

It is quite another matter to suggest that, after the Bill has passed, a General Election should take place before it has come into active operation. Parliament will then have completed, or nearly completed, four out of its possible five years; and if the country were either on general or particular grounds averse to the Government, the new Parliament would consider, before anything irreparable has been done, whether to repeal or to amend the Irish Government Act. If, moreover, it were known beforehand that this would happen, any outburst of disorder in Ulster would everywhere be regarded as premature and inexcusable.

There remains the proposal, to which Lord Loreburn has during the last week given his authority, for settlement by Conference. I wrote to Lord Loreburn, as soon as I read his letter in *The Times* to ask him to tell me precisely what he meant. I expressed sympathy with the spirit of all that he had written, and acquiescence in the reasoning of much, though not the whole, of his argument. But I pointed out that the parties concerned in this controversy, including Sir E. Carson and Mr. Redmond, are not likely, at the moment, to accept an invitation (from any quarter) to come into a room and sit round a table, for the purpose of talking in the air about the Government of Ireland, or about Federalism and Devolution. It is no good blinding one's eye to obvious and undeniable facts, and one of those facts, relevant to the present case, undoubtedly is, that there is a deep and hitherto unbridgeable chasm of *principle* between the supporters and the opponents of Home Rule. It is a question not of phraseology but of substance. Four-fifths of Ireland, with the support of a substantial British majority in the present and late House of Commons, will be content with nothing less than a subordinate legislature with a local executive responsible to it. They insist, moreover, that (whatever may be done with Devolution elsewhere) the claim of Ireland is peculiar, and paramount in point of time and urgency. A settlement which ignored these conditions would be no settlement at all. But within these conditions—so I said to Lord Loreburn—there is (so far as I am concerned) no point—

finance, Ulster, Second Chamber, representation of minorities, etc., upon which I am not ready and anxious to enter into conference, and to yield to any reasonable suggestion.

For a Conference to be fruitful, there must be some definite basis upon and from which its deliberations can proceed. I fear that at present (it may be different nearer the time) no such basis can be found. I shall be only too glad if that fear can now or hereafter be satisfactorily dispelled.

I feel bound to add, that after the experience of 1910, when there was on both sides perfect goodwill and a sincere desire for agreement, that an abortive Conference would be likely to widen differences and embitter feeling.

H. H. A.

INDEX

INDEX

A.

S2

Victor Emmanuel, King of Italy, 391
Victoria, Queen of England, 83, 87, 190;
    and 1892 administration, 59-60, 61,
    72; critical of Asquith, 64, 65, 66-7;
    death of, 123
Viviani, René, 233
Vizetelly, Henry, 47

Walton, Sir John Lawson, 170
War, 1914-18: coming of, 148, 239-45;
    outbreak of, 264, 322-31; War
    Council, 344-5, 349, 352, 353;
    replaced by Dardanelles committee,
    370, 375; reformed, 375-7, 382-6,
    387, 417; re-creation of General
    Staff, 383-4; demand for a small
    War Committee, 420-43, 446, 449-
    50, 453, 454-5, 456, 458; War
    Cabinet established, 459; Easterners
    v. Westerners, 349-51, 380-2, 387,
    416; Dardanelles campaign, 351-6,
    372, 375, 378, 381, 384-6; inquiry,
    410-11; shell scandal, 355-60; cam-
    paigns in France, 349, 355, 357,
    372-3, 387, 400-1, 410, 412-13, 416-
    17, 468; for end of, see Peace
Warren, Sir Thomas Herbert, 24
Watts-Ditchfield, J. E., Bishop of
    Chelmsford, 480
Weardale, Lord (Philip James Stan-
    hope), 115, 246
Webb, Sidney, Lord Passfield, 518n
Wedgwood, J. C., Lord Wedgwood,
    471
Week's Survey, 147
Wells, H. G., 379
Welsh Church disestablishment, 56,

66-7, 84-5, 86, 256, 278-9, 289, 329,
    344
West, Sir Algernon Edward, 70, 75
Westminster Gazette, 118
Whiteley, George, Lord Marchamley,
    125
Wilde, Oscar, 379
Wilhelm II, Kaiser of Germany, 148,
    327
Willans, Emily see Asquith
Willans, John (Asquith's uncle), 16
Willans, William, 15
Wilson, Admiral Sir Arthur Knyvet,
    241, 242, 350, 360, 361
Wilson, Sir Henry, 239, 240, 308, 312,
    383, 422, 468
Wilson, President Woodrow, 416, 475,
    477, 478
Wimborne, Viscount (Sir Ivor C. Guest),
    396-7, 402
Winterton, Earl (Edward Turnour), 225
Women's suffrage, 57, 186, 245-51, 256,
    282, 467, 486
Wood, Thomas MacKinnon, 237, 239,
    267, 304, 325n, 341, 345, 397, 458,
    478
Wordsworth, Archdeacon Christopher,
    Bishop of Lincoln, 19
Worth, Charles F., 77-8
Wright, Sir Robert Samuel, 35-6, 36n
    37, 47
Wyndham, George, 76n, 134, 229, 461

Yeats, William Butler, 267

Zola, Émile, 47